The great need of the Church in the West is for God the Holy Spirit to come in power as He has done so often in the past – ravishing hearts, enlightening minds, inspiring purity of worship, sending out into mission, mollifying hardened souls. Contrary to the wisdom of the age, it is not ... techniques or new schemes we need with pastors mas... ...or is the solution to our spiritual dearth a ... he return of spectacle. It is what many nin... Scottish Christians, whose experience of t... mented book, knew: the awesome God of ... people and setting mind and heart ablaze ... and pray!

Michael A.G. Haykin,
Professor of Church History and Biblical Spirituality,
The Southern Baptist Theological Seminary, Louisville, Kentucky

Spontaneous local revivals of religion in Scotland did not virtually disappear, as some have supposed, with the arrival of mass evangelism led by Moody and Sankey in the 1870s. In this fair-minded and thorough book, Tom Lennie has shown that there were evangelical awakenings in many parts of the land down to the inter-war years.

David Bebbington,
Professor of History, University of Stirling

Tom Lennie's *Glory in the Glen* is a welcome addition to the literature on the evangelical history of Scotland. He has researched the sources – both oral and written – thoroughly, and has assessed the evidence thoughtfully. I trust that the effect of the material gathered here will be to revive a new interest in our evangelical legacy, and to revive a new hunger for the God whose footprints are all over Scotland. Above all, I hope it will dispel the myth that genuine revival is marked by strange phenomena; the testimony both of Scripture and history is that it is marked by a return, through the Word of God and by the Spirit of God, to the Christ of God as the source of all spiritual life. I wish it a wide circulation.

Iain D. Campbell,
Free Church of Scotland, Back, Isle of Lewis

Glory in the Glen: A History of Evangelical Revivals in Scotland 1880–1940 is an intriguing, judiciously balanced, and often inspiring account of movements of the Holy Spirit in Scotland in a period that we do not normally think of as characterized by revivals (except for the 1949–52 Lewis Revival, which occurred later). This volume is carefully researched, often in old newspaper accounts and in fairly obscure church records and diaries. I appreciated its accurate distinction between 'revival' and 'revivalism', and its realistic appraisal of times of 'new measures' and excitement which led to no true revival. In times of true revival (life-changing outpourings of the Holy Spirit in large areas, accompanying the preaching of the Word and fervent prayer, marked by powerful renewal of faith in Christ, deep repentance, and moral fruit in the culture), there were at times (though certainly not always) unusual emotional outbursts and other 'outward manifestations' (trances, swoonings, visions, etc.). Following the wise assessment of the noted Free Church minister of Stornoway, the Rev. Kenneth MacRae, it is noted that while some of these 'manifestations' could no doubt be attributed to a sort of mass hysteria, nonetheless, the Lord was at work making men and women vividly aware of eternity and of their desperate need to get ready for it. Reading these accounts of conversions and personal renewal of thousands brought to mind the insight of Archibald Alexander, a founder of Princeton Theological Seminary. He had been converted in revival as a young man, and lived through another revival in 1830s Virginia. He stated that revival is primarily a supernatural 'speeding up' of the effectiveness of the ordinary 'means of grace' given to the Church (preaching, prayer, the sacraments and worship), rather than something different in type or quality (see his *Thoughts on Religious Experience*). It would appear that in true revival, people are suddenly 'sobered up' from almost total absorption into their daily, worldly affairs in this passing scene, and see in shocking clarity what really matters most about their life: a holy God, their own ugly sins, the beauty of the atonement of Christ, the awful and awesome bliss of eternal joy or horrors of everlasting hell, and thus, the need to cast their all upon the Lord immediately, and to follow Him in love and obedience, no matter what the cost. One of the encouraging aspects of this volume is the connection it traces between longing prayer and the granting of the Holy Spirit in reviving power (in terms of Jesus' promise in Luke 11). It has encouraged me to pray with new expectancy for God to revive His work among us.

Douglas F. Kelly,
Richard Jordan Professor of Theology,
Reformed Theological Seminary, Charlotte, North Carolina

What place have revivals had in the life of the church in Scotland? How widespread have they been and what has been their impact? These and many other questions are addressed in *Glory in the Glen*. Extensively researched and engagingly written, Tom Lennie's work is to be commended for bringing to life an element of Scottish church history that has not received the attention it deserves. *Glory in the Glen* reminds us that God is at work and we should pray that His Kingdom will continue to grow and prosper.

Alexander (Sandy) Finlayson
Professor of Theological Bibliography
Westminster Theological Seminary, Philadelphia, Pennsylvania

Reading this book, I felt a profound sense of thankfulness to God tinged with a holy fear. I had no idea that so often in so many places God has touched areas of the land of Scotland with the fire of His Presence! Tom has done us all a great service in writing this book. The research is detailed and meticulous and this is good, for as Duncan Campbell said when speaking about his own witness to the moving of God, 'Facts are powerful things.' Here you can read about what our God has actually done. My prayer is that as we read this we will learn something of the handprint of our God. No doubt even this well-researched book traces only a few lines of that handprint. We can never tie God down, but here we can learn what regularly happens when God visits a church or community in power. I know that I have come through the pages of this book with a prayer forming on my breath again and again: 'Come, Lord, once more to this land. Visit us with another day of Your Power.'

Kenny Borthwick
Holy Trinity Church, Wester Hailes, Edinburgh

As Mr Lennie contends, there is a good supply of primary and secondary literature about Scottish revivals up to the time of the Moody and Sankey campaigns in 1875. But there is a serious shortage of both kinds of information about spiritual movements in Scotland since that time. Indeed some of the localised revivals in that period seem not to have been noted much at all in published literature. Although a few of the revivals between 1880 and 1940 were fairly widespread, most were localised only, and many of these were in isolated communities. As a result, a good comprehensive survey of the Scottish revivals in this period is very much needed. Our author has delved into a wide range of little-known sources, and conducted many personal interviews, to gather as much accurate and first-hand information as he could. Some of the published sources are very hard to find. The chance to interview most of the people involved is now largely past, because they have now passed from the scene. The author pays special attention to the Lewis Revival in the 1930's, because he believes this revival to be particularly significant, more than movements which were better known, and better documented.

This is a serious piece of research. It is not light reading. It not only fills a serious gap in the annals of Scottish church history, but it will inspire us to pray for more and better revivals in Scotland in the future. In this way God may be the more glorified in the cities, countryside, highlands, islands and glens of Scotland, and Scottish society may be more purified.

Rev. Robert Owen Evans
Uniting Church in Australia

Glory in the Glen

A History of Evangelical Revivals in Scotland 1880–1940

•

Tom Lennie

ISBN 978-1-84550-377-2

First published in 2009
by
Christian Focus Publications, Geanies House,
Fearn, Ross–shire, IV20 1TW, Scotland

www.christianfocus.com

CIP catalogue record for this book is available from the British Library.

Cover design by Daniel Van Straaten
Printed and bounded by Bell and Bain, Glasgow

CONTENTS

DETAILED CONTENTS

Part Two: Fire Among the Fisherfolk

ABBREVIATIONS

ARC-FCS-SR&M	Appendix to the *Report of the Committee of the Free Church of Scotland on the State of Religion and Morals*
ARC-FCS-H&I	Appendix to the *Report of the Committee of the Free Church of Scotland for the Highlands & Islands*
BHMSR	Baptist Home Missionary Society Records
BW	*Bright Words*
CoS	Church of Scotland
DSCH&T	*Dictionary of Scottish Church History & Theology*
FC	Free Church (of Scotland)
FH&NCI	*Fraserburgh Herald and Northern Counties' Advertiser*
KGLCR	*Kirkintilloch Gazette, Lenzie and Campsie Reporter*
MR-UFC	*Missionary Record of the United Free Church of Scotland*
MR-FCS	*The Monthly Record of the Free Church of Scotland*
NE	*Northern Ensign and Weekly Gazette for the Counties of Caithness, Ross, Sutherland, Orkney & Zetland*
NIDP&CM	*New International Dictionary of Pentecostal & Charismatic Movements*
PGA-FCS	*Proceedings of the General Assembly of the Free Church of Scotland*
PGA-FCS-H&I	*Proceedings of the General Assembly of the Free Church of Scotland for the Highlands & Islands*
PGA-UFCS	*Proceedings of the General Assembly of the United Free Church of Scotland*
RJ&GANC	*Ross-shire Journal and General Advertiser for the Northern Counties*
RC-FCS-H&I	*Report of the Committee of the Free Church of Scotland for the Highlands & Islands*

RC-FCS-RM&T	*Report of the Committee of the Free Church of Scotland for Religion, Morals & Temperance*
RC-FCS-SR&M	*Report of the Committee of the Free Church of Scotland on the State of Religion and Morals*
RHM&CEC-FCS	*Report of the Home Mission and Church Extension Committee of the Free Church of Scotland*
RHM&CEC-UFCS	*Report of the Home Mission and Church Extension Committee of the United Free Church of Scotland*
RC-UFCS-H&I	*Report of the Committee of the United Free Church of Scotland for the Highlands & Islands*
SBM	*Scottish Baptist Magazine*
SBYB	*Scottish Baptist Year Book*
SCHSR	*Scottish Church History Society Records*
TC	*The Christian*
UFC	United Free Church (of Scotland)
UPC	United Presbyterian Church (of Scotland)

Acknowledgements and Dedication

THIS longstanding labour of love has relied on the ongoing generous co-operation of many people, not least those who provided me with information on specific revivals (particularly the Lewis revival of 1934-9). It would be impractical to list here the names of all who gave such assistance, though I have endeavoured to provide individual credits in the footnotes of the pages that follow. Sincere thanks to them all, as well as to those who loaned song lyrics, poems and old portrait photographs. I have sought to ensure that permission has been granted to reproduce all such photos included in this volume, as well as the scenic prints, each of which dates approximately to the period under review. Apologies to anyone with a title to the few images whose ownership I was unable to trace, or which I was led to believe were copyright free. My heartfelt gratitude also extends to a number of publishers who graciously granted me permission to quote from their authors' works.

I am much indebted to Paul Kenyon for his invaluable assistance with the creation of the many maps that accompany the text, and to David Miller and Pauline A. Graham for freely offering words of wisdom to a myriad questions. Special thanks are due to the Rev. Donald MacDonald, formerly of Carloway, who gave guidance to my research of the 1930s revival in that parish; also to Dr David Bebbington and Dr Robert Evans, who picked up on textual errors I had overlooked, Dr Bebbington also offering much further advice, for which I am deeply appreciative. A number of extremely busy individuals agreed to read through a draft copy of the manuscript and went on to provide endorsements – I am hugely thankful for their generous contributions. I am also very grateful to The Strathmartine Trust, whose benevolent grant enabled me to finance this venture, as well as to research Scottish awakenings of both earlier and later periods.

A personal thanks, lastly, to Christian Focus for their commitment to this project (not least Alex Macaskill, whose patience and dedication are greatly valued) and to everyone who spoke words of encouragement as I worked on it. In its completed form I wish to dedicate *Glory in the Glen* to Alex Muir, Inverness, who has consistently longed, prayed and wept for a genuine, widespread, Spirit-breathed revival in Scotland more than any person I know.

Tom Lennie
November 2008
tom@linnadale.fsnet.co.uk
www.scottishrevivals.co.uk

Foreword
by
Rev. Richard Owen Roberts

THERE are always two immensely consequential aspects of revival that urgently demand our prayerful concern and consideration. First, the manifest presence of Christ in the midst of His people, bringing both incredible conviction of sin and marvellous release from the bondage of corruption. Second, the extraordinary empowerment of the Word of God and the depth of its impact and the rapidity of its spread.

Both of these benefits of revival are clearly discernible in the Book of Acts' account of the day of Pentecost and the glorious things that followed. Through the power of the Holy Spirit, the resurrected Christ indwelt and profoundly impacted each believer. Their lives were radically and permanently changed and their labours were suddenly and gloriously full of life and joy. The Word of the Lord, which previously seemed to have had but small impact, went rushing forward as a mighty tidal wave of divine blessing, first upon the Jews in Jerusalem and then upon multitudes in widely scattered places.

Both of these beautiful features of revival are desperately needed today. The crippled Church, looking more like a dying refugee camp than a militant and victorious army, needs once again the manifest presence of Christ in its midst. Long ago the Psalmist cried, 'The nearness of God is my good' (Ps. 73:28), but we seem to know so little of that. Today's Church has busied itself with new methods and politically correct messages, but what is really needed is the living Christ in our midst. The world has heard our claim that God is with us, but the absence of holiness in our lives and the lack of spiritual power in the Church prove the idleness of our boast. Moses stated it correctly when he told the Lord, 'If Thy presence does not go with us, do not lead us up from here,' and asked, 'For how then can it be known that I have found favour in Thy sight, I and Thy people? Is it not by Thy going with us, so that we, I and Thy people, may be distinguished from all the other people who are upon the face of the earth?' (Exod. 33:15–16). The message of the Gospel can never be made attractive enough, nor the ingenuity and zeal of men sufficiently effective to rescue a degenerate Church and to save a dying, sin-cursed world. Only the manifest presence of Christ in the midst of His people can do this.

The Apostle Paul clearly understood that the Word of God does not always run with the same speed or impact its hearers with the same mighty strength. Thus, when addressing the Thessalonians, he pled with them, 'Finally, brethren, pray for us that the Word of the Lord may spread rapidly and be glorified, just as it did also with you; and that we may be delivered from perverse and evil men; for not all have faith.' (2 Thess. 3:1-2). Every thinking Christian must realise that we live in a situation that demands such praying once again. The Word of the Lord is not spreading rapidly. In fact, in countless churches, it must be sadly stated, the Word of the Lord is not spreading at all. Thousands of sermons are preached every week that appear to have no real impact. Countless occasions of personal witness result in no discernible advancement of the kingdom of God. The church desperately needs to be delivered from perverse and evil men, both from within its own ranks and from those who surround and influence it. Only God can quicken His Word, make it mighty, and cause it to spread again like a mighty tidal wave of blessing upon the world's peoples.

Just as Pentecost was desperately needed at the beginning of the Christian era, so another season of God-sent revival is the urgent need of this hour. A careful reading of 'Glory in the Glen' will help in many ways.

First, revivals are not just ancient history. The revival under Moses as recorded in Exodus might be considered ancient but spiritual awakening on the Isle of Lewis in 1950 is not. Furthermore, the stirrings of the Holy Spirit in China today and in other parts of the world are not 'past events'.

Second, God has already invested much of His grace and goodness in Scotland, as Tom Lennie's book, as well as 'Scotland Saw His Glory', clearly testifies. It is very sound to plead with God for another investment of His grace in those places where He has already given so much when we have reason to believe that it will be an investment providing a wonderful return. Think of the whole of Scotland once again ablaze with the Glory of God and plead with Him to do it again!

Third, at a time when discouragement is so common and when pessimism seems to have gripped so many, it is well to be reminded of those many times when God has made bare His mighty arm, when He has drawn near to His people, when His word has spread rapidly and with great impact. Between the covers of this book, you will see many such occasions. Let them quicken your faith and inspire confidence in the God who does not change!

Fourth, we must face again the solemn fact that we can save neither ourselves nor others. As the overwhelming evidence of our failures piles around us, this book should inspire and even drive us to look to Him who has so often met His desperate people and moved mightily on their behalf. Surely the time is upon us when we must abandon all hopes but Him!

Fifth, as is so clearly seen in the Book of Acts, the awakening was spread on the wings of testimony. The disciples went everywhere telling what God had done. Even as they spoke, time after time, God did it again. Throughout history, the reporting of God's mighty deeds has resulted in further precious acts of God. Mr Lennie has clearly indicated how frequently in the past the reporting of revivals led to additional revivals. As you read these lively accounts, may you be personally quickened and revived, and may an overwhelming longing for another great day of grace grip you.

Sixth, set your heart to draw near to God and expect Him to draw near to you (James 4:8). Covenant to pray that the manifest presence of Christ will once again fill your church, your community, and your nation.

Seventh, heed the Apostle Paul's prayer request. Pray effectually, pray fervently, that the Word of God will once again cover the earth as the waters cover the sea. Pray that millions will be profoundly converted and that the nations will recognise the authority of our mighty King, Jesus, the Christ. Pray over every page of this book and ask and expect God to move powerfully once again. Begin even now to thank Him for doing so!

Finally, the ancient paths are still valid. While the times are changed and the circumstances very different, God is still looking for a people who will humble themselves, pray, seek His face and turn from their wicked ways. He still can and will hear from heaven, forgive their sin and heal their land.

Rev. Richard Owen Roberts,
International Awakening Ministries

Introduction

SCOTLAND arguably has the richest heritage of evangelical revivals of any nation in the world. This bold claim may seem somewhat dubious given that it is Wales, and not Scotland, that has traditionally been termed 'The Land of Revivals'. I am first to acknowledge Wales as owning full rights to the epithet assigned to it, not least given both the smaller size and population of that land. However, the contention reached from my own extensive studies is that no nation on earth has a more varied, colourful or longstanding heritage of evangelical awakenings than Scotland.[1]

Intense and extensive awakenings such as that of the mid-eighteenth century (which had as its central focus Cambuslang), the Kilsyth and Dundee revivals of 1839 (which spread out during succeeding years through many parts of the country), and the even more widespread 1859–61 awakening, are deeply entrenched in the annals of revival history. Furthermore, fresh accounts of their progress or biographies of key leaders have been composed in recent decades, or reprints of past works made available. Details of events surrounding Moody and Sankey's visit to Scotland in 1873–4 are also easily obtainable.

When it comes to post-1880 awakenings, however, there is only one Scottish movement that generally stands out: 'The Lewis Awakening' of 1949–53.[2] Most people, even within the Scottish Church, are largely unaware of the many 'seasons of blessing' – albeit generally of a localised nature – that have occurred all over Scotland during the seventy-year interval between the 'Moody revival' of 1873–4 and that famed Lewis movement of the mid twentieth century.[3] Thankfully, in some cases this deficiency has been partly corrected in recent years. For example, separate studies, from differing angles, on the 'Fishermen's revival' of the

---

1. Another possible contender would be America, though, given the size and population of that country, along with its shorter evangelical legacy, comparisons are hardly adequate. To date no serious history of evangelical revivals in America has been compiled. However, for a unique two-volume academic reference work devoted to the study of revivalism in America and Canada, see Michael J. McClymond (Ed.). *Encyclopedia of Religious Revivals in America*. Westport, Connecticut 2006.

2. Stories of this revival spread largely through the relating of events by Duncan Campbell, the evangelist at the centre of the movement. Campbell became a popular speaker on revival at churches and conventions throughout the U.K., Canada, America and beyond.

3. Commonly regarded as the 'Lewis revival of 1949–52', accumulative evidence shows that it was still burning in one place or another throughout most of 1953 (Victor Maxwell. *A Mission to Millions: The Story of Ernie Allen and the Every Home Crusade*. Belfast 1999 p. 48; Colin and Mary Peckham. *Sounds From Heaven: The Revival on the Isle of Lewis 1949–1952*. Fearn 2004 pp. 68–72; Duncan Campbell. *The Lewis Awakening 1949–1953*.Edinburgh 1954).

early 1920s[4] by Ritchie, Griffin and Mitchell were published in 1983, 1995 and 2000 respectively.[5]

But other than these few significant awakenings, very little in the way of studies of post-Moody revival movements in Scotland has been undertaken. Several popular collections of reports of Scottish revivals were compiled well before 1880.[6] Later narratives offer little or no information on movements after 1875. William Couper, in his superb study, *Scottish Revivals*, which draws frequently on Lundie's project, is an extremely rare work, being printed in a limited edition of only thirty-seven copies. Though published in 1918, it only records movements up to the Moody campaign of 1873–74.[7] Alexander MacRae, in his *Revivals in the Highlands and Islands*, does include some post-1880 material, but the documentation is scanty and stops at 1905.[8] W.D. McNaughton, in a brief overview of his exhaustive studies on Scottish Congregationalism, reveals that 'We hear next to nothing of revival after 1874.'[9] Ian Muirhead composed an insightful paper on revivals in Scotland, but he, too, draws a line under Moody's first Scottish campaign, which, he believed, 'has still the old flavour [of early Presbyterian revivals], but the "use of constituted means" was there, in a vast concentration on detail which lacked little but the more developed scientific technology of a Billy Graham campaign. It is at least arguable', he concludes, 'that this was, for Scotland, the revival to end revivals.'[10] The popular belief is that very few genuine revival movements occurred in Scotland after Moody's 1870s visit. This book seeks to debunk that theory.[11]

---

4. Of which, as short as nine years after its outbreak, it could be said was, 'but a memory of the past' (Peter F. Anson. *Fishing Boats and Fisher Folk on the East Coast.* London 1930 p. 46).

5. Jackie Ritchie, *Floods Upon the Dry Ground*, Peterhead n.d.; Stanley C. Griffin, *A Forgotten Revival: East Anglia and NE Scotland – 1921*, Bromley 1992; George Mitchell, *Revival Man: The Jock Troup Story*, Fearn 2002. In 2000 an account was at last presented of a revival in North Uist in the late 1950s – John Ferguson (Ed.), *When God Came Down: An Account of the North Uist Revival 1957–58*, Inverness 2000.

6. e.g. Mary Lundie, *The History of Revivals of Religion in the British Isles, Especially in Scotland*, Edinburgh 1836; John Gillies, *Historical Collections of Accounts of Revival*, Kelso 1845 (reprinted Edinburgh 1981); Glasgow Revival Tract Society, *Narratives of Revivals of Religion in Scotland, Ireland and Wales*, Glasgow 1839 (reprinted Fearn 1989).

7. W.J. Couper, *Scottish Revivals*, Dundee 1918. This scarce work was recently republished, with additional material, by Richard Owen Roberts (Ed.), *Scotland Saw His Glory: A History of Revivals in Scotland*, Wheaton 1995.

8. Alexander MacRae, *Revivals in the Highlands & Islands in the 19th Century*, Stirling 1906 (reprinted 1998).

9. William D. McNaughton, *Early Congregational Independency in the Highlands and Islands and the North-East of Scotland*, Glasgow, 2003, p. xxix.

10. Ian A. Muirhead, 'The Revival as a Dimension of Scottish Church History,' in *SCHSR* Vol. 20, 1980, p. 196. Speaking of Britain generally, Dr Martyn Lloyd-Jones wrote that before 1870 revivals were frequent in the Church, whereas after that date, 'revivals became rather exceptional phenomena' (D.M. Lloyd-Jones, *The Puritans: Their Origins and Successors*, Edinburgh 1987, p. 4).

11. Globally, J. Edwin Orr wrote of the years 1882 to 1899 as a 'resurgence of the mid-century revival', with a great 'evangelical resurgence' in the Western World, and many outstanding revivals on the mission fields (J. Edwin Orr, *A Call for the Re-study of Revival and Revivalism*, Los Angeles 1981, pp. 33–40).

Often, information on these lesser-known movements has been uncovered only from long out-of-print or relatively obscure books, or from material hidden away in the columns of dusty old newspapers and journals. For some of the movements recorded in these pages, unfortunately, only the barest of information is known. It is very frustrating and disappointing to find allusion to a spiritual awakening and then to be completely unable to obtain more information on it because no fuller record was kept.[12] There have no doubt been many localised Scottish awakenings, perhaps some even in the twentieth century, about which nothing has been passed down and which are now lost in history. There may be others that were not uncovered in the research undertaken for this book. The author would be very grateful to obtain details regarding any such movement.

Information on one major revival movement in particular was gained by means of personal communication. I am referring to the Lewis revival of 1934–9. Although undoubtedly one of the most powerful Scottish revivals of the twentieth century, very little has been written about it and no general study has been compiled. Although at the time of writing most eyewitnesses of this fascinating movement have long passed away, I was yet able to glean a considerable amount of previously unrecorded information from some elderly islanders who had firsthand knowledge of the revival (including several who were converted at that time), and from those who had received firsthand accounts of the movement, such as sons and daughters of those involved in it.

Many evangelical authors, unfortunately, offer naïve, starry-eyed treatments of revivals, ignoring any negative aspects, which as a result often get lost in history. This work seeks to provide as objective a treatment of its subject matter as possible, taking into account any known criticism or negative attribute. For as another revival historian has stated, 'The work of the Holy Spirit can never suffer from fair scrutiny'.[13]

While to read of individual revivals can be most instructive, their grouping together helps to make comparisons, contrasts, and a host of other helpful observations.[14] The author was further encouraged in compiling this volume by the assessment of world revival historian Richard Owen Roberts that a 'more definitive account' of twentieth century movements was greatly needed.[15] Finally, history well attests that the retelling of past revivals can help in the promotion of further periods of spiritual blessing.[16]

---

12. I.H. Murray expresses similar regret when relating the scantiest of details obtainable on a time of refreshing in Dornoch in the early 1830s (Iain H. Murray, *Pentecost Today: The Biblical Basis for Understanding Revival*, Edinburgh 1998, pp. 71–72).

13. Joe Ridholls, 'Spark of Grace: The Story of the Haldane Revival', unpublished paper 1967, p. 40.

14. These observations are studied in Chapter 14: An Appraisal.

15. Roberts, *Scotland Saw His Glory*, p. vii.

16. For instances of this in Scottish history, see Part 5, 'Other Channels of Revival'.

ESTABLISHING A THEORY OF REVIVAL

THE great majority of extant publications on spiritual awakenings have been written by evangelicals and focus on their historical progress or their moral and spiritual aspects. Few of these, comparatively, are of an academic nature. J. Edwin Orr, in his PhD study *The Second Evangelical Awakening*, included a short chapter on 'revival psychology', and, while concluding that the movement followed 'recognisable sociological patterns', believed that these in no way detracted from its divine instigation.[17] Non-evangelical studies tend to see revivals and revivalism as one and the same.[18] William McLoughlin, in *Revivals, Awakenings, and Reform*, speaks of major nationwide awakenings as times of 'revitalisation', reactions by religious conservatives to significant changes in societal structure.[19]

Since the late 1970s, especially, an impressive volume of academic studies on religious revivals has appeared. Many of these have focused on individual scenarios, providing a penetrating insight into the constitution of revivals in particular locations.[20] The most formidable of these in a Scottish context is Kenneth Jeffrey's analysis of the 1858–62 revival in the north-east of the country.[21] There has also been, in recent years, an increasingly revisionist contribution to periods of awakening, especially to the Great Awakening of the eighteenth century.[22]

Almost every book on revivals begins with a definition of terms. Revivals as documented in this book have all occurred within the evangelical tradition.[23] There is general consensus in that tradition

17. J. Edwin Orr, *The Second Evangelical Awakening*, London 1949, pp. 246–250.

18. See Iain H. Murray's discussion of this in *Revival & Revivalism*, p. xix.

19. William G. McLoughlin, *Revivals, Awakenings and Reform: An Essay on Religion and Social Change in America, 1607–1977*, Chicago, 1978, pp. 10, 2.

20. For example, Paul E. Johnson's *A Shopkeeper's Millennium: Society and Revivals in Rochester, New York, 1815–1837*, New York 1978; Edith L. Blumhofer & Randall Balmer (Eds), *Modern Christian Revivals*, Urbana 1993; Kathryn Teresa Long, *The Revival of 1857–58: Interpreting an American Religious Awakening*, New York 1998; Janice Homes, *Religious Revivals in Britain and Ireland 1859–1905*, Dublin 2000.

21. Kenneth S. Jeffrey, *When the Lord Walked the Land: The 1858–62 Revival in the North East of Scotland*, Carlisle 2002. In the same period an increasing number of academic papers on individual revivals have been written, e.g. D.W. Bebbington, 'Revival and the Clash of Cultures: Ferryden, Forfarshire, in 1859,' unpublished paper 2004; Neil Dickson, 'Scottish Brethren and the Welsh Revival,' unpublished paper 2004.

22. See Frank Lambert, *Inventing the Great Awakening*, Princeton, N.J., 1999, who claims that, through preaching and through print, 'skilful and enthusiastic religious promoters' 'created' the phenomenon of national awakening. John Kent's *Wesley and the Wesleyans: Religion in Eighteenth Century Britain* (Cambridge 2002) assumes 'no large-scale religious revival during the 18th century' (back-cover).

23. Communal awakenings with the same characteristics as those considered in this book have also occurred among groups viewed by evangelicals as non-orthodox: e.g. in Ethiopia in the 1970s through missionaries from the United Pentecostal Church (Nona Freeman, *Unseen Hands: The Story of Revival in Ethiopia*, Hazelwood 1987), and through the teachings of a Hindu mystic in India (Francis Younghusband, *Modern Mystics*, London 1935). A series of awakenings also occurred in various Adventist colleges in America between 1967 and 1971 (R.E. Davies, *'I Will Pour Out My Spirit': A History and Theology of Revivals and Evangelical Awakenings*, Tunbridge Wells 1992, pp. 205–206).

that the term 'revival' refers to the quickening of spiritual life among believers, whereas 'awakening' has to do with the conversion of non-Christians in the community. Generally, however, both these scenarios occur together during a move of the Spirit – this was certainly the case in most of the following accounts. Generally, though, I reserve the term 'revival' to occasions that most fit Jones' definition below; often using synonymously, or ascribing to less intense movements, the word 'awakening'; and at other times variably employing phrases such as 'work of grace', 'spiritual outpouring' or 'season of blessing'.

Iain H. Murray states that 'Revivals are larger measures of the Spirit of God.'[24] Duncan Campbell calls revival 'A people saturated with God'.[25] Mark Stibbe regards revival as essentially 'a falling in love with Christ ... like love, it is a mystical, even miraculous, phenomenon requiring more than a merely cerebral explanation.'[26] Arthur Wallis, in his inspiring study *In the Day of Thy Power*, suitably defines revival as 'divine intervention in the normal course of spiritual things. It is God revealing Himself to man in awful holiness and irresistible power. It is such a manifest working of God that human personalities are overshadowed, and human programmes abandoned. It is man retiring into the background because God has taken the field. It is the Lord making bare His holy arm, and working in extraordinary power on saint and sinner ... it has the stamp of Deity upon it, which even the unregenerate and uninitiated are quick to recognise.'[27]

Of all definitions, I think I most like that given by R. Tudor Jones: 'A "religious revival" involves a spiritual "awakening" or "revitilisation" within churches or within an area which contrasts with the smooth flow of daily life. From the Christian perspective, it should be understood as the specific activity of the Holy Spirit deepening people's commitment to God and intensifying their concern about their eternal destiny. Individuals are converted often in large numbers, churches are revitalised and the excitement spreads to surrounding localities. These newly converted or revival Christians become infused with missionary spirit and dedicate themselves to a holy life and not infrequently to cultural and social service.'[28]

It is also the case, however, that 'visitations of God's Spirit' vary in potency and extent. Some revivals are much more sudden and dramatic, and draw far more sinners into the Kingdom, than others. Some revivals are institutional, others regional, and some national

24. Murray, *Pentecost Today?* p. 17.

25. Brian H. Edwards, *Revival: A People Saturated with God*, Darlington 1990, p. 26.

26. Mark Stibbe, 'Seized by the Power of a Great Affection' in Andrew Walker & Kristin Aune (Eds.), *On Revival: A Critical Examination,* Carlisle 2003, p. 25.

27. Arthur Wallis, *In the Day of Thy Power,* Alresford 1956, pp. 20, 23.

28. R. Tudur Jones, *Faith and Crisis of a Nation: Wales, 1890–1914,* Cardiff 2004, p. 283.

or even international. Outpourings of the Spirit vary in degree of influence rather than essence of nature. The accounts that follow are wonderfully varied in time, location, classes of people influenced, extent of impact, and a host of specific features. Each one, however, carries the same essential attributes – many of these are discussed in Part 5 under 'Characteristics of Revivals'.

Because the word 'revival' has so loose a meaning, and is constantly employed by Christians to describe events so diverse in duration, theological meaning and geographical spread,[29] Steve Latham and Andrew Walker have identified six 'R' levels in understanding the term.

- R1: a spiritual quickening of the individual believer.
- R2: a deliberate meeting or campaign especially among Pentecostals to deepen the faith of believers and bring non-believers to faith.
- R3: an unplanned period of spiritual enlivening in a local church, quickening believers and bringing unbelievers to faith.
- R4: a regional experience of spiritual quickening and widespread conversions, e.g. the Welsh, Hebridean, East African and Indonesian revivals
- R5: societal or cultural 'awakenings', e.g. the transatlantic First and Second Awakenings.
- R6: the possible reversal of secularisation and 'revival' of Christianity as such.[30]

The vast majority of revivals considered in this book fit into categories R3 or R4.

REVIVAL AND REVIVALISM

THE majority of textbooks on revival begin with a discussion of what it is not.[31] It is almost universally emphasised that revival is not a series of special evangelistic meetings, whether in a local congregation or on a mass crusade-type scale.[32] Nor is it mere emotional extravaganza. Rather,

29. Rob Warner, 'Ecstatic Spirituality and Entrepreneurial Revivalism,' in Walker & Aune, p. 232.

30. Steve Latham, *God Came from Taman*, in Walker & Aune, p. 172.

31. e.g. Richard Owen Roberts, *Revival,* Wheaton 1991, pp. 15–16; Selwyn Hughes, *Why Revival Waits,* Farnham 2003, pp. 11–16; H.H. Osborn, *Revival, God's Spotlight: The Significance of Revivals and Why They Cease,* Godalming 1996, p. 15; Malcolm McDow & Alvin L. Reid, *Firefall: How God has Shaped History through Revivals,* Nashville 1997, p. 4; Edwards, *Revival,* pp. 25–6.

32. Usage of the term 'revival' in this sense has always been more popular in the U.S.A. than in the U.K., though there are some British examples. A definite revival was noted as having taken place in Lothian Road UFC, Edinburgh in the first two weeks of November 1887, when special nightly meetings were held. The genuineness of this 'revival' has to be doubted, however, for it was also recorded that 'no one could be specially pointed out as having been brought under Christ's saving power for the first time at these meetings' (Alexander H. Mitchell, *The History of Lothian Road United Free Church Congregation,* Edinburgh 1911, pp. 52–3).

revival is seen as an extraordinary movement of the Holy Spirit, something that is 'prayed down', not 'worked up'. Revivalism, on the other hand, is initiated, encouraged and prolonged by the methodology of man.

But such distinction is by no means always clear cut. For one thing, what are often regarded as genuine revivals sometimes appear as a *consequence* of a series of organised evangelistic meetings (at other times it is only after first signs of awakening have become apparent in a community that an evangelist of tact and experience is secured to reap the harvest that seems *already* ripe). Further, as Nigel Wright has shown, 'Divine agency is mediated agency. When God acts, God acts in and through the natural that has been created and given.'[33] One obvious effect in regard to a move of the Spirit is to lessen the truly 'divine' nature of the movement, as both God and fallible humans are involved, making revival 'a mixture of flesh and spirit'.[34]

Related to this, it is important to remember that we all view revivals through particular theological frameworks, or, as Steve Latham puts it, 'We make revival in our own image.'[35] What is seen as 'a genuine move of the Spirit' by one person, group or denomination may be viewed in an entirely different light by another. A secular historian may regard all revivals as mass hysteria or in other sociological terms, ruling God completely out of the picture.[36] Believers from a strong Calvinist tradition view many of the post–1830 evangelical movements in both America and Britain – such as those connected to the ministry of Charles Finney or Dwight Moody – as 'Arminian' in origin and therefore as instances of revivalism rather than Spirit-induced revival,[37] whereas many other evangelical writers place them completely within the framework of authentic revival. While it is usually easy to distinguish between a genuine revival and a successful evangelistic campaign, at times, especially when details are scanty, such distinction is more difficult. The more information one has on a movement, the easier it is to make a valid judgment.

REVIVAL IN THE BIBLE

IRONICALLY, the word 'revival' is never used in the Bible, although the verb 'revive' does appear, viz., Psalm 85:6: 'Will you not revive us again?' The concept of community 'revival', however, finds numerous biblical

33. Nigel Wright, 'Does Revival Quicken or Deaden the Church?' in Walker & Aune, p. 125.

34. Latham, in Walker & Aune, p. 183. See also Carwardine, who argues that the difference between revival and revivalism does not centre on the use of means to an end, but rather on 'the type of means to be employed legitimately' (Richard Carwardine, *Transatlantic Revivalism: Popular Evangelicalism in Britain and America 1790–1865*, Westport 1978, p. 9)

35. Ibid. p. 174.

36. e.g. Bernard Weisberger, *They Gathered at the River*, Chicago 1958, p. 275.

37. Iain H. Murray, *Revival & Revivalism: The Making and Marring of American Evangelicalism 1750–1858*, Edinburgh 1994, p. xviii. Indeed, as its title suggests, the entire book is a discussion of the traditional Reformed distinction between 'old revivals' and 'new [Arminian] methods'.

precedents. Old Testament writers attest to revival during the times of Samuel (1 Sam. 7:1–13:3), Elijah on Mount Carmel (1 Kings 18:1–36), Jonah in Nineveh (Jonah 1:1–4,11), the reforms of Kings Asa and Josiah (2 Chron. 15:1–18 and 2 Kings 22:8–23:3) and the combined post-exilic leadership of Ezra and Nehemiah (Neh. 8:1–11:2). However, it can be argued that while the Holy Spirit was certainly active among God's people in Old Testament times, the abundant outpouring of the Spirit lay in the future.

Hence a better appraisal of revivals in Scripture can be found in the New Testament, beginning with the events of Pentecost, when 'All of them were filled with the Holy Spirit and began to speak in other tongues as the Spirit enabled them' (Acts 2:4). The next few chapters of Acts depict a period in Jerusalem of 'vigorous life, sustained growth, new accessions of spiritual power through new infillings of the Holy Spirit, and the presence of God experienced in an unusual way in miracles of both blessing and judgement'.[38] It is with reason that Dr Martyn Lloyd-Jones noted that 'every period of revival is a returning to what you can read in the book of the Acts of the Apostles'.[39] The remainder of this action-packed Biblical narrative is the story of one revival after another – with resulting persecutions – as the disciples spread out from Jerusalem to surrounding areas, where a dramatic turning to God was experienced throughout Judea, Galilee and Samaria, and, via Paul's tireless endeavours, through the areas of Galatia, Achaia and Macedonia.

HISTORICAL REVIVAL TRADITIONS

CENTRAL to the reasoning of Kenneth Jeffrey's excellent study of the 1858–62 revival in the north-east of Scotland is the proposal that revivals have evolved over time. He argues that three basic models of revival have appeared in Scottish Church history, with all three finding expression in different areas of Aberdeenshire during the period pertaining to his study. In the earliest of these traditions – in rural seventeenth-century Presbyterian Scotland – revivals were seen as spontaneous outbursts of divine favour. They were local community-based movements led principally by the parish minister, whose main tools of employment were the preaching of the Word and the infrequent and profoundly solemn Communion[40] season. Such revivals tended to be fairly protracted affairs (usually lasting many months or even a number of years), as too did the conversion process of individuals affected, which often involved physical

38. R.E. Davies, *I Will Pour Out My Spirit: A History and Theology of Revivals and Evangelical Awakenings,* Tunbridge Wells 1992, p. 50.

39. Dr Martyn Lloyd-Jones, *Revival – Can We Make It Happen?,* Basingstoke 1986, pp. 27–8.

40. Special times in the year when the sacrament of the Lord's Supper was celebrated. In Presbyterian churches, these generally biannual events were of great significance, and were held over a number of days.

manifestations such as weeping and prostrations, though generally in a fairly orderly manner. The typical convert within this tradition might be a church-attending, unmarried female in her early twenties. A brief survey of the Scottish revival movements of the seventeenth and eighteenth centuries, as outlined in chapters 1 and 2 of Jeffrey's book, suggests that the majority of these fall broadly within this early tradition.

A second genre of revival began to appear with the approach of the nineteenth century, and the accelerated growth of Independent congregations such as the Methodists, Baptists and Congregationalists. Awakenings in this category developed with the increased itinerant travels of lay, and often local, preachers among the largely superstitious people of the remote Highlands and Islands, where little or no evangelical presence existed. Generally coming from the same social and intellectual background as their audiences, these evangelists often contextualised their message to fit with the particular conventions of the community. Though the process of conversion was still often a protracted affair, the actual experience of 'new birth' was increasingly viewed as sudden and climatic, based on a 'decision' made by the sinner. This type of revival was invariably short in duration and intense in nature, nearly always involving spontaneous and noisy outbursts of religious enthusiasm. As such, they attracted considerable criticism, and were confined to remote areas such as fishing communities along the north-east coast, where they remained popular till the beginning of the twentieth century.

While the first two models of revival continued to co-exist, by the mid-nineteenth century a new form of evangelistic initiative had developed in Scotland, derived largely from Finney's controversial but incredibly popular 'revivalist' teaching and methodology in the United States. Finney wrote in his *Lectures on Revival of Religion* that, 'a revival is as naturally a result of the use of the appropriate means as a crop is of the use of its appropriate means ... it consists entirely of the right exercise of the powers of nature.'[41] As such, the term 'revival' became increasingly synonymous with a special evangelistic crusade, centred in fast-expanding urban settings. Led by professional itinerant evangelists, these were highly organised affairs, tailor-made to fit in with the working patterns of city-dwellers, and often with special effort made to target specific groups of people. The movements were short in length, and involved the use of the 'anxious seat' at the front of the church, towards which those concerned about their spiritual state were strongly encouraged to move; or an 'inquiry room', where, after the main meeting, they could be counselled individually or as a group. In Scotland, this modern form of revival found its expression in the larger towns and cities during the 1859–61 awakening, but gained almost

41. Murray, *Pentecost Today*, p. 8.

universal acceptance following the visit of Moody in 1873–4. While, as we have seen, revivalism is essentially a different entity from revival, the two may nonetheless co-exist, as would appear to have been the case in some Scottish locations during both the 1859–61 and 1873–4 scenarios. Revivalistic methods saw repeated expression in Scotland's urban centres during the period considered in this book as well as in more recent times.[42]

Overview of Scotland's Revival Legacy[43]

SINCE the Protestant Reformation of the 1500s, itself regarded by historians as a national spiritual awakening, Scotland has witnessed numerous seasons of revival in each successive century right up to the end of the last millenium. Two of the most famed of seventeenth-century revivals were those that occurred in the Ayrshire town of Stewarton in 1625 and that five years later in Kirk O' Shotts, to the east of Glasgow. The latter, like many of Scotland's early revivals, centred around the soul-searching occasion of the Presbyterian Communion season.

A remarkable revival movement commenced the following century in Cambuslang, served by William McCulloch. Associated with it was trans-Atlantic evangelist George Whitefield, who preached to over 25,000 at a Communion in July 1742. Soon the movement had extended to Kilsyth, where its progress was equally dramatic; to Glasgow and the south-west; to Perthshire; and as far north as Sutherland and Easter Ross.

The tireless evangelistic tours of Perthshire-born aristocrat James Haldane were a significant influence in the awakening that coursed through much of the Highlands and Islands from the turn of the nineteenth century. Revival broke out in Moulin, near Pitlochry, in 1799, being followed some years later by a deep movement in Perthshire's Breadalbane district, as well as in the islands of Arran and Skye. From the late 1820s a powerful flood of spiritual outpouring largely dispersed the cloud of spiritual darkness engulfing other western isles, particularly Lewis and Harris. The labours of John MacDonald of Ferintosh (the *'Apostle of the North'*) had significant impact on several of these movements.

It was not until 1838 that a further marked and widespread movement took place in the Lowlands. Beginning in Kilsyth, it quickly spread to Dundee and subsequently radiated through most of Scotland, from Aberdeenshire to the Western Isles; from the Borders to the Northern

42. e.g. in the work of William Ross of Cowcaddens (1883–1904), in the urban campaigns of Gipsy Smith, Torrey and Alexander and Wilbur Chapman (all referred to in this study), and more recently during the Billy Graham rallies of the 1950s.

43. For a detailed, comprehensive study of evangelical awakenings in Scotland from the Reformation up to the close of the decade of Moody's visit in 1873–4, see the author's forthcoming work, *Scotland: Land of Revivals – Evangelical Awakenings in Scotland 1527–1880.*

Isles. A young William Chalmers Burns played a pivotal role in the spread of this movement, hot on the heels of which, and strongly connected to it, came the Disruption of 1843, which was itself accompanied by several significant revivals, especially in West Highland and Island areas like Knapdale and North Uist.

The general awakening of 1858–61, greatly influenced by revival fires sweeping across Ulster, is by far the most extensive revival movement in the history of Scottish evangelical awakenings, extending to every county in the land. Locations especially blessed were Aberdeen, Saltcoats and Ardrossan, The Wynds (Glasgow), Carrubbers Close (Edinburgh), North Ayrshire, Annan and Dumfries, Cellardyke, Ferryden, the Moray and Banffshire coast and Sanday (Orkney). For the first time in Scotland, laymen, such as Reginald Radcliffe, Duncan Matheson and Brownlow North, undertook a large share of the work.

The dominant revival movement of the late 1800s was, of course, that connected to the labours of Moody and Sankey in 1873–4, first in Edinburgh and Glasgow, then in many towns throughout the country. Revival also spread to many localities the Americans did not visit, such as the quiet Aberdeenshire parishes of Cornhill and Drumblade, and the Western isle of Tiree.

The purpose of this book is to show that Scotland's striking revival heritage did not stop with Moody and Sankey's visit, but continued well into the twentieth century. This account of Scottish evangelical awakenings from 1880 to 1940 is not exhaustive, but does seek to provide a reasonably comprehensive account of the most significant movements that then occurred, representing instances of genuine spiritual revival as opposed to merely emotion-based revivalism. Diverse in nature as well in geographical location, these spiritual movements take in, variably, each of the three revival traditions referred to in the previous section. Most of them were localised affairs, confined to one or two communities, while one or two were considerably more widespread. It is significant that revivals in the Western Isles continued to occur right through our period of study and beyond. Here, more alert to the dangers of revivalist activity, with its emphasis on human will and emotions, the Church remained relatively unaffected by the changing religious culture prevalent elsewhere.

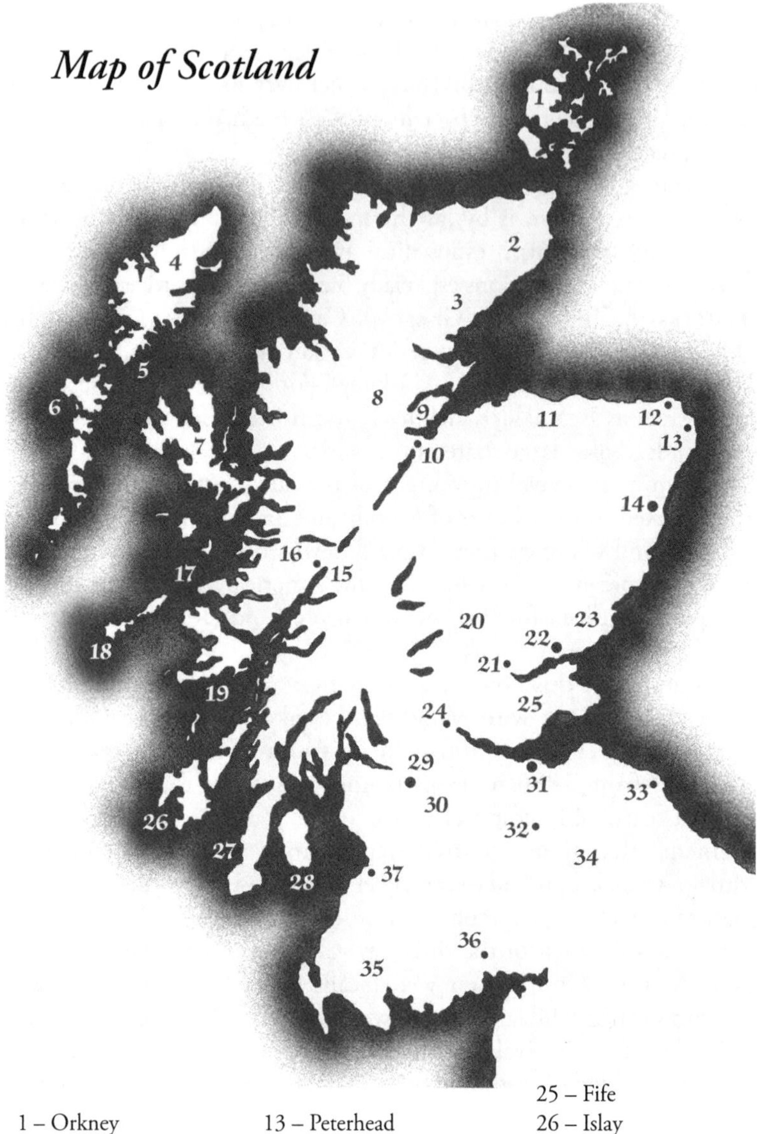

1 – Orkney
2 – Caithness
3 – Sutherland
4 – Lewis
5 – Harris
6 – North Uist
7 – Skye
8 – Easter Ross
9 – Black Isle
10 – Inverness
11 – Moray Coast
12 – Fraserburgh
13 – Peterhead
14 – Aberdeen
15 – Fort William
16 – North Argyll
17 – Ardnamurchan
18 – Tiree
19 – Mull
20 – Perthshire
21 – Perth
22 – Dundee
23 - Angus
24 – Stirling
25 – Fife
26 – Islay
27 – Kintyre
28 – Arran
29 – Glasgow
30 – Lanarkshire
31 – Edinburgh
32 – Peebles
33 – Eyemouth
34 – Borders
35 – Dumfries & Galloway
36 – Dumfries
37 – Ayr

Part One

GLORY FILLED THE LAND

In this dear land, in days of yore,
God moved in mighty power.
His Word He blessed, and souls found rest
When Scotland was on fire.
Once more, Lord, once more,
As in the days of yore.
On this dear land Thy Spirit pour,
Set Scotland now on fire! [1]

1. A popular chorus sung by Scottish believers in the 1920s (James A. Stewart, *Opened Windows: The Church and Revival*, Asheville, NC 1958, pp. 123–4).

Introduction

THE Church in Scotland at the start of the 1880s was in a state of flux. The Established Church had made up some ground in the forty years since the mass exit from its ranks in the Disruption of 1843, although throughout the Highlands the Free Church retained the allegiance of the vast majority of inhabitants. But the Presbyterian Church faced a number of problems – particularly the steady erosion of Calvinism, the theological structure that had undergirded Scottish Presbyterianism since the Reformation. Certainly Arminianism had made its unwelcome presence north of the border ever since John Wesley's first visit in 1751. But the filtering of Finney's revivalist techniques from the late 1830s, along with the rise of lay preaching that attended the 1859–61 revival, led to Arminianism making more serious inroads on Calvinism.

The strongest blow of all came with Moody's campaign in the 1870s. Though claiming to be essentially a Calvinist, much of his methodology came from the New School of theology. Although he still taught the necessity of repentance, gone was the hell-fire preaching for which Scottish evangelists were renowned. In its place were shorter sermons with a warm appeal to come to a loving Saviour, and emphasis on assurance of salvation through faith and the certainty and joyousness of heaven as a result. In addition, Moody helped give the doctrine of universal atonement a wide appeal where it previously never had such. He also made use of inquiry rooms and emphasised 'immediate salvation'. Each of these features was hugely controversial, and John Kennedy of Dingwall went as far as claiming that Moody's message constituted 'another gospel'. But each feature was nevertheless to become more frequently employed in the Scottish Church in the years ahead.

Similarly, while 'human hymns' had been the source of heated debate in Presbyterian circles for some time, the popularity of Sankey's hymns was a leading factor in their widespread acceptance in Presbyterian worship. Likewise his use of a 'kist of whistles' proved to be hugely popular wherever he travelled, and just two years after his Scottish visit the Established Church gave its formal sanction to the use of the organ in public worship, while by 1880 organs were being installed in most Presbyterian churches. The enduring results of the Americans' visit were therefore very considerable.

Presbyterianism was also facing growing competition from all sides. The Baptists, previously a small and uninfluential group, were becoming increasingly popular and respectable, and they exerted a strong evangelistic thrust in the late Victorian period. Equally vigorous in outreach was the Brethren, who had gained huge ground through the revivals of 1859–61 and 1873–4 and who continued to labour tirelessly for new recruits. Other groups rearing their heads in the closing decades of the nineteenth century were the Salvation Army and the Faith Mission, while, in the early years of the following century, a string of Pentecostal groups began to appear. All were fervently evangelistic.

Each group found the going tough, for there appeared a growing disinterest on behalf of the public generally. For one thing, increased opportunities for educational betterment resulted in improvements in literacy, and the combined effect of these was more independent and critical reasoning. The popularising of Darwin's theory of evolution and its discussion in the Press and popular literature was another source of growing mistrust in a plenary interpretation of Scripture. Added to this was the strengthening of geological understanding that the earth's creation could hardly be explained in terms of the literal seven-day period assumed in Genesis. Another major cause for concern was developments in biblical scholarship. The discipline of Higher Criticism had, by the late 1800s, largely undermined the fundamental belief that the Bible was a single inspired text to be recognised as the inerrant word of God. Advances in other disciplines, too, such as anthropology, psychology and comparative religions, all served to cast doubt upon standard evangelical beliefs.

Other explanations suggested for increasing apathy towards the Church were the controversial system of pew rents, which discouraged those on low pay, and, for those living in cities, the general conditions of urban life, where poor housing, poverty and alcohol addiction left families feeling too demoralised to even desire any association with Church, whose congregations and ministers were in any case predominantly from the middle classes. Drinking was seen by the Churches as the main cause of poverty and crime among the lower classes. Though vigorous campaigns by the church and some secular groups helped to dramatically curb the level of alcohol consumption by the 1860s, drinking remained a substantial problem in Scotland. Temperance societies became prolific; the Band of Hope, which had both a secular and religious face, had only seven branches in 1871. By 1887 this had increased to 570, and to 700 (and 147,000 members) by 1908.

A further reason for increased disassociation from Church was the extra leisure time that increased prosperity brought. Cinema, theatre and music halls were all gaining appeal around this time, while the working class amusements of football and dancing became a central focus of attack. Football had already attracted a massive following from the late 1870s, and, as the 'new opiate of the people', was especially frowned upon, probably because it created the same quasi-religious feelings of enthusiasm and loyalty that the faithful felt ought to be directed solely to the Church.

It is important to remember, however, that most of the concerns so far discussed led to a gradual ebbing away of church attendance rather than a sudden landslide. In fact, Church statistician Dr Peter Brierley has estimated that overall church adherence, based on membership or active involvement together with Sunday school attendance, all relative to population, reached its peak as late as 1905.[2] At that point over half the Scottish population belonged to some Christian body.

In fact there existed great optimism among evangelicals, especially during the first half of our period of study. The religious excitement created by the 1859–61 revival, with its resulting swathes of conversions, served to engender confidence and enthusiasm. This, combined with the recent obvious success of the Moody campaign, led to a proliferation of lay evangelists making repeated preaching tours around the country during the latter part of the nineteenth century and into the early decades of the twentieth. There was a great pervasive longing to capture something of the magic of the 'golden days' of 1859 and 1874. Revivalism, with its reliance on methods and its appeal to the emotions, had become a mighty force. But while to many this suggested a healthy religious condition, in truth it was a determined attempt to combat increasing indifference to the Church from the populace at large.

What is generally overlooked in regard to this era is that, although revivalist forces had become the new, popular and easier way to pull in converts, the old style 'outpourings of the Spirit', which had rained on sections of the Scottish Church from time to time from centuries past, had by no means altogether disappeared.[3] On the contrary, evangelical awakenings of a more spontaneous and orthodox nature (Jeffrey's models 1 & 2) continued to arise in one part of Scotland or another almost without intermission right up to the mid 1920s.[4] From that time onwards they appeared on a much more irregular basis, except in Lewis, where they continued through the 1930s and 1940s, and indeed, right up to the 1980s.

---

2. Peter Brierley and Fergus MacDonald, *Prospects for Scotland 2000: Trends and Tables from the 1994 Scottish Church Census,* Edinburgh 1995, p. 16.

3. Contrary to the view of one Scottish minister who remarked that 'no one born after World War 1 has witnessed a genuine revival' (related by John Armstrong in *Revival, What is it Really?*, quoted in J.D. King, *Written Not with Ink But With the Spirit: Introduction to Revival Literature with Anotated Bibliography,* Kansas City 2005, p. 69).

4. Globally, J. Edwin Orr wrote of the years 1882 to 1899 as a 'resurgence of the mid-century revival' (*A Call for the Re-study of Revival and Revivalism,* Los Angeles 1981, pp. 33–40). This assessment accords well with the situation in Scotland, where, almost without intermission from 1859 to the close of the century and beyond, there was a steady stream of revivals occurring in one place or another.

1
The Glorious Eighties
1880–9

1880–5

South Lanarkshire 1880–3

WHEN James McKendrick surrendered his life to Christ at the age of twenty-two, he little realised what major effect such decision would have, not just upon himself, but on the lives of thousands of others throughout Scotland and beyond. Born in 1859 in the coal-mining village of Old Carnbroe, Lanarkshire, and raised in the Haughead district of the more prosperous mining centre of Hamilton, McKendrick, like so many boys of his time, left school to take up work in the mines at the age of just nine. Mining was a hazardous occupation for even the most experienced of workers and James was never far from danger. Once he miraculously escaped death when the roof of the coalmine he was working in fell in.[1] In those days mining accidents, often of a fatal nature, were commonplace

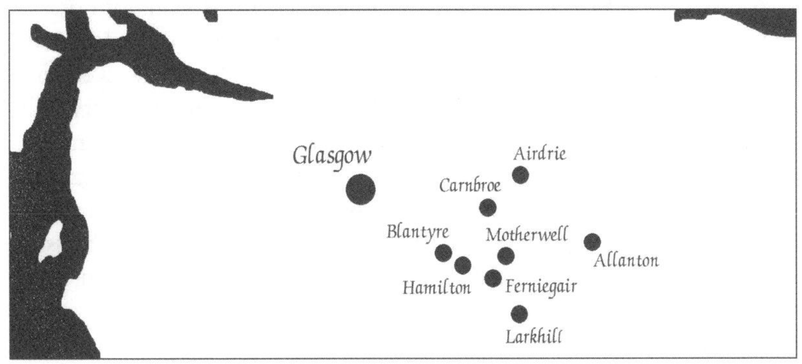

and miners were well aware of the precarious nature of their vocation. Indeed, in October 1877, nearby Blantyre – birthplace of renowned missionary and explorer David Livingstone – re-entered the history books as being the unfortunate location of the worst ever Scottish mining disaster, when a tragic explosion in Pit 3 killed 216 men and boys.[2] This

1. James McKendrick, *What We Have Seen & Heard During Twenty-Five Years' Evangelistic Labours*, Arbroath 1914, pp. 17–20.

2. Ibid. p. 32. McKendrick suggests the death toll in this accident was as high as 350.

was followed, just five months later, by an overwinding accident in the same Lanarkshire colliery, snatching a further six lives. Then, a year later, in July 1879, there occurred yet another tragedy, when nearly thirty men and boys met early deaths. These chilling events shocked the Scottish nation and remained fresh in people's minds for years afterwards.

The transience of life was further brought to McKendrick's own youthful mind when, in May 1881, his beloved father was killed outright under the falling impact of a huge stone several tons in weight. Startlingly aware that if it had been he who was taken, he would have died without Christ, and feeling keenly his responsibilities as eldest son to his mother and six siblings, James underwent deep conviction regarding his own unrighteousness and need for God. Coming through to a place of spiritual peace soon after, McKendrick immediately became an eager witness for the gospel. His first attempt at public preaching – among his very own neighbours – left him utterly embarrassed. 'I was speechless, and could not find a word to say. Yet my soul was on fire for their salvation. My first relief was a flood of tears, not words. At length I cried out; "All unsaved in this house are going to hell."'[3] Urging them to find immediate rest in Christ, McKendrick yet knew that never was there a more imperfect attempt at preaching but also that never was there anything more sincere. However much lacking in tact, his direct words and obvious passion made strong impact on those listening, and 'that night the work of God's grace had begun in many hearts'.[4]

A season of revival ensued with almost daily conversions, and in the space of seven months over 100 had professed Christ as Lord. This in one small village, the entire character of which was altered. McKendrick said that until Haughead's first church was erected shortly afterwards, it was a sight to behold over 200 people making their way to Hamilton to attend one of the Sunday services held there. Revival blessing soon spread to Ferniegair, Allanton and many other villages in the area that had hitherto seemed impervious to the gospel message. Such blessing continued right through to 1887, with considerable impact also being made on the town of Hamilton itself.[5]

One early case which greatly encouraged the young evangelist in his efforts was that of a young man who had been brought up 'amidst scenes of deepest darkness and awful wickedness. I knew him from his boyhood', recalled McKendrick. 'He may be said to have revelled in sin. His oaths and cursing often terrified and chilled me, and before he was twelve years of age I have seen him go down on his knees, and clasp his hands, look up to heaven, and blaspheme God in a way that made one

3. Ibid.

4. Ibid. p. 33.

5. Ibid., pp. 34–47.

shudder. When his stock of oaths and imprecations were exhausted, he would repeat them backwards. By the time he was sixteen years of age he was only sober when he could not get drink, and he just revelled in fighting, drinking, and blaspheming. His conversion and transformed life were, therefore, arguments that none could gainsay, and it filled us with the confidence that, since God had saved J.H., we need not despair of even the most hardened sinners.'[6] This movement served to act as a foretaste of things to come in young McKendrick's life. For the zealous evangelist quickly developed as a preacher of some renown and went on to ignite a glorious wave of revival right across the north-east coast of Scotland (see pp. 206–13).

Larger neighbouring towns in South Lanarkshire also partook of revival blessing in the early eighties. George Sharpe, then a seventeen-year-old clerk from the village of Craigneuk, records that in and around Motherwell in the spring of 1882, 'a revival was on. Street marching and street meetings were in evidence every day of the week. Miners, steel workers and factory hands were testifying to salvation and preaching the gospel of the grace of God.' Sharpe was 'virtually drawn into a hall with unwashed floors, ungarnished walls and dirty seats. … One could not consider the crowd that filled the place reverent. The preacher was neither scholastic nor eloquent, but he believed in the Bible and tremendously stressed the need of salvation for all men through Jesus Christ'.[7] Sharpe found himself moving to the penitent form, kneeling on the dirty floor and giving his life to Christ.

In 1880 churches in Wishaw were suffering from the general depression of trade in the area, to the extent that fully half of the eleven elders in the Free Church had been removed from the town in the past eighteen months. Although almost nightly evangelistic work was being carried on, the outward result remained small. Despite this, and the great devotedness and earnestness of a large number in the congregation, Free Church officials visiting the place in 1880 reported that, 'the result is not so great as might be expected, apparently because of the want of church interest and a tendency to prefer merely spasmodic efforts to those of regular and organised church life on the part of many who ought to be the strength and activity of the congregation'.[8] Later that year there was

---

6. Ibid., pp. 36–37.

7. Rev. George Sharpe, *This Is My Story*, Glasgow n.d., pp. 8–9. Over the next few years, up to the time of his departure for America in 1886, Sharpe attended an annual Christian conference, where he was 'thrilled again and again as the preachers gave their reports telling of great revivals in their churches, of transformed lives and of additions to their membership. These were great days for the Kingdom of our Lord Jesus Christ. The emphasis was ever on salvation for sinners and holiness for believers.' He believed, however, that with the steady advance of moderatism, especially from the mid-1880s, 'the fervour of evangelism waned' and 'revival fires burned with less intensity' (pp. 12–13).

8. Appendix to the *Report of the Committee of the Free Church of Scotland on the State of Religion & Morals* (hereafter ARC-FCS-SR&M), 1880, p. 21.

a significant change in the spiritual atmosphere, and in May 1883 the Wishaw minister could declare that, 'For the past two years and a half a work of grace has been going on in the congregation under the ordinary preaching of the Word. I have a list of over 100 who have continued to give satisfactory evidence of a real change. Among that number are some very striking cases – cases of men and women who had never been in a place of worship from childhood, and of others who for 15 years and more were drunkards.'[9]

Meanwhile, in nearby Larkhall, a visit by Brethren evangelist William Montgomery in 1883 was long remembered. 'Quite a revival took place when both saint and sinner received blessing. And not only were young converts seeking to be baptised but a few believers who had come into fellowship unbaptised were stirred up to the realisation of a joy which up to that time had not been theirs. One Sunday afternoon 14 brethren were baptised in the River Avon at Millheugh, when a vast crowd gathered on the bridge and along the banks of the river to witness this unique spectacle. People came from the neighbouring villages and it is estimated that about 2,000 people were present.'[10]

MULL 1881

WITH the spread of reports of a dramatic revival in Stornoway in 1880 under the ministry of Donald John Martin (see pp. 267–72), the Stornoway minister was invited to preach in various places, including Ardnamurchan and Mull. Soon after his visit to Mull a state of expectancy was more or less awakened in Kilmore Free Church, and special services were initiated. Of the numerous professions of faith, nearly all were from young men, 'some of them occupying important positions'.[11] A considerable number of these began to meet every Sabbath morning for pre-church prayer. Similarly, across the sound, in Ardnamurchan, where special services were also held, 'a deep religious feeling' prevailed, and Rev. Campbell of the local Free Church gave interesting accounts of conversions of which he was aware. As to the effect of the awakening, Rev. Ross of Tobermory opined, 'If eagerness to hear the word of God, and apparent meltings of

9. Ibid., 1880, p. 21. Around the same time twenty miles further west, the minister of Nitshill FC claimed that 'while there has been a decrease of population there has been an increasing interest in spiritual things. During the month of September last, a series of special meetings was held, when the church was filled night after night; and since then the manse has been visited time after time by anxious inquirers after salvation, and in several cases it has been the birthplace of souls' (RC-FCS-SR&M 1883, p. 5). The fruits of this movement were noted to be still in full blossom in 1888 (ibid. 1888).

10. From that time considerable development marked the forward movement of the testimony of this Lanarkshire stronghold, a pleasing feature being a progressive work amongst the young. In 1940 the register of the joint Sunday schools contained the names of nearly 1,000 children (David Beattie, *Brethren: The Story of a Great Recovery*, Kilmarnock 1940, p. 210.)

11. *RC-FCS-SR&M* 1881, pp. 4–5.

soul under it, are signs of a revival of God's work, then certainly we have these in Kilmore. I have heard some old people say that they never saw the people there so eager to hear the word preached.'[12]

In similar manner, Oban was spiritually stirred following Martin's week-long visit in February 1881.[13] Thirty-seven professed 'to rest on Christ and his blood', this number rising to around fifty by April. At the May Communion, twenty-five people were added to the Roll of the Oban Free Church, where the Rev. John MacKay was minister.[14] Special services in Connell Ferry, six miles distant, were also wonderfully blessed. Indeed, one minister stated his belief that the whole west coast was at that time in a very hopeful state spiritually.[15] Meanwhile, a work of grace was reported from Kilchrenan, on the banks of Loch Awe, in the winter of 1880–1. The Free Church station there had reached a low ebb of spiritual life, but the tide of blessing was seen to turn and the meeting-house at Dalavich became regularly filled to overflowing.[16]

Falkirk 1882

A MOST interesting movement spread through West Lothian in 1882. In Armadale, within the Free Church (the denomination most strongly affected), that year was described as 'the most pleasant we have spent'. Whereas, usually, around half-a-dozen would join the church at each Communion, the figure for May 1882 was 22 and for November, 29; making 51 hopefully converted in all. Another congregation reported 'a great stirring up among Christians', with one old man who had been a member since 1843 only then brought to the Lord. One minister reported 'quite an awakening' within his flock, where, by special meetings conducted mainly by himself, 32 joined his church, 21 being from the non-church-going community. Another minister noted that membership and attendance at ordinances were larger in 1882 than during any previous period in his ministry.[17]

---

12. Ibid.

13. In a letter to *The Christian*, Martin professes that 'the blessing seems to be all round. Inverness, Oban, Mull are sharing in it.' Of his visit to Inverness it was recorded that 'On Tuesday, Jan 25th, especially, the Word was with great power, and a goodly number of stricken ones remained to the after-meeting and found peace in believing.' Martin's visit was followed by a three-week campaign by John B. Bain (*The Christian*, 4 April 1881, p. 15).

14. John J. Murray, *The Church on the Hill: Oban Free High Church: A History and Guide,* Oban 1984, p. 11. Indeed, there was remarkable growth in this congregation during MacKay's ministry there from 1876 to 1883, when he transferred to Cromarty. In that seven-year period the Communion roll grew from 150 to 272, a rise of 81%. It was during this same period – in 1877 – that C.H. Spurgeon paid a visit to Oban, where he preached to a congregation of 3,000 on the slopes of Oban Hill, next to the Free Church. Further 'tidings of revival' were reported from this Highland town in 1893 (*RC-FCS-SR&M* 1894, p. 12).

15. Ibid. 1881, p. 5.

16. *Proceedings of the General Assembly of the Free Church of Scotland for the Highlands & Islands* (hereafter *PGA-FCS-H&I*) p. 9.

17. *RC-FCS-SR&M* 1883, pp. 8–10.

The most notable 'work of revival' seems to have taken place in Falkirk. Previous to 1882, the discouraged Free Church minister spoke of 'scarcely a young man' in his congregation 'manifesting any desire to do anything to advance the cause of Christ in the place.'[18] Prayer was strongly encouraged and as he sensed God moving among the people, the minister invited any who were anxious to visit the manse. A large number did so – especially young men – including many from the 'better class'. Deeply convicted, all bar one seemed to enter into true rest in Christ. When over thirty such cases had been dealt with, special services were conducted under auspices of the Y.M.C.A., being led by converted actor George Williams. It was said that no deeper spiritual movement had ever occurred in the town. Ninety-four people joined the Free Church in one year, most for the first time, including five members about to be struck off the roll by the Kirk Session if no improvement in their character was found. In each case the proposed action now proved unnecessary.

Recorded the minister, 'A miner and his wife were admitted to the Lord's Table with us yesterday. He had been a rough, wild fellow, but underwent a decided change about three months ago. He had not been baptised, but was willing to confess Christ anywhere. Last Sabbath I baptised him in public. It was a solemn service, and made a deep impression upon the people.'[19]

It was during this same time that independent evangelist John Livingstone was working with untiring energy in Camelon, just outside Falkirk. Here soon the Mission Hall, which had previously been next to empty, became teeming with new life. The movement in Falkirk increased further the demand for Livingstone's assistance all over the area. Instead of standing alone on the streets to witness, Livingstone soon was joined by a band of eager believers; young men and women keen to share in the trying work. One of these fellows was to prove an able helpmeet once again in Livingstone's closing years, as he laboured 'with the powers of darkness in the Gallowgate of Aberdeen'.[20]

In Camelon, 'one of the open-air meetings was held in a place where the dwellers showed very little interest. Sabbath after Sabbath the songs and words seemed to beat simply upon blank walls and closed doors and windows. Nobody looked or seemed to listen, and nobody seemed to care; but the missionary refused to be discouraged, and week after week the meeting went on. One of the houses was a licensed grocer's shop, the owner of which was a widow who had developed a taste for her own wares, and was fast drinking herself into bankruptcy. The unexpected often happens. She was probably in many respects the most hopeless case in the street. Yet it was to her that

18. Ibid. pp. 8–9.

19. Ibid. p. 10.

20. Anonymous, *A Faithful Minister: Being Memorials of the Rev. John Livingstone, Gallowgate U.F. Church, Aberdeen*, Aberdeen 1910, p. 22.

the Word of God came with saving power. She related afterwards how she gradually became interested; how the word of truth pierced her conscience, until, with a burdened heart she used to weary for the hour of meeting. Sabbath after Sabbath she used to sit on the floor of her parlour, behind the window curtains, and wait for the singing and preaching to begin. At last the word of deliverance came. She was set free from her galling bondage, and openly confessed her faith in Christ. ... It was worth years of toil to win such a trophy for the Saviour, to make a sin-laden life a new centre for the cleansing and healing influences of the Gospel.'[21]

DUNKELD 1882

DWIGHT L. Moody and Ira D. Sankey returned to Scotland at the close of 1881, eight years after their remarkable first visit. With an initial schedule not dissimilar to that first campaign, they stayed for six weeks in Edinburgh followed, at the start of 1882, by five months of outreach in Glasgow. In both cities their return was greeted with 'an outburst of popularity'.[22] *The Christian* reported that the crowd 'blocked the streets for hours and the excitement penetrated the meeting to such an extent that an inquiry meeting was not even attempted'. The article continued: 'other revival movements seem to have flourished on excitement, but this is at once killed by it; and instead of taking advantage of heated occasions, Mr Moody waits for the night of quiet power and the whisper of the still small voice.'[23]

From Glasgow, Andrew Bonar noted that 'beyond question now another wave of blessing has come'.[24] He spoke of 'several localities in the neighbourhood in which the work of God has been remarkably helped forward within these few months ... and the rain is still falling'.[25] Sabbath meetings were held in St Andrew's Hall, exclusively for women in the afternoons, and for men in the evenings. Both meetings were regularly packed to capacity, i.e., with around 5,000 people. Inquiry meetings would follow the main service, and there, Sabbath after Sabbath, for many weeks, hundreds of earnest seekers after rest and peace were pointed to Christ.[26] A great effort was made to follow up professions of

21. Ibid. pp. 22–3. It appears to have been during this period of awakening that 'Mr T.C.', later a successful evangelist with the Evangelisation Society and remarkably used in Busby in 1885 (for more information, see www.scottishrevivals.co.uk), was converted (John Wood, *The Story of the Evangelisation Society*, London 1907, pp. 100–102). He was arrested initially by the sound of a group singing hymns on the street, then brought to the truth through a gospel service and after-meeting in the Evangelical Union Church, led by the Rev. G. Bell.

22. John Pollock, *Moody Without Sankey*, London 1963 (reprinted 1995), p. 228.

23. *The Christian*, quoted in ibid. p. 228.

24. Marjory Bonar, *Andrew A. Bonar: Diary and Life*, Edinburgh 1893 (reprinted 1961), p. 333.

25. *RC-FCS-SR&M* 1882, p. 5.

26. Ibid. p. 6.

faith, and several thousand names were thus registered, many promptly attaching themselves to a church.[27]

Despite the success of this mission, virtually all revival historians and Moody biographers agree that there weren't nearly 'such outward and visible results'[28] in 1881–2 as came from the 1873–4 campaign.[29] Regarding the later visit, Principal MacGreggor of Trinity College, Glasgow accepted that 'there was the prestige of the former triumphs. There was a quickened expectation and desire, and yet, in spite of amazing things done at that second visit, there was nothing like the same sweep and spontaneity as in the earlier mission.'[30] R.W. Dale of Birmingham agreed. According to him, Moody, in his earlier mission, 'exulted in the free grace of God', whereas now the emphasis seemed to be more on 'repentance', which had a far less dramatic effect on his audience.[31] 'And where are the shining faces we had before?' he asked.[32]

During the early summer of 1882, Moody travelled to a number of towns in northern Scotland. There are no reports of revival in connection with this tour, although a movement in Perthshire was very much related to his mission in Scotland during this period. Rev. MacPherson of the Free Church in Dunkeld gave a report to the General Assembly in 1882 regarding the 'manifestations of divine favour' which his congregation were currently enjoying. During the previous twelve months he had seen more earnest, united, believing prayer in his church than in any past year of his ministry, and an increased spiritual interest, generally.

The work had its beginnings about the end of March 1882, when MacPherson paid a week-long visit to Glasgow in order to witness

---

27. Ibid. p. 10. J.G. Govan, later founder of the Faith Mission, remembers as a boy attending around forty of Moody's 1882 Glasgow meetings with his father, who was 'closely associated' with them. These meetings greatly stirred the young Govan, and for the first time he began to speak to people about their souls and to feel his own need for greater spiritual blessing (J.G. Govan, *In the Train of His Triumph: Reminiscences of the Early Days of the Faith Mission,* Edinburgh, n.d. p. 9).

28. Pollock, *Moody Without Sankey,* p. 228.

29. As plain evidence of this see the contrasting reports given of the 1873–4 campaign and those of 1882, as well as of Moody's third mission to Scotland in 1891, in J.M., *Recollections of Mr D.L. Moody and his Work in Britain, 1874–1892,* Edinburgh 1901, pp. 11–54, 106–52, 260–70.

30. Various, *Report of the Proceedings at a Great United Meeting Held Under the Auspices of the Glasgow United Evangelistic Association, the Christian Churches and the Christian Organisations for Youth Welfare in the St Andrew's Hall, Glasgow on Monday, 8th February, 1937 to Celebrate the Centenary of the Birth of Dwight L. Moody* (Moody Centenary Celebrations), Glasgow 1937, p. 44.

31. Quoted in Harry Sprange, *Kingdom Kids: Children in Revival,* Fearn 1993, pp. 260–61. A revised edition of this book was reprinted in 2002 as *Children In Revival: 300 Years of God's Work in Scotland.*

32. As a dramatic witness to the contrast between Moody's first two British missions, Dale reported that in 1875 he added over 200 converts to his Birmingham church as a result of Moody's mission there; whereas less than a dozen members were added following the 1882 campaign. 'Of course,' he continued, 'that period did not wholly lack its shining faces, but there was not the same striking demonstrations of the power of God Himself. The lesson which comes to us from it all is the lesson of profound humility, and of this need of looking up simply towards God. … We may organise and plan and often with sadly small results; but "Except the Lord build the house, they labour in vain who build it" (Various, *Moody Centenary Celebrations,* p. 44).'

the work carried on by Moody. (He had been unwell and thus unable to attend meetings during the Americans' first visit to Scotland in 1873–4.) Greatly impressed with what he saw in the metropolis, and taking a little part himself in the work, MacPherson returned home to begin a series of evangelistic meetings, at which he shared his impressions of the Glasgow movement, and at which the evangelist Major Oldham of India also spoke. 'After the first night or two,' wrote MacPherson, 'when scarcely any responded to the appeal, considerable numbers remained under deep conviction of sin, some sobbing bitterly, others oppressed with the burden of guilt and sin, and several Christians, of whom we had little doubt that they were God's children, earnestly seeking refuge from doubt and assurance of salvation. One could not but be deeply impressed with the altered countenances lit up with radiance and joyfulness as soon as the soul embraced Christ in the fullness of His grace and love.'[33] In almost every family an interest in divine things was awakened, and in virtually every one at least one member professed to have found Christ, sometimes two or three. Other Presbyterian churches, and even the Episcopal Church to an extent, shared in the blessing, while the Free Church ministers of Cargill, Strathbraan, Cluny and Markinch also gave aid. In all, 62 were added to the Communion roll of Dunkeld Free Church between 1882 and 1884.[34]

DUNS 1883–4

THE Berwickshire parish of Chirnside can claim a spiritual pedigree reaching back to the Covenanting times, and there the Covenanters held their largest Communion service, with no fewer than 3,000 communicants. The county seat of Duns is remembered for being the birthplace of three eminent churchmen of different centuries: Franciscan theologian and philosopher John Duns Scotus (1266–1308), Calvinist theologian Thomas Boston (1676–1732) and Scottish Church historian Thomas McCrie (1772–1835). During the nineteenth century Duns became a stronghold of the UPC, who formed three congregations in the town. But the Free Church was also prominent in the area, and in 1880 there existed a total of eleven congregations within the Free Church Presbytery of Duns and Chirnside.

With the hope of spiritual blessing in an area with a meagre record of revivals, a series of evangelistic meetings was arranged for each of the eleven Free Church congregations during 1883–4. Spiritual life in virtually all of these places was quickened and deepened. In Duns, where the meetings were carried on for five weeks under auspices of the Evangelistic Association in the town – the outcome of a season of revival some years previously – the work was one of extraordinary power and extent. 'Not only the

33. *RC-FCS-SR&M* 1882, p. 2.

34. Ibid. 1885, p. 17. See also *PGA-FCS-H&I* 1882, pp. 159–60; Dunkeld FC Minutes 1882.

townspeople, but persons from all parts of the surrounding country came under the influence of the work; and many of the large farms in the neighbourhood, communities of 12 and 15 families, were literally swept by the wave of blessing, till scarcely a household in each community was without some new-born, or newly revived soul.'[35] In Greenlaw, despite the worst of weather, 'the soul-hunger of the people showed itself in the large attendances and anxious faces that nightly filled the hall'. Similar meetings in Chirnside continued for fifty nights in succession, with open-airs and cottage meetings also proving most beneficial. In all communities affected, the movement appears to have borne 'precious fruit' of lasting effect, and deputies visiting these townships in October 1884 were impressed with the spiritual life existing in the congregations.[36]

GIRVAN AND LOCHGILPHEAD, 1885

IN the spring of 1885 a time of 'remarkable spiritual blessing' descended on the West coast fishing crews who were gathered in Girvan, Ayrshire for the herring season. The men came mainly from Argyllshire fishing ports – places such as Lochgilphead, Loch Fyne, Ardrishaig, Carradale and Campbeltown. Seemingly sensing a deepening in the spiritual atmosphere, the Campbeltown fishermen sent for their missionary to come over and help them, and he arrived on 19 February. Meetings were commenced on 21 February, but nothing out of the ordinary took place until Monday, 23 February, 'when the Spirit of God descended upon the fishermen'.[37] Many strong men were moved to tears, and remained at the after-meeting to be spoken with.

The awakening continued night after night for two weeks, during which time the weather was so stormy that fishing was stopped. Every night the fishermen filled the little church in which they had their meetings until, at the end of the two weeks, about 200 spiritually-anxious men had been dealt with by Christian workers in the after-meetings, nearly all professing to believe on the Son of God. On the Saturday many gave testimony to the saving grace of God in their lives, also expressing a desire to spread the glad tidings amongst friends and neighbours on return to their home communities.

A number of Campbeltown fishermen were based eleven miles south of Girvan, in the village of Ballantrae. It was observed that they were keen not to break the Sabbath as they had previously often done thoughtlessly. Some of them left their boats rather than go out fishing on the Lord's Day. It was also observed that instead of playing cards in

---

35. Appendix to the *Report of the Free Church of Scotland on the State of Religion and Morals* (hereafter ARC-FCS-SR&M) 1884, pp. 60–1.

36. Ibid. 1885, pp. 40–2.

37. *The Rosshire Journal and General Advertiser*, 27 March 1885.

their lodgings, many passed the time by singing hymns and studying the Word of God. One of the most remarkable features of the movement was that the local Girvan fishermen were totally bypassed by this wave of blessing. Christian workers present stated that as far as they could ascertain, none of the town's natives seemed to have been awakened by the power of God so apparent in their midst.

Many of those whose lives were deeply touched did indeed testify to their Saviour on their return home, and the Spirit continued moving among them. As a result, in at least one Argyllshire township, a work of grace sprang up later in the year. This occurred in the fishing port of Lochgilphead, and one of the workers called to help in the movement was John Colville. A native of Campbeltown on the remote south of the Kinytre peninsula, Colville became a full-time evangelist shortly after his conversion at the age of seventeen. He was deeply involved in the 1859 revival in his home town[38] – one of the first places in Scotland to be affected – and again during a movement there in the spring and summer of 1874.[39]

By the autumn of 1885, after many years labouring across the length and breadth of Scotland, as well as in England and Wales, the evangelist's health was beginning to fail. His strength not returning, Colville was advised to take a trip to the Mediterranean or to rest for some time on the south coast of England. He delayed this journey, with permission from his doctor, on the exciting news that a small awakening was taking place in Lochgilphead, chiefly among the fishermen of the town. The sound of 'anxious souls' was to him as the sound of battle to the warrior, and when a friend wrote from the Argyllshire town that the numbers were more than they could deal with, his spirit was stirred within him, and he was soon on the spot. Colville threw himself into the work, making a strong impression on the young folk at the Saturday meeting and being greatly privileged to see a good number of souls born into the kingdom. The doughty preacher returned home refreshed in body and mind.[40] But this was to be his last evangelistic work for the Master and he passed to his eternal home later that same year.[41]

---

38. Mary A. Colville, *John Colville of Burnside, Campbeltown, Evangelist: A Memoir of his Life and Work,* Edinburgh 1888, pp. 91–112.

39. Ibid. pp. 201–5.

40. Ibid. pp. 250–1. This is the only record of deep spiritual blessing among west coast fisherman in our study. Fishing along Scotland's west coast was not nearly as big an industry as that along the east coast; for example, west coast fishermen did not follow the herring down to East Anglia. This partly explains why spiritual awakening among this group was not as prominent as among their colleagues from eastern fishing towns. It is possible, however, that other revival movements occurred in west coast communities which have not come to the notice of the author (see, e.g., pp. 239, 302).

41. Ibid. pp. 262–4.

1886 – YEAR OF GRACE

THE year 1886 appears to have been attended by special blessing in numerous localities all across Scotland, nearly all of them in complete independence of the others. Apart from the marked revivals narrated in the following reports,[42] other movements to have occurred in this favoured year include that in Kirriemuir, when forty people made profession of

faith;[43] a gracious movement in most congregations of the Free Church Presbytery of Kirkcaldy, particularly Pathhead Free Church, where around sixty communicants were added to the membership roll, the majority of them dating their conversion to the recent work of grace;[44] and the ongoing work of the Edinburgh Students Holiday Mission, through whose labours there spread 'an unwonted spirit of inquiry abroad throughout the land', most notably in places like Kilmarnock, Stirling, Greenock and Wick

42. For accounts of awakenings in several Glasgow neighbourhoods in 1885–6, as well as in Dunblane in the latter, favoured year, see www.scottishrevivals.co.uk.

43. *RC-FCS-SR&M* 1889, p. 7.

44. Ibid. 1887, p. 18.

(see pp. 415–6).[45] We must not forget that awakening was also underway in certain parts of Lewis and Harris during this year, as well as in various north-east coast fishing communities, especially among young women (see Chapters 6 and 8). Clearly, 1886 was a wonderous year of grace.

AVOCH

IN 1885 the Rev. George Moir of Aberdeen became pastor of the Congregational Church in Avoch[46] (colloquially known as *'Och'*), on the south coast of the Ross-shire peninsula known as the Black Isle. Within weeks he saw some encouraging manifestations that the Lord was working with him. Urgent prayer for divine blessing was offered up and two evangelists with combined experience of 100 years in gospel work were invited to come and help. They arrived on Saturday, 20 February, and, with 300 gathering in church to welcome them, it quickly became evident that the Lord had heard and was answering their united and believing cry. The people were so eager to hear that the next day four public services were held in the large chapel, which was filled to capacity on each occasion.[47]

So mightily was the Lord working that the whole population of the village became more or less interested. On Monday Moir and the two visiting helpers engaged in door-to-door visitation – not entering a single house without finding either some young believers rejoicing or those who were deeply anxious and ready to be conversed with. Public meetings were held nightly, with many anxious enquirers stepping forward. By the end of the week several hundred people had been personally dealt with, the vast majority professing Christ as Lord and obtaining peace in their souls.

At the close of one afternoon prayer meeting, after the blessing had been pronounced, one young convert could contain himself no longer, and stood to his feet in prayer and praise. The fire caught the others who were present, until seventeen of the young converts engaged in prayer, one after the other; and so eager were they that sometimes two or three were on their feet at one time. So short and pointed were their requests that the seventeen prayers did not occupy more than twenty minutes.[48] At a praise and testimony meeting the next morning, one of the young converts started to his feet and thanked the Lord that he was one day old; another that he was three days old; a third, an elderly man, that although he had lost one of his bodily eyes, and the other was fast following, 'the Lord had opened both the eyes of his soul to see the precious Saviour'.[49]

45. *The Christian,* 23 April 1886.

46. McNaughton, *Early Congregational Independency,* p. 259.

47. *TC,* 18 March 1886, p. 12.

48. Ibid.

49. Ibid.

For some weeks a large number of fishermen did not go out to sea, preferring to attend to spiritual interests or desirous of securing the salvation of their loved ones.[50] One tall, strong fisherman, previously a frequent patron of the local drinking establishments, got hold of a good-sized bell and brought it to the manse, seeking blessing for his proposed *'bell mission'*. After prayer, he proceeded from one end of town to the other, boldly sounding his gong – most deliberately in front of the public houses he once frequented – and announcing the time of that evening's meeting![51]

Another fisherman belonged to the Royal Reserve Naval Force and had been in Inverness for a few days doing his drill. In his absence his wife had got converted, and on his return home she embraced him with beaming countenance, *'Oh Sandy, man, there's nothing in the world worth having and living for now but Jesus.'* This was music to the ears of her husband, who, the very night his wife had found the Lord in Avoch, had also come to saving grace in Inverness![52] One delightful feature of the awakening was the longing of young converts for their friends and relatives to be saved. At the close of one meeting a young lad returned home in tears. Looking up to his father he cried, 'Father, I'm saved, and mother is saved,' then, naming others in the family who had also been converted, he continued, 'but father, you're not saved, and so how can I help crying'.[53]

Country districts adjacent to Avoch also shared in the reaping. One convert from the parish of Rosemarkie was sixteen-year-old Alexander MacLennan – already a lad of 'studious ways, earnest mind and blameless conduct', but who now found a new love for and dedication to the Saviour. MacLennan shortly after went into the ministry, serving as pastor of Canmore Congregational Church, Dunfermline until his untimely death at the age of 35.[54]

While previous New Year's Days were almost a pandemonium for drunkenness and fighting in the village, New Year's Day 1887 was like a Sabbath for peace and quiet, with two well-attended chapel services being held. One year after the movement began it was reported that of the hundreds who professed Jesus during the awakening, only two or three were known to have gone back. Many who opposed the initial work in the village were brought in during a series of meetings held the following year (1887), the first being the man considered the most

50. Of the three congregations in Avoch at that time, the fisher-folk belonged mainly to the Congregational Church. The FC was, however, also noted as being 'very well attended' (*RC-FCS-SR&M*, 1894, p. 18).

51. *TC*, 1 April 1886, p. 12.

52. Ibid.

53. Ibid.

54. Hugh Jenkins, *Alexander MacLennan of Dunfermline: Memoir and Sermons*, Leith 1906.

intelligent fisherman in the village, followed by another tall, burly but very shy man who was now addressing crowds of neighbours in the open air, urging them to come close to Christ. A conference on *'Waiting, Walking and Working with God'* was also held at this time, several of the neighbouring ministers taking part, and the good work continued.[55] But this was not, as we shall see, the last spiritual awakening to occur in this small, favoured community.[56]

BONAWE

A WORK of grace was evidenced at Bonawe, by Loch Etive, near Oban, towards the end of 1885 and into 1886. An evangelist arrived there around Christmas time and began meetings in the school-house, but these were transferred to the larger Free Church, whose minister, Rev. MacKenzie, gave his hearty co-operation to the work. Such was the interest shown that meetings continued for seven weeks, the church being packed night after night. Some travelled a number of miles along heavily snow-covered roads, all of them more or less evincing in a quiet, earnest manner a deep hunger for the things of God. Personal visitations were conducted during the daytime, and not a few under anxiety entered into safe pastures through faith in the Lord. After-meetings in the church were a new innovation to this part of Scotland, and, along with public testimony and the singing of hymns, made great impact on the people.

The work was greatly blessed and encouraged by the arrival of a band of young believers from the granite quarries on the other side of the long, narrow loch. These men came over in their small boats to give testimony at the meetings to what the grace of God had done in their own lives just over twelve months previously. At that time, the Lord visited the workers in the quarries and, by the instrumentality of the same evangelist as came to Bonawe, so shook the place that souls dead in trespasses were brought to completely new life, becoming living monuments to God's grace. Whole families were among those converted to Christ on that occasion.[57]

Further south in Argyll, the Free Church congregation of Ardrishaig also shared in a time of blessing in 1886, which affected not only church attendance but also increased the number of communicants, all of whom were still standing two years later.[58] Meanwhile, around the same time

---

55. *The Ross-shire Journal and General Advertiser for the Northern Counties* (hereafter *RJ&GANC*) 18 March 1887.

56. A few miles west, in Dingwall, Rev. Donald Murray set up home after retiring from the FC at the age of 81. Here he held a service in Gaelic every week. 'People crowded to his house, where rooms and staircase had attentive and delighted hearers' (Rev. Norman C. MacFarlane, *Apostles of the North*, Stornoway, n.d., p. 88).

57. *TC*, 25 March 1886, p. 13.

58. *RC-FCS-SR&M*, 1888, pp. 3–4.

and still in the West Highlands, 'a remarkable work of grace' occurred in Ullapool Free Church under the ordinary preaching of the Word. 'Great earnestness, solemnity and manifest impression were apparent,' wrote the minister, the Rev. McMillan (a man said to have been normally very guarded in his statements), 'among whom were young people who gave me as much satisfaction as I ever received.'[59]

CANISBAY

A PERIOD of local awakening occurred in the northern Caithness parish of Canisbay, just a few miles south of John O'Groats, in 1886. Minister of the Free Church was the much loved Roderick MacGregor, who had come out of the Established Church over forty years previously during the difficult Disruption times. MacGregor had travelled to Ulster in 1859 to observe the great move of the Spirit in progress there, longing to see a similar revival in his home country and parish. Within months of his return, much of Scotland, including parts of Caithness, was also gripped by revival power.[60]

One weekend in February 1886, Alexander Harper, the North-East Coast Mission worker from Wick, addressed a soiree to the Sunday school children as well as, on subsequent evenings, a temperance and evangelistic address to adults. Interest was noticeably quickened and Harper agreed to return to hold a fortnight's meetings in the church.

From the first, great crowds filled the church while public interest continued to increase. Wrote J.M. Baikie, 'The parish had never been so roused, yet all was order and quietness. Both the land and seafaring classes were reached. It embraced as its trophies the youth of only 14 sweet summers, up along the ladder of life until its heavenly influence won the man of feeble step and hoary hairs, as he was ascending the other side of fourscore years.[61] At first MacGregor (and his elders) were said to have been a little diffident, but at length he said that, although the course of procedure was not on his usual lines, yet he was glad to take up the apostles' position of old, and 'be all things to all men that I might by all means save some'.[62] As such, he threw himself into the work.

> Sabbath services were particularly impressive. Early at 10 o'clock the Sabbath school met, and next a young women's class, while at noon the Rev. Mr MacGregor himself preached in his usual

59. Ibid. 1887, p. 16.

60. Baikie says that Rev. MacGregor 'ceased not to warn every one day and night with tears (in the most literal sense); only the usual results followed' (J.M. Baikie, *Revivals in the Far North*, Wick n.d., p. 62). In fact the names of thirty-five people were added to the FC roll at that time.

61. Ibid. pp. 62–3.

62. Ibid. pp. 63–4.

> winning yet solemn manner. The audience was all attention, and many gave signs of deep feeling. For the service at 6 p.m., crowds assembled an hour before the time and literally packed the church. At the close a second meeting was usually held, and many remained to be spoken to, when a long time was spent in devotional exercises, prayer and singing. Mr MacGregor joined in his favourite hymn, 'Rock of Ages,' with beaming countenance.[63]

At first the people were reluctant to share with the leaders their spiritual difficulties, but as conviction grew stronger they gained confidence and some even ventured to the manse for conversation. After a second series of special meetings had ended, Sabbath evening services were begun, and continued throughout the spring and summer. The minister often received help with these from church leaders from Wick or Thurso. A new method was adopted at the start of the New Year, by way of the elders, along with other interested church members going through the parish, holding meetings in the cottages and farmhouses. In this way the whole parish was visited. As a result, many heads of families were induced to initiate times of family worship in homes where it was previously unknown.

The Rev. John Sinclair of Bowden in Roxburghshire, a previous minister in Canisbay Free Church, gave a detailed account of the summer Communion, in which he went to assist in his former parish. He was astonished to find hardly any of the changes he had expected in regard to the number and length of services.[64]

> The Communion, which in olden time used to absorb the interest of the people for five whole days, does the same still; outside work by a great many almost entirely suspended, and the time devoted to the services of the sanctuary. Thursday brought with it a number of people from other parts of the country, and as the days advanced there came with them a number more. … Saturday found a large congregation. … On Sabbath the church was crowded throughout the whole service, which lasted about six hours; and on Monday there was a very large audience. …The Thursday, Saturday and Sabbath evening meetings were conducted chiefly by the elders and 'men'[65] from other places. These meetings consisted almost entirely of prayer and praise, into the spirit of which the large gatherings seemed thoroughly to enter. The fact is that from any of the meetings the difficulty was to get the people to go away.[66]

---

63. Ibid. pp. 62–3.

64. The one exception was that there were no longer any outdoor services to accommodate believers from neighbouring congregations, as these now had their own services on that day.

65. Longstanding Christian laymen in a community, who, by tradition in the north of Scotland, excercised considerable authority among the people.

66. *The Monthly Record of the Free Church of Scotland* (hereafter *MR-FCS*), September 1886, p. 262.

Sinclair described the Communion as a scene

> never to be forgotten. As young and old came slowly forward together to the front pews and took their seats, each bowing the head the moment he sat down, the impression made on us who looked on was such that it was with difficulty any one could offer prayer. Prayer was offered by Mr Sage of Keiss who also preached that day. Mr MacGregor delivered one of the most thrilling addresses I have listened to from two expressions in the seventeenth Psalm – 'Hold up my goings in thy paths' and 'Keep me as the apple of the eye' – and after two more prayers the tokens were put into their hands. They had previous to this received the right hand of fellowship from the session.
>
> As they went away I believe we all felt inclined to express our feelings in the words of Jacob, 'Surely the Lord is in this place … this is none other but the house of God, and this is the gate of heaven.' As we left the church one of the 'men' made the remark, 'We have seen strange things today.' It was truly a strange sight in Canisbay.[67]

Sinclair was particularly impressed with the disparity in communicants' ages. 'The youngest there was barely 12 years old, and the oldest 81 years. About 20 would be between 12 and 24 years of age, with a seeming gap then till 40 was reached; a number between 40 and 60 years of age, with a few above that; and the list closed with an old man of fourscore and one.'[68]

It was unusual in the north to see so many communicants of such tender age, but Sinclair fully trusted MacGregor's sound judgment – he had well known these youngsters, and even their parents, since their youth, and he had heard the minister's story of his and the session's cautious dealings with them. Sinclair took the opportunity of conversing with several of them after the service.

> Two features which I liked, both characteristics of the north, stood out prominently in them all. The first was a pervading sense of sin. A young man with whom I shook hands outside the church immediately after the Communion took the first word with me by saying, 'I am afraid everything is not right with me yet. I felt all the time I was at the Table as if I were one mass of sin.' And in broken accents as he went away he added, 'Oh, be putting a word up for me.'
>
> The second was the lack of bold assertions about the surety of their salvation. Not one of those with whom I came in contact would venture to say, 'I know He is mine.' An elderly man said, 'There is not a day but I have my doubts and fears still, but I just

67. Ibid.

68. Ibid., pp. 262–3.

come to Him; again every day. ... The minister told me he had never before seen such a deep interest taken in spiritual things in the parish, and such earnestness listening to the preached word; whilst he himself seems as if had renewed his youth in witnessing the fruits of nearly a 40 years' faithful evangelical ministry.'[69]

MacGregor exuded in his diary for Communion Sabbath, 20 June 1886, 'I believe that this has been one of the most remarkable and blessed days that ever occurred in the history of Canisbay. No less than 60 sat down for the first time at the Lord's Table – and were it not that many of the people were away at the coast fishing, the number would, I have no doubt, been 70, if not upward. O my God, "Keep them as the apple of the eye"!' Altogether, 'no less than 80 souls professed their faith, and have been wonderfully kept' in the Free Church alone.[70] This was a huge addition to a membership of just 150, where no more than two or three were normally added at a time.

The Lord being no respecter of denominations, the Church of Scotland also reaped from this 'great wave of blessing which passed over the district'.[71] Then in the following spring, 'a similar work was begun, and services kept up in Duncansby, Brabster, Gills and other places, to the conversion and comfort of many of His people.'[72]

Cromarty

A REMARKABLE and spontaneous season of blessing developed in Cromarty, Easter Ross, in the spring of 1886, chiefly in the landward parts of the parish, which was served at that time by the Rev. John MacKay, a Highlander converted during the powerful revival of 1859–60. Entering college, MacKay had been sent on vacation placement to Skye, where he had come under the influence of Roderick MacLeod of Snizort. MacKay greatly admired this worthy preacher, but, being non-controversial by nature, was unimpressed with his temperament.[73] In Edinburgh over a decade later, during D.L. Moody's influential 1873 mission in the city, MacKay felt constrained to go and hear the American evangelist. While initially 'very doubtful' of Moody's methods of evangelism, MacKay was persuaded by

69. *MR-FCS,* September 1886, pp. 262–3. This revival was the most powerful of several 'times of refreshing' that McGreggor's church enjoyed in the later period of his ministry. McGreggor died a few years later, in 1890 (*MR-FCS,* February 1890).

70. The text is from Psalm 17, and was part of the Communion sermon. (Article by Alex Muir, quoted in Anne L. Houston [Ed.] *Lest We Forget The Parish Of Canisbay,* Canisbay 1996, pp. 333.)

71. *Harper the Missionary,* p. 19, quoted in MacRae, *Revivals in the Highlands & Islands,* pp. 143–4.

72. Baikie, p. 64.

73. MacKay 'disapproved of the undue influence placed upon secondary matters, to the exclusion of the main theme of preaching Jesus Christ and him crucified'. His own motto was, 'In essentials, unity; in non-essentials, liberty; in all things, charity' (Rev. Alexander MacKenzie, *The Rev. John MacKay, M.A., Student, Pastor, General Assembly's Highland Evangelist,* Paisley 1921, pp. 29–31).

his girlfriend to go and hear him preach regularly. Soon he 'parted with prejudices against such evangelistic work, to which he afterwards devoted so many years of his life'.[74] Ordained in this same year (1873), the young pastor found his first charge in the Glen Lyon district of Breadalbane, the scene of stirring revival times in days past;[75] then moved to Oban just a year later, before taking his position in Cromarty in 1883.[76]

The Cromarty Free Church Session noted that, 'during the winter and spring of 1885–86 a spirit of earnest prayer for special blessing was given to the praying people [of Cromarty]. They longed, prayed, and looked for a shower of blessing. An unusual earnestness and seriousness pervaded the meetings for public worship, showing clearly that a deep work of the Spirit was being experienced by not a few.'[77]

It was resolved to hold meetings in two country centres before beginning a mission in the town. At the remote Peddiston School MacKay conducted an evening service, and while addressing his audience, noticed one of his hearers holding his head down. After the service had concluded, MacKay observed that the floor was wet with the broken man's tears. Others, in view of this and of the deep impression made by MacKay's address on the audience generally, sensed that the time for blessing had come, and they urged the minister to come and conduct a week-long series of meetings in the area. MacKay consented.[78]

After three nights, so great was the interest – with an increasing audience each evening – that it was found necessary to prolong the services and to acquire more speakers. The Free Church ministers of Fortrose and Killearnan came to help, and a second and a third week passed, 'and still the same and even greater interest was apparent everywhere. Over the moors and up the braes, an hour before the time, crowds of people, old and young alike, wended their way to the meeting-place, some, of course, to look on, but others with a great interest in their hearts.'[79] The schoolroom was regularly crowded and many were content to stand.

About the end of the second week, at the dismissal, any anxious ones were asked to remain for a little, and everybody present stayed back. Alexander MacKenzie records that, 'The whole district was moved, numbers were awakened, and led to joy and peace in believing. The numbers of parents blessed were very striking. Every household, and in some cases, the whole household, shared in the bountiful blessing. In

---

74. Ibid. p. 36.

75. Ibid. pp. 38–42. These pages give an interesting overview of the spiritual history of the Glen Lyon area.

76. Ibid. pp. 72–7.

77. ARC-FCS-SR&M 1887, p. 60.

78. MacKenzie, *The Rev. John MacKay*, p. 112.

79. Ibid.

the town during the weeks that followed, the blessing was also enjoyed richly, but not to the same extent as at Peddiston.'[80] It was a 'time of special power, when impression was almost universal in the country district.'[81] All who made a public profession were said to have still been consistent in their faith many months later.

Mr More, one of the elders in the congregation, used to come to the meetings almost every night, and some remarked on his power in prayer, and how, in answer to his earnestness, barriers were removed and souls were freed. Many young men and women came boldly forward and acknowledged their Lord, 'and the wonder of the work was the chief topic of conversation in the homes, on the field, and at the bench'.[82] As a result of this movement, ninety-five members were added to the church on profession of faith in Christ as Lord and Saviour.[83]

1887–9

Kilbrandon and Kilchattan 1888–9

KILBRANDON and Kilchattan was a parish in the South Lorne district of Argyllshire consisting of a section of the mainland, along with the inhabited islands of Seil, Luing, Easdale and a couple of smaller isles. Seil was connected to the mainland by the famous humpbacked Clachan Bridge ('the bridge over the Atlantic'). The total population of the parish

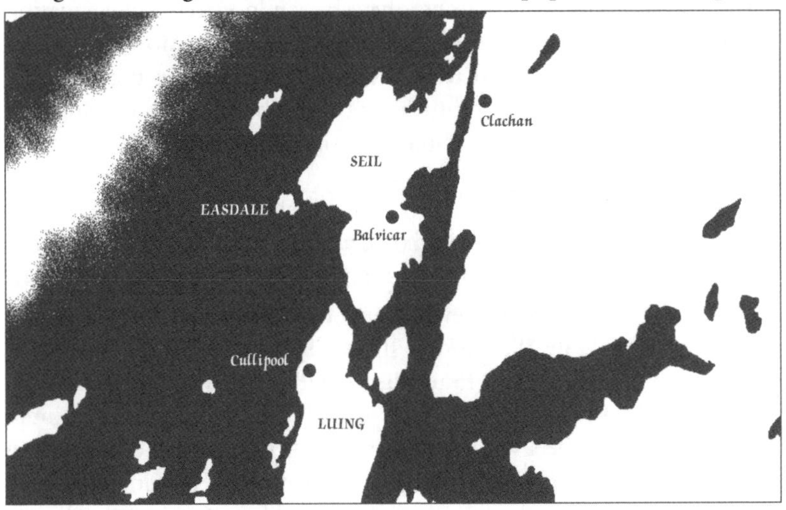

80. ARC-FCS-SR&M 1887, p. 60.

81. Ibid.

82. MacKenzie, *The Rev. John MacKay*, p. 113.

83. Ibid. 85 joined at one single (June) Communion (Cromarty FC Minutes 1886). The record of MacKay's ministry in Cromarty was summed up by one man who said, 'He worked earnestly, his people loved him, and the cause of Christ prospered' (p. 113). MacKay later relinquished his charge at Cromarty to become FC evangelist to the Highlands, during which time he again witnessed revival (see page 71).

was around 1,700. The Free Church minister in the district was Donald MacDonald, a man held in great respect in the area. The islands were famous for slate quarrying, which became a massive industry in the area. The tiny island of Easdale alone turned out up to nine million slates annually at the height of its productivity in the nineteenth century. It was said of MacDonald that he was so genuinely concerned for the welfare of his parishioners that on pay-day at the quarries he would spend hours walking up and down in the vicinity of the public house. He was so highly respected by his people that few would dare to enter the unholy place to squander money and health so long as he was there![84]

One hundred years previously, in 1786, this parish became the first location in the Western Highlands to experience an evangelical revival.[85] Now, in November 1888, following a season of deepened interest and expectation among the people, special services were commenced in the Free Church. Writing over a year later, MacDonald said, 'This continued night after night for about four months. Sometimes there were meetings throughout the day. People who had been non-churchgoers for years came out regularly and sat for hours without the least sign of weariness.' He further reported that the work, which 'went very much in families', was marked by 'calm earnestness and deep solemnity'. As to results, 'professors got a quickening and refreshing which is very remarkable', while 'upwards of 60 new members have been added to the congregation since December 1888'. In addition, three Sabbath morning prayer meetings which were started around this time were still in progress over a year later.[86] Interestingly, a further season of blessing fell on this west Argyll district just a few years later (see pp. 69–70).

EARLY WORK OF THE FAITH MISSION 1885–9

IRVINE

THE surrender to Christ of a teenage Glasgow boy in 1873 proved to be highly consequential for the development of rural evangelism in Scotland and beyond. Born in 1861 into a strict but happy West End Glasgow home, John George Govan found peace with God while on holiday in Arran at the age of twelve. The closing words of his dying father to him in 1883 – 'You are to be a witness for Christ' – left a profound impression on the young convert, as too did the active witness of his elder brothers, and the following year he further yielded his life to Christ.[87] Strikingly

84. H. Austin Stirling, *Duncan MacColl, an Apostle to Highlanders. Memoirs of the Founder of the Highland Mission, Glasgow*, Edinburgh 1932, p. 91.

85. Gavin Struthers, *History of the Rise, Progress and Principles of the Relief Church*, Glasgow 1843, p. 395.

86. ARC-FCS-SR&M 1890, p. 55. Kilbrandon and Kilchattan FC Minutes, 1888–90.

87. I.R. Govan, *Spirit of Revival: Biography of J.G. Govan, founder of the Faith Mission*, London 1938, pp. 23–30.

successful work among factory girls in Pollokshaws and in the tough Water Street district – when on top of his day-time job he was involved in mission work virtually every night of the week – proved from the start that Govan was a highly dedicated and formidable evangelist. Soon after, Govan gave up his business career and began a ministry of preaching the gospel wherever he was invited.

One of the most remarkable of these pioneering missions was in Irvine, Ayrshire. Govan spent a number of days in deep prayer, setting out for the Friday meeting assured that victory had been granted. The church was packed; there was a solemn sense of God's presence, and a

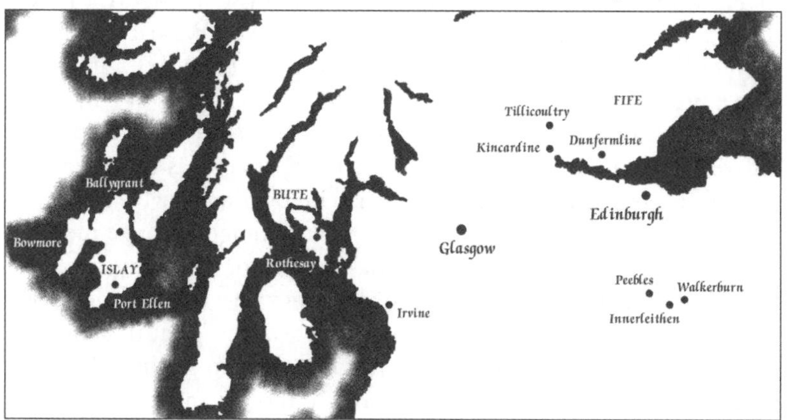

stillness that could be felt. He took as his subject 1 John 1:9 and spoke on 'the horrible, black and filthy nature of sin'. Conviction spread over the gathering, and when the benediction was pronounced everyone remained seated. Again he attempted to dismiss the meeting but still no one moved. 'If any of you are anxious about your soul, you can meet me in the hall downstairs,' he said. There was a movement, and then the people poured out of their seats and downstairs, until the hall was crammed. It was a night of salvation. 'Revival started, Hallelujah!' he entered in his diary when he went home. Before long there were hundreds of converted young people marching the streets, full of exuberance and the joy of a wonderful salvation.[88]

The effects of such changed lives were immediate. Two prayer groups were started, one for young men and the other for young women, and 'kitchen meetings' in folks' homes were also begun. The dancing school had to close due to lack of interest; instead the town seemed full of spiritual activity. On Sundays there was an early morning prayer meeting, led by a young convert, who, due to lack of confidence, relied on reading a portion of Andrew Murray's *In the School of Prayer* at each meeting.

88. Ibid. pp. 33–34. See also J.B. McLean, *Faith Triumphant: A Review of the Work of the Faith Mission, 1886–1936, by Those who Have Seen and Heard*, Edinburgh 1936, pp. 20–1.

This proved very popular, but soon interest in prayer became so deep that there was room for neither reading nor speaking. There was a further meeting for prayer at half-past-one, then converts went out in twos for house visitation and to hold hospital services and other activities. An open-air meeting and gospel service rounded off a very busy day, the good work continuing long after the Pilgrims' four-week mission was over.[89]

PEEBLES

GOVAN unceremoniously founded The Faith Mission in 1886, with initially only himself and colleague George Colvin as workers, soon after joined by two 'sister Pilgrims'. One of their early missions was to the Border town of Peebles, where 'a glorious revival' occurred.[90] Backed by hours of prayer, the two young evangelists went out to the main street and stood alone, proclaiming God's goodness in song. 'The coldness of Christians, the apathy and indifference of unsaved were banished by a breath from Heaven,'[91] and within a couple of nights the street was thronged with eager listeners. Before long the largest hall in town was unable to contain all who came to hear the gospel message; accordingly separate meetings were conducted for the children. Special services for Christians were held each Sabbath afternoon and testimony meetings were also conducted. Mr Govan, who spoke on several occasions, wrote of the 'great times here. It is impossible adequately to describe it. One needs to get into the midst of it to realise what it is, and to experience the joy and blessing of the presence and power of the Lord.'[92] The Congregational minister wrote: 'We expected great things but we must confess that we did not expect to see "the arm of the Lord revealed" in such a mighty manner.'[93]

The Pilgrims moved six and eight miles down the Tweed valley to the villages of Innerleithen and Walkerburn, where rich blessing again ensued. In the latter place the whole population of 1,200 was reached, 500 being present on the first meeting and over 600 cramming into the building on some nights. One evening over sixty professed salvation, while 260 professions were made in just one week.[94]

FIFE

A CONCERTED advance was made in 1888 on the 'Kingdom of Fife', of which county it was said that 'the mining towns were irreligious, and drinking and gambling abounded; there was little life in the fishing villages,

89. Ibid. p. 34.

90. *Bright Words* (Faith Mission Publication), 1906, p. 106.

91. Govan, *Spirit of Revival*, p. 44.

92. Ibid. p. 46.

93. *BW* 1906, p. 106.

94. Ibid. The establishment of Brethren assemblies in both Walkerburn and Peebles in 1886 and 1889 respectively may have been an influence of this movement (Neil T.R. Dickson, *Brethren in Scotland 1838–2000: A Social Study of an Evangelical Movement*, Carlisle 2002, p. 102).

while the industrial towns were full of a cold formal religion that is more damning than open sin.'[95] 'The Devil's Seat' was how someone nicknamed the region. Opposition – from both religious leaders and local yobs – was intense in many places. One night, just as a meeting started, a female Pilgrim went to open the barricaded door in response to knocking, and received a volley of rotten eggs full in the face. 'Praise the Lord!' she called out, 'and the next night the roughs came into the meeting to see this cheerful person!'[96]

The open opposition, however, soon gave place, in many cases, to serious conviction of sin, 'as a breath from God began to sweep over the county, and village after village was visited by a great spiritual awakening'.[97] It was notable how converts manifested interest in succeeding missions in other areas. Many worked from 6 a.m. to 6 p.m., yet still found strength to march alongside a wagonette – known as the 'Hallelujah Chariot' – into nearby villages, singing all the way songs like 'I love Thee because Thou hast first loved me.' Half-nights of prayer were common – these were times of sober dealing with God. Pilgrims would meet from 10.30 p.m. to 2.30 a.m., 'to be searched and humbled by God'. Said one, 'I can never tell you how near He came, broke us down in His presence, and then changed our mourning into joy.'[98] Mr Govan often said that much of the blessing in Fife was owing to the prayers of the remarkable Annie Bowie from Kincardine, 'a little woman on an invalid's bed, from whence she reached out in prayer to the world'.[99]

In midsummer 1888, a 'Thanksgiving Demonstration' was held in Dunfermline and was attended by over 750 Faith Mission Prayer Union members from all over central and southern Scotland. Two special trains were run, one from the east of Fife, the other from the west, gathering the faithful to the meetings. 'The first train brought the saints from Tillicoultry – nearly 100 strong – Coalsnaughton, 40 from Kincardine, and about 60 from smaller places, and the second train had contingents from Auchtermuchty, Strathmiglo, Ladybank, Kettle, Dairsie, Freauchie, Falkland, Leslie, Markinch and Lochgelly.'[100] Remarkably, around thirty people flocked to the penitent form on the very first night. Such a gathering was an amazing achievement considering that this was within eight months of the Pilgrims' first entering the inititally resistant 'Kingdom'.

---

95. Govan, *Spirit of Revival,* pp. 48–9. A work of grace had already commenced in some parts of Fife before the arrival of the F.M., e.g. in several FC congregations, especially in Kirkcaldy's Pathhead FC in 1886–7, where 57 young communicants joined the church in less than a year (*RC-FCS-SR&M* 1887, p. 18).

96. Govan, *Spirit of Revival,* p.51.

97. McLean, *Faith Triumphant,* p. 30.

98. Govan, *Spirit of Revival,* p. 55.

99. Ibid. pp. 55–6.

100. Ibid. p. 66; McLean, *Faith Triumphant,* p. 34.

ROTHESAY 1888–9

THE most notable revival with which Faith Mission workers were involved in the late 1800s – and indeed one of the most remarkable in the entire history of the organisation – was that which occurred in the fashionable Victorian holiday resort of Rothesay (population 8,500) on Bute in 1888–9, later spreading to other parts of the island. The Faith Mission began operations in October 1888 when 'two unassuming young women', as a local paper termed them, began to preach and sing the gospel in the West End Halls. 'It was little thought that shortly the whole place would be stirred.'[101]

A meeting among Christians was conducted, which was followed by a time of prayer that lasted several hours, being blessed by 'the coming of the Spirit to His own people'.[102] The town's inhabitants quickly sensed the joyous transformation in the lives of these believers, and before long the entire town seemed to be stirred. Attendance at weeknight meetings varied from 400 to 800, while on Sundays, 1,500 or more packed into the beautiful, commodious New Public Halls from all over the island. J.G. Govan, who felt 'utterly tired out' when he arrived from Glasgow, soon felt stronger than he had for months notwithstanding all the speaking and singing. Personally touched, Govan wrote, '*He* came near, and revealed the name of Love, and oh, I felt I had so little of His love, and was quite broken down at His feet.'[103]

Despite the unfavourable weather, so many Christians turned out for the open-air marches that they had to split into two groups, thus reaching different parts of the town. A further striking feature of the revival was its widespread nature, both rich and poor being affected. It was said that one could observe at the penitent form both drunkards and businessmen, as well as ladies in their fur coats.[104] One notable conversion was that of a renowned drunkard who had a crutch. A strong man, he exited a pub one night to find himself intrigued by the Pilgrims' singing nearby. Moving towards them, he raised his crutch to hit one of the ladies over the head. She carried on in song and the blow never fell. Soundly converted shortly after, this man carried a wonderful saving testimony for many a year.[105]

However, as in most revivals, the work was not without its critics, and the most severe came from within Christian ranks. The Faith Mission's teaching was attacked for promoting 'perfectionism' due to its emphasis

---

101. Ibid. p. 71.
102. Ibid.
103. Ibid. p. 72.
104. Ibid. p. 73.
105. Colin N. Peckham, *Heritage of Revival: A Century of Rural Evangelism*, Edinburgh 1985, p. 24.

on sanctification (the Mission attempted to clarify the matter by stating that no-one could attain absolute perfection this side of eternity). The Rev. C.A. Salmond of Rothesay published a forty-two page booklet in which he criticised the Faith Mission's emphasis on sanctification. By reference to the Scriptures and to Church history, Salmond sought to show that this teaching was unorthodox. It also left believers on the island, he wrote, 'confused and perplexed … coming to me in tears, asking what these things mean, and questioning their own interest in Christ, because they cannot honestly profess that complete conquest over sin, which some have been telling them is so easy of attainment to him that believeth.' Salmond had met privately with Govan to share his concern at this and other of the Mission's teachings and practices, but they failed to agree on a number of issues. While to Salmond Christianity was a joyous religion, he felt that 'somehow there is rather a forced mechanical look about the hand-clappings and other demonstrations of joy adopted by the Pilgrims in their more recent meetings'. And he was disturbed by their use of 'hackneyed secular tunes', such as singing the refrain, 'There will be an awful judgement day; Prepare to meet thy God,' to the music of the secular Scottish folk song, 'Jock O' Hazeldean'.[106] But Salmond insisted he was not speaking against the Pilgrims personally, or against revivals or evangelistic work. 'What one desires to do is, to appreciate and encourage the good, while not conniving, even by silence, at the evil.'[107]

The team came under attack too – for example, in the letters column of a Christian publication – for the methods it employed; the penitent form, song tunes as hymns, using musical instruments in church services and the employment of women preachers (the correspondence in a local newspaper also became 'very hot'). The Mission saw none of these as being contrary to Scripture, only to the religious practices of the day. Further, they felt, such methods were clearly used by the Lord in giving spiritual arrest and help to the ordinary person. Worse still was when what Govan termed 'the old Jesuitical plan of personal attack was resorted to',[108] though the Chief knew that however hurtful, these could only draw the accused closer to God. In any case, all forms of opposition resulted in the work becoming more widely known, and genuine supporters rallied to its defence.[109]

---

106. C.A. Salmond, *Perfectionism, The False and the True: A Lecture Delivered by Rev. C.A. Salmond, M.A., Rothesay, on 30th December 1888, with Special Reference to the Teaching of the 'Faith Mission Pilgrims',* Glasgow 1889, pp. 8, 10. Meanwhile, the FC reported very favourably and in some detail on the movement (ARC-FCS-SR&M 1889, pp. 47–8).

107. Salmond, pp. 39–40. He quoted Asahel Nettleton – 'one of the most largely used and greatly blessed of all revivalists' – who said, 'A powerful religious excitement, badly conducted, has ever been considered by the most experienced ministers and best friends of revivals to be a great calamity.'

108. Govan, *In the Train of His Triumph,* p. 48.

109. Govan, *Spirit of Revival,* pp. 73–4.

Afternoon Bible studies were a helpful part of the movement,[110] as too were praise and testimony meetings. Several hundred professions of faith were recorded during the three months of the campaign,[111] and the noticeable reduction in crime on the island was attributed by the chief magistrate to the Mission's work.[112] Other parts of Bute also received deep blessing. At the close of the mission, 260 people united to form a Prayer Union in Rothesay, and the town became the headquarters of the Faith Mission, also hosting its popular annual convention.[113] Eight converts of the revival later joined the organisation while others served overseas, as well as in various parts of Britain, in full or part time ministry.[114]

OTHER SIGNIFICANT MOVEMENTS IN THIS PERIOD[115]

Leslie 1880–90
Glasgow 1885–6
Dunblane 1886
Clydebank 1887–8
Early Work of Faith Mission
  Unnamed Location
  Islay

110. *BW*, January 1889, quoted in 'A Report From This Magazine, 100 Years Ago' in *Life Indeed* (the later title of the Faith Mission Publication), January 1989, p. 22.

111. ARC-FCS-SR&M 1889, pp. 47–8; Peckham, *Heritage of Revival*, p. 24.

112. Peckham, *Heritage of Revival*, pp. 24–5.

113. To many these were 'days of heaven on earth' (McLean, *Triumphant Evangelism*, p. 45), 'when a measure of power and blessing was felt by many' (John Long, *Journal of John Long*, previously unpublished work, 1927, published on www.home.earthlink.net, Chapter 5).

114. Peckham, *Heritage of Revival*, p. 24.

115. Full accounts of these movements can be found on www.scottishrevivals.co.uk.

Miners Row, Ferniegair, Lanarkshire – p.36

Hamilton – p.36

Avoch – p.47

John Colville – p.45

John MacKay – p.53

J.G. Govan – p.56

Cromarty – p.53

Rothesay, Bute – p.60

2
The Turn of the Century
1890–1904

Footdee 1891

THE small fishing village of Footdee (known locally as 'Fittie') is situated at the mouth of Aberdeen harbour. Built in 1808, it comprises two areas of fishing cottages built in two squares. This tight-knit community experienced no fewer than three dramatic bursts of revival during the 1860s – first near the beginning of 1861, again early the following year, and yet again in the early months of 1869. A new Mission Hall was opened, while all three of Footdee's public houses closed down in a few years. A report written in the 1870s remarked upon how the whole village had become 'a picture of tidiness such as is seldom to be met with among classes of the population reckoned higher in the social scale … this external order is only the index of a still more important change in the habits and character of our fisher town, the population of which has within the past few years undergone a remarkable change for the better in a moral point of view.'[1]

Once again, in 1891, revival swept through the community. In May of that year the Free Church Presbytery of Aberdeen made reference to 'a remarkable work which has been in progress for about two months past among the fisher population of Footdee, a work resulting, under God, from the labours of one of the north east coast missionaries. The whole place has been moved. There has been no excitement, but a deep and solemn feeling has pervaded the movement. The number of those who have professed faith in Christ is above 200 – the majority of whom are young men and women. One remarkable fruit of the work has been the fact that those who have been brought to the truth for the first time, and those who have received a fresh quickening in the divine life, are giving themselves diligently to the study of the Scriptures. It is the belief of competent judges that a genuine and most blessed work of grace has been and still is in progress.'[2]

---

1. Anson, p. 142. Many Footdee inhabitants would also have been among the 20,000 who heard Moody's stirring address on the nearby Links in June, 1874 (Rufus W. Clark, *Moody & Sankey in Great Britain*, London, 1875, pp. 144–5).

2. *RC-FCS-SR&M* 1891, pp. 16–17.

LISMORE 1895

WHEN Duncan MacColl moved south to live in Glasgow towards the close of the nineteenth century, it was not because of any outward attraction to city life, but rather due to 'the still, small voice of the Holy Spirit calling, calling, calling him to labour amongst the teeming multitudes of sin-burdened souls somehow, somewhere' in that city.[3] He obtained a day-time job as City Officer in Glasgow's City Chambers, but true fulfilment came when he founded the Highland Mission, in attempt to reach the thousands of Highlanders resident in the city. Over the next thirty years MacColl laboured zealously in the open air in all weathers with a team of co-workers, also acquiring a Mission Hall in Oswald Street, where many were to enter into new life with the Saviour.[4] With all his spare time taken up in gospel work, it is remarkable that MacColl should also devote his annual leave each summer to carrying the gospel to needy places throughout his native Highlands.

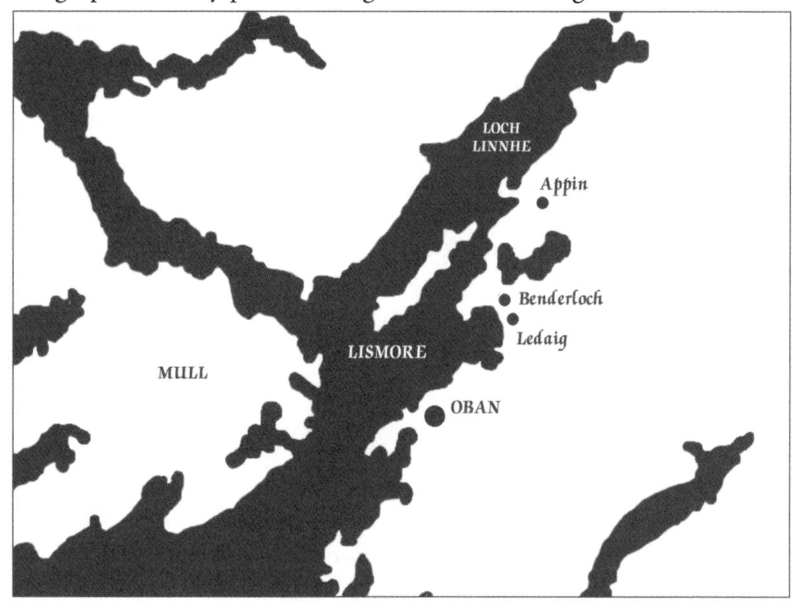

Such ventures being always preceded by much earnest prayer and deliberation, it was decided in 1895 to bear witness on the small island of Lismore – the place of MacColl's birth – near the mouth of Loch Linnhe, just a few miles north-west of Oban. MacColl journeyed north with two fellow-labourers, leaving Glasgow at 4 a.m., yet only arriving

3. Stirling, p. 29.

4. One writer has suggested that the evangelistic and social programme provided by the Glasgow Highland Mission, along with those of other lowland para-church bodies, was to some extent 'a sacred counterbalance to the secular ceilidh circuit frequented by émigré Highlanders' (Donald E. Meek, 'Religious Life in the Highlands since the Reformation,' in Michael Lynch (Ed.). *The Oxford Companion to Scottish History*, Oxford 2001, p. 520).

in Lismore as darkness was falling. After trudging six miles they reached a schoolhouse where some people had been waiting all evening for them, and who now pleaded with them to deliver an address.

While only a few people attended the first scheduled meeting – a good proportion of whom were MacColl's own kith and kin! – the Spirit was at work from the start. When one of the helpers returned to his lodgings he was asked to speak with the maid, who was in great agony of soul. The daughter of the house – also being under deep distress – listened intently to their conversation from a distance, and 'passed from death unto life just where she was'.[5] Two of MacColl's own relatives were also among the first converts of this mission.

As they walked to the local church on the second Sabbath morning, MacColl pondered deeply why it was that evening meetings were generally more markedly blessed than those held in the morning. Persuaded that a preacher should expect definite results from ministering the Word at any time of day, he immediately shared this conviction with his colleagues, and all three at once dropped to their knees in heart-felt intercession that God would use their ministry that very morning to the revival of His work and the salvation of lost men and women.

> The result was more blessed than pen and ink can describe. In the course of the service the preachers were conscious of unprecedented liberty in the proclamation of their messages, and it was very soon manifest that God was working in a special way. Many in the congregation were moved to tears. All conventionality seemed to be forgotten. Under the gracious guidance of the Holy Spirit, the service gradually took the form of a great enquiry meeting. It was long after the usual hour ere the congregation dispersed that forenoon. Many had already sought and found pardoning grace. Others remained behind in earnest conversation and prayer with the evangelists.[6]

Thus began a great movement in Lismore. So deep were its effects that people were being saved at their cottage doors or while attending to their cattle. Convinced that a movement of enduring nature had begun, MacColl at once called for assistance in the work from the church in nearby Appin. Dr McKay and Rev. Munn gave hearty response, crossing to the island each evening in a small boat, also being the means of carrying the blessing back to their home parish.

There was much evidence of deep conviction among the people, some men and women being literally prostrated under the burden of their sins. One man was in a terrible agony night after night. 'Oh, this hard heart,' he would say in Gaelic. MacColl and Dr McKay both tried repeatedly to lead

5. Stirling, p. 63.

6. Ibid. p. 65.

him to the Saviour. On the night of his conversion he threw himself on the floor in almost unbearable agony of soul, while much prayer ascended to God on his behalf; nor did he rise until the Lord had spoken peace to his storm-tossed soul. As the light of the Gospel shone into his heart, he rose up, his face all aglow with the joy of the Lord. Gripping MacColl's hand, he poured out his heart in gratitude for God's pardoning mercy.[7]

Another remarkable conversion involved a tall, handsome man who was at first strongly opposed to the gospel and would scowl angrily at MacColl. Before the end of the mission, however, he came out brightly for the Lord and was a few months later the means of saving McKay from drowning during an accident at sea as the doctor was returning by boat from a Sunday service in Lismore. This man in fact developed into an excellent gospel worker, organising a Christian Endeavour Society – with beneficent results – amongst the young people of Appin.

McKay confessed that whereas previously he had had little success in personal conversation regarding spiritual matters, now, such was the effusion of the Spirit that he became greatly used; constantly speaking with others on the boat to and from Lismore, and seldom bringing anyone to the meetings without their being led to the Lord. Further, as both he and Rev. Munn continued to cross over from Appin in all weathers from September to February inclusive, it seemed to be providential that during the many evenings he was engaged in gospel work during this six-month period the doctor was never called upon for medical help in his home parish. From the end of February, the nightly meetings were at last reduced to less-frequent services in the little chapel, which McKay and Munn conducted alternatively for a number of years. After the departure of the evangelists, it was noted how Gaelic became the especial medium through which God reached the people. 'Meetings in English seemed to be comparatively powerless, but as on the great Pentecostal Day the Word of Life came with power in their own tongue wherein they were born.'[8]

On the mainland the revival touched not only the district of Appin, but also the country area of Benderloch to the south. Here the local minister was initially unsympathetic to the movement, but before long changed his mind and threw his energy into it, opening up a Bible-class for the young converts and remarking years later that it was one of the finest pieces of work he had ever been privileged to do for God.

The movement also came to the 'preaching cave' at nearby Ledaig. This innovative sanctuary was inaugurated by John Campbell, who was 'graciously influenced and led to devote his life to Christ in the revival of 1843'.[9] Campbell had intended to enter the ministry, but, relinquishing

7. Ibid. pp. 66–7.

8. Ibid. p. 67.

9. Ibid. p. 2.

his studies for health reasons, was forced to return to Benderloch after a brief business career in Glasgow. Back home he became the local bard, doing a great work for Gaelic and English poetry. He also became an elder in Ardchattan Free Church, though his greatest work was the transforming of a natural cave amongst the rocks into a snug little place of worship capable of seating around fifty people.[10]

In this natural auditorium Campbell maintained a fruitful ministry for around forty years. He was particularly gifted in work amongst the young, teaching, in English and Gaelic, the simple truths of salvation in Sunday school, Bible class and week-night meetings. Here hundreds of young people received their early religious instruction and heard the gracious call of Jesus Christ.[11] Campbell was an old man when the revival of 1895 reached Benderloch, but he quickly opened up his Bible class in the 'preaching cave' for the young converts.[12] The awakening in Lismore appears to have had lasting effect, and when a minister visited the island in 1908 the memory of the meetings was vivid amongst the older inhabitants.[13]

KILBRANDON AND KILCHATTAN

THOUGH the combined parish of Kilbrandon and Kilchattan in Western Argyll had received a quickening touch of the Spirit in 1888–89 (see pp. 55–6), a further 'season of revival' accompanied a mission held in the parish a few years later.[14] Donald MacDonald was still the Free Church minister in the area and subsequent to the period of blessing, Duncan MacColl decided to assist this Highland friend for a weekend. Following an eighteen-mile hike from the train station in Oban, a warm welcome and full programme of meetings awaited MacColl as he arrived in Easdale. He crossed with MacDonald to the island of Luing, where they found a kitchen full of people waiting for a service, and as many more standing outside, unable to get in. A larger room was secured, but the same problem occurred here. Ultimately they adjourned to the open air, where an impressive meeting was held in the moonlight, and where, best of all, 'souls were born into the

10. A pane of glass in the roof kept out the rain while also admitting natural light from sun, moon and stars. A solid wooden floor was constructed and seats fitted to the curve of the rock. The only items of furniture were a bookcase and a table, said to have been made from a tree on which King Robert the Bruce leaned for rest after his fight with McDougall of Lorne! A natural window in the wall looked across the sea to Mull.

11. One of the earliest among whom impression was made was Duncan MacColl himself, his family having recently moved from Lismore to work a small farm in the Benderloch region. Indeed it was in this cave that MacColl signed the temperance pledge, to which he remained totally faithful throughout his life. In later years, MacColl would reminisce tenderly about 'dear John Campbell' and 'dear, dear Benderloch' (Stirling, p. 4).

12. Some years later this consecrated cave was ruthlessly demolished to make way for a railway line extension to Ballachulish, although nearby a hall was erected at Altnamara to commemorate the work of this saint and bard. Here for many a year Campbell's daughters carried on the ministry of their beloved father.

13. Stirling, p. 70.

14. Regrettably, MacColl's biographer does not record the exact date of this awakening.

sunshine of God's salvation'.[15] After taking the Sunday morning service in MacDonald's church while the latter was engaged elsewhere, MacColl returned with MacDonald to Luing in the evening. Here, more than one crowded meeting had to be held, so great was the eagerness of the people, and a large number professed faith in the Lord.

As MacColl left Easdale for Oban around midnight, with no human companion, his heart was so overflowing with the blessing of the Lord that he was conscious of no fatigue. His joy was such that he could not contain himself. That all-night walk was described by him as the 'happiest open-air meeting' of his life. As he walked, he shouted the praises of God with all his might, until at last he became conscious that he was giving himself a headache. 'What shouting it must have been!' wrote his biographer. 'Only those who knew his voice can form anything like an adequate estimate of it.' At one point on the journey he knelt down to pray, and so intense was he in his intercourse with God that he failed to notice that the ground was wet. Only after prayer was over did he realise that the legs of his trousers were soaked through. About 5 a.m. he arrived in Oban. By 11 a.m. he was back in uniform at the City Chambers.[16]

CAITHNESS 1897–9

TOWARDS the close of the nineteenth century it became evident that an unusual work of grace was going on in various parts of the north of Scotland. For years the faithful in Caithness had been entreating the Lord

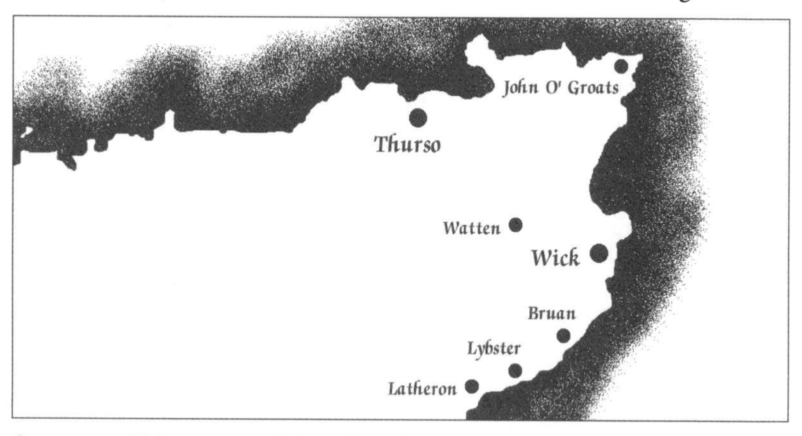

for times of blessing, and the Church in general was in high expectation that such favour was in store. The Rev. George H. Morrison of Thurso noted that over the course of many years he had rarely heard the public prayer of any believer throughout the county that failed to include simple,

15. Stirling, p. 93.

16. Ibid. pp. 94–5.

heartfelt petition for a season of spiritual harvest. The seed was sown through faithful preaching of the Word of God over many years. However, in a more immediate sense it was largely through the efforts of Highland evangelist John MacKay, Mr Cameron from the Highland Committee, and Mr MacPherson, missionary at Thurso First Free Church, that the fruits of blessing were made manifest. Excerpts from Morrison's diary give intimate expression of the day-to-day work at this time.

> Sabbath, 7th Feb. 1897 – Today Mr Cameron and I walked from Lybster to Bruan. Mr Cameron conducted the service in Bruan Free Church at noon. A very large gathering. At the close of, Rev. Mr Murray[17] announced the meetings for the ensuing week. He spoke a little on 'The harvest is past, the summer is ended,' etc; many were in tears. It is very evident we are on the eve of blessing here.
>
> Wednesday, 10th Feb. – While visiting today we came to a house where we found a young woman in great anxiety of soul. After some conversation, she yielded herself to Christ. Tonight we had our first inquiry meeting. Our unbelief has been rebuked. Four persons (adults) remained and professed to have received Christ. A most solemn time.
>
> Monday, 15th Feb. – Called at a house this forenoon, and found the father of the family under deep conviction. After talking to him for some time, he asked, 'Oh, how am I to come to Christ?' Our answer was, 'Come just as you are, with your sins, with your weakness, and cast yourself entirely upon Christ.' We quoted John 1:12 to him, and he there and then yielded himself to Christ. I shall never forget that scene; after we had prayed together we tried to sing Psalm 31:5, but all our hearts were too full. The mother and daughter of the family (earnest Christians) had been praying for him long, and great was their joy now as they saw him enter the kingdom. A father told us about his son who seemed anxious. We arranged to see him this afternoon; we found him in the field working. He was just waiting to be spoken to, and under the sky we together prayed, he asking God, for Christ's sake, to receive him as a poor sinner.
>
> Thursday, 18th Feb. – This has been a memorable day and evening. We visited all day, and many have entered into liberty, we have every reason to believe. There is no outward noise, but an earnest seeking after the truth. It was like a Communion Sabbath tonight. Old and infirm people were driven in carts to the church – some who have not been before for years. … Some of the people are coming eight miles every night to hear the simple story of the Cross. Tonight I was alone. I spoke on Isaiah

17. Minister of Bruan FC. Eight years later, in April 1905, following an ecclesiastical row, Murray was evicted from his church, to the great indignation of a huge number in the north of Scotland, among whom he was held in high honour during all of his more than forty years' ministry.

> 4:6. I had hardly spoken about ten minutes when the power of the Spirit was felt so great that nearly the whole congregation, including myself, broke down. It was indeed a place of weeping (Judges 2:1). Some wept on account of sin. Some wept for joy at seeing God's gracious work. One woman brought her husband to the meeting tonight. She has long pled with God on his behalf, and with him on God's behalf; and tonight he was given unmistakable evidence of a saving change.[18]

It was said of Bruan that everyone who could come was in church each evening and young men who went to sea made a point of being back in time for the services. Cameron wrote, 'It is very evident we are in the midst of a great revival here; we cannot get the people to go away when we intimate our after meeting.'[19] Altogether, over eighty people testified in Bruan to having received Christ. Of these, thirty-six joined the Church at the following Communion. In nearby Lybster too, the reaping was bountiful – around 200 standing up in the parish hall on the closing night of meetings conducted by the Rev. John MacKay, with no fewer than thirty-seven being admitted to membership of the local Free Church at the summer sacrament of 1897.[20]

Rev. Morrison commented on the movement's lasting results: 'If new love for the Word and for the House of God, if change of life, if the voice of prayer and praise in family worship, if the springing up of charity out of pure hearts and good consciences and faith unfeigned, if these things, and such as these, are to be taken as tests of a spiritual work, I would most respectfully submit that they are all present in this case.'[21]

Morrison also commented on the results of the move of grace on the very lay agents who were instrumental in channelling it. They had been humbled, and caused to hunger and thirst all the more for His righteousness. In turn this was invariably of humbling effect on the minister in whose church they were helping. The awakening also had a pronounced effect on preaching, all ministers finding it a renewed joy to preach from the Word. 'It is not that the preaching is more learned. It is not that it is more original. But it is that the very simplest and dirtiest text has flashed and sparkled again, as the dusty hawthorn by the hedgebank flashes under the dew of a May morning. We have learned, what is so hard to learn, that Jesus of Nazareth is far more original than we are. And all have determined again to know nothing among their people save Christ and Him crucified.'[22]

---

18. *PGA-FCS-H&I*, 1897, pp. 86–7.

19. *Report of the Committee of the Free Church of Scotland for the Highlands & Islands*, 1897, p. 7 (hereafter *RC-FCS-H&I*).

20. W.G. Mowat, *The Story of Lybster*, Lybster 1959, p. 19.

21. *PGA-FCS-H&I*, 1897, p. 88.

22. Ibid.

The blessing made manifest through the deputies of the Highland Committee spread also to other areas they visited in Caithness, and into Sutherland, in succeeding weeks and months. The far north of Sutherland generally had not shared in the great revival of 1860, nor in the blessings that flowed in many parts of the nation in 1874–5. However, during 1897–8 there seems to have been a moving of the dry bones all the way along the north coast as far as Cape Wrath. John MacKay noted that during his visit to north Sutherland, he found at Strathy, Farr, Tongue and Altnaharra, 'such earnestness among the ministers and office-bearers, and such a crowding to the meetings, as would cheer any heart. Our ministers in those wide districts are doing a good work. Mr Ross of Rosehall kindly responded to my appeal to him for help at Scourie, and our young minister there reported tokens of the Lord's presence were abundantly manifest.'[23]

In both counties old and young alike shared in the blessing, it being uniformly attested that wherever minister and congregation had been previously engaged in united, earnest and expectant prayer, early and abundant blessing was graciously vouchsafed. In Dornoch on one night as many as thirty persons stood up to testify that they had received Christ as personal Saviour.[24] In another place thirty-one new communicants were added within a few months of the mission. In Watten the number was twenty-four, more than double the number ever added at one time in the history of the congregation.[25] There were several instances of the families of elders receiving unusual blessing. In one place, noted MacKay: 'An aged grandmother, palsied in body, but firm and steady in faith, had the joy of seeing her aged husband and four of the grandchildren brought to the Lord. I shall never forget the long pew in which the three generations sat, four who had experienced a saving change before, and five who had just professed to pass from death to life.'[26]

Kirkintilloch 1897–8

IN the Dumbartonshire town of Kirkintilloch a quiet yet effective work was in progress throughout the winter and spring of 1897–8. It began in a simple and unassuming way with two or three gathering together for prayer. Soon the room they met in became too small for the numbers attending, so they adjourned upstairs to the Town Hall, which in a little while also proved inadequate. Finally they applied to the Rev. J.Y. Reyburn for the use of the Free Church building, which was cheerfully granted. Scores of young

23. *RC-FCS-H&I,* 1898, p. 6.

24. Ibid. p. 5.

25. Ibid.

26. Ibid. p. 6.

folk came out for Christ through the meetings that were held, and William Ross of Cowcaddens reported the joy he experienced in fellowship with those who had taken such a stand on a recent visit to the town.[27]

ARRAN 1897–8

IN the Shiskine district of south-west Arran a genuine work of grace attended the labours of John MacLean, known as *am Ministear Ban* ('the fair-haired minister'), who served the parish between the years 1880 and 1885. A decade later, the west and south of Arran again experienced exceptional blessing over a full two-year period when, in 1897–8, the labours of evangelist Mr Corsie were blessed to many. Areas visited were Lamlash, Whiting Bay, Kilmorie, Sliddery and Shiskine, and it was the latter two districts that were particularly affected, with over fifty people – many young – professing new-found faith at that time.

A minister who visited the island provided an interesting account of the work, all the more striking given that his visit occurred in 1904, seven years after the awakening broke out. 'As far as I can see it was a movement for which any man should have been thankful, and one should consider it forever a privilege to have been through it, though it were only as a door-keeper. The Lord was at work, and sinners were turning away from their sin. The fruits left are good. As might be expected, some fell back, and others are becoming moribund; but still the larger number of those who had then professed are living proof of the good done. I had the pleasure of attending the meeting, kept on still in this place by these converts, and I felt indeed refreshed among them. No man with Christian sympathy could but feel that there was reality there. I do not think for a moment that the movement is becoming exhausted. No, it is today bearing good fruit beyond the Rocky Mountains in America, and as far off even as New Zealand.'[28]

KINTYRE 1897–8

ACROSS the Kilbrannan Sound from Arran, God was also doing great things among the people of the elongated peninsula of Kintyre. The minister of the Lorne Street Free Church in Campbeltown was Alexander Bain, and it was to his church that the youthful Alexander Frazer went for a period of six months' assistantship in October 1896. Frazer conducted meetings in Campbeltown as well as many rural communities, such as Dalintober, Peninver, Kilkenzie and Strabane Farm. But it was Drumlemble in particular, a mining village about three miles inland from Campbeltown, which constituted 'the most important bit of the Assistant's work'.[29] Here a weekly Bible class had been held the previous

27. *TC*, 1898.

28. MacRae, *Revivals in the H&I*, pp. 36–7.

29. *RC-FCS-H&I*, 1896, p. 19.

winter for the benefit of miners and farm servants, being attended by men and women from all denominations. Frazer was keen to continue this good work, carefully teaching the Catechism and expounding its doctrines.

Both in town and country areas throughout the winter much expectant prayer had gone up to God, and there was a hopeful spirit among believers that God was going to bless the land, though when and how was not foreseen. Then, the following spring, during a week of special meetings at the close of this class, there was a deepening of interest and it became clear that the Spirit was moving. Souls were

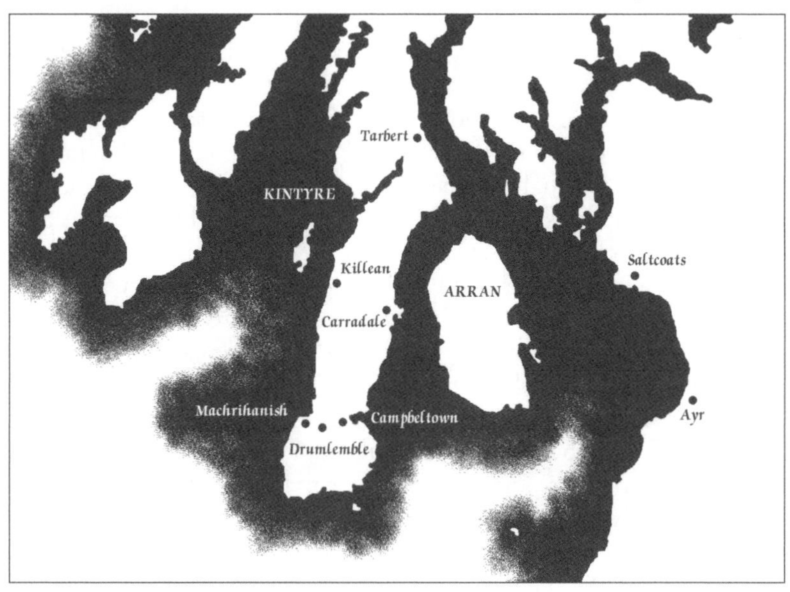

coming out for Christ in growing numbers as the nights progressed, and the week's campaign was extended to a fortnight, then to three weeks. The services were friendly and lively, with the singing of Sankey hymns, short prayers, a brief exposition of God's Word, and a short, pointed address. The schoolroom in which the meetings took place soon became 'crowded to the door', providing 'abundant signs of a great revival in the Laggan district'.[30] One night over twenty entered the inquiry room out of an audience of less than 200, overwhelming those giving spiritual assistance. Another night forty-one were dealt with, and all later professed conversion. Folk came from all around, many on a 'brake' (large horse-drawn carriage) put on specially to convey people from Campbeltown each night, and fully taken advantage of.

30. *The Campbeltown Courier*, 10 April 1897.

With a large number of farm lads and lasses coming through to a place of peace in Christ, there was occasion for great joy throughout the countryside, and spiritual issues were the main topic of conversation up and down the Strath. One of the first converts was a well-known and intelligent young farmer and a member of the Established Church. In the local coalmine almost the entire fifty workers attended the meetings, but all, too, seemed initially opposed to them. However, there came a break in their ranks so that, 'with the exception of two or three, every miner in the village, which was formerly a Sabbath-breaking, godless place, was enlisted under Prince Emmanuel's flag. The coal-pit that used to ring with vile song and savage blasphemy now resounded with 'psalms and hymns and spiritual songs. The day's work done in the darkness begins with prayer and ends with song.'[31]

News of dramatic conversions spread fast, and it was no time before many in Campbeltown itself were agitating for a similar mission in their own vicinity. Accordingly, an opening meeting was arranged in the largest venue – all 2,000 seats being taken – where some from Drumlemble gave testimony to God's saving power in their lives. For four weeks following this, nightly meetings were held in the large Y.M.C.A. structure, which, again, was packed every evening. As many as twenty and thirty would publicly profess Jesus on one night, close to 200 making public profession in all. Thankfully, virtually every church leader in the area was wise and gracious enough to spread his sails in awareness that the Spirit of the Lord was blowing, and to support this young apprentice who was reaping in apparent effortlessness and with public appraisal what they themselves had so patiently sown. Churches of all denominations benefited greatly in membership from the movement, with the number of communicants that year being the highest ever in Campbeltown. Nearly all converts already had connections with the Presbyterian churches, one exception being an engineer from Leith, whose boat happened to be in harbour over the Sabbath.

The local newspaper proclaimed that, 'the services have been productive of a widespread religious awakening greater than that of the celebrated evangelist Mr Moody. There can be no doubt that the good will be lasting.'[32] And lasting it was. One man, reminiscing on these stirring times many years later, testified, 'It was 68 years ago and it has lasted that length of time with me and there must be hundreds like me all over Scotland.' Among other pointers to the work's genuineness,

> the veterans of 1859 showed a beautiful Ananias-like spirit toward the young recruits of 1897. The village corner, where on Sabbath

31. *PGA-FCS-H&I*, 1897, pp. 84–5; *RC-FCS-H&I*, 1897, p. 16.

32. John T. Carson, *Frazer of Tain: The Rev. Alexander Frazer*, Glasgow 1966, p. 22.

> mornings the football matches of the preceding day had been discussed and plans made for the poaching raids of the day, was now deserted, the lads being at Church. … Farmers told of the wonderful transformation wrought in the ploughman's bothies. Masters and mistresses spoke of the change in the servants, while parents were full of gratitude for the conversion of their children. Some men resigned from jobs they found incompatible with their new-found faith, while 'Professing Christians' and even office-bearers of long standing have come out of their barren, useless formalism into the light and activity of a new-found joy.[33]

Everywhere the revival took hold, a striking yearning for the Word of God could be found, while in the country converts seized every opportunity for humble, earnest, united prayer, especially at mealtimes. Prayer meetings in Lorne Street Church rose from ninety to over 200 while the Christian Endeavour group more than trebled in size. There was a zealous desire to witness for Christ and even children were known to have led their parents to the Lord. A young carpenter could be seen night after night leading his fellow workers into the inquiry room, while one licentious miner who was recently converted was the means of saving change in the life of his dying father.[34]

The movement spread like a burning fire throughout the Kintyre peninsula. Mid-west of the district, in Killean parish, over fifty people confessed Christ. In the spiritually neglected area of Carradale, increased quickening had been gathering with the induction of George MacLeod to the UPC some years previously. However, it was through the visit of Samuel MacKenzie, under engagement of the Free Presbytery of Kintyre, that a peak was reached. High attendances induced a removal to the Free Church, and after two weeks a break came. Night after night for the next fortnight, many souls, both young and old, were brought to the Throne of Grace. It was said that such was the presence of the Lord that it felt like a cloud was hovering over the place, and the air was charged with spiritual forces. The vast majority who attended the services professed a saving change, and in one township of seven families, every soul, except the very young children, claimed to have become partakers of the blessing.[35]

Further north in the Skipness district, fruit was seen from the very beginning. MacLeod testified that the whole district was moved and

---

33. *PGA-FCS-H&I*, 1897, p. 85. The biography of Hector MacKinnon, who was inducted to Cambeltown's Highland Church in March 1897, also refers, albeit indirectly, to a significant united mission held in the town around this time (Mrs MacKnnon, *Hector MacKinnon*, London 1914, pp. 39–71).

34. *PGA-FCS-H&I*, 1897, pp. 85–6. Less than a year later Frazer was instrumental in heralding another season of blessing, this time in Queen Street FC, Inverness. (See www.scottishrevivals.co.uk)

35. Ibid. p. 86.

that such times had not been seen there since the days of the Haldanes a century earlier. Here, as in Campbeltown, there was some 'determined and bitter opposition' to the movement, 'and several cases of heartless persecution'. But much good was accomplished, and a Society of Christian Endeavour was set up in Carradale with 100 new members, and another in Skipness attracting over fifty.[36] With very few exceptions, the converts were said to have been 'doing well' a year later, and where no fellowship group existed, believers still came together for regular prayer and Bible study.[37]

TIREE 1885–1904

TIREE'S legacy of spiritual awakenings in the quarter-century from 1880 to 1904 follows closely on the heels of the 'great revival' of 1874.[38] Another factor conducive to spiritual quickening during this twenty-five-year period was the holding of special missions in various parts of the small isle by a number of visiting preachers, including Pilgrims from

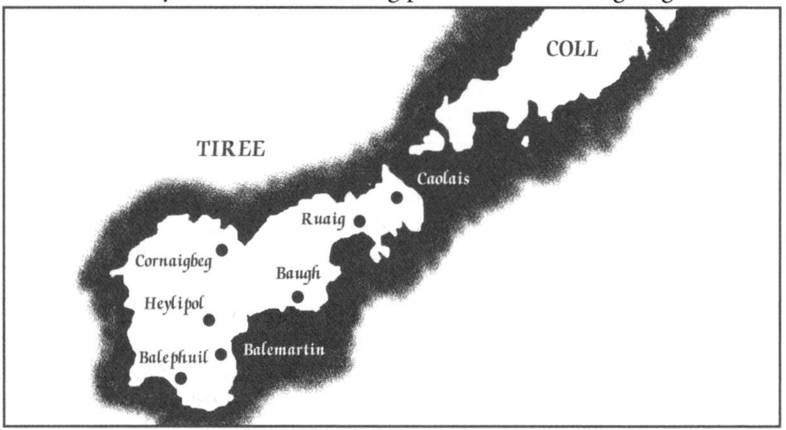

the Faith Mission, who visited regularly from 1895. While all the island's four denominations participated in these movements, the Baptists benefited most. Tiree-born Church historian Prof. Donald E. Meek states that, 'the period from 1880 to 1920 was punctuated by powerful revival movements in the Tiree (Baptist) church. Indeed, the current of revival flowed so strongly after 1874 that it is difficult to talk about revivals as isolated events in the life of the church.'[39] Peaks in activity (in the Baptist Church) occurred in 1885, 1895, 1898 and 1901–3, and onwards to 1914. Thereafter, of course, people in Tiree and elsewhere

36. *RC-FCS-H&I*, 1898, p. 7; ARC-FCS-H&I, 1898, p. 34.

37. *RC-FCS-H&I* 1899, p. 22.

38. Meek, Donald E. *Island Harvest : A History of Tiree Baptist Church 1838–1988*, Tiree 1988, pp. 16–20.

39. Ibid. p. 30.

became consumed with war events, although even then, 'the vision of an abundant harvest remained'.[40]

1887–8

WHILE the other denominations in Tiree were affected by a movement that occurred in 1887–8, it was particularly to the Free Church that blessing came at this time. It was preceded by much earnest prayer for an outpouring and also by the visit of a preacher who had just returned home from America, Cape Breton and Prince Edward Island, where he had seen God moving powerfully. The preacher testified to hundreds of Highlanders having been savingly changed in these faraway lands they had made their home. Many conversions had occurred via the instrumentality of R. MacLean, a young Free Church minister labouring in Prince Edward Island. In June 1887 the evangelist Duncan Drysdale paid a visit to Tiree, and both his preaching and his singing were effective in the conversion of some. A deep movement was now in progress. Six male students were converted and immediately became prominent helpers by speaking to the anxious, exhorting, singing at meetings, and similar. Others, as old as seventy and as young as thirteen, professed salvation. For two months two or more largely-attended meetings were held daily.

One remarkable conversion was that of a young girl whose conviction was so deep that for several days she felt unable to go to meetings. A Free Church correspondent takes up the story.

> On the day she next came she had to leave the meeting before dismissal. Some went with her and prayed for her earnestly. Then as we came out, the people were around her, and she seemed almost ready to die, when, suddenly, as they were praying, light dawned on her most wonderfully from heaven, and she exclaimed, with great emphasis, clapping her hands, 'I have found Christ; how good he is!' She is now a devoted, earnest Christian young woman.
>
> Some of them were very much awakened; and we had to pray and speak to them for a long time; but as a rule, there was not much outward demonstration or excitement. An old man of 65 years was in great distress, and had to be helped home and prayed with for some time. He could not sleep for two nights; but at length he found peace from the text; 'The blood of Jesus Christ cleanseth from all sin.' He gives evidence now of a saving change of heart. Another lad of 24 or 25 years was in much distress. At first he resisted the strivings of God's Spirit, and went to a vain neighbour's house to shake off his impressions. One night he was in terrible agony, and felt the burden unbearable. It

---

40. Ibid.

> struck him that he was putting a Crown of thorns on the head of the Saviour. He found rest from the verse, 'Behold the Lamb of God who takes away the sin of the world.' He is most earnest and powerful in prayer.[41]

As a result of the work of grace, weekday meetings were drawing as many in attendance as did formerly the Sabbath. On New Year's Day both a church and mission hall were full, not just for the morning service, but also in the evening. Family worship was eagerly set up; in some cases by young men who had never seen their parents pray. In one part of the island where locals had formerly met for music and dancing, the only songs to be heard were gospel hymns, including a number of new songs composed by recent converts.

1895

IN March 1895, as an agent of the Free Church, Dugald Matheson visited Tiree, the island of his birth, and found the place very much alive. Holding meetings in Balemartin, Cornaig and Ruaig, Matheson was delighted to find the halls full night after night, with approaching 200 people, of all ages, present. Towards the close of each meeting the Free Church deputy would ask how many were willing to stand on the Lord's side. Most of the congregation would stand up. As the evangelist and minister moved around speaking to those anxious about their souls, the congregation would sing a number of home-composed hymns. The meetings lasted around two-and-a-half hours and brought to Matheson's mind evening meetings on the island of a similar kind during the 1859–61 revival. He was very reluctant to leave the place, having felt, 'unless I am deceiving myself, the presence of the Master in a very marked way'.[42]

1898

ANOTHER movement occurred in 1898, when Baptist minister, Duncan MacFarlane, a native of Tiree, held meetings in the chapel at Baugh, midway along the island. MacFarlane preached every night for five weeks, assisted by co-workers from Tiree and by visiting Baptist ministers from Oban and Tobermory. For a short time local ministers from the Church of Scotland also participated. People gathered from all over the island, crowding into the church, and at least fourteen decisions were recorded by April. Further services, again well attended, were held in the Independent chapel in Ruaig, further to the east. 'We were looking for it and praying for it,' wrote MacFarlane, 'and the seed sown for years

41. ARC-FCS-SR&M, 1888, pp. 58–9, pp. 26–7.

42. ARC-FCS-H&I, 1895, p. 42.

is now bearing fruit. The revival of 1874 was on a larger scale, but not more interesting.'[43]

Assisting closely in the work at this time was Donald MacArthur, one of the first converts of the 1874 awakening. Known as an outstanding Gaelic preacher and pastor, he also laboured fruitfully in places like Islay, Mull and parts of the Scottish mainland. MacArthur became assistant to MacFarlane in 1898, and his ministry was characterised by as much zeal for the salvation of the lost as attended that of his pastor, whom he succeeded after the latter's death in 1908.

1901

MACARTHUR, 'whose praise in the Gospel is throughout the churches,'[44] was the human instrument in a revival in Balephuil, to the far south-west of Tiree, in 1901. This was the district where MacArthur was born, brought up and still resided, and it was of utmost joy to him that, apparently, almost everyone in that township was led to rejoice in Jesus as their Saviour at that time. In direct outcome of this harvest, it was for the occasion of a public baptism in May 1901 that A.A. Milne, the Baptist minister in Cambuslang, sailed over to Tiree to assist. Milne provides the following graphic account of such event.

> The weather was all that could be desired. The water was clear and beautiful under the beams of a blazing sun, and the bank of the loch, which forms itself into a crescent, was lined and thronged with spectators. Nine candidates for baptism appeared on the spot, accompanied by Messrs MacFarlane and MacArthur, Tiree; Brown of Bunessan, and Milne of Cambuslang; and after praise and prayer, a short address from Mr MacFarlane followed, to which the vast congregation listened with sympathy and respect, for the power of God was present to solemnise their spirits; and then one by one the candidates were led out by Mr Brown about 30 or 40 yards into the water, and baptised. The spirit of the Lord was moving amid the crowd on the shore, among whom were many converts of years' standing unbaptised; and from these an elderly woman, who had walked two or three miles to see the ordinance, was seen pushing her way through the crowd, and, stepping into the water, she begged to be allowed to follow her Saviour into the watery grave. Her request was readily granted, and after baptism she returned on the journey home without waiting to change her clothes. Then another, the head of a family, stepped into the water, saying, 'I have too long disobeyed my Saviour in this command,' and after he was baptised he thanked God, and testified that he had now peace of conscience. Another and another followed suit until, instead of nine, 17 were baptised.

43. Meek, *Island Harvest,* p. 30.

44. Ibid. p. 31.

> The following Sabbath, under the same favourable circumstances, and with as large a gathering of people, we met with four candidates on the same spot, but other four were moved to come forward 'at the troubling of the water', and these were baptised with them; and one of them, while wading out in the water, said to the missionary by whom she was led, 'I feel so much of God's power in my soul that I would not only follow my Lord through water, but even through fire if need be.' There are more yet to be baptised on the same ground, and several applications are on hand from the other end of the island, so that the Lord has done great things for the Church there to cause them gladness.
>
> There is no outward attraction whatever to explain these additions to the little cause. The buildings in which the little Church worships are probably the plainest and oldest-looking occupied by the denomination. There are no wealthy or influential members, but all are on one level, drawn from the cottar and crofter classes. Neither are amusements held out, such as soirees, conversations, or clubs, for only one soiree has ever been held in connection with the Church, and that as far back as 1874. It is Jesus who is the centre of attraction. 'In all things He has the pre-eminence.' The services are short, in Gaelic, and interspersed and brightened by hymns of their own composition; and at the close of every evening service a prayer meeting follows, which is always full and lively. And though the shades of evening lengthen on the fields outside and darkness gathers within, still the people are loathe to leave the place where God is blessing them. And he would be but a dull Christian who, on hearing them and understanding their spirit of prayer and praise, would not feel nearer heaven, and constrained to confess that God, of a truth, was in their midst. May the Lord continue to bless them and multiply such centres of usefulness in our Highlands and Islands.[45]

Such was the depth of interest aroused by the movement that it caused one of the missionaries on the island to make the light-hearted complaint that the 'people of Tiree are ill to serve now, because they will not be pleased unless they get meetings every night of the week!'[46]

1903–4

A FURTHER work of grace commenced in November 1903, receiving the hearty co-operation of Duncan MacFarlane, T.S. MacPherson and D.T. MacKay of the Baptist, established and United Free Churches,

45. *SBM*, July 1901.

46. Derek Murray, *The First 100 Years: The Baptist Union of Scotland*, Glasgow, n.d. p. 89.

respectively.[47] By January 1904 the movement became general throughout the island and a good number of young men and women were gathered in by the power of God, while many more were convicted but made no profession of faith at the time. Evangelist Samuel MacKenzie was called to assist in the work and his labours were gratefully received and blessed to not a few. One person commented: 'Looking back on these months since November, we can only say that the Lord's hand has been in the work and His blessing richly given.'[48] Yet again the following year, 1905, and perhaps influenced by reports of the revival in Wales, marked blessing attended meetings held on Tiree during May. Along with the tidings came a request for evangelistic deputies to visit the area.[49] As late as 1908, the Rev. John MacKay, assisted by the Rev. MacLauchlan of Coll, could report 'a considerable movement in Tiree. Ministers and people were greatly cheered, and the audiences seemed to have been in every case satisfactory.'[50]

While these recurrences of revival did much to boost church membership, this was greatly offset by emigration from Tiree for economic reasons during the latter half of the nineteenth century and well into the twentieth – mainly to Manitoba, Canada. The consequential struggle to hold the church together, and his constant travels on foot of up to twenty-five miles several times a week, had a serious effect on the health of Donald MacArthur during his period of ministry. Working largely alone, his health finally broke down in 1922, and Francis William Taylor, then pastor of the Baptist Church in Broadford, Skye, was sent to fill the gap.

Pre-Welsh Revival movements[51]

Nigg 1903

NIGG was considered a favourable spiritual location ever since John Balfour's days there in the early eighteenth century. The preaching of Rev. Swanson, whose ministry in the area lasted twenty-seven years,

47. D.T. MacKay was a tireless evangelist who reaped an enormous harvest throughout the Highlands and Islands over many years. It was said of him: 'He is not to be held in leading strings nor driven to any place; he is not to be counted an apostle of man, or by man. Like King Alfred, he desires to be free as his own thoughts. And yet he is ever on the Gospel front, plunging in where the need seems greatest, bringing strength where the line is likely to be broken' (*RC-UFCS-H&I,* 1923, pp. 9–10). As the reader will discover, his name crops up repeatedly in the present study.

48. D.P. Thomson, *Iona to Ardnamurchan by Mull, Coll, and Tiree: A Pilgrimage Through the Centuries,* Crieff 1956, p. 22.

49. *Missionary Record of the United Free Church of Scotland* (hereafter *MR-UFC*), 1905, p. 252.

50. ARC-FCS-H&I, 1908, p. 35.

51. There were, in fact, also pockets of pre-Welsh revival movements in Wales itself, as early as eighteen months before the 'official' outbreak under the ministry of Evan Roberts in October 1904; e.g. in a district in Glamorgan in the spring of 1903, and at New Quay, Cardiganshire, from February 1904 (Jessie-Penn-Lewis, *The Awakening in Wales,* London 1905 (reprinted 2002), pp. 48–50, 53–55; R.B. Jones, *Rent Heavens: The Revival of 1904,* 1931, pp. 31–3).

had a powerful effect on his hearers, as too did various succeeding ministers. After a period of several assistantships, Donald C.C. Gollan of Lochaber was ordained and inducted into Nigg's newly formed UFC in January 1902, a charge he was to retain for nine years. Remembered supremely as a pastor par excellence, his capacity to connect with and relate to his parishioners during times of trial and suffering was a gift he possessed to a remarkable degree. Regarding proclamation of the Gospel, Gollan's pulpit style was said to reflect a 'placid river rather than the mountain torrent. … He persuaded rather than compelled, and retained the interest of his hearers from his opening sentence to the last winsome word of the appeal.'[52]

It was into this setting that a season of spiritual renewal washed over the district in the spring of 1903, as reported by the weekly Ross-shire newspaper.

> The religious life of Nigg has been experiencing a time of remarkable spiritual quickening. Night after night for the past ten weeks the scattered population of this rural parish have gathered together under the guidance of the Rev. Donald Gollan, and in such numbers as to leave no standing room in the place of meeting. Boys of school age were there; rows of seats were occupied by young men and women from the surrounding farms; while sitting on the front benches were aged folk who could recall earnest ministries and religious movements of bygone days. Old men prayed; so also did the young; men long on the Way; and men newly entered upon the narrow path. No division! No jealousies! No suspicions! And today in Nigg there are seen glad evidences of the Grace of God.[53]

Westray 1903–4

IN the spring of 1902, evangelist Charles Robertson came to assist A. Campbell Sievewright, the local Baptist minister, on the tiny island of Burray, since linked to Orkney's mainland by the Churchill Barriers causeway. Through this ministry the 'interest rapidly spread beyond the limits of the church until the whole island was stirred' and 'some of the children of the school were amongst the first to experience blessing in the revival'.[54] This was due to the work of 'a little band of faithful and devoted teachers'. But an awakening of considerably greater intensity was soon to sweep over an island further north in the Orkney group.

52. Various, *Leaves of Remembrance of the Life and Work of the Rev. Donald Charles Campbell Gollan,* Coatbridge 1930, p. 28.

53. Ibid. Despite additions to membership, the overall figure rose only slightly between December 1902 and December 1904, due to an unusually high number being lost due to death or for other reasons (Nigg FC Minutes, 1902–4).

54. Burray Baptist Church Minute Book, 1904.

Westray, one of Orkney's most northerly and populous islands, has a strong evangelical heritage dating back to the closing years of the eighteenth century and the ministry of James Haldane.[55] A century on, in the winter of 1903, a fresh move of God's Spirit began to spread across

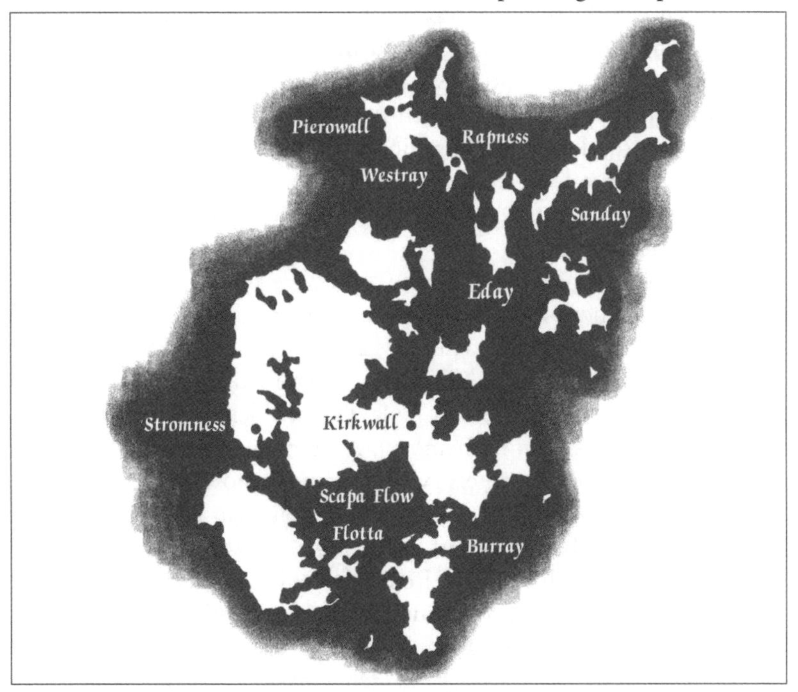

this northern isle. It was preceded by fifteen months of earnest, expectant waiting on God for revival, such outcome being strongly predicted by a deacon in the Baptist Church, who also took a great interest in cottage meetings in the area. Before he was to see his prediction come true, this man was killed through an accident involving his horse. His death was greatly lamented by many and no doubt induced deeper spiritual concern in the island. It was a great joy that two of this man's sons were converted during the awakening that ensued.[56]

It began largely through the capable ministry of the young A.Y. McGregor from Edinburgh,[57] who was invited to hold a mission in

55. In those pioneering days, the congregation worshipped in the open air, or met in barns or places like Noltland Castle, before establishing their own small Baptist Church. A 'deep work of grace' was seen on the island in 1843 and again in 1859–60.

56. *The Scottish Baptist Year Book* (hereafter *SBYB*), 1904, p. A16.

57. Griffiths described 'Young' McGregor as 'a godly, earnest, faithful and capable evangelist' who 'presents the truth in a most striking form … he exalts the Christ, makes much of the blood, presents the cross, and magnifies the grace of God by which men are saved and kept.' He was a member of Argyle Place UFC in Edinburgh, where his father was a much respected elder and treasurer. But he was also a baptised believer, and so felt quite at home labouring among Baptists. As part of his training for the ministry, McGregor had studied at the esteemed Moody Bible College in America.

the small Baptist chapel in Pierowall. As well as preaching the gospel, McGregor sang it, accompanying himself on his small organ. From the outset the work was deep and all churches on the isle – Baptist, Brethren, CoS and UFC – in whose buildings meetings alternated, benefited much. Such unity was most welcome, as ongoing strife had been evident following a church split in the late 1860s. The effects of this could still at times be felt. Once, while 400 packed into church for a united meeting, two or three stalwart members of another congregation resolutely sat alone in their own place of worship, until eventually they relented and went to the packed meeting house, slipping in as unobtrusively as possible, to the surprise and delight of all who noticed them.

Initially it was mainly the young who were touched, but gradually those more advanced in years also became affected. The work advanced steadily, despite the severe winter weather, with folk travelling many miles to attend meetings, walking unsheltered roads in terrific wind and rain (following an earlier season in 1903, considered to have delivered the worst weather in living memory). A number of individual cases of conversion are worthy of note. A young woman whose mother was dead, and whose final words to her daughter had been 'Trust in God and make Him your Guide' but who had never done so, was awakened by the hymn, 'Tell mother I'll be there'. Reminded of her mother's dying words, she was brought to Christ.[58] A young man, after trusting Jesus, returned home and burnt his pack of cards – 'the Devil's testament' – then induced his companions to do likewise. One merchant on the island found every one of his employees – about ten in number – to have been converted, while an unsaved hotel proprietor railed against the mission because of lack of trade.[59] Months later, while considerable preparation went into brewing, baking and cooking for the annual 'Harvest Home', much of it was wasted as hardly anyone turned up for the occasion![60]

On New Year's Day, 1904, the Baptist Church held three open-air services, two all-night prayer meetings, a watch-night service, and three further meetings. Aware that the work was of God and in His control, the Rev. A. Griffiths said one could only 'stand still and see the salvation of God as we saw in our Westray Baptist chapel more than 300 people of all ages leave their pews, walk up the aisles, and go into the inquiry room to seek and find their Saviour. We shall never forget the sight, and never cease to adore the grace so abundantly manifested to us in this nine-weeks' mission.'[61] Altogether, well over 400 – a quarter of the

58. *TC*, 14 January 1904, p. 25.

59. *SBYB*, 1904, p. A17.

60. Personal conversation with George Rendall, native of Westray, 12 September 2003.

61. *SBYB*, 1904, p. A16.

island's already religious population – confessed to trust in Christ, while many believers were quickened in faith. In the following months two baptismal services were held, during which twenty-four passed through the waters and into active church membership. A further nine became members shortly after, while others were waiting to be received or baptised. Concluded Griffiths, 'every church has benefited and Westray itself is like a new place in every way'.[62]

Some months later, in August 1904, the well-known London Baptist minister F.B. Meyer visited Westray,[63] reporting that 'the power and joy of those days linger yet, and as I went into the homes of the people, sat with them at their meals, sailed with them, walked with them, opened their old family Bibles, and spoke to them or knelt in prayer, it seemed that the breath of revival was still fragrant, like balmy air fragrant with the scent of heather'.[64] Meyer described the 'splendid Christians' of Westray as men and women of 'grace and grit', in an island 'where the people hardly care to don their Sabbath clothes unless you promise them a sermon of not less than an hour, full of good theology; where they believe the Bible from cover to cover; ... where there are no politics, no newspapers, and letters only thrice a week; where there are no public houses, no swearing, no magistrates nor police, no Sabbath-breaking; where the women are shy, the children modest, and the men religious'.[65]

A stone's throw from the Baptist Chapel, the Brethren assembly in Westray also shared in the blessing at this time, albeit providing a short-lived thaw in the tense relationship between the two groups, which had existed from the origins of the Brethren Assembly in the 1860s. Within this group, too, blessing was experienced in both Eday and Sanday, both of which had Brethren assemblies.[66] A work of grace was also experienced in the small south isle of Flotta. Ministers would row across Scapa Flow in small boats during the summer months when the weather was amenable. Griffiths visited the island and found God to be at work. Returning to his lodgings after one meeting, there was a knock at the door – a number of those attending the meetings were in distress of soul and earnestly sought the minister's advice. Griffiths was to liken the wave of emotion felt at this time to scenes from the recent Welsh revival. McGregor and Groat had visited Flotta in 1902, and, returning in 1908, found the work sustained. A beautiful little hall had been built

62. *Scottish Baptist Magazine,* 1904, p. 66.

63. Meyer was to claim some credit for the genesis of the Welsh revival which broke out just a few months after his Orkney visit (Eifion Evans, *The Welsh Revival of 1904,* Bridgend 1969, p. 169).

64. *British Weekly*, quoted in *The Orcadian*, 4 September 1904.

65. Ibid.

66. Neil Dickson, 'The Welsh Revival and the Brethren in Scotland,' Unpublished Paper, 2004, p. 5; (see also Dickson, *Brethren in Scotland,* p. 122).

to continue the work, meetings were blessed with numerous decisions, and prayer meetings were described as 'intense'.[67]

In counterflow to the great revival of 1860 (to which many likened this present one), which began on the nearby isle of Sanday, then spread to Eday and thence to Westray, the order seemed to be beautifully reversed with this breath of the Spirit. McGregor, accompanied variously by Griffiths and Orcadian colporteur and evangelist Thomas Groat, travelled from Westray to these other islands, the work back home being continued by a four-week mission from Mr Allan of Kelso. In Eday the united mission was extended due to a deepening of interest. In Sanday, A.C. Seivewright, the Burray minister, found great liberty and some folk came to church night after night who had rarely if ever attended before. He reported 'with safety that at least over 40 professed at my last meeting',[68] and well over seventy altogether.[69]

Other Movements

TIREE and Westray were not the only Scottish islands to experience significant blessing in the months prior to the outbreak of revival in Wales in October 1904. In February 1903, 'a work of grace' was reported among the Brethren in Lerwick, Shetland. 'Meetings have been held for a month, lasting three or four hours each meeting; the little hall became so crowded that the meetings were removed to a large fishing shed, with boxes, planks etc, for seats.' Other parts of Shetland were affected in the weeks following.[70] Around the same time a powerful interest pervaded the Strathspey district following meetings led by Samuel McKenzie. In one small church, '26 young persons have come out for Jesus'.[71] In a neighbouring parish, 'faithful dealing as regards prevalent forms of sin and worldliness had aroused some opposition, but ere long manifest signs of contrition were abundant, the whole district being singularly stirred. … A remarkable power has come upon the boys and girls over the district. A number from 12 to 16 years of age were completely broken down.'[72] Also in 1903 several villages along the north-east coast enjoyed a time of significant blessing, particularly Findochty and Portessie, while

67. *SBYB*, 1908.

68. Ibid., 1904, p. A19.

69. Westray's evangelical heritage remained strong through the next few decades, and stories were passed down of a short-lived but intense revival centring on the island's UFC., probably in the interwar period, when it was common to see the road 'black with folk', as islanders thronged to services in the kirk, which was regularly packed full (personal communication with Icy Harcus, Westray, 12 September 2002).

70. Dickson, 'The Welsh Revival and the Brethren in Scotland,' p. 5. Exactly a year previously at the other end of the country, in Stranraer and Lochans, both in Wigtonshire, the witness of two itinerant Brethren evangelists led, in February 1902, to 'scenes similar to the moving times' of 1869 in the area, when a spiritual movement had spread through the region over several years.

71. *RC-UFCS-H&I*, 1903, p. 8.

72. Ibid. p. 9.

the following year there occurred localised awakenings in Fraserburgh and Nairn (see Chapter 6).

Around the turn of the twentieth century, American Reuben Archer Torrey was starting to make a name for himself as a powerful evangelist. In 1902 he began an extensive world-wide tour with Charles M. Alexander as song leader. Their first mission in Britain took place in Edinburgh in January 1903. One night as many as 200 men walked down the aisle and confessed their acceptance of Jesus. One church that reached its highest membership figure as a result of many young people influenced by Torrey's campaign joining it was Broughton Place Church, led by the Rev. Dr John Smith.[73] From Edinburgh the two Americans, like Moody and Sankey thirty years earlier, transferred to Glasgow, where they remained for a month.[74] Here, one evening, 2,000 of 'the less fortunate class of people' gathered in from the streets of the Candleriggs district, and around sixty made professions of faith. Altogether, around 3,000 'decisions' were recorded in the city. William Oatts, Secretary of the Mission, had been an active worker in Moody's Glasgow campaign. He wrote that Torrey's work in Glasgow was 'in many respects even more remarkable than the work of grace in 1874', especially given that it lasted only a month, compared to Moody's five.[75]

Torrey and Alexander returned to Scotland some months later, in the autumn of 1903, and held a mission in Dundee. Although it rained almost every day of the campaign, Torrey insisted on holding an open-air meeting to reach the non-church-going people, despite the 'common-sense' objections of the mission committee. The time was set for two o'clock in the afternoon. Torrents of rain descended all through the morning, and much prayer was made for the rain to cease. At ten to two the rain suddenly stopped. A forty-five minute service was held, and within five minutes of the benediction, the rain came down in torrents once again! [76]

As with Moody, there was considerable opposition to Torrey's policy of public invitations. The Free Church believed that 'Dr Torrey's methods of constraining faith and urging men to confess Christ are mechanical to

73. Indeed, a member well acquainted with the church spoke of 'a spiritual awakening' having taken place in Edinburgh that year (1903), presumably as a result of the Torrey and Alexander mission (Anonymous, *Thirty Years of Broughton Place Church*, Edinburgh 1914, pp. 44–5).

74. It was at one of Torrey's meetings in Scotland that Kenneth MacRae first came to regard himself as a Christian, though the profession of faith he made at this time proved to be temporary (Iain H. Murray (Ed.), *Diary of Kenneth A. MacRae*, Edinburgh 1980, pp. 9–10). Writing at a later date of American evangelists such as Torrey, MacRae made note of 'the most unsatisfactory subsequent conduct of many of their professed converts' (p. 452).

75. John K. MacLean *Triumphant Evangelism: The Three Years' Missions of Dr Torrey and Mr Alexander in Great Britain and Ireland*, London 1906, pp. 19–29; see also George Davis, *Torrey and Alexander: The Story of a World-wide Revival* , London 1905, pp. 92–100.

76. Roger Martin, *R.A. Torrey : Apostle of Certainty*, Murfreesboro, Tennessee 1976, p. 167.

a degree.'[77] Characteristically, Torrey was adamant that public confession of faith was God's method, and he considered no other. There was also concern over the American's teaching on baptism in the Spirit and on hell.[78] Torrey spent a total of thirty months travelling around the British Isles, and while he and his supporters could glibly speak of 'two and a half years of revival work in Great Britain', in fact their missions were notably less successful than Moody and Sankey's in the 1870s, and it appears that nowhere – north of the border at least – did they act as the initiators of genuine revival.[79]

Alexander Frazer, hardly a stranger to spiritual awakenings (see pp. 74–8), witnessed a further move of the Spirit during the first decade of the new century, this while in charge at Tain UFC, Ross-shire. In the spring of 1904 a three-week mission was led by the Rev. John Ross of Aberchirder, whom Dr D.P. Thomson referred to as a 'real evangelist of the Highland type'. That year's report to the UFC General Assembly records that in Tain, 'There has been an abundant harvest of souls, over 150 have undergone a saving change and over 60 members were added to the Communion roll. A great outflow of generous giving has also followed.'[80] Though perhaps there was no general revival at this time, it was said that Tain had seen nothing like it since the days of Moody's visit thirty years previously.

COWCADDENS, GLASGOW 1883–1904 – A SPECIAL CASE[81]

THE son of a godly Caithness miller, William Ross entered the ministry in 1867, serving as pastor of Rothesay Free Church, Bute, until 1883. During these sixteen years well over 1,000 were added to the church, which

77. *MR-FCS*, 1903, p. 98. One writer, who heard Torrey in Edinburgh and in general approved of his preaching, gives this narrative of how Torrey would close a meeting: 'The following was the exact method that he pursued: 1) He invited all who wished to be saved to come forward to the front seat. 2) After which he read John 1:12, "As many as received him, to them gave he power to become the sons of God". The Dr then asked them if they were willing to receive Christ, and they replied in the affirmative. 3) Next he read Romans 10:9, "If thou shalt confess with thy mouth the Lord Jesus, and shalt believe in thine heart that God hath raised him from the dead, thou shalt be saved". Again they replied in the affirmative that they believed with their hearts, when he commanded them to turn to the audience and confess him with the mouth. This was all.' (ibid.)

78. A professor later constrasted Torrey's meetings to the Welsh revival of 1904–5, considering the latter to be more sincere, direct and spontaneous, while Torrey's methods were mechanical and hard, lacking both the joy and love which were most evident in the Welsh movement (Peter and Dorothy Bennett and Courtenay B. Harris, *Do We Consider the 1904/05 Revival as Just Water Under the Bridge?: Read the Reports From the Newspapers of the Day*, Llanfairfechan n.d., p. 44).

79. Greatest success was in London in 1905 – in the wake of the Welsh revival – where Torrey laboured for five months.

80. *RC-UFCS-H&I, 1904*. In fact a stirring of the Spirit seems to have been underway in Tain UFC as early as 1903, for 21 people were added to the church during each of the July and November Communions that year (Tain UFC Minutes, 1903–5).

81. Events in Cowcaddens FC cannot be fitted into any single time period considered in this book as it covers the entire twenty-one years of Ross's ministry among this north Glasgow congregation, which experienced almost continual bouts of revivalist activity from 1883 to 1904.

experienced 'wave after wave of blessing',[82] especially between 1880 and 1882. A call to Cowcaddens, Glasgow – a slum area reported to be 'one of the toughest arenas for the church in the United Kingdom'[83] – resulted in more spectacular growth still, with an incredible 1,050 new members in the three years up to the end of 1886.[84] Indeed, it was in May of that year that Andrew Bonar noted in his diary, 'the manifested power of God … has been shown for some months' in Ross's congregation[85] – such blessing also spreading to Bonar's own church. Among the young of Cowcaddens, a marked movement had commenced in October 1884, but became truly prominent in March 1885. A Children's Church Society was formed immediately after a visit from E.P. Hammond and numbered over 150 by April 1886.[86]

Ross's success was influenced by many factors. He was essentially a revivalist,[87] believing, controversially, that 'we may not be able to command wealth or friends, or sympathy or comfort, and it may be hard even to gain our daily bread. But, so long as God is true, we can command a blessing.'[88] As such, he laid plans for what his biographer-son calls 'a more or less perpetual revival' ('the trees on the banks of the river of God bear fruit every month, not every 20, 30 or 40 years').[89] Thus, he arranged for several missions every year, usually including one on temperance grounds and a long summer campaign in the open air.

The special missions were generally very fruitful in results. For example, at the close of a three-week mission in 1892, nearly 300 people over the age of fourteen professed Christ.[90] Ross said that for several weeks prior to Jewish evangelist Emilia Baeyertz coming to conduct a mission the following year, 1893, 'we felt first indications of coming blessing'. The church was 'right up against a thick stratum of hard rock' so 'we set ourselves to prayer, to lay hold on God for the blessing'. They also

---

82. J.M.E. Ross, *William Ross of Cowcaddens: A Memoir,* London 1905, p. 33.

83. Geraint Fielder, *Grit, Grace and Gumption: The Exploits of Evangelists John Pugh, Frank and Seth Joshua,* Fearn 2000, p. 62.

84. 218 people were received into church fellowship in the first few months of Ross's pastorate. Around half of these professed to be fruit of evangelistic efforts in the months preceding his arrival, when the church became crowded during Moody's 1882 campaign in the city, followed by the equally successful work of Major Colquhoun under auspices of the Glasgow United Evangelistic Association. Many of these converts soon went on to become office-bearers and workers in the Cowcaddens church.

85. Bonar, p. 349

86. ARC-FCS-SR&M, 1886, p. 62.

87. Ross had a keen interest in revival history and theory, and was once asked to write a handbook for revivals, sketching past revivals and defining conditions and methods necessary if old experiences were to be renewed. The book never took shape – his work at Cowcaddens instead became his volume on the subject – though he did, occasionally, speak on revivals at church conferences. (Ross, *William Ross,* p. 244.)

88. Ibid. p. 127.

89. Ibid. p. 120. One whose outlook on revivalism was contemporary to and comparable with that of Ross was Edward Last. Last's aggressive evangelistic ministry took place in Kelso and Glasgow (see www.scottishrevivals.co.uk for more information).

90. *RC-FCS-SR&M,* 1892, p. 13.

discovered around 140 families in the vicinity who had no visible church connection (many had recently moved to the area). These were targeted for special care and several pioneer missions were conducted. Then came the 'Glasgow Fair', when some 250,000 people were said to have left the city for ten days or more. Despite such unfavourable conditions, a mission was deemed appropriate, and Mrs Baeyertz – 'an evangelist of exceptional power' – came for a two-week mission. This was extended to three due to its remarkable success. Of one night towards the close of the campaign, Ross wrote, 'Altogether it was such a Sabbath as we had not experienced before for the manifested power of the Holy Ghost. …' [91] Mrs Baeyertz returned at the same time the following year, when it was said, 'No deeper or wider movement has been experienced in the history of the congregation.' [92] Indeed, interest was said to have been even greater than the previous year. About 240 persons were dealt with, a great many having no church connections, 'although many connected with other churches, far and near, were partakers of the blessing'.[93]

Perhaps even more remarkable than the special missions, Ross planned nightly meetings in the church which were directly evangelistic or spiritual in nature; his point being that the innumerable pubs and theatres in the area were open every night, so the Church ought not to be behind them in zeal and constancy.[94] Thus, night after night for the duration of his ministry the meetings went on, with faithful missionaries, office-bearers, and helpers from the congregation assisting in the work.[95] This was on top of a plethora of other meetings and services in regular operation – totalling around sixty meetings per week within a few years.[96]

This number increased greatly with the inauguration of three Pioneer Missions; these consisted of two women volunteers going to live in the very heart of the slums, in basic – but clean and pleasant – accommodation,

91. *TC*, 10 August 1893, p. 12.

92. Ibid. 26 July 1894, p. 26.

93. Ibid. 23 August 1894, p. 12. The 'work of grace' in Glasgow continued when Baeyertz moved from Cowcaddens to conduct a campaign in Trinity FC. Meanwhile, regarding a highly successful mission conducted by the Jewish evangelist in the Ayrshire town of Dalry in November 1895, one old missionary told the Rev. Alexander Aitken of Dalry FC more than once, 'This is what my wife and I have prayed for for years – a revival in Dalry, and I thank God that He has permitted us to see it' (*TC*, 5 December 1895, p. 12). For more on Mrs Baeyertz, see Robert Owen Evans, *Emilia Baeyertz, Evangelist: Her Career in Australia and Great Britain*, Hazelbrook, 2007.

94. Special effort was directed at delivering addicts from alchohol. Drink was the major scourge of Cowcaddens. As many as twenty-two pubs and licensed grocers were located in the vicinity of the church, and in a great many family circles of those who attended church were to be found at least one member beset by this social cancer (ARC-FCS-SR&M, 1887, pp. 60–1).

95. By 1890 there were 94 office-bearers (46 elders and 48 deacons), apart from other workers, serving in the church.

96. The wide array of organisations offered by the church included Sabbath schools, Bible classes, Christian Endeavour Societies, prayer-meetings, mothers' meetings, Boys' Brigade, children's classes, boys' and girls' industrial societies, church choir, literary societies, communicants' classes, medical missions, office-bearers and workers' meetings.

making themselves the friends of the people, visiting them and aiding them in sickness and trouble, and also conducting meetings for them in one of the rooms of each Mission-house. These Christian homes became a proclamation of hope and a defiance of despair, and soon won the hearts of many, also resulting in a steady stream of additions to church membership. As with the church, so also these centres enjoyed repeated seasons of spiritual blessing.

Ross describes one such divine visitation in 1901:[97] 'When I went over I found the little hall quite filled, there being about 100 present. … I asked those who had received blessing during the mission and who wished to be on the Lord's side, if they would stand. The sight was very striking – two thirds of the meeting were on their feet in an instant. There were a good many, I could see, undecided. Then I got all those who professed decision together in the front seats. There would probably be about 45–60 professing the Lord, and of these from 40–50 professed to have been brought in during these last few weeks.' Ross directed some probing questions to them regarding their commitment to Christ, to His Word, and to the Church. All were answered in the affirmative, causing Ross to exult, 'I have seen many touching sights since I came to Cowcaddens 18 years ago, but I never saw one approaching this.'[98]

Ross mentioned one notable case, among many, 'whom we have hunted for three years and could scarce get within gunshot of, and was brought in the first week, and has been very helpful with the anxious night by night since. Last night he was dressed like a gentleman. … I may say that the whole of this blessing is traceable locally to their 8 o'clock Sabbath morning prayer-meeting, where I asked them some months ago to pray for definite revival.'[99]

At a second Pioneer Mission, during the annual social of the Girls' Bible Class, 'There were 40 of them present and nearly every one of them had yielded their heart to Christ. They are both beautiful and bright for Him. They grew up in our Mission as children, and now have developed into this delightful Bible Class. I am quite satisfied that, if one had means, the condition of the sunken masses in any of our cities could be adequately met in a few years. It was one of the most delightful nights I ever spent. I can understand a little of the joy of the Lord.'[100]

---

97. The early months of 1900 also proved a time of marked blessing in the church, when, in the first seven weeks of the year, 'the workers deemed that they had seen about 170 cases in which, so far as man could judge, a real change of life had taken place' (Ross, *William Ross*, p. 229). Three years earlier, between May and June 1897, nearly 300 souls were conversed with at after-meetings.

98. Ross, *William Ross*, pp. 223–26.

99. Ibid. Indeed, the entire Cowcaddens work was founded in, and grew in, prayer, it being Ross's ideal that every evangelistic service be preceded by a prayer meeting, however few might be gathered for the purpose.

100. Ibid. pp. 227–8.

Even in each of the last seven years of Ross's ministry, an average of 115 new additions were made to Cowcaddens membership, with a further thirty-one per year transferring from other congregations.[101] During the latter part of this period – until his death in 1904 – Ross was also serving for half the year as an itinerant evangelist throughout the Scottish Highlands. Here, and elsewhere, he won the admiration of leaders from all evangelical denominations, developing, for example, a close friendship with Dr Hugh Pugh of Cardiff, who said that the first suggestion of the Welsh Forward Movement, which developed into great influence and was a contributing factor to the 1904 Welsh revival, came to him from what he saw on some of his repeated trips to Cowcaddens.[102] It was following a visit from a leader of the Forward Movement, evangelist Seth Joshua, to hold a fortnight's mission in Cowcaddens Church – and not in direct consequence of the Torrey mission in the city – that a deep work of grace was underway in Cowcaddens from the beginning of 1904. Over 100 professed conversion, while there also began a deep work of consecration in the lives of many believers.[103]

OTHER SIGNIFICANT MOVEMENTS IN THIS PERIOD[104]

Ayrshire 1896–9
Dumfries and Kilmarnock 1891–2
Kelso, Glasgow and Edinburgh 1888–1900
Spreading Branches of the Faith Mission
  Cellardkye 1890
  Western Highlands 1895–1902
Inverness 1898
Haggs 1902

---

101. The church minutes during the entire time of Ross's leadership suggest a perpetual revival in progress, as quarter after quarter (sometimes bi-monthly), impressive lists of additions to membership are stated. This is at times deceptive, however, for additions in a given year were sometimes more than offset by removals. E.g., while 144 new members joined during 1898, 241 were removed (153 by certificate, 51 without, 12 by death and 25 by discipline), giving a net loss during the year of 97 and a membership at the year end of 1,177 (Cowcaddens FC Minutes, 1899). Other churches in Glasgow also saw marked growth in the latter part of the nineteenth century. Rose Street FC grew remarkably from almost nothing to 1,000 communicants. Indeed, while in 1853 there were only 30 congregations in Glasgow and its suburbs, this had increased to 84 by 1893 (Norman Walker, *Chapters From the History of the Free Church of Scotland*, Edinburgh 1895).

102. Was it Dr Pugh also who stated that Ross's 'short visits to Wales have done more to awake our congregations and to inspire our ministers to aggressive work than that of any other man I know'? (Ross, *William Ross*, p. 283).

103. T. Mardy Rees, *Seth and Frank Joshua, the Renowned Evangelists*, Wrexham 1926, p. 62.

104. Full accounts of these movements can be found on www.scottishrevivals.co.uk.

Easdale, Argyle – p.69

Duncan MacColl – p.66

Alexander Frazer – p.74

Carradale, Kintyre – p.77

Balephuil, Tiree – p.81

Pierowall, Westray – p.86

Reuben A. Torrey – p.89

William Ross – p.90

3
General Awakening
1905–6

The Spirit Moves Throughout the Land, 1905

MORE has been written on the Welsh revival of 1904–5 than perhaps any other specific revival in history. A century on and still new information and assessments are being published.[1] The revival was, as R. Tudur Jones stated, 'one of the most remarkable events in twentieth-century Welsh history'.[2] Its seemingly spontaneous outbreak and rapid spread throughout much of Wales, especially south Wales; the deep conviction, fervent vocal prayers and enthusiastic singing of converts; and not least the influential part played by the charismatic, highly unpredictable and enigmatic Evan Roberts, have all combined to fascinate generations of believers and non-believers alike throughout the whole of the twentieth century and into the new millennium.[3]

News of sensational activities in Wales spread quickly throughout the British Isles and continental Europe, and, in time, to far-flung places of the world. Indeed, one of the striking facts of the Welsh revival was its virtually global influence. 'Within a comparatively short time,' wrote Eifion Evans in his foreword to Noel Gibbard's 'On the Wings of the Dove', 'people were flocking to this little-known country on the Celtic fringe of Europe from neighbouring countries and across Europe. A decade later and all five continents had experienced the ripples of revival.'[4] Within weeks of its commencement, news of the Welsh awakening came trickling through to believers all over Scotland. A very considerable number of Christian leaders went to observe the revival in Wales for themselves. Noel Gibbard states that

---

1. e.g. Noel Gibbard, *Fire on the Altar: A History and Evaluation of the 1904–05 Welsh Revival,* Bryntirion 2005; Jones, *Faith and Crisis*; Rick Joyner, *The World Aflame,* Pineville, NC 1993.

2. Jones, *Faith and Crisis,* p. 283.

3. Amidst the many reports coming in from all over Wales of revival being experienced in their congregations came one from Windsor Place (Presbyterian), Cardiff, stating, 'No result yet; but this is not surprising having regard to the nature of the congregation, largely Scotch people' (Gibbard, *Fire on the Altar,* p. 57)!

4. Gibbard, *On the Wings of the Dove: The International Effects of the 1904–5 Revival,* Bryntirion 2002, p. 9.

from Glasgow alone, people 'thronged to Wales during the end of 1904 and the beginning of 1905'.[5]

A number of stories were told of the involvement of Scotsmen in the Welsh movement. 'Let us have the fire in Scotland!' exclaimed one Scotsman in the gallery at Ebenezer Chapel, Cardiff. This was endorsed by the Rev. B. Logan from Glasgow, who fervently prayed that the revival might reach cold and parched Scotland. The congregation

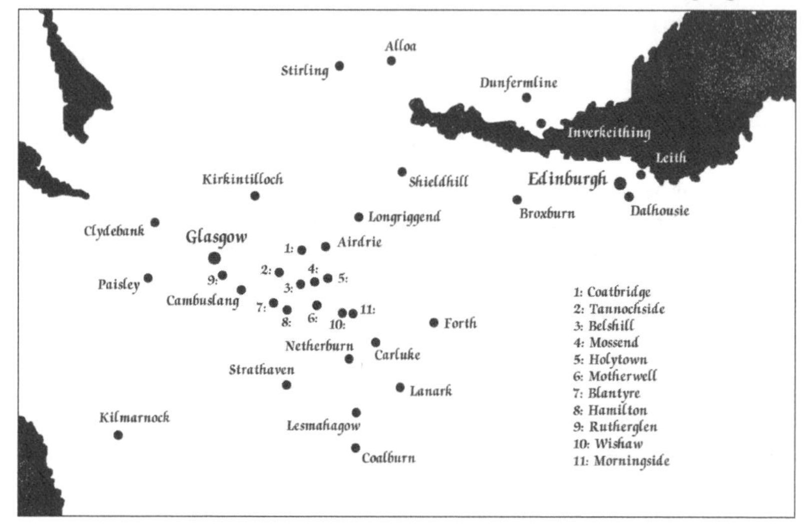

responded by singing, 'It is coming now.'[6] In the first week of 1905 a Scottish sailor implored a large gathering in a Welsh chapel to 'get back tae yer mither prayer', and with a pathetic simplicity he recited, 'Gentle Jesus, meek and mild, look upon a little child.' The people were deeply affected by the sailor's earnest, simple eloquence, and many conversions followed.[7] Brynmor Jones suggests that some people began compiling a 'map of revival blessing' in various parts of England and Scotland as a result of prayers made by Welsh believers for specific districts in these neighbouring countries.[8] In a personal interview granted to John Anderson of Glasgow, Evan Roberts made clear that while he had no desire to speak at meetings in big cities like London

5. Gibbard, *Fire on the Altar,* p. 114. One Glasgow minister who visited was Hugh Black – later Professor of Union Seminary, New York – who remarked, 'I am not come to judge the revival, for it is the revival that judges me' (Bennett and Harris, *1904/05 Revival,* p. 46). J.G. Govan, founder of the Faith Mission, also journeyed to Wales to experience the revival for himself, and was profoundly blessed by what he saw. In turn the Faith Mission was said to have been 'much influenced by the Welsh Movement' (Govan, *Spirit of Revival,* p. 137). Scottish theological students were also among those who came to observe the revival in Wales (Bennett and Harris, *1904/05 Revival,* p. 44)

6. *Glasgow Weekly Herald,* 14 January 1905.

7. Ibid.

8. Brynmor P. Jones, *Voices from the Welsh Revival 1904–1905: An Anthology of Testimonies, Reports, and Eyewitness Statements from Wales's Year of Blessing,* Bridgend 1995, p. 151.

or even Swansea, he had every intention of visiting Glasgow, probably towards the end of March.[9]

The remarkable events witnessed by Scottish visitors to Wales often helped to renew spiritual enthusiasm in the leaders' home congregations. From the start of the New Year special services were being held all over the land. Some of these were missions conducted by travelling evangelists; others were spontaneous gatherings or meetings organised by individual churches, aware that the Spirit was hovering over the nation. Indeed, in virtually every county in the land there was a charged spiritual atmosphere, with an extraordinary expectancy among believers and a heightened spirit of prayer, along with an increased openness and yearning among the unsaved. While a number of favoured places experienced full-blown revival at this time (e.g. Motherwell, Charlotte Chapel, Cockenzie and similar – see Chapter 3), general awakening developed throughout much of Scotland – with all denominations reporting growth. Unquestionably it constituted the most widespread time of spiritual awakening in Scotland in the twentieth century.

Glasgow

MEETINGS were held in halls in Glasgow from the start of the New Year. The Rev. B. Logan from the Glasgow Tent Mission had journeyed to Wales, and on his return home in January 1905 arranged special meetings in the capacious Tent Hall, 2,000 gathering for the first event.[10] These meetings progressed 'on the same lines as that in Wales',[11] in that they were 'left largely to the audience, and are not dependent to any great extent on the leaders. The people start the hymns, and prayers are offered just as the Spirit moves the people; and preaching or giving addresses forms but a minor part of the proceedings.'[12] The crowds weren't attracted by special evangelists, for none came, and there 'was no organisation except what grows out of the work as it goes on'.[13] Well over 5,000 inquirers were given instruction in the first six months of 1905 at this location alone.[14]

A 'revival party' from Wales travelled to Glasgow in March 1905, eager to see the rich blessing so abundant in south Wales spread also to other parts of the U.K. The group was made up of four men and ten women, the majority from Cardiff, including the leader, A.W. Morris. Among

9. *Glasgow Weekly Herald,* 21 January 1905.

10. Gibbard, *Fire on the Altar,* p. 114.

11. J. Edwin Orr, *The Flaming Tongue: The Impact of Twentieth Century Revivals,* Chicago 1973, p. 33. Logan believed, however, that the revival in Wales was a stream that flowed into an existing river of blessing in Scotland.

12. *The Revival,* 16 March 1905, p. 6.

13. *The Christian Herald,* 25 May 1905, p. 455.

14. *SBM,* 1905, p. 64.

them also was Mary Davies, a friend of Evan Roberts and one of the five popular lady singers from Gorseinon. Pastor Jack Findlay invited the group to minister in his St George's Cross Tabernacle. Amazingly, this large auditorium, which held around 6,000, could not accommodate all who wished to hear news of the Welsh revival. One witness, seeking to describe meetings, wrote, 'Voices throb with emotion and prayers rise above song, but the chief blessing has followed when the old Gospel has been preached. At all meetings tears ran down hundreds of cheeks, and perfect showers of requests for prayer are sent to the platform speakers, who carry on till exhaustion calls a halt.'[15]

One of the team announced that 'Scotland is on the eve of a great religious awakening.' As many as 1,200 assembled for the afternoon prayer meetings, while hundreds had to be turned away from the Lord's Day services as well as some week-day meetings. Findlay wrote of the 'gracious outpouring God has been pleased to send upon us. ... The meetings have been marked by much heartiness and freedom – prayer, song and testimony flowing on in an almost endless stream, leaving little time for anything of the nature of "ministry".' While most of the Welsh party remained in Scotland for some time, Morris returned to Cardiff after two weeks, rejoicing in the fact that 700 had professed faith during that time.

To reach a wider and larger circle, Findlay rented Hengler's Circus in Sauchiehall Street and held services twice a day for a week. The pastor wrote that 'those eight days ... will live in the memories of many. Alike for the numbers attending, the eager interest, and the apparent results, it was one of the most remarkable weeks we have known. Several hundreds of persons of all ages and both sexes (although males were in the majority) professed to surrender to Christ, and many of them were undoubtedly cases of genuine conversion. The converts' meeting on the Monday night was a remarkable occasion. The Tabernacle was full, and filled with joy and overflowing enthusiasm. Upwards of 200 of the converts gave testimony.'[16] On the last Sunday evening of the Welsh team ministering in the large circus hall, a second meeting had to be held for those who couldn't get in to the earlier service and were still waiting outside – constituting the sixth meeting of the day in that venue![17]

Findlay made a still greater effort later in 1905, which arrested the attention of the community at large. He once again engaged Hengler's Circus, this time for the month of September, to hold a mission to be led by evangelist Hugh Paton. Attendance, including large numbers of young men, increased steadily until hundreds were being turned away. On Saturday night a 'moral

15. *Glasgow Weekly Herald*, 25 March 1905.

16. Alexander Gammie, *Pastor D.J.Findlay: A Unique Personality*, London 1949, pp. 33–4.

17. *Christian Herald*, 30 March 1905.

street sweep' took place, when two processions of workers, one headed by a brass band, the other by bagpipes, moved along the city's main streets at pub closing time, and many men under the influence of alcohol were gathered and directed into the Circus, where 'a very fruitful if not a very orderly' meeting was held until the wee hours of Sunday morning. The spiritual results were said to have been remarkable, a larger number of non-church-goers being reached than during any mission of the kind. At the same time the regular meetings in the Tabernacle were largely attended, 'and the power of God has rested on them to a marked degree'. Many of the Circus converts, including some converted during the Saturday 'sweep', found their way to the Tabernacle, and were soon 'witnessing for their new Maker'.[18]

Meanwhile, a second team of Welsh revivalists was at work in various parts of Scotland from April 1905. The group was led by Thomas A. Davies, revival correspondent of the Welsh *Western Mail*, who used the pen-name 'Awstin'. The team worked with W. Breckenridge in Glasgow and with D.W. Roberts, a Baptist minister from Helensburgh. At one Sunday service Awstin jotted in his diary, 'Scotsmen and Welshmen full of the fire of the revival.'[19] The Rev. William Clyde and members of his Baptist Church at Glasgow's Tollcross had persevered in prayer for a fortnight before a visit of Maggie Condie, a member of the Welsh party, who worked heartily, both in church meetings and in street evangelism. During the first week 70 professions of faith were recorded, followed by 80 more during the second week, when an extra effort was made by many to bring people to the meetings. Parents would bring their children and children their parents. Many bore testimony to the grace of God in their lives, some of their stories being especially dramatic.[20]

A deep work of grace took place in Cowcaddens Church after Welsh evangelist Seth Joshua conducted a mission there in January 1904 (see page 94). When William Ross, the church's charismatic pastor, died in April of that year, a small band of people began to meet together in a private house to plead definitely for a spiritual outpouring on the district. Times of trial within the denomination (UFC) served to strengthen their prayer efforts, as too, many months later, did news of revival in south Wales. 'Abounding, passionate, agonising, persevering prayer for the Lord's revival in Scotland, not a man-made copy of that in Wales', was engaged in, while addresses on the same theme were also given. Blessing seemed to come spontaneously on 8th January 1905, and for many weeks following not a day passed without someone making

18. Gammie, *D.J.Findlay*, pp. 35–6. Yet another highly successful campaign, again led by Hugh Paton, was conducted in 1906, when congregations of over 3,000 were drawn from all parts of the city and suburbs. Thus concluded, wrote Gammie, 'a great period in the history of the Tabernacle'.

19. Gibbard, *Fire on the Altar*, p. 117.

20. Ibid. pp. 117–18.

profession of faith, either during regular services or at open-air meetings, and the like. The work of consecration among believers had continued through the previous year, as many workers 'passed through the most sacred and searching process of being crucified unto all sin and to subtle self before they received their baptism of power. Wonderful it is indeed,' noted one observer, 'to behold workers coming back to something that for power and delight transcends even their first enthusiasm of youthful faith and love.'[21]

When Awstin and Findlay ministered at Henderson Memorial Church in June 1905, the crowds were so large they had to close the gate to stop them rushing into the chapel. A prominent place was given to singing both Welsh and English hymns.[22] Not all meetings ran so smoothly, however. One day *The Weekly News* reported that 'the feeling was so high the other night that the police had to stop the religious meeting at Station Square. It was the miners' pay night and matters had become rather lively owing to the Catholics questioning the speakers.'[23]

In one area of south Glasgow, a number of people connected with the liquor trade had approached ministers and professed great interest in the revival work, wishing to find some way whereby their connection with the traffic could be broken.[24] In Govanhill and elsewhere, football teams were disbanded due to players being converted and caught up in more 'worthwhile' pursuits.[25] In Port Dundas, to the north of the city, there was a deep work of grace following six months of prayer for revival. Leaders were plain working men who pled for their fellow citizens and were astonished at the results. One night, out of thirty new converts, only two were found to have had previous connections with the Church.[26]

Four years after being born of the Spirit in 1886, teenager John Harper experienced a baptism of power and an increased passion for souls. The next day he took his stand on a street in his native village of Houston, Renfewshire, and strongly entreated all in his audience to become reconciled to God. For the next five or six years he carried on his day-job as a mill-worker but in the evenings and weekends would be found street preaching in Houston and nearby communities such as Bridge of Weir, Kilbarchan, Elderslie, Linwood and Johnstone. Impressed by his obvious gifting, the Pioneer Mission supported him in forming a church in 1897 with twenty-five members. Growth came quickly, and a corrugated iron hall was built at Kinning Park

21. *MR-UFC,* 1905, pp. 113–14.

22. Gibbard, *Fire on the Altar,* p. 119.

23. Quoted in Gibbard, *Fire on the Altar,* p. 118.

24. *United Free Church of Scotland Conference on Revival and Evangelistic Work*, 1905, p. 173.

25. Dickson, *Brethren in Scotland,* p. 123; *The Welsh Revival and the Brethren in Scotland,* p. 14. See also Orr, *The Flaming Tongue,* p. 34.

26. *Christian Herald,* 23 November 1905.

dockyards in 1901, seating 550.[27] While a born expositor, Harper was pre-eminently an evangelist whose entire ministry was soaked in prayer. When he spoke, 'the words came hissing hot from his heart ... he lived and preached as if Christ died yesterday, rose today, and was coming tomorrow.'[28]

One colleague spoke of 'constant revivals' in Harper's church, with overflowing crowds and hundreds of souls saved and blessed. The most memorable season of blessing was in 1905, being preceded by many months of earnest and united prayer for such occasion. W.D. Dunn, a native of the Borders and, since the mid-1870s, one of Scotland's most popular evangelists,[29] testified to seeing after-meetings looking 'more like a battlefield than anything else. Saints sobbing on account of their unwillingness to Christ, and poor lost sinners crying out for salvation.'[30] Scenes were compared to those of the Welsh revival ... 'crowds so great that it was difficult to get in, and after getting in still more difficult to get near the platform. Then, before anyone could speak 10 minutes, souls crying out for mercy under the mighty power of God. It was not excitement. It was the Holy Spirit convicting of sin.'[31] In just five months, over 1,000 professed faith in Christ, with over 230 joining the fellowship. Whole families underwent a change – as many as fourteen relatives in one family circle alone.[32] This called for an enlargement of the church premises in the same year – to seat 800 – by which time membership had risen to 445.[33]

Elsewhere in Glasgow's Kinning Park, 1905 was recorded as a 'year of revival' in the UFC, during the first year of the Rev. Lamont's pastorate. 'Prayer has been the secret of it,' he recorded. 'Besides meetings for prayer on Sabbath mornings at 10 o'clock and at the close of the evening service, our office bearers and workers lately entered into a solemn covenant of daily private prayer. There have been special missions with marked results, but in quiet weeks when there were no missions the ordinary means showed the continuous working of the Spirit. In all, about 140 in the congregation have professed conversion during the year, and the additions to the membership number 142.'[34] There was also considerable blessing among the Brethren in this district, who reported 200 conversions.[35]

---

27. Rev. George Yuille, *History of the Baptists in Scotland*, Glasgow 1926, p. 175; John Climie, *John Harper, a Man of God*, Glasgow 1912, p. 75.

28. Climie, p. 75.

29. For a profile on Dunn see *TC*, 7 June 1906, p. 16.

30. Climie, *John Harper*, p. 66.

31. Mr Malcolm Ferguson, Anniesland, quoted in Climie, pp. 74–5.

32. *MR-UFC*, June 1905, p. 252.

33. Harper died in 1912 while on the fateful *S.S. Titanic* en route to America, where he was to conduct an Evangelistic Mission in the world-famed Moody Church in Chicago. Later, in 1921, the Harper Memorial Church was opened in Glasgow in memory of this outstanding pioneering evangelist (Yuille, p. 175).

34. *MR-UFC*, 1906, p. 62.

35. Dickson, *Scottish Brethren and the Welsh Revival*, p. 12.

For Glasgow's Highland and Open-air Gospel Mission, 1905 was also a year of spiritual awakening. Their recently-acquired premises in Oswald Street, capable of seating 1,200 people, was oftentimes crowded to utmost capacity, and the Mission's founder, Duncan MacColl, entered into a deeper experience of the fullness of the Holy Spirit around this time. The years 1906–7 showed a further increase in the work, with so mighty a spirit of prayer prevailing among believers that it was no uncommon thing for the pre-arranged evangelistic service to be abandoned in favour of prolonged and passionate intercession.[36]

Lanarkshire-born George Sharpe came under the influence of the Holiness movement while ministering in America between 1886 and 1901, where he experienced several notable revivals. Shortly after being ordained into the Methodist Episcopal Church of America, Sharpe returned to Scotland. He wrote that during the year following his induction to the Congregational Church, Parkhead, in September 1905, 'every department in the church was ablaze with new interest. The membership grew every month while the growth of the Sabbath school was phenomenal.'[37] Dissension over Sharpe's emphasis on entire sanctification led to his eviction in October 1906. Independent meetings were promptly started in Great Western Road Halls and these became immensely popular. 'A new day had dawned in Parkhead, and a new interest in spiritual things had begun in the places round about. The following weeks the altar was filled with seekers, and for many, many months, week nights and Sabbath nights, and at times on Sabbath mornings, seekers were at the altar, six, seven, eight, nine, ten, eleven, twelve and thirteen at a time. They came from different parts, from Uddingston, Shettleston, Dalmarnock, Bridgeton, Springburn, Tollross, Dennistoun, Townhead and other places.'[38]

NORTH LANARKSHIRE[39]

MOTHERWELL

A NUMBER of factors led directly or indirectly to a remarkable move of God in the Lanarkshire town of Motherwell – the centre of Scotland's iron and steel trades – at the beginning of 1905. One visiting convention speaker – Dr Stewart MacColl from Australia – was led to predict, even

36. Stirling, pp. 45–7.

37. Sharpe, *'This Is My Story,'* pp. 69–70.

38. Ibid., p. 76. Soon thereafter a new church was built, Parkhead Church of the Nazarene, opening in December 1907. Offshoots were planted in the nearby towns of Paisley, Uddingston, and Blantyre. In 1909 The Pentecostal Church of Scotland came into being, with Sharpe as its leader. The church continued to grow and became a stronger advocate of holiness. (Anonymous, *The Church of the Nazarene in the British Isles,* n.d.).

39. For an account of revival movements in Bellshill and Clydesdale in 1905, see www.scottishrevivals.co.uk.

before there was any word of awakening in Wales, that revival would surely come to this town soon, and he even asked a colleague to telegram him 'when the thing breaks out!'[40]

For around twenty years Motherwell had been the home base for the Lanarkshire Christian Union, providing a rallying point for evangelical thought and activity amidst the throbbing life of the town. Playing a significant part in the L.C.U.'s activities was John Colville, a large employer in the district, chief magistrate for the burgh and Member of Parliament for the area. He was seen as a tremendous witness for Christ in Motherwell, pleading with listeners at the town cross one Sunday night in August 1901 to 'yield yourselves unto God';[41] this just four days before he passed to 'glory'.[42] Such was Colville's popularity that his very death brought about a degree of spiritual awakening in Motherwell, as well as in the Bellshill and Newarthill areas.[43]

Friday evening prayer meetings were begun in September 1904, whereby concerned Christians met between 8 p.m. and 1 o' clock the following morning to plead with God to move powerfully in their locality. At a convention in October, fervent prayer was again in strong evidence, and enthusiasm was soon to be enhanced by first reports of goings-on in Wales. A New Year conference saw the Christian Institute choked to the door with people from all parts of Scotland. With the topic 'Hindrances to Revival', the speaker stated frankly that many Christians were stuck up with pride, while with others 'bigotry was as prevalent as the mumps among children. Until the mudholes were swept away there would never be a revival.'[44] The crowds parted to their homes with heightened desire for the things of God, and deeply humbled and convicted of their self-righteousness, carelessness and general lack of spirituality.

Early in 1905, the Rev. Williams, a Bible teacher from America, began working at the Institute. His addresses on sanctification and heart cleansing brought further conviction to his audiences – to such extent that some Christians were unable to sleep at night. 'Judgment begins at the house of God' was his biblical stance. 'I do not concern myself so much about power,' he said, 'as about purity. When they get purity, the power will come all right.' Williams' preference was for God to deal with cases of anxiety directly rather than for them to be 'counselled' by fellow-Christians. As a result, many men were delivered from smoking, young women renounced their 'worldly fashions and adornments',

---

40. *BW,* 1905, p. 130.

41. Ibid., p. 131.

42. With similar spiritual aptitude, Alexander Finley, MP for East Lanark, also gave his full support to the revival that came to Motherwell a few years later (Gibbard, *Fire on the Altar,* p. 118).

43. *TC*, 19 December 1901, p. 23.

44. *Lanarkshire Examiner and Upper Ward Advertiser,* 7 January 1905.

long-overdue debts were repaid and longstanding relational disputes were healed through forgiveness. It was a sore struggle for many to get 'through', but when deliverance came, their feelings of peace and joy were uncontainable, and there were occasions of people leaping up and praising God for their newfound liberty.[45]

Shortly thereafter, revival broke out in the town. Initially, crowds attending nightly meetings at the Institute provoked such a spiritual stir that ministers from several denominations in the town came to help. They would sit amongst the people or oversee from the platform. Soon, these ministers opened their own buildings – several UF Churches, the Congregational, Baptist and Methodist chapels, the Hallelujah Mission, the new Mission Church in Muir Street, and similar – for prayer meetings and evening services. The Salvation Army and the Brethren also became engaged in the movement. The first hour of the meetings at the Institute was devoted to prayer, praise and the fervent testimony of young men recently converted. It was not uncommon for forty or fifty young people to profess conversion in one night. Although there was a visit to the area of Welsh revivalist J.J. Thomas, the Institute made no deliberate attempt to copy events in Wales, and meetings were more systematic than those in the south. Nearly always, a short regular address was delivered, though occasionally this was dropped. Nevertheless, as in Wales, there was an openness of spirit and a remarkable sense of worship, and at times leaders found it difficult to keep such vocal praise within reasonable bounds so as to attend satisfactorily to the anxious.[46]

Impressive numbers of young lads and men became involved in the movement, the great majority from the non-church-going class. Many of these had initially gone to a meeting simply for the fun of it, but in no time had themselves ultimately been persuaded to accept the gospel. Said one minister who was invited to preach at services, 'In the revival meetings in the Institute there were happy choruses, hallelujahs, bursts of praise and wonderful prayers, but behind it all, and through it all, and sometimes in a somewhat overwhelming measure, there was that consciousness of the presence of a Higher Power that constitutes the difference between a real revival meeting and what is merely an imitation.'[47]

The Baptist Church, led by the Rev. Joseph Burns, also quickly became another main centre of the revival. Prayer meetings had been held here nightly since January 1905. Indeed, in the first five months of the year, this church was only closed on three occasions. At a meeting of the town's ministers, it was agreed that those in their congregations whose churches lay beyond Airbles Street should assist in the Baptist Church

45. *BW*, 1905, p. 133.

46. See *SBM* 1905, pp. 66, 86; *MR-UFC*, May 1905, p. 213.

47. N.W., *History of the Lanarkshire Christian Union Institute 1882*, Strathaven 1937, pp. 46–47.

services, and the rest should take part in the work at the Institute. But in no time numerous other churches were throwing open their doors on a nightly basis for evangelistic services. By the end of March, the meetings were becoming more organised. At those in the Institute, for example, doors were closed as soon as the hall was filled, and no one was permitted to stand in the corridors.

One Sunday in March was described as 'a real religious gala day'. The work was inaugurated with a prayer meeting at 8 a.m., and gatherings were held continuously thereafter until 10 at night. The Primitive Methodist Church recorded nearly 100 conversions, while a similar number assembled in front of the choir rails of Brandon St UFC for a prayer meeting at the close of its afternoon service. On one Sunday evening, although all the places of worship in town were open, the Town Hall was crowded out, and an overflow meeting filled the Christian Institute to the doors. After the Town Hall meeting finally concluded, an extraordinary scene was enacted outside the building, where an order was given by someone to sing '"Crown the Saviour". Such was the inspiring influence of the proceedings that some thousands of people congregated and took part in the singing. The roadway was entirely blocked up, cars having to slide gently through the centre of the crowd, which remained till nearly ten o' clock.'[48] Some prominent church members, deeply touched, were among those making profession of conversion that evening. On the following day, the doors of the Institute had to be closed early against the besieging crowds who wanted to get in.

John Bissett, secretary of the Lanarkshire Christian Union and a zealous evangelist, stated that although he had personally been to meetings in Wales, he had not found the feeling so strong and remarkable as in Motherwell. A few, such as John Anderson of Glasgow's Bible Training Institute, who spoke at some meetings in Motherwell, testified that they never witnessed anything like the Motherwell revival since the days of 1859. A party of twelve students from Anderson's B.T.I. led several meetings in Motherwell during the revival, witnessing also in the back-courts of the vicinity of the church where they spoke.

While local ministers were most prominent in leading the Motherwell movement, a host of evangelists came to speak at meetings in the town. Among these were Mrs Colville, wife of the recently deceased M.P., John Colville; Mr Clinie, Glasgow, 'the evangelist Motherwell seems to appreciate most';[49] Mr Harkness, organist for Torrey and Alexander's campaigns; Dr McIntyre of Glasgow; and the Rev. Arnold of the London City Mission. The fame of the revival quickly spread and, as if ministers

48. *The Revival,* 23 March 1905, p. 7. See the comparable report in *The Lanarkshire,* 8 May 1905.

49. *The Lanarkshire,* 8 April 1905.

weren't overloaded enough with work, they were soon receiving requests to speak at meetings all over the country. Several church leaders went to nearby towns, such as Airdrie and Coatbridge, to testify to the blessings their churches had received.

Converted workmen carried their enthusiasm to the local steel and bridge works, where 'monster prayer meetings' were held night and day during meal-breaks.[50] One observer witnessed hundreds of 'big-boned, swarthy steelworkers gather round the furnaces and pray earnestly'.[51] Local ministers regularly addressed mass meetings of waggon workers, for example, including night-shift men. On one occasion 200 converted workers from surrounding districts marched with their wives and children upon Motherwell with band, banners and joyful song, creating a great sensation as they proclaimed salvation with their Motherwellian neighbours. Meanwhile, in some public offices, clerks began meeting half an hour earlier in the morning for prayer; in time these meetings extending throughout the town. One young man found himself unable to focus on his work due to deep soul concern. As he stood at his place of business, he made the decision to accept the Gospel offer. Lifting his cap, he rushed down to the church manse and agreeably surprised the minister by bursting into his study and exclaiming, 'I am saved!'[52]

In March signs of revival became apparent in Palace Colliery Rows, about three miles from Motherwell, so it was agreed to direct a grand march of witness to that populous centre. The rain fell in torrents, but this failed to dampen the enthusiasm of around 250 marchers, who held a magnificent open-air meeting on arrival at the Rows. Another unusual development in the revival was the sending of postcards with suitable texts to local businessmen. The most popular card bore the inscription, 'Get Right With God.'[53]

It was estimated that at the height of the movement as many as a dozen nightly open-air meetings were conducted simultaneously within a distance of no more than a few 100 yards. 'Half a dozen brass bands assist and deputations of converted carters, steelworkers, bridge builders and other labouring men give testimonies.'[54] The most popular was that held at the head of Airbles Street between 9 and 10 at night. Originally promoted by steelworkers on their way to work, it often attracted an audience of up to 1,000. By the end of May there were still over twenty meetings being carried on every day in the town.

---

50. Ibid., 15 May 1905.
51. *The Revival,* 6 April 1905, p. 7.
52. *The Lanarkshire,* 25 March 1905.
53. Ibid., 1 April 1905.
54. *TC*, 4 May 1905 p. 388.

Noon prayer meetings at the men's 'Pleasant Sunday Afternoon' (P.S.A.) were particularly popular.[55] These were of a rather informal nature; men of all ranks would drop in for ten or fifteen minutes before returning again to business. Another agency through which revival work was accomplished was the 'Y' branch of the British Women's Temperance Association, founded in Motherwell just a few weeks previously. Meetings were held in various other places, including the gymnasium of the Y.M.C.A. Institute.

By the middle of April, it appeared to some that the revivalists were experiencing a revival themselves, for they began plunging into the work with renewed vigour and enthusiasm.[56] By this time, too, several other of the town's churches had opened up to the movement, such as the Craigneuk UFC and St Mary's Parish Church.

Prize pugilists, wrestlers and numerous footballers (both professional and members of a local junior team) were among the many whose lives were transformed. The two young daughters of one notorious drunkard sought out Mr Bissett, to 'come at once to see our father, and get him saved'. Although in no way disposed to hearing the gospel message, the inebriated parent allowed Bissett in to his home, and before long 'he is smitten to the floor by the power of God's spirit, and lies writhing and crying aloud to God for mercy. Within 15 minutes he is perfectly sane and sober, and still in the deepest anguish of soul.' Soon the man came through to a place of peace and assurance, much to the delight of his wife and children. Promising his kids that 'ye've got a new feyther now', the new creature in Christ emptied his drink down the sink. He had become loosed from his addiction, and, wonderfully, such testimony still bore true months later.[57]

On another occasion ten young men were discussing the meetings, and ultimately turned in to witness one. Four of the company had previously professed conversion, and that night three more gave their testimony. A few nights later another two decided, and within a week the tenth man was brought in![58]

Around seventy men from the Hamilton Palace Colliery professed conversion at the Motherwell meetings – half of them sharing their testimonies in public one memorable Saturday night.[59] One of these colliers was an occasional concert comedian at local functions. Both he and his wife went and gave themselves to Christ at one meeting. Not

55. A men's Christian group which met each Sunday afternoon in the Town Hall, membership of which speedily rose to over 1,000. These events were thoroughly evangelical, to the point that no admissions were allowed into the choir without good account of saving testimony.

56. *The Lanarkshire,* 15 April 1905.

57. *BW*, 1905, p. 185.

58 *The Lanarkshire,* 8 March 1905.

59. *BW*, pp. 185–6.

only so, but all three of the lodgers staying at this couple's home were also converted, while another male friend was deeply touched on hearing them sing 'Tell mother I'll be there'. Eyes streaming with tears, the words of the chorus brought home to this man an unfulfilled promise he had made to his dying mother seven years previously, that he would meet her in heaven. The young couple had the joy of leading their friend to the Lord there and then. As if all that wasn't victory enough, the small band of believers immediately set off, Andrew-like, in search of other acquaintances, and before the night was over, three more had decided for Christ![60]

An equally remarkable case concerned a man who bought some bottles of beer, but on opening one at home, found there was something wrong with it, for it wasn't to his taste. Summoning a neighbour, he solicited his opinion. The friend, a Christian, replied that it was not so much the beer that was wrong, but the man himself! Further conversation led to the beer-drinker being led to Christ, the cause of much joy in his household.[61]

As to other notable results of the awakening, local officials reported 'a vast improvement in the behaviour of the townsfolk'.[62] Restitution was made in cases of fraud, homes were transformed, and there was a marked decrease in drinking, gambling, sporting and theatre-going. The police acknowledged that their work had been considerably lightened since the revival began, and that many who formerly required their almost constant attention were now well-behaved and sober citizens.[63] Christian workers of long experience were greatly encouraged by evidences of the genuineness and stability of the great majority of converts. Altogether, thousands of conversions were recorded in Motherwell, with ministers speaking of 100 here, 120 there, being added to their churches.

WISHAW AND MORNINGSIDE

EARLY in 1905, prayer meetings sprang up in Wishaw, the work being carried on largely by the working folk of the town. By March, numerous special missions were being held, including those led by an evangelist from Penzance, a boy-preacher from Motherwell, and a month-long campaign in the Town Hall led by A.Y. McGreggor, through which converts were added to all congregations in town.[64] The most notable work took place at the Steel Works, where prayer meetings were held night and day, and several remarkable conversions occurred. The local Press interviewed three local ministers on the 'Prospects of Revival in

60. Ibid.

61. *The Lanarkshire,* 25 March 1905.

62. Ibid., 18 March 1905.

63. Ibid., 1 April 1905.

64. *Wishaw Herald,* 5 May 1905; 2 June 1905.

Wishaw'. Expectations were clearly high and further meetings were planned, but it was agreed that droppings of blessing only were falling, rather than the showers so longed for. Only when believers manifested 'sacrifice, blood-shedding and tear-dropping on behalf of our fellow-men', said the Rev. Stott, would they 'see Wales repeated in Scotland'.[65]

The Brethren and Salvation Army proved particularly active in the Wishaw work, the latter especially endearing themselves more and more each day to the ministers and regular church-going people, replacing previous suspicion. 'Many who may not see the necessity for coal-scuttle hats and other distinguishing features of the Army' now saw that they were reaching a class that other churches seemed unable to reach. The Brethren, too, 'had a real wonderful manifestation of God's presence among them' in the early months of 1905.[66] By mid-March they had recorded over 100 professions and this once small group was forced to engage the large Town Hall for several Sunday evenings. At these, typical of Brethren meetings, excitement was notable by its absence.

In March 1905 a correspondent from a small mining community just outside Wishaw reported to *The Lanarkshire* that 'the "fire", which seems to be spreading all over the county, seems to have caught hold this week, for the first time in real earnest, in the quiet little village of Morningside'.[67] Following meetings led by a visiting evangelist, people had been greatly stirred, and prayer meetings were being regularly held. A few days later the same newspaper received a postcard, which read, 'Will have visitors from all parts coming to see the Lord's working. The Lord is doing great things in our midst – the mighty and wise confounded! Twelve souls saved last night. Talk of catching fire. We are burning! Glory all the way. Glory night and day. Never experienced such a meeting.'[68]

Just three days later the same correspondent noted, 'Over 50 persons have now surrendered to Christ, some down the pit, others in the brickwork, others in the home, and others on the road. God has opened His hand, and the work is increasingly and gloriously interesting. Christians are all the spree, filled with the new wine, hardly knowing whether it is night or day. St Columba's Mission Church is but packed every night with anxious souls.... The remarkable thing about the work is that the decent, respectable, kirk-going folks are being saved too, but the sublimest picture is to see those who never were in through a kirk door in their lives now among the saved. One man who tried his very best to enjoy himself in pleasures of the football world, drinking, dancing, etc, and his first two hours spent in the kirk this

65. Ibid., 31 March 1905.

66. *The Lanarkshire,* 18 March 1905.

67. Ibid., 25 March 1905.

68. Ibid., 29 March 1905.

week were worth all his past. A great spirit of conviction is abroad, so much that the football has been left unkicked, and a calm awe pervades the whole village. The devil has evidently drawn himself into his den or left the place.'[69]

A few days into April and a further postcard intimated, 'Fire continuing to spread. Church packed last night. About 70 of the young converts had to leave the church to make room for strangers. They marched through Morningside, thence to Newmains, paraded the principal thoroughfares, and found themselves in a field, and there conducted an open-air service. Came back to Morningside singing "Glory all the way!" Everyone satisfied that it was a glorious march. A complete conflagration expected this week.'[70]

AIRDRIE AND COATBRIDGE

AS in south Wales, where revival began so dramatically the previous year, the majority of Lanarkshire towns and villages where awakening flourished were mining communities, and hundreds of miners became caught up in the work.[71] An article in the *Christian Herald* gave particular mention to this class of worker. Not just in South Lanarkshire, but also from places like Longriggend and Airdrie in the north of the county, 'deep interest' was said to have been kindled in the hearts of miners. Still in Airdrie, 'the spirit of revival' was felt among the Salvation Army, and a number of people, young and old, professed conversion.[72] By April it was reported that 'fire is beginning to manifest itself in Coatbridge'.[73] Great effort was made to kindle the flames, causing one CoS minister to emphasize that 'revival would not come by trying to transplant Wales into Scotland and advertising the meetings'.[74] In the Baptist Church 37 new members were received in the early months of 1905, 31 by baptism.

One man active in rural Lanarkshire throughout the period 1903–8 was William P. Nicholson, a fiery young evangelist from Belfast, who went on to help ignite tremendous revival in Ireland in the early 1920s. Itinerating under the auspices of the Lanarkshire Christian Union, Nicholson often found that victory was only achieved after a period of hard travail, later stating, 'When we began a mission in a town or village, we weren't there long before we had either a riot or revival. Sometimes we

69. Ibid., 5 April 1905.

70. Ibid.

71. J. Edwin Orr also takes notice of awakenings 'of the Welsh pattern' being reported in mining communities in the Midlands and the north of England, while, on the continent, similar blessing occurred in mining districts 'as far apart and different as Silesian Teshen and Belgian Wallonie.' (Orr, *Flaming Tongue,* p. 64.)

72. *War Cry,* 15 April 1905.

73. *Coatbridge Express,* 12 April 1905; Orr, *Flaming Tongue,* p. 33.

74. Ibid. 24 April 1905.

had more riot than revival but never a revival without a riot'! [75] In March 1905, he spoke at a conference on revival in Shotts, which deepened the interest of many.[76] Towards the end of that year, in places such as Greengairs and Riggend, a few miles from Airdrie, a progressive work of grace was experienced well after Nicholson's mission had ended, and the Christian life of the district was greatly quickened as a result.

South Lanarkshire [77]

Cambuslang and Rutherglen

MEETINGS in Cambuslang, renowned in revival history, centred on the comodious Argyle Hall, which became so packed that people were content to stand in ante-rooms and passage-ways. Overflow meetings were also held in the Masonic Hall. Leading the movement was John Ferguson, an English sailor converted at sea nineteen years previously. On more than one occasion at sea off some distant land, unbelievers had sought to make him to suffer for his faith. As an evangelist in Cambuslang, too, his fearless preaching and straightforward manner raised the ire of some who held opposing beliefs. Despite suffering from a severe cold, Ferguson preached in the Argyle Hall with extraordinary zeal, painting a vivid picture of 'the fate that most inevitably befell the wicked', and exhorting people to unburden themselves of their sins there and then.[78] Ferguson also took time to pray aloud for sick believers, whose names were handed to him on a list.

Towards the end of March, Ferguson was forced to leave for Birmingham. He was accompanied to the Railway station by an enthusiastic crowd, who gave him a hearty send-off. The meetings continued, however, and in May, R. Hugh Jones from Neath, Glamorgan arrived.[79] A decorator, also training as a Methodist preacher, Jones led a procession up and down the town's main street each night before conducting a packed service in the Baptist Church. One newspaper stated that Jones' meetings were conducted 'very much on the Welsh ideal'.[80]

The benefits of the revival in Cambuslang became apparent on all sides. In all, the Brethren reported 200 conversions[81] while another minister reported 42 from his Bible class professing conversion or

75. Stanley Barnes, *All For Jesus: The Life of W.P. Nicholson*, Belfast 1996, pp. 40–6; Mavis Heaney, *To God Be the Glory: Personal Memoirs of W.P. Nicholson*, Belfast 2004.

76. *Wishaw Herald*, 7 April 1905.

77. For an account of revival movements in Hamilton in 1905, see www.scottishrevivals.co.uk.

78. *The Lanarkshire*, 18 March 1905.

79. Rev. Robert Howie tells the extraordinary story behind Jones' coming to Cambuslang in *The Lanarkshire*, 17 May 1905.

80. *Cambuslang Advertiser*, 20 May 1905.

81. Dickson, *Scottish Brethren and the Welsh Revival*, p. 12.

deeper consecration as believers.[82] There were also some notable moral effects. The sale of intoxicating liquor was said to have diminished to a considerable extent all over the district. A local grocer was astonished to receive a letter from someone who said he had come under the teaching of Titus 2:11–13, and enclosed stamps to the value of 3d, 'the value', the writer explained, of a 'small article taken from one of your shop counters some time ago'! [83]

A good work seems to have commenced in Rutherglen before news of the Welsh revival came through, for one 1904 report speaks of over 100 'lads and girls of thirteen years of age and upwards' being converted. The 1905 movement commenced early in the year with evening meetings at the Greenbank Street Institute and elsewhere being devoted to prayer for revival. The initial result was the deepening of spiritual life of God's waiting people; this was followed by an increasing number of enquirers seeking salvation. In spring, D.L. Roger conducted meetings for young people. With attendance each night at well over 1,000, 744 boys and girls professed Christ and signed the Covenant paper, receiving Covenant cards. This was the fruit of just five nights, with a large number of papers still to be returned. Then came the arrival of Welsh revivalist R. Hugh Jones to conduct a mission in Greenhill UFC in April. Within ten days there were over 200 professions of faith, while the names of 180 more were in the hands of workers (of whom 98 had connections with a church in Rutherglen, 5 were from Glasgow churches, and 77 had no church connection). To the minister's delight, most of the previous years' young converts rendered service at the meetings as 'orderlies', showing they were still standing firm. It was reported with much delight also that 'all the scholars in the Senior Sabbath School without exception profess to have accepted Christ'.[84] Meetings were held on the streets, in churches, and even in Cathkin Laundry, which was crowded by 'neatly-dressed laundry maids, all eager to benefit by the teaching of the revivalists'.[85] By the close of Jones' mission, over 360 people had apparently accepted Jesus as Saviour.[86]

CARLUKE AND FORTH

IN April a special service was held in Carluke's Baptist Church, when a number of recent converts were baptised. Wrote a correspondent, 'Day by day the revival movement, which is stirring the country to its depths, gains ground in Carluke. Nightly the band of Gospel workers which holds

---

82. *MR-UFC* , 1905, p. 213.
83. *The Lanarkshire,* 22 April 1905.
84. *Lanarkshire Examiner,* 29 April 1905.
85. *The Lanarkshire,* 17 May 1905.
86. *Lanarkshire Examiner,* 6 May 1905.

its meetings at the Cross, is being augmented. From its ranks speakers are never wanting – some eloquent, some otherwise – but all earnest and sincere. Now and then a local minister is to be seen in their midst, but this is the exception, not the rule; the speakers being mostly drawn from the working classes. There is scarcely a night but some new convert gives his testimony. A noticeable feature of these meetings is the unity of the different sects. There is scarcely a phase of Christianity which the town contains but has its representatives in these open-air meetings. There can be no doubt that if a clear understanding of and a close contact with the condition of the so-called lower classes are essential elements in the propagation of Christianity, then it is to these revivals, and not to the churches, we must look. The one is acquainted with humanity from the inside, the other mostly from the outside.'[87]

Meanwhile, further east, in the moorland village of Forth, fervour was noted as being 'deep and strong'.[88] Never, in the history of the village, it was said, had there been such a religious awakening. For many weeks, services were held every night, and 'brilliant testimonies' were delivered by both men and women at the regular open-air meetings.[89]

Lesmahagow, Coalburn and Netherburn

AS already suggested, there was considerable quickening among Lanarkshire's Brethren assemblies during this period. Many conversions were recorded in Strathaven and neighbouring villages following five weeks of nightly prayer.[90] It was to this town that the hire of a special train was required to transport 1,100 children – members of Lanark's five Brethren Sunday schools – on an annual excursion.[91] A mission in Lesmahagow towards the close of 1904 added 52 names to the membership roll. A campaign in nearby Coalburn the following year led to 47 members from Lesmahagow leaving that assembly to form a meeting there. This, however, had little overall effect on numbers in the Lesmahagow congregation since as many were added to that assembly during 1905! [92] The revival was general in the village, for many converts were also added to the UF Church.[93]

The Lanarkshire reported that 'the religious awakening has also stirred Netherburn (near Larkhall) to its profoundest depths'. For three months from January 1905, two lady preachers addressed crowded meetings

87. *The Lanarkshire,* 15 April 1905.
88. *Christian Herald,* 4 May 1905, p. 388.
89. *The Lanarkshire,* 15 April 1905.
90. Dickson, *Brethren in Scotland,* pp. 122–3.
91. Ibid., p. 135.
92. Ibid., p. 122.
93. *Proceedings of the General Assembly of the United Free Church of Scotland* (hereafter *PGA-UFCS*), 1905.

nightly, with blessed results. This was followed by impressive scenes at Bentrigg Colliery, where William Noble led the devotions of many converted pick-and-shovel welders. Both hymns – sung enthusiastically – and testimonies were features of the impromptu meetings. It was claimed that 'Netherburn, Draffan, Crossford and Kirkmuirhill are entirely permeated with the revival spirit.'[94] Meantime, the work also spread, to a lesser degree, to other communities close to Hamilton, such as Blantyre and Ferniegair.

BORDERS COUNTIES

HUGE interest was shown throughout the Borders region. John Shearer of Galashiels Baptist Church spent two weeks in Wales in February 1905, during which time he met with Evan Roberts and participated in some meetings. He found it impossible to convey a true picture of the meetings, but described them as 'strangely solemn, yet ineffably joyous'.[95] Shearer returned to the Scottish Borders 'with a new heart and a new bible'. Nightly meetings were held from 3 April to 8 July 1905, and soon revival broke out, with a real 'bending' of some believers in the Baptist Church. No evangelist was employed; there was simply a 'naked dependence upon God'. During these eight weeks of nightly meetings, not a night passed without professed conversions.[96] Altogether, Shearer reported, 120 people were converted, while 37 baptisms were held in the Stirling Street Church during 1905.[97]

On his visit to Wales a short time before, the Rev. D. McNicol of Hawick's Baptist Church was given an opportunity to speak with Evan Roberts. Informing him that people in his Borders town had been praying for at least three months for revival, he asked what they should do now. After thinking for a time, Roberts replied, 'Tell them to pray on'! To a crowded audience in Hawick's Town Hall, McNicoll urged congregations to provide expenses for their ministers to travel to Wales as his own church had so kindly done for him. He had ventured south, he said, with a great love for the people of Hawick in his heart, longing for them to be 'lifted from their sordidness and their indifference,

---

94. *The Lanarkshire,* 25 March 1905.

95. Shearer also spoke of 'great waves of unseen power' which evoked 'prayer like a torrent. ... God is felt to be very near, and hot tears tell of deep repentance and reawakened love. ... Strong men [are] broken down in an agony of remorse' (*SBM,* 1905). One meeting Shearer attended was that in Cwmavon, Port Talbot, when Evan Roberts made the declaration that there was an irredeemably lost soul in the congregation. On another occasion, at 5 o'clock one morning, Shearer descended the shaft of Morfa Colliery to the sound of 'Diolch iddo' ('Praise Him') and worshipped with the colliers underground (Gibbard, *Fire on the Altar,* pp. 113–4).

96. *The Revival,* 11 May 1905, p. vii.

97. Kenneth B.E. Roxburgh, *The Fundamentalist Controversy Concerning the Baptist Theological College of Scotland,* 2001.

wakened out of the sleep of death, which would by and by end them in eternal hell if they were not awakened.' Though claiming that Hawick was 'ripe for revival', when McNicoll asked those who truly wanted one to raise their hands, 'a considerable number did not' (though a large number did).[98] A few weeks later a Welsh revivalist led nightly meetings 'of a free and open nature' in the town. These proved 'hearty and spontaneous' and numerous conversions were recorded.[99]

In Eyemouth, 'the need of spiritual quickening was felt by all the clergy and not a few laymen'. Thankfully, most of the town's ministers at the time showed 'a beautiful spirit of toleration', despite differing on many points. The Rev. W.B. Kennedy of the Established Church, for example, was said to have believed 'in Christian unity as apart from uniformity' and was 'ever ready to unite with his brother-ministers in any movement which has for its object the common good of all'.[100] A united mission was held in the Town Hall in December 1905. With the aim of securing good audiences, the parish was divided into six districts, and the town's ministers – Established, UFC, Congregational, Primitive Methodist and Episcopalian – undertook individually to visit every house in the district allocated to them.

At a packed meeting in the Town Hall in Lockerbie, the minister suddenly felt a 'strange trembling all over. The sorrows of hell seemed to encompass me, and as I spoke the people quailed. The dying love of Christ melted our hearts, and the people sobbed. For a few moments we were quite speechless. The Lord was at hand and I felt He must carry on the meeting, so I quietly left. The people were riveted to their seats; the Spirit moved. Prayer, hymns and testimony went on for an hour and a half, then I returned and closed the meeting. It was a never to be forgotten night, and we are reaping the fruit of it now.'[101] Meanwhile, in Dumfries itself, the Revds C. McNeil and W.J. Street gave exciting and detailed accounts of a recent visit to Wales but there was no mention of any impression made on the congregation. *The Revival*, however, reported in condensed form that 'the quiet town of Wigtown is showing signs of revival. Messrs J.M. Hamilton and John McEwan had to take the Public Hall; largest gospel meetings ever held in the place; preached above the cell in which the Wigtown Martyrs lay the night before they were drowned.'[102]

---

98. *The Border Telegraph*, 28 February 1905.

99. Ibid., 28 March 1905. Hawick's UFC Presbytery also reported 'a revival of religion – particularly among the young' in some districts of the region (Presbytery Minutes 1905, p. 126).

100. Rev. Daniel McIver, *An Old-time Fishing Town – Eyemouth: Its History, Romance, and Tragedy*, Edinburgh 1906, p. 307.

101. Ibid.

102. Ibid.

CHARLOTTE BAPTIST CHAPEL, EDINBURGH

THE revival that broke out in a Baptist church in Edinburgh's city centre in the aftermath of the Welsh revival is one of the best-known Scottish twentieth-century revivals. But as with the Motherwell awakening, there were a number of premonitory signs that awakening was in the air before any news of a mighty revival in the Welsh valleys. Charlotte Baptist Chapel in Edinburgh's Rose St had benefited from the 1859 revival and also from Moody's visit to the city in 1873. By the turn of the twentieth century, however, the church had sunk to its lowest ebb. Membership stood at just 108, while in practise attendance was only around forty-five. Some felt the church should close down. After all, situated in the centre of Edinburgh and with no public transport on a Sunday, most people would have to walk, often a considerable distance, to attend. The building itself was in a poor state, run down, poorly lit and with boxed-in family pews that discouraged visitors. Further, Rose Street had sunk to slum level, the haunt of drunks and prostitutes, and containing no fewer than nineteen public bars.

Thankfully, however, there were a few hardy believers who refused to give up hope. One was Andrew Urquhart, the church secretary, whose faith and radiant optimism were a great inspiration. Sometimes, when walking to church, he would stop and, as if peering into another world, remark prophetically to his young son by his side, 'Don't you see the crowds flocking into the church?' The boy was perplexed, for the street was practically empty.

Another who envisaged a future blessing against all circumstantial odds was Mary Binnie, a convert of the 1859 awakening in Kelso.[103] She had later moved to Edinburgh with her husband and became a member of Charlotte Chapel through baptism due to the influence of her godly uncle, a deacon there. A woman who habitually lived in deep communion with God, Mary received in 1864 a promise through Psalm 45:16 that, 'Instead of the fathers shall be thy children.'[104] She understood this as a word that revival blessing would attend the moribund Charlotte Chapel. Moving back to Kelso through financial necessity after her husband's sudden death, Mrs Binnie also prayed that a Baptist church would be built in that small town. Having implicit confidence in God to answer prayer, she was little surprised to meet a wealthy and titled lady on the street one day who told her that God

103. Binnie was the grandmother of the wife of J. Oswald Sanders, author, Bible college principal and General Director of the China Inland Mission (later the Overseas Missionary Fellowship). Her story is told with affection in J. Oswald Sanders, *This I Remember; Reminiscences*, Eastbourne, 1982, pp. 92–5; and in Rev. William Whyte, *Revival in Rose Street: A History of Charlotte Baptist Chapel, Edinburgh,* Edinburgh, n.d., pp. 30–2.

104. Whyte, *Revival in Rose Street,* p. 31.

had laid it on her heart to build a Baptist chapel in Kelso! A new church was constructed soon thereafter.

First pastor to this church was Joseph W. Kemp, a recent graduate from the Glasgow Bible Training Institute, who saw membership grow to 150. He also conducted gospel services in the local theatre, which attracted large congregations. In due course Kemp married one of the twin daughters of Mrs Binnie. Still fully believing for revival in Edinburgh, this godly widow sensed the time was near when, three and a half years later, in 1901, Rev. Kemp was invited to become pastor of Charlotte Chapel.

In the course of the invitation, Urquhart had written to Kemp, stating, 'One should never venture to prophesy, but I feel almost inclined to do so and to say that you will, by God's help fill Charlotte Chapel inside of eighteen months and that it will be, after the first month or two, a centre of evangelical life in Edinburgh and increasingly a birthplace of precious souls.'[105] Disheartened by the status quo but greatly encouraged by the word of prophecy, Kemp began his ministry in February 1902. Prayer became his key focus. He had once had the privilege of hearing Dr Andrew Murray of South Africa speak at a convention, where he cried out, 'Wanted: men who can pray!'[106] This was to influence Kemp's whole life and ministry. At Charlotte Chapel, he called his people to intense, fervent, continuous prayer, and they responded in a remarkable way. Prayer meetings were started at 7 and 10 o'clock on Sunday mornings and again at 5.45 in the evening, while more often than not the evening service was followed by a prayer and testimony meeting.

Kemp's second strategy was open-air preaching. If people would not come to church, then the church would go to the people! The corner of South Charlotte St and Princes St became a favourite pulpit – and the birthplace of many souls. Kemp was also a keen Bible expositor, and began a School of Bible Study on Sunday afternoons, which, by 1906, was drawing well over 200 young believers to its meetings. The energetic pastor also set about reviving the appearance of the building – cleaning it from top to bottom, repainting, and fitting a new lighting system both inside and out (the large outside lights contrasted so starkly with dark Rose Street that the Fire Brigade was once called in, being told the building was on fire!). By the end of Kemp's first year, membership had risen to 142, in the next to 226, and it continued to increase year by year, while many other converts never formally joined the church.

In April 1904 evangelist A.Y. McGregor conducted a mission in the church, which was followed by a conference on revival.[107] McGregor no

105. Ibid., p. 33.

106. Ibid., p. 36. Murray was the son of a Scots-born missionary to South Africa, and he became a key leader in a revival movement that began in the parish of Worcester in 1860, spreading quickly to other areas.

107. *TC*, 21 April 1904.

doubt reported on the exciting awakening which had swept through the Orkney isle of Westray during his visit there a few months earlier, encouraging the congregation and stirring them to keep praying. (A midnight march through the city centre was also conducted at this time.) And pray they did. Inspired by Kemp's strong faith and passion for souls, prayer meetings were held night after night throughout 1904, steadily increasing in numbers and intensity and deepening in interest.

1905

KEMP'S health broke down towards the close of the year, and he was urged to take a holiday in Bournemouth. Previous to his arrival there, he heard of the revival taking place in Wales, so, disenchanted with his respite home, which he found depressing, he left after just one day in Bournemouth and made his way to south Wales. Here, he records, 'I spent two weeks watching, experiencing, drinking in, having my own heart searched, comparing my methods with those of the Holy Ghost.'[108] Kemp returned to Edinburgh, along with J.J. Thomas, a worker in the revival, and immediately began to share what he had seen. A conference on 22 January 1905, where reports on the movement in Wales were shared, began at 3.30 p.m. and went on till midnight.[109] This was the day that the fire of God fell, and His Spirit continued moving in revival power, as indeed He had surely promised.

As in the time leading up to the awakening, so too the entire movement that ensued was characterised by fervent prayer, and 1905 virtually became one long continuous prayer meeting. During almost the whole of that year the chapel was open every single night and there were few nights without anxious souls seeking the way of life. Sunday evenings were the busiest. Services often began well before the appointed time, with spontaneous prayer and praise. All 750 seats were quickly taken, the aisles were packed (100 folding campstools were purchased in September for placing in the aisles), while some even had to stand in the pulpit itself, or on the pulpit steps.

There was often little preaching, for even on the Lord's Day it was not uncommon for the pastor to go into the pulpit only to find the congregation so caught up in a spirit of prayer that preaching was impossible. Kemp wrote,

> I have yet to witness a movement that has produced more permanent results in the lives of men, women and children. There were irregularities no doubt; even some commotion. ...

---

108. Whyte, *Revival in Rose Street,* p. 34.

109. A second conference was held on 25 February, when Kemp concentrated on the characteristics of the Welsh revival, elaborating on what he had said before. (Gibbard, *Fire on the Altar,* p. 111).

> The people poured out their hearts in importunate prayer. Such a movement with all its irregularities is to be preferred far above the dull, dreary, monotonous decorum of many churches. Under these influences the crowds thronged the Chapel, which only three years before maintained a 'sombre vacuum'. After the first year of this work we had personally dealt with no fewer than 1,000 souls.[110] Who had brought it? God during the prayer meetings.[111]

A work of grace commenced in the Sunday school too, with twelve out of fourteen children in one class committing themselves to Jesus. The older children were also blessed, and before long these young ones had started their own prayer groups, with a sympathetic leader appointed to guide them. Ten children were baptised at one baptismal service on profession of their faith in Christ.

Balfour well describes the overall impact of the revival on the congregation: 'There was a holy abandon, a spiritual glow, and a deep, overwhelming sense of the presence of God. There was uninhibited liberty, abounding unspeakable joy and an outflowing of Christian love. There was heart-warming fellowship and radiant communion with the Lord. At the same time, there was a keen sensitiveness to the awfulness of sin and worldliness, and a deep desire to be right with God and with one another.'[112]

1906

INTO 1906, and it appeared that the intensity of the awakening was about to ease to a more manageable flow. Thus, arrangements were made 'to reorganise the work on generally accepted church lines'. But then 'again the revival fires blazed forth, and the meetings became marked by a deeper outgoing of the soul to God in prayer than ever; and a passionately expressed desire for the salvation of men was a dominant feature'.[113] Day after day and night after night the chapel remained open; the prayer meetings continued, and souls constantly sought the way of life. Indeed, Kemp described 1906 as 'a year of salvation. During the whole year the church has been stirred like a military camp on the field of war, alive with martial music and the tramp of fighting men. It has waged a good warfare, and although the fight has been often hard, victory has crowned the day. Many souls have been converted to God, backsliders have been restored, and many believers have received a fresh endowment of the Spirit and an equipment for service they never before

110. Balfour is less cautious, stating that 'about 1,000 were born again in 1905' (Ian L.S. Balfour, *Revival in Rose Street: Charlotte Baptist Chapel 1808–2008*, Edinburgh 2007, p. 100).

111. Mrs W. Kemp, *Joseph W. Kemp: The Record of a Spirit-Filled Life*, Edinburgh, n.d., p. 30.

112. Balfour, p. 100.

113. Kemp, pp. 31–2.

enjoyed.'[114] 1906 was therefore a year of considerable advance, though not, according to Kemp, with the same quality of blessings received the previous year.

The best was yet to come, however. Towards the end of 1906, the burden for prayer became if anything even stronger. The Sunday morning prayer meetings, which used to commence at 7 a.m., 'now begin at six o'clock and go on for almost seven days a week, with occasional intervals to attend to business, household duties, and bodily sustenance!'[115] Attendance at this meeting and those held on weeknights increased, as too did the intensity of the spiritual atmosphere experienced. On Saturday, 20 December, at a monthly conference held at the Chapel, students from Glasgow's Bible Training Institute – who had received a quickening in their own hearts after hearing of revival at the Moody Bible Institute in Chicago – spoke on revival. This was followed by the evening meeting, when testimonies of those recently converted came across with something of a divine unction. Both meetings greatly stirred those present, having such marked influence on them that some were unable to sleep that night. One man spoke the next day of strongly sensing that a new wave of revival power was about to be unleashed. This was confirmed by many others who had not been present at these meetings, yet who independently received impressions that God was about to move in a mighty way.

Kemp gave a description of a late prayer meeting held that same Sabbath, 21 December, when

> the fire of God fell. … There was nothing, humanly speaking, to account for what happened. Quite suddenly, upon one and another came an overwhelming sense of the reality and awfulness of His presence and of eternal things. Life, death and eternity seemed suddenly laid bare. Prayer and weeping began, and gained in intensity every moment. As on the day of laying the foundation of the second temple, 'the people could not discern the noise of the shouts of joy from the noise of the weeping of the people' (Ezra 3:13). One was overwhelmed before the sudden bursting of the bounds. Could it be real? We looked up and asked for clear directions, and all we knew of guidance was 'Do nothing'. Friends who were gathered sang songs on their knees. Each seemed to sing, and each seemed to pray, oblivious of one another. Then the prayer broke out again, waves and waves of prayer; and the midnight hour was reached. The hours had passed like minutes. It is useless being a spectator looking on, or praying for it, in order to catch its spirit and breath. It is

---

114. Ibid., p. 42.

115. Charlotte Chapel *Record* 1907, quoted in Balfour, p. 106.

> necessary to be in it, praying in it, part of it, caught by the same power, swept by the same wind.[116]

Plans for Watch-Night and New Year's Day services had to give way before this Divine visitation. 'What the closing hours of 1906 meant to many, only the Eternal Day will reveal. Crushed, broken and penitent on account of the defeated past, many of us again knelt at the Cross; and as the bells rang in the New Year, we vowed by God's grace to press into our lives more service for Him, to be more like Him in spirit and walk, and win to Him our fellow-men.'[117]

1907[118]

THREE services were held on 1 January 1907, and God drew near at each meeting, His presence seeming to rush like a mighty river through the souls of men and women. Services were marked by a stream of testimonies, songs and confession that forbade any prearranged order. Men and women with grudges against one another literally rushed from their seats to have them put right. People were bowed in prayer, heart-searching and contrition, while in the inquiry room there was much sobbing, and a number of decisions were made. Christians present from outside Edinburgh pled with God to move in power on their own localities, while Kemp himself, wisely allowing all to bend to the Spirit, moved all over the sanctuary in a ministry of helpfulness.[119] Speakers had been arranged to address the evening meeting, but it became clear that no sermon was to be given – the Lord was addressing his people directly, the burden of the day's meetings being that judgment must begin at the house of God.

Meetings like these continued for several months, deepening as the weeks passed, with prayer ever at the fore. The 5.45 p.m. meeting was put forward to 5.30 p.m. However, such was the power of God at this early evening occasion that it was still impossible to get to the open-air meeting on time – the upper vestry, pastor's vestry and library all being crowded with praying people. Such prayer, 'of a tumultuous sort', was always spontaneous, from the heart, and expressed aloud or silently in simultaneous manner by the scores of people present. But, Kemp explained, 'the confusion never gets confused; the meetings are held by invisible Hands. … God save us, lest we civilise the Holy Spirit out of our churches.'[120]

---

116. Kemp, pp. 32–3.

117. Ibid., p. 33.

118. Although the 1907 and 1908 movements in Charlotte Chapel occurred outwith the period of the General Awakening (1905–06) they are included here for sake of continuity and convenience.

119. *TC*, 10 January 07.

120. Kemp, p. 34.

At one prayer meeting, approaching midnight, a request was made by one disquieted soul that grace might be granted to give up a relationship with an unconverted partner. 'No fewer than four similar cases were the subjects of prayer that night, and in each case these unholy attachments were dropped.'[121] The gift of prolonged intercession was given to certain Christians in particular, such men and women praying audibly and at great length for the salvation of others, oblivious to their present surroundings. One man, unknown to church members, prayed in agony for over one and a half hours for those of his own town. Sweating profusely, he was virtually too weak to stand when the time came to close the chapel, and he had to be carried out of the building.

On 13 January a half-night of prayer took place, and Kemp was at a loss to describe adequately the resulting scenario. 'The spirit and scenes ... baffle description' he wrote. 'It was given to some of us to know what Isaiah meant when he said "The posts of the door moved at the voice of Him that cried."'[122] Three nights later, 200 attended an all-night prayer meeting, which lasted from 10 p.m. to 8 a.m., in which three quarters of those attending remained for the whole duration. 'From the beginning to the close the prayers ascended in one unbroken continuity. At times the prayers rose and fell like the waves of the sea. At half-past three in the morning the scenes were bewildering to behold. It seemed as though everybody in the meeting was praying at once. There was no confusion, nothing unseemly. The passion of prayer had caught the people, and we felt we must pray.'[123]

Kemp's biography fails to remark on the immediate outcome of this night of prayer. The chapel's 'Record' reports that the following morning, Sunday 24 February, the congregation gathered together 'with high hopes and expectancy; but as is often the case, our faith was put to the test, for the Lord's Day passed without any seeming blessing. We had looked for a great ingathering of souls, which did not come.'[124] Though clearly discouraged, the church was delighted when, a week later, over twenty souls professed faith in Christ. Balfour provides good evidence to suggest that this second intense, spontaneous phase of the revival, which had continued unabated for around eight weeks, was by now drawing to a close, although conversions and the deepening of believers' spiritual lives continued for the rest of the year. By February 1907, membership of the chapel had increased to 609,[125] making it the largest Baptist church in

121. Ibid., p. 37.

122. Ibid., p. 35.

123. Ibid., p. 36.

124. Charlotte Chapel *Record* 1907, quoted in Balfour, p. 110.

125. Of whom over 150 were men and the remaining 450 women.

Scotland (although it has been calculated that less than one in four of those converted during the revival period at the start of 1907 settled into Charlotte Chapel).[126]

One activity engaged in during the course of the revival – as and when led by the Spirit – and which continued through the spring of 1907, was the March of Witness. This had the three-fold effect of strengthening the faith and unity of the marchers, acting as a potent witness, and making room for unconverted people to get into the chapel! The March – usually in two companies – proceeded along Princes Street to the Scott Monument or up the Mound, folk singing and testifying en route, before returning to Charlotte Street corner for a 'monster open-air meeting', and back to the chapel for a prayer and praise time. The police were always sympathetic and helpful in directing traffic on such occasions, and the local Press reported positively on such pageants. *The Edinburgh Citizen* reported that after returning from one such March, the chapel was well-filled and the service 'somewhat lively', given the attendance of many drunks who had been picked up on the way. These men listened attentively to 'The Redeemed Drunkards' Band' giving short, pointed testimonies, their stories being described by the journalist as 'simply marvellous' and their Christianity 'a religion worth having'.[127]

Keen that the blessing they had received should not be kept to themselves, but shared throughout the land, Kemp invited ministers from all over Scotland to a united prayer meeting in his church in March 1907. Many were profoundly convicted and encouraged by such an occasion and at the earliest opportunity sought to share with their own congregations what they had learned and experienced. In an attempt to follow up decisions made at the chapel, the ever-growing list of converts was divided into districts, and thirty-four helpers were appointed to visit new believers in their homes, to learn of their progress and provide any encouragement and prayer as might be needed. This proved a most important and fruitful activity, and the helpers were themselves blessed by such engagement. The visits also showed up those disappointing cases who, it seemed apparent, had never been truly converted, here providing an opportunity for personal evangelism; while the large percentage who were found to have been genuinely saved were encouraged to keep looking to Christ.

1908

BY the beginning of 1908 Kemp feared that his church had entered into a 'cooling process', when, partly through exhaustion, partly through the falling of interest among some believers, activity was slackening and

126. Balfour, p. 112.

127. Charlotte Chapel *Record,* 1907, quoted in Balfour, p. 111.

meetings were losing their freshness and power. The pastor wrote of his fear that 'the holy fire is burning very low with some of us'. But just as the turn of the years 1904–5 and 1906–7 brought peaks in the waves of God's blessing upon the chapel, so too, near the start of 1908, a reviving work became apparent within the fellowship. At the morning service on Sunday, 28 December 1907, several testified to the blessings they had experienced during the past twelve months. A half-night of prayer was commenced that evening, reminding many of a corresponding night of prayer almost exactly a year previously, following which great blessing had poured down upon them. The Watch-Night service that New Year's Eve was attended by over 400, and was followed by the traditional open-air meeting on the corner of South Charlotte and Princes Streets. The next day all three meetings were well attended and each was preceded by an open-air outreach on the street corner.[128]

This was prelude to another season of grace among this favoured fellowship – in Kemp's words, 'raindrops' rather than 'showers' of blessing. One Friday in February, a spirit of prayer came upon the evening meeting 'in uncontrollable power', and for two hours believers remained broken and humbled before the Lord. 'Experiences, all too sacred to put into cold print, were given to many.'[129] A similar pattern followed each of the two prayer meetings the following Sunday. No open-air meeting was held after the evening service that weekend. Instead, the people felt compelled to continue in prayer, which they did till after 10 p.m. and again the following Thursday from 2.30 till 8 p.m. in the upper vestry. Both occasions were attended by many instances of conversion and the fuller surrender of believers.[130] Kemp wrote of these meetings in the March *Record*, 'Much warmth has been felt … reminding us of the gracious seasons enjoyed a little over a year ago.'[131] Then again, on Sunday, 1 November, a large group prayed from 9.30 p.m. till midnight. 'God's power was manifested amongst us. Many entered into blessing, and habits which had been hindering Christian progress were, by God's grace, broken off.'[132] Even this was not the last season of spiritual blessing to touch this prominent Baptist congregation during Kemp's ministry (see pp. 155–6).

As in the previous century, emigration took a heavy toll on membership, and although 1,148 new members were received during Kemp's twelve years, the membership when he left was 850. During the years 1907 to 1911, 850 names were registered as having accepted Christ (exclusive

128. Balfour, p. 117.

129. Ibid., p. 111.

130. *TC*, 5 March 1908.

131. Charlotte Chapel *Record*, 1907, quoted in Balfour, p. 110.

132. Balfour, p. 111.

of scores more whose names were not recorded) – an average of 170 per year.[133] Kemp himself emigrated to New York in 1915 and then to New Zealand.[134]

Leith

IN Leith, three UFC ministers and a Baptist pastor who had all journeyed to witness the revival in Wales spoke at a crowded meeting in Ebenezer UFC.[135] A season of prayer followed the service. Explained the Rev. J.D. Robertson,

> We have had a yearly gathering (united) for prayer for four years past, but we never saw anything like what followed my announcement. We usually had the long and awkward pauses, which are common when a meeting is thrown open. All was different. With an amazing spontaneity prayer followed prayer from all parts of the church. Hymns were interspersed in the Welsh manner. It was a soul-stirring time. At 12 o'clock the people showed no sign of going away and I announced that a similar meeting would be held next evening. Again the church was crowded, and we had the same scene over again. The fervour, enthusiasm and spiritual power have carried us right on through three weeks. All else has had to be put aside. On Friday last we reached our high water mark; the experience was inspiring and solemnising.
>
> There is a delightful spirit of harmony among the brethren in the ministry. Every Friday afternoon we have a meeting for conference and prayer and we never had such attendances for any purpose before. There have been many conversions. Every night we have decisions for Christ. The life of our churches has been quickened. It is easy preaching now. There is a new joy in it. The people are eager to hear. All the ministers speak in the same way of the blessing that has come. Our meeting in the church is followed by a march along the street to the foot of Leith Walk, where a service is held. There have been conversions here too. Some of the younger and stronger ministers are taking part. On Friday four were present, and the last of them to speak was giving a gospel message to a large crowd at 11.15![136]

'It is the work of God and we must be willing to stand aside and let Him do it,' said Robertson of the movement, which had flowed spontaneously,

---

133. Despite strenuous efforts to establish new converts in their faith and encourage them to settle into the Chapel, only 101 of these 850 people (12%) joined Charlotte Chapel; some joined other churches while all trace of others was lost.

134. In the 100 years since then, Charlotte Chapel has regularly been filled to overflowing, both morning and evening, on Sundays, during the ministries of succeeding pastors: Graham Scroggie (1916–1933), Sidlow Baxter (1935–1953), Gerald Griffiths (1954–1962), Alan Redpath (1964–1968), Derek Prime (1969–1983) and Peter Grainger (1992 to date).

135. 'A very zealous group' from Leith, including several ministers, had also attended a 'revival conference' in Charlotte Chapel in January 1905 (Gibbard, *Fire on the Altar*, p. 111).

136. *MR-UFC*, 1905, p. 113. See also *TC*, 23 March 1905, p. 17.

requiring no advertising. Those with over thirty years of experience in gospel work said they had never seen anything like it, he said, adding that the movement's main influences had been the interest awakened by news from Wales and the prayer and expectancy that had existed in Leith for some time past, when some from his and other churches had met together in groups to pray.[137]

The meetings in Ebenezer Church were packed nightly for twelve weeks,[138] and among those who attended were a number of fishwives from Newhaven who were keen in their support. A visiting evangelist from Wales, Thomas A. Davies, also spoke at a number of meetings. Special meetings for women were also held; one was addressed by a seventeen-year-old and saw no fewer than sixteen making profession of faith.[139] The minister of South Leith Baptist Church rejoiced that, 'a new spirit of enthusiasm has broken out among us', and at some meetings extra seats had to be put in the aisle. Within a year the church had received the names of 300 men, women, boys and girls who had professed faith in Christ at its meetings.[140]

COCKENZIE

FOR some years there had been a free and open gathering in the small east-coast port of Cockenzie, in what was then Haddingtonshire (now East Lothian) every Sabbath evening, when fishermen and their friends assembled in large numbers. Here exhortations, testimonies and prayers were offered – most spontaneously – by veterans of the 1859 revival and by converts of more recent missions held in the area. The Faith Mission conducted 'two stiff but not fruitless' campaigns here in 1904, and at the close of the second one, in December, meetings were continued for some weeks by local believers. 'Not a night passed without numerous decisions being made.'[141]

Then, on receiving assistance from Sinclair and Craig, believers who worked at the General Post Office in Edinburgh, and from others, the services grew in both attendance and earnestness, until the building was crowded, with

> windows, aisle, and small hall sometimes being fully occupied. The scenes witnessed at some of the gatherings almost baffle description, and will never be forgotten by those who were present. One night a mother could be seen rising from her seat and going forward to where her son was sitting; tears of joy were running down her cheeks, and taking hold of his hands, she shook them again and again; thanking and praising God.

137. *MR-UFC*, ibid., p. 113. See also *TC*, 23 March 1905, p. 17.

138. Orr, *Flaming Tongue*, p. 34.

139. *Christian Herald*, 22 June 1905, p. 543.

140. *SBM*, 1905, p. 65.

141. *The Revival*, 1 June 1905, p. 7.

> And well she might, for he was indeed a brand plucked from the burning. In another part could be heard a shout of 'Hallelujah!' from a woman who had just been informed that her husband was among those who had decided that evening, and who said that her prayers had now been answered. ... Every night, for months, both young and old were pressing into the kingdom.[142]

Soon a spirit of revival filled the whole village. Not only at the meetings, but also in the fishing boats, in the homes and on the street, people were impressed, and numerous conversions, including several very striking cases, took place. Some men testified that, just 'as of old when He entered a fishing boat and taught, so, on the Firth of Forth, He came aboard their craft and won them to Himself'.[143] Young fishermen who had been notoriously careless in their behaviour began to regularly attend church and take part in Christian work. The local constable also reported an ease in his workload, with the rowdiness of Saturday nights now banished; while the discord of many a home was exchanged for an undreamed-of peace.

Regarding the earlier and more successful Faith Mission campaign in 1904, one local Christian leader said, 'we can lay our hands on nearly every one that came out for Christ then.'[144] The Pilgrims were also able to witness over 200 believers marching in the open air on a Sunday as a form of testimony. Preaching almost seemed conspicuous by its absence. A week of special prayer meetings was arranged, which, a Faith Mission worker remarked with not a hint of regret, 'we simply have not been able to stop'![145] Meanwhile, it became impossible to close Sunday meetings for a full half-hour after time was up, as 'expectant and wholly yielded' Christians were so deeply 'imbued with an earnest desire to pray'.[146] One mother, on being asked what difference had taken place in her home, replied 'It's like heaven below,' as nearly all the members of her family had been converted.

Soon the departure of the boats for the herring fishing would carry the quickening influence to fishing centres as far away as Stornoway and Ireland. The extent of interest in spiritual matters within the community is seen in the dilemma over the newly-opened church, which seated 240 more than the old building, but was already proving too small for the number of people attending!

---

142. Ibid.

143. *BW*, 1905, p. 60.

144. Ibid., p. 83.

145. *BW*, 1905, p. 181.

146. Ibid.

ELSEWHERE IN CENTRAL SCOTLAND

OTHER than Charlotte Baptist Chapel (see pp. 118–23), there is a notable absence of reports of revival activity in Edinburgh itself during this period, although there were some signs of encouragement. At Bristo Place Baptist Church, 'a quickened spirit' developed and deep interest attended a conference on the Welsh revival in March 1905, where it was noted that all the speakers 'had been to Wales'.[147] Though evangelistic meetings were held frequently in the neighbourhood of Lothian Road Free Presbyterian Church, 'Regret' was the keynote of each annual report until the year 1906, and then, through the moving of the Holy Spirit, a remarkable change took place. 'Pleasant Sabbath Afternoon' meetings, established in Fountainbridge a few years previously, were initiated, and they met with instant success. 'In place of a handful, consisting chiefly of members of the congregation, there has been a packed attendance of men from the district who hitherto had had little or no church connection.'[148]

Just south of Edinburgh, at Dalhousie, near Bonnyrigg, many were converted under evangelist Joseph Kerr. These, consisting of a score of young men and eight girls and young women, were baptised by full immersion in the South Esk river one Saturday evening in April 1905. A large crowd took part in the service from the riverbank, while hundreds more watched from a distance. Earnestly imploring spectators not to mock the ceremony, Kerr dipped one after another convert, attired in bathing costumes covered with waterproofs, in the bed of the river. 'The dipping over, there was further singing, and the quaint ceremony came to a close.'[149]

Paisley, in Renfrewshire, experienced what was described as 'a year of continuous revival',[150] with one Baptist Church in particular seeing spectacular growth, from sixty new members in September 1902 to over 300 in March 1905.[151] Kirkintilloch, Dumbartonshire, saw a beautiful work of grace commence quite spontaneously, 'when numbers of young men and women pressed into the Kingdom'. The movement reached such proportions that a local newspaper described it as 'a miniature Welsh revival'.[152] Further south, a movement in the North Ayrshire town of Kilmarnock took especial hold of young men in the community, a band of whom conducted an open-air meeting every night prior to a main service in church. Meanwhile, it could be said that, 'in the engineering shops in town, religion is the subject of earnest conversation'.[153]

147. *SBM*, 1905, p. 65.

148. Mitchell, *History of Lothian Road UFC*, pp. 117–9.

149. *Glasgow Weekly Herald*, 15 April 1905.

150. *Christian Herald*, 6 April 1905, p. 301.

151. Orr, *Flaming Tongue*, p. 34.

152. *TC*, 15 June 1905, p. 18.

153. *MR-UFC*, 1905, p. 213.

As Baptist minister in Stirling, George Yuille had seen no quick results, even after concerted efforts over several decades. After travelling to Wales to witness the revival there, Yuille urged his own congregation to pray that such an 'extraordinary movement' might be witnessed also in Scotland, and particularly in Stirling.[154] As a result, not only of prayer, but also of 'enormous exertions on the part of church members to recruit new members to the cause', nightly meetings began in Stirling Baptist Church in April 1905 and continued for around two months. As the movement spread also to the town's other churches, one of these was opened for united meetings. After just a few weeks it was noted that, numerically, the results were 'already far in excess of any movement in Stirling within our recollection'.[155]

Upwards of 600 professed conversions resulted from the mission, though in January 1906 the church evangelist and assistant minister, William Ashby, a former Salvation Army officer who had been obliged to leave his post in 1905, having been convinced of the need for believers' baptism, could report 'only' 397 conversions, of whom, on visiting them, only 48 professions 'were entirely unsatisfactory'. Thus 348 individuals professing conversion were deemed to be making good spiritual progress. However, this remarkable statistic was only partially reflected in the Stirling Baptist membership roll, which showed an increase of 58 members in 1905 and a further 34 in 1906 (compared to 11, 15, 11, 5 and 29 in the years 1900–1904 respectively and 19 in 1907).[156] Follow-up conferences were arranged to reflect on the impact of the revival. Along with Yuille, Duncan MacGregor, principal of Dunoon Baptist College, spoke at one such convention in June 1905. In other Baptist

154. Fresh from his campaign in Westray, A.Y. McGregor had led meetings in March and April 1904 in Stirling's Public Hall, where around 1,000 people attended his final service.

155. Orr's study quotes a periodical of the time, which stated that 'all the churches in Stirling were filled' when special meetings were held (Orr, *Flaming Tongue*, p. 34). Welsh evangelist Seth Joshua also spent some time in Stirling around this time.

156. These figures certainly suggest that Stirling Baptist Church was deeply affected by the general awakening of the time, and supporting evidence clearly confirms this. However, there is good reason for believing that the Welsh revival was not the exclusive reason for growth in this and other Scottish Baptist churches during 1905. Brian Talbot shows that there were 1,352 additions to Baptist Union of Scotland churches during 1905, a significantly higher increase than the annual average. However, he points out that there was also a remarkable increase nationally in 1902 (1,265 additions) and a high level of consistent growth in 1903 and 1904 (657 and 542, respectively), building on healthy growth figures in earlier years (99, 337, 394, 171 and 223 in the years 1897–1901 respectively). Clearly other factors were in force. In the preceding decades there had been 'unprecedented levels of church-planting' by Scottish Baptist congregations, with 26 new causes formed in the last decade of the nineteenth century alone. An additional factor was the Twentieth Century Fund, a sum raised in previous decades to support church planting and other evangelistic work among Scottish Baptists. The advent of the new Baptist associations also encouraged greater team-working in mission activities in the first decade of the new century. Concludes Talbot: 'the evidence nationally presents a more complex picture and confirms that in the majority of congregations it was regular outreach initiatives rather than a dramatic revival that was the cause of significant growth in numbers' (Brian R. Talbot, *Standing on the Rock: A History of Stirling Baptist Church, 1805–2005*, Stirling 2005, p. 55).

congregations in central Scotland, such as Maxwelltown, Dundee[157] and Clydebank, meetings were held virtually every night over several months from the New Year of 1905. Two months' continuous missions were also held in Orangefield Baptist Church, Greenock and in Victoria Place Baptist Church, Glasgow.[158]

In Shieldhill, near Falkirk, a movement developed gradually and without the aid of any outside evangelist. 'Everybody is speaking about religion. … The reality of Jesus Christ has taken possession of the whole district. … There have been several conversions amongst the middle aged, but no fewer than 100 young people in this one congregation have come out for Christ,' during nightly services that were conducted in an orderly and quiet way.[159] In the shale-mining town of Broxburn, large open-air processions were held and the Brethren reported that on occasion, assembly members had been woken up during the night by distressed souls.[160] There were some 200 professed conversions.[161] Meanwhile, the Baptist Church in Denny reported a 'revival in embryo', with over seventy conversions as a result of a short mission.[162]

All the while Welsh revivalists were busy visiting a number of locations. In Dundee, J. Tudor Jones had a very warm welcome, especially from ministers, and many hundreds attended the prayer meetings.[163] The meetings in Dunfermline had been preceded by two years of effectual prayer for God to move in the town. Believers had initially met in private several times a week before moving to the larger Town Hall for a united prayer gathering. Conduct here too seemed to be along 'Welsh lines', with praise breaking in 'upon speech and prayer almost unconsciously, while many prayers may be in evidence simultaneously. … As the prayers gathered way, what can only be described as a holy thrill passed over every heart, sufficiently so to force the admission that we never felt the power of prayer this way before.' Both dinner-hour prayer times and half-nights of prayer for Christians of all denominations were popular, with an emphasis not only on intercession for the unsaved, but equally on the cleansing and deeper consecration of believers.[164]

---

157. Indeed, under the ten-year ministry of John Dick in Maxwelltown from 1898, 321 people were baptised and 495 received into membership (Bebbington, *Baptists in Scotland,* p. 247).

158. As Brian Talbot noted, 'This was an extraordinary amount of religious activity by any standards and required a congregation to be totally dedicated to the work to sustain such an intensive schedule over what amounted to several months in some of these churches' (Talbot, p. 56).

159. *MR-UFC,* 1905, p. 252.

160. Dickson, *Scottish Brethren and the Welsh Revival,* p. 12.

161. *The Revival,* 11 May 1905, p. vii.

162. Bebbington, *Baptists in Scotland,* p. 207.

163. Gibbard, *Fire on the Altar,* p. 120.

164. *BW,* 1905, pp. 8–9.

In 1903, spurred by the Admiralty's decision to form a new naval base in Inverkeithing, Rev. Walker of Dunfermline was moved to inaugurate a Baptist Mission in the area. By early 1904 a Christian Endeavour Society had been formed, and indoor and open-air work was conducted with much enthusiasm. A work of grace began and continued throughout the year, with crowded meetings being held weekly. Among the many who turned to Christ were a number of quarry workers, some of whom came to a place of 'peace in believing' while at work. In March 1905 the Rev. Turner of Alva was invited to superintend the Mission, and, preaching nightly for over three weeks, saw tremendous results, with over 200 professed conversions, including some of the worst 'worthies' in the burgh. In those few weeks 44 baptisms took place and a new church was formed, membership of which increased to 113 within six months.[165]

In another region in Fife, many new converts were baptised in the Daft Mill Burn during a snowfall, in front of 1,000 people gathered under wintry skies.[166] During July 1905, Seth Joshua preached in David McIntyre's chapel in Alloa and in Bridge of Allan. At meetings in the former town, the preacher realised that many were nominal members only, but gradually the Spirit overcame all resistance. 'The meetings here ended in showers of blessing,' wrote Joshua.[167]

REVIVAL IN THE SALVATION ARMY

THE first note that the Salvation Army was being affected by the general awakening spreading across the country was when the *War Cry* recorded that 'on the first Sunday of 1905, the spirit of revival was felt in hundreds of Corps' throughout the nation. Many congregations in Scotland came under the influence of the movement, including Dundee,[168] Dumfries[169] and Muirkirk in East Ayrshire, where, by March 1905, there were sixty 'souls saved' since the Corps opened five weeks previously.[170] In Glasgow's suburbs there were movements in Govan[171] and Pollockshaws, from which latter area were reported 'remarkable manifestations of revival fire. Young people bursting forth the first time in glowing testimony and fervent song. Open-airs held nightly, Fridays excepted … 20 souls since Monday.'[172] More notable still were the definite outbreaks of revival which occurred in the lowland districts of Stenhousemuir, Clydebank and Newmilns.[173]

165. Yuille, pp. 147–8; *SBM*, 1905, p. 64.
166. *Christian Herald,* 2 March 2005.
167. Gibbard, *Fire on the Altar,* p. 120.
168. *War Cry,* 28 January 1905.
169. Ibid., 8 April 1905.
170. Ibid., 18 March 1905.
171. Ibid., 9 September 1905; 28 October 1905.
172. Ibid., 25 March 1905.
173. Regarding the latter two towns see www.scottishrevivals.co.uk.

STENHOUSEMUIR

AT Stenhousemuir, to the north of Falkirk, two female workers began a Salvation Army Corps in the autumn of 1904. For some weeks little progress was made, but when special meetings were held one November weekend, fifteen children made commitments of faith. People now started coming to the meetings in greater numbers, and on the following Sunday there were another fifteen professed conversions, including those of a number of adults. Thus commenced a work of revival in the small town, and virtually every week for many months more people were added 'to the Lord's side'. By the end of March 1905 the conversions of no fewer than 226 adults and sixty-eight children had been recorded.[174] It was noted that 'the good works of the Officers among the people began to influence

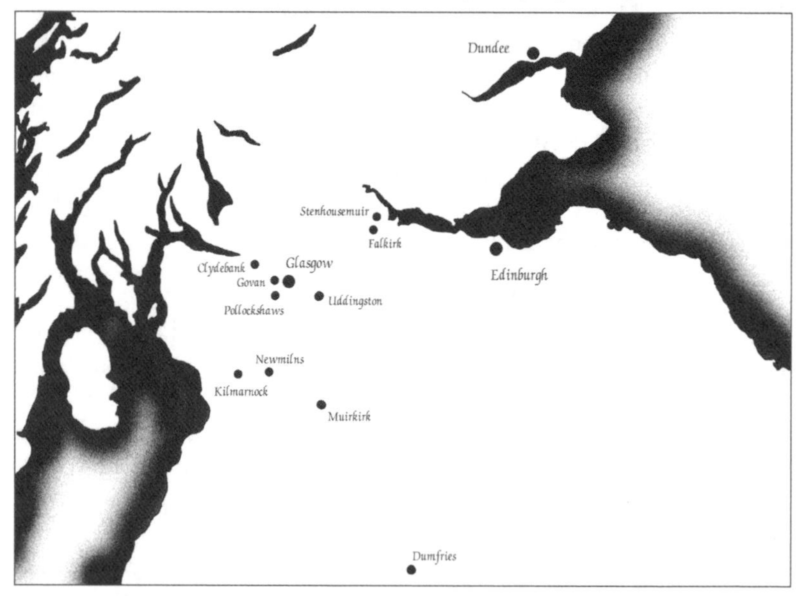

nearly everybody in favour of the Army. At least one of the local ministers has prayed in his pulpit every Sunday for the success of the work, while the house-to-house visitation by the Officers won the hearts of many.'[175]

One recruit, on being told that the Major would enrol him in two weeks' time, sighed, 'Oh, I dinna ken hoo I can wait a hale fortnicht; I wish he was comin' the morn.' When the day finally came, the recruit, who was too excited to sleep, went round to the Salvation Army Quarters and knocked up the Officers for knee-drill at 4.50 a.m.! Then he proceeded

---

174. While many Scots folk would have thought it presumption to say that they 'kent' they were saved, 'the Stenhousemuir soldiers are different ... and right boldly do they testify. They are also very enthusiastic' (*War Cry*, 1 April 1905).

175. Ibid.

to the Major's billet and sang about the 'Bright and Morning Star' until he, too, was aroused.[176] Around twenty married couples were among the revival's converts and all became Army recruits. In one family, 'an elderly man got converted one Sunday night. In the course of the Officers' visitation the next week, the man's wife also sought salvation. Their son followed on the Saturday, and his wife a week or so later. Then another son and two daughters were won for God, as well as the husband of one of these daughters. One of the married couples in this family now exercised their influence on a neighbour. The result was that another entire family was attracted to the Army, and one after another got converted.'[177]

Central Highlands

ONE of the first to return from a visit to revival scenes in Wales was William M. Oatts, a minister of the UFC in Glasgow who had recently retired as General Secretary of the Glasgow United Y.M.C.A. to devote himself to evangelistic work. His meetings in Blairgowrie, Perthshire from 8 January attracted large numbers and caused a great sensation throughout the district. Oatts spoke at length on the amazing scenes he had witnessed in Wales a fortnight previously on his visit there as a representative of the UFC. During that time he had been granted a short interview with the youthful Evan Roberts, who, in reply to a remark by Oatts that he hoped a blessing would come to Scotland, replied with a keen prophetic glance, 'It's coming!'[178]

As many as 1,100 people would at times crowd into Blairgowrie's Public Hall, with 200 having to be turned away. A change of venue was made to St Andrew's U.F. Church, the largest building in town, which became packed with an audience of 1,400 – a most significant number given the population of the community, suggesting that many had come from outside the town to attend.[179] At one meeting two companies of the Boys' Brigades were present, and when asked who wished to accept Christ that night, almost all of them stood up. Nearly 300 remained for the after-meeting, where 100 Boys' Brigade members and over thirty adults professed conversion. Oatts returned to Blairgowrie the following year for a two-week follow-up mission.[180] In the meantime, he also

176. Ibid.

177. Ibid.

178. *Blairgowrie Advertiser*, 14 January 1905, quoted in Sprange, *Children In Revival*, pp. 362–3.

179. *TC*, 26 January 1905; *Missionary Record*, May 1905, p. 213. The Rev. Malcolm White of Blairgowrie, who was converted under Dr A.N. Somerville of Glasgow and had taken part in the revival movements of both 1859–60 and 1874–5, was said to have been filled with gladness when this later wave of revival passed through his town, just one year before his death in 1906 (*Missionary Record*, 1906, p. 334; Orr, *Flaming Tongue*, p. 33).

180. *Blairgowrie Advertiser*, 14 January 1905; 17 February 1906, quoted in Sprange, *Children In Revival*, pp. 363–4.

conducted revival meetings in Kirriemuir and Perth, in each of which locations a beautiful work was initiated.[181]

A work of grace took place in the small fishing town of Ardrishaig on Loch Fyne, after a visit from a mission team from Glasgow in the autumn of 1905. As a result, some young male converts met for prayer on cold and dark evenings in an indent on the shore known as 'the cave'. Consequently, when a young evangelist came to hold meetings in the area, there was a significant number of conversions.[182] Writing from Fortingall, Perthshire at the start of 1906, evangelist Duncan Drysdale reported that God was doing a 'wonderful thing in the Highlands of Scotland'. In some places, he claimed, hundreds of people were weeping for their sins and yielding to Jesus. The lives of many 'ringleaders in every form of sin' were so transformed that they were now said to have been 'bold and open in the service of Christ'.[183]

ABERDEEN[184]

AS many as five ministers from Aberdeen journeyed to Wales to attend revival meetings, and each of them was convinced that the revival was of God.[185] One of these men was Baptist pastor Grant Gibb from the Gilcomston Park area of town, who made his visit to Wales in spring 1905. Testifying back home, he was disappointed at the lack of interest from among his congregation. Asking one Sunday school teacher if she had confessed the Lord at her workplace, she replied that she felt totally unable to. Now however, she yielded herself fully and within a week all seven girls in her workroom had submitted their lives to the Lord. Some began meeting twice a day to pray for revival; within a few days blessing came at a cottage meeting, and by the end of one month over fifty conversions had taken place. 'We let down our nets for a draught,' said a church officer, 'and soon enclosed a large number of souls.'[186]

In April, Gibb hosted a revival conference, only inviting speakers who had personally witnessed revival scenes in Wales. At the close of the meetings, on Saturday evening, a 200-strong procession marched to the regular open-air stance in Correction Wynd in the town centre. As they made their return journey, a team of 'sisters' split into pairs and proceeded to visit public houses along the way, personally inviting patrons to join them on the march. Many followed them out of the pubs.

---

181. *Lanarkshire Examiner*, 29 April 1905.

182. *TC*, 24 May 1906.

183. Ibid., 18 January 1906.

184. For information on the movements in Easter Ross-shire and Caithness, see www.scottishrevivals.co.uk.

185. Gibbard, *Fire on the Altar*, p. 120.

186. Anonymous, *These Fifty Years:* Anniversary Booklet of Gilcomston Park Baptist Church (1886–1936).

The road was black with folk, who then crowded into a packed hall, for what became known as the 'Saturday Night Rescue Meeting'. Numerous drunkards of both sexes were converted, and one street that long bore a name of disrepute was said to have been practically transformed. In March, Welsh revivalists Hugh Jones, who led later missions throughout Lanarkshire, J.J. Thomas, and others ministered in Aberdeen. The Press was generally kind, but some few 'cranks' criticised the 'gentlemen' who were responsible for the mission.[187] By the end of April, over 150 had professed to having accepted Christ, while the work showed no sign of abatement.[188] Popular evangelist Gipsy Smith harvested further fruit during his great mission in Aberdeen in 1906.[189] The Gilcomston Church continued to grow, and by 1908 membership reached its highest figure of 355.[190]

Cellardyke 1906

AN evangelist from a north-east fishing community held meetings in Cellardyke Town Hall in the closing months of 1906,[191] and from the start they were successful. The time was well chosen, for the boats had just returned from the 'south fishing' in East Anglia and the winter herring fishing did not start till January, so the men had free time to attend meetings. And attend they did, for night after night the hall was filled with 200 or 300, mainly young fishermen and women. A number of revival hymns, with their catchy tunes and sentimental words, were gustily sung, prayers for blessing on the meeting were offered and the traditional Bible reading was perfunctorily made – seen by most present as 'something to be got through before the real business of the meeting began'.

Belle Patrick, an 11-year-old schoolgirl present, remembered that the evangelist usually began his address 'in stilted English (certainly not recognisable as such by anyone from south of the border)', but 'soon lapsed into his mother tongue, to the great satisfaction of all his hearers'. The preacher carried his audience in an 'entrancing racy way', his message consisting of a 'calculated appeal to the emotions' with no exposition of Scripture. As such, it succeeded. Belle knew that 'the younger clan of school children' who filled the front benches had their heads turned round 'and behind the shading hands were wide-open eyes carefully noting every hand

---

187. Gibbard, *Fire on the Altar*, p120.

188. *Christian Herald*, 20 July 1905, p. 59; *SBM*, 1905, pp. 87, 105; Bebbington, *Baptists in Scotland*, p. 271; Yuille, p. 90; *TC*, 15 February 1905; Anonymous, *Together with God:* Centenary Booklet of Gilcomston Park Baptist Church.

189. Orr, *Flaming Tongue*, p. 35.

190. Shortly after followed a wave of emigration to Western Canada. Believers carried their testimony with them; and 'one church in Toronto became a colony of Gilcomston Park' (Anonymous, *These Fifty Years*).

191. Or possibly 1907.

raised, every tear or other sign of emotion, all to be recounted to admiring groups in the playground next day'. An after meeting followed for more personal dealing by the evangelist or other experienced believers.[192]

Belle wrote that 'as the days went by more and more people, including children, were "saved", and soon the playground at school held two separate camps – the sheep and the goats. I hovered unhappily between the two groups; of course I was not a goat; my father had been an outstanding figure, and all our family were "good living" so I could not be "unsaved". But I could not recount how long I had sobbed, how many tears I had shed in the reading room at the after meeting, so equally I could not claim to be "saved". One evening I went to the meeting with my heart set on one thing, and one thing only. I would be "saved" and join the elect. I have no recollection of the meeting at all, but I remember every detail of the after meeting. I was "dealt with" by the evangelist himself and so was greatly privileged and would be able to boast of this at school next day. But I would have to admit that, try as I would, I could not produce a single tear, and that I knew would bring grave doubt as to the reality of my conversion.' But despite her seemingly false motives, Belle's life was changed from that moment on, and she could say that 'never since that day, now nearly 60 years ago, have I had any doubt that I was then born again. … I was definitely committed to serve God and in His service I have found pure delight.'[193]

OTHER SIGNIFICANT MOVEMENTS IN THIS PERIOD[194]

Revival in the Salvation Army
- Clydebank
- Newmilns

Black Isle, Ross-shire
Wick and Thurso

192. Belle Patrick, *Recollections of East Fife Fisher Folk,* Edinburgh 2003, pp. 13–14.

193. Ibid., pp. 14–15. When still a child, Belle learnt by heart parts of the Bible, including the entire Book of Psalms, and she never forgot them.

194. Full accounts of these movements can be found on www.scottishrevivals.co.uk.

Tent Hall, Glasgow – p.99

St George's Tabernacle, Glasgow – p.100

George Sharpe – p.104

Motherwell – p.104

Rural Lanarkshire – p.111

Cambuslang – p.113

Edinburgh's West End – p.118

Joseph Kemp – p.119

Cockenzie – p.128

Blairgowrie – p.135

Cellardyke – p.137

4
Pre-War Ingathering
1907–14

Introduction

SPURRED on by the wave of blessing that disseminated over the country in 1905 to 1906, evangelists – mostly lay men and, to a lesser extent, women – proliferated in the pre-war period, and churches and Mission halls all over the country were saturated with special campaigns, lasting for anything from a week upwards. As an indication of their omnipresence, the 'Evangelists at Work' column in *The Christian* publication regularly overflowed with entries and in, for example, the issue dated 18 February 1909, no fewer than six special meetings or campaigns in Glasgow alone were referred to; no doubt others were advertised locally.[1] While perhaps the only outstanding revivals during this period took place within the Salvation Army, there were notable stirrings of spiritual activity in many places.

'An outpouring of God's Spirit in a very marked degree' attended the 'old fashioned' gospel ministrations of Samuel MacKenzie of the UFC on a visit to Islay in the early months of 1907, a mission that extended to eight weeks more than the three or four scheduled. The established and Free Churches co-operated and it became clear that many converts had been previously influenced by the ordinary preaching of the Word. Several weeks of nightly meetings were held in Port Charlotte, Bowmore, Gruinart, and Port Ellen. During the largest joint meetings ever held in this latter parish, 'there was a distinct influence for good over the whole community.'[2] Also in 1907, a significant work was carried on by the Faith Mission in the East Lothian village of Ratho, where 'quite a revival began'. Apart from women, close on eighty men professed faith over six weeks – all of them workers at the nearby quarries. These in turn sought to bring their fellow-workers to the Lord and it was reported that the 'tone of the local quarries is totally changed'.[3]

In 1908 – the same year that the town of Ayr experienced a dramatic move of the Spirit (see next section) – further north in Ayrshire a 'great wave of blessing' took place in Glengarnock. It started when evangelist George Cooke began a series of meetings in the Reading Room of the Iron and Steel

---

1. *TC*, 18 February 1909, p. 23.
2. Ibid., 21 March 1907; *RC-UFC-H&I*, 1907, pp. 242–3.
3. *BW*, 1907, pp. 7, 94–5, 115, 253.

Works, in which building Sunday gospel meetings had been held for some time. In the first week alone, some seventy to eighty people, besides children, turned to God. Thereafter, the larger Orange Hall was secured and 350 to 400 packed in to hear the gospel night after night. At one testimony meeting seventy witnessed to knowing the saving grace of God, over sixty of whom were new converts.[4] A good work was also done in the proximate village of Barkip,[5] while, the following year, 'an exceedingly interesting work of grace' progressed in the mining town of New Cumnock, where Duncan McNeil of the Ayrshire Christian Union was labouring.[6]

Also in 1909, the Fife colliery village of Hill of Beath, five miles from Dunfermline, experienced 'such a work of grace as is unique' in that community following a mission held by evangelist A.Y. McGregor.[7] Later that month, a campaign led by Mr and Mrs Andrew Cowie of Fraserburgh in the fishing community of Cellardyke – no stranger to spiritual awakenings – was so successful that it had to be extended again and again. Attendance at meetings, which carried 'no sensationalism', was aided by the fact that the fishing had come to a stop due to bad weather. Over 250 – mainly adults – professed Christ as Lord.[8] Glasgow, too, received a share of blessing in 1909. When William Oatts ministered in Anniesland it was said that 'for numbers and blessing, we have never had anything like it in the district'. The children's work alone increased fivefold in number, from 200 to over 1,000.[9]

The south Lanarkshire villages of Auchenheath and Kirkmuirhill played host to a 'season of spiritual revival' in the summer of 1910, when John Bissett, aforementioned Secretary of the Lanarkshire Christian Union, led a series of meetings. From here the blessing spread to other rural parts. Further north, in Bonnybridge, near Falkirk, there was said to have been 'an almost continuous revival' since the resuscitation of the Bonnyside Firebrick Works Mission some three years previously (at the time, brick manufacture was one of the main industries in this important industrial region). The 'whole district' was said to have been 'awakened in a remarkable manner', including some 'notorious evil-livers'.[10] During one week in February 1911 when W.D. Dunn spoke at meetings there, forty gave testimony to blessing received, and weeks later, others awakened during Dunn's visit were still being 'gathered in'.[11]

4. *TC*, 16 April 08, p. 26.
5. Ibid., 30 April 1908.
6. Ibid., 23 December 1909, p. 22.
7. Ibid., 8 April 1909.
8. Ibid., 22 April 1909.
9. Ibid., 8 April 1909.
10. Ibid., 21 December 1911.
11. Ibid., 16 February 1911.

REVIVAL IN THE SALVATION ARMY 1908

THE BIG ONE – AYR

'IF Robert Burns, the Scottish bard, were alive at the present moment, and dwelling in his little cottage at auld Ayr ... he would probably be swept with "Souter Johnny, his ancient treaty drouthy cronnie", into The Army Citadel, where many dry and thirsty Scotchmen are drinking of the Water of Life. For Ayr has been probed to its depths, and is at present in the throes of a well-sustained revival.'[12] So ran the opening lines of the *War Cry*'s first write-up of this remarkable revival, which began in November 1907. Amazingly the revival continued, in more or less force, for a full twelve months, and week by week the *War Cry* provided detailed reports of activities, making it one of best-documented religious revivals in Scottish history.[13]

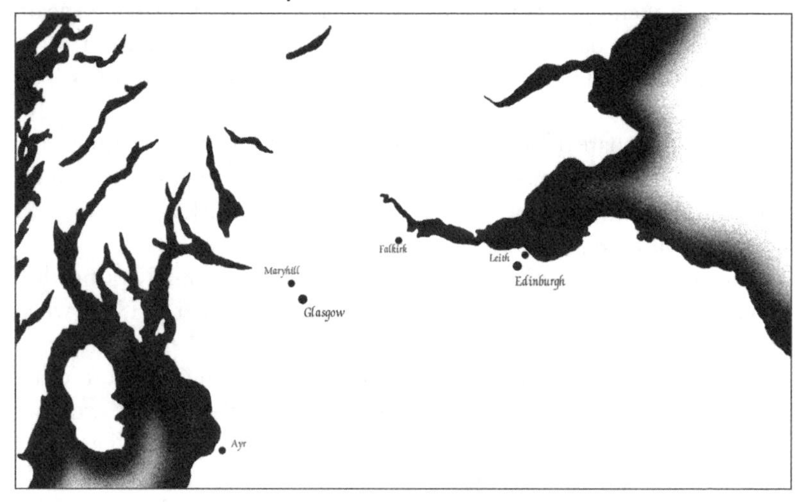

A variety of expressions were used to denote the significance of the movement. One Salvationist writer described it as 'one of the memorable spots in The Army's history'.[14] An ex-Army Officer with twenty-six years' experience of its work said the awakening was quite unique in his recollection.[15] Another reporter stated, more sensationally, of the movement that 'nothing like this has been seen since the days of the Covenanters'.[16]

---

12. *War Cry*, 18 January 1908, p. 9.

13. For a fuller account of this movement, see www.scottishrevivals.co.uk.

14. *War Cry*, 14 March 1908, p. 11. It was elsewhere noted, 'The scenes which are taking place nightly are just a repetition of those common in the early days of the Army, when not only the poorest, but also the roughest and lowest, were to be seen crowding our Halls and getting converted' (ibid., 22 February 1908, p.13).

15. *Ayrshire Post*, 17 January 1908, p. 5.

16. *War Cry*, 14 March 1908, p. 11.

From its inception and throughout its course, the revival was linked to the charisma, vision and evangelistic zeal of Adjutant Boyce, who came, with his wife, to serve as leader of the Ayr Corps in November 1907.[17] On his arrival he felt, in looking upon the soldiers, that he was gazing upon a disappointed people. 'And I made up my mind to try and help them. After being here a fortnight, I heard one of the Soldiers say, "this Officer preaches nothing but the love of God in his meetings". I felt that this was telling. Two or three good holiness meetings, and a half-night of prayer followed, and then we started Saturday midnight raids. Praise the Lord! The revival had begun.'[18]

The coastal town of Ayr had a population of around 30,000 at the turn of the twentieth century. Like most Scottish towns, it had its share of 'vice and misery and crime stalking side by side with formalism and indifference, and every other kind of sin'.[19] The area over which the movement was openly and admittedly active in its operations was said to have been 'to some extent circumscribed, covering the poorer portion of the town' – in particular the Auld Toon area.[20] It was among the poorest of the population that drinking was a particular problem, and it was among such a class that the revival had its greatest effect.

By mid-January, no fewer than 305 had sought salvation. On one occasion 81 recruits sang 'Rock of Ages, cleft for me' and were afterwards sworn in under the Flag. Amongst these were 12 married couples. That same weekend saw 125 souls dedicate their lives to God while 32 'sought holiness'.[21]

During one week in January, 'the number of penitents recorded at the mercy-seat' each night was

Monday, 51
Tuesday, 62
Wednesday, 51
Thursday, 26
Friday, 38 [22]

As a result, it was stated, 'on good authority', that while the average number of 'drunks' locked up in Ayr on a Saturday night before the revival was sixteen, by January the figure was just one or two.[23] The Police were said to be 'watching the movement with great interest as the sobriety of some "incorrigibles" during the past few weeks (Jan 1908) has been a revelation to them'.[24] One publican in town declared that it

17. The Salvation Army in Ayr began in the mid-1890s.

18. *War Cry*, 25 January 1908, p. 11.

19. Ibid., 1 February 1908, p. 11.

20. Ibid., 25 January 1908, p. 11.

21. Ibid., 18 January 1908, p. 9.

22. Ibid., 25 January 1908, p. 11.

23. Ibid.

24. *Ayrshire Post*, 31 January 1908, p. 5.

was good to see drunkards going to the Army, but another urged that 'the matter is going a little too far!'[25]

The *War Cry* printed testimony after testimony of men whose lives, along with those of their wives and children, had been utterly ruined by drink, but whose characters had been thoroughly transformed by the power of the gospel.[26] One man testified to a particular situation. 'We had been for several hours with the lifeboat, standing by a ship in distress. We were suffering intensely from the cold and the effects of the terrible storm. When whisky was brought to us, and passed round to stimulate the crew, the convert refused to take it, saying, "No, thank you, I am a convert of The Salvation Army". This made a wonderful impression on the men present.'[27]

A town councillor told how, in his business, he had had for weeks to call at a certain home, and almost invariably found the head of the family drunk on the floor, or, if able to sit up, blaspheming loudly. Now when he had called he found a really changed man who mentioned in confidence that his wife was getting his clothes back from the pawnshop! Another convert publicly proclaimed; 'this is the first Saturday night I have been sober for thirty years.'[28] So many lives were being transformed that a local doctor was known to send patients, victims of alcohol, to the Salvation Army for help, as he knew their methods were far more effective than any assistance he could offer!

One visitor spoke of meetings being so packed that the Treasurer had difficulty squeezing in the back door to see to the collection; a Salvation Army officer, accustomed to marching ten or twelve soldiers from the open-air to an inside week-night congregation of forty or fifty people, marching 150 converts to the Hall, only to find there was not even standing room in the Hall for them!

> And what are the congregations like? Just the class the Army delights to see in its Halls. Blear-eyed men, with drink sodden features, across which criminal instincts have written themselves large, and against whom conviction after conviction is recorded in the police-books near-by. Ragged men, unwanted men, evil men, whose very presence is a pain, and whose inner natures are, by long abandon to sinful lusts, infinitely worse than outside stains indicate. Others are regular workers, but unable to pass a pub with a penny in their possession, and, consequently, very poor. Yet, again, there are others, well clad, thrifty people, but

25. *War Cry*, 1 February 1908, p. 11.

26. One January edition of the *War Cry* also devoted its front page wholly to photos of over a dozen of 'the worst type of men' whose lives had been transformed. In the centre of the picture is a reproduction of Ayr Prison, sarcastically termed *The Summer Residence* by locals, where numerous converts had spent some time.

27. *War Cry*, 29 February 1908, p. 11.

28. *Ayrshire Post*, 31 January 1908, p. 5.

> hardened in the ways of the world, and not easy to move in ordinary meetings. … Scores of men of each of these, as well as other types, have knelt side by side at the mercy-seat, where God has saved them, and not only is there now the little bit of Army ribbon on their coats, but there is a new look in their eyes, happiness is not conspicuous by its absence from their tread, a stirring testimony on their tongues, and an open-mouthed wonder on the part of their old associates.
>
> Equally striking are the changes wrought among the women, a large number of whom are included in the converts, though men predominate. Bareheaded factory lasses, hard-headed housewives, ragged drunkards, and well-clothed respectable mothers, smartly-dressed young women, and small girls with bare feet have been so anxious to find mercy as to throw themselves down at the penitent-form, without regard to reprobate at one side or respectability at the other.[29]

'"This is undoubtedly the work of the Spirit of God!" declared a minister, as he walked out, after sitting in a meeting and taking in the extraordinary sights as a man takes in a view he never dreamed of seeing.'[30] Indeed, all societal classes in Ayr were quick to acknowledge that the Salvation Army was in the thick of the most remarkable religious movement that the town had seen in modern times.[31] Even in the Ayrshire county jail, 'the salvation of souls in such wholesale fashion' was the main topic of conversation.

'I have been saved six weeks,' said one recruit. 'Before my conversion I was a terrible drunkard and gambler. I used to get up on a Sunday morning and look at my four little children with scarcely any food or clothes, and my poor wife with a black eye. The children would keep away from me. But what a glorious change! When I arose this morning there was plenty of good food and every comfort, and all the family singing Salvation songs. The wife is also saved, and we praise God for The Army.'[32] When one worker brought home his pay-note and wages, 'it was the first his wife had seen for seven and twenty years'.[33]

Regarding the two primary leaders of the movement, *The Ayrshire Post* wrote that, 'nothing that influence and example can do is left undone by Adjutant and Mrs Boyce. The adjutant's energy is simply marvellous, while thanks to the buffetings and failures of the world, he has in a large measure the milk of human kindness.' Recognising the severe strain entailed by labour of this kind, a special officer was sent to assist Boyce

29. *War Cry*, 1 February 1908, p. 11.
30. Ibid.
31. Ibid.
32. Ibid., 18 April 1908, p. 9.
33. *Ayrshire Post*, 13 March 1908, p. 3.

in the work of reclamation. Ten visiting Salvationist sergeants were also hard at work daily.[34]

The extent of the revival can be seen by considering how one street in the town was affected. 'In No. 5 are two converts, three in No. 7, three in No. 9, two in No. 15, two in No. 16, six in No. 17, four in No. 18, eight in No. 21, four in No. 23, six in No. 25, and so on. And this street is by no means an exception.'[35] Just a few months later it could be recorded from another street that 'we have 300 names registered of people who have been to the penitent-form since the revival began.'[36]

Several top Salvation Army leaders came to witness the movement and to encourage converts, including, in January 1908, Commissioner Cosandey, Commissioner of the Salvation Army for Scotland. The British Chief Secretary of the Army, Colonel Eadie, visited Ayr early the following month. He wrote that 'there has been no religious movement in the history of Ayr since the days of the Reformation like this! It is not a revival in the usually understood acceptance of the term – it is a creation. The converts are not from the ranks of those who have been under religious influence – except when they have been in prison, where they are compelled to attend the church service. They are indeed gathered from among "the dead in trespasses and sins" – the heathen of Christian Scotland! … This is not a revival – it is a raising of the dead.'

He went on: 'There is no emotion in this movement; the people are not weeping, or laughing, or singing themselves into frenzy; they are demure, cool, deliberate. I have seen 58 persons walk out to the mercy-seat this weekend in a way I have never witnessed in all my life before. They came in exactly the same fashion that folks go into a shop to purchase goods. At the penitent-stool they have had to be taught how to pray, never having prayed before, but they have got up from their knees with a clear assurance of forgiveness that has made me feel emotional beyond the telling!'

Colonel Eadie concluded, 'Let the people who say the day of miracles is past, shut up! For this movement is miraculous!' [37] During the weekend of the visit of the Chief Secretary, the Hall was packed four times, while the Unionist Hall adjoining, holding 600 people, was also crowded out (this hall, plus another smaller hall, was used on a number of occasions as overflow venues). Also during one week in February, a particularly large number of youths sought salvation at the Young People's meetings. A special commissioner for the Army said of the revival: 'It does not resemble the Welsh revival in fervour. It does not bear any comparison

34. Ibid., 31 January 1908, p. 5.

35. *War Cry*, 1 February 1908, p. 11.

36. Ibid., 16 May 1908, p. 11.

37. Ibid., 22 February 1908, p. 11.

with the Cornish and North-West Scottish fisher Awakenings.[38] For a parallel you have to imagine a cross between Bulwell, an Army opening in a dense industrial district, and a Slum and Hooligan Corps.'[39]

The first 'promotion to Glory' of a convert took place at 5 o'clock one morning in early February when a notorious character, named Graham, one of three brothers, and converted only a few weeks previously, was called to his 'Heavenly Home'. Meanwhile, in June a wedding took place of two of the revival converts. The bridegroom was a nephew of a Brigadier in the Salvation Army, while the bride was one of a whole family of revival converts.

There were normally three meetings on Saturday nights. One for converts at 6 p.m., a revival service at 8, and a 'drunk-or-sober' meeting at 10.30 p.m.[40] Staff-Captain Ayers saw a banner announcing a 'Come-drunk-or-Sober' meeting held at 10.30 on Saturday nights.[41] He described one that he attended. 'Brothers to the front, with Band next, away they march at ten o'clock, watched by thousands. In the streets through which they pass they pick up drunkards by the score, and the new converts place them between themselves, until hundreds of drink's victims are marched back to the Citadel, cramming and jamming the galleries, aisles, penitent-form, and all the space around it. From the crowded platform can be seen the brave Bandsmen pushing their way through the crowd.' A drunk could be heard saying to another, 'Jock, dinna let them get a had o' ye or ye're done for! They'll hae ye, and ye'll hae tae get saved!'[42]

One Sunday was also full of incident: 'Sunday morning's open-air revealed something of the interest in the revival. Around the ring were gathered a large number of very poor women, with shawls over their heads, some with no boots upon their feet, and the tears running down their cheeks as they listened to the testimonies of their neighbours.'[43] As usual, a march-procession took place on Sunday afternoon – this was watched by hundreds from their windows, and it was said that at some points they gazed at it as they would some royal spectacle.

---

38. He is more than likely referring to revivals in north-*east* fishing communities. D.E. Meek seems to make a similar mistake when he refers to Scottish revivals being prominent among ' the fisherfolk of the north-west in the late 19th century…' (Nigel M. de S. Cameron [Ed.], *Dictionary of Scottish Church History and Theology*, Edinburgh 1993 [hereafter *DSCH&T*], p. 715).

39. *Ayrshire Post*, 31 January 1908, p. 5.

40. A Saturday night meeting in April began at 6 p.m. and continued till midnight, without a break. 'The midnight raid was a sight to behold – the whole town was alive with excitement and interest' (*War Cry*, 18 April 1908, p. 9).

41. A later placard prominently displayed outside the Citadel, which read 'Come and hear the converted Jailbirds, Drunkards, Wife-Beaters, Home-Wreckers, and Heart-Breakers speak and sing', attracted considerable interest (*War Cry*, 27 June 1908, p. 10).

42. *War Cry*, 22 February 1908, p. 11.

43. Ibid.

Into March, and rather than signs of the movement abating, it seemed instead to take a new lease of life. It was said of particular meetings in this month that, 'there has been nothing like it since the revival began. Tremendous crowds have attended open-airs and marches, and the Citadel has been thronged nightly. In every meeting souls have sought mercy, among them being some remarkable trophies. One, a sister, saved since the last report, got up in the Town Hall on Sunday night before 1,000 people and sang her experience. This caused a great sensation. The people looked, listened and wondered. Was it her whom they thought it to be? Yes! And when the Adjutant announced her name a storm of applause broke forth in token of approval. "Thank God", they were heard to remark, "Maggie saved at last!"' Several others, deeply impressed by her testimony, made commitments of faith. *The War Cry* urged readers to 'pray for Maggie, for the eyes of the whole town are watching her.'[44]

Once the power of the gospel had taken hold of people's lives, they were quick to witness to friends and neighbours. One man told Colonel Eadie that he had been saved eight weeks, and during that time he had won for Christ forty-nine others.[45] A woman approached the Adjutant in the street and announced that she was 'coming to get saved' for 'you have already got 24 of my relations during the revival'. She kept her word, and the Adjutant had the joy of seeing her at the penitent-form the following week.[46] Mr Boyce also had the delight of receiving into his ranks the local bookmaker, as well as 'the man who took the slips'.[47] A reporter for the *Ayrshire Post* wrote that, 'however critical I may wish to be, I cannot deny that … a great and good work is being done.'[48]

The revival was felt not just in the immediate area surrounding the Salvation Army Hall, but in all districts. It was said, 'One needs to be in Ayr only a very brief time to know that a revival is in progress. Its spirit can be felt in the very atmosphere.'[49] One March weekend the Army's presence was particularly noticeable – a great effort being made to raise funds for carrying on the work. It was further noted that 'nearly every place of worship in the town has benefited. Several ministers have, in fact, expressed to Adjutant Boyce their personal thanks for the influences of the revival. "In my district," said one, "the Army have done a great deal of good among a class of people who hitherto have not been reached".'[50]

---

44. Ibid., 14 March 1908, p. 11.
45. Ibid., 22 February 1908, p. 11.
46. Ibid., 18 April 1908, p. 9.
47. *Ayrshire Post*, 13 March 1908, p. 3.
48. Ibid., 31 January 1908, p. 5.
49. *War Cry*, 6 June 1908, p. 11.
50. Ibid., 16 May 1908, p. 11.

It appears, however, that the degree of inter-denominational co-operation in the revival was very limited. At a meeting of the Ayr UFC Presbytery in March 1908, the Rev. Donald Davidson of Wallacetown spoke of his delight in the revival but felt that, overall, the work was a hindrance to congregational life in the town. Salvation Army officers, he observed, worked independently, desiring no help from other local ministers. This was particularly apparent at baptisms, marriages and funerals. He quoted from the *War Cry*, 'The revival is essentially salvation, the ministers are not in it, and perhaps they had better leave it alone.' He regretted the truth of this comment, remarking that the Army was glad enough to get monetary help from other churches. Finally he said he had been at one of their meetings, and was neither asked to speak nor invited to come back again.[51]

In response, the Rev. A. MacCallum of Dalrymple said that Rev. Davidson's remarks were not the feelings of the Presbytery. 'The Salvation Army had their own class of work, and they were the people to do it. If it was indicated plainly that the Army did not want their help, then the ministers did not want to be so thin-skinned as to imagine that there was any harm in that. The Presbytery ought to rejoice, and rejoice whole-heartedly, that they were doing the work and doing it successfully, and if ministers could learn anything from them, let them do so, but by no means throw out criticisms.'[52]

The *War Cry* proudly testified that 'the effect of the revival on the town is marvellous. Requests are continually being sent to the [S.A.] Officers to visit people who are concerned about their souls' salvation, and who, as a result, have either got saved at home or at the Citadel.'[53] The testimony of the police also was that the revival had done a great deal of good. Within the Salvation Army itself every section of the Ayr Corps benefited from the revival: the Band increased in numbers and enthusiasm; so, too, did the Songsters, and also the workers associated with the Juniors.

As a result of the widespread influence of the awakening, people attended meetings from miles around. The Provost of Troon, Mr Logan, attended one Friday night meeting in April. During his speech he said: 'for the time being I put off the dignity of a provost, and hold it a very great honour to be assembled with the ex-jailbirds and drunkards who have been converted during the revival.'[54] A UFC elder decided to spend

---

51. *Ayrshire Post*, 20 March 1908, p. 3. Indirect confirmation of the lack of inter-denominational co-operation in the revival comes from Edward Last, who served as Baptist pastor in Ayr during this time. Though he refers to successful evangelistic events by his church during the period that revival was flourishing elsewhere in Ayr, he makes no mention whatever of this movement (Edward Last, *Olive: The Story of a Brief but Beautiful Life*, Glasgow c. 1911, pp. 19, 30–3).

52. *Ayrshire Post*, ibid.

53. *War Cry*, 6 June 1908, p. 11.

54. Ibid., 18 April 1908, p. 9.

his holidays in Ayr in order to see the work for himself, later remarking on the 'spirit of reverence and a great desire to listen and drink in the Word of God'.[55] General Booth also arranged to visit the town, being guest of the Provost and Council at a civic reception.

The Bailiff of Ayr also spoke positively of the influence of the revival, being deeply impressed at Boyce's interest in those charged with criminal offences. As a typical example, the Adjutant visited in prison a man who had received 129 criminal convictions – each one for drunkenness. He met him at the prison gates on the day of his release and took him to his home. The man attended meetings in the Citadel the following week, and was soon seen at the penitent form giving his soul to Christ. It was later reported that 'the landlady of the house where he lodges speaks of the remarkable change that has taken place in him since conversion'.[56]

The *War Cry* gave evidence in May 'that the Ayr revival still rolls on' by showing that 'five months ago the weekly average for open-air meetings were 250; inside 790. The average open-air attendance weekly now is 1,100 and inside 7,500.'[57] One Monday night in May, for one hour, converts could be seen streaming into the Town Hall to take part in what was called a 'Revival Tea' and, by 7.30 p.m., 1,250 persons had presented their tickets. This was said to be the largest public tea ever held in the town. During one weekend the following month, 'From 6 o'clock Saturday night until 10.30 Sunday night 22 Senior meetings were held, outside and in.'[58]

Numerous poor revival converts were among those who, in accordance with custom, were privileged during what was known as the 'May term' to flit from poverty-stricken areas to comfortable homes in other parts of the town. Although many who did not flit helped those who did, the numbers attending Army meetings during this period did not fail to let up.[59]

In July, progress of the converts was said to be 'very satisfactory.... They can be seen wearing the red guernsey, or the bonnet, and nightly taking their stand in the open-air and testifying in the very streets where they live. The neighbours readily accept their testimony, and give their enforcement to the reality of the change.'[60]

One man testified that he got so drunk on his wedding day that he woke up the next morning to find himself in a prison-cell, and that was where he had to spend his honeymoon! 'Thank God, the past six months,

55. Ibid., 12 September 1908, p. 11.
56. Ibid., 27 June 1908, p. 10.
57. Ibid., 16 May 1908, p. 11.
58. Ibid., 27 June 1908, p. 10.
59. Ibid., 6 June 1908, p. 11.
60. Ibid., 11 July 1908, p. 11.

during which time he has been saved, have been the happiest time of his seven years' married life. His wife also is a convert of the revival.' [61] Ms Sloan, 'the Y.P. Treasurer', was the only Salvationist in her factory, but soon a great work was wrought in several of her female colleagues. Soon they, too, were proudly wearing their shields or badges to work, where they held a Bible study during lunch-hour, as a result of which several of their unsaved work-mates came to the Citadel 'and got gloriously converted'.[62]

In June the Newton area of town was supplied with a 'hot bombardment' of Brigade workers to witness and testify.[63] Later in the summer a number of open-airs were held on the sea-front, attracting large crowds. Other open airs were held at the Fish Cross. At one, 'a man who got off his bicycle to listen to the testimonies was so taken hold of by the Spirit of God, that, while the meeting was proceeding, he rushed into the centre of the ring, fell on his knees and cried for mercy. God saved his soul, and he went away rejoicing in his Saviour.'[64]

The Ayr races were held in September, when factories closed down, and thousands of people from all parts of the country converged on the town. Drinking was a prominent feature of the festivities as too, of course, was gambling. Realising that many of the converts were formerly drunkards and gamblers, Adjutant Boyce arranged for a host of innovative counter-attractions for young converts who might otherwise be tempted to go to the races, saving many a young convert from temptation.[65]

Week by week, under headings such as 'Ayr's Wonderful Revival', 'Scotch Revival Fire' and 'Ayr's Remarkable Awakening', the *War Cry* carried reports of the revival's progress. Such reports in themselves helped influence the movement. In just one week in late summer 1908 one man sold four dozen of the *War Cry* in a part of Ayr where they had never been sold before. Meanwhile, a letter arrived from a town in England from a man who worked as a publican. He bought the *War Cry* regularly and became deeply interested in reading the testimonies of converted drunkards and jail-birds. He was so taken hold of, that he was compelled to leave his situation and get converted. He became a S.A. soldier (he enclosed his photo in full uniform) and got a job as a collier.[66]

In November 1908, a full year after its commencement, the revival was still in operation. One night that month, Dan Christie, an ex-international football player, had the joy of leading his brother to Christ. The newly-converted's testimony was greeted with great applause. On the

61. Ibid.

62. Ibid.

63. Ibid.

64. Ibid., 8 August 1908, p. 9.

65. Ibid., 26 September 1908, p. 11.

66. Ibid., 12 September 1908, p. 11.

same night, the Young People's Campaign was launched. A thousand young folk were present. Among the seekers were several who were children of revival converts.[67] November 21st saw the last *War Cry* report on the Ayr awakening.[68]

ARMY BARRACKS, GLASGOW

BY February 1908, the *War Cry* could observe that 'the same spirit which had its kindling at Ayr is being aroused throughout the whole of the Northern Kingdom, and is manifesting itself in unexpected directions. There is a swelling of public sympathy towards The Army, and a turning to God on the part of the vicious and the prodigal.'[69]

At the military barracks at Maryhill, Glasgow, Leaguer Gilfillan, a member of the Salvation Army, wrote that the weekly meetings that he was allowed to hold among his comrades produced stirring scenes, and in less than three weeks 25 penitents, including a married soldier and his wife, had sought salvation. 'The little schoolroom at the barracks is crowded every night,' wrote Gilfillan. 'One of the converts was a lion-tamer with a travelling menagerie, and on the way to France. To sever his connection with them he came to the barracks and enlisted. On my last visit I found him diligently studying the Bible on his cot. Three other converts have gone to Dublin to join the regiment. While going round the rooms the other day I found a young fellow, who was holding religion up to ridicule and creating a bad impression among other lads. After I had talked to him for some time about salvation, he promised to come to the meetings. He, too, was among the converts.'[70]

LEITH AND FALKIRK

A MOVEMENT commenced in the Edinburgh port of Leith in the late summer of 1908. During one week at the beginning of September, as many as 500 attended the nightly meetings in the Salvation Army Hall, and 33 seekers found their way to the penitent-form in search of salvation (as well as 18 'for holiness').[71] 'Times of great spiritual activity' were still being experienced towards the close of November, when large numbers were still attending the meetings, indoors and out.[72]

---

67. Ibid., 21 November 1908, p. 11.

68. From Ayr, revival spread to Beith, a small manufacturing town twenty miles to the north, with a population of around 5,000. It was recorded that during 24 days from mid-April 1908, '40 souls have been recorded at the mercy-seat, 34 for salvation and six for holiness' (*The War Cry*, 16 May 1908, p. 11). Awakenings, of various strengths, also sprang up in various other Salvation Army Corps – notably in Penge, South London (beginning in late autumn 1907), Leyton, East London (from February 1908), and Torquay (from July 1908). None, however, were as intense or as long-lasting as the dramatic series of events that unfolded in Ayr.

69. *War Cry*, 22 February 1908, p. 9.

70. Ibid., 28 March 1908, p. 11.

71. Ibid., 5 September 1908, p. 11.

72. Ibid., 21 November 1908, p. 11.

Commissioner Coasandey of the Salvation Army noted that in each of Scotland's large corps, drunkards' raids were being conducted every Saturday night. At Falkirk 'we had a striking demonstration. The whole hall seemed filled with whisky,' and there was much commotion. But when soldiers contacted some of the drunks the next day and invited them to that day's meetings, several came along 'and got converted. That started a sensation. On Monday night nine souls, including some of the most vicious characters in the locality, gave themselves to God. On Tuesday, several more, and so on throughout the week. And this,' continued the Commissioner, 'is not unripe fruit that falls and dies and is no good, but ripe fruit that promises to be of untold value to the Army.' Still in Falkirk, over 800 people attended a meeting in the Theatre one Sunday afternoon, while good reports also came in from Greenock and Dundee.[73]

LATER MOVEMENTS 1913–1914

THE year 1913 saw a move of the Spirit in the fishing town of Ferryden,[74] a location repeatedly favoured with Divine blessing.[75] Towards the close of the year, Westray experienced a definite 'time of blessing' when Brethren evangelist W.J. Gerrie came to preach, the Baptist Church also sharing in the harvest and receiving around twenty additions to membership.[76] In the same year – 1913 – the Brethren assembly in Galston, Ayrshire saw about sixty conversions when Percy Beard held a campaign – about half of them being young female textile workers from the same factory.[77]

In the capital, Charlotte Baptist Chapel yet again experienced divine blessing during the later ministry of the Rev. J.W. Kemp. A new church building was constructed in 1911–2. Officially opened in October 1912, Kemp could rejoice a year later 'in the fact that the Lord's blessing has continued with us amid our new surroundings. The same spiritual atmosphere which pervaded the old chapel fills the new one.'[78] Kemp began a series of sermons on revival. Services became crowded each Sunday evening and it was reported that 'there is to be found that spiritual atmosphere which true preachers long for'.[79] Prayer meetings became imbued with 'the power and presence of the Lord in a very real manner', and throughout 1913 there were spontaneous gatherings for prayer from 9–11 p.m. on Sundays after the other busy work of the day

73. Ibid., 22 February 1908, p. 9.

74. *The Revival*, 6 March 1913, p. 24.

75. e.g. in 1859, 1867, and again in 1891 through the labours of Hay MacDowall Grant of Arndilly, Duncan Matheson and James McKendrick respectively.

76. *The Revival*, 22 January 1914, p. 22.

77. Dickson, *Brethren in Scotland*, p. 131.

78. Balfour, p. 146.

79. *The Revival*, 8 January 1914, p. 25.

had been completed. Kemp delighted in such impromptu development, for which about 100 people assembled, the meetings being 'reminiscient of the days when the Church was in the throes of a glorious revival'. At one Sunday evening service, 'there was a complete breakdown, and fully 12 persons sought and found salvation.' The Chapel co-invited Gipsy Smith to conduct a mission in March 1913. As many men were turned away from the Sunday afternoon meetings as would have filled the Assembly Hall twice over. Scores testified conversion. Then, one Sunday in November, two dozen men and women accepted Christ.[80] Altogether, during 1913, around 130 were added to the membership. At the Watch-Night service on the closing Sunday of the year, quite a number, mostly young men, found their way to the inquiry room and some forty people gave testimony to having received Christ in the preceding twelve months. Then, with a call for all to rise who had been converted in the chapel previous to 1913, 'a great company stood to their feet – a never-to-be-forgotten sight.'[81]

Still in Edinburgh in the same year, 1913, and in the same denomination, a movement took place in Abbeyhill Baptist Church, then pastored by Albert Griffiths, who had seen much blessing during his ministry in Westray at the beginning of the century.[82] Meanwhile, from June to December 1913, in Cambridge St Baptist Church in Glasgow, where Edward Last was serving a second term of ministry, 105 people made profession of Christ – 'a work surely remarkable and encouraging'.[83]

In October 1913, American Presbyterian evangelist John Wilbur Chapman opened a crusade in Glasgow, which continued for eleven weeks. Some 12,000 'decisions for Christ' were recorded. In 1914 Chapman moved to Edinburgh before heading to cities in England. During one day at the Olympian Hall in Scotland's capital some 18,000 heard Chapman speak in three services. He frequently preached six times a day and it was said that citywide interest was aroused 'to an astonishing degree'.[84] The much-loved Gipsy Smith also saw 'great blessing' during his 1913 campaign in Edinburgh.[85]

Meanwhile, another American evangelist (along with his singing companion) blitzed southern Scotland with a series of evangelistic campaigns during the two immediately pre-war years. From February to May 1914 Messrs Stephens and Storrs, and their wives, held a concerted

80. Balfour, pp. 147–8.

81. *The Revival*, 8 January 1914, p. 25.

82. Ibid., 10 April 1913, p. 24.

83. Ibid.

84. Wikipedia online Encyclopaedia; Unknown, *John Wilbur Chapman, 1859–1918, Evangelist*, www.believersweb.org

85. *TC*, 27 March 1913, p. 24.

campaign in Annan and Dumfries. In the former town a massive wooden Tabernacle was especially built (on the same ground where Richard Weaver preached to crowds in 1861). The town was at first a hard field. 'They came among a naturally shy and conservative people, whose spiritual life was at a very low ebb.' However, at the end of two weeks it was evident that 'the spell was broken, and that God was working in a wonderful degree in the town'. Storrs performed as 'genial chorister and soloist', while his wife counselled at the after-meetings and also had the courage to 'interview every man and woman in the local market, and deal personally with each'.[86] Over 400 made profession of faith, while in Dumfries itself, where 'the whole town was thoroughly aroused', and folk came from miles around, professions were twice that number.[87]

THE WAR YEARS 1914–19

MANY evangelists continued to itinerate in Scotland during the First World War, while others took full advantage of the opportunities it provided for evangelism. There was, though, relatively little in the way of revival activity during these long, hard years. There were, however, a few notable exceptions, particularly among the Brethren, who continued intensive outreach during the period and formed a number of new assemblies. In November 1916 a movement took place among fishing girls from around the coast who were staying at Lochee, Dundee, when between seventy and eighty of them turned to the Lord. The following month another forty professed conversion during meetings in the city's Hermon Hall.[88] More significant still, and occurring over a greater time-scale, was a movement in the north and eastern parts of Harris, which continued throughout the war years (see pp. 303–4).

ARRAN 1916–18

FURTHER south off Scotland's west coast, another area where a 'never-to-be-forgotten' awakening occurred during the First World War was the Southend district of Arran. The minister of Sliddery Free Church, Rev.

86. Ibid., 12 March 1914; 19 March 1914.

87. Ibid., 21 May 1914; 28 May 1914.

88. Dickson, *Brethren in Scotland*, p. 186. An army chaplain was asked if there were traces of revival at the battlefront. 'There was not what is known to us as a revival,' was the padre's considered reply, 'but the good were better and the bad were worse.' He added, however, that 'instances abound of young men on the battlefield finding the Rock whose clefts afforded refuge in the midst of the pains and terrors of death' (*PGA-FC*, 1914, p. 308). In fact a little-publicised and largely unknown movement occurred during these years among soldiers on the vast training grounds of Salisbury Plain in Wiltshire (see www.scottishrevivals.co.uk). In addition, after being seriously wounded in action in France during WW1, Duncan Campbell was taken back to Scotland and spent the next thirteen months in hospital in Perth. He is said to have referred to this time as '"months of revival". He saw the gracious movings of God in the hospital. He said that he would just speak a word about Jesus and that would do it, people would be saved' (Brad Allen, *Catch the Wind: The Story of Spiritual Awakening on the Hebrides Islands*, Tarentum, Pennsylvania 2002, p. 35).

MacEwan, had long yearned for an awakening in his south-west Arran parish, but had been so dismayed at the apparent lack of fruit from his ministry that he had seriously intended resigning, that the Lord might send someone more useful. His elders, however, insisted that he remain. So, with the approach of the Communion in June 1916, the earnest pastor pleaded with his congregation to entreat the Lord that He might send to them a messenger through whom an awakening might occur in the district. Thus it was that the Rev. Kenneth MacRae of Lochgilphead, then a man of 32 and soon to be married, arrived on the island. His first service on Thursday morning, 1 June was well attended and he enjoyed it 'pretty well. I felt the place warm – spiritual warm – and that made all the difference to me.' At the close of the meeting the minister invited any who wished to become communicants at the Lord's Table to go forward to the Session. MacEwan's voice faltered with emotion as he spoke, and MacRae noted, 'This was the first evidence I had of anything of unusual life in the place. Yet despite his emotion and his earnestness no one came forward.'

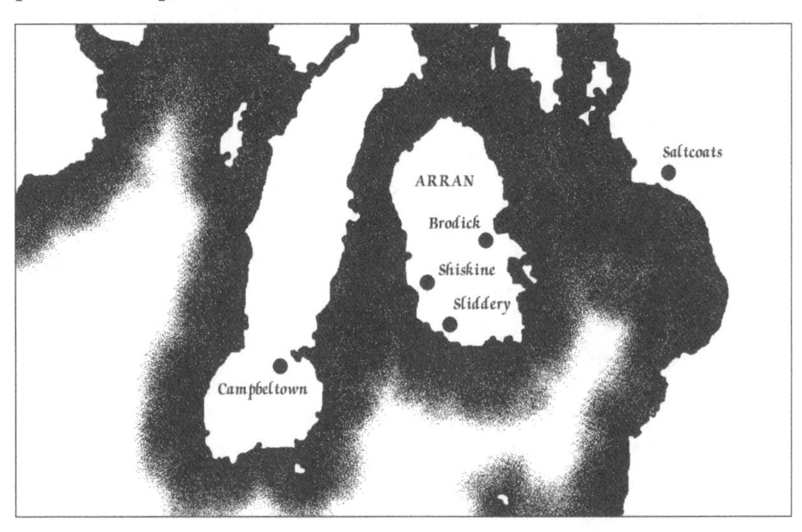

At the evening meeting, despite being less well attended, MacRae 'felt even more warmth than in the morning. Towards the end of the service, a woman in the front seat, a member and a good woman, burst out crying so unrestrainably that her sobs were audible even to myself. This was the second evidence of life.' The Friday evening meeting proved to MacRae to be 'still sweeter than anything that had gone before. I enjoyed it immensely and was given an earnestness which is not often mine. ...'

'Next forenoon,' MacRae wrote, 'I preached another topical discourse on "the Dew that descends upon Mount Zion" [Psalm 133:3]. This was a theme I had worked out in my own mind one dark evening, coming home from the Cairnbaan meeting some time before, yet I never had

had time to shape it and preach it until now. I do not know when I enjoyed anything so well. Tears were frequent. The two poor old women in the front seat were weeping. Jessie MacKinnon [an elder's daughter] was with her mother and sister near the front. If ever I saw distress I saw it in that poor girl's face.' Rev. MacEwan gave a final invitation to anyone who wished to apply for admission to Communion. Jessie MacKinnon rose and crossed to the vestry door. Wrote MacRae, 'I could have shouted for very joy, but I lost that when I saw the poor girl in the vestry. She was weeping and yet she was calm. I could see that her soul was face to face with eternal realities; nothing else mattered to her. Mr MacEwan was weeping too, but he gently led her to a chair and sat down beside her.' Jessie was questioned on her reasons for coming forward and directed 'to the One who alone can save'. She was then 'admitted a member of Christ's visible church and then, still weeping, she took her departure. Perhaps the most touching scene took place after that, as poor old Mr MacEwan tried to express his gratitude to the Lord for all that He had done. It was so wonderful; he had hoped for Katie [Jessie's sister, who had been awakened two years previously but had never made any profession], but he had no thought whatsoever of Jessie, and the poor old man broke down altogether. It was a moment of great stress.' Rev. MacRae wrote, 'I could neither restrain my tears nor my smiles of joy, and was constrained to cover my face with my hands.'[89]

Back at his lodgings later that evening, MacRae was greeted by his host Mrs MacAlister, who had been bereaved just six months previously by the loss of a son. 'She was a soft, gentle woman whose very look was love; one of the Lord's poor ones whom suffering has made meek.' Her other son, John, had been such a comfort to his mother since his brother died. She said he seemed to have changed and it made her heart glad. He was a very shy lad, yet he had offered his services as precentor when the ordinary precentor was called away for service in the army. He had also broken down earlier that day when sharing with a friend the news of Jessie MacKinnon going forward.[90]

On Sabbath morning MacRae 'got ample liberty' in preaching the Action sermon, which he normally felt poor at. But to him, 'the serving of the Tables was the sweetest of the lot. Jessie was weeping, Mr MacEwan was weeping, one poor woman made no secret of her tears; I could see them streaming down her cheeks and her black bodice shining wet with them. There was also weeping throughout the church, Katie MacKinnon and a married sister, I afterwards heard, quite breaking down. The Lord was very near to me and oh how precious it all was! I do not think

89. Murray, *Diary*, pp. 86–7.

90. Ibid., p. 88.

that ever I came nearer to being carried away altogether while speaking publicly. It took me all my fortitude to control my voice.'[91]

During the evening service, MacRae preached on John 6:40.

> From the very outset I felt a power and solemnity descend upon me which made me seem to lose sight of self, and all I knew was that I was preaching Christ to sinners. Almost at the very outset, poor Jessie MacKinnon bent her head and leaned forward upon the pew before her, and it was not long till Katie joined her and thus they remained throughout the whole evening. And they were not the only ones. Throughout the church here and there, there were bent and averted heads, and a stillness and solemnity prevailed, and the like of which I have never before experienced. Awe seemed to be written upon many of the faces which were turned towards me. As for myself, I was conscious that some mysterious Power was constraining me to preach as I never had preached before.
>
> We concluded by singing the closing verses of the second Psalm. In reading out the verses to be sung, something constrained me to repeat twice over the lines: 'Kiss ye the Son, lest in His wrath Ye perish from the way.' And that in itself seemed to increase the solemnity prevailing.[92]

John MacAlister, acting as precentor, rose and began the psalm. He hadn't completed the first line, however, when he ceased singing, overcome with emotion. He didn't sit down. He simply stood there, before the congregation, trying in vain to sing. From his seat, Sandy Robertson, the precentor from nearby Shiskine, took over in leading the congregation. He, too, came near to breaking point as he sang, while many in the church were also deeply moved. As for MacRae, he records that for the second time that day he almost broke down completely. As he stepped down from the pulpit, he found Rev. MacEwan, eyes brimming with tears. Without speaking he motioned to the precentor's box. 'To my mingled amazement and joy I saw there poor John sobbing like a child. I threw my arm round him and tried to comfort him, but it was long before he could check his emotion.'[93]

As they walked home, MacRae told John there was nothing for him but to leave everything with Jesus and to trust Him alone to save him. As they walked they met Peter MacKelvie, a volunteer in the Royal Engineers. MacKelvie was home on leave, but leaving for France the next morning. 'As he came nearer I saw that he was unwontedly moved. He shook hands with me and wished me goodbye, but I shall never

91. Ibid.

92. Ibid., p. 89.

93. Ibid.

forget the earnest look in his eyes and the evident sincerity in his voice as he twice repeated, "I'll never forget the sermons I heard from you when I am out yonder" (i.e. in France).'[94]

Back in his lodgings, MacRae found that the 'family worship was very solemn and filled with a strange unction. Oh what glorious days were these! We seemed to be away from everything except the things of the soul, and the Lord was very evident in our midst. Could those days have continued it would have been heaven upon the earth. We read verse about, but we were not half way through the chapter when John broke down again and Mr MacEwan considerately finished the reading himself.'[95]

Continues MacRae, 'I did not sleep much that night. I was too happy; too roused, but I had no wish for morning, for morning would witness my departure from a place which had become sweeter to me than any place on earth. Still, time will not tarry and the morning came. I would have given anything to stay for the Thanksgiving service, but I had to be at Minard on the following evening for the moderation in of a call to the Rev. John MacLeod, and that meant departure that very morning.'[96]

Mr MacAlister, another elder, arrived to pay the visiting preacher his expenses, insisting on giving two pounds, much to the protest of MacRae, who had purposely avoided expense by taking his bicycle with him, aware that the congregation was not a fully-equipped one. But 'Mr MacAlister gave me something else to cheer me, and that was that he was of opinion that his own son Charles had become impressed.'[97]

MacRae crossed to Kintyre by boat and began to cycle laboriously up against the wind on his way homewards.

> For the first 15 or 16 miles my way led along the shore and somehow I did not feel so downcast as long as I had the big Arran hills on the other side of the water from me, but when once I had climbed the long ascent above Claonaig, and the hills of Jura opened up before me, I felt a great loneliness enter my soul as I cast behind me a last look at the land I had come to love. But the brae was sloping before me. I free-wheeled down it and I saw the Arran hills no more.[98]
>
> Thus ended the most blessed time I have ever had in my life. I got a taste then from the Lord that was worth waiting for for 100 years, yet after it I can never rest content until I get another such. It has come not only as a blessing to me but as a lesson. I had been inclined to think that the Lord was so grieved away

94. Ibid., p. 90.
95. Ibid.
96. Ibid.
97. Ibid., p. 91.
98. Ibid.

> by the sins of the people that He had ceased to evidence Gospel power in any marked degree, but this came to show me that He is as willing and as able to save as ever He was, and that those who pray for it will get the blessing. This is its great lesson to me – the power of prayer. I believe that if the people of my own congregation would stir themselves up to plead for a blessing, as did the people of Sliddery, they would get it too. Blessed be His name for giving such a wretched sinner such a sight of His power.[99]

MacRae was invited back to Arran's Southend for Communion the following June (1917), and was delighted to find that the showers of blessing had by no means passed. Indeed at the evening prayer meeting on the Wednesday of his arrival, within five minutes of his address following the prayer time, 'tears were flowing copiously from all parts'. On the Friday MacRae had 'an evening remarkably sweet to my soul. After the sermon was over I would like to have shouted out for very joy.' He was no less delighted the next evening, to find as many as five new communicants coming forward to the Session. This time MacRae was able to stay for the Monday Thanksgiving meeting, when 'there was weeping all over the church. I never saw a congregation so moved, nor felt an assembly so softened and solemnised in my life.'[100]

MacRae prayed that it would not be 'the goodness which vanishes away as the morning cloud'. It proved not to be, for when the Lochgilphead minister paid a third visit to the parish in March of the following year (1918), at the Sabbath morning meeting, he 'had not long started before tears were in evidence in various parts of the church'. Attendance at the evening meeting was, as in the morning, large, 'and the service was very solemn. What a great treat it is for me to be in this place,' he rejoiced.[101]

OTHER SIGNIFICANT MOVEMENTS IN THIS PERIOD[102]

Revival in the Salvation Army – Beith 1908
Dunrossness, Shetland 1912

99. Ibid., pp. 91–2.

100. Ibid., p. 114.

101. Ibid., p. 130. When MacRae returned to preach in Sliddery in 1936, twenty years after his first memorable visit, he found the situation 'very sad', though not hopeless. 'A fortnight's intensive, judicious work might work wonders under God's blessing,' he wrote. 'The revival in Southend 20 years ago threw up material which now is the mainstay of the cause there. Were it not for that movement I am afraid that our congregation would have gone under' (ibid., p. 308).

102. Full accounts of these movements can be found on www.scottishrevivals.co.uk.

Ayr – p.144

Major and Mrs Boyce – p.145

Ayr converts – p.148

Charlotte Chapel, Edinburgh, 1912 – p.155

Sliddery, Arran – p.157

5
The Fruitful Twenties
1919–1929

Showers of Blessing, 1919–24

BY all accounts the horrors of the Great War had a hugely demoralising effect on a large proportion of the young men caught up in it. The faith of many was confused or even shattered, especially considering the unified and enthusiastic approval given to the Allied war effort by virtually all the Church denominations. By 1915 it was reckoned that 90 percent of 'sons of the manse' had volunteered for action and many ministers also signed up as chaplains and combatants. There was no truck for pacifism. But Scotland paid dearly for what has been seen as a disproportionately high price in casualties, a result of huge numbers of volunteers and the use of Scottish battalions as shock troops in the fighting on the Western Front and Gallipoli – young men whom novelist Ian Hay termed 'the vanished generation'. The cataclysmic reality of the staggering loss of life and the horrors witnessed by troops who survived the battlefront had a devastating effect on religion in Scotland. One investigation showed that despite a universal belief in God, only 20 percent of troops in Scottish regiments had a 'vital relationship' with a church, the figure being even lower for those in working-class battalions from the cities.[1]

Thus it was that many servicemen returned to civilian life demoralised, bitter and sceptical. Their mood was further lowered when the brief boom in the British economy that characterised the immediate post-war period quickly gave way to economic depression and mass unemployment. A young Brethren evangelist, active in Renfrew just after the war, noticed a hardening setting in during this period when, he felt, the preaching seemed too simple to the returning soldiers.[2] It seems remarkable, given this state of affairs, that stirrings of spiritual life should occur in many parts of Scotland – having particularly marked effect in many towns and villages along the east coast, from Thurso and Wick in the north to Eyemouth in the south. Factors that contributed to the increased spiritual interest during this period are discussed in Chapter 7.

---

1. T.M. Devine, *The Scottish Nation 1700–2007*, London 1999 (revised 2006), p. 385. These statistics were, however, higher than for English troops.

2. Dickson, *Brethren in Scotland*, p. 197.

1919 – EARLY 1921

WHILE some of the most significant occasions of spiritual blessing that rose up in the post-war era are detailed in the narratives that follow, it is important to note that many churches throughout Scotland that did not experience full-blown revival at this time yet had significant growth in attendance and membership. Irish Methodist evangelist John Long started a fortnight's mission in Haggs, then in Banton Baptist Church in October 1919. In the latter place, fifty children and twenty adults decided for Christ.[3] A six-week mission begun by Brethren evangelist John McAlpine in Coatdyke, Lanarkshire, in November 1920 resulted in 70 conversions and 28 baptisms, doubling the membership of the Assembly.[4] Further north, D.T. MacKay, evangelist for the UFC, said the work in the Highlands was 'promising and encouraging' during the year 1919–20, and he held packed meetings all over the north.[5]

Meanwhile, over the New Year period of 1919–20, a gracious work of revival accompanied the labours of W.D. Dunn at Carrubbers Close Mission, just off Edinburgh's 'Royal Mile', which had witnessed remarkable scenes sixty years previously, during the 1859–60 revival.[6] Dunn's work was followed by a nine-week mission by students of the Faith Mission.[7] Having been an itinerant evangelist for over fifty years, Dunn was yet empowered to give a discourse on 'the need for revival', which came over with freshness and vitality. There was blessing from the start, but during the second week of the mission came an 'abundant outpouring', with a burden coming on many either for their own salvation or for that of others. As a result, many were led to the 'inquiry room' – which on occasion was filled – with anxious souls falling down on their faces, sobbing and crying for blessing. This was the beginning of great things.

Every night after that wonderful scenes were witnessed. A large number of both young and old received salvation and many of the church's young folk received a baptism in the Spirit, which in turn set them on fire to see the salvation of others. Many of their prayers and efforts were rewarded. At one workplace in the city were four young men who had recently become Christians at Carrubbers Close Mission. Through their testimonies most other workers in the firm were brought to the meetings, and in due course the majority of these were also led to the Lord.[8]

---

3. Long, *Journal of John Long,* Chapter 14.

4. Dickson, *Brethren in Scotland,* p. 190.

5. *RC-UFCS-H&I,* 1920, p. 207.

6. During Moody's second evangelistic tour of Scotland (1882), he raised £10,000 to pay for a permanent home for the mission.

7. This was during the Faith Mission's ninth session, and resulted in what Colin Peckham called 'great blessing' (Colin Peckham, *The New Faith Mission Bible College,* Edinburgh 1994, p. 8).

8. *TC,* 19 February 1920, p. 20.

By March 1921, the Faith Mission was voicing indications of 'great blessing in Ireland & Scotland',[9] this before the powerful 'Fishermen's revival' and also before the remarkable outbreak of awakening in Northern Ireland through the dynamic preaching of W.P. Nicholson. Two months later, the Mission could also report 'tokens of revival' in Lowestoft, a spontaneous movement in the mining village of West Pelton, County Durham,[10] and a work of grace in the Ayrshire towns of Kilmarnock and Saltcoats. All of this was in addition to the Faith Mission's own work.[11] Further south still, on the border of East Ayrshire and Dumfriesshire, there was a 'breaking through of God in revival power' in the small town of Sanquhar when 86 people professed salvation during a Faith Mission campaign.[12] Sensing a deeper stirring to come during the remainder of 1921, the editors of *Bright Words* asked: 'Are we on the eve of revival?'[13] For many areas in Scotland, this proved exactly the case.

Late 1921–3

SIMULTANEOUS with the revival movement that blazed along the east coast of the country, a significant work of grace was reported from certain places in Glasgow and some south-west fishing ports. A movement occurred in Campbeltown, where attendance at a Bible class held for fishermen on Sunday afternoons increased from fifty to nearly 100, everyone showing marked enthusiasm.[14] Further south, Stranraer also had a share of blessing,[15] while from the isle of Arran, too, came hopeful notes.[16] Also in Argyll, in Achnacloich, Lorne, Baptist minister Alexander Brown testified to 'some young people who professed to have been impressed in our meetings and have begun to read their Bibles and pray in private'.[17] Likewise, in the Central Highlands, Neil McLachlan reported from Tullymet of 'several young people having made decision for Christ and others quickened to deep concern'.[18]

The Rev. Weir of Hamilton UFC noted 'a spiritual influence at work' amongst his people around the turn of the year 1921–22.[19] Membership of Rutherglen Baptist Church reached its peak in 1923, with 279 names

9. Ibid., 7 April 1921.

10. For more details on this movement, see *TC*, 27 January 1921.

11. *BW*, 1921, p. 79.

12. Peckham, *Heritage of Revival*, p. 48.

13. *BW*, 1921, p. 50.

14. *Report of the Home Mission and Church Extension Committee of the United Free Church of Scotland* (hereafter *RHM&CEC-UFC*), 1922, p. 36.

15. Ibid. 1922, p. 32.

16. *RC-FCS-RM&T*, 1922, p. 898.

17. *British Home Missionary Society Report* 1922, pp. 16–17, quoted in Sprange, *Kingdom Kids*, pp. 287–8.

18. Ibid.,1923, p. 13, quoted in Sprange, *Kingdom Kids*, p. 288.

19. *Glasgow Herald*, 11 January 1922, p. 12.

on the roll. During the period March 1922 – September 1923, no fewer than forty-eight people were baptised, a tent mission conducted by W.B. Munro of the Lanarkshire Christian Union no doubt largely contributing to this significant increase.[20]

GLASGOW 1919–23

GLASGOW remained in no way untouched by events of this time. While it cannot be said that there was a general revival in the city in the immediate post-war period, there was certainly a profound spiritual stirring, and genuine awakening in certain parts. Indeed, as early as the autumn of 1919 there was considerable activity in the city. The recently opened Cranston's Picture House, a large palatial building located in the city centre, was secured for Sunday evening services. The response was remarkable and the building was filled every Sunday long before the advertised hour. Alexander Marshall was one evangelist who preached frequently to the large audiences that gathered during the first and decidedly most fruitful of 'Cinema Services' held in the city.[21] Meanwhile, a tent mission held in the Crosshill district in 1920 by Brethren evangelist Fred Elliot saw 'intense interest and power' comparable, it was suggested, to the big revivals of the nineteenth century, with no fewer than 2,000 professions of faith and 120 baptisms being performed in a specially dug baptistry.[22]

As in other parts of the country, so, too, in Glasgow, the most concerted activity took place during or after the autumn and winter of 1921. Indeed it appears that it was the publicity given to the revival in the north-east of the country which gave a stimulus to mission enterprises in Glasgow, leading to a marked increase in attendance at the missionary meetings which were regularly held in various parts of the city. At some of these there was 'increased fervour on the part of the leading participants' and deliberate efforts were made to extend the movement.[23] For example, Salvation Army officers in various parts of the city reported large evangelistic meetings, while the meetings of the Gorbals Cross Mission were also 'exceedingly interesting and well attended'.[24] 'Revival meetings' were also held in Grove Street Institute, Bethany Hall, in Govan and in several churches in the city's East End.[25]

W.A. Ashby, a Baptist minister from Glasgow who had visited Fraserburgh to witness the revival there, spoke of his great joy on

20. Rev. R.E.O. White, *History of Rutherglen Baptist Community Church*, 1954.
21. Hawthorn, p. 137.
22. Dickson, *Brethren in Scotland*, pp. 188–9.
23. *Glasgow Herald*, 22 December 1921, p. 9.
24. *Christian Herald and Signs of Our Times*, 9 February 1922, p. 106.
25. *Glasgow Herald*, 9 January 1922, p. 10.

returning to his own church in late December 1921. He found that his own people 'had been touched by the power of the Holy Ghost. Young men and women had been visited by the spiritual quickening'. At his Watch-Night service in Glasgow about thirty or forty people came forward to dedicate their lives. He left the church at two in the morning, but the prayer meeting went on till 9 a.m., after which his people went home for breakfast and a warm-up, then returned to church at 10.15 to spend more time in prayer! Many conversions were recorded.[26]

It was in fact around this time that 'a remarkable work' began in the Seamen's Bethel, continuing for several months into 1922. Around 500 men from all classes and many nationalities would gather together for intercession, worship and to hear the Word, and decisions were recorded at almost every meeting. Meanwhile, at Dowanhill Christian Mission, Partick, there was a 'gracious movement', particularly among young men, while similar blessing was experienced in Govan, where 22 ministers united to pray together, also exchanging pulpits.[27]

The greatest work, though, was evidenced in some of Glasgow's many Mission Halls, which strongly influenced the evangelical character of the city. In pre-First World War years and again in the early 1920s, many of these Halls were packed to capacity. Evangelists could labour with marked success in the city for months on end, moving variably from church to Mission Hall. Special evangelistic campaigns in Glasgow usually lasted for at least a month, and open-air services were regular occurrences in many favoured locations. Indeed, it has been said that at this time Glasgow was the most evangelistic city in the world.

Largest and most prominent amongst these venues was the famous Tent Hall in the Saltmarket area of the city. Built in the aftermath of Moody's visit in 1874, this was a huge structure which conducted a whole range of 'ameliorative' functions such as Sabbath Morning Free Breakfasts, Poor Children's Sabbath Dinners, and the Crippled Children's League, as well as prayer meetings galore, open-air services and a plethora of other evangelistic activities. Peter MacRostie was Superintendent from 1908–34, and at meetings held during 1922 the hall, which held over 2,000 people, would regularly be packed. James A. Stewart remembers, as a young boy, seeing hundreds of people leaving a wealthy Presbyterian Church at 8 o'clock in the morning after having spent several hours at an early morning prayer meeting. At some meetings pipes, tobacco, playing cards, betting books and 'low novels' were given up by penitents, and these would cover the tables of inquiry rooms, despite the fact that little was said against such things in the messages delivered.

26. Ibid., 6 January 1922, p. 8.

27. *RHM&CEC-UFCS*, 1922, p. 32.

Owing to the sense of increased spiritual awareness throughout the city, a united effort was launched in January 1922 to extend and unify the movement. Nearly 1,000 gathered for an afternoon prayer meeting, when such was the intensity that several would make supplication at the same time. In the evening a procession of over 3,000 – composed largely of those connected to city missions – marched through the city centre – headed by bands and banner carriers.[28] Then over 5,000 packed into St Andrew's Hall for a demonstration, during which more than one speaker emphasised that they were not 'trying to manufacture a revival. … But God was moving in different places, and when the wind of heaven was blowing, they wanted to act their sails to catch the breeze.'[29] But despite sincerest efforts and repeated predictions from a number of revivalists and church leaders that a mighty movement of God was about to overtake the city,[30] no widespread awakening resulted. Localised movements in one or two district Mission halls continued to spring up, but the St Andrew's Hall meeting turned out to be the climax of the united revival effort and little subsequent activity of its kind was engaged in.

Yet blessing continued in some places. It was reported from the Free Church's Partick Mission during 1922–23 that 'there are many among us under soul concern. It is very evident that the spirit is at work. At our prayer meetings we have between 160 and 200 attending. Sabbath morning the attendance is twice what it was a year ago; at night between 500 and 600 worship with us, After this service we have a prayer meeting, to which nearly all our people stay.'[31] Hermon Street Baptist Church, which came into being in 1920 under the care of evangelist Duncan McNeil, saw considerable blessing from that date up to the time of McNeil's departure in August, 1923.[32] Meanwhile, James Wright served as minister of the prominent St Mark's UFC in Glasgow's city centre from 1921 till February 1925. During that period, he noted, 'a larger number of men and women were admitted to the fellowship of

---

28. Such activity promoted a negative word from the FC in a 1922 report: 'Some of the efforts of well-meaning people to promote a revival in the larger towns in the south resulted in things that were painful to witness. Processions carrying banners with strange devices, beating drums, blowing trumpets, and making a babel of confused shoutings are not for edification. God is not the author of confusion' (*RC-FCS-RM&T*, 1922, p. 899).

29. *Christian Herald*, 26 January 1922, p. 66.

30. One such prediction came from Fred Clarke, prominent in the beginnings of revival in and around Fraserburgh, who made a two-day visit to Glasgow in the latter part of December 1921, before returning to his native Wales for a brief holiday. Speaking in the Seamen's Bethel in Broomielaw, he, and other leaders present, gave assurances that Glasgow 'would soon experience this great spiritual epidemic. They were on the threshold of a great manifestation of the work of God'. Throughout the meeting there were manifestations of religious fervour; many knelt in prayer while others shouted 'Hallelujah' as Clarke exhorted (*Glasgow Herald*, 24 December 1921, p. 8).

31. *Report of the General Assembly of the Free Church of Scotland for the Highlands & Islands* (hereafter *RGA-FCS-H&I*), 1923, p. 1089.

32. Yuille, p. 176.

the Church on profession of faith than during any similar period in the history of the congregation.'[33]

Mid-Argyll 1921–3

Ardnamurchan 1921–2

IN 1920, Duncan Campbell, fresh out of the Faith Mission Bible College, where he had spent the previous nine months, and after a short stint at mission work in Northern Ireland, was posted to his native Scottish Highlands, and it was in this region that he laboured with much enthusiasm until 1925. Campbell recalled many years later, 'For five years I saw the hand of God in revival,'[34] a period which came to be termed, 'The mid-Argyll revival'.[35] Indeed, during these years, from 1919 to 1925, Campbell conducted about thirty missions in the Highlands and Islands.[36]

He knew that the first priority was to establish good relations with the locals of the communities visited.[37] On one occasion, when returning to a village where they were regarded with a degree of caution, the two Pilgrims came upon a poor elderly woman loaded with pots and pans and other wares that she was trying to sell. When the two young men offered to carry her burden the three remaining miles to the village, the woman at once consented. News of this kindly deed spread quickly through the small community, removing prejudice and softening hearts. In another community the crofters were busy trying to rescue a late harvest and had little time to come to the meetings. Duncan immediately postponed the mission for a week, took off his jacket, and joined the workers in the fields, helping to cut and stook[38] the corn. When the meetings resumed, the crofters faithfully flocked to hear Campbell speak, out of respect for a man whom they knew practised what he preached.

But the going was tough and behind each victory was a hard-fought battle. A rather self-righteous woman told Campbell that she didn't need him to preach to her as she had been through the Bible herself. 'Perhaps so,' was the Pilgrim's fitting reply, 'but have you allowed the Bible to go through you?' Some ministers, too, were critical of the Pilgrims'

---

33. John Ronald, *History of the Cairns United Free Church, Stewarton*, Ardrossan, 1926, p. 33.

34. Campbell also said that he could trace these spiritual movements in West Argyll to the experience of 'baptism in the Spirit' which he experienced when severely wounded on the battlefield in France a few years previously. (Duncan Campbell, *Revival in the Scottish Hebrides*, Audio Tape, quoted in Allen, *Catch the Wind,* pp. 40–1).

35. Allen, *Catch the Wind,* p. 40.

36. Colin and Mary Peckham, *Sounds From Heaven*, Fearn 2004, p. 41.

37. 'You must win the people to yourself first, before you can win them for the Lord,' he said. 'And the way to achieve this is by a practical demonstration of kindness and godliness'. (Andrew A. Woolsey, *Channel of Revival: A biography of Duncan Campbell,* Edinburgh 1974 (reprinted 1982), pp. 63–4).

38. i.e. set the sheaves of corn on end in groups of six or eight.

work. During one mission a local minister sent a letter to the young missionaries, saying they were disturbing the peace of the community, and that they should leave. After committing the matter to God, they sent a return note reminding the minister that while one may find peace in a graveyard, it is the peace of death! Happily, the minister later apologised and became a willing helper in the mission.

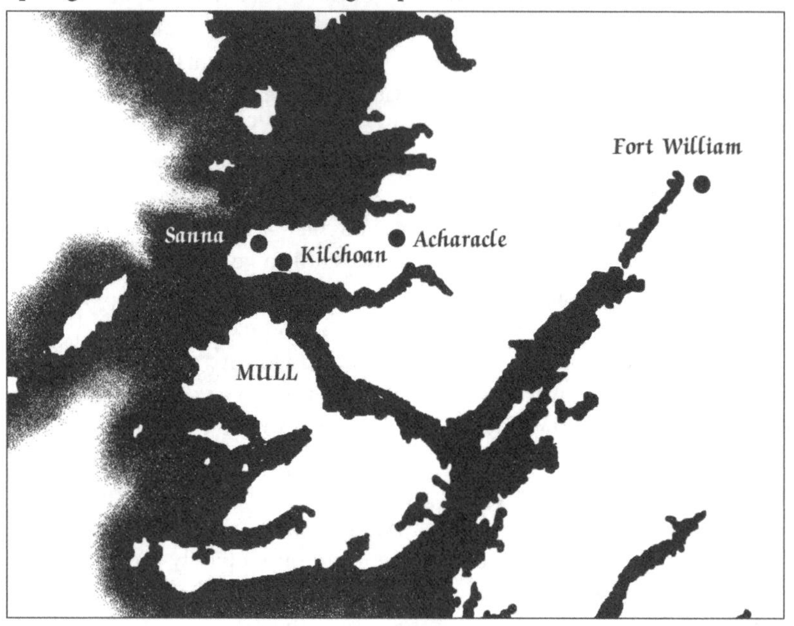

When Campbell and fellow Pilgrim George Dunlop came to conduct meetings in Sanna and Kilchoan, on the far west of Ardnamurchan, the most westerly promontory of the British mainland, during the first half of 1921, a gracious awakening went on for many weeks. Sunday evening meetings were packed and there were a number of conversions. One man, a farmer, spoke of 'scenes of great revival, such as the writer has not witnessed for the past 25 years'. A convert, asked if she would continue going to the local dances, replied, 'There will be no more dances; the promoters of these have been converted and are in the house of God.'[39] Prayer Unions were formed in both Sanna and Kilchoan, and, sixteen months later, when a Pilgrim returned to the former district, he was met by an old friend, 'a brother in the Lord'. After greeting each other, the Pilgrim asked, 'How are the lambs of the flock getting on?' In his own quaint way the man replied, 'There's none lame yet!' Not only so, but these converts were quick to win 'a goodly number' from darkness to light.[40]

39. *BW*, 1921, p. 103; Woolsey, *Channel of Revival*, p. 67.

40. *BW*, 1921, p. 212.

Back in Ardnamurchan towards the close of 1922, this time in the more easterly district of Acharacle, Campbell, along with fellow Pilgrim Steedman, witnessed another gracious move. 'The people flocked to hear the message, as many as 160, and up to 200 being packed into the schoolroom, and what was much more important than numbers, they came to listen with an interest and sincerity beyond what is often seen at such gatherings. Boys and girls in their teens, as well as men and women up to and over 70 years, were seeking the Saviour, and even people unable to attend the meetings were deeply concerned for their souls. A Prayer Union was formed with a membership of 60.'[41]

Kinlochleven 1922

THESE same two Faith Mission Pilgrims helped pave the way for further rich blessing in the West Highlands a year later. Kinlochleven was known as a hard place spiritually, and two sisters opposed to evangelistic endeavour adamantly proclaimed that the Pilgrims would be quickly chased away should they come near *their* house. However, having godly parents, the two siblings were much prayed for and spoken with. Besides, a few faithful saints had been praying for revival in the area for years, but even these believers couldn't contain their surprise when one of the two hardened sisters began to attend the meetings – after making a promise to a believing uncle that she would do so. There was even more surprise, and great joy, when this woman found her way into the Kingdom shortly after! Her sister scorned her decision, but within a week she too had found her Saviour. 'What changed your attitude so suddenly?' one was asked. 'These men are different,' she replied, referring to other preachers she had heard. 'They are concerned for our souls, and that man speaking tonight transmitted his concern to me, and I had to do something about it.' A deep conviction set in on many others too, and altogether twenty or thirty were added to the church.[42]

Mining Communities of Central Scotland 1921–2

AN increasing struggle had been underway between blue-collar workers and the British government since the First World War. In 1921 the government announced the selling off of mines, which led to coal owners instantly introducing wage cuts. This in turn led to a strike among outraged miners during the winter of 1921–2. In a desperate attempt to keep the peace, troops were dispatched to coalfields. With more sell-outs by union leaders occurring on what became known as 'Black Friday', sympathy strike notices were withdrawn, leaving the miners to be crushed

41. Ibid., 1923, p. 47.
42. Ibid., 1921, pp. 212–13; Peckham, *Heritage of Revival*, p. 53.

and wages cut by 10 to 40 percent across the country.[43] Despite previously being 'the workshop of Europe', Scotland after the war, according to war historian Trevor Royle, became 'an industrial and financial backwater'.[44]

Despite, or perhaps in part due to, the depression in the coal industry, revival movements began in some of the mining villages of central Scotland around this time. For a number of years no public worship service had been held in Blackbraes, near Falkirk, other than a Sunday school class. However, nearby, two miners had great times with God in the otherwise unused UFC hall, where they regularly prayed for the community, also holding open-air meetings two or three times a week. Pilgrims from the Faith Mission were invited to the village in September 1920, and from the start the presence and power of the Spirit were in evidence. Attendance steadily rose so that at one meeting 300 packed into the hall, fulfilling a vision given to the Pilgrims a year before of the hall filled to overflowing and a real revival stir among the people. In all, over forty adults and 100 children professed faith in Christ and a weekly Prayer Union meeting and Sunday evening service were begun.[45]

Also in Stirlingshire, while pitched battles erupted between gamekeepers and striking miners hunting for food as the economy went through a period of depression, the coal-mining village of Plean, six miles from Stirling, received a shower of spiritual blessing from mid-December 1921. Up to then the village, like many other mining localities, was more auspicious for its apathy towards anything religious. But since D. Gillies, a Glasgow evangelist, commenced a series of religious addressees under the auspices of the Stirlingshire Christian Union, 'a decided religious fervour, amounting in many instances to enthusiasm', characterised the meetings. These gatherings, which included late-night open-air prayer services, attracted predominantly young folk from the ages of twelve to twenty- five, while house-to-house visitation was 'presented with vigour'. In less than three weeks over 100 people had made public profession.[46]

The UFC took a prominent role in the movement and the Rev. Charles Robert spoke of being deeply impressed with the number of young male converts. His Presbytery – that of Stirling and Dunblane – considered 'various schemes … for the furtherance of the revival' and strongly recommended collaboration with ministers of other denominations.[47] The UFC minister of Cowie, Stirlingshire noted that the 'method

43. Things heated up again in 1926, when another miners' strike – and a subsequent general strike – took place.

44. Royle goes on to suggest that 'morale slumped in the face of economic stagnation and decline', leading to a 'sudden crisis of national self-confidence' (Royle, *The Flowers of the Forest*, flyleaf).

45. *BW*, 1921, p. 32.

46. *Glasgow Herald*, 6 January 1922, p. 9.

47. Ibid., 11 January 1922, p. 12.

followed is – meeting in church for one hour, then open-air for another hour – this in wind and wet, frost and snow. Next a Bible-reading and prayer meeting for enquirers in some kitchen in the rows, sometimes lasting till "the sma'" hours in the morning.'[48] Some in the area frowned upon such enthusiasm and on one occasion 'the village constable deemed it his duty to order the (open-air) meeting to disperse'.[49] Involved in the movement in Plean were some members of the Stirling Baptist Church, who held gospel meetings in the village every Sunday. So successful was the outreach that in April 1922, 29 local residents applied for baptism and membership of the Stirling Church. In September the work stepped up a gear, when an old army hut in Plean was purchased, 'for the use of the Mission'. By this time a Brethren outreach was also underway in the village, and this experienced even greater success than the Baptist effort, which pulled out before the year-end.[50]

There was also a significant movement in the mining villages of Lanarkshire in the 1920s amidst the continuing industrial tensions of the time. The Brethren assembly at Coatdyke saw its membership double following a six-week mission, when 70 conversions and 28 baptisms were recorded. Similar results were experienced in Shotts around the same time[51] – 300 years after outstanding revival first rained on this community (Kirk O'Shotts, 1630).[52] Spiritual blessing came to the Ayrshire mining village of Kilbirnie at the beginning of 1922. Here the Salvation Army and the two UFC congregations worked closely together. One UFC minister wrote that 'the great picture is the penitents in tears at the Mercy Seat, a comrade's arm around their neck praying with them – Oh, how homely, how real, how beautiful. The great joy is to be the means of grace to bring them there.'[53]

West Benhar 1922

'A WORK of grace had occurred amongst the miners' in Midlothian and also in the Lanarkshire communities of West Benhar and Shotts around the turn of the twentieth century, following visits from Faith Mission workers. One of the Pilgrims who 'saw great things' in this area was

48. *RHM&CEC-UFCS*, 1922, p. 37.

49. *Stirling Observer*, 12 January 1922, quoted in Calum G. Brown, *The Social History of Religion in Scotland*, London 1987, p. 215.

50. Talbot, p. 96. Both the Stirling Baptists and a Brethren team also competed in outreach missions in Fallin, a few miles south-east of Stirling. In October 1922, 12 converts applied for baptism and church membership of the former congregation.

51. Dickson, *Brethren in Scotland*, pp. 190–1. Among the converts of this movement was a grandmother of Neil Dickson's wife (personal communication, 24 July 2004).

52. A student at Spurgeon's College, London, who in the 1990s began researching the 1920s movement among Lanarkshire miners, tragically died of cancer and his work was never completed (personal communication with Dr Ian Randall, Church History tutor at Spurgeon's College, 28 March 2002).

53. *RHM&CEC-UFCS*, 1922, p. 34.

Ulster-born Margaret Livingstone, thought to have been a descendant of David Livingstone.[54] Among those influenced by the movement was Jackie Carter, whose home had been denuded of furniture and all his money gone to drink. He was converted while 'half drunk, and many others like him; and their families followed on, becoming good soldiers of Jesus Christ'.[55]

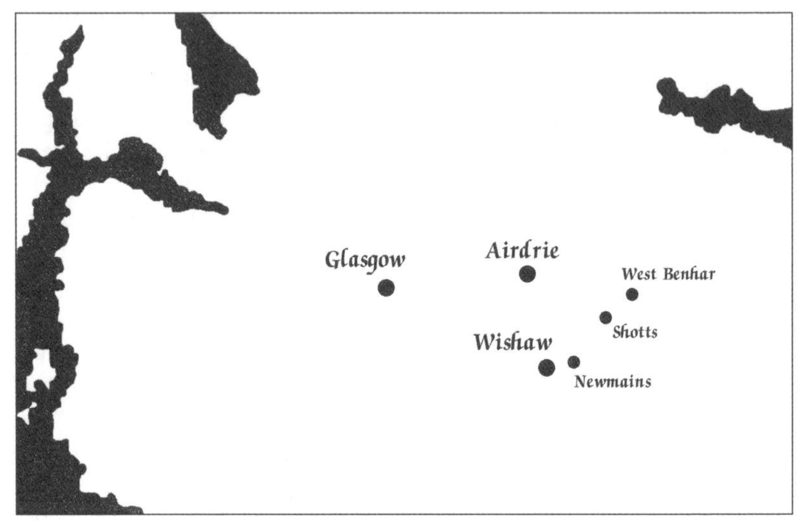

Two decades later, in 1922, in the tiny coal-mining village of West Benhar, a significant awakening began, occasioned once again by a visit from Faith Mission Pilgrims. One who attended the meetings was schoolgirl Margaret ('Pearl') Weir, whose father, Quentin Moore, had also been converted through the Faith Mission (back in 1903). Many decades later, Pearl recalled,

> I was the eldest of seven children. In 1922 when I was 13 years of age, the F.M. sent two lady Pilgrims to the village. Miss Woods was the senior Pilgrim. She came from Aberdeen. Miss Bruce, who was second in command, was a beautiful singer. Unfortunately, Miss Woods had burned her foot and could not walk to the meetings. Cars were few and far between in those days but my dad had a car and he brought the Pilgrims each night to the meetings. Miss Woods was the only Pilgrim I ever saw sitting to preach the gospel, but preach she did, and I remember her saying, 'You and your namby pamby religion! You need to be born again!' Men and women and young people were born again, night after night. Sometimes there were as many people outside

54. Margaret was born in County Antrim in 1873, and remembered that the atmosphere of the 1859 revival still lingered when she was a child.

55. I.R. Govan Stewart, *Abundance of Grace: The Story of Margaret Livingstone*, Edinburgh 1967, pp. 16–17.

> the hall as inside ... many people came from Shotts. The Rev. Mr Coull was the Baptist Church Minister there and he counselled people who got saved on their way home. Two brothers, Tom and Bob Murie who came from Shotts, played the concertina and the accordion together. The singing was excellent night after night and the hall was full to overflowing.
>
> One young miner who got converted was George Drysdale. He continued to work in the mines but later became pastor of the Pentecostal Church. Another young man, Tom Paterson, did a wonderful work among the deep sea fishermen in Shetland, especially during the 1939–45 war. After the war he was honoured by the King of Norway. Reflecting on the events of the mission, Mrs Weir concluded; 'It is apparent that we had experienced a real moving of the Holy Spirit in revival blessing. ... God only knows how far reaching were the results of this mission.[56]

Spreading in the Wishaw direction, the revival also touched other areas such as Newmains, in which town there was much conviction and turning to God.[57] Pearl became involved in the West Benhar Prayer Union, which began as a result of the revival, and she and her husband were founder members of the Benhar Evangelical Church, which sprang up in the area. As a result of her involvement in these organisations, and her warm and caring personality, Pearl came to be regarded as a 'spiritual mother' to many in the community.

Some exuberant converts of the Benhar movement went on to attend a Faith Mission conference in Peebles shortly afterwards. At one meeting they were so full of 'Amens' and 'Hallelujahs' that the Principal had to stop preaching until they had calmed down! At tea that evening Govan asked a quaint Scotsman who was present to give thanks. A little irritated by the exuberance of the Benhar converts, he began his prayer, 'Lord, we thank Ye for the conference this afternoon. We thank Ye for the converts frae West Benhar, and for their enthusiasm. But Lord, it must hae grieved Yer hairt tae see sae much o' the steam blowin' oot thro' the whistle that should had gang tae the piston!'[58]

Tiree 1922–4

WHEN Donald McArthur, pastor of the Baptist Church in Tiree, contracted a serious illness in October 1922, one of his own converts was asked to temporarily take his place. The Rev. Francis Taylor was a native of the Ross of Mull, and had been a shepherd until shortly after his conversion, when he began training for the ministry. After serving in

---

56. Mrs Margaret (Pearl) C.R. Weir (died March 1995), 'Revival at West Benhar', in *Life Indeed*, 1996, p. 66.

57. *BW*, 1923, p. 45.

58. Woolsey, *Channel of Revival*, pp. 173–4.

both Bowmore and Bunessan Baptist Churches for some years, Taylor accepted a call to Broadford, Skye, in 1920. Says one source, 'He is a big man physically, equal to the heavy demands of those seagrit outposts; and big in soul, earnest and sympathetic. Those who understand Gaelic consider him a splendid preacher.'[59] As such, Taylor was in popular demand and had visited Tiree numerous times over the years. Records Meek, 'In January 1921 Taylor preached at a mission in Tiree which resulted in a number of conversions and was followed in July by two memorable baptismal services in Loch a' Pahuill. At both services eight candidates were baptised. These events were the prelude to the revival which came in 1922–24.'[60]

Taylor immediately commenced a relentless preaching schedule in chapels around the isle but despite average attendances of 150 to 170, there were few apparent results to show for his eight weeks' preaching. However, by February around fifteen professions of faith had been made in different parts of the island, so that when Donald Dron, a missionary from Edinburgh, arrived in order to allow Taylor to return to his flock in Skye, he observed 'the extent of the field and the kind of service that was required – crowded meetings every night and intensive preaching'. His heart sank within him as he cried, 'Lord, I'm not able!'[61]

Aware of God's sacred blessing, Taylor felt impelled to remain on the island for some time. While six different stations throughout the island were utilised in the course of the mission, Taylor and Dron focused their efforts on the Independent chapel at Ruaig at the east end of Tiree; the former preaching in Gaelic, the latter in English. Recalled Dron,

> The little building stands on a slight prominence, and it was refreshing to see the people, a large proportion of them men, coming from north, south, east and west. The fact that they were in the midst of the spring work did not deter them, and very often it was after midnight when we parted. Ruaig district was considered a hard place, and the people non-church-goers, but now there is not one of its 60 or more homes that God has not entered with life and blessing. The little church is a hallowed place to many, and Taylor and I will never forget the sacred hours we spent in it, pointing awakened sinners to the Saviour.[62]

Meanwhile, the Rev. D.T. MacKay, now nearing his eighties, reported to the General Assembly of the UFC in 1924 that, 'about 60 or 70 young people in the east end of the island' of Tiree had recently professed the name of the Lord. Mr Livingstone, ordained missionary of the UFC,

---

59. *SBM*, August 1923, p. 101.
60. Meek, *Island Harvest*, p. 36.
61. *SBM*, August 1923, p. 101.
62. Ibid.

and others, had worked alongside Rev. Taylor in the work. 'We have been sowing the good seed here for over 26 years, and now the sheaves are taken in, and we hope and pray that many more will follow.'[63]

A number of the newly converted men grew quickly in faith, and soon began to preach locally. Unfortunately, while one or two went on to become ministers,[64] quite a few died in the prime of life due to tuberculosis or other illnesses – two of them while studying theology in Edinburgh. Further, while the revival – which continued until October 1924, after which time Taylor returned to Skye – led to a number of baptisms at three locations on the island, there was little overall addition to church membership as a whole in this period. This was largely due to adverse economic factors, which prompted many to leave Tiree in search of employment elsewhere.

Nevertheless, the island had experienced another significant awakening. Not only so, but when Taylor came back to Tiree to serve officially as pastor from 1928 till his death in 1939, further spiritual movements of some intensity took place in Cornaig (1929) and Ruaig (1933). It was at this time that Neil MacDonald, Taylor's assistant and successor and himself a gifted evangelist, said: 'Imagine Brother Taylor driving in an open governess cart four miles each way five nights in the week for 13 weeks. … Mr Taylor is unceasingly on the move among the needy, irrespective of church connection, and it is a marvel to many of us how he can accomplish his work in the pulpit with such efficiency and at the same time carry on the work of three ordinary men. He believes in carrying the heavy end of the yoke.'[65] Prematurely aged and exhausted from his labours, Taylor was forced to resign from his charge in 1938, to the great sorrow of his congregation.

KILMALUAG, SKYE 1923–4[66]

WHEN in 1919 Kenneth MacRae arrived in the Gaelic-speaking parish of Kilmuir – the most northerly district on the island of Skye – he came to a Free Church that had been vacant since the Union nineteen years earlier. During the intervening period, however, loyal missionaries and faithful elders in the congregation had carried on services in the three sections of the community (Kilmuir, Kilmaluag and Staffin). Indeed, since the striking revivals that had come here and to other parts of Skye early in the preceding

63. *RC-FCS-H&I*, 1924, p. 6.

64. Around the mid-1920s, just a year or two after this Tiree revival, D.P. Thomson met a man from Tiree, who stated that he was one of no fewer than thirty men in the ministry in Scotland at that time as the result of one unspecified revival movement in his native land. (Thomson, *Iona to Ardnamurchan*, p. 22.)

65. Meek, *Island Harvest*, p. 38.

66. Delightfully, though unusually, the memory of this localised awakening has been preserved by the day-by-day relating of its progress through the eyes of the man most intimately involved in it, Kenneth MacRae. Because of the uniqueness of this record, I describe the main features of the movement in some detail.

century, evangelicalism (in its Calvinistic form) characterised virtually the entire population, and church attendance was almost universal.

The parish covered a wide area, and the new minister had to travel up to eighteen miles from home on visits, either by horse and trap,

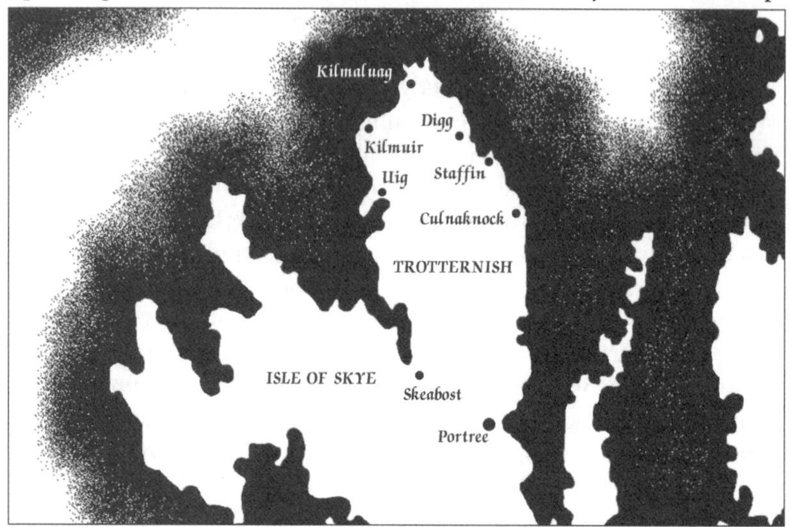

bicycle, or later, motorbike; or else on foot through the Bealach – a pass through the mountains – where he would meditate and pray as he walked. From 1921 to 1922, the spiritual situation in some parts of his parish, especially Kilmaluag, was showing signs of promise. A monthly meeting in one place attracted between sixty and ninety, while fourteen young folk turned up at his vestry after an invitation was made to those who were thinking about their soul and desiring to be put on the way of salvation.[67]

One evening at the beginning of 1923 MacRae gave a lecture in Kilmaluag (the first of three) on Dr Hodge's 'Way of Life'. 'The evening was very wet yet about 110 were present, including a carload from Staffin,' he wrote. 'I had no sooner begun the service than the atmosphere seemed to soften me, and during the prayer I could not keep the tears from brimming over my eyes and rolling down my cheeks. There was something, too, in the singing that touched me, a soft, gentle, broken note, as though there were a wistful longing among the people for the coming of Emmanuel to bless us. ... These young people of Kilmaluag seem to draw out my very heart. Surely the steps of the Lord are sounding among us as He draws near to bless! I came home with a full and a happy heart.'[68]

---

67. *MR-UFC*, 1922, p. 105.

68. Murray, *Diary*, p. 180.

Another sweet taste of things to come occurred during the summer, when, noted the Kilmuir minister, 'I took Spurgeon's advice and pleaded Isaiah 62:7. I got my answer in as delightful an evening as ever I had had. … Spoke from John 10:27 on Christ's sheep and, having especially in view these exercised lads from Kilmaluag, pressed home the marks and urged them to assurance's grip of Christ. Got great liberty both of speech and spirit, and there were visible tokens to show me that the message was holding the people. … It was an evening at the gates of heaven.'[69]

An event that lingered long in the memory of MacRae occurred at the close of a service in the Digg Schoolhouse near Staffin in October 1923. 'Despite the very pressing concerns of a late harvest over 60 were present. Among those who assembled I observed three young girls from another part of the congregation all about 15 or 16 years of age.'[70] One of these MacRae had previously described as giving 'evidence of having come under the power of the Gospel. I have observed how well she has been attending the means for the last two or three months. The Lord is wonderfully kind to motherless children – I have repeatedly observed it. Preached from Revelation 22:17 and was given wonderful liberty, clearness of thought, and unction of spirit, and the breathless silence of my audience told me that the truth had completely gained the ascendancy over them. If ever I felt the Spirit I did so then. What soul-melting views I had of Christ, and how my lips seemed to be opened to speak of Him!'[71]

MacRae continued: 'When the congregation were retiring, the girl mentioned above blurted out something about Christ and then fell a-weeping.' Later, after shaking hands with folk as they left for home, MacRae heard a commotion from the hallway.

> One of the Stoddarts hurried in for a lamp, and, on my following him, there I saw the girl standing in the middle of the cloak-room, with eyes fixed staring upwards and with a most heavenly look upon her face, yet unspeakably wistful. Miss Gillies, the teacher, had her by the arm, and behind, among the throng, one of her companions was convulsively sobbing. As I approached, and even when I spoke to her, her fixed look did not alter, and from her lips in most sad, yearning, appealing tones I heard the words, 'I want to see my Saviour! Oh Christ, reveal thyself to me!' The people were awed, my heart was so touched. I succeeded, however, in getting her calmed and taken round to the teacher's quarters, but she trembled all over and appeared to be so weak that she could scarcely walk.

Between 'a storm of extreme fury' that lasted throughout the night, 'and the sight of that poor girl's wonderful expression as I saw her at the

---

69. Ibid., p. 182.

70. Ibid., p. 183.

71. Ibid.

schoolhouse door – a sight which never left my mind', MacRae 'scarcely slept a wink all night. It was a wonderful and a most solemn night,' he wrote. The following evening the Free Church minister left for a Communion in Glasgow, 'in a very strange frame of mind; very anxious, very much impressed, thankful, and sorry to have to leave home at this particular juncture'.[72] Visiting the girl two weeks later, MacRae noted that she spoke intelligently, but felt impressed to encourage her not to focus on her emotions, but on Christ's offer of salvation.[73]

Meantime, blessing was also being experienced in other congregations in the area, where hopeful notes had in fact been sounded from some parishes as early as 1921.[74] D.T. MacKay, the UFC minister/evangelist, then nearing his eightieth year, visited north Skye during the year 1922–23. He reported 'a quickening time at Uig', where two of his colleagues were labouring. 'The fields seem to be white unto the harvest.' Also, 'in Skeabost and Arnizort the meetings were large and impressive.'[75] From Kilmuir parish, the same tireless evangelist spoke the following year of 'clear signs that God is working among the people here. They crowd the schools every night, and scarcely any leave the after-meeting for prayer. I preached on Sabbath at Staffin,[76] also in Digg and Culnacnock. Churches and schools were full to the door.' Regarding the children, 'in Kilmuir they attended the meetings regularly, and appeared to be much interested'.[77]

As the work in the Free Church intensified, attendance at prayer meetings in Kilmaluag increased to up to ten times the number at the start of MacRae's ministry, when it was normally eight or nine. An unprecedented number of young people attended, sometimes as many as twenty-eight, who, not content with waiting for their own service in Kilmaluag, would walk all the way to Kilmuir for the prayer meeting there. 'Wet, tired, and hungry,' wrote MacRae, 'with barely time to get a cup of tea, I had no right to expect them, and yet, though they came in late, there they were, every one of them. I have never seen any like them.'[78]

---

72. MacRae feared that, 'that poor girl will not be able to control herself, and if she gives way in Kilmaluag, since a number there seem to be in an exercised way, I fear such a general outburst as will perhaps injure more than help the true progress of the work. I dread the effect of unrestrained emotion. When emotion is accompanied by reason, it is good; when reason is thrown to the winds it can only be harmful. I have longed and prayed for a movement. Now, when it appears to be at hand, I dread it. Oh how anxious I feel about my poor congregation! But I must roll the burden of it all upon the Lord' (ibid., pp. 183–4).

73. Ibid., p. 185.

74. *RC-FCS-RM&T*, 1922, p. 898.

75. *RC-FCS-H&I*, 1923, p. 10.

76. MacRae makes mention of the UFC Communion Sabbath in Staffin on 4 June 1923, despite which event the FC 'had a good congregation there'. (Murray, *Diary*, p. 181.)

77. *RC-FCS-H&I*, 1924, pp. 6–7.

78. Murray, *Diary*, p. 186.

In his diary for 1923 and 1924, MacRae made an interesting outline of the personal journey to faith of several of his parishioners. On 3 May 1923, the minister, 'ere going out to visit in Kendram, asked that I might meet with something to hearten me and that prayer was answered. When I got near the house of Samuel Matheson I found him harrowing outside. At once he stopped work and came to me. After worship he came out with me and with the tears welling from his eyes asked me to remember him in prayer. He declared that he had no grace, that he still was as he had been when he came into the world, but that grace was speaking to me in that broken heart and contrite spirit was as clear to me as the noon-day sun. When I suggested that it was possible for grace in the soul to the one who had no assurance, I know no book more useful than Guthrie's "Saving Interest in Christ" and this I promised him. I could have danced with joy to meet such a case.' This man afterwards came out brightly for the Lord.[79]

MacRae's methods of gospel delivery during this reviving season are worth noting. He took particular notice of the view held by Dr John Duncan, that 'no extensive awakening has ever been produced by preaching on the work of the Spirit, but rather by awakening the conscience and setting forth Christ.'[80] He strongly believed that there 'is a kind of preaching which is peculiarly blessed to the awakening and conversion of sinners. I have often been much impressed with the statement that Paul preached the Gospel in power and "in much assurance" (1 Thess. 1:5). When this expecting spirit, this assurance of success, is given, the blessing will surely follow.'[81]

By October 1923 he felt that his message for the people of Kilmaluag 'was no longer: "Strive to enter in at the strait gate", but "Believe in the Lord Jesus and thou shalt be saved."'[82] It is perhaps strange that it was not until December 1924, when the movement had well nigh run its course, that MacRae introduced the subject that he intended to lecture on at future mid-week meetings – 'Revivals in the Highlands & Islands of Scotland'. This series was continued in the autumn of 1925 and into the following year, during which time he covered most of the recorded revivals in eighteenth and nineteenth-century Scotland.[83]

---

79. Ibid., p. 181. Another case was that of Angus Ross who, for three or four years after the Union of 1900, did not go to church, not understanding which side was right; and when once he began to stay at home he soon lost all desire to go out. In 1924 Ross finally wrote to the Kilmuir minister, seeking counsel. A couple of months later, MacRae rejoiced at an evening service to see Ross's face 'quite transformed in a wistful rapture of heavenly longing'. He later became a respected elder in the congregation.

80. Ibid., p. 178.

81. Ibid.

82. Ibid., p. 185.

83. Ibid., p. 197.

From the start of 1924 MacRae makes repeated diary reference to 'unusual liberty and power'[84] in his preaching. He also speaks repeatedly of personal and corporate blessing:

> Monday, 12 May 1924: 'I shut myself up in the study and began to seek Him. ... My cup overflowed, and so much did I realise His presence that for very joy I could scarcely contain myself. ...'[85]
>
> Monday, 21 July: 'My cup seemed to overflow and I got lovely views of the glory of Christ. I could have lingered in that pulpit for another hour. Seemingly the experiences of those who sat in the pews – at least the exercised ones – was somewhat similar to my own.'[86]

At a Communion service, held in the parish in the summer of 1924, MacRae heard Rev. Chisholm of Coll preach 'a sermon of extraordinary power from Isaiah 4:5. I was amazed at such a sermon. I have never heard such originality, such flashes of doctrine, such depth of experience, and such power. A number in the congregation were overcome, and he was overcome himself. I had to struggle my hardest to keep from betraying my feelings also.'[87] On the Sabbath day,

> Mr Chisholm had a well-filled church before him, about 550 being present. He spoke from Psalm 24, and once again his treatment of it, and especially his grasp of doctrine and the originality of his handling of it, amazed me. Surely I saw the glory of the Lord in that sermon and throughout the whole of his services, and the melted state of many of the people showed that they saw it too. His fencing[88] was unique and just as wonderful as unique. The people were manifestly impressed under it. During the period when the people were partaking of the elements I could hear him praying where he stood. When my turn came to address the second Table, I felt that I had nothing but the feeble utterance of a child. The concluding address was just as wonderful in its own way. What a service it was! I have never had such a happy time at my own Communion. He himself confessed to having liberty and such a sense of the holiness of the Lord as almost took his strength away and occasioned him the purest sufferings, mental and physical. The family worship at night was most sweet, but indeed this has been a feature of the whole Communion. Oh how thankful I should be for such a day![89]

---

84. Ibid., p. 188.
85. Ibid., p. 189.
86. Ibid., pp. 190–1.
87. Ibid., p. 192.
88. i.e. underscoring the profound seriousness of the sacrament and of membership vows, so as to exclude from these actions any who are not truly committed.
89. Murray, *Diary*, pp. 191–2.

On the Monday, 'We had a very good congregation of about 250. Mr Chisholm gave us another marvellous sermon from John 17:24. What glorious views he gave me of Christ and how he exalted Him in my soul! I do not think that ever I have had such a wonderful time under the preaching of the Word. I know not how to praise the Lord for all His kindness to us! I shall never forget this Communion season.'[90]

It was not all plain sailing, however, and towards the end of 1924 MacRae noted in his diary: 'I see once again that high seasons are followed by seasons of terrible backsliding and soul trials, and therein I discern two facts which seem to be obvious enough: - (1) That high seasons are preparatory; to fierce onslaughts by the Enemy, and mercifully bestowed for the upbearing of the soul during this dire period: (2) That high seasons generate spiritual pride, which is very effectively humbled by these very dark times of the swelling up of the tides of the heart's awful corruption.'[91]

Two means by which difficulties came to the parish during this time may in fact have deepened the effect of the awakening, though MacRae nowhere suggests this to have been the case. 25 September 1923 was marked as a Day of Humiliation throughout the Skye Free Church Presbytery, 'in view of the unfavourable harvest prospects'.[92] Soon after, an 'influenza scourge' raged through the district, debilitating many and causing the minister, too, to become 'very ill' and to be laid aside for a time.[93]

Throughout this period, and despite several conversions in the locality, the situation in Kilmuir, where MacRae had his residence, remained generally dark. MacRae had faithfully preached the gospel in Kilmuir since his arrival in the parish some years before, and had constantly looked for a general work of conversion among them. Increasingly, however, he became 'miserably disappointed' with their apathy.[94] Indeed it became evident that many of them had no expectation of blessing in this present generation. Persecutions, it was thought, would have to precede a great revival in the latter days and, as no such persecution had occurred, revival could not them be expected! This teaching they had gleaned from Lachlan MacKenzie, a minister of an earlier generation still highly revered in the Highlands for his prophetic gifting. In spite of MacRae's efforts to remedy this false teaching, it seemed as if he made little headway, and he

---

90. Ibid., p. 192.

91. Ibid., p. 195.

92. Ibid., p. 182.

93. Ibid., pp. 188–9.

94. 'I am more and more convinced,' he wrote, with particular regard to his Kilmuir flock, 'that the only hindrance to a revival of religion is the unbelief and unspirituality of the Lord's people, and that the only progress towards it lies in their awakening to their duty, and their earnestly seeking the reviving influences of the Spirit. It is vain to look for a work of quickening among the careless till the Lord's people first be roused' (ibid., p. 220).

was forced to note in his diary: 'exercised about the fact that working on the basis of new communicants since I came here, two out of every three of my hearers will be lost. It is a very solemn consideration.'[95]

Another hindrance in the Kilmuir congregations seems to have been an element of hyper-Calvinism. Because of the strength of MacRae's opposition to Arminianism this error was sometimes charged against him, but in Kilmuir, and indeed throughout all his ministry, he laboured vigorously against it. He recorded in his diary at one point: 'Today's sermons were very elementary but I feel that this is very necessary in Kilmuir, where ultra-Calvinism has generated a mysticism and a drowsiness that is strangling the Gospel; May the Lord bless his truth!" MacRae had no sympathy with the view that a minister should only tell sinners to 'wait upon the Spirit' instead of preaching the command, 'come to Christ'.[96]

Thankfully, in contrast to Kilmuir, other parts of MacRae's large parish were, as we have noted, blossoming like a rose. They were to him days spent, 'At the gates of heaven'. Regarding a meeting in Kilmaluag in October 1924 MacRae wrote:

> From the very outset I felt the atmosphere warm and reviving. I could not but marvel at the contrast from Staffin. I can scarcely pray in Kilmaluag now without shedding tears and it was especially so last night.[97] Surely the Spirit of God is at work among them. In the sermon got sweet liberty and my soul seemed to be drenched in heavenly dews. For the first time in my life I think I reached the point when I could honestly say that I would prefer to go away and be with Christ than remain in the world; not because the world of late had been made unusually bitter to me, but because of the glory of the One I saw and the longings of my soul after Him. ... During the closing singing, too, my soul was in ecstasy and I think that there were others also who tasted what I got.

It was little wonder that returning home by foot through the Bealach pass in Kilmuir parish, MacRae 'almost danced and praised God from the depths of my soul for His matchless Gospel and His wondrous love to my soul'.[98]

By the end of 1924 MacRae could report a good number in the Kilmaluag district showing signs of having passed from death to life,[99] including three from one family (two brothers and a sister), one of whom

95. Ibid., p. 220.

96. Ibid.

97. MacRae was often to refer to Kilmaluag in later years as 'Goshen'. Of all places in the world he loved it most (ibid., p. 227).

98. Ibid., p. 193. The fact that greatly increased financial offerings were forthcoming from the district was, to their minister, 'further proof of the fact which is almost daily becoming more evident, namely, that the Lord is working in Kilmaluag. I cannot shut my eyes to it' (p. 194).

99. Ibid., p. 196.

later became an elder in Portree Free Church.[100] Of these converts, all stood the test of time except for one: the same person, interestingly, who showed most signs of emotional excess during the movement; she never, in fact, made a public confession.[101] There were numerous others, noted MacRae, 'whose cases encourage me to hope that it is well with them, yet about whom I have heard nothing definite'.[102]

The minister also noted an average attendance at the prayer meeting of forty-five to fifty compared to just seven to nine in 1919. In addition to this, offerings were substantially increased, and, remarked MacRae, 'it has been proved impossible to organise a vain gathering in the Kilmaluag district owing to lack of support among the young people.' In summary, MacRae concluded, 'we have had what is undoubtedly a revival of religion without being aware of it, a revival which has been entirely lacking in the excitement usually associated with the idea of revival.'[103]

South-east Skye 1924 [104]

GOD had worked 'a great work of grace' through the Faith Mission in the parish of Strath in south-east Skye many years previously, but an 'unfortunate thing' happened since that time which had given evangelistic work a bad name. Thus when, shortly before his marriage, Duncan Campbell and a fellow Pilgrim arrived on the island in the winter of 1924, they were either largely ignored or directly opposed. Average attendance at meetings for the first fortnight was no more than thirteen, and one woman being visited shouted at her visitors: 'Clear out of this village … you servants of the Devil!' – considered to be one of the worst insults you could throw at a religious person in the Highlands. On another occasion, a local minister had to climb through a window to open the school for a service after the schoolmaster had locked them out.[105]

Such opposition spurred the evangelists to pray all the more, and they often walked the roads at night imploring God to intervene. Two young women, the fruits of the aforementioned mission, were also in earnest prayer and one of them boldly told Campbell, 'God is going to work in this place; souls will be saved, but we must fight the battle on our knees.' Duncan spent the night in prayer inside a barn; the women also prayed, and one of them ran to her friend's house between twelve and one in the

100. Some years later, MacRae noted in his diary that he had been aware of six cases in Kilmuir, along with eight in Staffin and eighteen in Kilmaluag, during his eleven years ministry there, which he believed showed evidence of saving change (ibid., p. 298).

101. Personal communication with Mary MacLeod, daughter of Rev. Kenneth MacRae, 21 September 2002.

102. Murray, *Diary*, p. 196.

103. Ibid.

104. Information on this movement is taken primarily from an account composed by Duncan Campbell and printed in *BW*, 1925, pp. 7–9. See also p. 29.

105. Woolsey, *Channel of Revival*, p. 105.

morning crying, 'God has come, but we must pray right through.' They prayed on till six in the morning.

The following evening the power of God fell on the meeting and one could hear souls groaning before the Lord in conviction of sin. One woman left crying, 'I am lost. There is no mercy for me!' But another woman brought her back, whereupon she threw herself down on the floor and, without human intervention, was gloriously saved. Attendance increased and soon the entire community was affected by God's presence. Rather than invite sinners to an inquiry room, people were left to work out their salvation with God. Thus a good number were converted in their own homes.

A cottage meeting was started in a township some distance away, to which one man came who hadn't been in church for nine years. Returning home under deep conviction, he spent hours on his knees crying out to God, sensing that God surely did not number him among the elect. Then, suddenly, he remembered God's promise of forgiveness in 1 John 1:9. Soon he was jumping with joy, waking up both his wife and daughter. Together the family praised God till six in the morning!

Another man – 'one of the big men in the district' – was originally opposed to the meetings. One of the two aforementioned young women, a member of the same church as this man, asked Campbell to remember him before the Lord. 'You pray, and I will pray, and we believe that God will answer,' she proposed. When the Pilgrims were invited to the church where these individuals were members, the man decided to attend the following Sunday. 'God met with him and convicted him. He went home miserable. Three nights after that,' records Campbell, 'God saved him and filled him. I believe God baptised that man with the Holy Ghost two days after his conversion.' About a week later, his daughter knocked on his door during the night and said she wanted to know Jesus. The father leapt out of bed and as the two of them knelt down on the floor, Christ was revealed to her soul, and together they wept for joy. Too happy to keep this joy to themselves, the two went to share the good news with the man's wife, who was asleep in bed downstairs. Hard of heart, and annoyed at being woken, she ordered them sternly to go to their beds! But at 5.30 that morning, she too was broken down by the Spirit of God and the gospel of Christ flooded her empty soul.

The old postman was a notorious drinker and no one even thought of inviting him to the meetings. Nevertheless, insulted that his wife and neighbours had gone without asking him, he went along 'just to spite them', and soon was himself wonderfully saved! On another occasion, returning from a cottage meeting, Campbell walked home alone along the shore, when he met three women. Asking one if God was speaking to her, she replied in the affirmative, and, kneeling among the rocks, gave her heart to the Lord there and then. At once the woman requested that Campbell go to see her sister, who had been wishing to speak with him for some time regarding her darkened soul. Campbell went and soon this woman, too, 'entered the Kingdom as the evening shadows fell across the distant Cuillins'.[106]

But this remarkable story didn't end there. A daughter of this woman had been anxious for six weeks, and was in such despair that an aunt often came to sit up with her till late into the night. One evening the girl was 'in an awful state'. ('Oh, it is awful to see a soul in agony,' remarked Campbell, 'and the awful thing about it is that you can do so very little for them.') But finally she quietened down and at two in the morning, 'Christ revealed Himself' to her. When her mother finally returned home two hours later, following her providential encounter with Campbell on the shore, she was overjoyed to find her daughter still up, with bright countenance and deep peace of soul. Eventually the mother entreated her daughter: 'The Lord has met with you, and He has met with me! We have not had sleep for several nights, and I think we should go to bed now.' But the young girl was too excited in the presence of God to even consider sleep, and rushed to the house of another aunt to inform her of her spiritual breakthrough. As she approached her home, the aunt came out to greet her, exclaiming, 'I got him too – at three o'clock this morning!'

As parish councillor, Neilag was a prominent figure in the community. He attended one meeting with pen and paper in hand so that he could write down his many objections to the services. Like numerous others who came to scoff, however, Neilag was soundly converted that night, also being immediately healed of a drink problem. He began to witness everywhere, even getting on his knees by the roadside to pray with people. Seen entering a lodge one evening with a bottle in his pocket, however, some locals became concerned that he was falling back. The reality was very different. It had been a family function and his relatives were hoping to see him turn his back on his wildfire religion. However, before eating, Neilag said grace, engaging in prayer for around twenty minutes in request that God would save those present! It being customary to bring a bottle of whisky to propose a toast, Neilag indeed produced a bottle from his jacket pocket, unwrapping it and pouring out the contents into glasses. Speaking later Neilag confided, 'I made them drink the toast … with the milk from the brown cow!'

Characteristically, Campbell was fearless in proclaiming the truth of God's Word as he moved from village to village. Speaking with a crofter one day he told him, 'Lachie, you're as hard as the devil can make you.' These plain words shook the big man, who went to his room to pray and passed from death to life. The Lord revealed Himself to a young girl as she was walking up the brae near her home. She was so overwhelmed by the reality of God's love as revealed in the death of Christ that for a time she could hardly speak.

106. Ibid., p. 74.

The work went on for eight weeks, and even beyond the shores of Skye relatives of those involved in the movement were converted. A young woman from the area who was working on the Scottish mainland became a Christian, and a man en route from Australia to his native island was gripped with conviction of sin on the boat, and was converted before he reached home.

While on Skye, Campbell suddenly took ill, and was confined to bed. A medical examination suggested tuberculosis – a dreaded disease in those days. Among those responsible for organising the mission was one resolute young woman. Having prayed much for it, and while watching by his bedside, she knelt before his bed and stated simply, 'Lord, you are going to heal him, and when you do, look after him, for the dear man hasn't the sense to look after himself!' From the moment she said 'Amen,' a change came over the patient. His strength returned and the following night he was back at the meetings, proclaiming with renewed vigour the truths of God's Word! After the Pilgrims left the island, meetings continued nightly for some time, and Campbell reflected: 'I believe that the work of grace, that wonderful work, came about through the prevailing prayer of those two sisters who knew how to pray and how to pray through.'[107]

LATER MOVEMENTS 1925–7

BY the end of 1924 the burst of revivalist intensity that had marked the first half of the decade had died down, but over the next few years there was still considerable activity. A mission in the Morningside district of Edinburgh near the close of 1924 had been preceded by a month of special times of 'waiting upon God', held variously in many homes and in a church hall. Subsequent meetings were 'packed to suffocation', the likes of which had never been seen before in the area, and among the many outstanding conversions were those of a dozen nurses from Craiglockhart Hospital and a recent police recruit from the far north of the country.[108]

The Faith Mission remained steadfastly active during this period. In Tranent, 'a score of converts took their stand in the open air'. A good work was done in other East Lothian communities, too, and several Prayer Unions were commenced. From these prayer cells and from the village of Wallyford, a subsequent work of grace was effected, for no fewer than seven young men entered the CoS ministry.[109] In East Stirlingshire, Camelon was swept by

107. Steve Taylor notes that, 'As a result of this and subsequent missions the work and ministry of the Faith Mission found a special place in the hearts of the Christian community in south Skye, an attachment which continues even today' (*Skye Revival*, CD-ROM, Chapter 20).

108. *TC*, 6 November 1924, p. 43.

109. One of them, the Rev. Dr James G.S.S. Thomson, did a period of training with the F.M., following his conversion, before working as a missionary in Algiers for some years. On his return home he studied for the ministry, graduating with high honours, and was awarded a scholarship to Oxford, where he was elected Casbred prizeman of St John's College. He later worked as a lecturer of Hebrew and Oriental languages at Edinburgh University, then at Columbia University in the United States. On returning to Scotland he was a parish minister till his retirement (Peckham, *Heritage of Revival*, p. 62).

'a great wave of revival blessing' in the spring of 1927. Hundreds regularly had to stand during meetings because every seat was filled, and older folk claimed: 'The days of Moody and Sankey have come again!' [110]

During 1927 also, 'a wonderful work' of 'real awakening' occurred in the northern tip of the country, in the John O'Groats district. As news of the work of grace spread, folk gathered in large numbers from as far as twenty miles distant. Ministers from Wick, Scarfskerry and Keiss assisted in the work, while Jock Troup came to preach and to sing. Among the many who gave testimony to blessing, received at a closing conference attended by over 250, was a married couple along with five of their children, three of whom were 'stalwart men', while yet another child, not present at this meeting, was also converted! [111]

Lambhill, Glasgow 1927

A KEEN footballer who had played for Scotland's national school team, James Alexander Stewart, was converted in Glasgow at the age of fourteen, through the ministry of Irish evangelist Tom Rea and via the earnest, expectant prayers of his devout mother. Following several absorbing years as a boy evangelist, Stewart teamed up with a door-to-door salesman from Edinburgh, and together they travelled round the towns and villages of the Borders region of southern Scotland, selling their wares, but also boldly witnessing for Christ. In time Stewart established the 'Border Movement', with aim of uniting and strengthening local believers and mobilising them to evangelise their own neighbourhoods. After a time he found himself amidst a spiritual awakening as he moved slowly and systematically from one place to another.[112]

But blessing was not confined to the Borders region. Stewart recalled how, at the age of just seventeen, 'in Glasgow, we were on the verge of a mighty spiritual awakening for the whole city, the largest in Scotland. All-night prayer meetings were held, and expectation ran high that God was going to do a "new thing".' The believers sang in great faith to the early hours of the morning:

> God answered the believing prayers of His people, and a spontaneous awakening took place, not in a big city church, but in a mission hall in the small mining town of Lambhill, on the outskirts of the city.[113]

---

110. *BW*, 1927, pp. 118–19; *TC*, 21 April 1927, p. 45.

111. *BW*, 1927, pp. 118, 189.

112. These spiritual stirrings occurred mainly on the English side of the Border.

113. This was the Lambhill Evangelistic Mission Hall, founded in 1895. There were a great many mission halls in Glasgow around this time; these included five Railway Missions, Artizans' Hall, Paddy Black's Mission, the Douglas Children's Mission, the Foundry Boys' Mission, the Canal Boatmen's Institute, the Seamen's Bethel, the Seamen's Chapel, the Church of Scotland Lodging House Mission, the Grove Street Institute, Braid St Mission Hall, Bardowie Mission, Gorbals Medical Mission, numerous mission halls run by Glasgow City Mission, the Tollbooth Mission, Duke St Mission, the Bethany Hall, YMCA/Christian Institute, and the 'flagship of the fleet', the Tent Hall in the Saltmarket (George Mitchell, *Comfy Glasgow: An Expression of Thanks*, Fearn 1999, pp. 68–73).

> My spiritual father, Mr Tom Rea of Belfast, was leading the saints there in a prayer crusade, asking God to rend the heavens and visit them. The presence of the Lord was felt everywhere, in the shops, in the homes, and even under the bowels of the earth where many miners were smitten by the Holy Spirit. Meetings went on for many weeks night after night. Mr Rea invited me to come down and help in dealing with anxious souls. It was an astonishing sight to me. It was impossible for us to leave the hall before midnight, owing to the deep distress among anxious souls. It was brother Rea's burden that the fire of God would spread to the city, which at that time was the greatest evangelical city in the world. We prayed together to this effect, but alas, we soon discovered that the evangelical leaders of the city were offended at the Lord that the revival had not begun in one of their great congregations. … I am deeply persuaded that the revival fires would have spread into the whole city and possibly to the whole nation had these evangelical leaders at that time not dictated to God as to where the revival should begin.[114]

Rea's mission lasted a total of eight weeks and was followed by a further mission in 1929. The Business Meeting minutes of the Lambhill Evangelistic Mission for October 1927 record that, 'owing to much blessing in an outpouring of the Holy Spirit of God, many souls were gathered into the Kingdom of God's dear Son during the eight weeks' mission from April till June. Over 200 souls confessing faith in Jesus Christ.'[115] An entry in the Minutes for January 1928 states further: 'We could not help but comment on the blessed year we had in 1927. The soul saving season, the strengthening and building up in the most holy faith season, spiritual and financial. It was a great year's blessing in the history of the Lambhill Evangelistic Mission.'[116]

THE SILENT THIRTIES

ALTHOUGH evangelical awakenings were not uncommon in one part of Scotland or another right up to the mid to late 1920s, after

114. Stewart, *Opened Windows*, pp. 123–4. Stewart contrasted this scenario to the position of a Bishop of the Lutheran Church in mainland Europe who, in later years, witnessed 'a great awakening in his land'. He said to Stewart, 'I do not care where the fire of God falls, whether it is in the Cathedral or in the Salvation Army Hall; for one thing I know – you cannot keep revival to yourself. If one group tries to control the fire of God it will burn them' (p. 124).

115. Business Meeting minutes of the Lambhill Evangelistic Mission for October 1927.

116. Ibid., January 1928. Stewart's involvement in evangelistic movements in these early days of his life stood him in excellent preparation for the years that followed. For, at only twenty-four years of age, this young man set off at the clear call of the Lord to minister in towns and cities throughout the vast expanse of Eastern Europe and the Baltic States. Remarkable revival followed him in virtually all these foreign lands, where the fields had truly been ripened for harvest. In Latvia, Estonia, Poland, Czechoslovakia, Hungary, Bulgaria and Romania, from 1934 to 1940, wonderful awakenings were experienced, preparing many young souls for the awful horrors of the Second World War and Soviet Occupation which took place soon after (*Ruth Stewart, James Stewart: Missionary*, Asheville, NC 1977, pp. 37–101).

that date they became much more infrequent.[117] During the whole of the 1930s there were virtually none at all on the Scottish mainland, in great contrast to the Outer Hebrides, where a powerful revival coursed through much of Lewis throughout the decade. In Scotland generally, however, evangelists and Faith Mission Pilgrims found themselves facing growing discouragement and apathy as they 'continued tenaciously, often plodding on in areas which yielded little fruit and offered scant encouragement'.[118]

One team active during this decade was the 'Oxford Group', consisting of Oxbridge undergraduates, clergymen and academics, and led by Dr Frank Buchman, a Lutheran minister/evangelist from Pennsylvania. Criticised by conservative evangelicals, sheer dedication moved this self-funded team to traverse the U.K. in the early 1930s, testifying to their own spiritual surrender with compelling sincerity. Their first big-city campaign took place in Edinburgh in March 1930 with around fifty men from Oxford and twenty from Cambridge taking part. Following the mission, one Oxford undergraduate spoke at a Methodist Bible class from 3 p.m. to 10 p.m. 'Numbers of young people gave themselves to Christ, continued to meet afterwards in weekly groups and carried the message to their Methodist churches in Scotland.'[119]

Other Significant Movements in this Period[120]

Balintore 1923
Partick Highland, Glasgow 1925–32
North Skye 1928–32
Avoch 1939

---

117. Two of the last localised movements in Wales to merit the term 'revival' also occurred in the late 1920s, viz., in Fochriw, near Methr Tydfil, in May 1928 (Selwyn Hughes, *Revival World Report*, July-August 1997, p. 2) and in Loughor, 1928–30 (Brynmor P. Jones, *Instrument of Revival: The Complete Life of Evan Roberts 1878–1951*, South Plainfield 1996, pp. 217–24), while another, also in south Wales, occurred very shortly after, viz. in Sandfields, Aberavon, 1930–31 (Iain H. Murray, *D. Martyn Lloyd-Jones, The First Forty Years 1899–1939*, Edinburgh 1982, pp. 203–27).

118. Peckham, *Heritage of Revival*, p. 72. At least one other UK location witnessed spiritual stirrings at this time, however. During a mission in 1935 in Belfast's Welcome Hall, 'God broke in in a mighty way'. The hall was packed, and crowds thronged outside the door. Then in 1939, with a visit from an Indian evangelist, again 'the Holy Spirit swept through the hall'. Preaching was set aside that souls could be dealt with, many crying out for forgiveness. 'Revival fires had been lit' (Victor Maxwell, *Belfast's Halls of Faith and Fame*, Belfast 1999, pp. 111-14).

119. D.W. Bebbington, 'The Oxford Group Movement Between the Wars' in W.J. Sheils and Diana Wood (Eds.), *Voluntary Religion: Papers Read at the 1985 Summer Meeting and the 1986 Winter Meeting of the Ecclesiastical History Society*, Oxford 1986, pp. 495–6; G.F. Allen, 'The Groups in Oxford' in R.H.S. Crossman, etc. (Eds.), *Oxford and the Groups: The Influence of the Groups*, Oxford 1934, pp. 24–5.

120. Full accounts of these movements can be found on www.scottishrevivals.co.uk.

Staffin, Kilmuir parish, Skye – p.181

Elgol, South Skye – p.187

Kenneth MacRae – p.179

James Stewart – p.191

Part Two

FIRE AMONG THE FISHERFOLK

Ye sons of the main that sail o'er the flood
Whose sins like a mountain, have reached unto God
Remember the short voyage of life soon will end
And so brother sailor, make Jesus your friend.
Look astern on your life, see your way marked by sin
See what dangers your vessel and cargo are in
If the hard rocks of death should grate on your keel
Can you say with assurance, your soul will be well?
Lay by your old compass, it will do you no good
It ne'er can direct you the right way to God
Mind your helm brother sailor and don't fall asleep
Or your vessel and cargo will sink in the deep.
There are treacherous shoals then on every hand
On the voyage of life, to that happy land
Consult your chart and compass every day
And your vessel will sail safely on all the way.
With the Pilot on board we can sail right along
Through calm and through storms till we reach our blest home
Then come unto Jesus, my dear sinner friend
For remember the short voyage of life will soon end.[1]

1. Song composed by John Innes during the 'Fishermen's revival' of 1921–2 (Ritchie, pp. 68–9).

Introduction

UP to the mid nineteenth century, the spiritual climate of many north-east coastal townships was said to have been desperate, and several villages were completely without any preaching station. In a succession of mini tours between 1859 and 1862, Peterhead-born cooper-turned-evangelist James Turner visited virtually all the fishing communities along the Buchan, Banffshire and Moray coast, while other evangelists held missions in the same or neighbouring localities. Almost everywhere a profound impression was made, and numerous communities were radically transformed by the gospel message. Many new congregations sprang up and the Church became an integral part of community life.

Revivalism, previously unheard of, became a dominant theme in these fishing ports to an extent unparalleled anywhere in Scotland during that era or since. For the following twenty years, especially in the coastal stretch between Cullen and Portgordon, fresh bouts of revivalistic activity flared up repeatedly, making particular impact in 1863, 1866, 1870–1 and 1874.

Such oft-repeated bursts of intense spiritual activity, as we are about to discover, were to continue to be a dominant force in the religious life of north-east coast townships through the remainder of the nineteenth century and well into the twentieth, although it has been suggested that as early as 1880 things had already begun to slow down.[2] The most widespread of these revivals occurred in 1921–2, being in part an extension of a movement that began in East Anglia shortly before. This movement proved to be the last in the unequalled sixty-year period of recurring revivalism in the region. Such unrivalled revival legacy has made the Inverness-Aberdeen coastline the revival 'hot spot' of the Scottish mainland in the period under review and for this reason alone it deserves to be considered in a separate section.

A number of reasons have been offered to explain why revivalism took so strong a hold of Moray Firth fishing villages. The inhabitants of these communities had long been highly superstitious, holding an inborn sense of the supernatural. James Turner, the central figure in the initial,

2. For example, writing in 1921, J.W. Walker, a native of Fraserburgh, opines that, along the north-east coast, 'since the eighties there has been a gradual decline in the religious fervour of the fishermen' and in regard to church attendance 'a sad and steadily increasing decline in this respect for the last 30 years' (Letter to *Glasgow Herald*, 16 December 1921).

dramatic revival that burst upon these shores, also possessed an acute sense of the supernatural, and these factors combined created a perfect context for intensely emotional revival to flourish.[3]

A more commonly noted reason why the fisherfolk received this revival so wholeheartedly was the physical danger they encountered virtually every day. A fisherman's work was one of the most hazardous of all occupations and in 1860 it was calculated that eleven out of every sixteen seafaring men died by drowning. Thoughts of eternity were therefore never far from the fisherfolks' minds, and it seems that the perils of their work turned them towards a combination of religious and superstitious beliefs. In relation to this, the sinking of a boat at sea and subsequent loss of life had a profound effect on the close-knit community the men came from and often acted as a stimulus for revival (see, for example, the Bullers o' Buchan account below).[4]

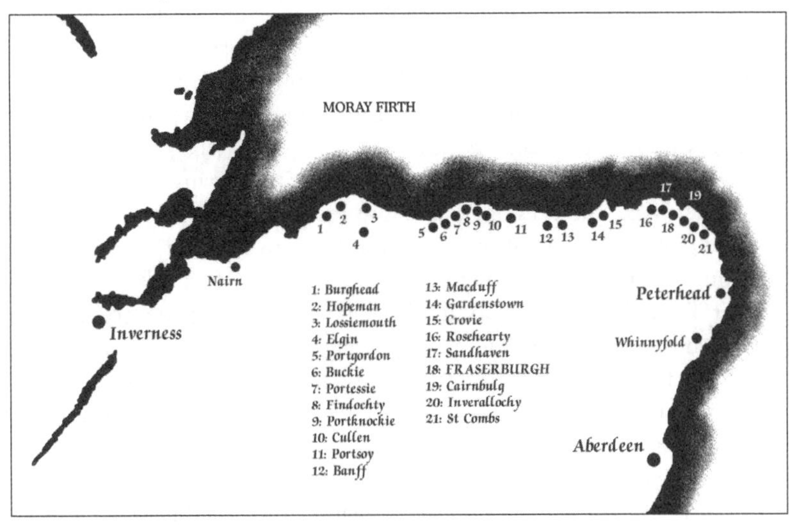

It is also significant that fishing communities depended totally on the success of the fishing seasons for their livelihood. This, in turn, was largely dependent on the weather and on general economic conditions (e.g. the cost of fuel for drifters). Several seasons of poor harvest would invariably prove disastrous for the fisher families, and would be severely felt by all classes of the community. (This was true, for example, in the lead-up to the revivals of 1860 and 1921.) The subsequent despair and hardship predisposed the people towards the consolation and hope offered by religion, or, as one journalist suggested, a poor fishing season was seen by fishermen as 'a visitation for unrighteous living'.[5]

3. Jeffrey, pp. 183–4.

4. Ibid., pp. 185–7.

5. *Glasgow Herald*, 12 December 1921.

The social conditions of the fisherfolk was another important factor which helped stimulate the outbreak of revival among them. They lived in extremely close proximity to one another (in some localities, such as Footdee, several families lived in separate rooms of one small house). Even in larger towns, such as Fraserburgh and Peterhead, the fisherfolk lived in well-defined areas known as the Seatowns. Thus, they both lived and worked alongside each other. A rough equality prevailed among the people, who were also fiercely loyal towards one another. The villages and seatowns were generally small, with populations of well under 1,000, creating ideal conditions wherein a sense of strong affinity could emerge among inhabitants. In addition, fishing communities tended to be cut off both geographically and socially from inland communities and bigger towns like Aberdeen. (There was even a code discouraging marriage to a person outwith one's own community.) They therefore existed as detached groups of people with an exclusive identity and a separate way of life. All these factors led to a strong sense of community, which affected the manner in which the people experienced revival.[6]

The way in which the gospel message was culturally contextualised to the fisherfolk is also significant. By accepting Christ the villagers were simply following in the footsteps of the very first disciples, many of whom were also fishermen. The message was more readily accepted because it was delivered, often, by one of their own class; a native from a nearby fishing community, such as a fisherman or cooper (barrel-maker). The revival was further diffused by ordinary local fisherfolk who had been converted. These were men whom the community could relate to and understand, and whom they knew they could trust. They would also have been aware of their former lives, and how much they had changed. Thus the evangelist was likely to be an uneducated man, who used simple language in their own dialect. He would make frequent use of seafaring imagery, such as referring to Christ as 'The Great Captain' or 'The Skipper'; ploughing through the sea of life, with its heights and troughs; the Bible being the chart; and being bound for 'the Port of Heaven'.[7] The most popular hymns among the fisherfolk were also abounding in seafaring imagery, an example being 'Will Your Anchor Hold?', while many new indigenous spiritual songs soon also became popular.[8]

Analysis of revivals along the Moray coast also requires consideration of the unique work patterns of the fisherfolk. The haddock season lasted

---

6. Jeffrey, pp. 196–9.

7. A message preached by Rev. Shirra of Linktown, Fife, included a message to mariners: 'We hae Christ for our skipper, the Holy Spirit for oor Pilot, an' God himsel' at the helm. Your boat, let me tell ye, is but a bit fir deal frae Norwa'; the keep o' oor boat was laid in Bethlehem, built in Judea, rigg'd in Jerusalem, launched on Mount Calvary, we hae the cross o' Christ for a helm, a cedar of Lebanon for a mast an' the Redemption o' mankind for a freight. ...' [Robert Shirra, *Remains of the Rev. Robert Shirra*, Kirkcaldy 1850, pp. 47–8].

8. Ibid., pp. 190–92; Donald E. Meek, 'Fishers of Men' in James Porter, *After Columba – After Calvin: Religious Community in North East Scotland*, Aberdeen 1999, pp. 139–40.

from March to May, while the more lucrative herring season began in June and continued until the end of October. Most of the fishermen and women deserted their village homes during these periods and spent the spring and summer working out of larger ports like Peterhead and Fraserburgh or Lowestoft and Great Yarmouth. During this time the work was constant and demanding and there was little time for social activities. After their return home, during the winter and early spring months, the men collected bait and only occasionally ventured out to sea. They had much more free time and they would often stay up late, socialising. Boredom might also set in, which partly would explain the eagerness with which they would rush to hear any preacher who came to their locality. It also helps explain why they were able to devote themselves to long hours of church services and late after-meetings in the event of an awakening. Indeed it was not unknown for some villagers to go for several days without sleep during the height of a revival, as they prayed, sang and exhorted their neighbours. It is worthy of note, then, that most revivals along the Moray coast have occurred between November and March.[9]

It has often been argued that the dangerous, unpredictable occupation of fishermen led to them developing a deep emotional disposition and that this in turn was a major factor in their inclination towards revivalism.[10] This, however, has been refuted by others, who suggest that fishermen tend to be level-headed and down-to-earth. In any case, it does not fully account for the fervour and excitability of coopers such as James Turner or Jock Troup, who showed up as important lay preachers. The fisherfolk were generally uneducated people, who had 'never been accustomed to the usages of society',[11] living, as they did, in complete cultural isolation from the 'higher' classes. It is also noteworthy that the more that revival was experienced among fishing communities, the more it became expected. According to Donald Meek, 'Revival was programmed in to the mind-set of many east-coast fishermen. In revival, they relived their origins as a Christian community; revival enabled them to grow as a community, and helped them to survive in the face of adversity. Revivals were a special reminder of the Lord's presence among them, taking them back to their foundations and giving them hope for the future.'[12]

---

9. Jeffrey, pp. 203–5.

10. e.g. Peter Anson suggests, rather simplistically, that the religion of 'the average cautious lowland Scot ... finds expression in moral action' while that of the fisherman will more likely find expression in emotion (Anson, p. 45).

11. Quoted in Jeffrey, p. 207.

12. Meek, *Fishers of Men*, p. 138.

6
Fires Along the North-East Coast[1]
1880–1913

Findochty 1880[2]

W.T. KER, Free Church minister of Deskford, Banffshire, had observed the stirring revival scenes of 1860 in the nearby villages of Findochty and Portessie, as well as the subsequent movements of 1863 and 1866. Having preached many times over the years in these localities, it was while again rising to speak at an annual 'Soiree' at the Wesleyan chapel in Portessie, on 1 January 1878, that Ker realised that many of the young men and women in the congregation would probably not be aware of his previous discourses on the distinction between genuine times of revival – such as 1860, when 'true life in Christ had begun for the village' – and periods of emotion-based revivalism (as he believed occurred in 1863 and 1866). Making this clear distinction again for his younger hearers, Ker urged that they 'seek that the glorified Jesus of Nazareth might himself return among them in the same way as at the first'.[3] The minister had to return home early due to bad weather, but his words brought back a deep sense of reminiscent longing among those who well remembered the 1860 revival, and all subsequent speakers at the meeting laid aside their prepared speeches to follow on from where Ker had stopped. The result was that groups of men and women in both villages decided to meet together in prayer until God should once again reveal Himself as He had done in days of yore. These prayer meetings grew in fervour and expectancy from that day on.

Ker felt certain that an answer would be given to their prayers. Anxious to remove any stumbling blocks that he could, while at the same time urging others to follow the example being set, he wrote a series of articles on revival, which appeared at intervals in *The Banffshire Herald* between

1. References in this book to the 'north-east coast' or 'Moray Firth Coast' generally relate to that stretch of coastal communities between Burghead and Peterhead, where religious revivals have been particularly conspicuous. Geographically, this stretch of coast includes parts of Aberdeenshire, Buchan, Banffshire and Moray.

2. J.W. Walker of Helensburgh gives a fascinating picture of religious life in the north-east in the 1880s. 'In my young days in Fraserburgh I had many friends amongst the fishermen, and used to go out with them to the herring fishing overnight. Many wonderful talks I had with them – the men from the village of St Combs being profoundly religious and remarkably intelligent. ... When I was a child we had to hurry up on the Sunday morning if we were to get a seat in the Free Kirk. My early recollections are of crowded services during the fishing season, pew upon pew packed with jersey-clad fishermen'. ('Letter' to *Glasgow Herald*, 16 December 1921.)

3. *TC*, 17 June 1880, p. 7.

August 1879 and January 1880. These helped to encourage believers and guard them against former abuses, while also making the subject clearer to those with little or no understanding of it. In addition, the articles strengthened those active in prayer, and before long it was reported among these that they had on several occasions been overshadowed by the power of the Holy Spirit. Then, as if out of the blue, that same power came down upon the whole village like the 'rushing of a mighty wind'. Ker, arriving at the scene a week later, was thrilled to witness a nineteenth century version of the Acts of the Apostles, as he

> met on the streets young men staggering under the influence of the new wine, their eyes filled with tears of joy, and their voices hoarse with suppressed emotion. It was very touching to hear at the meeting their attempts to tell what they were feeling. They were too full of matter, and their broken sentences were in fragments of unconscious eloquence, and of clear spiritual insight into the meaning of Scripture passages, that had greater power over me than the most laboured efforts of the learned. The help of man was very little needed, and great judiciousness was shown in the way of human oversight.[4]

For some days all manual labour was laid aside by the arresting hand of the Lord, and Ker and others ministered among the villagers with much earnestness. In Portknockie, meetings were held in the Free Church every night for six weeks, and thereafter in houses throughout the whole district. A good half-dozen kitchen meetings sprang up, led by the minister and office-bearers or by the office-bearers alone. With a measure of success they sought to gather to the meetings, not only believers, but also the non-church-going.[5] Soon, however, they were required to get back to work, and begin preparing boats and nets for the fishing season ahead – the herring fishing on the west coast. Promoted by their near departure, utterance was given to many of the young men whose lives had been so radically transformed, and they now had a boldness and freedom in sharing the good news with others. Ker noted among the workers an eagerness to be used as fishers of men in the places they journeyed to, as well as a deep reverence before the risen Lord of Glory. Further, they exhibited a humility of spirit, 'an entire absence of anything like a human exultation in such a work, such as has been seen in them on former occasions'.[6] These fisherfolk

---

4. Ibid. The revival was in great contrast to events in Ker's own parish, where there had been 'no special work of revival for many years' (*RC-FCS-SR&M*, 1882, p. 25).

5. ARC-FCS-SR&M, 1882, pp. 25–6.

6. TC 17 June 80 p7. Ker did not look favourably on revivalist movements that sprang up along the Banffshire coast in each of the years 1863, 1866 and 1870. They were, he said, 'accompanied by great intensity of emotion … (but) no such evidences of spiritual power as had before been so undoubted (i.e. in 1860) … no proof of anything higher than what may arise from earthly sources' (*TC*, 17 June 1880, p. 7).

were determined to maintain a strong Christian testimony wherever they went to lower their nets, a reputation built up over the previous twenty years, and also to show an example of diligence in business.

Preceding them to the fishing grounds, some older men made arrangements in Stornoway for the hire of suitable meeting halls for the incumbents. Over 6,000 men and women were estimated to have left the Moray coast for Lewis at this time and this season proved the most fruitful in a number of years.[7] This notwithstanding, there did occur an outbreak of stormy weather, but it only served to provide all the more time for outreach. And so, in time, a gracious work of revival was begun in Stornoway, whose striking testimony is related elsewhere (see pp. 267–72). The fishermen returned to their Banffshire homes full of praise to God for the obvious signs of spiritual blessings they had witnessed in the Western Isles and in which they had humbly played a part. Greatly encouraged, they looked forward with much expectancy to further signs of refreshing as they prepared to venture to east coast towns for the summer season, where much larger numbers would be congregated.[8]

Bullers o' Buchan and Peterhead 1880s

A FEW miles south of Peterhead is situated the Bullers o' Buchan, a spectacular series of carved caves and inlets, impressive bird life and some of the most striking cliffside views in Britain. Formerly a small but busy fishing village, a localised awakening took place in the Bullers near the turn of the 1880s, following the death at sea of Tammas Reid, a popular fisherman from the community. Not only were his wife and

7. Ibid., 29 July 1880, p. 6.

8. Neil Dickson suggests that awakening was more widespread throughout Buchan during this period, and many converts were drawn into Brethren assemblies (Dickson, *Brethren in Scotland*, p. 100). Among the converts in Peterhead were several fishermen from Cockenzie who had travelled there for the fishing season; they were later baptised in Lerwick Sound, Shetland. On their return home they formed a Brethren assembly in 1882 (p. 107). A few miles along the coast from Cockenzie, there was a spiritual movement in Newhaven in 1881. James Hood Wilson notes in his diary, 'Had to be at Newhaven by eight o'clock. Had a large meeting there, most deeply interesting. The whole area of the church was filled – the centre with fisher-people, men and women – the latter with white caps or bare-headed. There has been a most remarkable state of things for a few weeks' (James Wells, *The Life of James Hood Wilson D.D. of the Barclay Church, Edinburgh*, London 1904, p. 222). Elsewhere along the east coast, and possibly an extension of the Moray coast movement, two local fishermen, and others of similar calling, made a significant advance in both Anstruther and nearby Pittenweem in the early part of 1881. At first meetings were held only during stormy weather, when fishing boats were unable to go to sea. But as interest deepened, they continued every night. Christian helpers were almost overwhelmed with the responsibilities of providing assistance to the anxious. The whole community was touched by this memorable movement (*TC*, 7 April 1881, p. 15). This is probably the same movement as that referred to in an FC report that remarked on an awakening occurring in Anstruther around 1880, when attendance at the Bible class rose to 200. (*RC-FCS-SR&M*, 1888, p. 4). Further south still, significant blessing attended a mission in Eyemouth led by evangelists Scroggie and Dunn. A deep spirit of enquiry also spread to nearby Coldingham and Burnmouth, and it was said that 'throughout all the district there is scarcely a farm-steading or group of cottages to which one can go but one finds the Lord's hand has been at work, arresting the careless and awakening the dead' (*RC-FCS-SR&M*, 1881, pp. 7–8).

children deeply impacted by the tragedy, but so too the entire locality. Word was passed from one ship to another, and on the funeral day the Bullers' bay was full of boats, with no man at sea. The coffin was carried shoulder-high for a distance of over two miles to the kirkyard, and the following Sabbath the inhabitants of the village walked en masse to Tammas's church in Peterhead. Here, wrote John McGibbon, a native of the village, 'during the service our eyes were often wet with tears, and many an old grizzled veteran of the sea made many an excuse for wiping his spectacles that day in order to clear away the tears that would persist in flowing, for well we loved and respected Tammas.'[9]

At the meeting in the village chapel that evening a local Christian, Jeannie Bruce, shared how, just hours before his last trip, Reid had remarked how grand it was 'tae serve the Lord. I dinna mind o' anytime in my life when I felt Him sae near, or sae precious tae my soul,' he had said. The visiting preacher that evening called for someone to fill Tammas' place as an earnest worker at the chapel. In all, five volunteered, while ten young men and women went 'forritt' (a colloquial term for a sinner going forward to the penitent rail). McGibbon states that 'for many a Sabbath night after this our little mercy seat was filled with seekers, and quite a revival started amongst the young people.'[10]

This awakening followed close on the heels of more widespread gospel interest in the north-east of Scotland with the steady advance of the Salvation Army. Formed in the wake of the great revival of 1859–61, the first Scottish Corps began in 1879, and progress developed rapidly through the remainder of the century. In Aberdeen the Army acquired the old Castlegate site on Union Street to build their new impressive Citadel, modelled on Balmoral Castle. They worked on the maxim that if the sinful did not come to them, then they must take the gospel message into the streets. Within a short time, 'hundreds had been gathered into their ranks, some who had been the terror of Aberdeen, but now were sober, well-clothed, and industrious, and as energetic for good as they had formerly been for the evil.'[11]

When the Army rented premises in Peterhead, locals, not least believers, were highly suspicious, having heard of 'the bands, the drums, the flags flying … the tambourines playing'.[12] Having seen the large gory bill-

9. John McGibbon, *The Fisher-Folk of Buchan: a True Story of Peterhead*, London 1922, pp. 96–7.705.

10. Ibid., p. 98.

11. McGibbon, p. 81.

12. Ibid. p81. In another part of Scotland, long before the Salvation Army were established there, the aged Malcolm MacLeod of Lewis, a convert of the 1820s revival in Uig, was asked 'what he thought of the ways of the Salvation Army with its fiddles and drums'. He said, 'If souls are savingly converted I don't care one straw whether there be fiddles or not.' Said Norman MacFarlane, 'For one of Malcolm's spiritual upbringing and in those long ago days when the Salvation Army was everywhere decried, he showed remarkable breadth and enlightenment' (Rev. Norman C. MacFarlane, *The 'Men' of the Lews*, Stornoway 1924, p. 223).

posters announcing the Army's arrival, and their intent to 'bombard every citadel of Satan' in the town, the locals wondered 'how these innovations would suit us staid respectable-going people of Peterhead'.[13] Their warmth of personality and soundness of doctrine soon won over many, however, and numbers were converted on their first day of open-air meetings. Says McGibbon, 'another revival started that was the means of bringing many of our wanderers home and of stirring up the dry bones and the lukewarm ones to do their first works again.'[14] When General William Booth visited the town in May 1882, over 1,000 – plus 300 Army members, mostly women – crowded into the hall to hear him. However, as was often the case in these fledgling years of this religious group,[15] when Army supporters led a procession through town the following evening, considerable disturbance was incited, and several Salvationists were physically attacked.[16]

Attitudes began to soften, however, and as the captain went through the town 'like a fire-brand'; he got to know everybody, and all the town soon got to know 'oor captain'. 'Happy Tommie', as he was otherwise known, helped walk drunk men home, 'watched with the sick, buried the dead, and wept with the sorrowing', and 'some of the very hardest cases that we had in the town, and who had withstood the influences and the fires of the other revivals, were brought to their knees by the faith and the persistent effort of these officers.'[17]

McGibbon describes a typical afternoon meeting – sandwiched between the main morning and evening services – held in the old James Turner hall, which had now become occupied by the Salvation Army.

> The crowd of men and women who pack themselves into that building is tremendous, and often they will overflow from the hall onto the stairs, glad if they can get a peep inside and hear what is going on. This is also an open meeting for anyone who cares to speak or sing, or pray. The swinging sea hymns that the fisherfolk are so fond of singing, with the rollicking chorus that everyone can join in with, are being sung with all their heart and soul. Such grand old hymns as 'Rescue the perishing, care for the dying,' or one that has a chorus like 'Pull for the shore,

---

13. McGibbon, p. 82.

14. Ibid., p. 85. This movement paralleled equally dramatic awakenings that occurred as the Salvation Army made inroads into other parts of the United Kingdom around the same time, such as in parts of Manchester from 1878 (Glenn K. Horridge, *The Salvation Army: Origins and Early Days: 1865–1900*, Godalming 1993, pp. 154–181) and in the Rhondda Valley and other areas of Wales in 1879 (pp. 208–21). Another 'glorious work of grace' that accompanied the fledgling days of the Salvation Army in Scotland occurred in Coatbridge in 1882. John Bissett, later leader of the Lanarkshire Christian Union, was converted at this time (Bryson, *History of The Lanarkshire Christian Union*, pp. 41–2).

15. In the year 1882 alone, over 600 Salvationists were brutally attacked in towns and cities throughout the United Kingdom; and in several instances victims died as a result of their injuries.

16. Anonymous, *'It Happened in Peterhead': Extracts from The Peterhead Sentinel and The Corps History Book*, Peterhead n.d., pp. 17–18.

17. McGibbon, p. 86.

> sailor, pull for the shore,' are caught up and sung over and over again. As the testimonies and the singing are open to all, old and young throw themselves into these exercises with so much enthusiasm that there is scarcely time for all to speak who would like to. Orthodox people might say that to their taste it lacked solemnity, but our fisher-folk know when to be free and when to be solemn, and their reply to any such criticism would be, 'Man, it's graund; where the spirit o' the Lord is there is leeberty.'[18]

In a short time, the 'Sally Anne' had become a highly significant presence in the town, retaining such influential position right up to the Second World War and beyond. [19]

One young man who took part in this awakening in Peterhead was John Ross, later to become a minister in the Free Church and a popular Highland evangelist. In the early 1880s Ross, a student at Edinburgh's Free Church College, travelled independently to Peterhead in order both to study and engage in Christian work. He records,

> There was a revival movement of a very genuine type among the east-coast fishermen. On the Sundays and Saturdays, and other nights when the boats could not go to sea, Toppings' Hall, where the meetings were held, used to be crowded, so that late-comers could not get even standing room. These meetings were addressed by men from as far south as the Firth of Forth and as far north as the Moray Firth. They also had large open-air meetings. There was tremendous enthusiasm, and at that time many were added to the Lord of such as shall be saved.
>
> That was a great time in Peterhead. One night there a young man and I knelt on the ground and consecrated our lives to Christ's service; and that young man became a great soul winner'.[20]

Ross was amazed to see unschooled fishermen – like Peter and John in the Gospels – who were yet 'mighty in the Scriptures; orators (born-again orators) with a power I cannot explain. … I saw, too, that, even when men seem unusable, God can find use for them; and I was surprised at the number of anxious souls that came to me seeking the way Zionward.'[21]

Offering to pray with one fisherlad Ross engaged with, the man suddenly muttered in trembling voice, 'O Lord, you know my heart is like a cage of wild beasts; have mercy on a sinner.' Nearly fifty years later, Ross bumped into this same man at a railway station. He testified to Ross that the day they prayed together he passed from darkness into light, and

18. Ibid., pp. 126–7.

19. Elsewhere in the north-east, the FC parish of Belhelvie, eight miles north of Aberdeen, also enjoyed 'extensive revival' during the 1880s (*RC-FCS-SR&M*, 1888, p. 4).

20. Ross, *Reminiscences*, pp. 17.

21. Ibid., pp. 17–18.

that light had burned ever since. When Ross conducted services at a later date, that man was one of his best helpers.

MINISTRY OF JAMES MCKENDRICK 1882–96

EARLY MINISTRY ALONG THE EAST COAST c. 1882–93

AS noted elsewhere (see pp. 35–7) the early fashioning of the Christian life of South Lanarkshire born James McKendrick took place in an atmosphere of revival, and by his mid-twenties the young man had developed into an evangelist of considerable repute. Steadily developing in his abilities as a preacher, and with a deepening desire to see sinners saved, it wasn't long before McKendrick was conducting outreaches in far-flung areas of Scotland. Invited to help with a mission in the village of Bervie, south of Montrose, the miner-turned-evangelist witnessed a 'gracious outpouring of the Holy Spirit there and many were saved'.[22] Arbroath was next to be visited, resulting in what was considered by one to be 'the greatest awakening ever seen' in the town's history. When Mckendrick came to nearby Gourdon, he regarded it as 'the most spiritually neglected place I have ever known in Scotland'. However, after spending six hours a day in prayer for six full weeks, the place yielded much fruit, including the conversion of a man of ninety-eight years.[23]

The fishing village of Ferryden, near Montrose, had experienced repeated bursts of revival blessing since the first powerful movement rocked the community in 1859–60. In January 1893, however, 'the spiritual tone was low'. The Free Church minister, Rev. Mitchell, was ill and confined to bed so McKendrick's colleague James MacFarlane preached on Sunday morning, making a deep impression on most hearers except the choir, 'who seemed a giddy and frivolous lot'. This was no surprise to McKendrick, who had found choirs to be 'the devil's corner in many a church'. McKendrick preached a vigorous sermon that evening on being 'born again'. At last choir members began to feel the full force of the message applied by God's Spirit for themselves. McKendrick pointed at them as he spoke, and many literally trembled and went pale in the face. 'Tears rolled down many faces, and some sobbed aloud.' The following night 'the best singer in the choir' was among those who became 'truly born again' and 'ere that week closed most of the choir members were saved'. By the middle of the second week 'the whole village was

22. McKendrick, *Seen and Heard*, p. 51.

23. Ibid., pp. 53–61.

awakened', fishing was abandoned and folk came 'from all around to see the mighty power of God'. This was the greatest 'outpouring of the Spirit' McKendrick had witnessed to date and when MacFarlane returned to the village over several successive years he had the joy of seeing most of these converts still walking strong in their faith, although within a number of years some of 'the very choicest' had been drowned at sea.[24]

Revival Tornado – North-East Coast 1893

Introduction

McKENDRICK'S experience in Ferryden proved to be a foretaste of things to come. For it was on subsequent outreaches to the north-east fishing towns and villages that his most abundant harvests were reaped. From the beginning of 1893 till the close of 1896, McKendrick's autobiography turns into a revival chronicle of exceptional adventure, as it relates story after remarkable story of its subject (along with James MacFarlane) presenting the gospel message all along the coast, from the fishing communities of Angus, up around the Aberdeenshire coastline, westward into Banffshire and right along the Moray Firth towards Inverness.[25]

Fraserburgh and Rosehearty

IN Fraserburgh the evangelists held two six-week campaigns, during which local ministers were greatly encouraged at the 'evidences of the mighty saving grace of God'.[26] In nearby Broadsea, 'an unprecedented wave of blessing fell upon that place ... over 100 people were truly converted to God and the character of the place was completely changed.'[27] In Rosehearty, McKendrick's seven-week mission had been preceded by a visit a year previously, when he had felt strongly compelled to deliver a direct message on being 'born again' at the annual Free Church soiree, normally a purely social occasion marked by dressing-up, eating and humorous speeches. Despite the offence his message had caused to many upright citizens, McKendrick felt it helped pave the way for his later success. However, initially attendance was small, so the evangelist spent three hours one day walking through the village sounding a fisherman's boat bell and inviting people to the meetings.

---

24. Ibid., pp. 90–3.

25. For accounts of McKendrick's work in Gardenstown and Crovie, Hopeman and Portessie (1896), see www.scottishrevivals.co.uk.

26. It was said at this time that religious work among the fishing population of Fraserburgh was being carried on by an unusually large army of workers. The 'Fisher Girls Rest' system had recently been extended, and every denomination in town had missionaries catering to the temporal as well as spiritual needs of the fisherfolk (*Buchan Observer*, 25 July 1893).

27. McKendrick, *Seen and Heard*, p. 105.

The conversion of just one local man led to him boldly witnessing to all his relatives. Some of these were converted and in turn earnestly sought the salvation of others. Soon meetings were packed to capacity and a great work commenced. Meetings occasionally went on till 1 or 2 a.m. and even then people had to be asked to leave the hall. Meetings would then continue in folk's homes, where those converted sought to help any anxious soul … 'and the song of praise and the voice of prayer could be heard from many houses at all hours'. A remarkable feature of the work was that a number of prominent elders from various denominations, including the Free Church and UPC, were dramatically converted. Even more striking, over 100 married folk were brought to the Lord, besides about twenty unmarried, most of them over thirty years old and a good number over fifty. 'Our farewell was pathetic, as so many old people bade us goodbye with tears of gratitude running down their faces.' [28]

FINDOCHTY

PERHAPS the highlight of McKendrick's tour occurred in Findochty, then one of the largest fishing villages on the Moray Coast. The community had seen numerous waves of revival power since the season of 'great awakening' in 1860. By the time of McKendrick's visit in 1893 the younger generation were growing careless in their ways, causing older Christians to long for another season of grace. Meetings were initially marked by the earnest and striking prayers of such saints, but no breakthrough came. Unable to sleep one night, McKendrick and his wife made earnest intercession to God to grant Findochty a gracious visitation. The prayer meeting prior to the service the following evening was, noted the evangelist, 'a hallowed season such as I had never before experienced' [29] and sure enough, as he later preached from the stage, the power of God fell upon the audience and several men leapt up, crying aloud in deep conviction. Nine men professed to having found peace that night, including one who had previously left the hall in troubled mind, hoping his anxiety would pass away. Unable to sleep, he saw from his bedroom window that the hall lights were being extinguished. Throwing on his trousers but little else, he rushed back to the building in great distress, and fell full length on the floor before McKendrick. 'Needless to add, God saved him and for several days he seemed like a man under the influence of drink, as he went about the village telling all he met how God had saved him.' [30]

---

28. Ibid., pp. 106–19.
29. Ibid., p. 122.
30. Ibid., p. 124.

All fishing in the village was abandoned, and the only topic of conversation was salvation. Meetings became so overcrowded that for five weeks evening meetings began at 6.30 and continued for two hours. McKendrick then asked everyone to leave so that others might be admitted. A second meeting continued till about 10.30, then all were again asked to leave and a third meeting commenced, which continued till 2.30 the following morning! A custom in the area was for those recently saved to immediately go to their relatives' homes and tell of the good news. As friends united in prayer and praise, they would further rejoice by joining hands and singing a hymn with an upbeat rhythm, tapping their feet as they went. Termed by onlookers the 'Gospel dance', McKendrick found the sight of several hundred in such holy, joyful motion a truly unforgettable experience! [31]

McKendrick marvelled at the intense prayers of one aged woman at a prayer meeting near the start of the mission. From among her many relatives – each of whom she named and about whom she made a few remarks regarding their condition and needs – 'her six sons she went over, one by one, and all the while the big tears rolled down her face.' That woman was overjoyed to see all six sons being converted over the next few weeks. One of them, seeing his friends at the back of the hall, went to them, pleading for them to give in to Christ. One by one, they dropped to their knees, making earnest prayers of surrender. 'This young man had only been saved about four o'clock that afternoon, and by seven he was God's telephone, through whom the Spirit was speaking with irresistible power. He was naturally shy and very retiring, but filled with the Holy Ghost he was bold as a lion.'[32]

One woman, who by her appearance and manner McKendrick had judged 'to be half-witted', pushed her way into one already overcrowded meeting. The evangelist's worry at how she might disrupt the meeting was aborted when, suddenly, she sprang to her feet and pleaded with the people to give themselves to Christ. 'No pen could reproduce the scene,' McKendrick wrote later. 'Heavenly light shone in her face as she said "O Lord Jesus, Ye saved me – I'm born again. … O Lord, dae wi' them aw whit Ye ha'e din wi' me. … Oh, humble me," and suiting the action to her petition, she kept stooping down till her hands touched the floor, saying all the while, "Lord, humble me."' [33]

---

31. Ibid., p. 126. Interestingly, some trace of this practise has continued through the years. As recently as 1959, when a nine-year old boy came to Christ in the Brethren assembly in Portessie, he was first taken to a relative's house where prayer was offered, then to the home of another relative where they sang and rejoiced over his salvation (Sprange, *Kingdom Kids*, p. 228).

32. McKendrick, *Seen and Heard*, pp. 126–7.

33. Ibid., p. 129.

On the other hand there was the local baker, who, on being asked if he had eaten of the 'Bread of life', showed little enthusiasm for the gospel or its workers. This was perhaps not altogether unsurprising, for a result of the revival in the area was that very little food was eaten during the height of the movement, resulting in a worrying slackening of business for the grocer and baker! In summarising, McKendrick described the Findochty revival as one of the 'grandest works of God's grace I have witnessed'.[34]

Two stalwart Christians from Findochty came to help in the mission in Sandend, then a small fishing village with a population of around 350. Meetings were a bit stiff, so most of a whole day was devoted to pleading with God for His blessing, until assurance came. Sure enough, 'the grace of God swept through the small village and Sandend, so long dead and barren, now bore much fruit and blossomed as the rose'. McKendrick estimated that about half the population was converted.[35]

NAIRN

FURTHER west, in Nairn's Seaman's Hall, the spiritual break came with the conversion of a popular local fisherman, Sandy Main. His testimony at the next meeting became the main topic of conversation among the fisherfolk and soon the meeting place was packed out. Then, following the preaching of a businessman from Peterhead, nearly fifty people professed conversion on one night. 'For six weeks the grace and power of God reigned in Nairn' and a feature of the movement was that at least the first fifty converts were men. And not only was the fisher community touched, including the majority of a gang of youths known as the 'Rowdy Band', but also the 'up-town' people. Remarkably, about 500 confessed conversion in the town – 'the greatest wave of blessing my eyes had ever seen,' [36] wrote McKendrick, who received a personal note of thanks from the police for the change that had been effected in the town. Evidence of this change is seen in the following. A theatre group came to Nairn for three weeks each year at this time, always attracting good audiences. This season, however, no more than fifty turned out to the large Town Hall for their opening performance. Attendance decreased to a mere twenty-five the following evening, and the company was forced to abandon show and promptly clear out! [37]

---

34. Ibid., p. 136.

35. Ibid., pp. 137–42. As a result of the revival a Brethren Assembly was formed here the following year (Dickson, *Brethren in Scotland*, p. 121).

36. McKendrick, *Seen and Heard*, p. 150.

37. Ibid., pp. 150–1.

Portknockie

ANOTHER area that witnessed considerable outpouring was the village of Portknockie. Here a small band of men used to gather in a room above Jock Miller's shop to pray that God would send to their village an evangelist through whom blessing would come. One day there was a knock at the door. It was James McKendrick, wanting to hold meetings in the village.[38] This was promptly arranged. During the second week of meetings, 'the spirit of conviction was deep throughout the village, and there was an atmosphere of reverent solemnity everywhere that could be felt'. During an appeal towards the close of a three-hour meeting, a man with a severe facial skin disorder suddenly dropped on his knees, crying for mercy. Minutes later, he raised his head and his diseased face beamed with joy. He had found peace and proceeded to give an emotional testimony in which he shared of his intention the previous evening to take his own life, but he sensed a voice telling him to attend the service the following night. He was so glad he did. By this time it was nearly 11 p.m. so McKendrick felt he should close the meeting, which he did. Suddenly a man stood up crying, 'Oh, praise God, I'm saved!' He stepped on to a seat and with his face shining, appealed strongly to the people to trust in Christ and be saved.[39]

McKendrick continues the story:

> The scene that follows can never be described. ... The Holy Spirit of God seemed just to mow the people down, and in less than 5 minutes over fifty people were on their knees upon the floor, crying to God for mercy. Over 40 of these were men above thirty years of age. As one after another was born again and filled with the Holy Spirit, they literally danced for joy, and there was such a scene of excitement and religious fervour as no words can fitly set forth. I besought every saved person in the place to get outside, form into a procession, and give expression to their new-found joy by singing some hymns and marching through the village. I kept a few of the old and experienced Christians to assist Mr Brown and myself in helping all who were in distress about their soul, and as one after another found peace and forgiveness, they set out and joined the procession. This continued till 2.30 am, but even then many were too excited to go to rest. I have very imperfectly described that night, for it was the night of nights in my career, and in reviewing the extraordinary scenes of which I was an eye-witness on that occasion, I understood as never before how natural it was for ignorant onlookers on

---

38. Personal communication with Rena Mair, a native of Portknockie.

39. McKendrick, pp. 183–8.

> the day of Pentecost to imagine that those men on whom the Spirit descended were filled with wine.[40]

The dramatic sequel is recounted by McKendrick:

> By 6am the boats should have been off to sea, but some had not gone to bed, others for only an hour or two, so that the majority were not anxious for sea, the more so as it was Saturday, and the funeral of a resident was to take place at one o'clock. All turned back, and not a boat went to sea. At 8am a gale burst with almost the suddenness of a gunshot, and had the Portknockie boats been out, most probably not a single one could have escaped. Because of the position and formation of the harbour, not a boat could have entered in the face of such a gale. This was the unanimous verdict of the men, and it found confirmation in the large number of wrecks and loss of life in other parts of the coast. But for the great spiritual blessing in Portknockie on the previous night, the death-roll in the village would have been awful.[41]

CELLARDYKE C. 1897

McKENDRICK also paid visits to the fishing communities of Fife. He arrived in Cellardyke, the county's largest fishing village, about the end of November, just at the time that fishermen were returning from the summer herring season in East Anglia. A terrific gale had got up and at least three vessels from further north had gone down, taking all men on board. But despite some perilous experiences, the *Taeping* of Cellardyke arrived home safely in what seemed little short of a miracle. All this had an astonishing effect on the people and so they came to McKendrick's meetings as a 'prepared people'. The skipper of the *Taeping*, Henry Bett, got soundly converted and immediately got the rest of his crew to attend the services. Within a fortnight six out of the seven had been converted. These earnestly sought the salvation of others, with such effect that daily some were added to the number converted. After five weeks of meetings McKendrick was about to leave on New Year's morning when he was called to pray for a man in deep anxiety. This was the seventh member

---

40. Ibid., pp. 188–90. Alexander Mair, later a missionary to China, was a child living in Portknockie at the time of McKendrick's meetings and he gives the following account: 'Rev. Peter Brown, minister of the FC, sometimes planned for an evangelist to come [these were arranged for the dark winter evenings when fishermen were home from sea]. ... One of my most vivid boyhood memories is of a November evening in 1893, when I was nine years old. I was standing at the door of the church hall, and was amazed to see a crowd of men and women coming down the steps with a joy not of this world on their faces. I knew that something great had happened inside that hall, and later heard that over 40 men (and women as well) had been soundly converted that night, and I watched as they went home to tell their families and neighbours of what the Lord had done for them. There was little sleep in the village that night' (Alexander Mair, *Unforgettable*, London 1966, pp. 10–11).

41. McKendrick, *Seen & Heard*, pp. 189–90. Alex Mair confirms this report (p. 11). This is probably the same non-denominational 'evangelistic effort' referred to in the FC Report of 1895. Around 100 testified to good being received, fifty of whom joined the FC (*RC-FCS-SR&M*, 1895, p. 14).

of the *Taeping* and he was soon 'rejoicing in Christ as his Saviour' and went on to be an able preacher. Returning to the village some years later, McKendrick had the joy of 'seeing my children walking in the faith, and of hearing some of them preaching the good news'.[42]

Spiritual Stirrings 1904–5

RATHER ironically, given the oft-repeated seasons of spiritual blessing which occurred along the north-east coast from the 1860s onwards, there appears very little in the way of records of revival along this stretch for the months immediately preceding and following the dramatic outbreak of revival in Wales in the autumn of 1904, when other parts of Scotland saw notable blessing. One exception was when the Rev. George McLeod of Knock UFC in Lewis took up evangelistic duties in Fraserburgh towards the end of July of that year. 'From the day I entered upon the work till the never-to-be-forgotten 1st August,' he wrote, 'no former experience of mine could come up to the spiritual power felt in all our meetings – whether these were held on Sabbath or week days, in church or in the various rooms. I venture to say it was a time of much blessing to many.'[43] Meanwhile, 'much blessing' also resulted from a three-week mission held in Cullen in the spring of 1905.[44]

Fraserburgh and Peterhead 1910–11

IN 1910, Welsh revivalist Fred Clarke conducted a mission in Fraserburgh, which proved so successful that hundreds sought the Lord in anxiety of soul.[45] Shortly after, in the village of Sandhaven, while Clarke's mission was again fruitful, a deeper soul-saving work broke out after his departure. In Cairnbulg and Inverallochy, too, crowds wept their way to the Cross as interest and conviction increased. So strong were the meetings that Clarke found it almost impossible to close the mission.[46] Although neither Clarke nor any in his audiences could have

42. Ibid., pp. 177–82. McKendrick was a tireless labourer and through the years made no fewer than sixteen trips to the isle of Lewis, six journeys to Shetland and countless visits to villages, towns and cities all over Scotland and England. In 1909 he relocated to Australia, where, relentlessly, he held missions throughout that vast land. Yet nowhere did he see the obvious, outward success that he witnessed in those early years among the fisherfolk of north-east Scotland. Speaking honestly, yet without egotism, towards the end of his earthly labours, the evangelist shared what must help explain his amazing ministry of genuine anointing: 'I have preached on an average 450 times a-year for the last 28 years. Yet I can truly say I have spent more time upon my knees alone before God than I have spent on the platform before men. Fine talk and eloquence in preaching are not always power – indeed, such gifts are ofttimes a hindrance and a snare, and prevent true dependence upon God. A prayerless man must be a powerless man; a prayerful man is a powerful man. … It is this that makes life worth living' (McKendrick, pp. 259–60).

43. *RC-UFCS-H&I*, 1905, p. 17.

44. *TC*, 13 April 1905.

45. Ibid., 2 March 1911.

46. Ibid.

anticipated it at the time, such scenes, though wonderful in themselves, served merely as something of a foretaste of the astonishing events that would unfold in the very same communities and under the very same evangelist, a decade later (see Chapter 7).

Early the following year, 1911, a glorious movement began in Peterhead. Meetings were conducted in the Baptist Church by the powerful soul-winner A.Y. McGregor of Edinburgh, during which time around 300 people professed conversion. The whole town was said to have been stirred by the Spirit, and shortly after, when apologies for absence were reported to the Northern Baptist Association at their rally in Buckie, A.C. Sievewright, Baptist minister at Peterhead since 1909, wrote that he was 'happily prevented from coming' to the convention as he had 300 enquirers to deal with, owing to a revival![47] Sadly, Sievewright was hampered with ill-health and left in 1916 for New Zealand.[48]

OTHER SIGNIFICANT MOVEMENTS IN THIS PERIOD[49]

Moray Coast 1883–8
- Banff, Portknockie, Boyndie, etc 1883
- Fraserburgh, etc 1886
- Cullen, etc 1887–8

Ministry of James McKendrick 1882–96
- Gardenstown & Crovie
- Hopeman
- Portessie

Findochty & Portessie 1903

47. Ibid., 13 April 1911.

48. Yuille, p. 100. It is unclear if this is the same awakening referred to by P.F. Anson when he makes brief mention of a revival along the north-east coast sometime between 1880 and 1920, 'under the direction of the Baptists, who opened "bethels" and meeting-houses of every description in almost all the fishing centres' (Anson, p. 45).

49. Full accounts of these movements can be found on www.scottishrevivals.co.uk.

Findochty – p.200

Bullars O' Buchan – p.202

Peterhead – p.203

John Ross – p.205

James McKendrick – p.206

Ferryden – p.206

Portknockie – p.211

7
Fishermen's Revival [1]
1919–23

Introduction

AS previously noted, it seems remarkable, given the deeply demoralising effects the First World War had on many of the young men drafted into the Forces, that a powerful evangelical revival should rise up in many towns and villages along the east coast of Scotland and East Anglia in its immediate aftermath, causing hundreds of young people to flock to crowded church meetings night after night. It is, of course, significant that a large proportion of those caught up in the revival that spread through fishing communities at this time had not done active service in the war. Fishing was a reserved occupation as fish was a very important source of fresh food, so many fishermen were not called up for military service, although crews were depleted. In any case the bombardment of many British cities, and the dreaded recurrent arrival of news that a relative, friend or neighbour had been killed in action caused many in Britain to seriously consider eternal issues.[2]

---

1. Waves of blessing swept across many parts of the British Isles during the early 1920s. While, in England, the ports of Yarmouth and Lowestoft were particularly moved, awakening seems in fact to have been fairly general throughout East Anglia (see page 224 fn33). Independently of all this, a movement spread through parts of Cornwall and Devon from the spring of 1921 and into 1922, as Dave Matthews, a convert of the Welsh revival, preached to huge audiences (*Christian Herald,* 19 January 1922, p. 46). The 'last flicker of expansion' of modern English Methodism also occurred in the early to mid 1920s. Individual Methodist congregations in Ashburton (Devon), Chesterfield and in an unspecified location were reported in 1920, 1922 and 1923 respectively (Ian M. Randall, *Evangelical Experiences: A Study in the Spirituality of English Evangelicalism 1918–1939,* Carlisle 1999, p. 93).

In south Wales too, a time of awakening began in the Grangetown district of Cardiff as a result of prayer, Lionel Fletcher preaching on Sundays to a congregation of around 3,000. 'Touches of the 1904 revival' were also experienced during a mission in Swansea in the summer of 1921, with 300 publicly accepting Christ, while from New Year's Eve of that year, a 'striking movement of the Spirit' occurred in Newport, the majority of converts of which were married men and women (*TC,* 12 May 1921; 30 June 1921).

Across the Irish Sea, Ulster was already in the throes of 'three years of glorious revival' amidst strong disillusionment over unemployment, mass emigration and deep political turmoil when the abruptly-spoken W.P. Nicholson undertook a mission in his home town of Bangor in October 1920. From here, and from Portadown, Lisburn, Belfast and Newtonards, came a surge of converts, with lasting testimony, and the drawing of comparisons to the great revival of 1859 (Stanley Barnes, *All For Jesus: The Life of W.P. Nicholson,* Belfast 1996, pp. 60–8).

2. John Lowe Duthie suggests that the more 'generalised unease about the post-war world' led to many young converts of the fishermen's revival becoming puritanical in their faith. He mentions the strict intemperance which all converts adhered to, and the fact that 'marriage separations were looked on askance and there were a number of instances where couples were reconciled publicly through being converted' (John Lowe Duthie, 'The Fishermen's Religious Revival', quoted in *History Today,* December 1983).

But the war in fact created another factor that helped promote the spread of evangelism in Britain. Its apocalyptic atmosphere greatly encouraged prophetic speculation. A sharp increase in the popularity of pre-millennialism developed among evangelicals, according to which belief the Second Coming of Christ would be followed by his thousand-year rule with the saints. One of the several pre-millennialist groups that sprang up was the Pilgrim Preachers, formed in 1919. Based on Brethren principles, they conducted evangelistic campaigns throughout Britain, emphasising the Second Coming and the urgency of immediate salvation. Their teaching was especially well received among fishing communities.

Another newly-formed pre-millennialist group was the Advent Testimony and Preparation Movement. On their council sat Douglas Brown, an English Baptist minister who helped fan revival into flame in East Anglia in the summer of 1921. Brown reported to an Advent Testimony meeting that the ingathering of converts was 'largely through the preaching of the truth of the Lord's coming'. On thirty-one consecutive nights he spoke for fifty minutes on the second advent.[3] Similarly, it was said that in the twin villages of Cairnbulg and Inverallochy, 'every sermonette that is preached [by Fred Clarke] to them [the villagers] has as its theme the imminent Second Coming of the Messiah and the end of the world'.[4] This type of understanding took on a more prominent and urgent role among believers, particularly in communities in the north-east of Scotland, where the Brethren, who had long adhered to pre-millennialist views, were already strong. Thus, when churches started engaging in vigorous evangelism in attempt to replenish numbers following losses in membership due to war casualties, they met with a more positive response than might otherwise have been expected.

REVIVAL STIRRINGS 1919–20

WESTRAY

STIRRINGS of revival in post-war Scotland began, not in the fishing ports of the north-east, but further north still – in the remote Orkney island of Westray. With the induction of a new minister, the Rev. Edward Hogg, and following a special three-and-a-half week mission in February to March 1919, 'a gracious work of revival' went on in the island. In this the various fellowships participated, with 'as many as 12 young people on one evening giving their hearts to the Lord'.[5] In the months that

---

3. *TC*, 28 April 1921, quoted in D.W. Bebbington, *Evangelicalism in Modern Britain: A History From The 1730s To the 1980s*, London 1989, p. 193. Interestingly, any emphasis on an imminent Second Coming was completely removed from Brown's 1922 collection of *Revival Addresses*, published by Morgan & Scott (A. Douglas Brown, *Revival Addresses*, London 1922).

4. Duthie, p. 24. Similarly, Jock Troup proclaimed, *'The Second Coming is near. I know it! I can feel it within me.'* (*NE*, 21 December 1921, p. 5).

5. *SBM*, 1919, p. 48. See also BHMSR, 1920, p. 12. The latter report also notes an 'improvement in Sunday school attendance and in some places a quickened interest' during 1919 (p. 9).

followed church leaders knew there was still 'without a doubt a spirit of enquiry among us',[6] so a programme of special outreach to outlying districts and to the nearby isle of Eday was engaged in, resulting in numerous more conversions, including those of several Sunday school pupils. Altogether, well over twenty members were added to the Baptist Church alone in this year.[7]

Yet again the following year there was a movement in Westray's Baptist Church.[8] In September 1920, an 'earnest Christian named Captain Craigie, of Westray' invited the recently-formed Pilgrim Preachers, based in England, to pay a visit to Orkney as well as to Shetland. Ernest Luff, co-founder of the Pilgrims, felt led to promise that they would go, although the team lacked the funds required to pay the boat fares to these northerly isles. At the eleventh hour, as the group arrived in Thurso to depart for Orkney, an unexpected gift reached them, meeting the travel expenses and leaving a margin of just two shillings! In Westray, 'God worked mightily.' The Baptist church was opened to them for a few days' visit. 'At the closing meeting, the power of God was manifested, and some 15 or 20 souls publicly confessed Christ. Fourteen years later we revisited that place, and we were told that the blessing was deep and real. A happy father told us that his two daughters were among those saved at that time.'[9]

COCKENZIE

WELL before the north-east fishermen set sail for East Anglia, there were a number of further instances of spiritual revival in both north-east Scotland and various other parts of the country. One notable example was in the small Lothian fishing port of Cockenzie. Here a special prayer meeting had been held for two months prior to an evangelistic campaign organised by the recently-formed Charlotte Chapel Evangelistic Association in the spring of 1921. Graham Scroggie, minister at Charlotte Chapel, was one who spoke at meetings here.[10] Over 100 professed conversion, including many workers from the nearby coal-mine. Twenty to twenty-five of these men, lives transformed, began to meet at 11 every morning for prayer, and

---

6. Letter from John Craigie (Church Secretary) to Rev. J.B. Frame, 4 November 1919.

7. There was, however, no religious revival in Westray simultaneous with those occurring along the Moray Coast in 1921–2. Tom Rendall makes the general observation that 'Orkney did not participate in the fervent religious revivals that characterised some fishing communities.' He found instead that on many islands, 'religious observance lay happily alongside superstition', except in the case of Westray, where there was 'very little superstition' (Kate Towsey (Ed.), *Orkney and the Sea*, Kirkwall 2002, pp. 111–12).

8. It is not entirely clear whether this time of blessing took place in Westray or in Burra Isle, Shetland, but the evidence suggests Westray.

9. John W. Newton, *The Story of the Pilgrim Preachers and their Tours throughout Britain*, London 1939, pp. 39–40, 120–1.

10. Scroggie longed for God's blessing on his church, but he was said to have 'dampened revival fires' at Keswick in 1922 following passionate addresses given by Douglas Brown (Randall, p. 23).

again in the afternoon when the pits were idle. The pastor of Cockenzie UFC claimed that only two months previously these men would sooner have flown to the moon than attend a prayer meeting! [11]

MORAY COAST

AT the same time, the Methodist Church claimed a 'great revival' in its mission along the Moray coast,[12] where 'from Portgordon to Cullen' a movement was spreading with glowing intensity. The work began in Cullen and moved westward, stirring up much counter attraction, yet also gaining huge attendances in churches and open-air meetings in places like Buckie and Findochty. In Portessie, over 100 decisions were recorded, mainly made by 'sons of the sea', but also including children, one of whom, over sixty years later (Mrs Katherine Young), clearly recalled the occasion of her conversion at age eight, along with that of her eleven-year-old sister.[13]

WICK

SEVERAL visits had been made to Wick in 1919–20 by a small team of holiness Pilgrim Preachers from Wales. Scores of professions of faith had taken place at meetings in the Baptist Church and practically all churches in town shared in accessions to membership.[14] God had begun to move in power in this northerly town. Stepping up Scottish endeavours in 1921,[15] perhaps in anticipation of widespread outbreak of revival, the zealous Pilgrim Preachers returned to Wick in the autumn of 1921, holding open air services at the foot of a cliff near the bridge, from where interested listeners made their way to meetings in the Baptist Church. By this means around fifteen or sixteen people made professions of faith, these events occurring before the return home of high-spirited local fishermen from revival scenes in East Anglia.[16]

PETERHEAD AND FRASERBURGH

HOLDING meetings in Peterhead in the autumn of 1921, a missionary from South Africa sensed such concern for souls among some Christians as he had rarely seen before. Certain that God was going to move in a definite way, the missionary urged Brethren evangelist Alexander Marshall

11. *TC*, 21 April 1921.

12. Ibid., 28 April 1921; *Methodist Recorder*, 14 April 1921, quoted in Sprange, *Kingdom Kids*, p. 287.

13. Sprange, *Kingdom Kids*, p. 287.

14. *SBM*, 1922, p. 17. One man converted during the earliest of these missions was Angus Swanson, a CoS lay-reader in the town. Following his conversion, and after a time spent evangelising with Jock Troup, Swanson resigned his membership of the church. Returning to Wick, he met two Brethren evangelists, and in 1923, along with nine teenagers who had also been influenced by the recent revival, formed a Brethren assembly in the town (Dickson, *Brethren in Scotland*, p. 190).

15. *TC*, 27 January 1921.

16. Jackie Ritchie, *Floods Upon the Dry Ground*, p. 74.

to go and hold meetings in the town. He did so, and after four nights a break came when several came through to a place of peace in Christ.[17] Their testimonies were to long stand the test of time in different parts of the country.[18] After Marshall's departure from the fishing port, the work continued, helped on by David Walker, an evangelist from Aberdeen.[19]

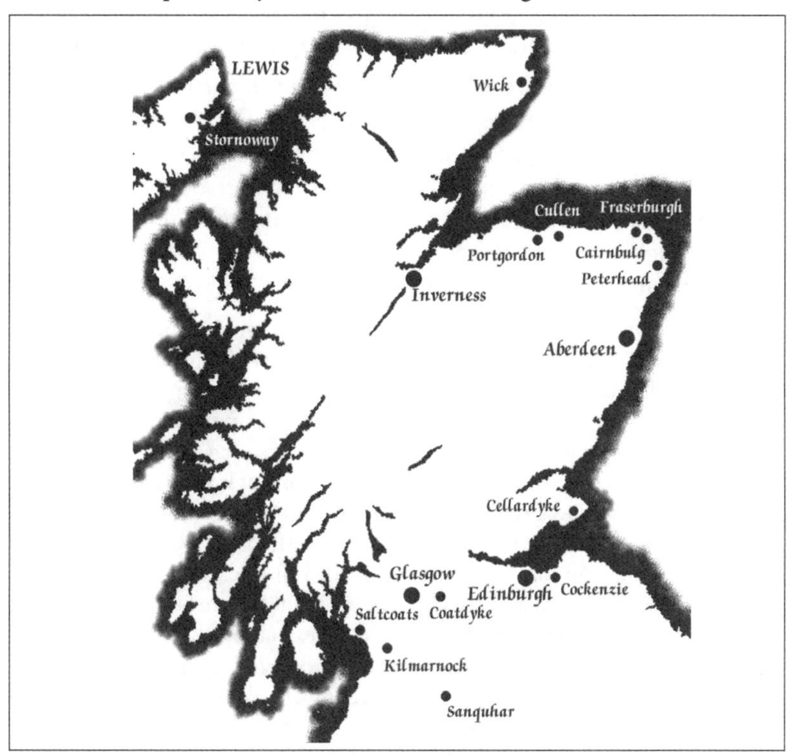

Working in Fraserburgh at the same time was Malcolm MacIver, a divinity student acting as Free Church deputy to the fisherfolk. MacIver's ministry in the town the previous year was so owned by God that some in his denomination considered that the real origin of the whole revival movement that ensued was 'not remote from these earnest and faithful services'.[20] Preaching mainly to the fishergirls, MacIver found so many attending the meetings that they had to remove to a section of the church that was 'in a deplorable condition, and certainly not safe to worship in'.[21] But into such accommodation they poured, with close on

17. Hawthorn, *Alexander Marshall*, p. 138.

18. One of these converts was an aunt of Jackie Ritchie, 'who went to live in St Monace, Fife, where she bore a lovely testimony for Christ during her whole lifetime' (Ritchie, p. 24).

19. Ibid., p. 24.

20. *RC-FCS-RM&T*, 1922, p. 880.

21. Ibid.

200 – almost all Lewis girls – attending the week-night services when work permitted.

MacIver reported: 'From the beginning, we could not but be conscious of the presence of the Eternal One … the new life is so evident in some fifty girls, that, having been brought from darkness into light, they form the most stirring and convincing report that can be given, that this is none other than the work of the Spirit.'[22] MacIver was astounded by the ignorance of Scripture exhibited by one girl in particular. 'She, poor girl, was in such deep distress for many days that some feared she would lose her reason. But the Spirit that convicts comes with comfort, and by Him she was led to the sinners' Friend,' as too, after a time, were many others who had 'wept bitterly, wrestling in agony of soul for the blood of sprinkling'.[23]

Baptist minister W. Gilmour wrote that

> It was in the early autumn when the mellowing influence of sunshine and breeze was bringing to maturity the fruits of the field that the earnest of another – a spiritual – harvest began to appear in Fraserburgh. A certain wistfulness upon the people when the Word was being preached; an increasing readiness to come under the Gospel appeal made the hearts of loyal watchmen eager. Prayer became markedly definite and expectation passed into realisation – surrender to Christ became frequent. Revival was on the way. All this had its full expression in the regular services of our own church and elsewhere in the town. The heralds of this glorious dawn were chiefly young people. Happy in their new-found Saviour they went forth to the streets and lanes and sang His praises. The usual open-air meetings of the fishing season became centres of a deepening spiritual interest also. God gave us the ears of the crowd. All this continued after the fleet left for Yarmouth. The number of the saved was steadily increasing.[24]

Environs of Fraserburgh

MEANWHILE, in the area around Fraserburgh, Welsh pastor Fred Clarke, accompanied by George Bell from Hamilton – 'the boy with the remarkably blue eyes' – conducted meetings in the winter of 1919, and a work that endured many months was begun.[25] In Cairnbulg, Clarke

22. Ibid., p. 881.

23. Ibid.

24. *SBM*, 1921, p. 15.

25. Despite previous visits north of the border, little was known of this 'man of mystery'. Clarke later revealed that his foster father was Major Rev. C.L. Perry, who ran a 'big religious place' in Newport, Wales. The story of Clarke's post-war visit to north-east Scotland began with a mission he had been conducting in Wishaw. His lung began to bleed due to an injury received in France during the War. He instinctively felt he should abort the mission and he moved south to London. Here 'the impression was so deep and so profound that his spirit seemed to demand that he should take the first train to Cairnbulg' (*Glasgow Herald*, 22 December 1921, p. 9).

found that the fishermen had become so materialised through the wartime success that there was very little desire for things spiritual. He persevered, however, and soon around one dozen souls professed salvation. Over a number of months, and continuing even after Clarke left the area, these young believers would meet together for days and nights to pray.[26] They were wonderfully to witness the answers to their prayers when they later became helpers in the larger revival movement that spread throughout the district on Clarke's return to the area in the autumn of 1921, when he led meetings in the same Bulgar Hall he had preached in previously.[27]

After several weeks in his earlier mission with few visible results, the Welshman felt ready to move on to fresh pastures. He continued till the Sunday night in October when the meetings were scheduled to finish. Then one local Christian, a godly man who lived in the 'secret place of the Most High', urged him to stay, claiming God had told him that blessing was going to fall down on the place. From that night on, the villages around Fraserburgh experienced divine favour, and Clarke stayed for four months. Conversions were most evident among the sixteen-to-eighteen age group. When youths from the dance hall next door to the Gospel hall came in to disturb meetings, Clarke spoke over them, claiming them for Christ. As a result, so many were converted that the dance hall had to close.[28] Clarke estimated over 200 conversions in a very short time.[29] One of this number was a young factory girl, whose first prayer included a cry to God to 'save every lass in the factory'. Since that time, colleagues in her workplace began coming to the Lord in ones, twos and threes. On occasion two or three in one family were saved, causing inexpressible joy in the factory. By this time, the Cairnbulg fisherfolk – including scores of new converts – were south at East Anglia, where 'with cries of "Hallelujah", they 'sounded the tooters of their boats and waved their handkerchiefs to one another to tell the gladness'.[30]

By this time also Alex Mair of Portknockie had been appointed Deputy Secretary of the China Inland Mission for Scotland. Part of his job was to organise meetings for missionaries as they came home on furlough. He records:

> In the autumn of 1921, I went to speak at the Seamen's Mission in Fraserburgh; this was carried on by three ladies who were well

26. One of these converts was a young fisher lassie who was used during the later 'times of refreshing' in 1921–2. Afterwards she joined the Faith Mission and sat under the ministry of its founder, J.G. Govan. Jackie Ritchie met her around 1980 when she was an old woman, still with a strong faith and fond memories of those early days of awakening (Ritchie, *Floods Upon the Dry Ground*, p. 21).

27. Ibid., p. 21.

28. Ibid., pp. 21–2.

29. *Glasgow Herald*, 22 December 1921, p. 9.

30. *NE*, 28 December 1921, p. 3.

> known in the town and along the coast. The leader was Miss Gladwell, and it was known locally as the Gladwell Mission. The meeting that night was packed, and the congregation listened with rapt attention as I told them how the Lord was working in China. There was already a spirit of revival in the atmosphere, as telegrams were coming to families throughout Fraserburgh from their people at the English fishing port of Yarmouth saying, 'Thanks God! I'm saved!' Jock Troup was being marvellously used as speaker among the fishermen, and this was to him, as well as to them, something altogether new and unexpected. Shortly after my return to Glasgow I received a letter from Miss Leach, one of the three Mission ladies, informing me that two of the girls on the way home from the Sunday night meeting had been so convicted of sin and their need of the Saviour that they knelt down in the street and there and then gave their hearts to the Lord.[31]

Fishermen's Revival in Scotland 1921–2

'Scottish Revival' in Yarmouth 1921

HERRING fishing being a migratory occupation, in the latter half of September each year at least 700 Scottish drifters (around 7,000 men[32]) would sail from all over Scotland to their autumn base in Lowestoft or Yarmouth in pursuit of the 'silver darlings', while around 3,000 women would travel on specially chartered trains to help with the gutting, pickling and barrel packing. In Lowestoft a revival had begun in London Road Baptist Church in the spring of 1921, following a series of meetings conducted by the Rev. Douglas Brown, a former seaman from South London.[33]

In nearby Yarmouth it was not until October that revival was unleashed in full power. Among the Scottish migrants to East Anglia in 1921 was a young cooper from north Scotland by name of Jock Troup. 1921 was an *annus terribilis* for the Scottish herring industry. The Government had revoked existing subsidies to curers, while a flourishing continental market suddenly dissipated. On top of this, meagre catches of fish in the summer and heavy gales in the autumn left the fishing industry in a state of depression. This had a double effect. It afforded the Scottish fisherfolk in East Anglia plenty of idle hours. The loss of livelihood and hence of financial security also influenced many to turn to God for solace and happiness.

---

31. Mair, *Unforgettable*, p. 48.

32. *MR-UFC* (1921, p. 48) suggests 20,000 men from Scotland.

33. Brown also witnessed an intense spiritual interest in the larger towns of Norwich, Cambridge and, especially, Ipswich.

Taking advantage of increased idle time, especially at weekends when many Scots fishermen refused to sail, Troup began holding open-air meetings. Sometimes for hours on end his booming voice would echo through the market square and beyond. On the third Saturday in October, the Spirit of God moved in power as Jock preached from Isaiah 63:1 and as a young fisherman from Cairnbulg boldly sang out his testimony in song. Scores of men and women were convicted, and many fell to the ground under His might. Over the next few weeks, dozens of men, women and children were brought to their knees in repentance of sins, and many telegrams were sent home to Scotland telling of wonderful stories of conversion.

For a short time in November, both Douglas Brown and Jock Troup worked together in evangelistic outreach in Lowestoft. Towards the close of the month the Scottish 'armada' prepared for the voyage homeward: to fishing ports in Fife, Lothian and Aberdeenshire, or further still to towns and villages along the Moray coast, or to even more northerly ports like Wick, Stornoway and Lerwick.

Fraserburgh

WHILE in Yarmouth, Troup experienced a vision of a man in Fraserburgh asking God to send Troup to his town. Resolving to obey the 'call', he travelled north, taking every opportunity to share the gospel message as he went. It was said that before his train reached Crewe, everyone in his carriage had been converted! Arriving in Fraserburgh in response to the vision he had received, Jock went to the Town Square, where he immediately began preaching. A large crowd gathered around him, but, owing to the rain, they decided to move to the Baptist Church nearby. As they approached, the pastor and his elders were just leaving the building after a specially convened meeting in which they had drafted a letter to send to Troup, whom they believed was still in Lowestoft, urging him to visit Fraserburgh at the first opportunity! Moreover, Jock immediately recognised one elder as the man he had seen in his vision a week or two before.

The town to which Troup had arrived was in a state of economic depression. The herring fishing, both at home and in East Anglia, from where many local fishermen had recently returned, had proved a failure, while a local toolworks had also recently closed down, depriving hundreds of men of a livelihood. A fifth of the town's population was unemployed and about a third of house rents remained unpaid. According to the local newspaper, 'the past year (1921) has been one of the worst experienced in the industrial history of Fraserburgh. … In fact, no community has suffered more from the depression that has afflicted the whole country.'[34]

---

34. *Fraserburgh Herald*, 3 January 1922, p. 3.

Despite, or perhaps partly because of this, people came to the meetings in droves, forcing a move to the larger Congregational Church and eventually to the Parish Church, which seated 1,200. Around 150 people – nearly all men, and the vast majority young – would gather for a two-hour prayer meeting each weekday afternoon in the Baptist Church. Open-air services continued too; indeed meetings were held at one place or another every hour of the day, with prayer sessions lasting till the early hours of the morning. There seemed to be a spirit of conviction everywhere, as if the whole town was in the grip of God's presence. On a number of occasions men and women would literally stagger into the inquiry room, broken and in tears due to conviction of sin. While most converts were from the fishing class, a good number were not. Age-wise, while most were young, several were in their seventies or even eighties. Particular impact was made on the town following the conversion of a notorious gang of fishermen known as the 'Dirty dozen', while, more generally, the town's three cinemas were said to have been empty during the duration of the revival.

The attitude of the churches to the awakening, both in Fraserburgh and elsewhere along the coast, was divided. Generally, the Baptist, Congregational, Methodist, United Free and Free Churches all openly welcomed the movement. In some sections of the Church, however, the revival was regarded as likely to do more harm as a result of its excesses than the permanent good which might remain when the excitement had subsided. Some Presbyterian bodies, particularly the Established Church, had initially been very cautious and even dismissive of the revival,[35] but in time began to promote revival meetings on their own account, in an attempt to carry the movement into channels where they believed most good would be done, and to free it from what they believed were the hectic and extreme features that had become associated with it.

Such attempts did not always meet with success. At one point it was intimated that Douglas Brown, the Baptist minister who had been so successful in Lowestoft, had announced his imminent arrival in the town for a short preaching visit, and this was greatly anticipated by the converts. The Parish Church, being the largest in town, was placed at his disposal and the four Presbyterian ministers invited the Baptist and Congregational ministers, as well as Jock Troup, to join them. Brown's visit was cancelled at the last minute, however, due to illness, and so Troup and company led their own meeting in the Congregational Church, which was packed full, while only a sprinkling turned up to the service conducted by the quartet of Presbyterian ministers, who

35. One Glasgow minister felt that 'if the churches in Fraserburgh at the inception of the movement had been more sympathetic it would have been helpful both to the churches and to the revival movement' (*Glasgow Herald*, 11 January 1922, p. 12).

were rather aggrieved by their colleagues' lack of co-operation, yet who hoped that 'their action would not ... cause a cleavage in the religious life of the community'. [36]

Troup was assisted during his time in Fraserburgh by Willie Bruce, a native of the town and a longstanding friend, having been converted through him five years previously. A former work-mate of Troup's, Bruce was 'a quiet, timid fellow', but his conversion turned this 'quiet,

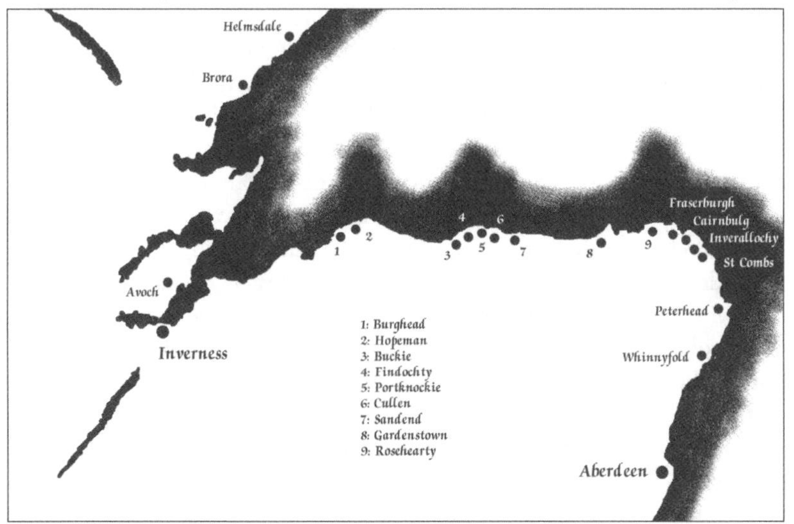

expert dancer and roller skater into a lion'. This, according to Troup, was the reverse of his own conversion experience. Troup had always been 'inspired with wildfire, but God tamed him into a docile creature'. That had been five years previously, and two years elapsed before he was able to utter a word about what had happened. But for the last three years Troup had been doing the Lord's work and claimed he had found a happiness that this world could not give. Another believer referred to Willie Bruce as 'a splendid young fellow, who, by his winning frankness and transparent honesty of purpose, had endeared himself to all, even to the bitterest critics of the evangelical campaign'.[37]

A journalist closely observed those attending a typical evening meeting in Fraserburgh. This took place in the Congregational Church, which was 'filled to its utmost capacity with men and women of the fishing population. The men predominated in number and a large proportion were of the age 25 to 30.[38] Many of them in all probability served in the

36. Ibid., 19 December 1921; 20 December 1921.

37. *Fraserburgh Herald and Northern Counties' Advertiser* (hereafter *FH&NCI*), 27 December 1921, p. 3.

38. At most other meetings, too, men were said to predominate, and it was said that, oftentimes, you never heard a female's voice.

Navy during the war. Older fishermen, with seamed and weather-beaten faces, wearing short blue coats, were also a considerable part of the audience. The remainder was made up of women, young and old. Some had shawls over their heads, and one old woman looked picturesque in a white cap or mutch. The whole gathering sang the Moody and Sankey hymns with great enthusiasm, and with a pleasing harmony. Mr Troup was in the pulpit, along with two ministers and a layman who was taking part in the service'.[39]

Two men greatly influenced by scenes in Fraserburgh were D.P. Thomson, then a student minister, and Alex Mair of the C.I.M. When Mair attended a meeting in Fraserburgh it immediately reminded him of the revival he witnessed as a boy in Portknockie in 1893. The church was crammed, upstairs and down, 'and even the pulpit steps were invaded by young men'. Many poured into meetings like these a full hour before they were due to begin, and they would sing hymn after hymn unguided, until the speaker arrived. Troup preached that night, then invited seekers to the inquiry room. 'There was no undue pressure, but the whole atmosphere was charged with power, and many responded,' noted Mair. As people left meetings, they would 'troop home by street and road, singing their favourite hymns'.[40]

A number of church dignitaries came to witness the revival for themselves. D.P. Thomson spoke of seeing 'Professor Paterson, one of the greatest theologians of his day in Scotland, sitting with tears running down his cheeks, and adds, "I have been in many prayer meetings, both before and since that time, but never in any in which there was an atmosphere and an audience quite like what we sensed and saw there".'[41]

The Baptist Union of Scotland offered aid to any of its churches caught up in the revival.[42] Towards the close of December 1921 Rev. Burns of Edinburgh and Rev. Ashby of Glasgow were sent, with the consent of their own congregations, to assist the Rev. William Gilmour in Fraserburgh. Ashby came for a ten-day visit to the northern port and was rather surprised to find that 'the revival does not meet you when you enter the town. The revival is there, but it must be sought. My first conclusion was that I had come to the scene of a very successful evangelistic mission. I gladly discovered my conclusion was premature and incorrect, for when I visited among the people in their homes, and as I listened to the story

39. *The Scotsman*, 21 December 1921, p. 9.

40. Mair, *Unforgettable*, pp. 49–50.

41. Ibid., p. 50.

42. While a number of congregations took up this offer, those in Peterhead, Buckie and Lossiemouth, though reporting deepening interest and good work, did not feel that special help was required, while the church in Hopeman, owing to the united character of the services being held there, felt it could not at the moment avail itself of the offer.

of sovereign grace, I felt the breath of the Spirit, and saw the grace of God.'[43] It was also noted that converts consisted mainly of 'young men and women from 16 to 26' years of age and that the movement was confined 'almost entirely' to members of the fishing community. Because of this, D.P. Thomson wrote, 'large classes here in Fraserburgh are still critical and in many cases even hostile'.[44] The Rev. George Burnett said that those who felt the revival was due to emotionalism were simply wrong. 'It had taken hold in the most stolid corner of all Scotland. They would find far more emotion at a football match any Saturday afternoon in Glasgow than they would get at the revival meetings.'[45]

A Christian publication wrote of Troup as 'utterly free from self-consciousness and withal wholly surrendered to God'.[46] A secular journalist saw him as 'the personification of the religious zealot. Of sturdy build, with a deep-set and a strong voice, he has the physical strength which enables him to speak for hours every day at the various meetings which he is conducting.[47] ... Gesticulating and perspiring, he denounces the sins of the world, calls upon men to repent before it is too late.'[48] The evangelist never ceased to speak till he became thoroughly exhausted, and sometimes the meetings were very prolonged.[49]

To a journalist from *The Scotsman* who sought an interview with Jock Troup during the course of the evangelist's campaign in Fraserburgh in December 1921, the reply came that he 'would speak no more with an ungodly man'. Eventually he consented to talk briefly with the journalist but he was very uncommunicative and his few short answers were vague. The interviewer noted Troup's 'overwrought appearance', and that such was his intensity that even in private conversation he showed considerable excitement. Shortly 'one of his colleagues, who approached and almost pulled him away, seemed anxious to save the evangelist from over-strain'.[50] In fact, at the beginning of the New Year Troup retired from all meetings, owing to a hoarseness in his throat due to his constant preaching and an abscess resulting from a slight injury to this thigh some nine months previously. He was operated on in Wick Hospital and forced to abstain from involvement in the revival.

---

43. *SBM*, 1922, pp. 15–17.

44. *BW*, 1922, p. 5.

45. *Glasgow Herald*, 13 January 1922, p. 10.

46. *SBM*, 1922, p. 15.

47. In Lowestoft and Yarmouth, Troup would start at six in the morning, praying and preaching for five or six hours on end; then, after a short rest, he would go on again, only finishing late in the evening.

48. *The Scotsman*, 21 December 1921, p. 9.

49. Ibid., 22 December 1921, p. 7.

50. Ibid., 21 December 1921, p. 9.

The Scotsman's 'Special Correspondent' continued to be fascinated with matters relating to the revival. One lengthy report began by noting the origins of the movement in Lowestoft and Yarmouth, where the Scottish fishermen 'came under the influence of a group of evangelists whose effect upon their minds was so strong that when the men came home, far from having forgotten what they had heard, it seemed to have riveted itself still more intensely upon their imaginations'. He had heard some exaggerated stories regarding the revival but was

> of no doubt that this revival is one of phenomenal intensity. … Meetings have been held nightly, not only in halls, but in private homes. Men and women of all ages have attended those meetings and avowed themselves converted by the emotional atmosphere generated at the first gatherings. Men who were never known to possess the gifts of self-expression to any extent have become almost eloquent. Men and women alike have risen up to confess, not only in general terms that they have sinned, but that they have been guilty of specific sins which they state plainly before their assembled neighbours.
>
> Young men between 20 and 25 years of age join in the singing of evangelical hymns in the streets of those villages. The gatherings are sometimes continued all night or far into the morning, for the people have shown themselves highly emotional.
>
> However, there have been no signs on their part of hysterical paroxysm. Old men show themselves affected just as much as the younger members of the population, but observers who have attended meetings assure me that, in spite of the intensity of feeling that prevails, the audiences never become extravagant in the way that has been known during other revivals.
>
> The mood in the villages I have mentioned may be described as one of intense religious emotion tinged with fanaticism. In Fraserburgh and Peterhead, where the revival spirit has taken firm hold of the fishing people, several meetings are being held every night. These gatherings are marked by great enthusiasm, which is wrought to white heat as the evangelists who are the leaders pour out their fervid oratory. Their efforts are now being reinforced by some of the rank and file of the fishing population, who have learned in the course of this revival how to sway the minds of their fellows. All along the coast – at Buckie, at Portgordon, at Findochty – the effects of the revival are being manifested, but its centre alike in regard to intensity and numbers of people concerned is the district of Fraserburgh. [51]

It was said that Troup won 100 converts in his first week in the north Aberdeenshire town, and 400 in five weeks. Soon though, he and Bruce

51. Ibid.

felt a call to go and preach in Dundee, and so a valedictory meeting was held in Fraserburgh's Congregational Church towards the close of December 1921. It was reported that

> at every reference to the departure of the two young evangelists adult men and women sobbed like children, and all the addresses were frequently interrupted by emotional exclamations from the congregation. Every pew was filled to more than twice its ordinary seating accommodation, and it would have been impossible for anyone to go along the aisles without walking over the heads of men and women sitting in the passage ways. Even the steps leading up to the pulpits were occupied, and the porch of the church was crowded. Hundreds of people were unable to obtain admission.[52]

During this remarkable meeting, Bruce stepped to the front of the pulpit and spoke of his conviction that there would be a 'burst' in Dundee and later on a 'burst' all over Scotland. At this stage many members of the audience interrupted with cries of 'Hosanna' and 'Hallelujah', and from different parts of the hall audible prayers were raised. Bruce vocalised his hope that the prophecy he had just made would prove as realistic as the one he made at Yarmouth some weeks earlier, when he declared to Troup, 'Jock, you are not bound for Wick this time, but for the Broch (Fraserburgh). You cannot get away from the call to go there.' Every time they knelt together in prayer, the picture of Fraserburgh somehow came into their vision. The way events had transpired, Bruce suggested, it was now clear to them they had indeed been hearing from the Lord. 'Pray for us every day while we are away,' beseeched the youthful speaker, whose address was frequently punctuated by 'Hallelujahs', 'Amens', and cries of 'Glory be' and 'All hail to you' from the body of the church.[53]

Shortly after, crowds thronged the railway station as the two men departed, weeping tears of joy and sadness, and singing 'God be with you till we meet again'. No one had any idea when that would be because many were aware that Troup and Bruce had expressed a desire to carry their missionary campaign to London, where they wished 'particularly to denounce the lethargy of the Metropolitan clergymen and the "moral faults" in the dress of the young women of the "Modern Babylon"'. There was also speculation that the two evangelists were beginning to sense a call to China. 'They have been telling their most intimate friends that in their prayers they have been shown pictures of Eastern Empires,' and at their farewell meeting in Fraserburgh, Bruce

52. *FH&NCI*, 27 December 1921, p. 3.

53. *The Scotsman*, 21 December 1921, p. 9.

stated off his own bat that indeed he would go to China if the Lord called him there.[54]

Mair states that D.P. Thomson 'and his friend arrived as interested observers, but soon found themselves taking a definite part in what was going on, so that when Jock Troup decided to go south in order to carry the fire elsewhere, they were asked to carry on the meetings, and were greatly used of God'.[55] Mair met Thomson again in 1945 when he came home on furlough from China. 'I happened to mention a certain man who "did not believe in revival", and D.P.'s immediate response was, "Send him to me! For I know of 200 people at least who went out as missionaries or entered the ministry at home as a direct result of the revival in Fraserburgh!"'[56]

CAIRNBULG, INVERALLOCHY AND ST COMBS

THE nearby twin villages of Cairnbulg and Inverallochy were centres of the movement from the start, strong religious excitement reaching almost a 'fever pitch' on the return of converted fishermen from East Anglia to a district already in the throes of revival through the preaching of Fred Clarke. Amazingly, out of a population of 1,500, it was estimated that around 600 professions of faith were recorded in a fortnight. Early morning prayer meetings were begun each Sunday from 6.30 to 9.30 a.m. in a net loft above a warehouse near the harbour. Ages ranged from mid-teens to about sixty, and the spirit of prayer evidenced there was potent. On Sunday afternoons, open-air services would attract almost the whole village, while large numbers also attended baptisms in the 'Water froth' burn near Cairnbulg Castle.

Clarke and his assistant George Bell were still active in the area. Clarke was described as an awe-inspiring figure wearing 'full clerical garb ... very like the costume of a Jesuit priest [with] the eyes of a mystic'.[57] An Aberdeen newspaper, describing one of his meetings in the neighbourhood, compared him to 'a heavy tragedian seeking to get a grip of his audience without delay. ... Without saying a word he raised his right arm and everyone in the hall, even those in the street, knelt down and prayed. ... Within a minute sounds of sobbing came from every part of the hall, and a woman's voice shrilled, "O Lord, forgive and forget." After a few minutes the congregation rose one by one to their feet and

54. Ibid. Troup spoke of a further visionary experience where the power of the Lord suddenly overcame him and he was told that Banff was the next to be drenched with revival showers (*NE*, 21 December 1921, p. 6). In fact, while Banff, like most other towns on the coast, did share in this awakening (services in its Methodist Church for example, 'eclipsed all previous standards'), it was not touched as powerfully as nearby communities.

55. Ibid.

56. Mair, *Unforgettable*, p. 51.

57. Duthie, p. 24.

in ever swelling tones sang the hymn "At the Cross, where I first saw the Light." Then came a perfect tornado of unsurpassed prayer, the voices so mingled that only here and there could the words be distinguished.'[58]

Other scenes were equally unforgettable – seventeen boys and girls kneeling in prayer in a circle in the middle of the street, a recurring phrase being, 'O God, save mammy and daddy.'[59] Or 200 fishermen by their boats at the harbour, listening as biblical parables were read to them. 'After each explanation, the men knelt down together on the shore and engaged silently in prayer, wringing their hands and swaying their bodies to and fro.'[60]

Intense emotion and a certain extravagance were more evident in this area than other ports, enhanced by the strongly millennialist teaching of Clarke. Constantly emphasising his conviction regarding the imminent Second Coming of Christ, Clarke urged his listeners at every opportunity to turn their backs on things of this world, as nothing could be held on to but their souls. A number of villagers made active disposal of dubious possessions by holding a bonfire on 17 December 1921, on which they burned cigarettes, pipes, tobacco, playing cards, dancing shoes and children's board games such as ludo and tiddley-winks, then knelt around the fire singing and praying. It was incredulously reported that some converts 'have been purchasing night-lights and sitting up in groups keeping vigil in anticipation of the great consummation of all things,'[61] and that some fishermen would not venture to sea in case they were separated from their families on the Day of Judgment. Some men withdrew the insurance of their fishing boats on the grounds that a shipwreck might be God's will and it was not for men to interfere with God's providence, while others gave up trade union membership in the belief that only an alliance with God was important.

Some locals lamented that even highly popular pastimes such as football and golf were 'having to take a back seat', as players and supporters abandoned these activities in favour of revival meetings. A reporter for the *Fraserburgh Herald* wrote that the Inverallochy Golf Club was a 'flourishing body till this upheaval made itself felt'. Just a few years previously the local team had travelled to London to play against a team from the House of Commons, and the fishermen had returned home with presentation clubs received from Mr Balfour M.P. and other distinguished politicians. This had all caused a great sensation in the community. 'After last year's large membership, and the enthusiasm manifested in the game, the prospects for the present year looked bright.'

58. Ibid.

59. *FH&NCI*, 27 December 1921, p. 3.

60. Duthie, p. 24.

61. Ibid., p. 26.

But all that had come to a standstill, for the present at least. This was true, not just of golf and football, but of 'all other games and pastimes. Nothing is thought about nor spoken about but spiritual things, and meetings are held all day long either in the open air or in the village halls.'[62]

One visitor described a visit to Inverallochy, where he made the acquaintance of a local minister, who, he said, was a very remarkable man, one of their most learned scholars, a man who got secret information from German camps during the war from the military authorities, and a good evangelical preacher. The minister took him to visit some of the youthful converts. There was one who was mending his fishing nets, and who came in to retell him his spiritual experiences, a 'splendid fellow of 17 or 18'. This youth told him that in the old days he used to spend most of the Sunday playing cards on the links or in a boathouse. He went down last year to Yarmouth meaning to be, as he said himself, 'as coarse as the worst o' them'. He said that after a fortnight of spiritual conflict he made the momentous decision, and now all his delight was in the Lord and in passing on the good news to his companions. He opened his Bible at Psalm 40, and he said that this was his psalm: 'He took me from a fearful pit, and from the miry clay, And on a rock He set my feet, establishing my way.'[63]

Every Sunday about 1,000 people could be seen marching between Cairnbulg, Inverallochy and St Combs, two miles east of Inverallochy, the processions being led by standard bearers and drummers. The UFC minister of Rathen, which parish included the three above-mentioned villages, reported an increased attendance at services, and that, since October 1921, he had conducted a fortnightly prayer meeting in the hall at St Combs with an attendance which grew from 60 to 100.[64] The *Fraserburgh Herald* stated that 'the revival in St. Combs has been attended by an (unspecified) occurrence which has cast a shadow over the district'.[65] Meanwhile, D.P. Thomson also led two meetings in St Combs; 'at the second we had nearly 150 adults on a week-day afternoon,' accompanied by 'real blessing'.[66] Remarkably, in the Fraserburgh area, including the communities of Cairnbulg, Inverallochy and others, over 700 people professed conversion and were brought into the Salvation Army alone.[67]

It was said that just a few miles inland from revival scenes in coastal communities, no trace of the spiritual movement could be found.

62. *FH&NCI*, 20 December 1921, pp. 1, 4.

63. *The Scotsman*, 5 January 1922, p. 7. The quotation is from the Scottish Psalmody.

64. *RHM&CEC-UFCS*, 1922, p. 36.

65. *The Scotsman*, 27 December 1921.

66. *BW*, 1922, p. 5.

67. *The Scotsman*, 24 December 1921, p. 11.

Around the end of January 1922, the UFC Presbytery of Deer asked all its ministers whether revival had touched their parishes. The answers from ten districts were of a negative character, very definitely so in the majority of cases, though less definitely in a few, where, although the movement had not yet extended to their district, many people were nevertheless much interested in it. Only in five parishes was there definite information regarding the spiritual movement (Rosehearty, Rathen, Peterhead and two congregations in Fraserburgh). The report concluded that the revival was 'very partial' and was 'confined to the coast towns and villages and to the fishing population in them, and that places only a mile or two distant were wholly unaffected'.[68] Thus, for example, although David Cordiner addressed several public meetings in New Pitsligo, just ten miles from Fraserburgh, a local minister had 'not heard of any result' other than that 'the roughs were out in full force and their behaviour was disgraceful'.[69] While this was true of many places, a number of other inland towns near to the coast did share in the spiritual blessing, albeit to a lesser degree. For example, special meetings were held among the UFC in Elgin, six miles inland from Lossiemouth.[70] Elgin's Congregational minister, David Dale, also spoke at length and in glowing terms to his congregation of the revival scenes he had witnessed on special visits to Fraserburgh and Hopeman.[71]

Sandhaven, Rosehearty and Gardenstown

THE villages immediately to the west of Fraserburgh did not experience the Spirit's touch so intensely as those already referred to. Yet when Faith Mission Pilgrims visited Sandhaven in January 1922, at least 'one remarkable meeting took place, when God the Holy Spirit worked Himself directly, and we felt we must keep our hands off. No message was needed, we were truly on "holy ground", and before half the meeting was over, several souls yielded to the pleadings of the Lord.' Following blessed times here and in nearby Rosehearty, the Pilgrims had 'a week of definite believing prayer with the Christians, most of whom were new-born babes in Christ'.[72]

In Rosehearty, revival meetings were carried on from November to December 1921 in the UFC hall while a Sunday morning fellowship meeting was also started, being followed occasionally in the afternoon by a largely attended open-air service at the Harbour Head. Yet it was not until Febuary 1922 that the UFC minister could report that 'the revival

68. *FH&NCI*, 14 February 1922, p. 4.

69. *The Scotsman*, 24 December 1921, p. 11.

70. *RHM&CEC-UFCS*, 1922, p. 36.

71. *Moray & Nairn Express*, 24 December 1921, p. 6.

72. *BW*, 1922, p. 211.

has just touched us'. The meetings, he said, were 'quiet and useful. The great result has been a keener and more general interest in what the Church stands for.'[73]

In the small village of Gardenstown, a few miles further west, wise Christian men who had known the power of God in their lives for many years gathered the young converts together for fellowship in the middle storey of a building known as 'Castle Grant'. Owned by a local fisherman known as 'Fish Francie', and used mainly as a net store, converts and sinners would sit on herring nets, eagerly drinking in the Word of Truth. The many conversions had a profound impact on the village and surrounding district, and it was not uncommon to hear from the street the sound of families in their homes singing out their thanks to God, accompanied by the family organ.

FINDOCHTY,[74] PORTKNOCKIE, CULLEN AND BUCKIE

FROM the three close-knit communities of Cullen, Portknockie and Findochty, whole families were converted while at the East Anglia fishing. Thankfully there were many seasoned Christians from these ports to encourage and direct them on their new path when they returned home, some of these having been fashioned during previous revival movements along the Moray Coast. Nevertheless, when the fishing boats set sail for East Anglia in the autumn of 1921, those attending church at Findochty that Sunday seemed to be sparse in number. Noting the spiritual apathy in the region, a Salvation Army Officer, along with a young mother and her daughter, were walking home from a Sunday service in September, when they suddenly stopped, and, falling down on their knees, cried out to God to do something to ameliorate the situation. Assured that God was about to work mightily they continued on their way, little realising that the following week, letters and telegrams would arrive home telling of amazing conversions in Yarmouth, including those of some of the most notorious characters from their home communities. There were spontaneous conversions at home too, so that by the following Sunday, attendance at church was noticeably improved.

On the return of the fishermen, the Salvation Army continued for many weeks to 'proclaim nightly the story of the Cross'.[75] On the first night the Corps and converts marched through the village, stirring up a sense of deep expectancy, following which souls at once began to

---

73. *FH&NCI*, 20 December 1921; 14 February 1922, p. 4.

74. Findochty, which crops up repeatedly in the revival history of Scotland, was well known for the high level of church attendance among its inhabitants. At one point there were no fewer than twelve different religious denominations in the village (Robert Smith, *One Foot In The Sea*, Edinburgh 1991, p. 79).

75. *Glasgow Herald*, 2 January 1922, p. 9.

surrender. Great rejoicing took place over penitents between November 17th and December 13th.[76] Other churches were equally active – A. Cameron, a young Findochty minister, could be found 'proclaiming the evangel night and day'. All this had 'graven a deep impress on the spiritual life of the community', bringing to many a heart 'the vision that time can never erase'.[77] As the harvest continued in abundance, groups of newly saved souls travelled to nearby villages to preach the gospel, with remarkable results. Even before the close of 1921 the Salvation Army had claimed 107 adult conversions, including seventeen who were married, and ten young people.

An evangelist by name of the Rev. Fourness J. Carr came to Portknockie in 1921 and held a mission in the Church of Christ. Sixty-three conversions were recorded.[78] In nearby Cullen, a group of girls was led to the Lord, and these were told to go home and ask their mothers to hold them in prayer. Heart-stricken, one mother's response was, 'My quinie (wee girl), I canna' pray for masel' yet!' Next day, an open-air meeting took place almost right outside this woman's house; she left her washtub, arms full of soap-suds, and, standing in the ring with uplifted hands, cried, 'I want you all to know I accept Jesus Christ as my Saviour!'[79] Her testimony electrified the town and a soul-saving work began. A few months later, a Salvation Army Captain and others were appointed to the town. At their first open-air service, eighty stepped forward [for salvation]. The town was buzzing with spiritual activity, as no fewer than twenty-six meetings were held indoors or out through the week. Indeed, the main difficulty these workers faced was that everybody already seemed to be saved! [80]

The revival also extended to Buckie, a few miles west of Findochty. J.R. Reid, minister of the Wesleyan Methodist Church, had devoted 'all his energies to soul-saving effort in church and open-air' and reported that over 300 people had been converted since the spring of 1921. Of these he further claimed that by mid-January 1922 'two thirds were still standing loyal and true'.[81] The only church they had failed to touch by the end of 1921 they were successful in touching within a fortnight of the New Year, when many women were among the number converted.

---

76. *War Cry*, 31 December 1921, p. 6.

77. Ibid.

78. Interestingly Carr returned to Portnockie in 1964, some forty-three years after his first visit, but there was no move of the Spirit at that time (personal communication with Rena Mair, whose father, Joseph Mair, was a convert of the 1921–2 fishermen's revival, going on to become an earnest evangelist in the north-east).

79. The Salvation Army played an active role in the revival, as, too, did the Brethren. It was said that in a few short years the chief evidence of revival having taken place was 'the number of meeting houses and "bethels" of the rival sects of the Brethren which have sprung up in nearly all the villages affected by this strange movement' (Anson, pp. 46–7).

80. *The Scotsman*, 24 December 1921, p. 11.

81. *Christian Herald & Sign of Our Times*, 26 January 1922, p. 66.

HOPEMAN AND BURGHEAD

BOATS from Burghead and Hopeman displayed the 'Inv' registration to represent the nearby town of Inverness, as too did those from Black Isle ports such as Avoch. In each of these places, a genuine work of grace took place. Special evangelistic services began in Hopeman on 27 November, and that evening some eight or nine people stayed behind and professed Christ as Saviour. 'And so,' writes the UFC minister, 'night by night, save Saturdays, the movement went on for six weeks with similar results; until in January, the second week, we added 169 to the membership of the congregation. It meant a gathering of 400 to 500 people right on to the end nightly; on Sabbaths of 600 to 700 people.'[82] Here the Baptist and UFC ministers stood jointly at the forefront of the movement.

In nearby Burghead, James Henry, the local Free Church minister, had exercised a faithful ministry since his induction in 1906, but he bemoaned the want of people being saved. As he attended the Saturday prayer meeting of the October sacrament in 1921 along with Rev. MacKenzie, the visiting minister from Nairn, Henry felt quite oppressed by the dearth of new witnesses. Suddenly a form stepped forward in the dark passageway next to the vestry. It was a young man, Alexander Tomlie, who wished to publicly proclaim his love to Christ on the Communion Sabbath. He was received and later went into the ministry (serving as pastor in Kirkcaldy and Lybster from 1937 to 1955). Thus began a considerable stirring among the dry bones in Burghead, and also in Yarmouth, where some local fishermen were deeply touched in November. The Kirk Session minutes record that so many men and women were converted that an additional Communion was held in December. Those present at the preparatory services remember how Henry wept tears of joy as he welcomed more than ninety first-time members into the church.[83] The minister was further delighted to see a father and son, neither of whom used to attend the prayer meetings, both attending and leading in public. One manifestation of the awakening was the relinquishing of dancing and other 'worldly amusements'. The local policeman told Henry that the public houses in town were practically deserted. The same was true in Hopeman. Publicans were to be found standing at the doors of their establishments looking for customers.[84]

ROSS-SHIRE AND SUTHERLAND

IN Avoch the lives of some of the most 'careless fellows' in the district were transformed as the result of a mission carried on largely by the fishermen

82. Anson, pp. 46–75.

83. Rev. John Keddie in *The Monthly Record*, 1993, pp. 56–7.

84. *MR-FCS*, 1922, p. 105. The marked decrease in public house trade was not confined to Hopeman and Burghead. The FC rejoiced that 'the licensed houses and places of entertainment in all the areas affected are having a very bad time, for they are banned by the fishermen' (ibid., 1922, p. 3).

themselves, aided by a Faith Mission campaign in March '22. Altogether, around forty individuals were brought to Christ, the Congregational work being supervised by the Rev. Thomas Kerr, who had also served as minister during the even deeper movement of 1906 (see page 138). The 'marked increase in sobriety in the district' was largely attributed to the revival. The UFC further boasted that 90% of its members, as well as 90% of the young people belonging to the congregation, now attended services regularly.[85] Cromarty and Knockbain also tasted of the awakening.[86] Meanwhile, an Free Church Report in 1924 indicated that a steady but quiet work of grace was evident in the 'west coast of Ross-shire, but the paucity of reports makes accurate summary an impossibility'.[87]

Further north in Sutherland, a work began in Helmsdale 'very early' in the course of the overall revival movement.[88] Converts led services there over the New Year of 1921–2 and when Jock Troup came to preach in the village, meetings in both the Fishermen's Hall and the UFC were filled to overflowing. Zealous converts were eager to share the good news in outlying districts. Brora became deeply affected. The UFC minister reported that 'for ten weeks now the work has been going on here steadily and increasingly. During that time we have had meetings practically every night. I was almost done out when Mr Dowie (the rural evangelist), I believe directed by God, came to help. At almost every meeting we have definite decisions for Christ, some nights as many as 30, some as few as two.' (One of these nights was described by one leader as 'the greatest victory and triumph for the Gospel ever seen in Brora'.[89]) 'The whole community, including the surrounding hamlets, has been affected; and every class in the community – servant girls, shop girls, clerks, fisher people and miners and students. Brora has a heterogeneous population and the revival has not singled out any particular class.'[90]

The revival had affected all churches in the district – Parish, Free and United Free – while local officers of the Salvation Army had also co-operated, having been given use of the Parish Church. Indeed, a growing spirit of unity and harmony was notable, and joint services between the Free and United Free Churches took place on Sabbath nights after the ordinary services. The minister of the UFC wrote: 'Another notable feature of the revival here is the complete lack of excitement. Practically in every case the decision is deliberate. Some come forward to the vestry while we sing the closing hymn, some come back to the vestry after the service

85. Avoch UFC Minutes, 1922.

86. *RHM&CEC-UFCS*, 1922, p. 32.

87. *RC-FCS-RM&T*, 1924, pp. 1329–30.

88. *Glasgow Herald*, 13 January 1922, p. 10.

89. *RHM&CEC-UFCS*, 1922, p. 33.

90. Ibid., p. 35.

is over, and some come to the manse to tell that they have decided for Christ; something altogether new in a Highland congregation.' A special Communion was held in the UFC on Easter Sunday to commemorate the work of grace that had occurred among them. The minister said that although he could not fully explain what was happening in their midst, he fully believed it was totally the work of God's Spirit, and as such he disclaimed any credit for its success, asking that his name be omitted from any reference to events in the community. As far as he was concerned, all he had done was that, 'with the help of a few of our praying people I opened the door of our church at the beginning of the year and have tried to keep it open since then, and the work has gone on increasingly week by week'.[91] Altogether, it was estimated that over 200 openly decided for the Lord in just ten weeks. Months later, when Rev. MacKay spent two weeks in the locality, he observed that the spiritual temperature of the place was still high. 'A good section of the young men confessed Christ publicly. … There seems to be an awakening among the people. The prayer meeting in both languages is well attended.'[92]

Peterhead and Whinnyfold

IN Peterhead the work was largely led by Davie Cordiner. A local man, Cordiner had been saved at the age of thirteen but his spirit had grown cold during the war years, when he served as a corporal of cooks. Being personally revived in East Anglia in 1921 while engaged as cook on the drifter *Energy*, Cordiner felt a definite commission by God to become a leader of the movement on his return to Peterhead. Rejecting the discouragement of the ship's mate and that of his mother back home, both of whom informed him that he was far too quiet a man to speak publicly, Davie was yet strengthened by his mother's prayers as he boldly took his stand at the town's Broadgate. On the second night, he was accompanied by several other young converts and a few lads from the Salvation Army, to which he also belonged, and soon a crowd of 200 was spellbound as they listened to the message of God's power to save. Cordiner, who was not as forceful a preacher nor as striking a personality as Jock Troup, identified closely with his fellow townsfolk, and appealed to them in their native Doric tongue. After two hours in the open-air the crowd adjourned to the Salvation Army Hall, where so many came forward in answer to the appeal that the inquiry room was said to have been packed full and extra space had to be found to accommodate the additional seekers who came forward.

91. *RC-UFCS-H&I*, 1922, p. 18.
92. *RC-FCS-H&I*, 1923, p. 1083.

Scores of Peterhead fishermen had been converted in Yarmouth, and these wholeheartedly engaged in the work as soon as they arrived back home. For six weeks open-air meetings continued every night, being followed by a march of witness through the town, in which well-known gospel songs were triumphantly sung. On one evening the dense crowd blocked several streets and the police were called to assist. On another rainy night when the appeal was made no one came forward to kneel in the centre of the open-air ring. Davie took off his coat and laid it on the wet, muddy ground, other helpers following suit. Such act of sacrifice proved to be propitious. Around ninety people had knelt in profession of Christ before the evening was through.

While the work was not as powerful as in the Fraserburgh area, hundreds made profession of faith. Cordiner took every opportunity to witness, even at the local Labour Exchange where many gathered daily, but he noticed that the fisherfolk were much more receptive to the gospel than the townspeople generally. An evidence of this was the testimony of one correspondent, who, casually strolling through town, observed a group of half-a-dozen young fishermen singing 'Will your anchor hold?' while accompanied by a colleague on a mouth organ. They were not holding a meeting, but simply giving vent to their new-found joy. Cordiner himself rejoiced that 'they canna get the dancing halls open in Peterheid,' while another thought it 'far better tae stan' here speakin' for the Lord than tae go hame every Saiterday nicht [from the dancing] wi' yer shirt soakin' for the devil'.[93]

At the point of Cruden Bay on the east Aberdeenshire coast lies the tiny isolated village of Whinnyfold. There was no church here so believers had to walk to Cruden Bay every Sabbath morning to attend the service there. Davie Walker, an evangelist from Aberdeen, arrived in the village in January 1922 at the invitation of a young believer. Meetings were held in a Christian home, which soon got crowded to the point that every room in the house was packed. Relocation was made to the village hall and here, one Sunday, a meeting was in progress. A group of young men were hanging around outside on return from a leisurely walk to Port Errol. One woman coming out from the hall noticed her son fooling around with his friends, and went over to reprove him, suggesting he should be at the meeting hearing how to get saved. At once, the whole group made for the hall where each lad was gripped by conviction. They all made genuine profession of faith, and each went on to spend his life for Christ.

General Impressions

IT was noted by some church leaders who came to observe the revival that there was no organisation for the continued shepherding of

93. *War Cry*, 31 December 1921, p. 6.

those who professed conversion, and that it was difficult to procure information as to the number of professed converts and the permanence of the impression made upon them.[94] Another criticism was that the revival led to cases of insanity among followers. Captain Rohu of the Salvation Army said there had only been four such instances and he condemned the exaggerations that had found vent in certain quarters regarding them. Two of the individual cases known to Rohu were, he claimed, mentally weak prior to the revival. The third was one whose life of dreadful sin before his conversion contributed directly to his mental breakdown, and the last case was one in which the person had suffered previously, and was still suffering from spinal trouble.[95]

The Scottish Press showed an interest in the revival from its early days. The *Daily Record* quoted a French psychologist as saying that the cause of the movement was unemployment. 'This hurricane of enthusiasm now sweeping over these communities will – as in the case of the Welsh revival – collapse when the workers are again merged in their daily toil.'[96] This negative attitude largely changed after the UFC and Baptist denominations sent Commissions of Inquiry to several of the main revival centres and published their predominantly positive reports.

Revivalists seemed desperate to extend the revival to the east coast cities of Aberdeen,[97] Edinburgh and Dundee. Evangelists visiting these cities, as well as Glasgow further west, boldly told audiences of their conviction that revival was coming to each place.[98] In Edinburgh, a sense of spiritual quickening was felt in Carrubber's Close Mission, where Clarke spoke in December 1921, but also in churches where no revival meetings were held. Crowded Sunday evening gospel services led by Graham Scroggie in Charlotte Baptist Chapel in early 1922 regularly saw the Lord 'present in mighty wonder-working power.'[99] Yet while

94. *The Scotsman*, 23 December 1921, p. 6.

95. Ibid., 24 December 1921, p. 11.

96. Which theory the Rev. Dale of Elgin felt was 'inadequate and fallacious.' If unemployment was the cause of religious revival, he posed, then the churches would have been thronged months ago, for unemployment was no new thing in Scotland. Furthermore, he stated, 'lack of work produces depression instead of elation...Again, idleness does not produce moral reform, but, on the contrary, moral degradation' (*Moray and Nairn Express*, 24 December 1921, p. 6).

97. As early as the first part of 1921, spiritual interest was aroused in the *Granite City*, as thousands attended evangelistic missions. Irish evangelist Tom Rea had to prolong his stay due to marked expressions of 'Christian singing, weeping, praying' (Dickson, *Brethren in Scotland*, p. 191). Also in regard to 1921, George Yuille notes the occurrence of a revival in Gilcomston Park Baptist Church, under the ministry of Rev. Gibb (Yuille, *Baptists in Scotland*, p. 90). It is unclear, however, whether this movement occurred before or after the start of the revival among the fishermen. It is surprising to observe, not that this populous city as a whole remained unaffected by the revival in progress in nearby northern ports, but that its close-knit fishing community of Footdee, with its remarkable legacy of revivalism, does not feature in revival accounts.

98. e.g., Fred Clarke prophesied that the 'greatest revival since Pentecost' was about to sweep across Britain (*The Scotsman*, 23 December 1921, p. 6).

99. Balfour, *Revival in Rose Street*, p. 169.

there were evidences of first fruits in one or two east coast city districts, and considerable excitement at meetings where revivalists preached, no golden harvest appeared in any of these cities, generally.[100]

Angus and Fife

ALSO in January 1922, Davie Cordiner made visits to coastal towns like Montrose and Arbroath, where genuine blessing was recorded.[101] Revival also touched the attractive fishing villages of south Fife, where, to Cellardyke, Anstruther, Pittenweem and St Monans, fishermen returned from East Anglia with the joys of new spiritual life. In St Monans, while some of these men joined the Congregational Church, others established links with the Brethren, and a new assembly was formed in 1924.

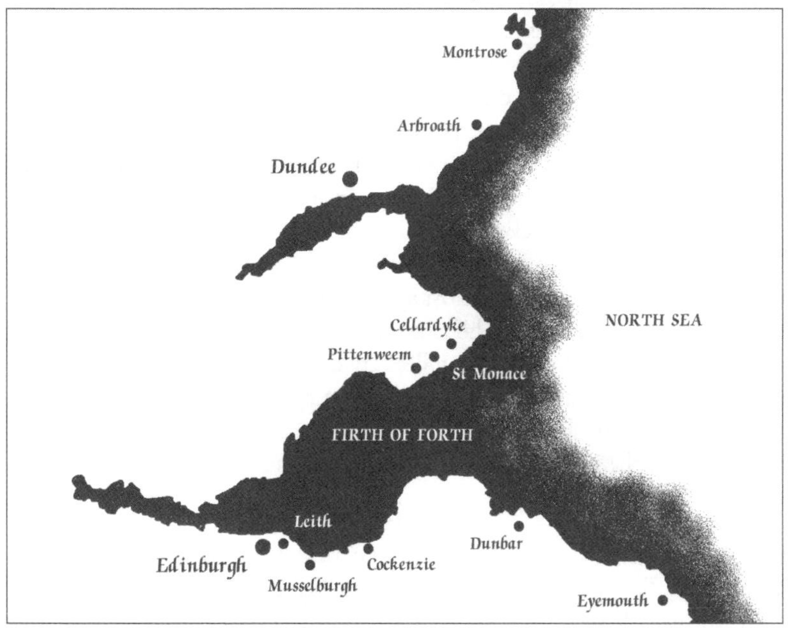

When the fishermen of Pittenweem returned home from East Anglia they immediately started evangelistic meetings each night in the local Baptist church hall. The local ministers were neither consulted nor asked to assist and at first they held aloof from the movement. However, a Baptist mission under the care of the Rev. J.B. Frame had been pre-arranged to synchronise with the return of the fishermen from England

100. On the contrary, strong criticism of revivalists in general came from some city ministers. Rev. W. Major Scott preached in Dundee's Ward Chapel at the same time as Troup and co. were speaking elsewhere in the city. In a hard-hitting address, Scott exclaimed that 'saviours of society must not be confused with professional revivalists, who too often were ignorant of nearly everything except the art of working upon the emotions of a crowd of people…The out-growth of such unhealthy emotionalism had no genuine connection with religion at all' (*The Scotsman*, 27 December 1921, p. 3).

101. I have, however, been unable to uncover any specific report of revival in Ferryden, that most spiritually favoured of locations during the latter half of the nineteenth century, during this period.

and the evangelist arrived to find the movement in full swing. The Baptist cause alone collected the names of 76 people who professed conversion during just one month, while 'there are still indications of deep anxiety in the hearts of others'.[102] A seven-year-old girl from the village came home from school one November day to find her mother crying. Thankfully, they were tears of joy, as she had just received a letter from her husband in Yarmouth testifying to his recent conversion. Sixty years later, this delightful scene was still firmly impressed on the daughter's memory.[103]

Meanwhile the Cellardyke men later followed suit with similar gatherings in the reading room of their local Town Hall. Hearing of the blessing on the town, two male Faith Mission Pilgrims came to continue the work in the village after the men left for the herring fishing in January 1922. For three months the meetings continued. As in Pittenweem, the local ministers held aloof to begin with but were gradually drawn in, and all of them were on the platform at the final meeting. At the May Communion in one Presbyterian Church, around forty young men and women were accepted as members and became the backbone of every department for the next thirty years or more.[104] A Faith Mission prayer group, led by Belle Patrick (see pp. 137–8) with no regular help, also grew during this period from six to sixty in number. In addition, a children's meeting, which had arisen almost spontaneously some weeks previously, grew in leaps and bounds. The reading room where they met could hold about eighty to 100 adults, but Belle had 200 children's names on her register, with an average attendance of about 150. Wherever she went in the village, she constantly had a train of followers around her, so popular was she with the children.[105]

LOTHIAN

ON the south side of the Firth of Forth, the small fishing ports of Cockenzie, Port Seton, Musselburgh and Fisherow were also moved by a strong breath of God's Spirit. Largely due to the reputation of the God-fearing fisherfolk, Musselburgh had become known as 'The Honest Toun', and, as in other fishing ports, biblical names were commonly given to boats.[106] Here the Scottish Coast Mission saw the public hall crowded for weeks on end, and on one night alone, forty enquirers were dealt with in the missioner's home.

---

102. *SBM*, 1922, p. 16.

103. Ritchie, pp. 39–40.

104. Patrick, p. 135.

105. Ibid., pp. 135–7.

106. W.M. Gibson lists a stream of such names, including *Jehovah Jirah, Green Pastures, Guiding Light, True Vine, Lily of the Valley, Rose of Sharon, Quiet Waters, Morning Star, Harvester, Crystal Sea* and *Christmas Star* (W.M. Gibson, *Fishing In Old East Lothian: Cockenzie, Port Seton, Fisherrow and Prestonpans*, Haddington 1994, p. 59).

While there were few signs of spiritual blessing in Edinburgh itself, in neighbouring Leith the situation was very different. Interdenominational meetings were held, and the UFC minister said of the movement that

> this is the greatest thing I have seen in Leith during my ministry; and I am thankful to have had some little share in it on the eve of my giving up active duty. The only event approaching it was in 1905 at the time of the Welsh revival, when Ebenezer Church was the centre of a remarkable movement and services went on continuously, nightly for 17 weeks, the fruits of which are with us now. … We had open-air meetings in fixed localities – before we had gone far in the week there were ten of these. Each section of campaigners – after a short meeting – marched to the foot of Leith Walk, where a final rally was held, before marching to South Leith Parish Church. The speaking was done by ministers (some of whom had never done the like before), workers from various missions, and others. The crowds were large and interested – especially at the foot of the Walk, where it was huge. … In this part we had the co-operation of the Salvation Army, who gave up most of their own meetings for the time. Their band did yeoman service.'[107]

Eyemouth

FURTHER south in the ancient port of Eyemouth, there was said to have existed 'a religious strain in the community that goes deep into the souls of the fisherfolk. It is in the very fibre of their being. The life they lead, with its dangers and frequent contact with elemental strife, tends to bring them to a vivid realisation of things eternal.'[108]

As in towns and villages along the north-east coast, so, too, in Eyemouth, revival broke out suddenly among the fishing class. 'There had been little of what is usually called preparation, and as little organisation'[109] prior to the revival, yet 'one day it was not and the next day it was. God held Eyemouth in the grip of His hand.' About a fortnight before the return of the fisherfolk from Yarmouth, and having heard of the remarkable work of grace in progress there, J.P. Barton, minister of the Primitive Methodist Church, along with just one or two helpers, went to the market-place and conducted an open-air service. 'It seemed that the people were just waiting for an opportunity,' he reported.[110] At the second meeting the impression was so deep that an after-meeting was held in a house nearby, when eleven professed conversion.

---

107. *RHM&CEC-UFCS*, 1922, pp. 34–7.

108. *The Scotsman*, 21 December 1921, p. 9.

109. *MR-UFC*, 1922, p. 47.

110. Ibid.

In Great Yarmouth, two Eyemouth fishermen in particular came under the influence of revival there in progress, and on their return home, and in conjunction with the energetic Barton, a man described as having 'all the fresh enthusiasm that is the possession of youth', prayer and testimony meetings were begun in the main street. These proved so successful that they were continued nightly from the middle of November to the end of February. During that time, often in biting cold weather, seldom did a meeting pass without some professing Christ. In time the movement gathered 'a large section of the community as active followers', and its effect on the town was unmistakable. Yet it was emphasised that while there had been some emotional elements to the movement, it had been conducted entirely without any remarkable outbursts or strange manifestations.

An Edinburgh-based journalist turned up for a dinner-hour prayer meeting in the Primitive Methodist Church, 'a simply furnished building, which seemed to assume impressive beauty from the devoted spirit of the worshippers'. About fifty gathered at the chapel gate – a number of fishermen 'in workaday garb, smoking placidly as they chatted,[111] vigorous-looking lads in full bloom of youth, and young women, some of them without hats'. Barton ushered the group into the chapel for forty-five minutes of spontanteous prayer and singing, during which he himself took little active part.[112]

This journalist noted also how 'the revival is distinctly musical in character. One of the converts has related how, after attending a meeting at Yarmouth he woke up in the night singing a revival hymn, and though he had never sung before he had been singing ever since. … As I write some young folks have just hurried past my window humming a familiar hymn tune. This forenoon a fisher lad passed me at the harbour, not whistling a music hall ditty, but a Sankey hymn. … Song is the readiest medium by which the converts seek to express their feelings, but in prayer also some have acquired wonderful faculty in simple yet strong expression of the new spiritual impulse they are experiencing.'[113]

The same journalist witnessed the 'normal proceedings' of at least two evening open-air meetings:

> On the stroke of seven two sturdy fishermen emerged from a low pend giving access to the market place, a small triangular space in the centre of the town. They carried a harmonium between

---

111. The journalist saw this as 'convincing confirmation of the fact that they, at any rate, have not yet gone the length of burning their tobacco pipes on the fervour of religious zeal. Such manifestations would be foreign to the movement here, which, while depending upon enthusiasm for much of its driving force, has been unaffected by undue excitement or excess' (*The Scotsman*, 22 December 1921, p. 7).

112. Ibid.

113. Ibid.

them, and were followed by several youths bearing shops' lamps, which burn acetylene gas. A few minutes previously the place had echoed to the shrill voices of children playing merrily, but as soon as the ring was formed by the revivalists the children's voices were hushed. The public street seemed to become consecrated to the cause of conversion. It was a bitterly cold night, when a rosy fireside must have had strong temptations; yet within a short time more than 100 of the converts were gathered round, lustily singing hymns.

Once or twice a chill wind has compelled the company to move from the market place to a 'hieldy' corner of the town, where the meeting proceeds in comparative comfort … by the light of a number of ship's lamps they are enabled where necessary to follow the minute print of the revival hymns with which the service usually opens. So familiar have most of the singers become with some of the hymns, however, that they sing verse after verse without a glance at the little cloth-bound hymn books. And it is inspired singing; not perfunctory mumbling of the words. The emotions of the revivalists are obviously stirred, and a great volume of robust harmony rises into the starlit night. The onlookers are drawn in, too, by this fervent praise.

Mr Barton, the Primitive Methodist minister, played the harmonium, but the notes could not be heard at a few yards, so heartily did the singers respond. The ring in the centre of the street received constant reinforcements. A husband and wife would come out of a side street and take their places, to be followed perhaps by an elderly fisherman with his daughter hanging on his arm. From the youngest to the oldest of the community were represented. The wind whistled through the streets and to remain stationary for a few minutes meant a fit of shivering, yet despite the discomfort they stood their ground here for the greater part of an hour. Most of the women wore shawls, which were wrapped round their heads and made a kind of frame in their faces, whipped by the cold wind.

The strains of 'The Lord's My Shepherd', 'Crown Him' or 'Why Not Come to Him Now' awaken many echoes in those curiously intricate alleys of the town, with their suggestion of mystery. Here were the haunts of smugglers of bygone days – the forefathers of the revivalists. … Those narrow passages disgorge men, women and children every night nowadays, who flock to the market place to take an active part in the services or linger on the pavement to hear what is passing.

A short evangelical address was delivered by the Rev. Mr Miller, in which he urged the youth of the town to take up the torch which had been lit. … There is no fire and brimstone, however. 'I am not here to frighten you into repentance' he told his hearers. As he moves about the little wooden platform he tells the crowd fringing the inner circle of the joy that is waiting for them if they will but pledge themselves to Christian service. 'Why does Laughy dance when he is on this board?' he asked, and revivalists and onlookers alike joined the hearty laughter which followed this reference to one of Mr Barton's lay lieutenants. Laughy is the local nickname for a well-known fisherman named Loch, who is prominently identified with the Congregational Church. Well up in years, he is in the forefront of the revival movement and his genial temperament makes him a general favourite. Another fisherman named Johnstone, who is a leading member of the Primitive Methodist Church, is also one of Mr Barton's right-hand men. 'It is the joy Laughy is experiencing that makes him dance', the preacher informs the crowd. 'He can't help dancing'. The 'dancing' is a symptom of a nervous temperament which keeps Loch smiling and always on the move when he is speaking in public.

After the address and some hymn-singing comes the testimony of the converts. There is little sign of backwardness. They follow one another into the ring to give their 'wee word' as one of them expressed herself, and with a sincere, humble diction that in some cases approaches eloquence, they tell the story of their conversion, and appeal to others to follow in their footsteps. A young woman came forward for the first time, and for more than ten minutes, with quiet, deliberate phrases, she gripped the crowd with her exposition of the new outlook she had formed on the doctrine of brotherly love. Incidentally, she alluded to the presence of public-houses in their midst as contrary to that doctrine, and hoped that when next the electors of Eyemouth had the opportunity they would go one better than 'limitation' and carry 'no license'. A stalwart, ruddy-faced young fisherman followed her with his simple little testimony. In his ears were little golden rings. Each time he turned, the ear rings flashed in the light, and it required little imagination to picture such a figure engaging in some bold smuggling venture of an earlier time. The briefest gap was filled in by the singing of a hymn. At the conclusion of one verse, which told of the peace to be found in Jesus, a bareheaded woman, with a shawl wrapped round her shoulders, sprang into the ring. 'I ken what that peace means noo, friends,' she cried, her face alight: 'I ken a difference noo. I've been washing and baking aa' day, but I'm able to get to the meeting, and there's no' a happier woman in Eyemooth.' This said, she hurried back to her place in the circle of converts. The majority of those who gave their testimony were women. Of the few young fishermen who stepped forward last night, one lad, with sincere conviction written across his face, appealed with fervour to those outside the movement to take the pledge of Christian service. He appeared to be labouring under emotional strain. 'It's wonderfil," he cried: 'It's mair than wonderfi', it's ...', but further words failed him, and he returned to his place.

There are prophets of gloom, too, amongst them. Recalling the fact that a revival took place in Eyemouth[114] some years before the great sea disaster of 1881, in which 129 Eyemouth fishermen lost their lives, one of the revivalists has sought to draw a parallel.[115] 'Before that great sorrow of forty years ago our men were prepared by the revival which took place in the town,' was his message. 'Perhaps He is preparing us for another visitation.' In the testimonies there is a strain that runs through each – an expression of gratitude to Jesus as the Saviour. In different ways many of the converts tell how they have been freed from indifference and worldly passions.

... Thereupon Mr Barton announced that they would go on parade. Forming into procession and with the lamp-bearers at the head of the column, they threaded their way through some curious old byways to a part of the town bearing the high sounding name of George Square, but which could only hold the meeting and little more. Some half-dozen quaint, old-fashioned houses made up the square. Here the short service was taken part in by a fisherman, who, in simple, unaffected language spoke for a few minutes. He was followed by Mr Barton, who observed, with some fire in his voice, that he had read a statement somewhere that the revival was on the wane. It was not on the wane in Eyemouth, he cried, amid 'Amens' from several of his hearers. Great joy had come into the hearts and homes of the Eyemouth people these last few days, and greater wonders would still be seen.

There was hymn-singing here also, and as the Revivalists traversed some more dark, narrow lanes on the next stage of their journeyings, their lamps casting strange shadows on the walls of the houses, they sang as they went. A halt was made, this time in the rear of a tenement near the harbour. The space available here was even more limited, but the crowd, numbering two or three hundred, were out of the cold blast. Clothes drying in the wind could be discerned on the third floor balcony, and occupants of one tenement leaned over the balcony railing, their heads pushed

114. This movement occurred in 1869–70. See Peter Aitchison, *Children of the Sea: The Story of the Eyemouth Disaster*, East Linton 2001, pp. 181–2. In fact there was also a later period of localised awakening in the fishing town, occurring sometime between 1880 and 1910, though the exact date is unknown. The Baptist Church, known as Sorella House, and which was first formed in the early 1800s, became extinct in 1879. For a while thereafter it was used by the United Presbyterians as a Sabbath school. Eventually Robert Scott, known at Evangelical Union Conferences as 'the Eyemouth Fisherman', took over the building, and, with it as a centre, 'led in a local evangelistic movement which greatly affected the non-church going'. Later, sadly, Sorella House was used as a place of business (McIver, *An Old-Time Fishing Town*, pp. 309–10).

115. Known in Eyemouth as 'Black Friday', this is the worst Scottish fishing disaster ever recorded. A total of 189 men lost their lives, leaving 93 widows and 267 children. Eyemouth alone lost 129 men, and one third of its fleet. Others were from the nearby villages of Burnmouth (24), Coldingham Shore (3) and Cove (11). Seven men were also lost from Musselburgh and 15 from Newhaven.

> through between the garments. Hymns were sung, and before the procession left for the service in the church at 8.30, Mr Barton apologised to the tenement dwellers. Amid laughter he expressed the hope that they had not wakened up the bairns, but they had friends there, he added, who would like to know they were adjourning to the church for prayers and testimony. A large number followed in the train of the lamp-bearers to the Primitive Methodist Church, where the nightly service was held.[116]

In an interview given to the *Scotsman* journalist around 20 December, Barton said he had unbounded respect for the honesty of the fisher folk and their kindly disposition. They were a rugged type, he said, but extremely gracious people to live amongst and very magnanimous in their response to an appeal of a philanthropic nature. Regarding the revival that had broken out among them, Barton sought to emphasise that it was entirely undenominational. It was in the interests of the religious life of the whole community, and he was hugely thankful, for example, for the invaluable co-operation of Rev. John Miller, minister of the UFC, as well as that received from numerous laymen connected with the Methodist and Congregational Churches.

Up till mid-December the weather had been suitable for open-air meetings, and in good weather these attracted around 500 people. The cold snap that followed compelled them to spend the larger part of the nightly proceedings indoors. Barton mentioned that he was keeping a record of all converts, so that when the movement had passed, he would supply each minister with a list of the names of those attached to their particular church so that they would be able to look after their own flock. Of the nearly 250 pledges to Christian service hitherto received, the minister noted that most were within the fourteen-to-sixty age range, the majority being married.[117]

Regarding lasting results, Barton said that the speech of the town had been cleansed of swearing, which had become far too predominant in the streets and the harbour. The transformation in the home life of the people had been remarkable. At the last General Election, for example, comparatively few had bothered to vote. Similar indifference existed towards governmental elections. Barton wished for people to see that the gospel of Jesus Christ embraced the whole of life. A healthy, vigorous Christianity was needed that would relate itself to every interest and pursuit in life.

As to immediate change, it had been noted that 'previously there was more room in the churches than people. Today there are more people than room.'[118] Most churches were now well filled on Sundays. Apathy

---

116. *The Scotsman*, 21 December 1921, p. 9; 23 December 1921, pp. 5–6.
117. Ibid., 22 December 1921, pp. 6–7.
118. Ibid., 22 December 1921, p. 9.

had been broken down. Attendance at the one cinema house in town showed a 'perceptible falling off' during the time of the revival, and even some educational evening classes had to be discontinued due to lack of attendance in preference of the revival meetings. Barton insisted that the leaders were doing their very best to safeguard against anything extreme as had been reported in one or two places further north. Enthusiasm, he explained, was essential to success, but excess had been rigorously avoided. A feature of their campaign had been the calm spirit of the people. That was what Barton liked about it. There was no semblance of undue excitement in the homes of the people. They wanted the people to make the decision with open minds and balanced feeling. The proper atmosphere had to be created if their appeal was to be successful, but they had no desire to work up feeling for feeling's sake. The response had been perfectly spontaneous.

Asked whether fishermen were more responsive to an evangelistic appeal than other members of a community, Barton responded, 'No. We had an evangelist here not long ago who laboured in vain amongst the fishermen for three weeks. It was the electrifying atmosphere at Yarmouth that has given our movement such an impetus. … There is no mistake about it,' he added. 'This movement was very much needed in Eyemouth. We are getting people into churches today who have not been across a church door for 10 and 15 years.'[119]

Altogether, over 300 people were said to have professed conversion. Ministers in the town were greatly stimulated in their labours and all churches benefited. One minister observed, 'At my last quarterly Communion, I had the largest number of young communicants received in the course of my ministry – a larger number than I had received in the course of a whole year. My prayer meeting has been a joy, both as to numbers and spirit. Family worship is observed as never before in my experience. Men and women take part publicly in prayer with reverence and power.'[120] Blessing was seen too, in nearby Burnmouth.[121]

Ten years later, when Jock Troup visited this town to hold meetings with James Stewart (see pp. 191–2), they found the spirit of revival still alive and well. It turned out that the local Methodist minister had been one of the first to be converted at the unforgettable meetings in Yarmouth in 1921. When Jock stood on the seat of his car to preach, with his head sticking through the open roof, it was – perhaps exaggeratedly – estimated that at least 30,000 were gathered to hear him – about one-and-a-half times the population of the town.

---

119. Ibid.

120. *RHM&CEC-UFCS*, 1922, pp. 31–8.

121. Ibid., p. 32.

WICK

THE four male Pilgrim Preachers from Wales were still active in the Caithness town of Wick when the fishermen returned from East Anglia (see page 220). No doubt greatly encouraged by stories of the dramatic conversions of at least a dozen of these hardy men, the mission exploits of the Baptist Church took on renewed vigour, and something like 100 conversions among townsfolk were recorded within just a few days.[122]

The revival among the fisherfolk themselves was to some extent a distinct work, and was led almost exclusively by the Salvation Army. Given, further, that the skippers of two or three local boats were members of the Salvation Army, it was natural that on return from Lowestoft most of the Wick folk converted there attached themselves to Army barracks. Within days of their return almost the entire population of the town was talking about the revival. At one of the first meetings led by the Salvation Army, over 100 went forward in penitent state. The following night, there were a further 120, and conversions were recorded nightly for weeks thereafter. At another meeting, on the Brae-head above the harbour at the Pultney side of Wick, a recent convert went over to two well-known fishermen coming out of a pub. Turning to one of them, he gave the prophetic word that if he got saved, then he would be used to lead many to Christ. Later that evening this man was indeed converted and became a keen witness for the Lord.

Open-air meetings were a striking feature. On one occasion up to 1,000 gathered to hear the gospel message and around half-a-dozen streets were blocked. Processions were also conducted through the town; these were led by a young Christian playing her melodeon and at times attracted over 500 to its ranks. On Sundays meetings commenced at nine in the morning and often did not conclude until 10.30 at night. Often there were no fewer than three big evening meetings going on simultaneously.

One convert had suffered since childhood from a serious speech impediment. Now, however, he was able to give his testimony without a single stammer. 'I don't understand it,' he exclaimed, 'the day of miracles is not passed, for my impediment is gone!' Traditionally, on Thanksgiving Day, a football match was played in Wick, which boasted some top-rate young players. This year, however, concerns of a spiritual nature took so much more precedence over sport that it was found impossible to get together a team. Indeed one fit lad said that though he used to love kicking a ball around, these days he was spending his time kicking the Devil!

---

122. The *Glasgow Herald* suggested that converts were 'mostly of the rougher types' (13 December 1921).

The effect of the revival was felt sharply by those in the liquor and tobacco trade. One tobacconist spoke of how he missed 'the most inveterate smokers these days. Young fellows who would get through twenty packets of cigarettes a day come no more.' Publicans who had appealed a recent, sensational 'No Licence' Election in the town suggested postponing the appeal for a month, in the hope that by that time many men caught up in the revival would have reverted to their former ways. One convert overhearing the publican's remark retorted, 'As long as there's a big God in heaven, we'll never go back!'[123]

Up to the start of the New Year, only the Salvation Army (and to a lesser extent the Baptists) had 'caught the flame' of the revival in Wick. As such it was described as an 'incomplete movement.' Indeed, when one local church held a mission in late December, none except accustomed members attended the meetings. Asked why they weren't participating in the revival, one church leader said that while all Presbyterian churches had 'the fullest sympathy and a lively gratitude' for the movement, they felt their co-operation wasn't required as the Army hadn't requested their assistance! In any case, he continued, 'there is a great difference between pastoral work and evangelical work, and the minister absorbed in the former is often unable to take up the latter.'[124] A greater spirit of co-operation resulted when the public Rifle Hall, the largest in town, was employed for meetings, though even that proved too small to hold all those who turned up.

A journalist describes an open-air meeting in Wick led by the Salvation Army 'in a gale on a roadway of mud. Within the ring strode one sturdy fisherlad after another, to announce in blunt, brief fashion that he was saved, that he was ever so glad about it, and that he recommended others to get saved too. As he stepped back, one of the women Officers gave out a hymn, whereupon a few verses were roared forth in competition with the wind.... The weather continued at a high pitch of freezing discomfort, but that al fresco Prayer Meeting continued aglow with enthusiasm.' The journalist mingled with a large audience stretched along the pavement two or three deep. All listened with close attention and earnest faces, as too did passers-by. 'Nowhere did I hear a word of criticism,' he wrote. 'From first to last there was not the faintest trace of hostility or derision.'[125] A nearby pub stood virtually deserted.

Presently, the converts marched in procession to the Army hall. Here, lad after lad (most aged between 15 and 19) bravely stood up in the bright light, within full view of chums and neighbours, and confessed that he had accepted Christ as his personal Saviour, most announcing

123. *War Cry*, 17 December 1921, p. 11

124. Ibid., 2 January 1922, p. 1

125. Ibid., 7 January 1922, p. 8

that the change had occurred three weeks previously, others a month, and a few less than two weeks. One lad 'with ruddy cheeks and twinkling eyes' said he spoke to everyone of his love for Christ – but someone a few days previously had told him to keep it to himself! 'That's just what I canna dae!' said the beaming boy. As he sat down, one of his mates sprang up and declared, 'We are the happiest people in Wick: the rest of you are a wash-out!'[126]

The Salvation Army Commissioner, Kitching, wrote that despite the evidence of unrestraint at meetings, the work in Wick was marked by close organisation. 'Registration is followed by visitation, and utilisation ensues, for parties of converts march off to surrounding villages singing as they go, to return with stirring accounts of open-air penitents and requests for established resident workers. 'If my sins had been put upon the ___,' said one convert, mentioning a cargo vessel in the harbour, 'they would have sunk her!' Kitching added that General Booth was greatly interested in the movement and was hopeful that it would tend to stimulate religious activity generally.[127]

Towards the end of December a number of fishing boats were leaving for the West Coast fishing based in Stornoway. One boat, the *Mizpah*, was manned entirely by professing Christians, and they sailed from the harbour with the Salvation Army flag flying from its masthead. The crew, along with many friends on shore, sang out revival hymns – a scene unexampled in the port of Wick. By the end of the month it was evident that although the revival was still proceeding, its intensity had subsided.

At the New Year bonfire, instead of the customary drunken revelry, Salvation Army choruses were sung at an open-air rally. Many young converts began witnessing in villages around Wick, and many also had the privilege of seeing their parents turning to the straight and narrow way. But the strain left its mark on some workers. The Captain of the Salvation Army was forced to rest due to ill health. And when Jock Troup arrived in his home town on 3 January 1922, his voice was so hoarse due to extensive preaching that he was required to undergo an operation on his throat. In no time, however, he was back in action, and crowds thronged to hear him preach as boldly and as inspiringly as ever. At times Jock would retreat to the harbour, and, alone on a boat, cry out to God in prayer. Reinvigorated, he too travelled to country districts along with a comrade, a recent convert of the Pilgrim Preachers. One night well after eleven in the evening, Troup felt led to hold an open-air meeting. Doors and windows opened as people were attracted by the singing and

126. Ibid.

127. *Glasgow Herald*, 24 December 1921, p. 8. Like fishermen converts elsewhere, new Salvationists used nautical terms in their conversation, such as referring to the Almighty as the 'Big Skipper'.

preaching. Soon a good number had gathered, the Spirit fell, and several men and women collapsed in the street under conviction, crying out to Christ from the gutters to have mercy on them.

The small community of Scarfskerry on the north Caithness coast 'was also feeling the throb' of revival and at the instance of the Baptist Home Mission Society, Rev. Hirst undertook some weeks of service there, also giving valuable help in Wick itself. Altogether, many hundreds confessed Christ during these few intense months – as many as 500 attached themselves to the Salvation Army alone. Among the converts were a number of students and a graduate science teacher from the local school.

INVERNESS

IN Inverness, the main burst of blessing began in late 1922, considerably later than that in most of the fishing villages further east. By this time, Troup had enrolled as a student at the Bible Training Institute in Glasgow. Here, the wholesome teaching and godly witness of the Principal, Dr David McIntyre (son-in-law of Andrew Bonar, and a successor to him as minister of Finnieston Free Church) was a major inspiration. Another blessing to him at this time was the friendship forged with fellow-student Peter Connolly, a former Roman Catholic from the north of England. Jock and Peter developed a close friendship, and during their college days, and for years afterwards, this fearless duo were called upon to conduct gospel campaigns throughout Britain. Towards the close of 1922, Troup and Connolly, along with another friend, Somerville Smith, took part in both pre-organised and independent missions in the Highland capital. They lodged on a boat on the Caledonian Canal and it became their habit at night to make their way to Bught Park, where they agonised on their faces in prayer before God. Wonderfully, blessing came to the town, and continued long after they left. It is said that during this season of spiritual refreshing the streets were often black with people as they made their way to church. The UF Church was filled three times a day for prayer, the largest hall in town attracted 1,600 in the evenings and the Baptist church conducted a series of baptismal services over several months.[128]

PORTSOY AND LOSSIEMOUTH 1923

INTERESTINGLY, while two or three fisherfolk from Portsoy had been converted during the autumn fishing season in Great Yarmouth, the north coast revival of 1921–2 almost completely bypassed this Moray Coast town. Indeed some folk boasted that their community

128. *SBM*, 1923, p. 46.

was impervious to revival and that even during the great awakening of 1859–61, fiery evangelists like Duncan Matheson and James Turner had failed to move the town.

Things were very different in Cullen, six miles to the east of Portsoy, where the Salvation Army had seen wonderful things in late 1921 and throughout 1922. Yet towards the end of that year, God impressed on them to believe for still 'greater things' in the following year. At the Watch-Night service on Hogmanay, all who truly shared such a vision were asked to sing with their hands raised. Said one, 'I see them now – the packed hall, uplifted faces, some tear-stained, hands outstretched to God – a sublime moment of childlike faith in God.'[129]

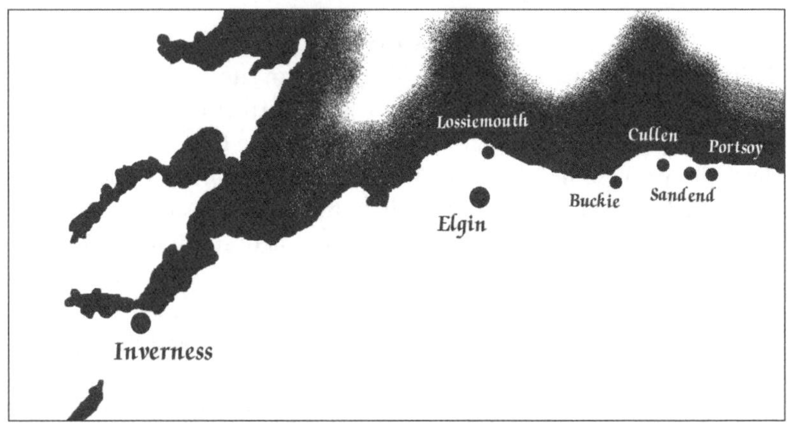

Early in the New Year, one or two believers from Portsoy implored Salvation Army workers to come and hold meetings in the town, and together they began to pray for the community. On many occasions Lieutenant Towns would weep all night for the place. At the first open-air meeting held in Portsoy one boy in his early teens came forward seeking salvation. Meetings in Cullen were turned into prayer meetings for Portsoy, and one night the Salvation Army Officer in Cullen sensed that souls were being won in that neighbouring town. Indeed, three more young men were saved during the open-air meeting that very evening, bravely giving immediate testimony before a crowd who knew them well (tragically, one of them was drowned at sea shortly afterwards). In the after-meeting that followed, six more professed Christ as Lord. The awakening in Portsoy had begun. Quickly the whole town was stirred. Services were moved to the Town Hall, which was packed nightly – floor and gallery – to its 500-seat capacity, with many unable to gain admittance. Ofttimes, people gathered at the penitent form well before the meeting had commenced. By this time prayer meetings for Portsoy

129. Ritchie, *Floods Upon the Dry Ground*, p. 99.

were being conducted by an eighty-year-old Salvationist, 'Granny Pirie', as all other helpers were fully employed among the seekers, who surrendered in numbers night after night.

The whole town seemed transformed, and a spiritual atmosphere was everywhere apparent. People came to meetings from all around. In one case an intense family dispute of twenty years' standing – involving acts of violence - was instantly healed, with long-term effect. An unusual number of older married couples also turned to Christ at this time. One elderly woman pulled an Army Captain into her home, begging for prayer. Her kitchen table became an altar that day as she found peace with God. Soon a Salvation Army Corps was established in Portsoy and was keenly attended.[130] One young fisherman converted at this time was Jim Slater, who gave his life to Christ following a meeting led by the Army at Portsoy's Shorehead. Slater became a prominent Salvationist and local historian, also being well-known for his poetry. He wrote:

It was in nineteen twenty three the
Army came along.
And on the Shorehead preached the word
And sang the salvation's song;
God blessed the message, simply told
I can still mind it fine
For on that day wi' ither lads I made
The Saviour mine.[131]

From Cullen to the west and Portsoy to the east, the movement spread to the fishing village of Sandend. From this small community one young man attended one of the meetings in Portsoy, and cried out to God for salvation. He arose sober and saved. His mother literally sang for joy when the young man arrived home that evening saying, 'Mither, here's a new man tae ye the nicht.' The Brethren more than any other group gathered the biggest harvest in Sandend – and their meetings soon became very largely attended. Two hundred and fifty would pack into their services in the old village hall, some being forced to perch on the windowsills and other unlikely places.[132]

Further along the coast towards Inverness, the port of Lossiemouth had also remained untouched by the revival wave that had recently stirred so many other fishing communities. But by 1923 the Baptist minister, sensing a spirit of inquiry, especially in his Bible class, proposed a series of special meetings, much to the indifference of his deacons. Without

130. Ibid., pp. 99–101.

131. Quoted in Smith, *One Foot In The Sea*, p. 83.

132. Ibid., p. 84; personal conversation with Sylvia McKay, 23 April 2007.

the assistance of any outside evangelist, these quickly grew in attendance, and conversions were now being recorded. Soon 1,000 people were crowding into the nearby UFC, the largest building in town. Assistance was offered from neighbouring Baptist ministers and from Mr Garden, a former member of the congregation, later a Baptist minister in Australia, home on a visit from that country. The adverse criticism evident at first in the secular Press and among some in the clergy gradually died down, as folk openly observed the 'civic righteousness which now obtains in Lossiemouth'. This included the transformation of many drunkards. Meetings were informal, with 'more dependence put upon the Spirit than upon form', and evidence of the genuineness of the movement was seen in the numbers attending the weekly converts' meeting in the Baptist Church, which regularly attracted 150 folk.[133]

OTHER SIGNIFICANT MOVEMENTS IN THIS PERIOD[134]

Cellardyke 1920–1
'Scottish Revival' in Yarmouth 1921
Aberdeen, Dundee and Edinburgh 1921–2
North-East Coast (Undated)

133. *SBM*, 1923, pp. 46–7, 63.

134. Full accounts of these movements can be found on www.scottishrevivals.co.uk.

Fraserburgh Harbour – p.221

East Coast Fishwives – p.222

Jock Troup – p.224

D.P. Thomson – p.228

Davie Cordiner – p.240

Cairnbulg – p.232

Helmsdale – p.239

Whinyfold converts – p.241

Eyemouth Harbour – p.245

Wick Harbour – p.252

Portsoy Brass Band – p.255

Part Three

'O'ER THE MINCH' – HEBRIDEAN HARVEST

Revival at Garry-bhard

Will you come to Garry-bhard with me?
The Spirit's gracious work to see,
Drawing souls to set them free
To shelter and security
Will you come to Garry-bhard with me?
When the news was brought to me
My tears were falling fast and free
But sorrow it could never be
But love constrained my blessedness
Will you come to Garry-bhard with me?
What a fellowship was there
The crowds appeared from everywhere
Some of them in great despair
For grace to save them hurriedly
Will you come to Garry-bhard with me?
Singing voices and praying men
From villages they came, and then
Their voices echoed through the glen
And night was turned to day for us
Will you come to Garry-bhard with me?
When God did lead His travelling band
In olden days in desert land
Heaven and earth at His command
Responded with alacrity
Will you come to Garry-bhard with me?
The Israelites were sore distressed
By enemies each day oppressed
The Lord of Glory brought redress

And sadness turned to happiness
Will you come to Garry-bhard with me?
This also was the very way
For those who gave themselves to pray
Invoking God to bless their day
When wearied with discouragements
Will you come to Garry-bhard with me?
But even when they were in pain
In barren land without the rain
The wood made Mara sweet again
Garry-bhard and Cabharsta!
Will you come to Garry-bhard with me?
Your work how wonderful to view
Coming in its time like dew
Changing death to life anew
And grace in place of ignorance
Will you come to Garry-bhard with me?
Resurrecting from the earth
The souls who were enclosed in death
And also giving life and health
To saints whose souls were famishing
Will you come to Garry-bhard with me?
The church at Park, who can deny
Has got a blessing from on high
Leac-Bhan church, and glad am I
Is crowded to capacity
Will you come to Garry-bhard with me?
Lemreway is budding fine
Awake and sing, O soul of mine
The gracious covering divine
Has spread for you its canopy
Will you come to Garry-bhard with me?
O! youth of Gravir, dear to me
At such a time, come hear my plea
And seek salvation full and free
And do not die in ignorance
Will you come to Garry-bhard with me?
O! that He would still nearer come
To all my friends, the ones I love
The Holy Ghost poured from above
To rouse you from your lethargy
Will you come to Garry-bhard with me?

May God's own Son be ever blessed
Although the cloud our souls oppressed
He did not leave us there to rest
But came to bring us blessedness
Will you come to Garry-bhard with me?
More growth, more victory be there
And still more blessing everywhere
This my chief desire and prayer
Till to my grave they carry me
Will you come to Garry-bhard with me?
So as my song is at its end
Let us to God our thanks extend
And at the throne, your poet-friend
Remember – in absentia
Will you come to Garry-bhard with me?[1]

1. Kenneth Nicolson, *Revival At Garry-Bhard*, translated from Gaelic by Rev. Dr John Ferguson; used with kind permission.

Introduction

THE island of Lewis slowly began to emerge from deep spiritual darkness shortly after the start of the nineteenth century. Several factors contributed to this. Of prime importance were the Gaelic Schools, which were started in 1811. These quickly spread and there were eight in operation by 1815 and fifteen by 1833; the sole textbook used being the Bible. The translation and circulation of the Gaelic Bible was a major influence in spreading scriptural knowledge. As literacy in the islands increased through the work of the Gaelic Schools, Gaelic translations of popular evangelical literature also began to circulate.

Lewis's first evangelical revival began in a township in Barvas in 1822, spreading from hamlet to hamlet, and also to other parishes. A number of lay preachers held impromptu open-air meetings in different areas, drawing great crowds. A strong degree of fanaticism attended the movement, with the occurrence of spasms, screaming and trances. As a result of such phenomena, 1822 became known among locals as 'Bliahna an Fhaomaidh' - 'the year of the swoonings'. Around this time, in 1824, Alexander MacLeod was inducted to the parish of Uig, where, through

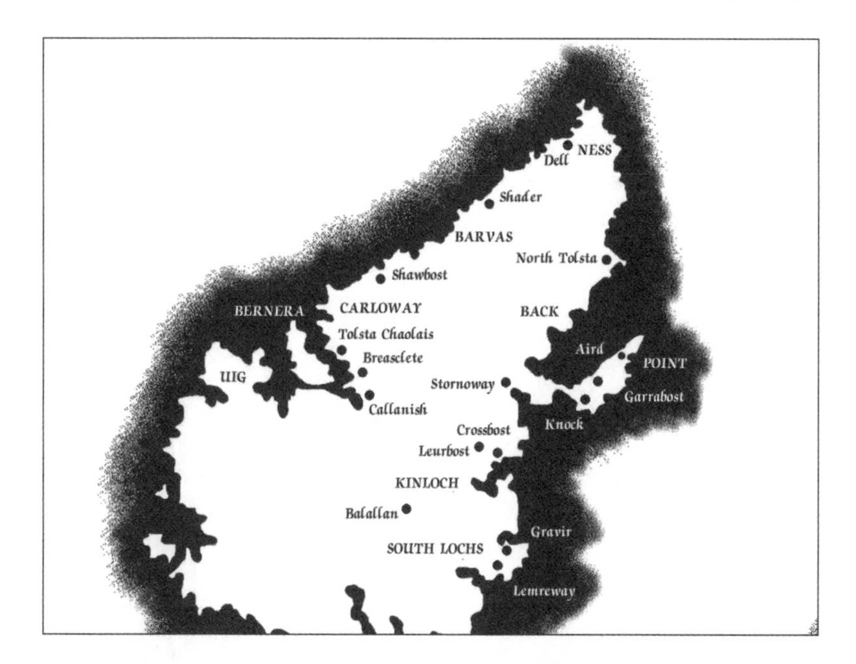

his powerful evangelistic ministry, a mighty revival soon emerged in the district. The movement intensified and seemed to be at its strongest between 1828 and 1830. The Rev. MacDonald of Ferintosh – en route to St. Kilda – participated in a Communion here, during which 'the great congregation was smitten as by a mighty wind and the people were laid prostrate on the earth'.[2] In 1828 an estimated 9,000 people from all over the island assembled for a Communion at this remote location. The movement spread to other parts of Lewis (notably Lochs, under Robert Finlayson) and also to Harris, where the preaching of converted local blacksmith and poet John Morrison carried great influence. North Uist was also witness to a significant revival in the 1820s, largely through the ministry of lay evangelist Finlay Munro. The Outer Hebrides were never to be the same again, retaining ever since a stronger evangelical identity than virtually anywhere else in Scotland.

There were stirrings of revival in several Lewis localities, particularly Uig, around the time of the Disruption in 1843, while a deeper movement spread through North Uist during the same year. Meanwhile, the 1859-61 revival, international in scope, which had potent effect in nearly all Scottish counties, did not fail also to affect the Outer Hebrides. This powerful awakening spread throughout Lewis and Harris, but was perhaps strongest felt in Ness, Lochs and Stornoway. While the movement can perhaps be termed Lewis's 'Forgotten revival' of the nineteenth century, an equally little known movement is one which sprang up in Ness in 1874, during the time of the widespread 'Moody revival' on the Scottish mainland.

2. *The Oban Times*', 24 September 1898, p. 3

8

Bringing in the Sheaves
1880s

Stornoway 1880[3]

AS you approach Lewis by ferry from Ullapool, the most prominent Stornoway landmark to greet you is the tall steepled Martin's Memorial Church, an impressive Gothic structure made of red Torridon sandstone, accommodating over 600. Opened in 1878, the church took its name from the first minister who served in it – Donald John Martin. Martin was four years into his pastorate when a most significant revival took place. Born in 1847, Martin worked in various occupations before entering full-time ministry in 1870. With strong Skye lineage on his father's side and Raasay and Lewis ancestry on his mother's, it was perhaps appropriate for him that a Hebridean island should constitute twenty years of highly fruitful ministry.

At the time of Martin's induction, membership of the Stornoway Free English Church stood at only forty, but this soon grew under the new leadership. A strong, burly man, Martin had an abundant supply of energy and a strong sense of humour. Though not remembered as the greatest of preachers, he was pre-eminently a man of prayer, and spent much time on his knees in his study or in the church vestry, or pacing the floor in dialogue with his maker. Martin communed with God as he walked to church, and, during the service while the congregation was singing, their minister would ever be in prayer in the pulpit. This gave an edge and power to his preaching that arrested the listener and went straight to the heart. 'It was in prayer,' wrote his biographer, that 'he developed the burning for souls which rose to a passion. He had his seasons, times when he reached the summer solstice and times when he touched the winter. But even his winter was never scant of prayer. His summer was all ablaze with it. Every visit was prefaced with prayer, every letter written with the breath of it on the page, every sermon drenched in it as in a fountain of healing. It controlled him.'[4] One friend who knew him well said that during one particular season, Martin was so burdened with a

3. Ronald Blakey suggests that this revival came as a result of Moody's second mission to Scotland, but this is impossible, as Moody only returned to Scotland in November 1881, over 18 months after the start of the Stornoway movement (Ronald S. Blakey, *The Man in the Manse*, Edinburgh 1978, p. 52).

4. Rev. Norman C. MacFarlane, *Life of the Rev. Donald John Martin: Preacher, Soul Winner, Social Reformer*, Edinburgh 1914, p. 80.

spirit of intercession that for days he could neither stand nor sit, but bowed prostrate on the study floor, crying out with passion for souls.[5]

Recalled Martin at a later date, 'Prayer preceded and prayer accompanied our work here. Before it commenced I had my mind wonderfully led to the fact of the Ascension of our Lord, and the promised Spirit, in Psalm 68 v18. If Christ be really now the Living Mediator, are not Pentecostal times possible for us, just as possible as at Pentecost? Jesus still lives, just the same as when He first ascended. I believe that still, as of old, according to our faith it shall be.'[6]

As to the beginnings of the movement, Martin was perplexed by the fact that not one communicant was added to the church at the February Communion, 1880. He and others took this as a sign that the Lord was putting the church to the test. From that point, a spirit of prayer was poured out on the people.[7] A weekly meeting to pray for the coming of the Holy Spirit was commenced,[8] during which 'we felt at times lifted beyond ourselves into a higher life'.[9] Then in the late spring came encouragement from believers among the fisherfolk of the Moray coast, who flocked into Stornoway harbour as they did each year at this time. This year, however, was different, for the visiting fishermen were especially full of joy and faith, having just partaken of a potent revival in their home communities (see pp. 200–2). Martin admitted that just prior to this, 'I did not know of one anxious soul in this distant region.[10] By this time some young folk were being brought to the Lord, and Martin cancelled his summer vacation, sensing that they were on the 'eve of blessing',[11] having had a cloud hovering over them all summer. In October John Bain,[12] an agent from the Evangelization Society of London, arrived for a fortnight's meetings. Up to then it had been mainly young women and children who had been brought in; now young men were being converted too. The cloud had broken and a shower of blessing was being poured out. A wonderful awakening had begun.

It was a quiet movement, with an 'entire absence of tumultous excitement of any kind'. It seemed to be mainly a manifestation of converting power, with whole households and classes being brought to the foot of the Cross. Various drunkards who had defied all other

5. Ibid., p. 81.

6. Ibid., p. 86.

7. *RC-FCS-SR&M*, 1881, p. 1.

8. This appears to have been in addition to the weekly office-bearers' prayer meeting and the ordinary prayer meeting for the congregation.

9. MacFarlane, *Donald John Martin*, p. 83.

10. *TC*, 7 April 1881, p. 15.

11. Ibid.

12. Bain was converted in the Wynd Church in Glasgow and had previously worked as an evangelist in Falkirk and among miners in Spain.

means of obtaining help were amazingly transformed. Some young men, deliberately avoiding the gospel meetings, were nevertheless mysteriously drawn to them and savingly changed. Letters of testimony came pouring into the manse. These were very precious to Martin, who preserved them all. One came from two young salesmen, 'country lads', who shared a room in town and who were converted about the same time. Both, like numerous others during this awakening, became full-time ministers of the gospel.

The work appeared to be so obviously of God that Martin felt all he needed to do was abide in Christ and allow Him to do the work. He spoke of how 'souls seem to glide into the kingdom when God blesses'.[13] At times he found it all so new, so strange, so seemingly easy that he was tempted to wonder if it was all for real. His main difficulty now was knowing how to deal with the large numbers professing faith – a dilemma many in church leadership might be only too happy to encounter![14] For many it was a time of inexpressible joy and even children shared in the blessing. The Sunday school was 'most wonderfully changed'. The teacher in the senior boys' class stated that he had reason to believe that every lad in his class had professed to having been enabled to receive the Lord Jesus.[15] The work wrought among these pupils resulted largely from an emphasis placed on the substitutionary work of Jesus.[16] Many young girls and expecially servant girls were also brought to Christ. In some instances whole families and households were brought in.

One of the firstfruits of the awakening was John F. MacFarlane, a former whaler turned local Inspector of Poor as well as Registrar of Births, and similar. For months he had been under tremendous concern of soul, though Martin's visits were as glimmers of light. When at last he came through to a place of spiritual peace, MacFarlane at once became a man of prayer, and ardent in service. His methods of Christian work were so unique that *The Scotsman* newspaper, on one occasion, gave him the honour of a special leading article.[17]

13. MacFarlane, *Donald John Martin*, p. 81.

14. Martin was so occupied with the revival that he had no time to get caught up in the ecclesiastical gale that blew through his denomination at this time, the Robertson Smith case. Some years after the revival had subsided, however, when a similar controversy emerged (the Marcus Dodds case), Martin did not fail to make his opinion heard.

15. *MR-FCS*, January 1881, pp. 9–10.

16. Martin said that he had felt pressed to make this truth a key-note of his teaching in recent months. Speaking of the blessing at a meeting of Sabbath school teachers, he noted how they all stated that they had observed in their own teaching over the previous twelve months 'a wonderful facility and clearness in expounding to their scholars the substitutionary sufferings of their Lord' (*RC-FCS-SR&M*, p. 3).

17. One form of service that MacFarlane carried on for many years was to hand to every fishing-boat in the harbour a bundle of religious magazines every Sabbath afternoon during the fishing season. Parcels were sent to him from all parts of Britain. With a fleet of 600 boats, this required some considerable organisation and labour. He also organised open-air meetings, acted as the church treasurer for years, and in numerous ways assisted his minister, whom he almost idolised, and the two were very closely linked.

The whole town seemed to be caught up in the movement, and several other churches also shared in the blessing.[18] Norman MacFarlane goes as far as stating that 'almost every person of any consequence in the town was swept by the wave into the Kingdom of God'. The minister from the UPC entered soul and spirit into the blessing, and for months had been praying for members of his own flock individually. Martin had begun to do likewise – interceding for those in his congregation and from others he longed to see converted – and in a short time he was able to stroke out scores of these names from his prayer list, as one by one they were led to the Throne of Grace. The Stornoway pastor had been praying for one entire household, soon to observe that 'that family seemed to jump into the kingdom'![19] Another method of Martin's was, as with William Haslam some decades previously,[20] to stand alone in his church praying individually for members of his congregation in the very pews they normally occupied.

In both his preaching and his private discourses, Martin emphasised the sinfulness of man and his utterly hopeless condition apart from Christ. This led to a peculiar feature of the movement in that many who had been living fruitful lives for God for years would find their way into the inquiry room as if they were seekers for the first time. So freshly convicted were they of personal sin that they sought to be prayed for all over again as anxious souls, a parallel experience to that of Hebrew scholar, Rabbi Duncan of Edinburgh's New College, many years before them.

Opposition struck against the work from various quarters. Some pointed to the crowds making for Martin's church and said, 'there go the play-actors to the theatricals!'[21] More commonly and disconcertingly, however, opposition came from certain ministers in the island, some of whom issued thunderbolts directly from their pulpits against both the movement and the man through whom it came into being. In this strict Calvinistic territory, evangelistic campaigns were seen as an Arminian method, and were thus viewed with suspicion and disfavour. However, one of Martin's co-presbyters, who had wildly railed on him for his 'revival methods', mercifully retracted all such charges in the days prior to his minister's transfer to Oban. Martin personally claimed strong allegiance to Calvinist principles, but knew that God's sovereignty 'does not exclude from the matter of salvation all will of the creature whatsoever'.[22] Other attacks were cynical and at times personal, but Martin said they

18. *MR-FCS*, January 1881, pp. 89–90.

19. Ibid., p. 85.

20. An English parson, converted through one of his own sermons, who had gone on to experience stirring revivals in at least two parishes in which he served; viz., Baldhu, Cornwall (1851–54) and Buckenham, Norfolk (1863–71).

21. MacFarlane, *Donald John Martin*, p. 88.

22. Ibid., p. 91.

only served to drive his people even more to their knees. In any case, he refused to resort to counter-attacks, even in his private correspondence.

Meantime, the work of grace went on flowing in abundant blessing till January of 1881, with drops still falling throughout February and March. Stornoway at that time was compared to Kidderminster during the ministry of renowned English Puritan Richard Baxter. Naturally, given the circumstances, several parties from all the congregations in town came to meetings, as well as people from other congregations on the island, all keen to enjoy something of the divine favour being poured out on the town. Martin mentions one 'very nice fellow from Back' who stayed to the after-meeting. 'Not one word of English had he, but he told me he had been praying for me all the time.'[23] Groups of young men gathered together in the open air for prayer; a favourite spot being the hayricks in the public park, around which they formed a chain, kneeling on the ground to pour out their hearts to the Lord in thankfulness for His mercy and in earnest supplication for the salvation of unsaved loved ones. Praise seemed to ascend from almost every house as its inhabitants gathered together for family worship.

As to the fruit of the awakening, Martin noted 'an entire change in the tone of the community'. The local librarian informed him of a marked change in the style of books being borrowed by those who had yet made no profession of faith. Then there was the dancing-school; at one time running in full-force, but now practically emptied. The teacher was forced to leave without paying the Hall rent. He said he would return, but did not. The Templars' Lodge now operated like a church prayer meeting, hymns and sacred songs forming the main element of the entertainment. Drinking clubs were broken up – 'the members now take their places at the Lord's Table, in place of the table of devils, as they once did.' A commercial traveller, returning to the mainland after a visit to Stornoway, was asked how business was in that town. 'Business,' said the man, 'why, there is no doing business there at all. Every shop you went into the first question was, "Are you saved? Are you converted?" And not a bit of business would they do till that question was answered. I could not stand it, so I had just to run.'[24]

During the Communion season in February 1881, sixty new members – mostly young – were admitted to the Lord's Table in the English Free Church.[25] Martin believed that many more would soon be publicly professing the Lord as Saviour, given the fact that, in the Highlands and Islands at the time, the Sacrament of the Lord's Supper was often regarded

---

23. Ibid., p. 81.

24. *RC-FCS-SR&M*, 1881, p. 2.

25. *TC*, 7 April 1881, p. 15. It was an unheard of thing in Lewis to admit to the Table converts still in their teens and with little Christian experience, and Martin came under a lot of criticism for this concession, not least by one or two of his own elders.

more as a mark of high spiritual attainment than a means of grace, and new converts were often reluctant to come forward as members. On the other hand, a good number of those awakened and apparently converted, yet who later fell away, did so through the trapping of alcohol.[26]

A Free Church Report for 1881 suggested that, 'over the whole of Lewis, but especially in Stornoway, a revival of religion has been to a large extent experienced'.[27] Further south in the more remote parishes of Uig and Bernera, for example, there was also a movement among the people, and eager anxiety manifested to hear the truth. In March 1881, The Committee for the Highlands and Islands sent the Rev. McLean of Shiskine there, to assist the local minister in conducting meetings.

News of the awakening spread throughout the Highlands. Martin himself was invited to conduct services in the Music Hall, Inverness, where a season of spiritual quickening and refreshing was experienced and folk were wonderfully drawn into the Kingdom. He also conducted a mission in Oban and Mull at this time (see pp. 38–9). Both were very fruitful, and he was delighted to see that some of the converts of the latter mission had become office bearers in Oban's Argyll Square Church by the time he moved there in 1897. In none of these locations, however, did such a movement ensue as most delightfully overtook the Lewis capital during that memorable autumn and winter of 1880. Wonderfully, Stornoway received further showers of blessing just seven years later, in 1887, when several thousand would regularly gather for open-air meetings in the town square, to hear north-east fishermen, as well as some locals, eloquently render profoundly moving testimonies (once again, this potent revival was strongly inter-related to one that broke out among Moray fisherfolk around the same time). To a lesser degree, yet another movement was experienced in Martin's church in 1896, at which time it was also testified that 'all over Lewis there is unusual interest in divine things'.[28]

NORTH UIST 1880

MEANWHILE, elsewhere in the Outer Hebrides, the island of North Uist also experienced a striking religious movement in 1880. This occurred in connection with the labours of Donald Stewart, a lay evangelist who laboured in promoting the gospel on the island for several months from the end of 1879. Stewart worked 'with characteristic earnestness, not

26. A strong advocate of temperance reform, Martin purchased two Stornoway public houses and turned them into a large coffee-shop.

27. RC-FCS-H&I, 1881, p. 9. It was also stated that 'this work in Lewis is not confined to Stornoway and its neighbourhood, but there are striking manifestations of it in other parishes in the island' (*RC-FCS-SR&M*, 1881, p. 3).

28. *RC-FCS-H&I*, 1896, p. 9. For more details of both movements, see www.scottishrevivals.co.uk.

only preaching in the church and meeting-houses and in his brother's barn, but also visiting the people in their houses'.[29]

The Rev. D.C. Ross, Free Church minister at Appin, crossed over to Uist to assist in the movement. He provided the following eyewitness account of the awakening:

> There is an uncommon eagerness to hear the Word of God, more especially how the blood of Christ makes atonement for the soul. Every night of the week but Saturday, with occasional day meetings, the people gathered from far and near to hear the gospel and such was the power of the truth that at times one and another were constrained to cry aloud – which was discouraged, as tending to distract the attention of the people – and others had a hard struggle to suppress their cries, while others still might be seen silently weeping. Some were awakened after returning home from the meetings, and one man was startled out of his sleep with the Word of God ringing in his ears. It was noticeable too, how boys and girls were in constant attendance; and cases are known of little ones lagging behind their companions, and slipping away to pray in the sandy hollows. Two boys threw their once fondly-cherished treasure – a profane song-book – into the fire of their own emotion, feeling, I suppose, that they were committing their dearest idol to the flames. Grown-up people, unable to read, have begun in several cases with the alphabet, and are now able to spell their way through the Word of God, searching it as for hidden treasures. Five or more district prayer meetings and Sabbath Schools have been started in addition to those previously existing. Not a few have applied to the minister for Bibles, of which he happened to have had for some time a considerable number for sale. There is a great temperance movement and one night we saw as many as 26 remaining to sign the pledge, another night 16, and in all somewhere about 200 have already given in their names.[30]

Ross continued:

> Some profess to have found the Saviour and are giving credible evidence that their profession is sincere. Some who neglected the house of God from one excuse or another for years are now in constant attendance, and neighbours who were once at variance are now living in amity. But while some have found the Saviour, more are 'under the sharp discipline of the law in their consciences', and asking the way to Zion, weeping as they go. Sabbath visiting – with its invariable accompaniment of vain conversation, a sin to which some of them were much addicted

29. *RC-FCS-H&I*, 1886, p. 171.

30. Ibid.

> – has been abandoned, with much sorrow for their past offences. In the services nothing but the psalms is sung, and there are no after-meetings, but the anxious are sought out and visited in their homes. The elders and maturer Christians are almost all in full sympathy with the work, and manifesting a spirit of the utmost tenderness towards the awakened; and we know of one woman who was awakened at a meeting while a venerable elder was reading the words, 'Repent, for the kingdom of heaven is at hand,' and she is now rejoicing in the Saviour. Her husband, at one time intensely worldly, who had the sharp arrows of the Almighty sticking in his conscience for two or three months, sat up on one occasion all night with a Christian shepherd reading and singing, and praying, when towards the dawn the love of God was so shed in his heart that he was filled with wonder that all the world did not believe in Jesus.[31]

Following his labours in North Uist, Stewart was called to Berneray, Harris, where he travailed for a number of months and saw many tokens of blessing in connection with his work. During this time he was repeatedly requested to go to other spheres of labour, but for the first part of 1881 he declined, as he felt that to leave would be injurious to the work in Berneray.[32]

BENBECULA 1882

PERHAPS related in part to the influence of spiritual stirrings in North Uist, a notable work of grace found its commencement in the neighbouring isle of Benbecula early in 1882. The small island, which sits between North and South Uist, had a population at the time of around 1,800 people, fully half of them being Roman Catholics. A deputy of the Free Church, visiting North Uist, Harris and Benbecula, gave a cheering and encouraging account of the spiritual condition of each island, but enthused particularly of the latter place, where, for a number of months, people had been showing unusual earnestness. 'They flock to the preaching of the Word whenever an opportunity is given them, and the impression under the hearing of the Word is very deep and solemn.' The deputy urged that a new church be built within the district to accommodate 400 people, and that a preaching station be immediately set up with a view to its being connected into a charge.[33]

HARRIS (AND LEWIS) 1883–6

BY the summer of 1883 it became evident that the Lord was owning His word and preparing Harris for times of refreshing. All over the district,

---

31. Ibid., p.2. Frustratingly, Mr Ross closes with the comment, 'But I must not be tempted into details'! (ibid.)

32. *RC-FCS-H&I*, 1881, p. 9.

33. Ibid., 1882, pp. 231–2.

and in some of the smaller islands, souls were being quickened into newness of life. The minister in Tarbert, the Rev. Roderick MacKenzie, was anxious to commence a season of special meetings throughout the parish. But this was difficult to arrange. The people were scattered and poor, roads were non-existent and tracks were often difficult to traverse.

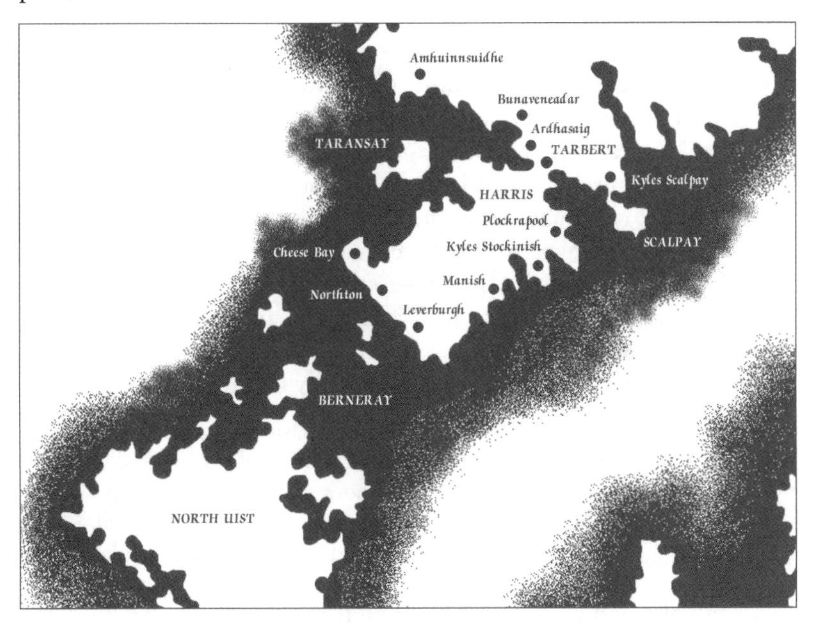

Besides, evening meetings would be almost untenable during this season due to people being engaged in necessary duties on their crofts.

In 1884 MacKenzie was removed and Donald Stewart, evangelist, came to occupy the vacancy till a permanent minister could be secured. Stewart knew the area well, being a native of Luskentyre in the west of the parish. In the south and west of Harris his family had been residents for three quarters of a century. Brought to saving knowledge of the truth nearly thirty years previously, he had devoted himself for the last twenty years to evangelistic work, being greatly used in Tiree, Benbecula, Grimsay, North Uist and adjacent islands, as well as on the mainland of Scotland. Soon he was able to find indications of blessing attending his labours in Harris, with people deeply interested and attendance at services large.

Stewart remained until September 1884, when in consequence of indisposition brought on by his many labours, it was necessary for him to take a time of rest. In spring 1885 he resumed his itinerary at Loch Stockinish, further south on the island, and here he continued with little interval for six months. As interest in divine things steadily quickened, the Board School often proved too small, so services were not infrequently held in the open air. People came long distances, and occasionally from districts upwards of twenty miles away, and the elderly as well as the young shared in the blessing. Despite a degree of nervous excitement in a number of cases where particularly strong feelings were concerned, most instances of saving change occurred without any undue excitement.

The meetings were kept up and the interest deepened, to the extent that Rev. McLean, the new minister, who became wholeheartedly involved in the movement, asked for others to be sent to help him. Mr MacDonald, catechist, arrived to assist, as too, in November 1885, did Free Church deputies Major MacLeod and the Rev. Lee of Nairn, and so the good work continued, with short intervals. The number of anxious souls was great and many were believed to have passed from life to death. D.J. Martin of Stornoway also came to the aid of McLean, with further gratifying results. At one point McLean's health, too, broke down due to his incessant labours.[34]

MacLeod reported to the General Assembly that he and Lee

> commenced at Tarbert, Harris. Their visit was during the Communion time. The day was very cold, and although he was well coated with a thick overcoat and a waterproof over it, he felt the cold. He went out of the village to look for the place of meeting, as the church could not hold the half of the people, but he could see nothing but rocks; there was hardly a house in sight, and when he asked where the congregation was, he was told they were up on the side of a rocky hill. He went up there and found a large congregation collected in that cold place in heavy rain that would have frightened any one from going outside, and much more from sitting on the side of a hill. He saw old men and women sitting there in floods of water and rain for four hours listening to the preaching of the gospel. It grieved his heart to see them. He got a chair himself, and he offered it to a man older than himself, but he would not have it. After the Communion, the people were dismissed, and the deputies hardly had time to take a bit of dinner when they were told that the church was filled again with the people. How they had managed to get dinner he did not know; he thought the most of them had had none. He need not describe the scene in church, but he wished Dr Rainy had seen it, for it was one thing to hear about it and another thing to see it. Some Highlanders thought their ways and affairs could not be understood by Lowlanders, which reminded him of the Irish soldier who said of his doctor who was an Englishman, 'What does an English doctor know

34. The information so far related is taken from a report given by William Ross of Cowcaddens to *TC*, 29 April 1886, p. 8.

> about Irish diseases?' He did not believe there was a dry stitch on the people, yet they continued there until 12 o'clock at night, and even then, if the deputies had not dismissed them (against their will), they would have continued there all night; for their wish was loudly expressed, to continue the service.
>
> At another place five miles from Tarbert, they met near the top of a hill, in a plain, primitive meeting-house, built in the shelter of a rock, and thus invisible until one came right upon it. The houses of the crofter fishermen, for whose accommodation it was erected, were at a considerable distance from it, along the sea-shore, but out of consideration for the minister, and to save him the trouble of coming to the town through difficult rocky paths, they chose the present location, being within a quarter of a mile of the public road. It was built out of common unhewn stone without lime, and roofed over by plain deals of wood. Here they met their minister in all weathers regularly far from their homes.
>
> In that wild moor they found the place crowded with men and women, Bibles in hand. And he really felt the electricity of divine love at that meeting, for he was moved in his inmost soul by the looks and sighs of the people, for the love of Christ was beaming in every face. The people crowded and pressed hard to shake hands with them, but lacked boldness to do so. He went to shake hands with them, and when he looked at his new glove he hardly had a rag of it left, for the people's grip was so strong that they had torn it to pieces![35]

Rev. Lee testified that 'we would gladly have exchanged turreted buildings and ornate churches for an experience similar to that (which) we then enjoyed'.[36]

On the Communion Sabbath, October 1885, Messrs Lee and MacLeod had services from midday until midnight, with an interval of two hours or thereby. The preaching in the evening was over by ten, but then a prayer meeting was held under MacLeod's superintendence, which continued 'until the clock struck 12. Prayer was engaged in during those hours by representative laymen from all the islands around. We found the congregation well organised. Some of the present office-bearers were added to the church during the ministry of Mr McKenzie; indeed they have had more or less blessing for years. Fourteen new communicants were added to the roll on the occasion of our visit, and as the result of the revival work which is still going on, we doubt not the present roll of 111 will be greatly increased.'[37]

---

35. *RC-FCS-H&I*, 1886, pp. 175–6.
36. ARC-FCS-SR&M, 1886, pp. 56–7.
37. Ibid., p. 57.

One fascinating illustration of the work relates to the island of Taransay, to the west of Harris, as reported by Principal Rainy to the General Assembly in May 1886:

> That island was held by one tacksman,[38] and there were perhaps a dozen families on the island. The tacksman's house was the only one he had remembered to have seen which was at all a comfortable and finished house, built on the peculiar architectural principles of the common block houses, and had walls seven feet thick. Well, some of the young men of Taransay had been over in Tarbert, and they told what they had seen. There awoke among the people a great desire that some portion of the blessing might reach themselves, and they began, without the assistance of any office-bearer or minister, to engage in prayer. While so engaged, there was a peculiar impression, and the person who was leading the devotions was unable to proceed. Well, as the result of the movement, he (Dr Rainy) was informed by letter that there was not a single family on the island in which there was not some hopeful appearance.[39]

The workers laboured under the serious want of suitable meeting places in Harris. Two such houses were needed – one on Loch Stockinish and one at Collam – and contributions were invited from any of the Lord's people who were able to help. Meanwhile, a Free Church worker quoted in the General Assembly reports for 1886 enthused that 'Harris is still ablaze spiritually, and in Lochs God is working his wonders. I expect soon to see our island aflame. The spirit of controversy has been kept out, and the blessings seem spreading!'[40]

While the movement was most notable in Harris, William Ross reported in April 1886: 'The parish of Lochs and other parts of the Lews are being moved already. I feel assured there is a great harvest of souls to be reaped.'[41] In fact awakening had spread to Lochs in the summer of 1885, where, for some time previously, the cry for God's blessing had gone up from a Saturday evening prayer meeting specially called for the purpose. They didn't have to wait long, for the young minister, the Rev. John MacDougall, and his Free Church people 'soon found themselves in the midst of a wondrous work of grace', which was still in progress at the end of the following year. A good number of both young and old joined the church, while some who had fallen back after the 1860 revival were re-awakened.[42] At the same time blessing was also being

38. Acting viceroy between landlord and farming tenants.

39. *PGA-FCS-H&I*, 1886, p. 175.

40. *RC-FCS-SR&M*, 1886, p. 7.

41. *TC*, 29 April 1886, p. 8.

42. ARC-FCS-SR&M, 1887, p. 38.

experienced in Kinloch, while, additionally, the minister of Carloway reported that in several districts within the bounds of his parish a deep work of grace was evident. A visit of Free Church deputies to Uig, too, revealed 'large and deeply-impressed audiences, and that the fruit of the time of blessing in Bernera, some time ago, is still being gathered in'.[43]

Point 1886–8

SUBSEQUENT to a spiritual movement in Back in 1886 (see www.scottishrevivals.co.uk), an unexpected movement began in Knock Free Church, Point, towards the end of an eighteen-month vacancy in the parish. In October 1886 Rev. MacKaskill of Dingwall Free Church visited Lewis, where, along with others, he laboured for some time as a deputy of the Committee on Religion and Morals. Two young men from Aird, in the Point peninsula, described as amongst 'the most careless and godless characters from the township',[44] were among the many who attended the Communion services at Back, where MacKaskill was preaching. Returning home after five days, one of the men, who, like his colleagues, had previously been thoughtless regarding spiritual matters, couldn't stop thinking about all that had been said and done during the long weekend, and instead of retiring to rest, went to a secluded place by the sea-shore and there sought, and it seems, found, peace in Christ – returning home in the morning with great joy in his heart.

George MacLeod was ordained and inducted to Knock parish at the end of 1886, two months after the awakening began. He takes up the story: 'This young man's conversion, or '"seriousness" as they termed it, soon spread over the whole place, as if a gentle breath of wind had entered in at the one end of the township and gone out at the other, rousing young and old to a calm, thoughtful inquiry about their eternal interests. Every house felt the influence to some extent, and realised that they were in the presence of some unseen Power. Young and old met and consulted together, and sent some of their number to one of my elders, a godly man, to help them in their difficulties, and preside over their prayer meeting. All this took place, I think, in two days.'[45] Within a few months that parish was said to have constituted a network of prayer meetings.

MacLeod led the movement with diligence and sensitivity over the ensuing months of its progress. MacKaskill later reported that

> when there last Oct. (1887), assisting at the dispensation of the Lord's Supper, the scene was most touching. After Thursday there

43. Ibid.
44. Ibid., p. 39.
45. Ibid., 1888, p. 59.

> was no church in the island that could hold the multitude that assembled to hear the Word, till on Sabbath the numbers reached to between 7,000 and 8,000. The aspect of the congregation all along was most solemnising. They looked as if all were concerned for their souls' salvation. Sabbath was an exceedingly cold and boisterous day, yet that vast multitude sat out the service with wonderful patience. There was an evident thirst for the Word, and cold indeed must have been the preacher's soul unless it was stirred to its very depth by the sight. Lewis was then, and is still, in a most hopeful condition religiously.[46]

'But it may be asked,' continued MacKaskill, 'how is that account consistent with the agrarian disorders[47] that followed? My firm conviction is that however much I sympathised with the people as to the causes that led to these, they were stirred by Satan to oppose this blessed work which promised such an abundant harvest, and which in spite of all that has happened, is still promising and producing hopeful results.'[48]

Reporting on the means employed in the movement, MacLeod remarked in 1888 that most of the elders took a deep interest, but that nothing was tried but

> the old-fashioned, orthodox preaching, praise and prayer. It was nothing uncommon to see our meeting-house literally packed, and keeping together for four hours, praying and singing. The reading of a chapter or a portion of a psalm has been known to give a blessing. On more than one occasion I began my service at 6 p.m. and continued till 9. On pronouncing the benediction, the people would sit still, wishing to hear more of 'Jesus and His love'. I would then call an after-meeting, and ask all those who were anxious to stay behind. Almost all would stay with us. Not being able to deal with so many personally, there was nothing for it but to hold up Christ to them as their Friend, Brother and Saviour. I had to preach daily, and sometimes twice a day, and used every other means of gathering them in, and for keeping them after we did get them.[49]

As to results, the Free Church deputy concluded:

> only one day can tell this. There are, however, ways of tabulating results that ought to cheer the godly, encourage the inquirer,

46. *PGA-FCS*, 1888, p. 101.

47. Disturbances caused by crofters agitating for greater rights from landlords. Allan MacColl provides strong evidence that by and large, and contrary to the accepted belief that the attitude of Highland clergymen towards land reform in the aftermath of the Clearances consisted of a mixture of callous indifference, cowering deference and fatalistic passivity, Highland Christians – both clergy and laity – were committed to land reform as an engine of social improvement and conciliation (Allan W. MacColl, *Land, Faith and the Crofting Community: Christianity and Social Criticism in the Highlands of Scotland 1843–1893*, Edinburgh 2006, p. 187).

48. *PGA-FCS*, 1888, p. 101.

49. *ARC-FCS-SR&M*, 1888, pp. 59–60.

> strengthen faith, and simplify prayer. The results of this movement have been numerous. The means of grace are appreciated and sought after better than I have seen anywhere else. Prayer meetings have been multiplied, kept up, and taken part in by the men and the young converts in a way that would satisfy the most cautious mind. When the principal prayer meeting would be going on the young men would go in bands to the houses of those in trouble, or indifferent about their salvation, and read and pray with and for them. Classes were opened and keep going. Men and women took their stand on the side of Christ. The work was chiefly among the young men. About 40 have come forward and joined the Church, and more than as many again have been following as faithfully as those who have joined. The happy point about the work is that not one of those who have 'gone aside' to follow Christ has turned back, and also that the work is going on still.[50]

Lewis, Harris and Uist 1888–91

THAT the promising work going on in several parts of Lewis was still in progress in 1888 is apparent from an interesting report given by the Rev. Angus MacDonald of Portnahaven Free Church regarding work at Peterhead during the summer fishing season of that year. Wrote MacDonald:

> A number of young men from Lewis took part in these meetings; and it was gratifying to see the hold they have of the truth, and the soul-moving earnestness with which they presented their petition. Several of these have been recently awakened, and are a clear evidence that the Lord has been working in Lewis. They were wisely called upon to engage publicly in prayer in their own congregations; and they had therefore more confidence to engage in that duty away from home. It may be remarked that it is generally the more intelligent part of the young people who seem to have received a blessing and it may also be stated that very few of the young women who came under the influence of the truth ventured to the fishing this season. They were, I am informed, afraid of the injurious influence of their surroundings away from their native homes.[51]

Blessing in Lewis continued during the following year and right into the early 1890s. In January 1890, minister of Kinloch Free Church gave testimony to 'a very marked work of grace' in his parish. 'I observed signs of the good work going on in my congregation just now as early as the time of our last Communion in September,' he said. 'Not, however, till later on, when Mr MacKay of Tiree visited the congregation and assisted

50. Ibid.

51. *RC-FCS-H&I*, 1889, p. 21.

in a series of gospel meetings, did so many come under concern. I am pleased to say that there are many promising cases, both among young and aged. The meetings continue to be well attended, and the work is steadily progressing.'[52]

During the latter part of 1890, from various districts in Lewis and, particularly, Uist, came reports of 'an amount of Christian vigour and activity in congregations, which augurs well for the future'.[53] For example, widespread awakening occurred in the village of Balallan in that year – the results of which were lasting, as witnessed by the numbers then admitted for the first time to the Lord's Table.[54] One church testified to 'a manifest increase of spiritual life, shown by increased liberality to the Lord's cause, especially to foreign missions, several recent additions to membership and some anxious inquirers'. In another parish there were 'seven weekly prayer-meetings and nine Sabbath Schools, well attended and taught by 26 teachers'. From yet elsewhere came news of 'a religious awakening throughout this district during the past winter and several interesting cases of what appears to be real conversions'.[55]

Meanwhile, the Free Church Presbytery of Harris reported in early 1890: 'In some of the congregations, and especially in Tarbert, Harris and Bernera, there has been of late an unusual interest manifested in spiritual matters, and many have been awakened to be concerned for their souls. They have added over 60 to their Communion roll within the year.'[56] In South Uist and North Harris in particular, the shower of blessing was conspicuous, and was partly influenced by a visit from D.T. MacKay of Tiree at the September 1890 Communion. In the Kyle Scalpay area of Harris several people were seriously impressed before the Communion. MacKay stayed for ten days after the sacrament. 'When preaching one day at Kyle Scalpay, there was such an outburst of feeling and weeping and crying, that he had to stop in the middle of his discourse. After he left Harris, meetings were held every evening in the district, and the impression continued for many weeks together. When preaching there afterwards it was difficult to get through with the service, owing to the cries and sobs of both men and women. Some very old men, 80 and over, are among the awakened, as well as not a few of the young.'[57]

In 1891, at such far removed locations as Lochs, Barvas and Uig, the Communion services had to be held outside, so great were the crowds

52. *RC-FCS-SR&M*, 1890, p. 13.

53. Ibid., 1891, p. 15.

54. *RC-FCS-SR&M*, 1890, pp. 12–13.

55. Ibid., 1891, p. 15. Frustratingly, the report does not name the individual parishes referred to.

56. Ibid., 1890, pp. 12–13. Twenty-seven were added to Tarbert FC for the first time in September 1889, and a further 29 the following March (Tarbert FC Minutes 1889–90).

57. Ibid.

that gathered. The facts with regard to Uig are all the more remarkable, given that it was the first occasion for twenty years in which outside services had been held in that congregation. Of Bernera, it was reported by the local Free Church elders that at every Communion in recent years some had been converted. The largest number ever admitted to the Lord's Table on one occasion on the island was at the Communion season of November 1891,[58] following which some of these new believers quickly matured in their faith and were soon taking part in the regular prayer meetings.[59]

Other Significant Movements in this Period[60]

Ness 1880s
Back 1880s
Stornoway 1887 & 1896

58. Of these eventful occasions, one correspondent wrote, 'Our Communion services are yet with us grand religious festivals – spiritual feasts. There are to ministers in the north no more joyous times, nor any more blessed opportunities of spiritual refreshment, than these Communion gatherings, and I am sure the people can say the same. ... I am more and more struck with the immense power of these as occasions of special evangelistic work. Friends not knowing the Highlands sometimes forget this ... but I am persuaded that no more blessed opportunity of preaching the glorious gospel is anywhere found than in our Highlands at such gatherings; nowhere will one hear that gospel more earnestly, lovingly and faithfully preached in all its fullness' (ibid., 1892, p. 15).

59. Ibid.

60. Full accounts of these movements can be found on www.scottishrevivals.co.uk.

Stornoway Harbour – p.267

D.J. Martin – p.267

Francis Street, Stornoway – p.271

North Uist – p.272

Harris 'Black-houses' – p.274

Loch Seaforth (separating Harris and Lewis) – p.282

9
The Union Awakening
1900–17

Union Controversy

TO gain a more considered perspective on the pockets of awakening that developed throughout Lewis in the first decade of the twentieth century, one needs to understand the wider ecclesiastical situation existing at that time. Official discussions on the proposed union of the United Presbyterian Church of Scotland[1] and the Free Church had begun as early as 1863, but were abandoned in 1873 due to resistance among a Constitutionalist minority within the latter party. Discussions resumed again in 1896 with more success, three years after the passing of the Free Church's Declaratory Act had pressed around 14,000 elders, members and adherents to leave that denomination with their two leading ministers to set up the Free Presbyterian Church. In 1900 the vast majority of remaining Presbyterian seceders were at last gathered into one body, the United Free Church, while a separate Free Church continued, mainly within the Highlands, professing loyalty to the Westminster Confession of Faith and to the establishment principle. At its formation, the United Free Church consisted of 593 former UPC and 1068 former Free Church congregations, giving an initial total membership of some half a million. The Free Church, by contrast, was reduced to 27 ministers and, while figures were hard to ascertain, claimed around 125 congregations and 70,000 members in 1904.

The Free Church minority held the newly-formed Union to be unconstitutional, and took out a long-threatened legal action for payment and transfer of the whole assets of the property held in trust for the Free Church. The resultant case was twice dismissed by the Court of Session, but an appeal to the House of Lords proved more successful and in August 1904 the property and funds of the Free Church were deemed to belong to the relatively small and largely provincial minority group. But pressure from the sorely wounded UFC led to the formation of the Churches (Scotland) Act of 1905, whereby a Commission was appointed to distribute the property between the two groups in an equitable manner, an arduous task that took several years to effectuate.

1. This overwhelmingly Lowland and urban denomination resulted from the Union in 1847 of the United Secession Church and the Relief Church, thus bringing together the two elements from both the first and second Secessions from the CoS (1733 and 1761).

In the lead-up to the Union being consummated, a deputation of pro-Union Free Church ministers conducted meetings in every parish on Lewis except Uig, urging parishioners of the advantages of the Union. Resistance to the Union was particularly strong, largely through the efforts of Hector Cameron of Back, who almost came to the point of despair in the process.[2] In the event, it was estimated that out of a Free Church membership in Lewis of around 20,000, only 1,600 joined the UFC.[3] The vast majority of these were from the Uig and Stornoway English-speaking congregations.

Unseemly squabbles over the occupancy of buildings became commonplace, however, both in Lewis and elsewhere in Scotland. The bitterness of feeling engendered at this time was very considerable. It seems somewhat remarkable that amidst such squabbling, anguish, bitterness and disaffection, both of the concerned Lewis Churches should find the Spirit of God moving in a deep way within their congregations. But such was the case. 'When the land was thus scorched and arid as the sandy desert, the hearts of believing men and women turned to the Lord, in earnest prayer, for the outpouring of His gracious spirit, and He sent His blessing "as the dew unto Israel".'[4] Ironically, in the Established Church, which remained aloof from the wranglings between these other two Presbyterian denominations, there were no reports of significant spiritual awakening at this time.

What G.N.M. Collins said of Free Church members was true also of those of other congregations. 'The "Shorter Catechism" they already knew, at least by memory. They were familiar with its masterly definitions of Christian doctrine even if they could not fully grasp their meaning. And if the "Confession of Faith" was widely regarded as rather beyond them, the pulpit message to which they were accustomed was impregnated with its teaching.' Many had also grown up under district catechising. So now, 'In their fireside conversations they kept themselves abreast of the trend of events in the ecclesiastical arena … and that man was indeed a "stranger in Jerusalem" who knew not "the things that had come to pass there in those days". The people took sides over the matters at issue, and felt it incumbent upon them to do so intelligently.'[5]

---

2. While some view Cameron as the Lewis Free Church hero of 1900, others see him as a deeply contentious figure (e.g. John MacLeod, in *Banner In The West: A Spiritual History Of Lewis And Harris*, Edinburgh 2008, pp. 199–200).

3. Meanwhile, in Tarbert, Harris, the whole congregation followed Rev. Nicol Campbell into the Union.

4. MacRae, *Revivals in the Highlands & Islands in the 19th Century*, pp. 159–60.

5. G.N.M. Collins, *The Days of the Years of my Pilgrimage*, Edinburgh 1991, pp. 29–30. Or, as Norman MacLeod put it: 'The heated controversy between pro-Union and anti-Union people produced knowledge of fundamental doctrines which had been of little interest to them before then. The result was that the Spirit of God moved over these troubled waters' (Rev. Norman MacLeod, *Lewis Revivals of the 20th Century*, Lewis 1989, p. 6).

AWAKENING WITHIN THE UNITED FREE CHURCH

1900–1

REMARKABLY, as early as 1901, Proceedings of the General Assembly of the newly-established United Free Church of Scotland reported that 'the tidings from Lewis of awakening work is exceedingly encouraging and hopeful. A spirit of expectancy and a deep longing for a season of special blessing were manifested in several parishes for some months past. The special strain and stress that some ministers and congregations recently experienced intensified this feeling, and earnest men and women betook themselves to special prayer for a revival of genuine religion.' The Rev. MacDonald of Stornoway confessed his delight 'that, amid much to discourage them, the Spirit of the Lord had blazed up, and testified to Himself'.[6]

A Report to the General Assembly in the same year spoke of how 'the remote south-west Lewis parish of Uig has felt the quickening breath of the Holy Ghost at various times during its fascinating history, not least in 1828, 1842 and 1859'.[7] Now, some decades later, in the autumn of 1900 and the spring of 1901, 'The Rev. D. MacArthur, the young minister of Uig, soon after his settlement was conscious of a spirit of anxiety among his people. He had special tokens of the Spirit's presence and power in connection with his first Communion in September,' whereafter D.T. MacKay was invited to come and help. As a rule, MacKay held two services a day for three weeks, 'with the most blessed results'.[8] Interestingly, and probably not without significance, this was the one Lewis congregation, 'which up to that point had not been disturbed over the Union question by the visit of men who felt strongly on the subject, but was allowed to pursue the work of preaching the Gospel and building up a Church for Christ'.[9]

MacKay wrote of his memorable visit to Uig, 'A large number of old and young have been convicted of sin by the Spirit of God, and turned from darkness to light, finding peace and joy in believing. The people have come out to church in a very marked way for miles every day. Indeed, all manual labour was for a time given up, and the worshippers returned home at night singing the praises of God.'[10] At the following Communion season, in March 1901, nineteen young communicants were admitted by the Church Session as a result of the awakening, while

6. *PGA-UFCS*, 1901, p. 208.

7. *RC-UFCS-H&I*, 1901, p. 11.

8. Ibid.

9. Ibid.

10. MacRae, *Revivals in the Highlands & Islands in the 19th Century*, p. 75.

the Rev. Donald MacArthur intimated that there were between eighty and ninety more whom they would as gladly have welcomed.

MacArthur was also the Interim Moderator of Bernera UFC at the time. A native of Staffin, Skye, he had been inducted to the Free Church in Uig at the age of 32, just a year before the Union, which he and many in his congregation entered into in 1900.[11] As a result, Mr A. MacLeod from Ness was posted to Bernera as Free Church missionary, described as a 'talented young man, whose labours are highly appreciated'.[12] Quickly, awakening spread throughout this small island, and as there were ministerial vacancies in both the Free Church and UFC at this time, the two joined together in the work, and the fellowship forged in the heat of the revival was so genuine and deep that strong ties remained between the two churches over ensuing decades. Some of those converted in both congregations were described as Christian men of outstanding gifts and grace. At the administration of the Lord's Supper in September 1902, an immense (and largely Free Church) congregation from the island and surrounding districts assembled in the open air and 'very hopeful tokens of divine blessing' were evident.[13] The Bernera movement, however, proved to be a fairly isolated incident of early co-operation between the two bodies.

Significant blessing was also experienced further north, in Barvas, while in Ness,

> during the Communion services, held amidst much discomfort in a school-house, it was felt that there was something unusual about the services. Those who spoke felt as if they had unusual liberty; those who listened that it was a time of blessing. On the Sabbath evening some of the Lord's people who stayed to a prayer meeting melted down, and many said that the Lord was in that place. On Monday there was a deep solemnity about the service, and the minister felt the interest to be so deep that he followed up the services with a series of meetings. At the second of these strong men had to leave the meeting, crying out, 'What must I do to be saved?' Their catechist, a level-headed man, not given to exaggeration, said he never remembered anything like it since the revival of 1859. The minister and the catechist kept up the meetings for six weeks, night after night; and at last 19 men and fully as many women gave signs of a saving change.[14]

Meanwhile, in Kinloch, 'whole families had been brought to Christ', and it was believed that 'there were at least 50 persons under deep

---

11. Uig FC remained without a minister until 1929, when John M. Morrison was ordained and inducted there.

12. *MR-FCS*, October 1902, p. 168.

13. Ibid.

14. *PGA-UFCS*, 1901, p. 208. See also MacRae, *Revivals in the Highlands & Islands in the 19th Century*, p. 77.

concern; unless it could be said that even already they had passed into the Kingdom'.[15] Peter MacDonald's congregation in Stornoway shared, too, in the revival, and during Communion Services held here and at Ness, Barvas, Kinloch and elsewhere in the spring of 1901, 'there was much blessing enjoyed; believers were greatly quickened and refreshed and souls were won to Christ.'[16] Indeed, speaking of the work at the UFC General Assembly that same year, MacDonald described it as 'one of the deepest spiritual movements that had ever been known on the island'.[17]

Special services were carried on in the different parishes of the Presbytery, to which UFC ministers from Ullapool, Tarbert, Dores, Avoch, Snizort and Kilmuir had all given assistance. D.T. MacKay also made a return trip to the island during 1901, as too did Alexander Frazer – well known for his connection with awakening work in Campbeltown and Inverness three years earlier – who began a mission in Stornoway at the urgent request of local ministers. A number of letters were sent to the General Assembly from brethren in Lewis testifying to the quickening being experienced in their congregations. It is, however, a great pity we are not told to which parishes each report pertains. One minister begins, 'I am delighted to inform you that we have a great revival just now. Scores of my people are being led to the Saviour. It is impossible for me to describe the great movement. Young men and young women, old men and old women, are brought to the light. In our after-meeting tonight there were over 100 present in great anxiety about their salvation.'[18]

Another testifies: 'During our series of special services the people were deeply moved, and scores of them, young and old, were turned to the Lord. We all feel that the Lord is with us and blessing us in a very wonderful manner.'[19] Another minister records: 'We had large congregations at all our Communion Services, but especially so on Sabbaths. Our church, which holds considerably over 1,000, was packed to the door. …'[20] Elsewhere in the island came a report: 'The Lord has been working amongst us for some time and our Communion season was one of the most enjoyable we have ever had. Quite a number have been brought under concern and there is unusual liveliness and attention to the word amongst us. …'[21]

In some places blessing continued throughout 1901, and the General Assembly Report for 1902 contains the following excerpt

---

15. *PGA-UFCS*, 1901, p. 208.
16. *RC-UFCS-H&I*, 1901, p. 11.
17. *PGA-UFCS*, 1901, p. 208; MacRae, *Revivals in the Highlands & Islands in the 19th Century*, p. 76.
18. *RC-UFCS-H&I*, 1901, p. 11.
19. Ibid.
20. Ibid., p. 12.
21. Ibid.

from a letter sent in by a Lewis minister in the ordinary course of communication on other matters: 'I am glad to say that the Lord has visited us in a merciful way. Anything and everything must give place to this work. We are having daily services for some time back, and except for some help given by local brethren, the catechist and myself are doing the work alone. The people asked me to plead for the assistance of Mr MacKay of Cromarty, but I understand he is not available.' [22]

1903–4

FOLLOWING visits to several parishes, the Rev. Walter Calder of Stornoway wrote in 1904,

> Here we are in Lewis as a Presbytery practically churchless. ... The congregations meet for worship in schools, manses, barns, and the open hillside ... . Yet, there is a spirit of prayer, of earnest expectation, and hopeful expectancy prevailing amongst us. The Sabbath services, which are well attended, are characterised by devout seriousness and bright joyousness. But still better is the fact that there is not a single parish within the bounds of the Presbytery in which there are not evident tokens of the Divine blessing. During the last three months many have been awakened and several have professed conversion, and we regard these cases as precursors of great blessing. The indications throughout the island are especially promising at present. I heard some of the elders say recently at a public meeting that they were coming to the Sabbath services not only praying for a blessing, but also looking forward to and expecting conversions every day. If we are passing through a time of trial, we are also enjoying a time of refreshing from the presence of the Lord. [23]

Members of the UFC Presbytery of Lewis declared themselves thoroughly satisfied with their visit to the Uig congregation in September 1904. 'It was with pleasure they found family worship in every family connected with the congregation and that special manifestation of the saving work of the Holy Spirit in the congregation in recent years was felt.'[24] The following year a Lewis minister, when writing about the trying prospect of eviction from his manse, added, 'This congregation is in a most promising state at present. Had we suitable places for meeting in, we might hope for a rich harvest of

22. Ibid., 1902, p. 9.

23. *RC-UFCS-H&I,* 1905, pp. 4–5.

24. John MacLeod, *A Brief Record of the Church in Uig (Lewis), up to the Union of 1929*, 2001 Stornoway, p. 38.

souls. We are doing all we can to spread and deepen the work, but we do not wish to enter into any details at present.'[25]

1908

DONALD John Martin, then of Oban, conducted an evangelistic tour of Lewis in September 1908. He noticed signs of encouragement in Leurbost, but,

> on reaching Callanish I got into a different region and atmosphere altogether. Here tokens of spiritual revival met me on every hand. My host for the afternoon and his wife had become communicants since my last knowledge of them, and when we met in the meeting-house immediately after the close of the F.C. service, many of those attending it turned in, and we had a large and attentive audience.[26] ... From Uig I went to Ness, calling at meetings at Callanish, Shawbost and Shaidir (Barvas) by the way. At Shader in the congregation of Barvas, I again came on the tracks of blessing. I was told that the most of my large audience there had either professed conversion or had come under religious impression. Mr Morrison, the minister, told me a story of remarkable blessing. One night after the first service, when they came out, they found the people standing round the door weeping, and they had to re-light and have a second meeting to deal with the anxious; and this continued for weeks, night after night. Whole families professed conversion, and are now sitting together at the Lord's Table.
>
> I cannot close without mentioning that the honoured instrument in these times of refreshment, so far as human agency is concerned, was the Rev. D. MacKay of Tiree. Mr Morrison,

25. *RC-UFCS-H&I*, 1906, p. 8. Speaking in 1909 of the difficult days following the ruling of the House of Lords five years earlier, the Rev. George MacLeod of Knock said: 'There is considerable difference between our position in the Highlands today and our position there some six years ago, when we found ourselves without house and home. Possibly, some of you think that we were somewhat sad and discouraged and disappointed at the situation as we found it. Well, I frankly admit that we were sad and sorry, but not for one moment afraid of the position in which we found ourselves. We rather rejoiced in it. We rather felt ourselves proud of it, and I am here tonight to tell it, that we have reason to look back to thank God that he honoured us by making us endure the suffering and taking our little part in the testimony to which this Church was called, to stand true in the hour of trial. We were, it is true, turned out of our manses and our churches, but we were never turned out alone. I said more than once, and I say it tonight, that it would have been well for many of the congregations north and south to have been in the same position and the same condition, to have gone through the same experience, in order to receive the same blessing that many of us in these days and years received and enjoyed from on high. The position is that we were turned outside to the hill, and found ourselves along the seashore. There were our people, almost one and all of them, under the influence of the Spirit of God. I asked on one occasion a man who is not given by any means to exaggeration, if he thought he need not tell if many or any of a certain congregation were under the influence of the Spirit. What was his reply? "I cannot," he said, "at this moment put my hand on a man or a woman of the congregation who is not, as far as I can judge, under the influence of the Holy Spirit." The result has proved the truth of that' (*PGA-UFCS-H&I*, 1910, p. 340).

26. Altogether, 41 members were added to the roll of the Carloway UFC in the first decade after the Union (MacLeod, *Lewis Revivals*, p. 9).

> Barvas, speaking to me of these times, said that Mr MacKay had come when the people were prepared for such times. He said that he thought that the real secret of these times lay in the fact that the people, in what they were called to suffer and to lose, were cast in utter dependence upon God, and were found waiting on Him and on Him alone; temporal loss had closed them in to spiritual gain. And God did not disappoint them. The one thing which our people now want in the Lewis is proper places of worship. [27]

Reflecting shortly after his visit on the spiritual harvest enjoyed in Lewis, D.J. Martin noted three fruits that especially impressed him. First, 'I had been long accustomed to see Communion Tables in Lewis filled with our older people. I was struck with the remarkable change that had passed over our Communion Tables there in a few years, when I saw young men and women filling them. And I would like our friends to know this, that the profession of Christ in Lewis has for its condition a distinct confession of conscious conversion. It may be that the subjective is pressed too far in the admission of communicants in the western Highlands, but I mention that to show what were the forces that brought these young people to the Communion Table.' Another feature was 'the increase of liberality. What a marvellous collection that was in Knock, £204, from a poor country congregation composed mostly of fishermen. The Foreign Mission collections in Lewis have been larger this year than ever.' The third thing he noted was 'not merely liberality, but liberty … people going home singing Sankey's hymns and meeting in the quarry for a prayer-meeting. All over the Highlands I find that text fulfilled: "Where the Spirit of the Lord is, there is liberty." They have shaken themselves free from all false traditionalism.' [28]

1910

BLESSING was still being experienced a couple of years later. When a minister from the mainland went to Lewis in 1910 he found that

> not only was there a considerable membership in our church, but that it was a constantly increasing membership. Lochs had 45 members, Uig 160, Barvas 181, and so on. But these are only the communicants. You have adherents to the number of 500 in some places, and in several cases there is a practical membership of about 1,000. But not only is our Church increasing in membership, it is also increasing in givings. The Central Fund contributions have gone up to £500 or £600. But more than that, we were made to feel that religion was a great reality among the

27. *RC-UFCS-H&I*, p. 1908, pp. 14–15.

28. *PGA-UFCS-H&I*, 1908, pp. 299–300.

> people; they seemed to be living almost in a revival atmosphere. There was no great excitement, but a spiritual movement was going on, and has been for long. … One said, "There has never been a week during all that time (since 1900) in which we have not had manifest tokens of the Spirit of God at work in our midst." It was the Communion season when we were there, and we got the full fruit of all that had led up to it. I wish you could have seen those congregations. … At these Communions you feel the atmosphere to be that of a truly spiritual kind, such as might have followed on a time of revival. It is something that you cannot explain. I don't know how many are familiar with the Gaelic singing. But if those who are not familiar with it would go to Lewis to hear it, it would be well worth their while. Nothing moved me so much; again and again it moved me to tears. It seemed as though all the pent-up emotions of these Highland hearts seemed to gather strength as they rose; they seemed to mount up through the rafters, and away out to the everlasting hills beyond. One felt somehow how real and deep their religious feelings are.[29]

Though scorned and shunned by many Presbyterians in Lewis, the Faith Mission doggedly persevered on this Calvinist stronghold during these years. Pilgrims reported briefly, 'Glorious time, prejudice broken down, UF Church packed, converts testifying and singing in Gaelic and English.'[30]

1912

NO stranger to the Outer Hebrides, itinerant evangelist D.T. MacKay was again drawn to Lewis in March 1912. In Balallan,

> the work was of much interest from the beginning; the session and minister were very keen on evangelistic work and by their prayers and efforts the people came out well. On Sabbath night we held the first after-meeting in the vestry, when three young people were awakened and found rest in Jesus Christ. The meetings went on for ten days in this way. It was a sight I can never forget – young people in their teens weeping for their sins and seeking mercy. In one family five were awakened – one of the young lads is most promising and wants to go in for the ministry. This is the fourth time that we have had meetings of this kind in Kinloch. Eight came forward at the Communion, but this represents only a small number who were impressed at the time.
>
> The same results were obtained at Leurbost. All the denominations attended the meetings, and a number of Free Church

29. Ibid., 1911, p. 296.

30. Govan, *Spirit of Revival*, p. 157.

> adherents professed conversion. The office-bearers in these places gave their services ungrudgingly. After Kinloch I went to Gravir where the meetings were also most interesting. The people were greatly impressed. The Communion roll was doubled at the next Communion. From Lochs I went to Uig, where we held two meetings daily. The springtime is always a busy time in the districts. The schoolhouses were full, and had good and very impressive meetings. Quite a number of young people came under the power of the Gospel message. They used to sing leaving the church going home in the evening. Five of these came forward to the Lord's Table for the first time. ... At a former revival in Uig (1906) there were two men at 80 brought to the Lord. One of them died very happy in the Lord. The other is 86 years of age and very bright; I saw him last year at Uig. He is rejoicing in hope.[31]

1916–17

EVEN during the war years, interest hardly diminished. Returning to Lewis in 1917, D.T. MacKay found the work to be 'very encouraging. Quite a number appeared to have come under the power of the truth, and our ministers were greatly cheered by their joining the church. In one district prayer meetings were held to the small hours of the morning – a striking evidence of the intensity of desire.'[32] Another interesting piece of information from this period comes from Murdo MacAulay, who relates that in Carloway, around the start of the war, the Revds Donald MacLeod and Neil MacLean Morrison were translated to the parish's Free Church and UFC respectively. The two ministers were said to have been 'great friends and were often seen walking around the Free Church manse arm in arm while their respective parishioners were at loggerheads!' Many converts were added to these congregations during the war years.[33]

Awakening Within the Free Church

THE hardships faced by Free Church congregations in the first few years after the Union were very considerable; the most obvious being that they invariably found themselves with no building to worship in. The Stornoway Free Church congregation had to worship in the Drill Hall, where Hector Cameron preached to over 700 people on the first Sabbath after the consummation of the Union. Of course, an additional handicap for this lone ranger was that other ministers were not readily available to assist at such Communion seasons. Rev. John MacLeod of Glasgow paid a visit to each of the island's parishes during 1901, accompanied by

31. *RC-UFCS-H&I*, 1913, p. 9.
32. Ibid., 1918, p. 6.
33. Murdo MacAulay, *The Burning Bush in Carloway*, Carloway 1984, p. 30.

Hector Cameron. He heard that, in Kinloch, the elders had approached their late minister for use of the church building for a special service, but it was refused. 'Consequently the large congregation, which had gathered from the different townships around, had to sit out in the open field, exposed to discomforts, within a few yards of the church and manse which have recently been erected, to a great extent, by the proceeds of the manual labour of the poor but industrious of members and adherents of this congregation.'[34]

1900–1

SUCH circumstances led to increased unity and resolution among Free Church people. It was soon reported that 'matters in Lewis are full of encouragement' spiritually.[35] At a service conducted by MacLeod and Cameron in Barvas, it was said that 'the people were most attentive in hearing the gospel preached to them in such an earnest and simple manner, and many of them were deeply impressed and seriously affected'.[36] In Carloway, the people had

> erected a tent, covered over with boat sails, at a beautiful spot between Carloway and the township of Tolsta Chaolais. From every side the people flocked towards the tent, all classes earnestly wending their way from different directions, until a very large concourse had gathered, who solemnly united to worship God. The singing here was re-echoed by the surrounding hills. On a beautiful summer evening worshipping under the canopy of heaven, the scene was resplendent and beyond description.
>
> This was one of the largest meetings held in Lewis since the Union controversy began; and the Rev. Mr Cameron, inspired by the responsiveness of the congregation before him, ably outlined in review church history since the Reformation. ... The whole audience was hanging on the speaker's lips ... for ability, lucidity, and earnestness Mr Cameron on this occasion excelled himself. Although the people sat for hours, there was not the slightest inclination to move though exposed in the open air. At the close of the service the Session was constituted on the hillside, at the same time Mr MacLeod was busy baptising a large number of children in the tent.[37]

By August 1901 it could be said that 'the harvest is truly great at present',[38] though, owing to the effects of the Union, the labourers in Lewis were few.

---

34. *MR-FCS*, August 1901, p. 142.
35. Ibid., May 1901, p. 93.
36. Ibid.
37. Ibid., June 1901, p. 110.
38. Ibid., August 1901, p. 142.

1903

STORNOWAY seemed to be at the centre of quickening activity in 1903. Alexander Murray was minister in the English Free Church in Stornoway at the beginning of the century. He had a special rapport with the fishermen of the island, amongst whom he found a congenial atmosphere. Their spontaneity, heartiness and openness to aggressive evangelistic methods strongly appealed to him, and he not only welcomed this class of men at church, but also spoke to them – often in large numbers – at the manse. Many of these fishermen attended his large and flourishing open-air meetings in the Town Square after the Sabbath evening service, a tradition inherited from D.J. Martin's ministry. In the spring of 1903 a storm prevented the fishermen from leaving the harbour, so meetings for prayer were initiated, and these continued every evening for five weeks, during which time only one address was given. 'The Spirit of God filled the place,' recalled Murray; 'old and young were converted, and joined in praise and prayer.'[39]

Meanwhile, William Ross of Cowcaddens reported of Stornoway in 1903 that 'a work which took its origin last June in conference and last January in special prayer, is still going on, and most delightful results are being seen. Two brethren from Glasgow have been assisting in the work, and they tell me of the remarkable presence of the Spirit of God.'[40]

Carloway 1903–13

BY 1903, if not earlier, Carloway was experiencing considerable spiritual awakening. The parish's Free Church had a ministerial vacancy as a result of the Union, and the burden of maintaining the church's witness was thrust upon an office-bearer, Murdo MacKay, whom his fellow-elders esteemed as the one most fitted to conduct the services. A tailor to trade, MacKay was 'neither eloquent in the estimate of human wisdom, nor forward in asserting himself, yet his personality conveyed the aroma of a deep spiritual experience'. It was largely through his ministry that awakening spread through the entire parish, and both young and old were touched. 'This,' noted a Free Church colleague, 'was too much for the enemy of souls, who saw his kingdom being disturbed, and Mr MacKay had to endure much obloquy, in the course of which he was fortified, however, by a like-minded Session, and by the young people, whose devotion to him was unbounded.'[41]

Not least affected by the revival was the village of Tolsta Chaolais. Of significance here is a visit by the Rev. George MacKay of Stornoway (later

---

39. Isabella B. Murray, *In Remembrance: Rev. Alexander Murray*, Edinburgh 1921, p. 73.

40. *PGA-UFCS*, 1903, p. 20.

41. *PGA-FCS-H&I*, 1939, p. 290.

of Fearn, Ross-shire), who began his ministry in the Free Presbyterian Church, but translated to the Free Church in 1905. As interim-moderator for Carloway, MacKay came to the village of Breasclete in 1904[42] to preach at some services and to conduct a wedding ceremony for a couple from nearby Tolsta. There were no bridesmaids at the wedding, but instead two men acted as witnesses. In those days no ring was given at marriage, but rather, a white band was placed around the bride's brow, known as the *currag a' bhreid*.

According to the customs of the time, the wedding party would walk in procession from Tolsta Chaolais to the crossroads at Breasclete, making their way in pairs behind the happy couple and accompanied by a piper. A dance was arranged for later in the evening, and, suspecting this, MacKay warned the group after the ceremony that unless their behaviour was totally circumspect, he would personally call along before the night was through!

Suspicious of their intent, and keeping to his threat, MacKay made his way to a farmyard barn in the district, in which location the party was under full swing. Not being able to find an entrance in the dark, the minister climbed up to the roof of the barn, and proceeded to make a hole through the thick thatch so that he could peer down into the building below. Noting from his vantage-point that entry to the barn was via a door from the dwelling house, the minister was inside the barn in a few minutes. Approaching one of the musicians, MacKay forcefully seized the melodeon from his arms, doing likewise immediately after with a similar instrument being played at the other end of the hall. Not a strong man, but carrying the authority of his collar, MacKay sat down with one squeeze-box on each knee, defying anyone to remove them.

Taken aback by the brazen behaviour of the intruder, the dancing stopped, but soon the merry-makers began to transfer to another barn nearby, where they hoped they could resume their amusements uninterrupted. But here, too, the unwelcome visitor made an appearance, demanding the piper to hand over his pipes. The owner of the prized instrument spoke up tersely, *Le fuil a fhuair mi iad, agus le fuil a chailleas mi iad* ('By blood I obtained them, and by blood alone shall I lose them'). He had been presented with the pipes by his army company for continuing to play them while wounded. Deeply proud of such presentation, the musician intended to hold onto them for dear life.

Leaving the party after a short exhortation, MacKay made his way to the bride's house, where he was to lodge for the night. In the course of conversation with his hosts, he remarked that soon several anxious souls would be wanting to see him. This seemed most unlikely, given the

42. MacAulay, *Burning Bush*, p. 28. Norman MacLeod sets the year at 1902 (*Lewis Revivals of the 20th Century*, p. 6).

affront he had caused and his consequent standing with the young folk of the parish. But so it turned out. Meantime, MacKay left the following morning for Bernera, returning the next day to Tolsta Chaolais, where he preached a powerful sermon, the test and substance of which have been wholly lost, except for the following snippet which has been repeated among local believers again and again. 'No worse judgement,' he is known to have said, 'could come upon a parish than a lame piper, a drunken schoolmaster, and a graceless minister.' The schoolmaster of the district was at that time addicted to alcohol, and the clerical reference was to the Rev. Dr Duncan MacLeod, latterly of Tarbert, Harris. MacKay's opinion that MacLeod was graceless was not shared by all who knew him. Norman MacLeod described him as 'in fact a humble evangelical preacher although rather eccentric'.[43]

At least two people later came to apologise to MacKay for their behaviour on the night of the wedding, and these were also evidently convinced of their need for a Saviour. Remarkably, one of these was Alistair Morrison, the piper who had been interrupted on the dance floor. Apparently, this young convert was to make a great impression on his colleagues, his unusual gifts adding lustre to his graces. He matured quickly, perhaps in the foreknowledge that he was going to die young (he died in active service during the Great War). Previous to MacKay's visit, awakening in the parish had already begun, during which several married couples and others attended the weekly prayer meeting for the first time; but the above incident certainly helped encourage the movement.[44]

This period of revival produced a number of young converts who later became stalwart office-bearers in a number of Carloway villages such as Callanish, Breasclete, Tolsta Chaolais, and Doune. There were 10 admissions to the Free Church in the parish in 1907, 11 in 1908, 8 in 1909, 8 in 1910, 8 in 1911, 3 in 1912, and 9 in 1913 (unfortunately, no records are available for the years 1903–7). Along with this, as previously noted, 41 names were added to the Roll of the UFC within a similar period.[45]

Another story from this period involves Norman MacDonald, colloquially known as *Tormod Sona* (Happy Norman), a man popular with believers throughout Lewis and one who was known to enjoy an unusual sensitivity to things of the Spirit. One day, after making the long journey from Galson (in Ness) to Tolsta Chaolais to visit a friend, Norman was understandably exhausted on arrival. Gathered in the house for an

43. MacLeod, *Lewis Revivals*, p. 8.

44. This story is recorded in MacAulay, *Burning Bush*, pp. 28–9.

45. Ibid., p. 28. MacAulay stated further that the movement spread to other parts of the island, such as Cross to the north, and Lochs to the east, the results of these also showing on comparable church records. (See also MacLeod, *Lewis Revivals*, p. 9).

evening meeting was a group of joyous and enthusiastic young converts, fruit of the awakening evident in the parish. Troubled by their loud and seemingly frivolous laughter, Norman went outside to pray. He speedily found a convenient nook in a cleft in a rock behind the house, and was not long there when the words came to him with power, 'These are not drunken as ye suppose, seeing it is but the third hour of the day.' Convinced that God had spoken to his situation, Norman returned at once to the house, where he entered heart and soul into the fellowship. Indeed, such was the felt presence of God at that meeting that Norman was eventually overwhelmed and collapsed in a swoon.[46]

Says the author of his memorial, 'Norman MacDonald was nothing if not original. He was a man all by himself. In manner, mind and experience he differed profoundly from most people.' It was not to be unexpected, then, that on occasion his mannerisms were seen as disconcerting to some. At another cottage-meeting, Norman 'sat beside a minister, and all the time he held one of his [the minister's] knees tightly in his strong hands – presumably by way of giving physical as well as spiritual support. When the meeting ended Norman said, "If I am not mistaken the power of God is present here tonight." In the after-meeting, as Norman was praying, two young women present were brought under deep spiritual concern which afterwards issued in their salvation.'[47]

So keen was Norman to partake in godly fellowship that he was regularly in the habit of walking many miles to meetings both in his own parish of Barvas (later Ness) and to other districts. This he did until well advanced in years. Said Murdoch Campbell, 'It was this intense desire to know more of God, and enjoy more of His blessing, that kept his feet in the footsteps of the flock. Once, after walking a long distance to a service he met a friend who remarked that he should rest his weary limbs. Looking down at his feet, soiled and dusty after his long journey, Norman replied, "They shall rest in the grave till the resurrection."'[48]

The story is also told of a young man, Donald MacAulay from Breasclete, who about 1910 became a member of Carloway Free Church, although for three years previously he had laboured under the persuasion that no sinner like him had any right to be a communicant. No sooner was he given the needed strength to become a church member than the 'Enemy' resumed the battle, and the odds against Donald appeared so great that he actually decided not to attend any more Communions. However, when a certain Communion came, he made up his mind to

46. MacLeod, *Lewis Revivals*, pp. 8–9; Rev. John MacLeod, *Happy Norman (Tormod Sona) + Gleanings of Early Days of Gospel Power in Lewis*, Stornoway n.d., pp. 33–4.

47. Rev. Murdoch Campbell, *The King's Friend: Memorial of Norman MacDonald or "Tormod Sona"*, Glasgow n.d., p. 17.

48. Ibid., p. 26.

at least go to the fellowship meeting. 'Whatever the question was asked, Norman, when called upon to speak, made the intimation, "You are here today and you have been telling yourself that owing to your state as a lost sinner this may be your last appearance at a Communion; but, according to the Lord's sure promises which he speaks at this very moment, you will continue to follow all the means of grace in which the Good Shepherd of your soul will make you lie down in the green pastures of His love and favour." Norman said no more, but what he had said filled Donald's heart with adoring amazement that the Lord should have guided him to the place to hear such a statement made in public, a statement that exactly described his own frame of spirit.[49]

Another keen believer who travelled by foot from north Lewis to meetings in other parts of the island during the revival at the start of the century was Murdo MacFarlane. This godly Christian would walk barefoot from his home in Ness to Communions in Uig – a distance of some 30 miles – carrying his shoes in his hands to avoid wearing them out. When he arrived at the church in Uig young girls were waiting with water and towels, ready to wash the feet of the saints of God as they arrived.[50]

1905–10

IN his Back parish, Hector Cameron often dissented at the Kirk Session against some of those desiring to go forward for the first time to the Lord's Table. But the Office-bearers just as often over-ruled him. Said a ministerial successor, 'I was informed of at least two instances in which he sent tokens to people whom he himself expected to appear but did not turn up.'[51] It was due to a time of spiritual blessing in Back in the first years of the twentieth century that no fewer than ten people came forward in 1906 to the Free Church Session to apply for church membership.[52]

From Malcom McIver's Free Church congregation in Stornoway around this time a group of young converts formed a committee in the period leading up to the Communion season, with the purpose that they might look out for other young persons coming under conviction of sin and that they might buy them new clothes and shoes to wear when they came out to the weekly prayer meeting. Such was the poverty in a lot of households at the time that many people felt unable to attend church due to a lack of suitable clothing. Despite the denominational strife existing as a result of the Union, it was said that on some occasions in

---

49. MacLeod, *Happy Norman*, p. 47.

50. Personal conversation with Mary Peckham, grand-daughter of Mr MacFarlane, 20 May 2003. See also Dr Brad Allen, *The Land God Chose to Love [An Tir a Roghnaich Dis a Ghradhachadh]*, Tarentum, Pennsylvania 2004, pp. 93–4.

51. Murdo MacAulay, *Hector Cameron of Lochs and Back, The Story of an Island Ministry*, Edinburgh 1982, p. 22.

52. Ibid.

certain places believers of different denominations met together in folk's houses in a spirit of unity.[53]

Remarkably, the first overt acknowledgement of a revival movement within the Free Church in Lewis in the twentieth century from General Assembly Reports occurs as late as 1909, when 'promising appearances of a spiritual quickening' through the ministry of the denomination's own agents were noted.[54] Word came in from Stornoway and from Lewis generally to the effect that much gratifying interest was being shown in the means of grace. It was reported that recent Communion services in Stornoway and all over the island were proving most encouraging and refreshing to both the ministers and the participants.[55]

By the following year, fuller accounts were being receieved of 'the impressive reality of spiritual quickening within the island. Not only so, but evidences are at hand that the spiritual life of the congregations in Skye, in some parts of the western sea-board of Ross-shire, and in Argyllshire show unmistakable signs of reviving influences.'[56] Testimonies of two ministers whose knowledge of Lewis was considered both extensive and accurate were recorded. One wrote:

> Strangers coming to assist at Communions in Lewis were overwhelmed with joy and inspiration by seeing the people in hundreds flocking to the House of God, some of them nearly two hours before the appointed time. It is quite evident that the Spirit of the Lord is working both among young and old in the Island of Lewis during the last five or six years. Prayer meetings are held when the people are at home, every night of the week except Saturday, from Dec. till March. In one congregation in Lewis not less than 22 were added to the Communion roll last year. The work of the Spirit is not confined to one congregation in the island. People are travelling from 20–24 miles from Communion to Communion seeking the Bread of Life.[57]

In like manner, the Rev. Nicol Nicolson wrote,

> It is quite apparent that at least for the last two years there is a hopeful movement at work among the young folks of Lewis, manifested by their earnestness and liveliness in attending the means of grace on Sabbaths and weekdays. Not a few of them are coming forward from time to time to make public confession of Christ.[58]

53. Rev. John J. Murray, *Revivals in Scotland*, Carey Conference 1990, audio tape.
54. *PGA-FCS*, 1909, p. 305.
55. *RC-FCS-RM&T*, 1909, p. 317.
56. Ibid., 1910, p. 475.
57. Ibid.
58. Ibid.

1913

THREE years later, immediately prior to the start of the Great War, a Free Church report noted that 'spiritual movements still continue, and the reality of these movements has been proved by many transformed lives that have been elevating factors in their native surroundings, and unmistakably so at the fishing centres. These desirable results are local, and not general, yet the Committee [of the Home Missions and Supply for the Highlands and Islands] have no doubt that the work of the Lord, which is being vigorously carried on, is everywhere bearing fruit which may as yet be hidden from the observer, and that, as one writes, "There are many more of the salt of the earth in our midst than we think."'[59]

HARRIS 1912–17

D.T. MACKAY had visited the Harris districts of Obbe (renamed Leverburgh in 1920), Northton and Manish in June 1912, where he 'received valuable help from the Established Church and Free Church missionaries. The after-meetings were well attended and a number professed to have found the pearl of great price.'[60] In all, MacKay preached no fewer than fifty times in Harris in these few weeks.

In November, this indefatigable evangelist went to the north and eastern parts of Harris, where he stayed for seven weeks. Here a movement had begun some months earlier, originating in the Bays area, a stretch of rugged coastline and small communities along the east of the island. MacKay travelled between Scarp, Taransay, Amhuinshidy, Scalpay, Bays and Tarbert, and all over this wide parish. He observed the 'remarkable work of grace' that was going on under the itinerating ministry of UFC catechist, Donald Smith. On different occasions when preaching, MacKay stated that he could not hear his own voice, so great was the emotion of the people. 'At Tarbert 15 came to the Lord's Table for the first time. Much blessing attended the meetings in Scarp, and several confessed the name of the Lord. I also conducted services at Tarbert on three different Sabbaths,' he wrote.[61]

In a report to The General Assembly in 1914, Nicol Campbell, minister of the UFC in Tarbert, reported that 'matters are more promising in the congregation just now than they have been since I came to Tarbert, Harris, years ago. The work in Bays is still going on, Mr Donald Smith, our catechist, labouring almost night and day. Many have professed faith in Christ, and there are some new cases every week. The

---

59. *Report of the Committee of the Free Church of Scotland on Home Missions and Supply for the Highlands & Islands*, 1913, p. 102.

60. *RC-FCS-H&I*, 1914, p. 9.

61. Ibid., p. 10.

Rev. D.T. MacKay lately went through the congregations, Scarp and Taransay first, then to Scalpay, Tarbert, and the outskirts. He was three weeks with us, incessantly at work – generally conducting two meetings a day. He is an extraordinary man. At Ardhasaig and Tarbert, especially, he was the means of bringing out the people wonderfully, and in his usual phrase saw "impressions everywhere". Of course he produces impressions himself by his extraordinary way of preaching. Undoubtedly the Lord is with him.'[62]

The movement seemed to continue in a quiet manner during the war years. When MacKay returned to Harris in September 1914, he found large congregations gathered for the Communion services, affording him special opportunities to make his customary intense appeals. At Scalpay, such were the indications of awakening that he confessed feeling 'sorry leaving this island with many evidences of a soul-awakening movement'.[63] Then, again, in 1917, MacKay found: 'In Harris there was much to cheer. We had crowded meetings and such was the power of the Gospel and the deep concern awakened that some could not refrain from crying out during the service. There were good results, praise the Lord. In one congregation between 50 and 60 have come to the Lord's Table during the past two years – the fruit of times of refreshing in these parts. The labours of the pastor, now retired from the ministry, are still bearing fruit.'[64]

---

62. *RC-UFCS-H&I*, 1914, p. 10.
63. Ibid., 1915, p. 10.
64. Ibid., 1918, p. 6.

Uig – p.288

Peter MacDonald – p.290

George MacKay – p.297

Balallan – p.294

Lochs – p.295

Stornoway Fish Market – p.297

Norman MacDonald
(Tormod Sona) – *p.299*

Northton and Scarista, Harris – p.303

10

Post-War Reaping

1919–28

Lewis 1919–21: General

THE total population of Lewis in 1914 approximated 30,000. Incredibly, from this number Lewis contributed 6,200 servicemen (including returning emigrants) to the war effort. Consequently, about twenty percent of the entire Lewis population was on active service in some capacity during the First World War – with approximately half of them serving in the Royal Naval Reserve (RNR). Many men returned home at the end of the war bitter, confused and disillusioned by the hardships they had endured, and shaken by the atrocities they had witnessed. The mood on the island was further shattered on 1 January 1919 by the tragic sinking of HMS *Iolaire*, which was ferrying home around 285 servicemen (and crew) on leave after the war. Just a stone's throw from reaching Stornoway, the ship struck rocks and went down, taking over 200 Lewis men with it and causing untold grief to every village and district on the island. The formerly staunch evangelical hold on Lewis was further weakened by the suffering and poverty that followed the war, and by a Church witness that, despite the awakening that occurred in its aftermath, some felt was noticeably diminished by denominational schism caused by the Union of the Free and the United Presbyterian Churches.[1]

These conditions, taken alone, paint a thoroughly depressing picture of the spiritual situation of Lewis in the years following the war. For many of the island's inhabitants, however, the reality was very different indeed.[2] An impartial observer, speaking in 1919, wrote, 'If one were asked to point to a tangible sign of the vitality of religion in Lewis, one would direct the inquirer, not to its full churches, but to its empty prisons. It

1. Kenneth MacRae believed from what he had seen that it was not so much the war experience that spoiled ex-servicemen and turned them away from the means of grace, but rather 'the outburst of pleasure and amusement that followed the war'. This notwithstanding, he still felt that if people in middle life and above attended church as well as the young men, he would be highly satisfied (*MR-FCS*, 1922, p. 105).

2. This was equally true of North Uist, where there also appears to have been a small movement around this time. Since the Union of 1900, the parish of Sollas, and nearby districts, had been served by UFC missionaries, and a 'new composite mission house' was erected in the area. After Murdo MacKay left his two-year charge there in 1914, Neil Munro came to fill his place. It is said that he 'was much encouraged by an awakening in the district'. After a short time he moved to the island of Coll. Malcolm Matheson, who had been highly respected when he previously served with the UFC in Sollas, returned there after MacKay's departure, and remained until 1924 (Rev. David MacInnes, *Kilmuir Church, North Uist 1894–1994*, Kilmuir 1994, pp. 34–5).

would be difficult to find elsewhere in the United Kingdom – or Ireland – a community of 30,000 souls with so clean a criminal record.'[3]

D.T. MacKay, attending a Communion sacrament in Lewis in the spring of 1919, noted how

> The Communion Services in Lewis, as elsewhere in the Highlands, may be compared to a Highland Keswick.[4] People even come from places twenty miles distant. They fill the churches both on Sabbaths and weekdays. So eager has been the spirit manifested at one of our recent services that one of the elders remarked to me that all day long that word came pressing in upon his spirit – 'The fields are white unto the harvest.' A like impression was made on the ministers present. One of the brethren felt so much the divine presence that he was constrained to speak to several personally about salvation, and had a prayer meeting at the end. In the neighbouring parish a like spirit was evident. Some waited behind to be spoken to.[5]

There were other indications of increased spiritual earnestness during the immediate post-war years. A Free Church Report in 1923 spoke of a movement having been in progress for 'the last two or three years'.[6] Rev. A. MacKay of Kingussie, who came to assist the Revds John Rose and R. McLeod in the Communion,[7] gave a detailed account of the services in Crossbost and Garrabost, on the east of the island, in March and April 1921. Each of the three district churches connected with the Garrabost Church was believed to hold around 350 people, and all of them were full, sometimes packed beyond comfort. The main church accommodated 1,800 and was nearly full every day, and though people of nine other congregations left for their homes after the Monday morning service, about 1,200 met that evening for public worship. Likewise, the Saturday evening prayer meeting in Crossbost made a rare sight, when the church – which held nearly 700 – was nearly full.

MacLeod wrote that

> At the Communions there was a manifest seriousness. A thirst for the Word roused people to attend the meetings so early that ministers sometimes began ten or 15 minutes before the appointed time; and though the services lasted from one and a half to three hours or more it was seldom we saw one go out

3. William C. MacKenzie, *The Book of the Lews: The Story of a Hebridean Isle*, Paisley 1919, p. 152.

4. The 'Keswick' reference relates to an annual Christian convention (begun in 1875) in the Cumbrian town of Keswick, attracting many thousands of evangelical Christians.

5. *RC-FCS-H&I*, 1919, p. 8.

6. *RC-FCS-RM&T*, 1923, p. 1098.

7. All three ministers had previously lived in Canada for a spell, where they resided in close proximity to each other.

> before the close. The singing was charming. A few present were: a young man, a returned soldier, who came 26 miles though he used a crutch and cane; another young man who was one of two who started a Free Church prayer meeting in Fort William, Ontario, in 1910, but who recently returned to live in Lewis on account of the greater gospel privileges found there; a woman who through "the secret of the Lord that is with them that fear Him" was enabled to intimate a week or more before Nov. 11th, 1918, that the war was to cease that day; and an aged elder who said that he felt such a longing desire for the salvation of the unconverted that he would if possible go between them and the bottomless pit if he would be the means of saving them.[8]

The following year brought further reports of encouragement from Lewis. Kenneth MacRae, Free Church minister at that time in Kilmuir, Skye, was aware of a movement in Back and a 'shaking of the dry bones in Shawbost and in Ness'. He said that people were attending the churches as they had never done in recent years.[9]

D.T. MacKay, reporting in early 1922 on the movement underway in Lewis, said,

> I have found it a great privilege to assist in the Revival[10] movement in the Island of Lewis. A large number of young men and women have come to the knowledge of the truth, and are now rejoicing in Jesus Christ as their Saviour and their God. The recent Communions in the congregations there were most inspiring and helpful. It was a joy to see so many of our dear Highland youths casting in their lot with God's people and beginning to run the race for heaven. There have been daily meetings held in these congregations for months past and the blessed result is a rich harvest of precious souls, the best experienced for many years back; and there is much reason to thank God and take courage. In Garrabost I spent four Sabbaths. The large church at Aird was full during the week.[11]

8. *MR-FCS*, 1921, p. 75. The Lord's Supper was observed in Lewis' 11 FC Congregations twice a year, beginning at Stornoway on the third Sabbaths in August and February, and ending in Garrabost on the first Sabbaths in November and April. Where observed, all outdoor work was suspended from Wednesday night till the following Tuesday morning, and schools were closed; so that the week-day meetings were nearly as large as the Sabbath services. Besides the numerous church services and Friday fellowship meeting, prayer meetings were held from 8 to 9 p.m. on Saturday evening, after the Sabbath evening preaching, and again after supper in private houses, sometimes on till midnight.

9. *The Monthly Record*, 1922, p. 105. In 1922, also, the FC commissioned a Report on Services for Scottish workers in the English Fishing Ports. This consisted of a number of individual reports from several ministers and lay deputies who went from Scotland to minister to the hundreds of Gaelic-speaking men and women who travelled to East Anglia each autumn in pursuit of the herring, including many from Lewis. Lay deputy Miss MacKay said in respect of Yarmouth: 'We knew of five cases of awakening during the season – two at the very beginning, and three near the close. Some, however, gave the number of awakened as ten – eight under FC preachers and two through the instrumentality of Mr J. Troup' (ibid., p. 886).

10. Rev. MacKay was not wont to make common use of the term 'revival'.

11. *RC-FCS-H&I*, 1922, p. 6.

Meanwhile, the minister of the Stornoway English Church wrote at this time, 'One fact in particular struck me as strange, or rather I should say, two, though they are closely related, and these were: first the youthfulness of the fishermen converts; and, second, the youthfulness of the converts among the resident population. The last night of Mr Moor's campaign saw about 20 (ages 15 to 18) profess their faith in Christ.'[12]

BARVAS 1920s

FOLLOWING a visit to the Lewis parish of Barvas in 1922, 'burning and flaming evangelist'[13] D.T. MacKay reported, 'The work here is most interesting and encouraging. Quite a number of young people of both churches have come out to the light, and the good work is still growing. Churches are crowded and full at the after meetings. The same has taken place at Ness … .'[14]

The awakening was thought to have been brought to the community through the conversion of a woman during a mission in the neighbouring northerly parish of Ness. However, the thoroughly evangelical ministry of the much-respected Rev. D.H. Morrison, minister of Barvas CoS at the time, greatly assisted the movement, as did the work of lay missionaries active in various parts of the parish, such as Borve, where several of the converts resided. Twenty-one people are believed to have been converted during this movement, the number corresponding to the year the revival began. This number consisted mainly of teenagers and men and women in their early twenties. One young woman who 'came through' at this time was Effie MacLeod, whose later offspring were at the centre of the 1949–52 revival in the same district.[15] Mrs MacDougall, the mother of Margaret MacLeod – one of the very first converts of the 1949 revival – was also converted during the early 1920s awakening. She held back as long as she could but eventually 'came through' in 1922 – at the tail end of the movement – when aged just sixteen. Mrs MacLeod remembers her mother telling her that one day, shortly after she had been accepted by the church session as a suitable candidate for membership, she and another young convert of the movement went to pay a customary visit to the manse – where Mrs MacDougall also served as a maid. Such was the reverence of the minister that, after welcoming them into the kitchen, he instructed that all should kneel down on the floor, in which position he engaged in earnest prayer for the young visitors.

An older relative of Mrs MacDougall – Katrina – was a much-respected Christian in the community, and she helped to 'mother' the joyful band

12. *RHM&CEC-FCS*, 1922, p. 35.

13. Norman MacFarlane, *Scotland's Keswick: A Sketch of the Message and of the Men*, London 1916, p. 100.

14. *RC-UFCS-H&I*, 1923, p. 10.

15. John Murdo, Donald John and other siblings in the Smith family.

of new converts, her wise counsel proving of great help to the young believers. One lad who was part of this group – he later worked in Lochs as a game-keeper – was keen to offer help to those who were under deep soul concern. He said to one of the number, 'Look, if you have any problems, just go to Katrina.' Others in the group laughed, for though new in the faith themselves, they knew that the spiritually anxious would be better advised to turn to the Lord for relief, not to a human aid. The movement went on for several months and it is interesting to note that many of the converts went on to become the nucleus of the Barvas CoS congregation in later years.

Amazingly, there was another spiritual movement in Barvas later in the 1920s. At one meeting in particular, a number of people came under concern of soul. Margaret MacLeod remembers being told of a grand-uncle visiting her grandparents after this meeting and saying to her grandfather, 'Why are you sitting there so restfully; don't you know there's a bunch of girls nearby earnestly seeking the Lord?' But Margaret's grandparents had also been at the meeting, and they were well aware of the state of anxiety that some were in. The grandfather replied to his brother-in-law that he personally had been with them earlier. He found in them a great longing to be directed onto the path of salvation. Indeed, such was their desperation that they crowded around him closely; so closely that as he prayed with and spoke words of encouragement to them, his long beard would touch and tickle their necks! 'Why else,' he asked, in jest, 'would they gather around an old, bearded man like me?!' [16]

These were days when even the unconverted had great respect for ministers and elders. The young folk in the community had, of course, to make their own entertainment, and in Barvas it was common for them to meet together at a nearby bridge which crossed a twisting burn. Here they would blether and share stories, eye up the 'talent' of the opposite sex and dance in the open air to the sound of a melodeon, which one or another in the group had brought along. There were yet no cars in Lewis and in the early evening there was little traffic of any form to disturb them. When, however, occasionally, an elder in the church passed their way he would stop and speak to them about spiritual concerns. Invariably the merry-makers would stop and listen attentively for the duration of the short address, and some, no doubt, would hold the things they heard close to their hearts, where it would perhaps lead to deeper soul-searching at a later date. Soon, the church officer would take his leave, the young would bid him farewell, and the dancing would resume!

---

16. Personal conversation with Margaret MacLeod, a native of Barvas, 15 September 2002.

LEWIS 1922–4: GENERAL

A Free Church Report compiled in early 1923 on the general spiritual conditions existing in Lewis referred to 'a movement preceding quietly and hopefully'. It continued,

> religious conditions of the island calls for more than a passing reference. Returns are to hand from all the congregations. They are in accord in showing that in Lewis the Sabbath is sanctified, church services and prayer meetings are well attended by old and young, there is close attention to the preaching of the Word, and a spirit of deep seriousness. The moral condition of the people is praiseworthy, and there is no license for the sale of alcoholic liquor in the island. Pernicious literature – the moral plague of many other districts – is practically unknown there. But behind all this, and resulting in this, there is the work of the Holy Spirit enlightening men's minds and setting their affections on things above. It is a good witness to the reality of the religious movement in Lewis that the young people leaving home for work in the industrial centres retain to so large an extent amid their new surroundings the good influence of home. Whatever justification there may have been in the past for the reproach that Lewis men away from home forgot their religious upbringing, that charge could not be generally levelled now. It will be readily admitted on all sides that in Glasgow, for instance, Gaelic prayer meetings are the only ones really well attended. It is for the Free Church a matter of satisfaction that her influence in the island is paramount, and that her pulpits there are excellently manned.[17]

In Kinloch around this time, there was a spiritual quickening among the youth within the UFC, and a number professed their faith in Christ by joining the Church in full communion, which was a source of great encouragement to the pastor, the Rev. MacKay.[18] Preaching in Balallan during the year 1923–4, the ageing evangelist D.T MacKay spoke of the church being crowded every night, 'and some professed to have received the pearl of great price, and came to rejoice in the Lord'.[19] Similarly, in Scalpay, Harris, MacKay's efforts were 'equally successful. Meetings were held for a fortnight and the large church was full to the door. A number professed to have received the Pearl of Great Price, and have since made a public profession of their love for the Blessed Redeemer.'[20]

In May 1924 a Free Church Report on the 'Religious revival' of the early 1920s in Scotland described the spiritual situation in Lewis as

17. *RC-UFCS-RM&T*, 1923, pp. 1098–9.

18. Ibid.

19. *RC-UFCS-H&I*, 1924, p. 7.

20. Ibid., 1923, p. 10.

'more or less what it was. The atmosphere is lively, and perhaps, after all, this may be more indicative of a real and lasting work of grace[21] than the somewhat noisy and excited revivalism which seems to be characteristic of modern times' (this was a reference to the emotionalism that at times characterised meetings in one or two of the north-east centres in connection with the recent 'Fishermen's revival').[22] In 1925 it could still be said that prayer meetings were better attended than formerly, a spirit of earnestness and concern was being manifested by many of the young people, and 'the situation continues to be hopeful'.[23]

NESS 1922–6

DURING the first two decades of the twentieth century Cross Free Church, in the Ness parish of Lewis, was served by just one pastor, who stayed there for a total of nine years. So a mood of expectancy greeted the arrival of a new minister in 1920. The Rev. Roderick John MacLeod was twenty-eight when he arrived in Ness. A Harris man and son of a lay-preacher, he received his theological training at Edinburgh's Free Church College. Here, he was subject to an unusual dream one night, whereby he was en route to his native Hebrides from the mainland. Arriving at the Kyle of Lochalsh, he boarded the passenger boat, noting also another ship bound for Lewis, which was carrying servicemen only. Approaching his home island, MacLeod observed in horror the other ship beginning to sink in the rough sea, and he watched helplessly as two sailors struggled frantically in the freezing water. He instantly exhorted them to look to Christ for salvation, before death eventually engulfed them.

Speaking in a church in Glasgow shortly after this dream, MacLeod realised that he had forgotten the text from which he was to preach that evening. Praying for divine assistance, he suddenly recalled his 'dream sermon' and the text on which it was based. He spoke with liberty and directness, and at the end of the service two men approached him, thanking him in soft, broken voices for his message, which had led them to embrace the Saviour. MacLeod recognised them as the two men he had seen in his strange night vision. Shortly after this, these same two men were among the many who lost their lives in the tragic *Iolaire* disaster, one of the worst peace-time catastrophes in British maritime history (see page 307).

On settling in Ness, MacLeod's message and warmth of personality particularly appealed to the young men of the parish, especially those recently demobbed. There had been general apathy in the congregation,

---

21. An example is the parish of Carloway, where, during a four-year ministerial vacancy from 1919, 14 were added to the Communion roll of the FC, and, on the induction of John MacIver in 1924, 'tokens of the Lord's favour' were enjoyed over a sustained period of time (MacAulay, *The Burning Bush*, pp. 30–2).

22. *RC-FCS-RM&T*, 1924, p. 1329.

23. Ibid., 1925, p. 153.

but very quickly MacLeod began to create a new interest through his earnest and scriptural preaching. In a poem written later by a convert of his ministry, MacLeod is portrayed as being a man who won the hearts of his people with preaching filled with 'hope and love'. He was a 'beloved shepherd', whose teaching was as a tree beside calm waters, deep-rooted and providing both shelter and food.[24]

Praised when he was dead, however, MacLeod was widely distrusted and miscalled while he was alive, this by a few suspicious and censorious elderly believers. One man, Angus Thomson, savagely rebuked MacLeod at the Session after he had seen the minister vaulting a fence rather than walk decorously through the gate. Such conduct, railed the elder, was unbecoming to the dignity of the Lord's servants! MacLeod smiled as he quoted from Psalm 18: *Le neart a mo Dhia thar balla leum is chaidh mi fhein gun stad* ('And, by my God assisting me I overleap a wall').

A short time after his arrival in Ness, the enterprising new minister suggested to his Presbytery that special meetings be held for the young people of the parish. This, however, was rejected, so in spring 1922, MacLeod decided to start them himself! Open to anyone, they particularly drew in local teenagers. Partly as a result of these, by the beginning of 1923 it was apparent that a revival was in progress in both the Free Church and other congregations in the parish. That the UFC was involved in the work is evident from a verbal conveyance by D.T. MacKay to the General Assembly in May 1923 that 'a number of young converts have come forward at the late Communion'.[25]

Cottage meetings were begun throughout the district and were well attended, worship often continuing into the early hours of the following morning. For a while these meetings took place virtually every night of the week, and, though there was no formal schedule, people would be 'led by the Spirit' to the next evening's meeting without having been told where it was to be held. Walking to and from meetings in groups, believers shared testimony, exhortation and encouragement with each other. The Spirit broke down traditional barriers; those of differing church traditions fellowshipped together, and it was considered quite appropriate, for example, for one man to walk alongside another's wife, as they shared some spiritual concern together. Fellowship was sweet among believers, who were bonded by the revival in a unique way.

24. His obituary says of him, 'He had the personal qualities that endear a man to his fellows – great sympathy, a genius for friendship and happy humour. There was nothing small or crabbed about him. He had a genuine and open-hearted nature and than he no man could be more loyal and true. … He had many natural gifts of presence, and fervour of utterance which made him a preacher generally admired. The Cross was his constant theme and the treatment of it always betokened careful study, preparation and originality. … He was beloved by his people, all, and by his Christian courtesy, … unobtrusive devotion and regard to the whole community' (*MR-FCS*, 1929).

25. *RC-UFCS-H&I*, 1923, p. 10.

Realising a lack of Gospel ordinances appealing to seekers and the unconverted outwith normal public worship and the twice-yearly round of Communion seasons, MacLeod instituted an annual winter diet of week-long evangelistic services, to which he invited especially winsome and gifted preachers well suited to addressing both the seeking and the careless. These *orduigean beagan* or 'little Communions', as they were termed, proved immensely popular, and were soon introduced in many other churches on the island. Indeed, so popular did they become that they are still in evidence today. In addition to these, and equally radical, MacLeod introduced a special children's address in the course of Sabbath worship, inviting young ones to come and sit at the front of the church to hear it.

By 1924 the whole parish of Ness was caught up in a spirit of revival. Later coined by some *Dusgadh Rodaidh* ('Roddie's revival') – a term MacLeod himself would have deplored – this movement is considered by some as one of the most significant Lewis revivals of the twentieth century.[26] In later years, converts were known as 'so-and-so, who was in Roddie's revival', and nearly eighty years later, when the last convert of the movement passed away, the revival was still well known in the community.

The awakening was not known for outward excitement, though there was considerable silent weeping and deep contrition of heart. One woman remembered these years as precious to her soul's experience. As a girl of fouteen, she walked with a friend to a meeting in Galson for the first time. On the way they met the well-known Norman MacDonald – *Tormod Sona* or 'Happy Norman', who in old age had recently moved to the area. Rejoicing to see two young girls seeking good for their souls, Norman stopped, and, waving his walking stick at them, cried with the Psalmist, *Bha aoibhneas orm trath thubhairt iad Gu taigh Dhe theid sinn suas* ('I joyed when to the house of God, Go up, they said to me,' from Psalm 122).[27]

One notable feature of the movement was that more men were brought under its influence than women. A number went on to become outstanding lay agents throughout the Highlands and Islands and several became ordained ministers. Among the latter was Donald MacDonald, later of Greyfriars Free Church, Inverness, considered to be one of the Free Church's best loved and foremost experimental Christian leaders in the Highlands and Islands. Similarly, Callum Morrison was converted in his late twenties, and went on to become minister of Scalpay Free Church and later Partick Highland Free Church in Glasgow. Morrison,

26. See Iain D. Campbell, *Revival in Lewis* (http://www.backfreechurch.co.uk/). Interestingly, a number of Ness folk living in Glasgow were also converted during the period of the revival.

27. Personal communication with John MacLeod, grandson of one of the two girls, 2 August 2002.

like many others, delighted to see believers of different denominations coming together in a spirit of unity during the revival. This engendered in the young man an evangelical ecumenism that remained with him throughout his life.

It was very uncommon for children at this time to attend church, nor did they attend cottage meetings, yet many of these, too, were converted during the awakening. Isabella Morrison,[28] thought to have been the last surviving convert of the awakening, was converted around the age of twelve. Bella, as she was known, remembered twelve children placing trust in Christ at this time, although some slipped back afterwards.[29] Another child-convert was Donald MacDonald. He came to the Lord in his early teens, and, along with his converted friends, was 'as happy as the days were long. The sun of God's favour was shining on our tabernacle and we were full of the joy of the Lord.'[30] However, when, at the age of fourteen years and nine months, MacDonald applied for admission to the Lord's Table, the Kirk Session was extremely reluctant to grant this privilege to one so tender in years. 'They maintained,' wrote MacDonald, 'that if you were sure of your interest in Christ, there was something wrong with you, and that if you doubted your interest in Christ then that was an evidence of grace.'[31] One had to be good enough, or old enough, to join the church, and evidence was required of an unusual work of grace in the heart, a special experience that made one worthy to become a communicant. It was only due to the intervention of a senior elder that the young believer was admitted to membership, but the hurt of this experience, along with the partial ingraining of this type of thinking, remained with MacDonald for a long time.

Another notable convert of the movement was George Murray, later to become an inspiring leader in the UPC (now the Newton Presbyterian Church) among the Cape Breton Scots community in Boston, Massachusetts. Murray was born in Ness in 1894 and had recently returned to Lewis from the trenches of France. He had 'a sense of conviction of his lost condition … eventuating in a great illumination of faith and knowledge of forgiveness of his sins as the words "He hath made Him to be sin for us who knew no sin that we might be made the righteousness of God in Him."' From that time on, Murray began his Christian testimony, first making confession before the Free Church Session of his home congregation in 1923.[32]

---

28. Isabella later married Angus Finlayson, minister of Tolsta FC, and from 1964, Moderator of the General Assembly. Bella, 'besides sympathising completely with her husband's aims and interests, possessed gifts of intellect and personality that rendered her eminently suitable as a helpmeet in the work of the Gospel' (Donald MacLeod, 'Tribute to Angus Finlayson' in *MR-FCS*, August 1974).

29. M. MacAulay and Rev. M.A. MacLeod, *Discussion on Revival*, audio tape.

30. Donald MacDonald, *Christian Experience: A Selection of Sermons*, Edinburgh 1988, p. viii.

31. Ibid.

32. MacLeod, *George Murray of the "U.P."*, p. 18.

The Ness Free Church membership roll shows interesting statistics regarding the revival. While there were 13 new members during the two Communions in March and October 1922, 10 were added in 1923, 12 in 1924, 27 in 1925, 21 in 1926 and 15 in 1927, before dropping down to just 7 during 1928.[33] In addition, there were thought to have been other converts who didn't join the church at that time. The significance of the revival is seen in the fact that in 1914 this parish had only 141 communicant members; yet, over the period of the revival, over 100 new admissions were received. The conversions ceased in 1926 when, shortly after his marriage, MacLeod accepted a call to the Dumbarton Free Church. Economic conditions in the Highlands and Islands were severe in the early 1920s and caused many young people to leave their homeland in search of a better livelihood elsewhere. In the space of just two years, 850 left Lewis, many crossing the Atlantic on ships that picked them up directly from Stornoway harbour. A good number of revival converts were among those who sailed overseas, including George Murray, who, when asked many years later why he had left family, friends and an exciting spiritual climate for a future unknown, replied simply, 'Hunger'.[34]

As for Roddie MacLeod, his first child died in childbirth, and he himself died tragically in 1929, aged just 37 and shortly before the birth of his second child. On hearing the sad news, Murray, who went on to compose much fine Gaelic poetry, wrote a moving tribute to his gifted minister: *Marcheanfal treud ri teachdair treud ri teachdair treum do'n tug sinn speis thar chaich* ('Strong were the bonds that existed between you and us').[35]

Harris 1925–8

WHAT progressed into a significant spiritual movement with enduring effect arose in Harris sometime in 1925. The Rev. Dr Roderick MacLeod,[36] Superintendent of the UFC Committee for the Highlands and Islands, gave the following report in the spring of 1926.

---

33. Ness FC Records. This is slightly different to the figures recorded by Norman MacLeod, who states that 15 new members were added to the FC in 1924, and 11 to 14 admissions during each Communion up to 1926, when, with the departure of MacLeod, 'the conversions ceased' (MacLeod, *Lewis Revivals*, p. 9). Both George Murray and Donald MacDonald became members in 1925, while Bella Morrison didn't join until 1928.

34. Donald E. Meek has observed that waves of spiritual revival tend 'to peak immediately prior to periods of more intense emigration' (Meek, 'Religious Life in the Highlands' in Lynch (Ed.) *The Oxford Companion to Scottish History*, p. 519). A similar pattern occurred in Tiree following a deep movement on that island during the same decade (see page 179; cf page 83).

35. MacLeod, *George Murray*, p. 18.

36. The UFC Superintendent led a team of 33 lay missionaries, 8 ordained preachers and missionaries and a ministerial itinerant evangelist (D.T. MacKay). Of these 42 men, 32 were Gaelic-speaking. MacLeod had a ministry of encouragement by visiting and writing, with concern not just for the missionaries but also for their families. (Frank D. Bardgett, *Devoted Service Rendered: The Lay Missionaries of the Church of Scotland*, Edinburgh 2002, p. 131).

> The Committee's Mission agents have come well out of a rigorous winter. It was trying enough on the western shores of the mainland, but in the islands, for days at a time, it made work impossible. In spite of the weather, however, the services, Sunday and week-day, were well attended. The Islesmen are used to rain-storms and wet clothes, and probably with the majority, Sunday weather has the least chance of keeping them at home. If church is not so far away as to ensure a soaking to the skin, they will be in their places.
>
> There are times, however, when that normal interest deepens and rises to a definite spiritual movement. Harris has had one of these visitations. It was, as far as one can judge, entirely spontaneous – the outflow of long accumulated impressions and impulses. It rose like a spring wind and blew over the island. The young people were most noticeably impressed, and what is unusual in the isles, they are making their profession young, and that out of a deep and searching but happy experience. Many of them, too, feel that their call to faith is also a call to service and perhaps we have here God's provision of a recruiting field for the thinned ranks of the Ministry.[37]

It is believed that the awakening arose from the prayer meeting held in the small community of Bunavoneadar in north-west Harris. While previously this had been very well attended, by the autumn of 1925 numbers were dwindling, largely due to increased pressures on the crofters' time during the harvest season. At one point the elder, advanced in years, who was in charge of the prayer meetings decided it was right and proper to stop them altogether, at least until the harvest was over. He went to the next meeting with the intention of making this announcement. But, although, again, only two or three people showed up, the godly elder somehow found himself unable to make the proposed intimation. The following week five people attended the meeting, which slightly increased number the elder took as a sign that he was right not to stop them. The following week a still greater number came out, much to the encouragement of the elder. A week later and revival had broken out in the parish.

Writing in general terms of a Highland missionary's work, the UFC Superintendent said,

> The work of the Committee's missionaries does not shine in a Report, for it is usually a long, patient sowing and a piecemeal harvest. In little sequestered townships and thinly-peopled areas striking increases in membership are impossible, 'shock-tactics' are impracticable, and the Guilds and Societies of a

37. *RC-UFCS-H&I*, 1926, p. 10.

> town congregation are unknown. Yet the Highlands and Islands Missionary has little time hanging on his hands, his work has compensations, and his 'uneventful annals' are rich for himself and his cure. He has few people, but he knows every one of them, and time and need conspire to make him father-confessor to them all. His five or ten miles' walk to visit outlying families is an event to them, and, to him, new interests. Then with the people nearer his Station he shares an unavoidable intimacy, and they see one another in all weathers and in all moods. They rarely lock their doors in the Outer Islands and along the West Coast, and with a man whom they trust they make sincerity the greater part of their courtesy. So whether he likes it or no, the missionary, in his witness and preaching and neighbourliness, submits to the acid test of intimacy. The Committee is thankful for agents who have stood the test again and again, and have come out approved.[38]

Beginning to focus on the work in Harris during 1926, MacLeod continued:

> But even in those little communities their 'uneventful annals' have red-letter days and periods; for now and always the wind bloweth where it listeth. Last year's Report referred to the religious movement in Harris. The movement still continues and keeps its original character. The same sober earnestness – 'too full for sound or foam' – is seizing upon a people instinctively religious, and is raising the instinct to conscious faith. This year, too, the greater number of the converts are young – on the threshold of manhood and womanhood.[39] Perhaps we are at the start of an era in Highland religion when faith will cast out misgiving and constrain thousands to venture confession of the Lord whom they love but still more fear to dishonour. For there are tokens that Harris will not contain the movement. From other centres there is news of quickened interest and expectation. Surely the Isles wait for Him.[40]

Though now well advanced in years, D.T. MacKay visited the various districts of this 'large and interesting congregation' in the summer of 1927. He said, 'The Lord has graciously revealed His power among them, and a large number of old and young have come under the power of the truth, and are now going on their way rejoicing in the Lord. It was a very great joy to see young men praying in the meetings, so full of faith,

---

38. Ibid., 1927, p. 8.

39. One young convert, the father of Kitty Campbell of Plockrapool, later became an elder in the Scarista CoS and a leader in a subsequent period of revival in Harris, in 1945–6 (personal communication with Kitty Campbell, 24 September 2006).

40. *RC-UFCS-H&I*, 1927, p. 8. One district to which the movement spread was Scalpay.

vigour and love. It was a quiet deep work of God's Spirit, – not much excitement; only a few cases seen in this way. The new converts entered into the spirit of the movement, and assisted with revival district prayer meetings, and their earnest endeavours gave much strength and stimulus to the good work.'[41]

From the start, a number of converts made clear their deep desire to engage in fulltime service for the Lord. MacKay firmly believed, 'The material is there, and we trust they may be aided financially. There are some attending school and college with a view to the ministry. They all seem very promising, excellent young men, able, modest and true.'[42] The evangelist continued, 'The prayer meetings are still well attended, and we hope and pray that the work may spread to every corner and to the surrounding islands, Uist, Skye and Lewis. The work began in one of the darkest townships in the island. The lads did not go to the church but to the hills on Sabbath, but the tide has now turned and quite a number in this village are now bright Christians praying in the meetings and assisting the work of the Lord.'[43]

'D.T.' returned to Harris in 1928, from where he reported that

> the good work is most inspiring and encouraging. Quite a large number of young men and women came under the power of the Truth, and are now praying and singing in the meetings and thus helping on the work of the Lord. A large number of the young men are coming out as preachers of the Gospel. Some are now at school and some at college. They are all very promising and gifted young men who will be a credit to the Island and to the Church. … I spent over a month in Bernera and Cheese Bay. Meetings are very promising, the church full, and all the meetings well attended. The Rev. Murdo Smith is now well settled at Bernera and doing a good work.[44]

One result of the movement, quickly put into effect, was the development of various building operations in the parish. The Rev. Duncan MacLeod of Tarbert, who engaged with 'much zeal and energy' in the work, secured the purchase and erection of a hut at Amhuinsuidhe, between Tarbert and Scarp on the northern shore of West Loch Tarbert, where the Land Settlements under the Board of Agriculture had brought new residents to the area. At Caolas Scalpay, on East Loch Tarbert, the UFC Session carried out the roofing and furnishing, at their own expense, of a deserted cottage for meeting

41. Ibid., 1928, p. 9.

42. Ibid., e.g., James Morrison, Scalpay, who was ordained in North Uist in 1942.

43. Ibid.

44. Ibid., 1929, p. 10.

purposes. Thirdly, at Kinresort, on the marshes between Harris and Lewis, the walls of a Ladies' Highland Association[45] School were rebuilt, roofed and equipped to house services for the township, for the salmon-fishers who worked there and for the people of the shielings (summer grazings) in the neighbourhood.[46] The movement had clearly made a deep impression throughout north Harris.

---

45. An Edinburgh-based organisation formed in 1850 to meet the deep educational and spiritual needs of those living in the Highlands and Islands. There were 160 L.H.A. schools in existence at the time they were taken over by the Education Authority (Mrs J.T.S. Watson, *Pathmakers in the Isles 1850–1949*, Edinburgh 1919).

46. *RC-UFCS-H&I*, 1927, p. 9.

Rural North Lewis – p.309

Roddie MacLeod – p.313

Donald MacDonald – p.315

George Murray – p.316

Habost, Ness – p.315

11
Layman's Revival
1930s

Introduction

UNDOUBTEDLY one of the most significant evangelical revivals to have occurred in twentieth-century Scotland[1] was that which took place in Lewis in the 1930s. It has often been stated that this revival, which sprang up in various parts of the island between the years 1934 and 1939, was generally an even more powerful movement than the famed Lewis revival of 1949–53 (Norman MacLeod, who was converted in the early stages of the 1930s movement, wrote that it was 'probably the most impressive and widespread revival in Lewis since the renowned awakening in Uig under the ministry of the Rev. Alexander MacLeod in 1824'[2]). This is ironic, given the notoriety which the 1949–53 movement has gained, not just in Britain but throughout the world. In contrast, the 1930s revival has been, at least until recently,[3] little known even in native Scotland, and to this day many Scottish believers are completely unaware of its occurrence.[4]

A number of reasons have been proffered for the lack of public disclosure on this movement – sometimes dubbed 'the Layman's Revival' due to the general lack of direct ministerial influence. Though often dramatic in nature, the revival became greatly overshadowed by the outbreak of the Second World War, which also led to a significant

1. 'unquestionably the most fruitful' according to Rev. John N. MacLeod (*MR*, September 2002, p. 12).

2. MacLeod, *Lewis Revivals*, p. 10. See also Black, *Revival: Personal Encounters*, p. 68. MacLeod suggests that the 1930s revival (of which he was a convert) was more widespread in Lewis than the 1949–53 awakening. The Peckhams (one of whom was a convert of the later movement) make a similar claim (Colin and Mary Peckham, *Sounds From Heaven*, p. 32). For evidence that this, from whatever source, is at least contentious, see maps and data in the following pages. Yet, as we shall see, while neither movement exerted much influence in places like Back and Stornoway, and in certain parishes affected by both revivals the first was stronger than the second (e.g. Carloway, Lochs) or vice versa (e.g. Ness), in other areas the later revival had considerable influence where the earlier had almost none (e.g. Uig, Harris, including Berneray).

3. Colin and Mary Peckham helpfully include a number of testimonies from the 1930s awakening in their 2004 book, *Sounds From Heaven*.

4. This revival would certainly have become better documented had it come to the notice of J. Edwin Orr, later the world's leading revival historian. Twice in 1934 (once on bicycle), as a young man of just 22, Orr made impromptu tours of Scotland, everywhere urging believers to pray for revival. Unknown to him as he traversed the length and breath of the Scottish mainland, a wonderful spiritual movement was progressing in Lewis. Orr sensed a 'rising expectancy of revival in Britain' around this time, but said this had receded within a few years (J. Edwin Orr, *An Apprenticeship of Faith*, Wheaton 1993, pp. 29–36, 64).

diminution in its progress. Further, there was no one person at the centre of the movement – as Duncan Campbell was a decade later – who would become a spokesperson for the revival at church services and conferences on the U.K. mainland, and via written accounts of its progress. Thirdly, due to the bizarre physical phenomena that were sometimes manifested at meetings – which many saw as excesses, and therefore to be deplored – many church leaders and lay people preferred not to publicise the movement. In any case, there was felt little need to broadcast goings on; people were well aware that the more that attention was brought to unusual incidents, the greater likelihood of glory being diverted from God to man. Further, the Lord had sovereignly chosen to pour out His Spirit on these Hebridean isles. He wasn't dependent on man's testimony of His work elsewhere in the country. If he wished to bless particular places, He would do so in His own way and in His own time. Lastly, some people felt that their experiences in the revival were too personal, too precious, too holy, to be shared abroad. They had been given primarily for their own encouragement and were not to be spoken of lightly.[5]

I have read all the scanty documentation relating to this thirties Lewis awakening. I have also conducted personal interviews with dozens of people who were either personally involved in the movement in the different parts of the island that were affected, or who obtained firsthand information from others who were themselves involved. It will be observed that I have given more space to this revival than to any other movement documented in this book. I have done so because of the significance and potency of this movement and also because it constitutes a first serious attempt at providing a detailed account of its progress. In the following narrative, therefore, I seek to present for the first time an accurate and fairly comprehensive record of the remarkable revival that occurred in Lewis in the six years prior to the outbreak of the Second World War.

CARLOWAY 1934–8

HOME to the inspiring Druidical stones of Callanish, which attracts thousands of visitors each year, in 1934 the parish of Carloway also played host to a significant spiritual movement, particularly in connection with the Free Church. Before it began, there was an air of apathy in the district, and almost no one under the age of forty was a church communicant. Instead, most of the district's young were caught up with 'worldly pleasures, such as football, badminton, concerts and dances, while the ceilidh was as popular on Sabbaths as on weekdays'.[6]

---

5. e.g., a woman hoping to interview a convert of the 1930s revival for local hospital radio found a deep reluctance among believers to share their stories. In conducting my own research, too, there have been instances where people have been reluctant to share incidents that they consider personal and sacred. See also the experience of Angus MacLeod (page 352 fn55).

6. MacAulay and MacLeod, *Discussion on Revival.*

The work in the Free Church occurred during the ministry of John MacIver, a native of Point, Lewis, and later a student at both Edinburgh University and the Free Church College in that city. Ordained and inducted to Carloway in August 1924, MacIver quickly proved to be a powerful preacher, declaring the whole counsel of God, often with such unction that left his congregation in tears.[7] So popular was his preaching that he was in great demand at Communion seasons in other parishes, and during his term in Carloway he was to receive several calls from other congregations.[8] The motivations that lay behind his preaching were a love for Christ and a love for souls, and wherever he preached his hearers thirstily drank in every word. MacIver was also a faithful pastor, tending sensitively to the needs of converts, old and new, and a Carloway man recalled how, just as a teacher taking a group of children on a field trip requires all his skills to keep them safe and under control, so MacIver carefully shepherded all the young revival converts in his parish.[9] More than half a century afterwards, converts could still fondly reminisce on how he 'was always with the people of the Lord, feeding the flock, taking us nearer to the Lord'.[10]

An average of four new communicants were added to the church roll during each of the first ten years of MacIver's ministry – tokens of the Lord's favour, yet insufficient to keep the pastor from becoming at times extremely despondent.[11] Even while at theology college, he had thoughts of leaving the ministry entirely. Such feeling of inadequacy was deepened on meeting, one day in Stornoway, his ministerial colleague, Malcolm MacIver of Crossbost, Lochs, the latter informing him that a spiritual movement had begun within his own congregation. Soon after this, Malcolm MacIver had a dream in which he and John were together in the Carloway church listening to a sermon delivered by Donald MacLeod, the previous minister in Carloway. John turned to his colleague and informed him that this was the seventh time MacLeod had preached from this text. Malcolm responded by saying that seven is the 'perfect' number. Just then, weeping broke out throughout the congregation. Someone remarked that the 'time of weeping is over'; then Malcolm woke up. From that day on, the Crossbost minister was convinced that revival was coming to the parish of his dear friend John MacIver. The following morning Malcolm's

7. See Murray, *Diary*, p. 361. On one occasion, when MacIver preached an 'able sermon' at a prayer meeting in Stornoway, there were tears on the faces of at least two in the congregation.

8. One call was to Ness, which he decided to turn down. Another was to Stornoway, which was eventually taken by Kenneth MacRae.

9. Quoted in Iain D. Campbell (Ed.), *Heart of the Gospel: Sermon Notes of Rev. John MacIver and Rev. John MacKenzie*, Fearn 1995, p. 9.

10. Personal communication with Duncan John MacLeod, Carloway, 24 September 2002, thought to have been the last surviving male convert of the Carloway revival. Duncan passed away in late 2007 at the age of 92.

11. Indeed some believe that the weight of his ministerial burden and the initial spiritual dearth in the area drove MacIver to the verge of a breakdown.

wife noted her husband hurrying to finish his breakfast and asked him what the rush was about. He told her of his meeting with John MacIver the previous day, of his discouragement on hearing about the movement in Crossbost, and of his own dream during the night. He wanted to travel across to Carloway without further delay, to relate the dream to his ministerial friend, with the hope of encouraging him.

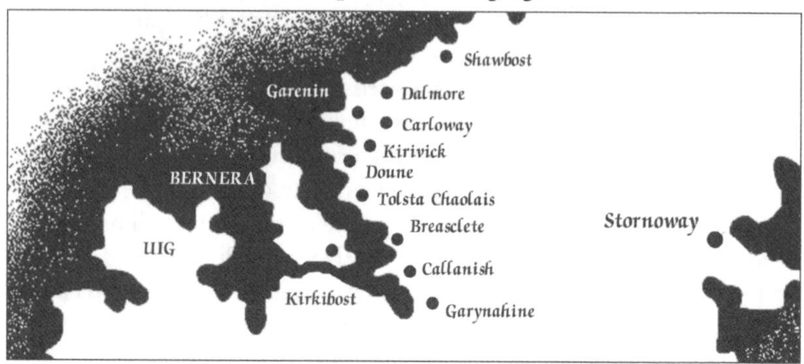

Indeed, the revival began very shortly afterwards, when attendance at meetings increased notably. There was a corresponding increase in the liberty enjoyed by MacIver in preaching as well as by the believers in praying. Among the first converts was Duncan MacLeod from Garenin (Donnachadh an Oighre), who later became an excellent precentor; John MacLeod from Upper Carloway, later an elder in Carloway Free Church; a man from Breasclete nicknamed 'Russian', and two or three more from Carloway. When one experienced Christian saw Duncan and John MacLeod attending a prayer meeting for the first time, his immediate reaction was to burst into tears of joyful emotion. Conversely, the reaction of his wife, also a believer, was a feeling of her heart being as hard as flint in comparison with the two new believers. Wonderfully, all but a few of this initial crop of converts remained steadfast in their faith,[12] a telling indication of things to come – for it has been well attested that the vast majority of converts from the overall revival movement in the parish (i.e. between 1934–9) remained true to their profession of faith.

MacIver sent an account of the movement, up to early November 1934, to Kenneth MacRae of Stornoway. MacRae wrote that

> Indications of an awakened interest in eternal things became manifest immediately after the Spring Communion, and up to date 14 men and 8 females appear to have come under the influence of the truth. Some of the former were ringleaders in frivolity, with the result that concerts, etc, in that district cannot receive sufficient patronage to ensure their continuance. Besides the effect upon

12. One of these firstfruits, who appeared an extremely bright believer, being ahead of most people in knowledge and doctrine, sadly fell away in later years.

> the community is such as to discourage all such gatherings. These young men now are organising and carrying on prayer-meetings among themselves. The movement is distinctly encouraging and there is much reason to plead that it would increase and spread.[13]

The revival thus far was confined to the Carloway district. Chrissie MacAulay was one of the few females converted at that time, coming to faith in mid-March 1934, when she was only seventeen, shortly after the revival began. A more widespread movement took off during the early spring of 1936. This was deeper and much more extensive, spreading through all the villages in the Carloway area, then on to Callanish, to Breasclete, and to Tolsta Chaolais. (During the later phase of the revival quite a few in their mid-teens were converted, although no accounts have been recorded of the very young being touched.)

One who was converted at an early stage was Donald MacIver, a native of Dalmore. A profound impression had been made on MacIver around three years earlier when, as a young boy, his Class 6 Form had gone for a school picnic to a beach on the western coastline of Carloway. A few boys moved away from the group, and soon, with the tide moving out fast, one lad was snatched away by the strong current. MacIver rushed to help and almost drowned trying to save his friend, who tragically lost his life in the accident. This incident had a profound effect on the young MacIver, who, as a result, almost had a breakdown, and suffered from strong bouts of depression over the following three years. By this time revival stirrings were being observed in Carloway, and, hearing two women talk of their experiences, MacIver felt the Spirit speak deep into his soul. Quickened, he went along to a local church service for the first time in his life. It being Communion season, he attended not only services in Carloway, but also travelled to meetings in Back the following week and to those in Ness the week after. By this time MacIver realised it was time for him to publicly proclaim his faith in Christ. Soon after, the keen young convert took the bold step of attending a prayer meeting in his home parish, during which five others also came out for the first time. MacIver became a church member shortly after.[14]

The work of the Spirit progressed steadily but calmly, arousing few incidents of emotional excess but with clear evidence of an even deeper interest in the preaching of the Word. Soon the whole parish was caught up in a revival spirit, and wherever people met, whether in a house or by the roadside, at the peat-banks or in the fields, at fanks (sheep enclosures) or on buses, even at funerals, the subject of conversation seemed to be centred on

13. Murray, *Diary*, p. 280.

14. Personal communication with Donald MacIver. Blind and bed-bound due to a weak bone condition, Donald was aged 94 when I visited him in his New Valley home (just outside Stornoway) in September 2002. Sitting up in his bed, he took great delight in fellowshipping with another believer. He literally bounced up and down as he shared stories of the revival and of his precious Saviour. Donald passed away in 2004.

one thing – the revival in the area, and who had been converted. Christians prayed eagerly for the salvation of others, and on certain occasions they would converse with someone for whom they were praying, and the next day find a wonderful answer to their prayers by bumping into the same person, who by now was a totally new creature in Christ! Some families had four or five from within their number converted, others one or two, yet, remarkably to those caught up in the movement, there were also several families who remained dark even in the midst of this glorious awakening.

Church services were generally packed – *Bha 'n aite air ghoil* ('the place was agog')[15] – with an air of solemnity attending them. 'The whole counsel of God was declared from the pulpit, and no attempt was made to cater for the stirred feelings of the listeners.'[16] The Word of God stole as fiery darts to the consciences and hearts of both the converted and unconverted. Often, both minister and congregation would be affected in clearly visible terms, and the services became 'veritable Bochims'.[17] The congregation would often be unwilling to leave such a 'Bethel' ('house of God'), and would linger around the door of the church, singing verses from their most-loved psalms, the sound of their uplifted praise echoing throughout neighbouring villages. On Sabbath days, especially during Communion season, droves of people could be seen making their way to Carloway Free Church from Doune, Kirivick, South Knock and all the other villages in the district.

Initially people were taken by surprise by certain individuals who showed signs of saving grace. When Murdo MacAulay was a baby, it was prophesied regarding him that he would become a preacher of the gospel.[18] Word of this prediction got around and throughout his youth he was sometimes referred to as *Murchadh am Ministeir* ('Murdo the Minister'). However, as he grew up, Murdo became what he later overstatedly termed a 'leader of evil' in the parish,[19] among his worldly pursuits being the enjoyment of badminton and football, for which latter sport he was the local team captain. As he eagerly attached nets to the goal-posts of the new football pitch one day, a friend commented that it would be unlikely MacAulay would ever play a game there, what with

15. MacAulay, *The Burning Bush*, p. 33.

16. Ibid., p. 34.

17. A place of weeping. Bochim, located near Gilgal, was the biblical location where the angel of the Lord reproved Israel for its sins.

18. The Carloway woman who made this prophecy made two similar bold predictions around the same time. A sister of Norman MacLeod died in a tragic accident as a child. When this girl's mother became pregnant again, the woman visited her and told her that her child would become a servant of the Lord. Norman, born in 1912, was ordained as a FC minister in 1950, in which capacity he served till his retirement in 1988. The third prediction was also given to an expectant mother. But when it transpired that the baby was a girl, some felt it cast doubt on the authenticity of all three prophecies. However, this girl indeed became a deeply committed Christian and served for many years as a missionary in India.

19. MacAulay and MacLeod, *Discussion on Revival.*

all the spiritual activity going on in the area. At first MacAulay sought to cynically explain the conversions among his peers in naturalistic terms – 'Well, that lad lost his mother recently … that girl has been ill for some time … .'[20] In all honesty he himself felt no desire to be converted. However, attending church one Sabbath, the young man was convicted under the preaching of the Rev. Murdo McIver of Shawbost.

After suffering a prolonged illness, he had to give up his work in his uncle Calum's shop. Murdo was now spiritually awakened, though for a time he sought to keep this hidden from family and friends. He eventually identified himself as a believer while attending a Communion in Point in the autumn of 1935, and on his return home, attended the weekly prayer meeting for the first time. He was never to play football again, giving up all such sports for a greater love and commitment. Other young sports-loving converts, too, gave up their worldly amusements. Church adherents were said to have been nonplused as to what all this religious fanaticism would come to, since football, badminton, concerts, and dances had lost their most ardent supporters![21]

MacAulay later spoke of the conviction that many came under.

> As they cried for mercy and grace to help in time of need, some felt as if they were groping in the dark to find true peace in Christ. Some were in this state for a considerable time so that, if they heard any speaker at a fellowship giving marks which they could not follow, they were ready to conclude that there was little hope for their salvation. Others were carried as if on the crest of a wave into the haven of peace, comfort and felicity as they closed in with Christ in full assurance of faith. Many felt like the father of the epileptic boy, crying, 'Lord I believe, help thou mine unbelief' (Mark 9:24). They could well understand the apparent contradiction in his request through their own experiences, as they felt more conscious of their unbelief than of their faith. The effect of the life and conversation of the young converts was remarkable – a hatred of sin, an abandonment of their former lifestyle, a longing for holiness, with a dread of bringing any blemish on the cause of Christ.[22]

A surprising convert of the movement was Murdo MacLeod, known as Murdigan. Although brought up in a church-going family, Murdigan was considered, even by close friends, to be an 'out and out enemy of the truth' and 'beyond redemption'.[23] Yet, though rough and intimidating in character, this opponent of the Gospel was to come forward to the

---

20. Ibid.

21. Personal communication with the Rev. Donald MacDonald, minister of Carloway FC from 1964 to 2002, 4 December 2007; MacAulay, *The Burning Bush*, p. 33.

22. Ibid., p. 34.

23. MacAulay and MacLeod, *Discussion on Revival.*

Cross like a lamb. The Spirit was clearly stirring within his soul by the spring of 1936, when Murdigan decided to attend an evening service in church, hoping to get a seat near the back so that he could get out quickly without being noticed! But his spirit was quickened further by that evening's sermon, and a few months later, Murdigan experienced a vision of the glorified Christ; a vision so profound that for the rest of his life, and despite the reasoning of more 'balanced' Christians, he was convinced he had seen the risen Lord with his own two eyes.

Murdigan was at times so affected by the Spirit's working in his life that one could not tell if he was weeping or rejoicing and his emotions often caused him to leave his public prayers unfinished. Whenever, especially, he or someone else quoted John 1:14 – 'And we beheld his glory, the glory as of the only begotten of the Father' – Murdigan would invariably burst forth in sobs and tears, or, equally characteristic of this unique figure, in that familiar giggle that was truly his own. Another product of the revival who underwent a similar experience to Murdigan was Aohnghas Ian Ghraidhean (Angus John). Aohnghas testified to soaring in his spirit with Christ, till he had to ask the Lord to withhold His hand, as he could not take any more of His presence. He spoke of seeing Christ as clearly as he could the person standing next to him.

Yet another convert was John MacLeod ('An Cor') from Garenin. Like so many others, John had emigrated to Canada during the depression times of the mid 1920s. But on seeking entry into the United States some years later, he was refused passage, and so felt little option but return to Scotland in the early 1930s. John was a jolly, amicable figure, liked by everyone in his home community, not least the young lads, who loved to tease him. During a spell of heavy rainfall one autumn, the stream that flowed through Garenin broke its banks and some crofts were partially flooded, ruining stooks of corn and haystacks, including those belonging to John. The boys of his village teased him, advising him that the following year, his stooks, too, would be taken away. This slightly rattled the crofter, leading him to respond resolutely, 'God will have to be very smart before he will catch me out'! He was determined that his stooks would remain safe and dry.[24] Although he believed in God, John sometimes felt he was fighting against Him, and he did not enjoy personal assurance of faith. Things were soon to change, however.

After cycling with a friend to the Shawbost Communion in February 1936, John casually asked to be woken up at the end of the sermon so he would not be left alone in church! But the preaching, on Christ's crown of thorns, went straight to the heart of 'An Cor', and he became

24. Personal communication with the Rev. Donald MacDonald, 7 December 2007.

disturbed. Back home, he found himself increasingly praying for peace, being delighted when at times his burden was less felt, so that he could indulge in gambling with his colleagues. On one occasion when he was sorely stricken, a neighbour felt led to visit his home, with the words, 'Today I must abide at thy house' (Luke 19:5) impressed on her mind. She comforted him by quoting from John 11:4 – 'This sickness is not unto death …' – and, soon after, John came to a place of inner peace with Christ. He and his sister Effie attended the prayer meeting for the first time on the same evening shortly after. John went on to live a life of powerful witness to his Master, sharing the gospel message far and wide as he travelled in his work with the merchant navy.[25]

Mary MacDonald, a native of Kirivik, never tired of telling the dramatic story of her conversion. As a teenager she was intelligent, happy and carefree. She had many interests and was involved in a host of local activities – such as the Gaelic Society, the Debating Society, ceilidhs, and badminton. But life for her family hadn't always been easy. Her mother, Christinna, had been widowed while still a young woman. She had three hungry children to raise, the oldest of whom later died at the age of just twenty-one. Though not yet a believer (she found the Lord at the grand age of ninety!), Christinna, like most people in the community, was a regular church-goer and she expected her family to attend with her.

Though not a church member, Christinna nevertheless opened her home to accommodate relatives (not all necessarily Christians) attending the Communion from other parishes, particularly Bernera. She would spend much time in advance of the weekend baking, cooking and making sleeping arrangements. Being a great social occasion as well as a time of spiritual refreshment, it was often late before folk got to bed.

The Sunday evening of a Communion weekend always had a strong evangelistic thrust and to this service a great many non-church-goers also found their way. Mary was still tired when she arose one Communion Sunday morning during the revival, but she got on with preparing lunch while other family members went to church. As evening arrived she felt particularly tired, but pushed herself to make the ten-minute walk to church. Being a Communion weekend, the church was especially busy, so young people were expected to sit upstairs to allow the older folk to fill the downstairs area. John MacIver took his place in the pulpit, which towered well above the congregation. Seated next to him was William Campbell of Point, the guest preacher that evening. Campbell was highly respected throughout Lewis but his sermon delivery was often known to be heavy, not always coming over as exhilarating, especially to the young.

25. Right up to being 'called home to his heavenly reward' the Lord was first in his thoughts, and his final words were 'To be with Christ is far better' (Philippians 1:23). (MacAulay, *The Burning Bush*, pp. 49–50.)

As he began preaching, Mary, already quite exhausted, strained to keep her eyes open. But all the time McIver was keeping a watch over the congregation and he, no doubt, would notice if anyone appeared not to be paying attention. Mary held her minister in high regard so, in an attempt not to appear disrespectful, decided to put her arm on the desk in front of her, on which she lay her weary head. Others, she thought, would assume she was in a posture of meditation. Instead she quickly fell into a deep sleep!

By and bye she was startled out of her slumber by hearing Campbell quoting from the book of Malachi: '… and the day that cometh shall burn them up, saith the Lord of hosts, that it shall leave them neither root nor branch' (4:1). The words seared her heart in a way no verse of scripture had ever done before. Clearly she was being awakened not only from a physical, but also from a spiritual sleep. Now in tears, Mary remained head on arm for the rest of the sermon, afraid to sit up lest anyone see that she was under conviction. So embarrassed was she that as she left church she constantly turned her face so that even her closest friends couldn't see how deeply she had been affected. How ironic, she thought. Throughout the previous week the girls had frequently pondered amongst themselves: 'Who will be missing from our camp tonight?' (i.e., who would get converted and so withdraw from the group?). One friend had joked, 'You might be the next, Mary!' 'No fear,' was the defiant reply, 'I'm too hard boiled!' The girls all positively resisted conviction and conversion – it was seen as being suggestive of a weak constitution. Strong-minded girls like them had the ability to shrug off any conviction! But now, for the first time, Mary was wondering why she, of all people, should become so emotionally affected. As they walked up the road together, Mary's closest friend turned and said, 'See you tomorrow at badminton.' Mary retorted, 'Please don't talk about that tonight.' 'Oh,' replied her friend, 'has something touched you?' Mary felt compelled to briefly explain how the sermon had moved her, but pleaded with her not to tell any of the others.

As she opened the door of her home Mary knew she had yet another hurdle to cross. The house was full of relatives attending the Communion and she had no desire to explain to them how she was feeling. She helped serve everyone their suppers, following which a time of worship was held. Among the gathering was Mary's cousin and close friend. Since his conversion some months previously, Mary had taken great delight in teasing him about his faith (as she did, too, her brother Neil, who had also come to faith during the revival). That night, however, Mary was in no mood to tease anyone. As worship started, she found a stool and placed it next to the door leading to the hallway. Afraid that the Spirit might touch her again, she was prepared for a quick getaway! Sure enough, as the group began singing, her heart was again pricked and she became deeply moved. The minute worship concluded, she went straight through the door and up to her bedroom, where she quickly changed and dropped into bed. She was upset and confused, aware of being up against something much stronger than herself. She began calling out to the Lord. Shortly, though lying face to the wall, she became aware that her bedroom door was opening. Someone crept stealthily into the room, without turning on the light. 'It's my cousin!' was Mary's immediate thought. 'He must have sensed that I was under conviction and now he's coming to pay me back for the tough time I've been giving him since his conversion!' She didn't move or say a word, hoping he would turn around and leave. Instead he came closer. Sensing her haughty, rebellious spirit, he touched her and said, 'There you are, on your own! Now take your fill. I hope not a bone will remain unbroken by morning!' With that he walked out, leaving Mary to weep at her hopeless condition.

Initially, her cousin's words made her all the more resistant. Defiantly, she went to play badminton the very next evening. As she walked into the hall her friends turned to her, wondering what she was doing there. 'We heard that you were converted last night!' said one. They seemed to her like Job's friends, whom the devil was using to harangue her. Determined to prove she was still in full control of her life, she grabbed a racket and exclaimed, 'I'll show you whether or not I'm converted!' As she focused firmly on the game in hand, all soul concern left her and she played furiously, in a brazen attempt to prove to all present that she was no weakling. Sure enough, she won her game, but as she left the hall that night her spiritual burden came back to haunt her and she knew deep down that she would never be back. There was to be no more fighting.

Mary gave her life wholeheartedly to the Lord and the following Thursday attended the prayer meeting for the first time, giving public testimony to her conversion.[26] The transformation was immediate and obvious. The minute she gave in to Christ, she gave in fully. Just as she had had both feet firmly in the world for most of her life, she now jumped with both feet firmly into the Lord's camp. The states of being and not being a Christian were so different to her that she knew she simply could not doubt. On the contrary, she became very confident in her new-found faith (in contrast to her brother Neil, for example, who wasn't quite so sure of the Spirit's work in his life). She never again had any desire to go back to her old ways, or engage in the activities that at one time so enthused her. After her conversion and apart from working on the croft, Mary had virtually no time for anything that wasn't directly related to her Saviour and His people. The Lord was her life. And while

26. Shortly afterwards she became a communicant member, which day was especially memorable as a considerable number of other converts also joined the church on that occasion.

she never fell out with those former friends who remained unconverted, there was no doubt at all in her mind that she had to go her separate way. Such radical turnaround was true, not just for Mary, but for the vast majority of converts of the Carloway revival.

It was more than ten years later that Mary heard a corollary testimony to her own. After she got married (1944), two Christian friends from the neighbouring village of Doune were in the habit of visiting the MacDonalds. They would cycle over and often stayed till the early hours of the following morning, so much did they enjoy fellowshipping together. Indeed, while Mary was more than happy to provide supper for her visitors, she was reluctant to go and make it since it interrupted the sweet fellowship they were enjoying. So she compromised by leaving the door between the kitchen and living room wide open so she could hear all that was being said! One of the visitors was Hugh MacLean. Mary had heard his testimony before but not the exact details or the timing. She was in for a pleasant surprise one evening when she heard Hugh recount his story while she was making a bite to eat.

At the time of the revival much of the pasture-land in Lewis was not fenced into fields, but lay open. In the summer months the sheep and cattle that grazed on the land were watched over by the young folk of the neighbourhood. It was a responsible and time-consuming job, and Hugh was one youngster who saved a little hard-earned cash over a number of months from this employment. With the money he made, he bought a brand new suit. But he wasn't really a dancer and few other social occasions cropped up, so the suit lay around in his bedroom, rarely getting an airing. At this time Hugh had never been in church, but as Communion came near it occurred to him to go to the Sabbath evening service to make use of his lovely suit. He went along early and sat upstairs as was the custom. His mind was hardly on spiritual things, however. Instead he became engrossed with the joinery work inside the building, which he considered particularly well crafted. No one had told him how impressive it was or he would have been to church much sooner! By this time the service was well underway, but Hugh was oblivious to who was in the pulpit or what was being preached. Instead his eyes were working their way round the church, examining the woodwork like those of an official inspector.

All of a sudden he bolted upright. The preacher was quoting from a book in the Bible and the words shot home to Hugh like an arrow dead on target. The text that particularly spoke to him was, '... and the day that cometh shall burn them up, saith the Lord of hosts, that it shall leave them neither root nor branch' (Malachi 4:1). This verse Hugh had never heard before in his life, but somehow the words now struck home with poignant meaning. Mary had been listening all the while to Hugh's story as she prepared sandwiches in the kitchen. But now she stopped and, going through to where the men were seated, asked Hugh, 'Was it William Campbell who was preaching that night?' 'Yes it was,' Hugh replied, asking how she knew. 'Because,' she exclaimed, 'it was through that very same text that I, too, was powerfully awakened!' It turned out that both Hugh and Mary had come under conviction through the same sermon and even the very same text, preached on the very same night, but it had taken more than a decade for them to realise it. Many of the young folk in Carloway had thought of the Rev. Campbell as a rather laborious preacher, but clearly the Spirit had been working powerfully through his message that particular night.

Like Mary, Hugh became a bright, lively Christian. He had several remarkable experiences in his early days of walking with the Lord. One evening, after a hard day's work, he hurried his dinner before rushing off to Carloway Free Church, determined to make the prayer meeting. He loved to pray and fellowship with other believers and he took advantage of every opportunity to do so. He was rather late that night, however, and as he turned the handle of the church door, he found to his dismay that it was locked. Being a wild and wintry night, the door had been locked from inside to keep it from blowing open. Hugh didn't want to knock for fear of disturbing those engaged in prayer inside. Instead he silently cried, 'Lord, I'm loathe to turn back. You know how great my desire is to be here.' He tried the door once more before taking his leave. To his surprise, it opened. Hugh walked in. The elder who had locked the door was astonished, knowing full well it was securely fastened and that nobody else had a key. Hugh explained why he had been late, and his earnest prayer outside the door. Everyone agreed that the Lord himself had surely provided a supernatural answer to his heart cry.

Hugh worked at home on his father's croft. After his conversion, relations between the two men were at times strained because of the latter's aversion to the Church and to his son's recent religious fervour. So opposed was he to Hugh attending church meetings that he would 'invent' jobs in attempt to keep him at home. Early one evening, just as Hugh was about to set off to a cottage meeting, his father, who also owned a small fishing boat, said he needed help preparing a fishing line by the shore. Hugh had expected such decoy, but it didn't lessen his deep disappointment at missing out on being with the Lord's people, whom he dearly loved. Nevertheless, it would have been considered unseemly to disobey his father while still living at home, so, reluctantly, he set off for the shore. After they had been working a while, Hugh decided to slip away and spend a few moments in prayer, his favourite activity. Finding a secluded spot, he knelt down on the sand and poured out his heart to the Lord. He wished he had a Bible with him so that he could hear from God as well as speak to Him. After a time he opened his eyes and to his amazement, saw an open Bible lying by his side on the shore. At once he picked it up and began to read, enjoying a marvellous time of spiritual blessing.

Greatly refreshed, Hugh closed the holy Word and set about hiding it safely so he could find it again. Though he made no mention of the incident to his father, as they travelled home he could hardly contain his excitement at the Lord's wonderful provision. The next day, Hugh returned to his hallowed spot, anticipating another time of sweet communion with the Lord. But search as he did, the book was nowhere to be found, despite Hugh knowing exactly where he had hidden it. He returned to the shore a number of times to renew his search but all to no avail. He was led to conclude that the Lord had miraculously provided his Word for that one specific occasion when he was feeling depressed and in great need of encouragement.

Mary fondly related times when she made the journey to Bernera to attend Communion seasons. These were exciting occasions – Bernera was itself in the midst of a glorious awakening (see pp. 349–52), and revival converts delighted in coming together in fellowship. It was no small event; the joyful pilgrims usually left home on Thursday or Friday, returning home on Monday. At that time, of course, there was no bridge connecting Bernera to the Lewis mainland, so folk crossed by boat from Doune or elsewhere along the coast. Despite the effort required to get there, people didn't even consider not going. For them it would have been much harder to stay home than to go along with the others. A great many believers regularly made the journey.

Mary's husband, Donald MacDonald, came from Tolsta Chaolais. Although he lived in the same parish and attended the same church as Mary, throughout their school years they had little connection with each other. Converted around 1936, a few months before Mary, Donald used to tell of one occasion at a Communion in Bernera during the revival when his own minister, John MacIver, was also present as the visiting preacher. Donald had a fine singing voice, and although men as young as he were not usually called upon to precent at meetings, his gifting was such that following his conversion he was regularly requested to do so (it was through his precenting that he got to know Mary). To his surprise, he was called upon at the Bernera services. The Bernera Free Church was a very old, single storey building. Being so low, the pulpit was situated almost immediately above the precentor's box, with only a few steps up to it. McIver was known to preach with considerable unction, and during his sermon that day he was so emotionally affected that Donald, who even as a young man was almost bald, felt drops of tears on his head as they fell from the face of the minister above him![27] Donald died in 1984 while Mary survived him by more than 30 years, attaining to the ripe old age of 93. Despite many trials she remained remarkably strong in her faith to the very end.

Services were held only in Gaelic; and though many were unable to read in Gaelic when first converted (it wasn't taught at Primary School, though everyone spoke it), they made rapid progress through studying the Bible and learning texts and sermons by heart. One of McIver's favourite books of the Bible was the Song of Solomon and he often preached from this portion of scripture. One member of the Carloway congregation used to mark in her Bible all the texts in the Song of Solomon that her minister preached on, and people were amazed afterwards to find that more verses were underlined than not! It is perhaps no surprise that McIver should turn so frequently to this Old Testament book, considered an allegory of God's love. For the Carloway minister never preached the Law solely – the emphasis of his sermons was always the love of Christ.

Prayer was central to times of informal fellowship. But opportunity was also given for discussion. For example, the previous Sabbath's sermon would be discussed, or the message given at the Thursday prayer meeting. New converts would question any elders present as to the meaning of particular verses referred to during these services or during times of their own personal Bible study, and to matters relating to their own life experiences. And they would not be satisfied with shallow answers; they wanted to discover the truth.

Sometimes, when young believers tripped, they were apt to conclude that they had sinned against the Holy Ghost. When pressed repeatedly by one who wished to know what the unforgiveable sin was, an elder, after several failed attempts to satisfy his questioner, finally told them to read Guthrie's *The Christian's Great Interest* (a copy of which he produced) and they would find their answer there![28] Chrissie McIver remembers that at another cottage meeting questions were fired at a particular elder from all directions, causing him to repeatedly look up this verse or that in both the Old and New Testaments in order to provide a satisfactory response. Finally, he turned to the eager questioners and said with a glint in his eye, 'I hope you realise that after all this wear and tear to my Bible, you're going to have to buy me a new one!'[29]

---

27. All through the later part of his life, Donald retained an amazing ability to recall the details of McIver's sermons, right back to the days of the revival. It was thought that he could recount around three-quarters of his sermons as he heard them. He particularly delighted in retelling them when groups of Christians were gathered together in his home, and when he did so, his words came over with an unction similar to that which attended McIver's original delivery, so that those present keenly sensed the spirit of those revival days. It was not uncommon at such times for both Donald and his audience to be moved to tears.

28. Ibid., p. 35.

29. Personal communication with Chrissie MacIver, 23 September 2006.

In actual fact, the elders delighted in the questions raised by young converts, which had the double effect of building up both the faith of the new believers and that of the more experienced Christians, who were constrained to search the Scriptures for themselves. As a result, office-bearers 'were quickened in the inner man, some more than others, and this was very noticeable in their public prayers'.[30] For these, and other experienced believers, it was unbridled joy to see so many previously careless individuals in the parish turning with such zeal to the Lord and advancing speedily in their new-found faith. MacIver himself regarded the new converts in his parish as the most intelligent youth on the island, and other ministers visiting also noted how particularly enlightened in mind and spirit these folk were.

Joy filled the lives of converts. MacAulay noted that 'during the revival itself visiting ministers were greatly uplifted, and older Christians were on the top of Pisgah'. Duncan John MacLeod remembers a man, an old deacon, who presided over some meetings, always concluding with the singing of the last three verses of the 148th Psalm. All those present at the cottage meeting gathered around him, keenly relating to the words being sung. People sang from their hearts and everyone was greatly stirred and blessed.[31]

Sometimes non-Christians would be eager to attend prayer meetings, being mysteriously drawn to places where the atmosphere was spiritually charged. MacAulay remembered one unconverted person who stayed at a meeting till seven in the morning, listening intently to the discussion and soaking in all that he could. It was said that even the unconverted could tell when the Spirit had withdrawn from a meeting, sensing an indifference and coldness in the atmosphere. There were even occasions, as with a particular gentleman in Glasgow, when people outside the island were aware of the unusual events taking place in their homeland, without ever being told of them.

One Lewis girl working in Glasgow when the revival started returned home to Carloway in the springtime to help her mother in the family home. Despite having been informed by letter of events in the parish, she admits to getting

> a shock on arriving there. Every available seat (in the church) was full. Sad to say I was not very happy with the carry-on – I wasn't getting on with my spring-cleaning! In the morning a crowd would be there round my father at the family worship. Sometimes one would get up to pray without being asked. One morning I just let go and said, 'This is terrible, my holiday over and I didn't get half of my spring-cleaning done!' That night they

30. MacAulay, *The Burning Bush*, p. 35.

31. Personal communication with Duncan John MacLeod, 24 September 2002.

> had planned to go to a neighbour's house because there was a housebound invalid there. They started pleading with me to go with them. In the end I said, 'All right, I will go with you and you will see that I will come back as I went' – but I didn't. If I am a Christian now it happened that night. I had only a few days of my holiday left. I went back to Glasgow and worked my notice in my job and went back home. I stayed nearly two years and what an unforgettable time I had.[32]

One man greatly revived during the revival was Duncan MacPhail, a deacon in the Free Church, then in his eightieth year. As with others, the revival was to him almost as a 'second conversion'. As a shepherd would conclude, on noticing a lone sheep leaving the rest of the flock and skipping along with the lambs, that this sheep was in better condition than the rest, so it appeared with Duncan. He would eagerly join with young converts going to meetings, who in turn were happy to walk him home, often late at night. His prayers were fervent and wide in scope, often covering all the nations of the world in a single petition! When requested to ask God's blessing on a cup of tea, Duncan would stand with cup and saucer in hand, and as his mind and spirit focused on the wonders of God's grace, he would shift cup and saucer from one hand to the other – everyone in the room giving a sigh of relief if he ended his thanks with both items of crockery still intact! It is said that whenever young converts visited homes, tea was immediately prepared, mainly with a view to hearing the converts asking a blessing or returning thanks. MacAulay notes that 'of this tea recent converts were quite apprehensive'![33]

Whenever people gathered together during the revival, prayer became spontaneous. MacAulay writes,

> At worship, where a death had occurred, the names of two people were called on to pray between singings, and it was not unusual to hear 12 to 15 prayers during worship. I remember one house prayer meeting where 17, almost all recent converts, were called upon to engage in prayer. Today (1984) I would feel two or three longer than the 17! There was such an earnestness and freshness about these prayers that they gripped the attention of all, some of whom audibly prayed with them.[34]

Often young converts found their questions answered directly from the pulpit, sometimes with such clarity that they felt someone must have told the pastor about their specific situation! John MacIver, in particular, seemed to have hold of the pulse of his congregation. On

32. 'Testimony' in Steve Taylor, *Lewis Revival 1934–1941*, Kensaleyre n.d., pp. 2–3.

33. MacAulay, *The Burning Bush*, p. 33.

34. Ibid., p. 33.

one occasion, after a meeting in church, some converts arrived at the home of a lady who had been unable to attend the service as she was looking after her aged mother. Boasting in jest as to how excellently McIver had preached that night, there was a knock at the door. In walked the minister, whose first words were, 'I think you're going to extremes when I'm not there'! Those gathered inside were amazed at his able discernment.

MacIver gave guidance as to how to conduct the house meetings. At first men kneeled to pray, but as houses got more and more packed, this was deemed inappropriate, and men stood to speak with God, while others remained seated. New converts found it especially difficult to make public prayer at first. Some would end their prayer in despair with a shake of the head and without even adding the customary 'amen'. Others would be so moved that they were unable to finish their prayers due to their eyes becoming wet with emotion. Given their inexperience at public praying, a group of young male converts, not yet church members, began to meet by themselves in an empty cottage, where they 'practised' prayer on their own. Women were not allowed access, nor were experienced Christians, apart from one person who was called on to lead the informal gatherings. Murdo MacAulay came to one such meeting well prepared. When called to pray, he eloquently reeled off a string of texts that he had previously committed to memory. Sitting down, there was an uneasy silence, before someone quipped, 'Who's going to get up to pray after that?!' [35]

Marion Morrison became a believer and church member some years before the Carloway revival but was greatly blessed when many of her friends 'came out' during this exciting season as well as some in her family. She recalled that nothing would keep the young folk from walking the several miles to the many meetings in Carloway throughout the week. Life at that time was a constant schedule of church and house meetings, and some were determined not to miss out on anything. Many professions of faith were made during these informal cottage meetings, although some people who were under a degree of conviction but hadn't yet made a profession needed considerable encouragement before they found the courage to attend them. For Marion and her friends, it was a great excitement to anticipate who from their neighbourhood might turn out to the Thursday prayer meetings for the first time! Marion worked for a while as a maid at the manse, where, among other duties, she would milk the manse cow. She had a deep respect for McIver, but

35. Considerable information has been provided about how cottage meetings were conducted during the time of spiritual awakening in Carloway, the apprehension of new converts in prayer, as well as other general aspects of the revival. Many of these characteristics were common to the revival movement throughout Lewis in the 1930s and are therefore not reiterated in the subsequent sections on this revival.

noted his periods of melancholy and depression, especially in later years.[36] While preaching, however, McIver always seemed strong of faith and his sermons came over with the power and unction of the Holy Spirit. This notwithstanding, there were a few occasions when he felt so weak that he was unable to enter the pulpit at all.

The revival seemed to spread from Carloway, where it so dramatically started, to Tolsta Chaolais, then to Breasclete, and on to Callanish. In Breasclete, the work deepened following the spring Communion of 1936, at which time it was reported that 'matters have been exceedingly bright'.[37] The movement here seemed to follow a different pattern to that in Carloway, with more evidences of extravagance. Kenneth MacRae, on hearing of the Breasclete work, decided to 'suspend judgment' on the movement, though privately noted that 'it seems to be the same sort of thing as is going on in Point – people affected by a strange concern which appears to bear no relationship to the truth. It seems to catch hold of those affected by it for no apparent reason ... this is an aspect of the movement for which I do not care.'[38] In fact converts were reported in all the ten villages within the Carloway district, which covered a length of about nine miles.

TOLSTA CHAOLAIS

THE work became more intense in Tolsta Chaolais, too, at the beginning of 1936. Here, the testimony is given of Roderick MacKay, one whose life was wonderfully changed at this time.

> I was born in the little village of Tolsta Chaolais on the west side of Lewis in the district of Carloway. Loch Roag was a stone's throw from my door. I was the third youngest of a family of seven, six boys and one girl. When I look back now on my very young years I often think what anxious moments our parents must have had bringing up a family of seven, being so near the sea and climbing rocks and being such wild characters as we were. Our parents were not Christians at that time and had a very tough time trying to keep all seven of us in order.
>
> I left school at the age of 14 and at that time work was very hard to get apart from our own croft work and a few shillings a day helping others in the village with their Spring work. When I was fifteen I got my first job and that was in the month of May, keeping the sheep away from the crofts of the village and

36. Personal communication with Marion Morrison, 26 September 2007. MacIver's Carloway congregation worried for his health. Once when he went missing, some anxious young folk went out looking for him – eventually finding him safe and well up in the hills near Doune.

37. Murray, *Diary*, p. 299.

38. Ibid.

driving them out to the moor three times a day from May until November. My pay was £30 for six months' work. I had two dogs and they hardly understood anything but swear words. I was really a wild character, every hillock on the moor heard me cursing and swearing at my dogs and at the sheep and I was not very nice to some of the men in the village either. I remember one man giving me a row for swearing when an elder in the church was hearing me, standing outside his house. That gave me a few thoughts at the time; I did not forget it altogether. I sometimes thought that God's judgement would come upon me and if God had permitted me to carry on like this who knows what depths I would have sunk to.

The Revival started at the beginning of the year of 1936. I was just over 18 years old and my past began to give me some concern. The devil was putting me through dark patches too. The revival started over on the Lochs side of the island around the village of Garyvard and it spread like wildfire to the west side. It made a big impression from Garynahine to Shawbost and across to Bernera. I knew that God's Spirit was striving with me and although I didn't know how to pray and nobody ever heard me pray, I tried to ask God for forgiveness and to have mercy on my soul, to forgive me for all my cursing and swearing and the other sins I had committed when I was keeping the sheep away from the crofts.

By this time it was the spring, April 1936, and every day we heard of somebody new coming out to the prayer meetings. There was hardly a day passed without hearing of somebody being converted. I was very much troubled in my soul by this time and I believed that the Lord was awakening me and calling me to come out on His side, but I did not have the courage to come out to the prayer meeting, although I had the most strong desire to do so. I remember saying to my mother on the Wednesday morning that I thought I would go to the prayer meeting that night. Well her answer was not that encouraging; she said if I did go, I would have to keep going, so I did not go that night.

My parents were adherents of the Church of Scotland, and I knew little or nothing about the church, but my desire to know more was growing. There were only about half a dozen families belonging to the Church of Scotland in the village, and at that time none of them were showing any interest in the things of the Church. There was only the one meeting place in the village and both churches shared it. The Church of Scotland minister had a service there once a month. He was a very good man; his name was the Rev. Murdo MacLennan.

In a way I felt on my own as there was nobody in the village of my age with whom I could pal around, but there were many in the surrounding villages of Breasclete, Callanish, Garynahine and Carloway. The church was, and still is, in Carloway. Both churches are there now. The majority were in the Free Church and they were still coming in and being converted, there were twos and threes from the same family being dealt with by God's Spirit. There were not many households between Garynahine and Carloway that the Spirit of the Lord did not touch, and here I was with the deepest desire to be among them, feeling on my own in one sense and afraid to take the next step. I was praying to the Lord to show me what to do and to give me the courage I required to come out to the prayer meeting; it didn't matter what Church. The Lord answered my prayers when I could not hold out any longer. I finally plucked up courage to go out to the Free Church prayer meeting on the Wednesday night.

On my way to the prayer meeting that night the devil was trying to make me turn back, telling me I was a fool and that the Free Church elders at the door would ask me what did I want, and what was I going to say to them? But that was the devil trying to stop me from coming out on the Lord's side. When I got to the door I was welcomed with open arms. We had a house meeting after the prayer meeting in an old Christian's house, and he asked me when I went in, 'and what are you doing here?' Well I can tell you I felt very small, I did not know what to say, but that I had a strong desire to be there, and they soon put me at ease.

There were two or three old ladies from Doune there and they were praying for the young fellow who was with them that night. On the way home that night I felt as if a load had fallen off me, and although I still had my burdens, I felt very glad to have had the courage to be in the prayer meeting. I was at the receiving end at home with criticism from my brothers. They were saying to me that it was because I was hearing of others being converted that I went to the prayer meeting; with that and my doubts, it did not help. However the Lord gave me the strength to go on with my desire growing stronger to be found in Christ. The following Sabbath I got up early, dressed, took my bike and cycled to Carloway to the Church of Scotland. On my way to the church that morning I caught up with other younger people with the same feelings, doubts and fears as myself. Words fail me to tell of the joy I experienced that day in Church. I did not know how the minister and his wife got to know, but they spoke to me after the service and told me that they heard I was converted. I did not know what to say, I felt as if I was walking on air.

For a full year after that I can never explain or find words to tell of the glorious transformation that took place in my life, how wonderfully the Lord was working in Lewis at that time, to be caught up in the Spirit of revival. I got to know young people and old in the surrounding villages by going to house meetings

> nearly every night in the week, especially in Breasclete and Callanish. It was the most glorious part of my life; I even thought there was something of the Spirit of revival in the animals around me. We had two cows and a few sheep at that time, and I also thought it was in the glorious weather; I was seeing God at work in everything. Although we were in the house meetings nearly every night we didn't seem to get tired at all.
>
> I remember one night being in a prayer house meeting in Breasclete until six o'clock in the morning and, without having any sleep, I started working on the croft as soon as I reached home. I was getting a lot of criticism from my brothers and also from my parents for coming home at all hours of the morning. I learned that every Christian must expect to be criticised and in some cases to be persecuted by the devil and world, but praise the Lord, He enabled me to carry on when I thought of what He had done for me. The Lord was working wonders every day and a great change was taking place in many young lives and some very rough characters too. There were very hardened men and women softened by the Lord's Spirit. They could be seen with tears streaming down their faces in repentance for their past sins and some of them felt the Presence of the Lord so strong that they were overcome and went into trances; it was glorious to be with them, and feeling part of it was beyond words.
>
> The years 1936, 1937 and into 1938 were glorious years of spiritual awakening in Lewis and quite a number became ministers of the Gospel in both Churches (Free Church and Church of Scotland). I have had the Lord's presence without number down the years since then, but I cannot find words for that most glorious and special time in my life. When I look back at these days of Revival I thank the Lord with joy in my heart for the love with which He loved me and died for me, and gave me a real hope of eternal bliss on the other side. Quite a number of those who started on the road with me are now in Glory and in possession of the blessings to which there will be no end. To God be the glory, great things he hath done. He is the same God who is still on the throne and able to save to the uttermost those who put their trust in Him.[39]

But the revival was to come to a rather abrupt stop. In September 1939, many converts from nearby Carloway, and indeed from all over Lewis, came to Shawbost for the autumn Communion. On the last day of the month, in the early morning, while many were still in their beds, a messenger lad from Breasclete cycled up from Carloway to inform the majority of the young men that they had been called into the armed services. It wasn't by any means unexpected, and some boys had joined

39. Testimony of Roderick MacKay (died 2007), now in the public domain.

the Territorial Army some time before, partly in preparation for such event, partly to earn some extra cash. But that didn't lessen the shock and sorrow experienced by many of these men, not to mention their families, and many tears were shed by those in both groups. The actual point of departure, when farewells were movingly made, was to many almost unbearable. That evening, the young men made their way to Stornoway to sign up, before moving on to Harris to spend some time in preparatory instruction.[40]

Sometime later while in France, Murdo MacAulay comforted his Breasclete comrades who were stationed with him by proclaiming prophetically, 'Don't worry, none of you will perish.' He reminded them that this was not just his own wishful thinking, but what he believed the Lord was saying. Nevertheless, such was his love for these dear friends, most of whom he had known since childhood, that he was in tears as he prayed for them. Sure enough, every one of those young men was brought home to Lewis safe and sound. Indeed, of all the men from Carloway who were called up to fight in the War, only two did not return home alive. The two who were lost – at least one known to be a committed Christian – were in the navy, and were killed in action in separate incidents when the ships they were stationed on were torpedoed.

Converts joining the war effort brought their faith with them and many were not afraid to let their light shine. For Norman MacLeod, the trauma of the war served as an acid test of the reality of his Christian experience. He often organised and conducted religious services in the naval barracks when stationed there. Posted on the destroyer *HMS Veteran*, he had to take his turn as night watchman. One night with little happening, he whiled away the time, precenting and singing one of his favourite Gaelic psalms in loud, if hardly melodic tones. Next day on meeting his commander, he was asked who had had the middle watch. Admitting it was he, Norman was firmly advised to practise his raucous gibberish singing elsewhere so that the commander could sleep undisturbed in his cabin by the bridge!

It was reported that the Carloway revival was especially genuine, and apart from a small falling away near the beginning, almost all the converts continued in their faith. Thirty-five years later, a native of the parish returned home from the Scottish mainland to find that the entire football team, every player in which was saved during the revival, had become, and still were, members of their local church; and the team captain, Murdo MacAulay, one of the best known

40. For more information on the effect of the outbreak of the Second World War on the revival in Lewis, see pp. 389–92.

of all converts, was now the much respected minister of the more northerly parish of Back.

Carloway Free Church records show:

5 new members in 1934,
9 in 1935
16 in 1936
14 in 1937
29 in 1938
8 in 1939
21 in 1940
3 in 1941

This gives a total of 121 over the eight-year period.

Though the above figures are highly significant in themselves, it is important to remember that a number of Carloway converts never joined the Church. Others moved away in their late teens or early twenties to seek work on the mainland, some of whom joined churches in the localities to which they moved. Of those who remained in Lewis, quite a few only became members years later. Donald MacDonald remembers one woman who was converted during the 1930s awakening, only joining during his own ministry in Carloway Free Church between 1964 and 2002.[41] If one includes converts from within the CoS in the parish, it is estimated that there were at least 200 conversions in all.[42]

POINT 1935–6

IN the 1920s and 1930s, Knock Free Church in the district of Point (also known as the Eye Peninsula) was the largest Free Church congregation on the island. William Campbell, a native of Arnol on the island's Westside, was inducted to the Knock parish in 1926 and quickly won the hearts of his parishioners with his emphasis on the love of Christ for repenting sinners. Campbell proclaimed the earnestness and power, the demands and terrors of God's law and the need for conviction of sin, and then he directed awakened, helpless sinners to a Saviour who was perfect, willing and able to save to the uttermost all those who came to Him in their need. As time went by, new faces began to appear at the weekly prayer meeting. One who was saved early in Campbell's ministry was Alexander MacLeod – known as *Sandy Mor* ('Big Sandy') – who, like the other young people of the district, used to sit in the gallery, which went round three sides of the church.

Campbell quickly established a close relationship with John MacIver of Carloway. Both were eminent men of prayer who longed for God's

41. Personal communication with the Rev. Donald MacDonald, 24 September 2004.

42. Given the magnitude and effect of this awakening, it is interesting to find that MacIver's notes in the Church records for these years make no mention whatever of the spiritual movement in his congregation, nor, is it thought, did he ever preach directly on the topic of revival.

glory to be revealed in their lives, as well as in the lives of those in their congregations. The two ministers often shared fellowship in each other's homes, encouraging and learning from one another. They also swapped pulpits on numerous occasions. Obtaining first-hand information on the awakening in Carloway, Campbell longed to see a similar work of grace among his own people, for there was much spiritual darkness in the district at that time. In late autumn, 1935, the Point minister had a time of great liberty in prayer, and strongly sensed that the Spirit was about to move in his congregation. This note of expectancy was heightened by an equal liveliness and thrust in the prayers of certain church members at the prayer meetings. Campbell began a series of nightly services in his church in Garrabost, when he invited ministers from other Lewis districts to assist in sharing the Word.

At the beginning of the second week, Campbell preached from Ezekiel 37:1 – the valley of dry bones. Noted one who was present: 'Half-way through his sermon he (Campbell) stopped preaching and began to pray. I have never known this to happen before. The Spirit was outpoured among us and I don't think there was a dry eye in the congregation. The power of the Spirit was evident in a wonderful manner.'[43] Indeed there was such unction to Campbell's message that about forty people professed conversion that night. Revival in Point had begun. When asked later what difference there was in his preaching during the revival, Campbell admitted that his sermons carried the same evangelistic thrust as always. The difference was that during revival he felt almost a compulsion to preach, and his words seemed to carry a special sense of unction.

Soon the movement had spread to Shader, Knock and Aignish, and indeed throughout the whole region. *Sandy Mor* testified: 'The first awareness of a change in ourselves and in others was when we met together in the prayer meetings. There was a oneness of spirit as we engaged in prayer and an increased burden as we interceded for an outpouring of the Spirit in the community. This led us, as the Lord's people, to have more gatherings together. There seemed to be a compulsion to pray, and we all felt it.' Sandy also had a vivid recollection of coming from a meeting and finding young men and women by the roadside weeping and praying that the Lord would have mercy on them.[44]

Plans were afoot in the early 1930s to build a community hall in the district in order to hold dances, concerts and the like. The church opposed the plans and many homes added their signatures to a petition against the building project. The Land Court did not honour the petition, however, and preparations were made to begin construction. But when the revival began, people's interests lay in church and cottage

43. Testimony of Alexander MacLeod (*Sandy Mor*), audio tape.

44. Ibid.

meetings and interest in the building project dwindled. The plans were laid aside and the hall was never built.

Says Alexander MacLeod:

> The amazing thing was that there were those who spoke against the awakening – ministers, elders and deacons and others. I recall William Campbell making a statement from the pulpit in Sheshader, Point, about those who opposed the work of the Spirit of God. 'I will say this to you,' he said, 'that the children of God have never done anything more offensive to the Lord than to go against the work of the Spirit of the Lord among His people; inevitable consequences will follow. It will be the judgement of the hardening of the heart. You will be fortunate; indeed it will be a miracle, if this judgement does not overcome you until the day of your death. You may salvage your soul but you cannot escape the judgement of God.' We saw this happening before our eyes where some were never moved again by the gospel until the day that they died.[45]

Stornoway 1936

STORNOWAY remained largely aloof from the revival taking place in some of the country areas. One exception relates to a small movement of a very different nature that occurred in the town when a band of Pilgrim Preachers arrived from the mainland at the beginning of 1936. Of that two-week campaign the visiting evangelists recorded three years later, 'We had memorable meetings, and a band of young men and women were led to the Lord.' With the motto, 'Out and Out for Jesus', they formed a Christian society for mutual help, instruction and testimony, and through their witness others were added to the Lord. Eventually, some left to work or study on the mainland; one young man entered ministerial studies while a young woman began training for other Christian work.

In 1939 the Pilgrim Preachers returned to Lewis, and were delighted to find that 'those remaining of the "Out and Outers" stand by us in our open-air meetings, helping us to win other precious souls. To see the joy in the faces of these three-year-olds, as more young folk accept the Saviour, is at once an inspiration and a joy to us all.'[46]

---

45. Ibid.

46. Newton, *The Story of the Pilgrim Preachers*, p. 122. Kenneth MacRae expressed a contrasting impression of the movement. Of the Pilgrim Preachers' work among schoolchildren in Stornoway he stated pointedly, 'I have no faith in it. It has resulted in additions to the Communion rolls of at least two of the other Churches, but its products seem to be characterised by a cock-sureness and self-sufficiency that is very far removed from the humility and brokenness one associates with the genuine work of the Spirit. These young "converts" were never heard of as being under concern and gave no evidence of any such thing, and even now, so far as those connected with the FC are concerned, have never put in an appearance at the prayer meeting, while such inconsistencies as attendance upon concerts and "the pictures" mark them off as the victims of a religious delusion which is claiming only too many nowadays.' He went on, 'I write thus, but, oh, my own religion is eminently unsatisfactory! And yet I can honestly say that, apart from the work of the ministry, I have no interest in life, and would not wish to live unless I could get to preach Christ to sinners' (Murray, *Diary*, p. 297).

Pilgrims from the Faith Mission also visited the island during the period of the Thirties revival.[47] In 1937, before the movement had reached its height, they reported that many had been brought into the Kingdom of God through their regular missions and special conferences. The Highland Superintendent wrote that on a visit there he had found 'full halls, good spirit, converts bright, some walking about 20 miles. Escorts of singing converts for miles seeing us home. Generous giving and hospitality. Never had so much liberty in my soul. Hallelujah!' [48]

Generally, Stornoway was little affected by the spontaneous revival movement that so deeply affected country areas. How much this had to do with Kenneth MacRae's outspoken views against certain features of the movement is unclear. Church of Scotland congregations in the town seem to have remained largely unaffected too. However, Kenneth Nicolson, a student on leave from the Free Church College in Edinburgh, remembers preaching in Stornoway on one occasion in 1938, when, during the singing of a psalm, he strongly felt the presence of the Lord. So affected was he that he thought he was going to fall over. Not wanting to create a scene, he prayed for sustenance. Looking towards the congregation, Nicolson noticed that some of his hearers, too, were overcome by the Spirit.[49]

There were other evidences, too, of Stornoway church-goers being affected in their emotions. Converts never became church members on the basis of profound or unusual experiences, but were quizzed carefully by the Kirk Session on their knowledge of the Word of God. Even Kenneth MacRae, while insisting he would 'give the swooners no latitude', was nevertheless very pleased with one woman who, although subject to emotional outbursts, was able to give clear and Scriptural evidences for her faith. Another woman of like disposition, however, 'while her life appears to be changed, and while she appears to have some sort of knowledge of sin in the heart ... had no Scripture for anything and seemed most ignorant of the Word', and hence was refused admission to the Lord's Table.[50]

Bernera 1936

AS a young man, John Morrison, a native of Leurobost in North Lochs, went to the Scottish mainland to train for the ministry. He had been in the habit of supplying Kiltearn Free Church, near Dingwall in Ross-

47. A group that MacRae viewed in similarly disparaging terms to the Pilgrim Preachers. He called them 'an organisation thoroughly Arminian in doctrine and in practise unmistakably of the school of Finney' (Kenneth MacRae, *The Resurgence of Arminianism*, Stornoway 1950, p. 24).

48. *BW,* 1937. The Highland Superintendent also noted considerable interest in the Gospel in Tiree at this time.

49. Personal communication with Kenneth Nicolson, Crossbost, 15 August 2002.

50. Murray, *Diary*, p. 372.

shire, when he received a call to move there. The call was tempting, not least because a new manse had recently been built in the parish and it was to be partly furnished for the new minister moving in. Meanwhile, the charge on the small island of Bernera, off the west coast of Lewis, had been vacant since the Union with the UPC in 1900. Travelling there to assist in a Communion season, Morrison noted the small congregation and the desperate needs of the parish. He felt strangely drawn to the place. Shortly after he received a call from the Bernera congregation, and, around the same time, yet another call from the Kiltearn Church. The young minister was forced to his knees to seek God in earnest. As he did he sensed the small, still voice of God – a voice he had matured in discerning over the years – assuring him that his service in Bernera would be blessed.

Before long, the young minister was back in Lewis, serving God and the people of Bernera. However, despite his conviction that he was where he was meant to be, things did not look encouraging on any front. For one thing, he had to renovate the manse, which was cold and damp due to a prolonged vacancy. Coming out of a prayer meeting with several office-bearers one evening, Morrison admitted that things were grim and that he was angry with the Lord for not fulfilling His promise of blessing.

There also existed on the island a notable disinterest in the gospel and, especially among the young, a growing passion for worldly pursuits. For example, football was becoming a relatively new craze on the remote island, although both the new minister and many of the older churchgoers were strongly against it. As if in direct defiance of Morrison's views, work was commenced at setting up a pitch in the field next to the manse. Morrison boldly proclaimed that no game would be played on it. Some mocked the minister's prophecy, but things turned out exactly as he predicted. Indeed, one boy who was seen playing on the new pitch was later converted. Returning home to the manse one day, the scriptural verse, 'Behold the Lamb of God', came strongly to Morrison's mind. He felt it was of God and his heart was encouraged. Sure enough, two people were converted in the parish that day, a cause of great joy to the minister. This was one of the first signs of the fresh wave of God's grace that was to breeze over the district. The revival that Morrison had so long awaited had at last arrived.

Another man who had precognition that blessing was coming to Bernera and that he would be personally involved was Donald Smith, a native of the island. Converted at the age of eighteen, Smith was eager to study the Word of God, but was unable to do so as he was illiterate. However, his next-door neighbour agreed to teach him to read passages from the Scriptures, and the young man learned quickly, in time becoming a zealous lay evangelist. He began to hold meetings in folk's houses, where many heard the gospel for the first time, and where believers were built up in their faith. One young lad whom Smith helped lead to the Lord was Angus MacIver, who later studied divinity at Glasgow University before translating to Canada, where he began a Christian college in Toronto.

Smith was a man who had a remarkable closeness to his Father. It has been recorded with some detail how he publicly announced the death of Charles H. Spurgeon, several days before official news came to the island that this famous London Baptist minister had indeed passed away. A powerful preacher, Smith had a fruitful ministry in Harris and the Uist islands. In 1936, when semi-retired and living in Uig, he looked over to Bernera and cryptically prophesied: 'I'm going across one day with a sledgehammer to break those hard stones over there!' [51] Two weeks later he went across and the revival began, Smith being significantly used during the time of blessing that was then in progress.

In the days of revival in Bernera the island had a large population and the churches were often packed with worshippers. On Sunday mornings (as well as on other days during Communion times) the road leading to the church was black with folk dressed in dark Sunday clothes wending their way to or from the place of worship. As people left church those going northward walked home together, musing on that morning's sermon or engaging in other meaningful discussion. By and bye they would reach a road junction; one branch leading north-west to the village of Croir and the other north-east towards Tobson. The believers were loathe to split up, disgruntled at the thought of discontinuing the fellowship that so strongly bonded them. It was said there occurred at this juncture something akin to a tug-of-war, with believers vying amongst themselves in attempt to entice each other to go home with them for lunch and more fellowship! No one wanted to return to their own homes alone. A visitor from Carloway who witnessed this almost comical scenario on at least one occasion used to tell others that unless they saw it themselves they could never understand how touching it was.[52]

Kenneth MacRae, often wary of revival movements, was to note in his diary: 'It seems to be a more rational work and to have more relation to the preaching of the Word than that of which I have heard in another area. I have heard of no extravagances in connection with it.'[53] John MacIver of nearby Carloway was often invited to preach at Communion services on the small isle. He and a number from his congregation travelled across by boat from Doune in the west of the parish. The large

51. Colin and Mary Peckham, *Sounds From Heaven*, p. 228.

52. Personal communication with Chrisanne MacDonald, 21 January 2008.

53. Murray, *Diary*, p. 299.

Bernera fishing vessel would cross on the Friday, Sunday and Monday of the Communion, and it was said to have been a memorable sight to witness it sailing towards Carloway Pier after an enriching Communion season on Bernera, with the sound of Psalm 122, verses six to nine, ringing out from many united voices across the calm autumn water. Of the many revival converts from the island, some were later lost in the war, while, in more positive vein, four Bernera converts went on to become ordained ministers.

LOCHS 1938–9

BY 1938 a new wave of revival had arisen, commencing in South Lochs, which soon became powerfully affected. Minister of Kinloch Free Church at the time was Murdo MacRae, who was inducted to the parish in 1927, and remained there till his death in 1961. A spiritually-minded man, MacRae was deeply concerned by the low spiritual condition of the parish in the early years of his ministry. So serious had things become that on occasions when the minister was not present, the precenting, preaching and all other church activities were left to just one dedicated elder. As MacRae and this same elder were walking towards the manse one day, the elder remarked on the spiritual darkness prevalent in the parish. 'Ah, yes,' replied the minister, 'but I think you'll find that the tide is about to turn!'

This wasn't the only prediction that revival was coming to Lochs. Shares Annie MacKinnon: '… a godly man had a significant dream before the revival commenced. He saw an angel passing over the villages, and the villages where the angel tarried were the villages where revival came and the ones the angel bypassed were not visited.'[54] Also in Lochs, spiritual fire was evidently seen above a church before the awakening commenced and the man who saw it indicated that revival was coming.

The movement began through a young man in the village of Garyvard, by name of Murdo McKinnon, later an elder in the local Free Church.[55] McKinnon and his aunt were two of the very few professing Christians in this community; indeed there was such spiritual apathy that out of a total village population of around seventy people, only four or five regularly attended church. Returning home one Monday from a Communion in Knock, Point, where revival was already being experienced, McKinnon felt persuaded to share the good news of salvation with his mother and his sisters. All were visibly moved. That same evening an elder from the neighbouring congregation of Kinloch arrived unexpectedly at their

54. Annie MacKinnon, quoted in Colin and Mary Peckham, *Sounds From Heaven*, p. 251.

55. Many years later, Angus MacLeod, a native of South Lochs, in a quest to obtain first-hand information on the revival, sought to interview Mr McKinnon to ask more about his experiences in it. Unfortunately, the modest elder refused to talk, leaving Angus so discouraged that he set aside his tape recorder and made no further attempt to investigate this unique Lochs movement.

home. He was asked to conduct a time of worship and several people from the village were invited to join them. Several people were convicted of sin at this impromptu service, and news of the fledgling awakening quickly spread through the community.

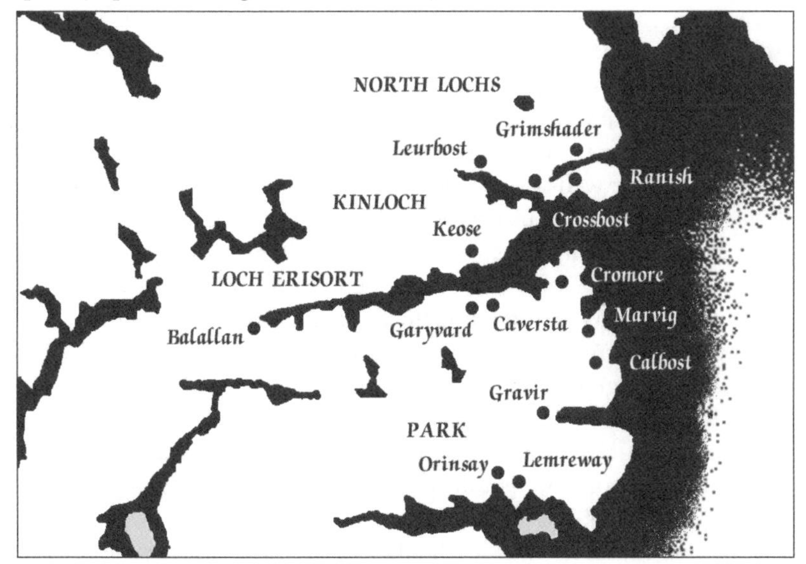

The spiritual awakening of some who attended the meetings was gradual. Others were awakened quite suddenly. Donald MacLeod was working away at his shoe-repair business in his small bothy in Garyvard when a friend from the nearby village of Caversta dropped by for a blether. The main topic of conversation was the meetings being held in the home of Mrs McKinnon (who was in fact a sister of Donald). Following strong encouragement from his friend to 'go down with him and see the goings on', Donald hesitatingly went along to that evening's meeting. He came under deep conviction, coming through to a place of spiritual peace in Christ soon after. His friend, however, seemed unaffected by the meeting he attended and indeed by the revival in general. While Murdo's mother was not converted at this time either, several others in the family were.[56]

Soon a season of contrition and awakening was spreading through the congregation, and also into neighbouring Kinloch and North Lochs. In Garyvard itself, meetings in the McKinnons' home grew to such an extent that they soon had to be transferred to the Mission House, sometimes called the 'prayer house' – a hall in the village that held over 100 people. When this finished they would move on to one of several cottage meetings which were held in folk's houses every night.

56. Personal communication with Murdo MacLeod, Garyvard, 13 September 2007.

Villages in South Lochs were spread out along lonely twisting tracks, but people travelled from all over to attend meetings, often walking or cycling long distances. At the height of the movement, teenagers from Marvig cycled the four or five miles to Garyvard and back again to be at the evening meetings. As was customary in Lewis at this time, younger children didn't attend any meetings. Angus MacLeod remembers that two elders would regularly make the journey from Garyvard to Calbost to meet with believers there. Others would travel by a small boat across Loch Erisort to attend services and oft-times the eager pilgrims would gustily sing out well-loved Gaelic psalms. Their voices would carry harmoniously across the surface of the sea, resonating like the sound of an angelic choir in the ears of fellow believers returning home from meetings on foot.[57] In like manner, people would come out of their houses, miles away across the loch, on a calm summer's evening, and stand and listen to the people singing at the close of meetings in the church or cottage meeting.[58] Many people also attended meetings in Lochs from the island's Westside districts such as Carloway and Barvas. For example, a building contractor in Shawbost – MacLean to name – used to transport lorries full of folk along bumpy twisting roads to meetings in Gravir.

Christina Matheson was a schoolgirl during the time of the revival. Brought up in Stornoway in a church-going family, though not a thoroughly religious one, she delighted in going out to South Lochs for the whole duration of the summer holidays to stay with her granny, Mary Ann Montgomery, who had been widowed some years previously as a result of the *Iolaire* disaster (see page 307), leaving her to bring up eight children on her own. A Free Church member, Mrs Montgomery was a godly woman who never neglected to 'take the books' (lead a short time of family worship) in her home each morning and evening.

Christina quickly became used to this routine. But she remembers one summer in particular that was somewhat different to the rest. Although she didn't fully realise it at the time (because adults didn't normally speak to children about spiritual concerns) a fully-fledged revival was in progress in the summer of 1938, and the Stornoway schoolgirl arrived in the middle of it. She did become aware, however, that people were being unusually affected, because she remembers that one day an aunt, who was working as a maid to the minister, came into the house in tears. It transpired that the woman was under conviction of sin.

Christina also recalls the cottage meetings in the district, which were held virtually every night at the height of the revival. In the summer months when there was much work to be done on the croft as long as daylight persisted,

57. Personal communication with Angus MacLeod, Marybank, 24 September 2002.

58. Colin and Mary Peckham, *Sounds From Heaven*, p. 263.

the meetings often didn't start until well into the evening, by which time young children were already in bed. Such was often the case when meetings were held in the home of Mrs Montgomery. When these were held in other people's homes, Mrs Montgomery and others in her family were always keen to attend, so the younger children were 'boarded out', i.e. looked after by an adult in the community who, for some reason, was not able to attend the meetings. The houses in Lochs consisted mostly of small 'buts and bens' (small two-roomed stone cottages), yet it was amazing how many people crammed into them for these informal gatherings! In compliance with her understanding of Scripture, Mrs Montgomery always covered her head with a piece of cloth during times of prayer. At a later date Christina was told by her aunt of the swoonings – usually of young women – that often took place at these house meetings, and also that at such gatherings several people were known to speak in tongues.[59]

Kenneth Nicolson,[60] a native of Gravir, was converted before the revival started. Although he was studying at the Free Church College in Edinburgh in the late 1930s, he was at home for a spell during the progress of the revival. He later wrote of the beginnings of the movement in his parish: 'Initially only one or two seemed interested in the gospel. Prayer meetings were held and more interest was shown, and a number came under the influence of the Holy Spirit. Thus when the movement spread, people from all surrounding areas and further afield gathered and it became obvious that many who before were indifferent were now anxious to be saved. The power from on High spread and then in the village of Lemreway His power was made manifest and the atmosphere seemed heavenly … .'[61]

Kenny used to cycle miles to attend meetings along with a friend, Alistair MacKay from Stornoway. Alistair was converted during the revival, and was staying with Ken at the time. (MacKay was soon to be called up into the Royal Air Force, and was killed in service during the Second World War.[62] It was this tragic incident that moved Ken to compose a poem, in Gaelic, about the Garyvard awakening – see pp. 262–4.)

Cottage meetings in particular were regularly full. Believers and those anxiously seeking God loved to meet and seek the Lord together and, at such times, Kenny reminisced, 'time didn't mean anything'. Yet the local Free Church minister, Murdo MacRae, was normally very strict

59. Personal communication with Christina Matheson, 28 September 2006.

60. Later to become FC minister of Portree (1944) and Barvas (1957), officially retiring in 1979. Nicolson became a popular preacher throughout the island, and was still ministering when in his nineties.

61. Personal communication with the Rev. Nicolson, 25 September 2006.

62. Alistair kept in touch with Kenny while out of the island, and over sixty years later, Kenny was still deeply moved to read his dear friend's letters. Though the deceased's mother believed that her son had been killed over land, Kenny sensed in his spirit that though his soul was in heaven, his body was drifting in the sea. Sure enough, after a long period of grief, Alistair's body was washed ashore on the island of Islay, 150 miles south of Lewis. He was brought home and buried in Stornoway.

about meetings being held within regular hours, it being considered imprudent to allow them to continue till late. Once, however, when cycling home from a cottage meeting in the remote village of Lemreway around two o'clock in the morning, who should Kenny and Alistair meet coming in the other direction but the Rev. MacRae. The minister was returning from a house-meeting elsewhere in the parish! It was apparent that he had rethought his position and recognised that when there was evidence of the Spirit moving in power then, it was totally appropriate that meetings should be allowed to continue.

As a student minister, Kenny was invited to preach in various places in Lewis during his short stay home. He remembers preaching in Lemreway, among other places, where some were overcome with emotion. He also spoke in Habost, where, from one single family, three brothers were soon to be killed in the war. Crossbost and Ranish, he recalls, also shared in the blessing. Looking back, Kenny became convinced that at least part of the purpose of the revival was to prepare young men for eternity, prior to the tragedies they would face during the imminent war, which snatched away so many young lives.

Kenny's sister was married in Bayble, Point, and, while the revival in Lochs was in full flow, he remembers going to stay with her so that he could attend a Communion there. Some others from Lochs were also present, and although the services in the Garrabost Church were powerful and affecting, the Lochs folk couldn't help wondering what they might be missing back home in their own parish!

Some unusual phenomena accompanied the awakening in Garyvard. Pantings, prostrations and even uncontrollable screaming would sometimes attend church services or, more frequently, cottage meetings. The most common of these was fainting fits, often referred to as swoonings or trances. Usually those affected passed out quietly and without disturbance, and would lie prostrate and motionless, oft-times with their faces transfigured and in a state of obvious peace and enjoyment. Others cried out incoherently, quoted Bible texts, or preached and prayed with great fervency. Sometimes those affected would be carried out into the open air. Either way, they generally regained normal consciousness within a short time. On doing so, some who had been affected would talk about the unusual sense of calm they had felt, while others related visionary experiences or messages they had received. Many said they were simply conscious of the majesty of God and their own insignificance. Others still admitted they had experienced nothing unusual at all, and in no significant manner did their character or spirituality change afterwards.

While some who witnessed these prostrations felt uncomfortable with the phenomena, others recognised that the Spirit of God was at work. When someone passed out, Murdo McKinnon was known to say,

'Leave them alone, they've never been happier in their lives!' Some non-Christians were among those who experienced prostrations, and, to the disappointment of many, these were not always converted as a result, nor, indeed, even at a later date. It is also important to understand that swoonings were prominent only for a relatively short season, whereas conversions continued over a much longer period.

These phenomena particularly affected young women (Kenneth MacRae put the female/male ratio at four to one). A few were established believers, but the large majority were new converts, and, as has already been suggested, some were affected who made no religious profession at all. In Garyvard, one of those especially influenced by bodily manifestations was the young man through whom the revival was thought to have begun. Murdo McKinnon was well-respected in the community and not normally readily excitable, yet on occasion he, too, had to be carried out of a meeting due to fainting. Physical phenomena came to be expected occurrences at meetings, and when, during one cottage meeting, nothing out of the ordinary happened, the man leading it incorrectly concluded that the Spirit of God had not been with them. Kenneth Nicolson remembers one remarkable occasion when two or three women seemed to be levitated from their seats at a meeting. Although church services, with a minister presiding, tended to be more orderly, Kenneth MacRae spoke of attending a service in Lochs at which he had been invited to preach, where, from the pulpit, he could see some girls lying on the floor of the church, kicking against the gallery. Such was the commotion that the minister felt unable to think, let alone speak.[63] MacRae also observed, both in Lochs and elsewhere, that the singing of particular psalms tended to produce more acute behaviour than did others.

Meanwhile, an elderly woman in Lochs who, up to then, had no particular interest in religion, suddenly claimed that she had received a heavenly message requiring her to remain in her attic until her village was converted. She became regarded as something of a special messenger and people flocked to her home for personal conversation and counsel. Some of the most unusual phenomena to occur during the revival had connections with natural elements. It was said that on one occasion the congregation in a Mission House in Park heard a tremendous shower of hail rattling on the roof until the whole place literally 'dirled' (shook). Those inside were understandably perplexed, for, when they opened the outside door, they discovered it was a fine evening and there hadn't been even a drop of rain.

An equally perplexing incident took place during one of the many meetings held in Mrs McKinnon's house in Garyvard. As the meeting wore on, several people became aware of a noticeable presence – the

63. Personal conversation with Mary MacRae, 20 September 2002.

atmosphere seemed spiritually charged. Then an echoing sound resonated through the house – a booming sound heard by everyone present. It was reported that the house actually shook from its foundations, as if by a tremendous wind, and those present felt an extraordinary power, causing many of them to fall into trances. One man, a brother of Mrs McKinnon – who was at the time, and afterwards remained, unconverted – exclaimed excitedly, 'It's judgement day!' Others also trembled, wondering how to account for the strange noise.[64]

Such was the spiritual atmosphere at these meetings that the very character of some in attendance appeared to be radically affected. An elder from an adjacent congregation was present at one meeting, and in due course, was called upon to pray. Known normally to be very quiet in prayer, as he stood to petition the Lord, others in the room could distinctly hear his voice getting stronger and stronger. The elder spoke with unusual anointing, and indeed, seemed to be lifted to the heavens in prayer, becoming completely indifferent to his earthly surroundings.

One fascinating story that recalls the powerful way in which people were affected came from the district nurse, Christina Smith. In the course of her duties, Ms Smith would visit an elderly bed-ridden woman in the area, to assist with her needs. One day there was a knock at the door, and another elderly woman from the same village came into the house. Both women were Christians but had fallen out many years previously and they had had little dealings with each other since that time. But now, the visitor decided, it was time to let bygones be bygones. 'It's fourteen years since I've been here,' she said, 'but that's not important anymore.' With the coming of revival forgiveness seemed so much easier.[65]

Allan MacArthur has fond memories of his childhood in South Lochs. He grew up in the village of Marvig till he was eight or nine, when his family moved west to Barvas. Even then Allan would return to Lochs to spend much of his summer holidays at the home of his grandfather. This friendly old man was not particularly religious, yet like the head of many Lewis families, he conducted family worship every morning and evening. Allan remembers that even the postman, if arriving with mail during the hour of worship, was invited to join in. In the school playground, the revival and the *curam* became the main topic of conversation. Allan recalls asking a classmate, Roddie Finlayson, what the word *curam* meant. Roddie replied simply, 'It's something that comes on you.' Of

64. One man in the district, while not having heard the first of these two stories, remained totally sceptical on hearing the second, and sought to give natural explanation to it by saying that there were probably about 200 people crowded into the building at the time, and since it was such a flimsy structure, it might well have shaken and even have been liable to collapse altogether under the pressure.

65. Personal communication with Donald MacKay, Lochs, 12 March 2007.

course, this did nothing to satisfy Allan's enquiring mind, but, as he was later to appreciate, it was a rather good description.

Several unusual incidents connected with the revival in Lochs stuck firmly in Allan's youthful mind. He recalls the bodies of several people going 'stiff' during a service in church, and them having to be carried out into the fresh air. During one particular service in Garyvard, a woman from Marvig saw flames of fire coming down on the pulpit. This caused a stir among the congregation, and the woman herself, being much affected by her vision, had to be carried outside by some elders. Possessing a strong mind and not known for emotional expressions, this woman was considered to be the most unlikely person to have an experience of this kind. Strangely, she was not thought to have been converted at the time of her vision or at any time during the progress of the revival. However, decades later, when Allan visited her in the old folk's home in Stornoway, it was evident to him that by that time she possessed a clear heart knowledge of her Saviour.[66]

From Garyvard the movement spread out into the villages of Gravir, Lemreway and Orinsay. In all these places the more outward manifestations were again in much evidence during the early stages of the movement, as well as 'loud and appealing cries for mercy as people became aware of their need of salvation'.[67] In Lemreway both men's and women's emotions were affected as they sang psalms in meetings. One resident of the district wrote: 'There was a godly woman in Lemreway. She was not able to attend church but on the night of the prayer meeting she was at the well to fetch a pail of water. The prayer meeting was about to start and she was looking at the meeting house and saw a cloud resting above the building. That was the night when the revival broke out in the prayer meeting in Lemreway.'[68] One man, just a boy at the time, recalls that his mother started going to meetings in this remote village around that time, and that, like other young women, she passed out occasionally during their progress. As a young lad, her son, Dan, witnessed this scenario on one occasion and admits he found it 'a bit scary', even wondering if his mother was having a serious fit and needed a doctor. Looking back on the revival decades later, Dan said he would describe these emotion-charged events simply as 'hysterics'.[69]

The revival also spread north to Crossbost and Grimshader – and to a lesser extent, Ranish – in the North Lochs district by early 1939. 'There again … men and women were moved by a strange power to engage in public prayer and exhortation. They seemed burdened with a

66. Personal communication with the Rev. Allan MacArthur, Lochcarron, 15 February 2007.

67. Rev. M.M. MacSween, quoted in *Stornoway Gazette,* 2 June 1939, p. 8.

68. Annie MacKinnon, quoted in Colin and Mary Peckham, *Sounds From Heaven,* p. 251.

69. Personal conversation with Dan MacLeod, Lemreway, 15 November 2006.

responsibility for the salvation of others and they possessed an uncanny amount of freedom in prayer and pleading. The people in the district came together to the services in private houses, the ministers and office-bearers of the two churches took part together, and for the time being at least all sectarianism was lost sight of. As one after another became influenced, he or she in turn became an ambassador of the "Good News of Jesus Christ" to somebody else, and thus the work still went on.'[70]

There was some stiff opposition to meetings being set up in both Crossbost and Ranish. In Ranish, such an attempt by two elders had to be aborted altogether,[71] while in Crossbost some elders insisted: 'No, there will be no prayer meetings! It is a busy time of the year, and people need their sleep!'[72] Refusing to be defeated, one resolute elder decided to ask a resident in his home village of Crossbost if he would open up his house for meetings. To their delight, Murdo MacDonald readily consented.

'There were only eight of us,' said Mary Jane, recalling the first meeting in Murdo's house, 'but the singing was out of this world!' That night, four out of the eight were converted, including Mary Jane herself. 'It was a sensational revival,' enthused Annie MacKinnon; 'just before the war and many of our lads left for the services and some did not return. The two elders who originally arranged the prayer meeting in Crossbost never lost their desire for a repeat of the revival but prayed continually to their dying day. They kept the fellowship meetings going. Those who are saved in revival never seem to lose the glow.'[73]

Annie recalls that in 1939 she was just sixteen and working in the deer shooting lodge in Lochs. 'I will never forget how the "gillies" used to come home in the morning – radiant. "We were not in bed last night," they said. "We had an all-night prayer meeting and we are not even tired."' Indeed, recalled Annie, 'There were prayer meetings every night in the home of one of my relatives during that revival.' A wonderful atmosphere attended both cottage meetings and church services. In fact, continued Annie, 'Sometimes ministers could not preach. There was such a sense of the Lord's presence! Some people had such visions of hell and a lost eternity that they were even collapsing on the dance floors. These were never seen on the dance floor again.'[74]

Annie wasn't converted at that time – indeed not until she was twenty-nine – but she still couldn't resist the power of the Spirit drawing her to the centre of worship. One night she refused to be persuaded to stay

---

70. Rev. M.M. MacSween, quoted in *Stornoway Gazette*, 2 June 1939, p. 8.

71. In the testimony of Mary Jane, Murdo MacDonald's daughter, 'the Lord turned them back' from Ranish (Colin and Mary Peckham, *Sounds From Heaven*, p. 250).

72. Ibid.

73. Annie MacKinnon, quoted in ibid., p. 251.

74. Ibid., pp. 250–1.

home despite her mother's objections and the fact that there was a gale blowing outside. 'I will never forget that atmosphere,' she said. 'It was the presence of the Lord! The conversation centred on the revival and my memory is that I felt as if the Spirit of the Lord was in the very air one was breathing – and it was just wonderful! The atmosphere was not just in the church but everywhere. ... And yet I did not get saved! You can be in a move of the Spirit and miss out!'[75]

Mrs MacKinnon has another unique story from the revival. 'In 1939, the people were poor. They had to pray for every meal. I recall being on holiday at home in Lewis. I met a godly widow who later lost three beautiful sons in the war. She was left with two daughters. She was known in the community as the elect lady. Her daughter met me and said to me, "You must come and visit my mother." So I went with my brother. Her five children were in school and she told us that on a certain day she had potatoes for their meal but she had nothing in the house to cook with the potatoes. About midday she had a conviction that if she went down to the shore she would find a skate on a certain rock. In obedience to this conviction she sent the boys to the rock – and there they found the skate! The meal was provided for the children.'[76]

Point 1938–9

CONVERTS often made the journey to neighbouring parishes – and, indeed, to districts further afield – to taste of the awakening there, especially during Communion seasons. For example, many trips were made from Point to Lochs and vice versa. New friendships were formed, and there was a joy and warmth in these relationships that never died.

Communions became highly popular occasions, as converts young and old, invigorated by the spiritual power at work in their own lives and in their community, came under the teaching of local and guest ministers in their own and other districts and enjoyed deep fellowship with likeminded believers from all over the island. Their young hearts bounded with joy as they keenly shared testimonies with their friends and caught up with the exciting news of God's gracious revival work in these other districts. Duncan John MacLeod fondly remembered such occasions, when as a young man he and his colleagues would be away from home from Thursday till Monday, at times sleeping in the barn of a host family, with corn sheaves as a mattress. The older Christians would get to sleep in the house, where often a large number of people would be

75. Ibid., pp. 250–1. John Murdo Smith makes a similar testimony: 'At meetings when revival was taking place, a year or two before 1939, I was young at the time, yet, the amazing thing was, that although I was unconverted, I was conscious of the presence and power of God in the meetings – explain that as you will, but I was very conscious of God's power' (ibid., p. 269).

76. Ibid., p. 252.

accommodated and where two or three might sleep side by side in one bed. 'Lewis was one congregation during the revival,' recalls Duncan John, and 'all visitors were received as from the Lord.' [77]

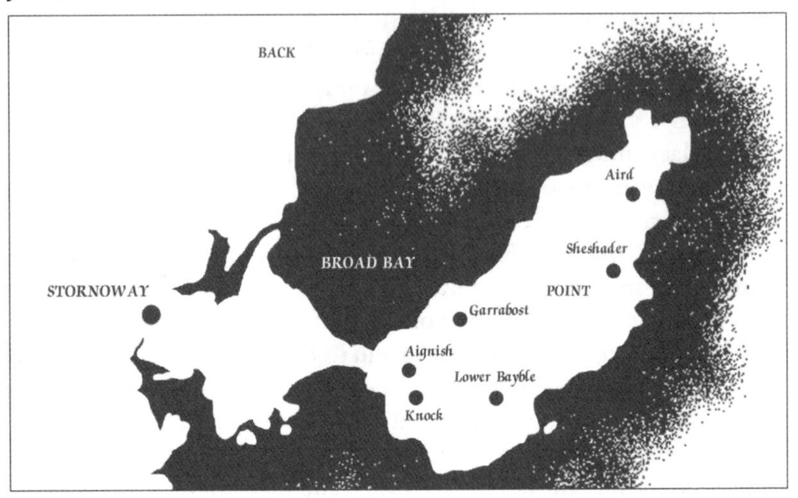

In the spring of 1938, a young schoolteacher from Point attended Communion services in North Lochs. A member of the CoS, the young man had made a profession of faith several years before, but during the awakening found a new lease of spiritual life. As he got ready to head for home on the Monday morning his stomach turned at the thought of leaving the Lord's people behind. As he made his way north by motorbike across the moors, the very scenery around him seemed transformed, and on arrival at the school where he worked, even his pupils sensed something different about him – something they could not quite pinpoint. Arriving home from work that afternoon, the young man at once suggested to his sister that they begin meetings in their house that very evening. Surprised by the obvious change in her brother and by his sudden proposal, his sister felt she could not but acquiesce.

The teacher went to see a Free Church elder in the village, who was very willing to come and preside. He also called on the CoS missionary – a godly man, greatly respected in the district – and also on a young man gifted with a musical voice of exceptional sweetness. Word quickly went round the village and even before the appointed hour of the prayer meeting the house was packed. One of the first to be affected was the teacher's sister. Soon there were many crying out aloud and some were prostrated on the floor. The earlier revival fires in Point, which had partly abated, were now being re-ignited.

After that night, meetings were also held in other houses in the area, and people began to gather from other villages. Some came out of curiosity or

77. Personal communication with Duncan John MacLeod, 24 September 2002.

to scoff, but left sobbing. Converts testified how difficult it was to describe the spirit present at these gatherings, or the effect of the heartfelt singing. The old Free Church elder continued to preside over the meetings. Being wise and diligent, he helped by choosing readings and psalms that were appropriate to the spiritual needs of the converts. He himself was rejuvenated in his faith, as were many other older Christians. On the other hand there were those who were sceptical and who remained bitter and censorious, so losing the blessing. They wanted others to start in their faith the same way as they had; any other way they considered wrong.

Church of Scotland minister Harry MacKinnon had only arrived in Lewis in 1937, but soon found himself in the midst of this glorious religious awakening.[78] MacKinnon worked alongside his colleague, William Campbell of the Free Church, and the two congregations became almost as one, a most unusual feature in Lewis at this time. Both leaders, along with other ministers on occasions, would attend the meetings. Campbell was overjoyed to see many in his parish turning to the Lord. Some were more sceptical, advising that assessment be withheld until the fruit of any profession of faith became evident. But Campbell publicly exhorted: 'We should all rejoice when we see and hear sinners seeking the Lord. That rejoicing is to his glory. If we wait to see that they will not fall, we cannot get the rejoicing then.'[79] Norman Campbell said of his Free Church pastor that 'Rev. William preached until the perspiration flowed down his face. His face seemed to change as the sense of the presence of God decreased, his preaching was not as dynamic. He spoke quietly, but when the Holy Spirit came upon him he was authoritative and dynamic. Souls came to know the Lord and lives were changed.'[80]

In a nearby village[81] there were some who had been assisting Campbell by their prayers for a fresh outpouring of the Spirit. One day in April, a few of them were discussing the revival that had now come as an answer to these prayers. Alexander MacLeod (*Sandy Mor*) proposed that they hold a meeting in a part of the village where there were very few Christians. He decided on the house of a woman who occasionally attended public worship but whose brother never darkened the door of a church. Sandy sent word to the woman to say that there was to

78. He was described by a local journalist as a 'gentle, sensitive soul' who 'saw good in everything. He lacked the dry toughness of Kenneth MacRae' (James Shaw Grant, *The Gaelic Vikings*, Edinburgh 1984, p. 83).

79. This was Campbell's second experience of spiritual awakening in his parish since his induction there in 1926, the first having occurred just a few years previously (see page 346). In fact this faithful preacher went on to enjoy two further periods of revival blessing during his ministry in Point – in 1949–50 and again in 1957–8.

80. Colin and Mary Peckham, *Sounds From Heaven*, p. 188.

81. This is possibly a different account of the commencement of meetings in the village mentioned above.

be a prayer meeting in her home that evening! He and others then approached the elder in the village to ask him to preside at the meetings. The elder was a bit lukewarm as he felt it was all rather unorthodox, but he eventually agreed to officiate. The deacon in the village, however, was most enthusiastic, and at once agreed to attend; he was a deeply spiritual man who was known to spend considerable time praying alone on his knees in his barn.

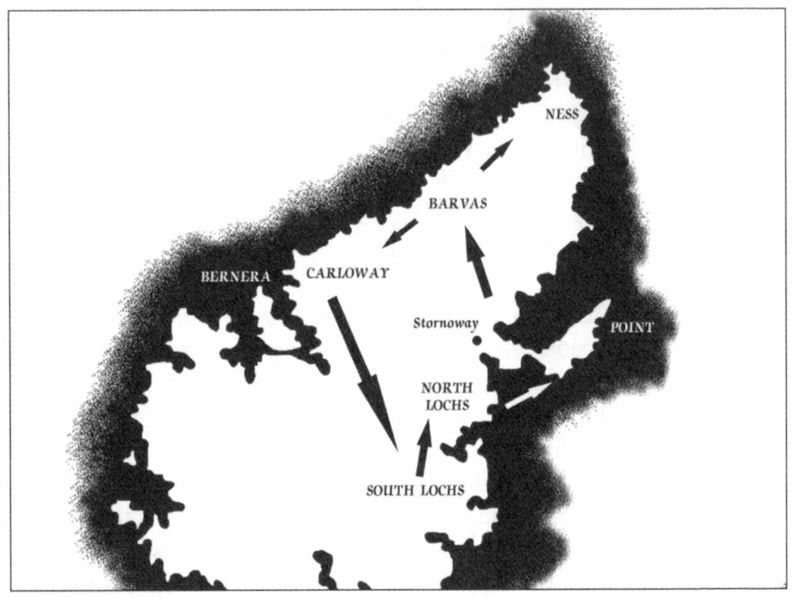

The elder began the meeting, with Kenny MacLeod (the singer mentioned above) precenting the line.[82] The woman of the house was the first to go into a trance. This was followed by audible sobbing from many, especially three sisters, one of whom seemed to have convulsions. The elder asked the deacon to pray. The poor man, being startled by the commotion, prayed honestly, 'O Lord, you know that we were praying for revival – but not like this!' Then he stopped and began again on a different track. This time he praised the Lord, sensing strongly that, although the phenomena he was witnessing were unusual, the Spirit of the Lord was marvelously present, and in full control. After that night, meetings were held in other houses and, wonderfully, the brother of the three sisters came out. More and more attended the meetings, and their spiritual eyes were opened. Some elderly men were also converted.

There was an old Christian who had been wrestling with the Lord, imploring Him to have mercy on the inhabitants of that part of the village. His grandchildren used to eavesdrop on him crying out to the

82. The practise undertaken in some Presbyterian churches, whereby, in the absence of musical instruments or a choir, the song-leader (precentor) strikes up the tune for the congregation.

Lord and were touched by the intimacy and obvious sincerity of his prayers. When the revival started, this man was frail and confined to bed, and thus unable to attend the revival meetings he had so faithfully prayed for. In part-consolation for this, his daughter used to help him out of bed and take him to the window to see the crowds passing by, en route to the weekly prayer meeting. The old man rejoiced at the sight.

For a time special services were held every night in Point in private houses on a kind of rota basis. These were joint services, attended by ministers of both congregations (Free Church and CoS). Frequently attendance was so great that worshippers had to stand around the doors and windows, unable to gain attendance. The meetings would begin around 9 p.m. and continue till midnight or even later. When the ministers left, meetings were often continued, mainly with the singing of psalms and prayer, and it was normally during this part of the service that worshippers were most likely to be affected physically.

Sometimes more than one house meeting was held on the same evening. *Sandy Mor* said that, in his home village, 'we held services at 10 p.m. after the prayer meeting on Sunday nights. These were house prayer meetings. We also held these meetings every Tuesday and every Friday until the houses proved too small for the number of people attending.'[83] At times house meetings would continue right through the night. Yet few people felt any ill-effect from a night with little or no sleep. Young girls walking home from meetings at dawn were yet able to work throughout the following day at the peatbanks or in the tweed mills in Stornoway, without feeling the worse for wear.

There was a deep thirst for prayer and worship, not to mention an insatiable desire to hear the Word of God. Although the converts were at times downcast and concerned lest their beginnings in the journey of faith were somehow not normal and therefore not acceptable to God, they were gently and wisely taught from the pulpit, and warned against relying on their own feelings, or, on the other hand, taking their salvation for granted. There was a lot of heart-searching and many tears were shed. Meetings were also held in a shed, situated in the proximity of both the CoS and Free Church buildings, which are located very near to each other. After services in their respective places of worship, people would come together in this informal meeting hall and enjoy wonderful times of prayer, worship and fellowship.

There was to some extent a seasonal pattern to the movement. Fishermen were away for extended periods of time during the spring and summer, whereas in winter the fishing was more localised, so the men were more at liberty to attend meetings. There was always a liveliness of spirit during the

83. Testimony of Alexander MacLeod (*Sandy Mor*), audio tape.

revival, but blessing was more noticeable during the winter months when the fishermen were home. One moonlit night a crowd of converts and older Christians, including an Free Church elder, stopped on the top of a hill for prayers and singing. One convert commented: 'Our hearts were so full then! How good to remember the days when our hearts were melted under the preaching of the gospel and wished to do something for him. Those of us who are left remember these times, and wish they would return.'[84]

Kenneth MacDonald's parents both came to the Lord during the 1939 revival. 'At that time, to attend the meetings,' he said, 'they would walk all the way from Garrabost to Shader, Point, and back, arriving home at 4 a.m. This they did many times but it had no ill effect on their health. They were thrilled to be involved in the glory of those days.'[85] In the village of Bayble, residents scoffed at those in neighbouring villages such as Shader, where revival had broken out. Soon, however, the movement had spread to Bayble as well, and the same emotional manifestations were taking place there as elsewhere in the parish.

Another couple, both teenagers, whose lives were transformed during the Point revival, were Roderick Stewart and his future wife, Ms MacDonald. Although one was a year older than the other, both were in the same class in school, and both were attached to the CoS. Stewart had always felt an inability to sing and so was shocked when, at one meeting, the Rev. MacKinnon handed him a hymn-book and asked him to lead the singing! Terrified, yet seeing no option but to comply with his minister's request, the young believer launched into the hymn, only to find, to his own amazement and the congregation's delight, that he was given strength and ability to keep the tune. Indeed, such was the unction on him that instead of singing the customary two or three verses, he stretched it out to a full eight! From that time on, Stewart delighted to join with fellow-believers in singing praises to his Lord. And sing they did. It was said that such was the power of the singing at open-air gatherings in Point that their melodic tones could be heard all the way across the expansive Broad Bay (*Loch a Tuath*) in the parish of Back!

Just as believers from all over the island would congregate in Point at times of Communion, so too did Point believers travel to meetings in other parishes. One deeply spiritual woman in Carloway – known as 'Praise-the-Lord-Mary-Anne' – told of Stewart and a friend sitting in front of her at one meeting in Carloway, when suddenly the two young men fell out of their pew 'in the Spirit', and onto the floor, where they remained stationary until they had the strength to get back up. After the

---

84. Testimony of Kenina MacLeod in *Associated Presbyterian Church Magazine*, November-December 1996, Vol. 37, p. 8.

85. Testimony of Alexander MacLeod (*Sandy Mor*), audio tape.

revival, Roderick studied for the ministry and went on to serve as CoS minister in Dennistown (Glasgow), Gardenstown and Clydebank, before moving back to Lewis in 1975 and taking up the charge of Bernera.[86]

MacKinnon related one incident of a cottage meeting in which a girl cried out that there was someone present who did not accept Christ. The meeting then became uproarious. Seven or eight people were on their feet shouting, 'Who is it? Who is it?' A young lad in another room broke down, weeping violently, and those who had been shouting stood up rejoicing that he had just become saved. They shook him by the hand, congratulating him, while he cried out repeatedly the refrain, *Na balaich eile, c'ait a bheil iad?* ('The other boys, where are they?'). On another occasion, when an elder prayed that they might have a peaceful meeting, some of the younger men reproved him, asking whether it was better to have a peaceful meeting or one at which souls were saved. At yet another gathering, when members of the congregation were affected by violent shaking, MacKinnon felt as if there was an electric shock passing through him. It seemed to come from the table on which he was leaning, but even when he lifted his elbows off the table, the sensation continued.[87]

Sandy Mor recorded that he, and others who occasionally went into trace-like states, were certain that it was the Spirit of God who was at work in them. 'The first time I ever fainted in a meeting was on one occasion when I was last to pray,' he recalled. 'As I prayed, I was suddenly made aware of the state of the lost in our district. A great burden fell upon me as I interceded on their behalf. Eternity seemed to open up to my view and I felt my strength leaving me. I simply passed out, the intensity of that burden has left me but I have never forgotten those moments.'[88]

Sandy also records being at a cottage prayer meeting one night, and feeling burdened for a particular young man. The next night he felt constrained to visit him and invite him to the service, which was shortly to begin. The lad happened to be in a state of deep anxiety of soul and so his mother suggested that he should be left alone. At once, however, the young man jumped to his feet and made for the door, scoffing when his mother advised them to go down by the beach road so that they wouldn't be seen! 'What does it matter to me who sees me?' the lad replied. 'That is not the way Christ came to save me – a lost soul!' It being most evident that the Spirit was striving with him, Sandy knew that it wasn't necessary

86. Personal communication with Donnie Stewart, son of Roderick Stewart. Donnie became a Christian in the late 1970s and went on to form the New Wine Church, an independent charismatic fellowship based in Stornoway.

87. Grant, *The Gaelic Vikings*, pp. 83–4.

88. Testimony of Alexander MacLeod (*Sandy Mor*), audio tape.

to discuss spiritual matters as they walked along the road to church. Under profound conviction, all his friend could say was, 'I'm going to hell.'[89]

Sandy continued,

> The minister had unusual liberty that evening and six or seven came to the Lord. The elder asked another man to lead the singing of three verses of a psalm but he declined, asking the elder to do so himself. The elder did so, but instead of singing three verses, he led the congregation for seven verses. We felt as if we did not ever want to stop. The singing was beautiful. The young man and I set off on our way home and as we walked we came across a number of people by the side of the road crying. "We didn't get anything!" they said. "This one and that one is saved, but we didn't get anything! What must we do?" We went on a little further and we heard singing and then further along the road another group was crying and asking the Lord to have mercy on them. What a wonderful night that was!
>
> I accompanied the young man to his home and as I returned I saw a light in one of the homes. It was between midnight and 1 a.m. I thought that I should go into the house in case there were people there who were seeking the Lord. I glanced through the window and, yes, there were people inside, so I entered. Six young girls sat on a bench by the window. The lady of the house requested that I should conduct the worship, but I was rather shy and did not wish to take the lead in front of so many people, so I declined. She then said that we should pray for someone to come who would lead us. 15 minutes later the door opened and our prayers were answered. A relative of mine had gone home after the prayer meeting and was drinking a cup of tea when suddenly he felt a burden coming upon him. He set down his cup and stood up. His mother said to him, "You mustn't go out any more tonight," to which he replied, "I won't be long."
>
> He felt that he should go to Lower Bayble to the first house where the light was on. And so it was that he came, in answer to our silent prayers. There we sat, waiting on the Lord when suddenly the house shook! It shook! There are witnesses still alive who will confirm this. The six girls on the bench fell to the floor. The daughter of the home called out to her parents who were in bed, "Get up, get up, the house is falling!" An unsaved man who was in the meeting began to cry to the Lord for mercy. "O God," he cried, "have mercy on me," and then he added in unbelief, having come to the conclusion that he was not one of the elect, "You won't!" His sister, who was saved, cried out to him, "O Calum love, He will! He will! Don't stop until you find Him!"

89. Strangely, Sandy makes no mention of when or even whether this lad eventually came to a place of spiritual rest – presumably it didn't happen that evening or it would have been stated.

> He repeated his cry and his sister encouraged him to seek the Lord. I will never forget that night as long as I live, and yet there were Christians at that time who did not believe that this work was genuine.[90]

Sandy fondly recalled the 'springtime, the time of year when folk were busy out on the moors, cutting peat from the bogs for fuel. Sometimes, because of the meetings, we did not go to bed at all, yet we did not feel tired. We would arrive home from the meeting at 3 a.m. or even 5 a.m. We used to sing as we worked on the moor, and the singing could be heard a mile away. It was wonderful!' Sandy concluded: 'Usually when the postman called he would bring all the local news, of sickness, or trouble, or glad tidings of any kind, but at that time the question asked would be, "Have you heard if anyone was converted last night?" This was the focus of conversation at that time.'[91]

Barvas and Shader 1939

FROM Point the movement, with accompanied phenomena, spread westward to Barvas and Shader in early 1939. The story of its beginnings in this district is well-known in Barvas revival folklore. A busload of people from the Westside attended the spring Communion in Point and two young people came under deep conviction of sin on the homeward journey. This resulted in the loud and joyful singing of favourite psalms by the Spirit-filled group.

When they arrived back in Barvas, the joyous band of believers gathered together in the home of the Smiths in Ballantrushal, who were among the crowd that had been to Point. Nicknamed the *Gobha* ('the blacksmith'), John Smith was an elder in the Barvas CoS and a man well respected for his godly life and spiritual leadership, as well as being a noted precentor. Also among the number was a missionary's son, a student minister then living in Borve. Margaret, a young woman from the parish who hadn't been to the Point Communion, arrived at the impromptu meeting and was introduced to the student minister. As they shook hands, Margaret felt a strong current flowing from him. She said later that if she hadn't been leaning against a table she would have fallen to the floor, such was the power that surged through her. It was apparent that the believers had brought back the 'power' from Point.

Margaret lived not far along the road from the Smiths, and decided to run home briefly to check on something. As she came near to the gate of her house she heard footsteps some distance behind her, so she stood

90. Testimony of Alexander MacLeod (*Sandy Mor*), audio tape.

91. Ibid.

and waited. It was her brother, John. John had also been to Point, where he had come under deep conviction, and had just arrived home off the bus. The two siblings went back to the Smiths' house and as soon as they entered, Margaret fell flat on her face and for some time was unable to get up. When she eventually did rise, she felt like a new person, and it became apparent that she was indeed a new creature in Christ. Revival had finally come to Barvas parish.[92]

While the movement came as a most welcome surprise to many in the parish, some had been eagerly expecting it. One godly old woman, ill and confined to bed, prophesied that revival was going to come to the district and she even announced the names of some who were

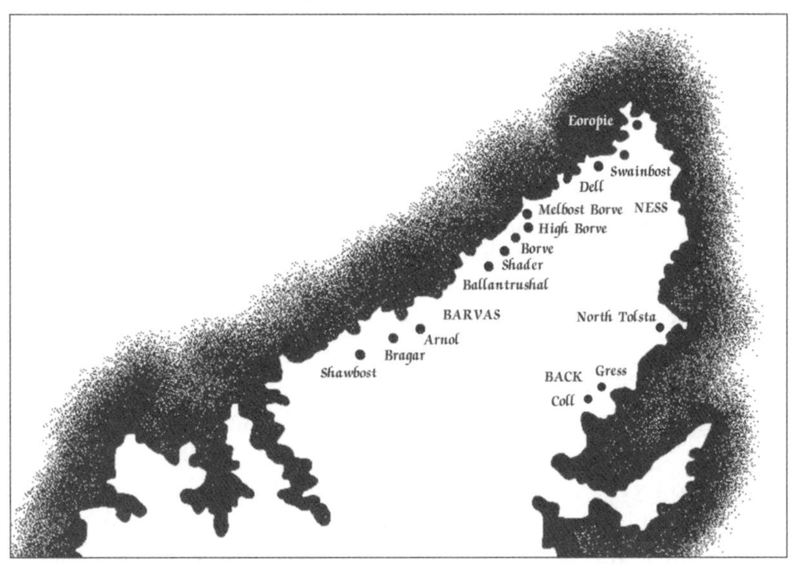

going to be converted as well as others who, she said, would oppose the movement. As it turned out, her predictions proved to be uncannily accurate, although, unfortunately, the woman herself didn't live to see them come to pass.

But there were others, too, who foresaw revival in Barvas. Margaret MacDonald was staying with a sick and dying aunt in Shader at the time revival began in the area and remembers her aunt predicting that revival was coming. So confident was she that she shared it in detailed form with the church missionary. 'She spoke very naturally of those who would be saved,' recalls Margaret. 'What about this fair-haired one?' asked the missionary, pointing at me (then aged sixteen). 'She will be one of the first,' she replied, and I left the room very quickly! I respected the things of God and the people of God. As I could not go to the church

92. Personal communication with Donald John Smith, son of the *Gobha*.

I paid careful attention to the family worship and, as Auntie had said, I was one of the first converts!' Margaret recalls also: 'There was a concert convened in the school hall on the Friday night of the Communions in Ness. I was only seventeen at the time and was asked by a local boy to accompany him to the concert. I could not even think of such a thing. My brother went but came home early.'[93]

In addition to these striking predictions, just weeks before the movement in Barvas began, a resident of Ballantrushal also received a clear prophecy that revival was coming to the area. Mary MacLean was converted in Glasgow in 1928 when aged twenty-three. Married and living back in Lewis, she said she began to 'preach to the unconverted that a revival was on its way. I told them to be out day and night at the meetings at Communion time and not to miss anything, that a great revival was coming.' Some were perplexed by the prediction, but Mary felt the presence of God so strongly that she even felt she was soon to be taken from this world.

> I wasn't worried for the family; I knew the Lord would get someone to look after the family. I was all prepared to be taken away – oh, the presence of the Lord was so strong, I thought no-one could stay in this cold world without the presence of the Lord. And there was a girl who lived near me, and she used to help me with the baby. 'Oh, Hetty!' I used to say. 'Be out morning and evening. Revival's going to come.' And after the Communions she came and said, 'I was out every morning and every night, and no revival came.' 'The revival is coming,' I said. 'You keep out. The revival is coming.' Anyway, the Communion in Point came about the end of March. And I was waiting for the revival, when the power would come.[94]

On hearing of the move of God on the east of the island, folk back in Shader had exclaimed how they wished that the blessing in Shader, Point would come to Shader, Barvas! In Westside Shader, the *Gobha* arranged for two girls to go round the district, house by house, announcing that he was holding a meeting in his home. Despite the short notice given, the house was filled to overflowing. Extra seats were made by setting planks of wood on concrete blocks. These were placed in the yard outside the house, the doors and windows being flung wide open so that all could hear. As many as eight were converted on that remarkable occasion, which became the first of nightly meetings in the area. Donald John Smith (the *Gobha*'s son) says he doesn't recall even one occasion when it rained during these weeks of semi-open-air meetings.

Three women from Borve and Melbost testified that they could hear the lusty singing taking place at the Smiths' home from as far away as

93. Colin and Mary Peckham, *Sounds From Heaven*, p. 169.

94. Hugh B. Black, *The Clash of Tongues with Glimpses of Revival*, Greenock 1988, pp. 144–6.

the school, which was situated about a mile to the north. Indeed, many testified that the beautiful heartfelt singing that took place during this season of spiritual awakening was like nothing they had heard before – it was unique to times of revival. Similarly, Donald John Smith remembers an incident in 1939, when some girls were walking up from Borve, past the school. They were able to hear singing from the Smiths' home.

> Under normal circumstances they could not have heard the singing for the hall was too far away, but this being revival, the people seemed to have an inspiration which gives the voice more power. It is spiritually rooted, and, as they sing, the reality of it seems to give the voice extra force. As you sing in revival you sense the Spirit's presence and know the reality of the subject of which you are singing, to the extent that you want to reach out and touch it. And of course we were singing the Word of God, for the psalms are the hymn-book of our church in the islands.[95]

A baby daughter was born to Mary MacLean on the 10th of March, a few days before the *Gobha* began his cottage meetings. Mary's husband was unconverted at that time. She records, 'He was planting potatoes when he saw the two girls at the door and came up and asked who they were. "The *Gobha* has sent two girls inviting everyone to a meeting in his house tonight," I said.'[96] Mr MacLean was sure it was Christians who were being invited, not non-believers like him. But Mary assured him that he would be welcome and strongly encouraged him to attend. At last he gave in, and decided to attend the meeting that night.

When he got back home Mary enquired of him as to what had taken place. 'Some were standing singing,' Mr MacLean replied, 'some were falling down on the floor, and some others were preaching away, preaching away: … And I'm thankful you could not go out, that you are not able to be out, what with the baby.' Sensing that her husband had felt out of place among so many praying believers, Mary said, 'Never you mind. All you have to do is close your eyes and leave everything you hear and see and just pray to God, "Oh, Lord, open my eyes and gain my heart for yourself"… don't be offended with anything you see, but pray away for your soul.'[97] Although he had made up his mind that the meetings were not the place for him, Mary again urged him to attend the next one the following evening, and, reluctantly, he consented to go.

Meantime, at home with the baby, Mary spent some time in prayer. 'The power came on me in the house here,' she said. 'I was forced to go on my knees. The power of prayer came on me for the meeting, and for the coming of revival to open the hearts of the unconverted. The

95. Colin and Mary Peckham, *Sounds From Heaven*, p. 220.

96. Black, *Clash of Tongues*, pp. 147–8.

97. Ibid., pp. 147-8.

burden wasn't just for one or two, but for the whole world.' When her husband arrived home he complained, 'They were worse tonight than they were last night. … I'm thankful that the baby's here to keep you in the house.' Despite feeling slightly uncomfortable at the meetings, there was something tugging at his heart for, on the third night, Mary didn't need to ask him to go to the meeting. He went of his own accord. 'And when he came home, I didn't venture to ask what was going on. I knew something was happening; I felt it. And when he took the Book to say prayers, the tears were running down from his eyes, and I never asked about the meeting. I saw that he had been converted.'[98]

On alternate nights meetings were held in the Smiths' home and in that of another local prayer warrior, Miss Barbara MacDonald. But these two homes couldn't hold all who came, so permission was granted to use the local Free Church, and this, too, soon became packed out. From the moment revival began in Barvas, it became the sole topic of conversation among the crofters who met together at the smithy.

Donald John Smith well remembers the packed cottage meetings held in his parents' house.

> We children were sent to bed upstairs but we didn't sleep. We would creep out of the bedroom, venture down a few steps of the stairs, and sit there to listen to what was going on in the meeting. Sometimes we would hear someone praying in one room and someone else in another room at the same time, for the Spirit was moving in a powerful way. We children were deeply affected by what we heard and saw. The cry of the penitent frightened us and we listened the following day to the older people as they spoke about those who were converted the previous night.[99]

Remarkably, given that the 1949–53 revival began and had its central focus in Barvas, it is commonly believed (though there are no means to prove or disprove such claim) that more were converted during the 1939 revival in the parish than during the latter, more famed awakening.

One well-known convert of the Barvas revival was Donald Saunders, who had served in the army in World War 1 and who was by now middle-aged. His son's distinct memory of him after his conversion is that he was constantly to be found on his knees in prayer. He was also given great joy, a joy which he brought with him into the '49–53 revival. Like other Barvas converts of 1939, Donald made it a priority to seek out and nurture converts of the later stirring movement. Sadly, Donald

98. Ibid.

99. Colin and Mary Peckham, *Sounds From Heaven*, p. 219.

died suddenly in 1952, at the tail end of that famed awakening, to the considerable distress of those he had so diligently mentored.[100]

Three further notable figures in the movement in Barvas were Colin MacLeod, Ruiridh (Roderick) Alex MacLeod and Kenneth MacDonald (known as *Coinneach Beag* – 'Wee Kenneth'). Roddy Alex had lived a colourful life before his conversion. He remained a lively and outspoken character after it, but now his life centred on Christ and till his death he retained a passion for the salvation of souls. *Coinneach Beag*, unlike Roddy, never got married, but like him, underwent a dramatic transformation of priorities following his encounter with Christ. Kenny lived in a low, thick-walled thatched cottage known in Lewis as a 'black house', and here many a believer gathered during both the 1939 and 1949 revivals for sweet hours of prayer and fellowship. A man of deep spirituality, Kenny was often affected emotionally in prayer, and Donald Saunders remembers that on visiting his parents, as he often did, Kenny never left the house without issuing a word of encouragement, most notably, 'Now keep seeking the Lord!' Such was Donald's respect for Kenny that he felt no stronger connection with anyone than with this esteemed man of God.[101]

Two women deeply involved in the Barvas revival were Jessie and Catherine Smith of Borve. The sisters spent much time in prayer and Jessie, particularly, had a remarkable ability to discern the future.[102] At one time during the revival the two women were so much at meetings that their cow went dry due to lack of milking, potentially resulting in her lactation ceasing. Clearly the sisters had other priorities.[103]

Christianne MacLeod was a teenager living in the village of High Borve (in Barvas parish) during the time of the revival. For some time she had yearned to encounter the Lord in a real and personal way, but she felt too timid to share her heart's cry with her Christian friends. Finally plucking up the courage, she approached one of her non-Christian friends and asked her to go with her to the meeting in Shader. Her friend gave her a strange look and told her it was a daft idea! With a bit of persuasion, however, she yielded, and off the two girls set for Shader, both apprehensive of what they might encounter there.

As it happened, two other of Christianne's friends had also turned up for the meeting, so all four girls sat together. The meeting was powerful,

---

100. Personal conversation with Donald Saunders (Jnr), 12 December 2008. Two of Donald Snr's daughters were also awakened during the 1939 revival.

101. Like his close friend Roddy Alex, Kenny was among the number who left the FC and joined the CoS (see page 381). The Smiths, on the other hand, were well established members of the CoS, their forbears being Free Presbyterians.

102. This persisted even in old age. While living in a home in Stornoway shortly before she died, she had premonitions of two deaths shortly before they took place.

103. Black, *Clash of Tongues*, pp. 133–4.

and all three of Christianne's friends came under conviction and wanted to stay for the after-meeting. Christianne was deeply concerned by the fact that, although her friends on either side of her had come under spiritual concern, she personally wasn't convicted. As she walked home alone, she thought to herself, anxiously, 'Perhaps if I go to sleep tonight a sinner, I will lose my soul.' Early the next morning there was a knock at Christianne's door, and news came that all three of her friends had been converted the previous night! On the one hand Christianne was overjoyed by this revelation, yet at the same time it made her feel all the more condemned.

Shortly after, a missionary came to speak in High Borve Mission Hall. He shared his belief that something good spiritually was going to happen in the community, and that the villagers should take heart. The verse came to him, 'Comfort, comfort my people, says the Lord' (Isaiah 40:1). The missionary also conducted worship in the MacLeods' house, and a real blessing was felt. He encouraged believers to continue meetings in the village. Sure enough, at the very next meeting held, two people were converted. The following evening another two gave their hearts to the Lord at the after-meeting. Christianne came through to a place of spiritual rest soon after, much to the joy and relief of both herself and her family.

Thereafter, she remembers going to a constant stream of meetings. One night a service would be held in the CoS, the next evening in the Free Church. After these finished, many followed on to a house meeting. Cottages couldn't hold all the people trying to pack into them, so great was the hunger for fellowship among so many. Christianne recalled, however, that many who flocked to cottage meetings never dared go to the main prayer meetings in church. They weren't yet ready to make a public declaration of faith in Christ. Some cottage meetings, she recalls, went on till three or four in the morning! Occasionally, one or two people were so overcome that they had 'spasms' and were carried out of the meeting. These gatherings continued on an almost nightly basis until the springtime, when people had to attend to basic duties, such as cutting peats and sowing crops, and it became simply impractical to attend numerous services and late after-meetings every week.

The preached Word of God spoke powerfully to many people at this time. Sometimes certain verses would have particular effect on those present. One Sabbath morning in Barvas Church, the congregation sang Psalm 45. Verses 14–15 seemed to come home strongly to Christianne, whose heart delighted in them: 'They are led in with joy and gladness, they enter the palace of the king.' One evening shortly afterwards, as Christianne slept, she dreamt that a man was standing beside her. He began to precent Psalm 45, including verses 14–15, which again came powerfully home to Christianne. The music, the words, the atmosphere – it all sounded so heavenly. When she finally awoke from her deep sleep, Christianne was disappointed to find that everything in this present world seemed so earthly in comparison. Thereafter, she longed to hear again music akin to what she had experienced in that vivid dream.[104]

Margaret MacDonald spoke of numerous instances of unusual manifestations during the revival. She claimed, for example, to have heard heavenly singing on the night she was converted. Another night, she said, 'I went with my brother to the meeting. I was afraid that he would be killed in the war. We sat on the stairs to the balcony as the church was so full. A bright light came through the door and passed between twins sitting in front of us. Then it seemed to pass through my brother. We could not speak of this experience, but later when my brother was killed in the war I looked back on the occasion and wondered! [105]

On another occasion,

> A group of us converts were walking together with linked arms. Ruaridh Alex was talking and I did not want to disturb him. I saw a light at my feet and at last I said, 'What is this light I see on the ground?' We looked behind us and the light was there. We looked upward and it seemed as if the sky was split open and we were encircled in this light. Everyone in the group saw it. I have never spoken of this experience [till over 50 years later] and have never understood its significance. … I have not felt free to speak of these things before as they seem too sacred to tell. … One cannot explain these things but there was something personal in it. That was how it was with revival.[106]

Some people were so overcome with the presence of God that they fell to the ground. They would fall 'unconscious through the fullness of the revelation they received through the Word, and their faces were radiant as they reflected the heavenly visions which they beheld.' [107] Margaret recalls, 'A group of people returning from a prayer meeting fell to the ground without warning. The presence of God was everywhere. At family worship one night, the atmosphere was so charged with the presence of God that one felt one could reach out and grasp that which surrounded us. Along with this came a sense of unspeakable joy.'[108] There were also reports of people claiming to have had vivid visions of Christ, and on at least one occasion a woman from the Westside reported having seen her Lord in physical form.

---

104. Personal communication with Christianne MacLeod, a native of Shader, 23 September 2006.

105. Colin and Mary Peckham, *Sounds From Heaven*, p. 170.

106. Ibid.

107. Ibid., p. 169.

108. Ibid., p. 170.

John Murdo Smith, later CoS minister in Lochmaddy, North Uist, remembers, as a teenager, house meetings during Communion season in Barvas when 'there was such power in the singing that people went out through the power of the Spirit'.[109] While the Rev. Kenneth MacRae was informed that in Barvas there were 'certain irregularities in the meetings, such as women praying and exhorting, and a good deal of disorder,' a Free Church convert from that area said she recalls no chaos in the meetings. Some who 'fainted' were supported by others around them and those affected might come round crying softly, but she could recollect no shouting or screaming at the many services she attended.[110]

A young girl converted at this time was Mary MacDonald (later Murray), whose life was greatly influenced by John Smith (the *Gobha*), who lived next door to her parents' home in Shader. Mary would walk with fellow worshippers to the church in Barvas on Sabbath mornings, while on Sunday evenings there was a service in their home village. After the close of this meeting, believers would make their way to a cottage prayer meeting. Mary would walk as near to Smith as she could, eager to pick up whatever helpful comments this godly man had to make on the minister's sermon. Believers would gather together in church or in friends' houses every night. 'We prayed and sang psalms till the small hours and when the meetings were finished we would all go outside and sing again. The singing could be heard throughout the village and beyond as it was springtime and the weather was favourable'. Mary attested that during the revival she felt as though she was living on a spiritual 'high'.[111] Another 'of the crop of promising young men whom the Gospel produced in Shader' during the 1930s was Roderick Morrison of Barvas. 'His light shone' during his six years' service as an elder in the Free Church before his premature death at the age of 36.[112]

Barbara MacDonald was already a Christian when revival came to the Westside. 'It was a wonderful time for some people,' she said, 'but for us it was also a terrible time. We were not in the meetings where the people were being blessed. We were called by God to the place of prayer and we would be in another room when the meetings were going on and the power would come and we would be filled with power and the burden of prayer would grow and grow. It was like childbirth. The pangs would come and the pain would come and there was a sense of delivery and joy as a soul was born into the kingdom

109. Sprange, *Kingdom Kids*, p. 288.

110. Personal communication with Christianne MacLeod, 23 September 2006.

111. Shortly after, though, she went through a period of spiritual despondency. Despairing, she cried out to God, imploring him to restore her peace. With clarity she sensed Him speak the words of Psalm 45:10 to her soul in Gaelic ('Listen, O daughter, consider and give ear. ... The king is enthralled by your beauty; honour him, for he is your lord'). She was relieved of her burden and continued her walk in joy. (Personal conversation with Mary Murray, a native of Shader, 18 September 2002.)

112. *PGA-FCS*, 1939, p. 288.

(as would be happening in the other room). And then the wind would come again and the pangs and the pain and the delivery. Again and again it would come. It was very wonderful but it was very costly.'[113] Such intense soul-travail was experienced by others too during the period of revival, and others noted that one could at times hear the moaning and travailing pangs subside as souls were birthed into the kingdom (Isaiah 66:8).[114]

Barbara was renowned in the community for her devotedness to prayer, and she was also known for sometimes going into a trance-like state. The following story is well known in Lewis: 'A man, Colin MacLeod, fled to the bar in the town to drown the convictions which so disturbed him, but he did not stay long. He took a lift home and came off near his house. Barbara knew that he had gone to the town and to the pub and came out to meet him. When he saw her he got down on his knees on the road and called on the Lord to have mercy on him.'[115]

The sense of the power of God's Spirit frequently rested upon Mary MacLean during these months and as a consequence she felt sapped of bodily strength. Another experience that Mary had only became apparent some years later when a Pentecostal minister from the mainland visited her. 'We talked a bit and turned to prayer,' the minister wrote. 'I laid hands on Mary and suddenly she began to speak in tongues and when we rose from our knees she looked at me and said, "That is what happened to me in '39 but I never knew what it was."'[116] During this time, also, Mary was unable to attend any of the meetings, because of her recently-born baby, whom she breast-fed. That other prayer warrior in the parish, Barbara MacDonald, too, frequently came under the power of the Spirit, and so her mother kept her away from Mary lest she, too, went again under the Spirit's power to the extent that she was unable to cope with the baby. 'But', noted Mary, 'when they heard that I, too, was under the power, Barbara was allowed in. The power was great. The revival had come.'[117]

It wasn't long into the revival before many of the praying folk of Barvas began to sense strong opposition. What deeply hurt John Smith was the fact that the most intense opposition came from within the Church itself. He felt burdened for having commenced the house meetings, and apparently even considered ending them.[118] The division regarding revival meetings commonly centred on the high degree of emotional activity

---

113. Black, *Clash of Tongues*, pp. 129–30.

114. 'Can a country be born in a day, or a nation be brought forth in a moment? Yet no sooner is Zion in labour than she gives birth to her children.'

115. Colin and Mary Peckham, *Sounds From Heaven*, p. 170.

116. Black, *Clash of Tongues*, pp. 121–2.

117. Ibid., p. 148.

118. Ibid., p. 128. Donald John Smith questions details of this story as related in Black's book.

that often attended them. The minister and elders of Barvas Free Church objected to the manifestations that were evident when, they claimed, the power of God came upon His servants in particular ways. Those so affected might be physically removed during a church service. Those who were opposed to the manifestations during this revival generally remained that way in later years. Thus, during the famed 1949 revival, it was largely those who had been involved in the previous movement that gave it their support. Others who had resisted in 1939 generally remained outside the later movement.[119]

Mary MacLean was another who quickly became aware of the counter-attack from within Christian ranks. Previously she had been hopeful that the whole community would be converted. Had the leaders moved with God, she believed, then the outcome would have been even more glorious.

> But Satan came. ... Satan had his own power among the people. Oh, yes. When I would send anyone for the young people to come in, I used to preach to them, and when my younger brother came in among the others, he would say, 'Mary, we don't know who to believe.' The young people were going to the meeting, to Barbara's meeting and to the *Gobha*'s. Some were saying it was the devil's work, and some were saying it was the Lord's. And the poor unconverted souls were standing between the two groups; between Satan and the Lord's work. And that was so hard. And the pressure for prayer for the Church of God came upon us now so heavily; the pressure for the people who were saying it was the devil's work. And there were ministers too against the revival.[120] But I was standing in the power of the Lord. And I wasn't afraid; I was telling everything that the Lord was doing. And there I was, I had to stay in. But when Baby grew well on in months I used to go to the Church of Scotland meetings here.[121]

After a time, as Communion came round, Mary felt the urge to go back to her own church. She first approached the Session, who interviewed her. Asked why she had stopped attending the Free Church, Mary confessed that she had at times come under the power of the Spirit; she knew church leaders did not look kindly on emotional expressions during services, and she didn't want to upset them. Boldly, she also remarked on the elders' failure to visit her during her absence from Free Church meetings.

---

119. Hugh Black recalls the testimony of one Lewis man, who deeply regretted going too far in opposing God in revival. 'I spoke against the moving,' he said, remorsefully, 'and from that time God has never spoken to me. I am lost and there is nothing anybody can do for me' (ibid., p. 161).

120. According to Mary, the local FC minister was against the revival. 'Oh, the battle I have gone through with that minister and the elders,' she exclaimed. 'I'll never forget it' (ibid., p. 149).

121. Ibid., pp. 148–9.

> And so I did go to the Table. But the power came after that, and I couldn't venture out to this church. And at every opportunity I had to go, I went back to the Church of Scotland. And mind you, what a battle; you can understand what I was going through. But the power was so strong from the Lord, and the presence of the Lord was so wonderful, and I was saying, 'Oh, well, as long as I am under this pressure, the Lord will give me all the words I need. I don't need to worry!' I stayed in at the next Communion. And do you know, I was so much under the power that the Communion bread and wine were brought to me here.
>
> At the next Communion the Lord's presence and power came strongly and I had to go again. I wasn't afraid, and I was prepared to speak openly to the elders in front of the minister. And the minister asked, 'Why didn't you come to the church after you had Communion?' 'Because when the power came upon me I was going out of the body and I didn't want to upset any of you. When the power of the Spirit came on me I was going off, and it was there I was seeing the visions.' They made no comment on this. 'Oh, well, you can come any time you feel the Lord is leading you to come to the Table.'[122]

Donald John Smith also spoke of opposition to the revival. 'A young man was converted in the revival a few weeks before he was called up to go to the war. He was in a meeting in the church one night when his father stormed in and tried to drag him out, for he did not want him to have anything to do with the revival. The young man left for the conflict in Europe and was soon killed in action. The attitude of his parents changed after the sad loss of their son.'[123]

It is said that the Free Church minister of Barvas, the Rev. John MacLeod, became a bitter opponent of the revival.[124] He was said to have been hostile not only to certain emotions that accompanied the movement, but also to the fact that people from both churches were mingling freely in the Free Church. MacKay is reported to have given instructions to the caretaker of the Shader meeting house not to give the key to anyone but him, not even to the elders of the church. However, on one occasion a man climbed into the church through a window and

122. Ibid., pp. 152–3.

123. Colin and Mary Peckham, *Sounds From Heaven*, p. 220.

124. There were also, it must be noted, some unlikely critics of the 1949–53 Lewis revival. Some of those converted during the earlier movement, just a decade previously, as well as some more longstanding believers, spoke against the latter movement. Some had genuine concerns. Others, having lived through revival, were certain as to how it should begin and how it should progress. The 1949 revival was in many respects very different in character to its forbear and so it was denounced by some as being other than a genuine work of the Holy Spirit. MacLeod was still minister of Barvas FC at the time of the latter movement. Again he opposed it, as well as its leader Duncan Campbell, and once again a number of people left the FC to join the CoS. However, it is reckoned that more people made the transfer from FC to CoS during the 1939 revival than during the latter movement.

opened the building to other worshippers from the inside. One of those awaiting entry was a church elder, the father of 'Sandy Alex' from Shader, who openly wept at being refused entry into his own church. 'I built this church with my own hands and now it is locked to me!' he cried.[125]

Young men and women within the Free Church, and the unconverted who had attended revival meetings, naturally found it very difficult to sit in their own place of worship and listen to their minister denounce a movement that they knew was proving such a blessing to so many. Amazingly, many such people stuck it and remained within their denomination. Numerous others stuck it for as long as they could, but after a time felt no option but to leave the Church to which they had been attached since childhood, and went to join the local CoS instead.[126]

It was during this earlier period of spiritual quickening that Mary MacLean experienced several striking visions. Some of them were of such duration that her mother had to come and look after the baby as Mary was unable to attend to her. Indeed her longest vision, which occurred in early 1939, lasted on and off for around two weeks. She vividly describes what she saw:

> a vision of heaven, and of hell. And hell – there was a plunging into hell as if sheep were plunging over a precipice, and I was hearing the gnashing of teeth and the crying. I saw the flames going through the people. … And I thought, with the furnace that was coming out of hell, that there wasn't a hair on my head that wasn't singed with the furnace. But then, a vision of heaven, and Christ. … I couldn't take my eyes off Him … I couldn't blink. And the vision of heaven was so wonderful. And the brightest day here is like darkness compared with the light that's there in heaven.[127]

During this vision, Mary's body went stone cold. Because she was in this lifeless condition for so long, and unable to detect a pulse, her sister assumed that she had died. She even looked out a white sheet to place over her body until a coffin arrived. But Mary's mother and her cousin Annie, both aware of Mary's previous visionary experiences when her body appeared as if in a coma, refused to accept that she had passed away. Indeed, after a while, Mary began to feel thin, warm streams coursing through her entire body, and, to the surprise of all present, she spoke faintly, asking to be brought a hot-water bottle. Annie later said it was

---

125. Colin and Mary Peckham, *Sounds From Heaven*, p. 170; Allen, *Catch the Wind*, p. 185. Yet John MacLeod notes, wryly: 'He must have been a very remarkable old man, Barvas Free Church was erected in 1850' (MacLeod, *Banner In The West*, p. 263).

126. CoS minister at the time was Donald John MacDonald, a native of Tarbet, Harris. MacDonald later emigrated to Cape Breton, and, following the death of his wife, remarried and settled down in Northern Ireland.

127. Black, *Clash of Tongues*, pp. 149–50.

the most wonderful thing she ever heard! Her right arm warmed first. 'And when I got as far as putting my arm to my brow it was like putting a hand on a dead body. My head was still cold. But everything else was warm. And I came back to life.'[128]

NESS 1939

WHILE revival was fairly widespread in Barvas, the movement in the large and more northerly parish of Ness was less intense. It seems that there was a general spirit of awakening throughout the parish, with more obvious pockets of revival in one or two areas. Free Presbyterian Church leaders were deeply suspicious of the revival. Therefore, in some districts of Ness where there existed a predominant Free Presbyterian presence, there was a notable absence of spiritual stirring. The Free Church minister of the parish was Alexander MacLeod, a dearly-loved pastor who was fondly remembered for many decades after his departure to Govan in April 1939. An occasion that was often talked about by two elderly folk in the congregation related to a sermon delivered by MacLeod in the Cross Free Church around 1937 or 1938, on the verse: 'Now one greater than Jonah is here' (Matt. 12:41). The church was nearly full, as it regularly was around this time, with many young, as well as older folk present. A considerable number of people were deeply moved that night, and some were reduced to tears, not least one godly elder from the community.

Although there was no widespread revival in Ness at this time, the villages of Swainbost and Europie each experienced a notable shower of divine blessing, ironically around the time of ministerial vacancy in the Free Church, and just before John Morrison was inducted in 1940. A number of people came under deep conviction, and a state of general excitement and expectancy prevailed in the area. So keen were people to grow in faith and to enjoy fellowship together that it was said that no one in the congregation stayed at home if they knew a prayer meeting was being held anywhere in the neighbourhood.[129]

CARLOWAY 1939

UP to this point, and unlike other districts, the movement in Carloway had been largely free of emotional excesses such as prostrations. However, these started to become more apparent in 1939 when companies of believers from the area attended special meetings in places like Crossbost

---

128. Ibid., p. 150. Because of their fascinating content, Mary MacLean's experiences have been related in some detail. It is important to recognise, however, that hers is a rather unique testimony. The majority of believers in Lewis were not affected by bodily weakness or powerful visions, and did not have disagreements with local church leaders.

129. Personal conversation with Norman Smith, elder and church secretary in Ness FC, 20 September 2006.

and Gravir in Lochs, and Barvas, in both of which parishes unusual phenomena were more evident. In April 1939, a party from Carloway visited Shader, Barvas, where, reported Murdo MacAulay, the 'raising of hands and praying aloud, almost shouting, had become the custom'.[130] At the weekly prayer meeting the following evening in Carloway Free Church, several worshippers fell into trances. The next night, a special meeting was held in the building, and again trances were experienced, both by Free Church members and some from the CoS.[131] Mrs Bishop, latterly of Benbecula, recounted one house meeting when a dozen young people – mainly those in their mid-teens who had met together for prayer, worship and Bible reading – all passed out.[132]

Some of the Carloway converts, however, felt as if they were 'being severely rebuked for having come to spy on these prostrations and activities'. Murdo MacAulay believed that the blessing on Carloway stopped at this point. However, it seems that many were still being touched by the Spirit, for it was claimed that on the very week that the Second World War broke out, there were nineteen new professions of faith in Carloway Free Church on the Sabbath day. The people knew the war had begun, and there was a feeling of both solemnity and brokenness before God. People began to pray and tears flowed copiously, to the extent that the cloth on the pews became wet as believers wept over the new converts, and over the uncertain days ahead, knowing their beloved ones were about to set off to war (for more on the connection between the war and the revival see pp. 389–92).

Extent of the Revival

AS we have seen, a number of parishes were deeply touched by the 'Layman's revival'. One newspaper reporter, after travelling seventy miles around Lewis, observed that the 'revival has its centres at four points of a square formed by Crossbost, Garrabost (Point), Barvas and Carloway'.[133] A number of other districts and villages on the island, however, were largely or entirely bypassed by the movement. As already noted, the northern parish of Ness was certainly affected by the 1930s awakening, but apparently not as deeply as other areas referred to. Meanwhile, the populous district of Back is almost completely absent in accounts of the pre-war movement, although even here there were stirrings.[134] The remote south-westerly district of Uig wasn't strongly

---

130. MacAulay, *The Burning Bush*, p. 33.

131. *Stornoway Gazette*, 5 May 1939, p. 3.

132. Sprange, *Kingdom Kids*, p. 288.

133. *Scottish Daily Express*, quoted in Murray, *Diary*, p. 365.

134. 'Religious Revival in Lewis,' in *Stornoway Gazette*, 28 April 1939. There was (and still is) no Church of Scotland in the Back area, and it was said that the FC minister in Back was very suspicious of the phenomena that accompanied the revival elsewhere.

affected either (ironic, perhaps, given its fame in Lewis revival history) and nor was Stornoway (see pp. 348–9), nor, strangely, Shawbost, even though situated midway between Carloway and Barvas, two epicentres of the revival. As for Free Presbyterian congregations throughout the isle, they didn't recognise the movement as being of God, and for its whole duration they remained officially outside it (although some individual members came under its influence by attending some cottage meetings).[135] The revivals in Carloway, Point, Lochs and Barvas continued over a period of months or years, and only began to abate when the war started. Naturally, however, awakening in these districts did not continue in equal intensity during the entire period of 1934 to 1939. Rather, the years 1934 (Carloway), 1936, and 1938–9 were years of most heightened spiritual interest and revival activity.

THE 'PHENOMENA' CONTROVERSY

BY May 1939 the whole island seemed to be talking about the extraordinary events that were taking place in mission halls and at cottage meetings in different parts of Lewis. For, as well as trances and shouting, numerous other bodily manifestations were also in evidence. Some people seemed to have muscular spasms that caused them to jerk forward suddenly, often groaning at the same time. Others stood rigid with arms upraised, sometimes for hours, without apparent fatigue. Some bounced violently up and down in their seats, in a way they would normally be unable to do. Norman MacLeod remembered attending one particular house meeting when, after a time of prayer in which he sensed a certain liberty, he opened his eyes to observe that the couch opposite him, on which a number of young converts had been crammed together, had keeled over onto its back, so that all he could see was eight youthful legs kicking in the air!

The intense emotionalism that accompanied the revival was unusual in an island like Lewis, where people were naturally reserved and undemonstrative. In some districts, elders and others tried to exercise a slight restraint on worshippers who appeared to be getting carried away in their emotions. This attempt was generally resented and criticised by lay worshippers. There were also, of course, as already noted, numerous reports of more spectacular phenomena taking place, particularly in

---

135. For example, two young men from the Free Presbyterian congregation of Breasclete (both later became elders) were known to 'have begun their spiritual pilgrimage' through the influence of the Carloway revival (personal communication with the Rev. D.J. MacDonald, Free Presbyterian minister of Dornoch, 7 February 2008). A native of Callanish, MacDonald stated that fellow villagers thought nothing of cycling seven miles to meetings in Carloway FC during these days of blessing, and a good number from his community were converted. He believed that, partly because the revival wasn't predominantly a 'church thing', people of different denominations, including Free Presbyterians, felt more free than under normal circumstances to fellowship with each other.

connection with the movements in Lochs and Barvas. It was because of events like these that the whole movement later became known as 'the revival of manifestations'.[136]

The large majority of young folk on the island who stood aside from the more unusual goings on poured scorn on those who were drawn into the movement. Some referred to the revival as the *cliobadaich*.[137] It appears to have been from such scoffing sources, and with typical Lewis humour, that a report spread round one district that the spring work in a certain village had come to a halt as the end of the world was expected the following Friday!

Thus it was also that many in Lewis who were not personally involved in the movement became wary of being seen as snoopers on the work. When Scottish novelist Neil Gunn came to Lewis to acquire material for his forthcoming book, *The Silver Darlings*,[138] he showed great interest in the religious enthusiasm extant. His host for one evening, a headmaster from Aird in Point, sought to fully accommodate his distinguished visitor, yet felt awkward about the two of them attending meetings, aware that they were 'outsiders' to the movement, and sensing that their presence might alter the flow of meetings.

In like manner, James Shaw Grant, editor of the local weekly *Stornoway Gazette*, felt it imprudent to attend revival meetings, believing that the presence of a stranger with notebook in hand would put a dampener on proceedings, and restrain the more timid worshipper by the prospect of publicity. He felt it would also 'play to the gallery', enticing the exhibitionists to 'go to town'. Acting on good conscience, Grant kept away from these services but was able to get good information of any newsworthy element from others, including ministers, who were directly involved.[139]

In fact, during the years 1934–8, the *Stornoway Gazette* showed little interest in the awakenings occurring in various places on the island. However, by the end of April 1939, with its spread to Point and Barvas and the increased intensity associated with it, the paper was printing detailed reports on activities.[140] The national Press, too, began showing great interest in the awakening, intrigued by the 'extraordinary mental and bodily excitement' that affected some worshippers. One reporter noted that house meetings were attended by between forty and fifty

136. Colin and Mary Peckham, *Sounds From Heaven*, p. 160.

137. An uncommon term suggesting a tremor or sudden movement, more commonly used in fishing, referring to a fish tugging at the end of a line.

138. This book, regarded by some as one of the finest Scottish novels of the twentieth century, includes a description of an imaginary revival in a Lewis village in the late 1800s.

139. Grant, *The Gaelic Vikings*, pp. 81–2.

140. The first detailed article on the movement was headed 'Religious Revival in Lewis: Services Attended by Unusual Events', in *The Stornoway Gazette*, 28 April 1939.

people, the majority of whom would rise spontaneously and pray. 'Psalms are interrupted,' he wrote. 'As hour succeeds hour the "atmosphere", I am informed, changes. Sometimes a woman will collapse, others will rise simultaneously, weeping, call in Gaelic on their relatives. Some lose all power of their limbs, have to be carried into an adjoining room and laid on a couch until they recover.'[141]

There also came investigative visits from a number of ministers who crossed over from the mainland, each intrigued by what he had heard and intent on discovering the truth behind the stories. Whatever the source of the outside interest, Lewis people remained somewhat wary, and were very reluctant to publicise it, aware that to do so might hamper God's good work. In any case, the experiences of many were deeply personal and seen as too 'holy' to be spread abroad.

Aware that events were following a course quite different to previous revivals in Lewis, many older Christians expressed apprehension at the shape the movement was taking, disapproving in particular of the physical manifestations and the shouting. While a few ministers may have viewed *all* the phenomena as a revelation of the same divine power that had brought the revival into existence in the first place, most church leaders, of both denominations, while recognising that a genuine work of grace was most evidently in progress, expressed concern over certain elements of the movement. It was generally accepted that those first affected were carried away by genuine religious enthusiasm, while many who subsequently joined in the demonstrations could have controlled themselves had they tried. Only once during a service did John MacIver of Carloway discern an instance of over-emotionalism. He at once spoke firmly against it and it stopped immediately. The blessing of God continued through the service. On seeing strong emotions in other districts, however, MacIver did not feel led to interfere.

Norman MacLeod, a convert of the Carloway revival, neither approved nor disapproved of physical manifestations per se. In later years he compared the phenomena that took place in Lochs and other places to 'similar symptoms (which) have accompanied revivals down through the ages'.[142] He emphasised that in the Lewis practice, as exercised by Kenneth MacRae, 'those who were affected by these agitations, and who

---

141. *The Scottish Daily Express*, quoted in Murray, *Diary*, p. 365.

142. He mentions like phenomena occurring under the ministry of Edward Bryce in Bread Island, Virginia in 1671, as recorded in the memoirs of John Livingston (of Kirk o' Shotts fame). 'Some people ... used in the time of sermon to fall upon high breathing as of those who have run long. But most ministers discountenanced these practices and suspected them not to proceed from the work of the Holy Spirit ... and accordingly few of these people came forward to any solid exercise of Christianity.' He goes on: 'John Wesley looked upon these physical agitations as proofs of the divine presence. Charles Wesley suspected and discouraged them. Whitefield was incredulous, while Jonathan Edwards puts in an apology for them' (MacLeod, *Lewis Revivals*, pp. 14–15).

later came before the Session for Communion, were carefully examined regarding their knowledge and if they satisfied the Session in that respect they were accepted without any note being taken of the phenomena which accompanied with conversion.'[143]

By far the most outspoken critic of emotionalism and physical manifestations was the afore-mentioned MacRae. Indeed the Stornoway minister expressed caution not only over the more extraordinary developments of 1938 and 1939, but also over aspects of earlier movements, such as that in Point (1936) and elsewhere.[144] He gave an address to his home Free Church entitled 'Unusual Features of the Present Religious Movement in Lewis,' which was printed in the *Stornoway Gazette*. After affirming his opinion that 'a really sound religious movement had taken place in Lewis and was testified by its fruits', MacRae noted that the physical manifestations 'affected both believers and non-believers; that they were not saving in their nature, that they were not accompanied by any sense of sin, that those affected could give no adequate explanation of their experience, and that they bore no relation to the preaching of the Word'. In addition, he suggested that manifestations distracted people from the much more important issue of new birth; that they may even be seen as a substitute for the 'one thing needful'. Also, they tended to lead to spiritual pride, causing those affected to think they belonged to a superior order of Christians. In considering the teaching of church leaders on manifestations during past revivals, MacRae said that none regarded these things as being of the Spirit.[145]

However, rather than seeing them as being demonic (although he believed they could be exploited by Satan to advance the interests of his own kingdom), MacRae saw such outward expressions largely as mass hysteria, a view that was supported by a medical textbook from which he quoted numerous symptoms of hysterial disorder:

(1) It is more prevalent in highly-strung people, especially young women.

(2) It is infectious.

(3) It is frequently associated with convulsions, tremors and trances.

(4) Attacks always come on in an audience, never alone.

143. Ibid.

144. It would have been most interesting to have known more about MacRae's thoughts on the progress of the movement in 1939, but unfortunately, his diary for this crucial year has been lost.

145. For example, Asahel Nettleton – whose experiences of remarkable revival in America in the early 1800s MacRae had carefully studied – discovered that when he tried to extinguish excesses during one revival in New England, he was criticised for having 'put a stop to it. They seemed very much grieved at my conduct,' he had lamented (Bennet Tyler and Andrew Bonar, *Nettleton and His Labours*, quoted in Murray, *Diary*, p. 370).

(5) Those affected can control themselves in spite of declarations that they cannot.

(6) Those affected are subject to delusions and hallucinations.

(7) Consciousness is not entirely lost.[146]

MacRae pointed out that every one of these criteria fitted the revival phenomena in Lewis precisely. In addition, he felt that late prayer meetings, protracted into the early hours of the morning, and repeated night after night, definitely did induce hysteria. These extravagances were likely to grieve the Holy Spirit and end the revival altogether. What was needed, he said, was a 'really solid work of the Holy Spirit, which would convince of sin, reveal the majesty and holiness of God and send sinners in secret to a Throne of Grace for mercy'.[147]

While some applauded MacRae's strong and considered stance on this subject, many others within the Free Church, and even – though more discretely – some from within his own congregation, criticised him for quoting from a medical textbook on a religious matter. They saw this, not only as heresy, but almost as blasphemy. Certain doctors on the island, however, without making public pronouncement on the issue, agreed with the minister. One stated: 'If a man had appendicitis they call a doctor, but when a man is tortured in his mind, they throw a party, call it a service, and all the neighbours come to gloat!'[148] Medical practitioners were concerned, too, that the intense and continued emotion under which many of the worshippers laboured was having an effect on those who were not physically robust. Indeed, there were cases where a breakdown in health did occur.

In a letter to the *Stornoway Gazette*, however, Highland-born Duncan M. MacRae, then a doctor living in Rhodesia, expressed much more optimism regarding some of the more unusual hallmarks of the Lewis revival. 'To the stress of religious emotion,' he wrote, 'different temperaments react differently, and who shall say which is the wheat and which is the chaff? Time alone can tell. The wind bloweth where it listeth, and it is not for us to dogmatise as to the ultimate meaning of such manifestations. The parable of the sower is the best commentary on the subject. "God moves in a mysterious way His wonders to

146. *Stornoway Gazette*, 12 May 1939.

147. Ibid. MacRae was, of course, not against revivals per se. He had already aided in the progress of two such movements (Arran 1916 and Skye 1923). James Shaw Grant acknowledged that 'there was nothing [MacRae] wanted more than to see a great religious revival in Lewis. But he wanted a revival of substance, in his terms, not froth.' Iain H. Murray, editor of MacRae's diary, also noted MacRae's belief that 'such were the prevailing conditions in the nation that only the unusual and widespread activity of the Spirit, witnessed in revival periods, would bring a turning of the tide' (Murray, *Diary*, p. 363).

148. *Stornoway Gazette*, 4 August 1939, p. 6.

perform," and surely the first word of adverse criticism should not come from a Scottish pulpit!' [149]

Close of the Revival

WHEN revival began in Lewis, there was no word of the war (although months before its outbreak there were striking premonitions of armed conflict breaking out – see next page). But the parishes in Lewis that had been so singularly blessed were soon to be plunged into anxiety and sorrow on seeing their young men being called into National Service, especially the Navy.[150] The date in late August 1939 when these men were to depart was one observed in Stornoway as a Fast Day in advance of the local Communion season, held traditionally on the last Sunday in August. The services of the day were solemn beyond description. 'The day was devoted to the worship of God and hearts were too sad and too full for mere words.' [151] After the services had ended, nearly 1,000 young men, mainly naval reservists, gathered onto the pier in Stornoway to board the *Lochness*, which was waiting to transport them to the mainland. *The Stornoway Gazette* movingly describes the scenes of that memorable evening.

> The crowd on the pier that night was probably the largest which has ever been gathered there in the history of Stornoway, and it was a strangely silent company. There was not even a hum of conversation. ... There was a steady stream of reservists through the crowd and up the gangway, but their leave-taking with friends was also silent. A quiet handshake, at most a simple word of farewell, then up with the kit bag and away. It was eerie to see the deck of the ship filling up until there was scarcely standing room, and not a whisper rising from the crowd.

---

149. MacRae continued, 'In all my experiences of life, I have looked back with a loved regret which I would not willingly resign, to my association with the loveable personalities who were the products of a previous religious revival in my beloved native island. Narrow and illiberal their attitude may have seemed to mere worldlings, but I at least still believe in them, and will always welcome any movement which tends to maintain amongst them the religious traditions of my early years. In a distracted world the truth of a thing, if old, may seem to be against it, but that is no proof that it is wrong. Gainsay it who will. Scotland's religion has made her great. Let it flourish!' (ibid.) Another correspondent, D.M. Lamont from Dervaig, Mull, claimed to have been 'from my youth, an eyewitness of revivals, both in Scotland and in America, of the same type as the present Lewis awakening'. He compared the Lewis movement to one that began under the ministry of Donald MacDonald of Perthshire among exiled Highlanders in Prince Edward Island in 1828. Owing to its 'hysterical' aspects, the Canadian movement was scoffed at by many believers, who termed it 'a passing phase' marked by 'fits of religious mania'. Yet, he claimed, the revival continued for 'more than 100 years'! The ruling principle in both the Prince Edward Island and Lewis revivals, Lamont noted, was not the sensational, but rightly 'eternal salvation through Jesus Christ' (ibid.).

150. A large proportion of Lewis recruits joined the Navy. It has been said that per head of population, more young sailors from Lewis lost their lives in the Second World War than from anywhere else in the U.K. During the early years of the war, the navy ship *Dunnotter Castle* was crewed almost entirely by young men from the Highlands and Islands, especially Lewis. The captain of the ship, himself spiritually minded, ensured that a certain compartment of the boat was set aside specifically for Gaelic prayer meetings. Prayer meetings in Gaelic were also held at this time in some other of Britain's main ports, such as Southampton.

151. Campbell, *Memories*, p. 9.

> Then suddenly the silence was broken. At first a single voice rising tremulously in the air of a Gaelic psalm – a precentor giving out the line. Some of the crowd round about the Fish Mart door took up the verse and the solemn words of the 46th Psalm swelled out to the tune Stroudwater:[152]
>
> *God is our refuge and our strength;*
> *In straits a present aid;*
> *Therefore, although the earth remove*
> *We will not be afraid.*
>
> The huge crowd took up the words till the sacred song gathered volume and wafted over the harbour and over the deserted streets of the town. This was not a mere display of feeling but an expression of that trust in God which dwelt in many hearts. The vessel then left the shore and passed out of view, while the crowd, in silent little groups, moved away to their homes.[153]

By the start of 1940 nearly 2,000 men, equivalent to between 8 and 10 percent of Lewis's population, was estimated to have been on active service or under training (a considerable percentage, yet lower than in the First World War, because by the late 1930s there existed a greater proportion of those whose active years were passed).

On the night of 12 March 1939, nearly half a year prior to the outbreak of the war, Mary MacLean received a terrifying vision, which made her literally tremble. She saw some ships lying at the bottom of the sea and bodies of men lying on them. On another occasion she 'saw' that her mother was going to be left alone in the house. When war broke out that autumn she knew at once that her vision related to events that were soon to occur.[154] Her husband and her three brothers were called up to serve in the Forces. One evening on her knees in prayer Mary 'saw' a ship, split in half, and her youngest brother lying lifeless. She tried to tell herself it was just her imagination. Soon, however, word came that her younger brother was missing, so Mary reluctantly told her family of the vision she had seen a fortnight previously.[155]

Just a month later, another brother was killed aboard his ship and he, too, was buried at sea. However, there was much consolation in this case, for it later transpired that he had conversed with another Lewis man on the ship – a young believer from Carloway. He had asked him if, when the war was over, he would accompany him to the weekly prayer meeting in church (a clear sign that he had been converted).[156]

---

152. *Stornoway Gazette*, quoted in Murray, *Diary*, p. 324.
153. Campbell, *Memories*, pp. 9–10.
154. Black, *Clash of Tongues*, pp. 144–5.
155. Ibid., pp. 150–1.
156. Ibid., p. 151.

The revival pretty much drew to a close with the outbreak of the war. Remarkably, however, cottage prayer meetings continued in many areas, albeit with a more subdued expression, until about the end of the war. The worshippers rejoiced whenever converts and older Christians came home on leave and joined them. There were a goodly number of additions to church membership in the early years of the war, but most of these pertained to people converted during the pre-war revival. Murdo MacAulay wrote regarding Carloway that 'by 1940–41 the movement had abated. … Although there were driblets in the following years as in the years prior to 1934, it is clear that the congregation had gone back to its status quo by 1940.'[157] MacAulay immediately observed on his return from the war in 1945 that the revival had run out of steam. In evidence of this, where previously on coming out from a church service people would linger in groups to discuss the sermon or where they would gather for fellowship that evening, now they walked straight home, and cottage meetings were few and far between.[158]

Outbursts of emotion were also decreasingly observable after the outbreak of war, although they still persisted to some degree. Even at a service in Stornoway Free Church in May 1940, the Rev. MacRae became conscious of 'the peculiar gasping sound characteristic of the religious movement in Lewis', so that all liberty forsook him, and he felt that he could not pray. Such emotionalism, he believed, had caused 'so much controversy and division throughout our congregations'. On mentioning his displeasure at such phenomena towards the close of the service, there ensued a chaotic scene.[159] In conclusion, MacRae stated: 'If any think that this is the evidence of a revival among us, then all the other, ordinary evidences are absent. It troubles me very much, but I shall give the "swooners" no latitude.'[160] After a time, such outward expressions of emotion died out altogether, only to rise again in some areas (though to a lesser degree) during the next major revival to come to Lewis, towards the close of 1949.

In fact many people in Lewis believe that the 1949–53 awakening, the most famous of all Lewis revivals, was in effect a continuation of the Thirties movement. Donald John Smith of Upper Shader is strongly of

---

157. MacAulay, *The Burning Bush*, p. 33. There were no admissions to the Lord's Table in 1940, two in March 1941, two in September 1941, none in March 1942 but five in September of that year. In 1943 there were no admissions, and in 1944 there were two, both in September.

158. Ibid.

159. MacRae noted that, 'the disturber … completely abandoned herself to this strange influence, until at last she was bawling in such a stentorian voice that I had forthwith to pronounce the Benediction. There was almost a panic in the crowded hall and at least two other females subject to these attacks became similarly affected. One old woman, in her efforts to escape from the Hall, climbed over the back of her seat. Eventually the young woman was carried out and placed in a country bus which happened to be at the door' (Murray, *Diary*, pp. 370–1).

160. Ibid.

this opinion,[161] while Catherine Campbell makes similar suggestion in stating that the spirit of prayer in which the 1930s revival was birthed continued during the war years and afterwards, 'eventually increasing until the 1949 revival broke out'.[162] The earlier revival, they claim, was somewhat rudely interrupted by the outbreak of war, but its embers were never quite extinguished, but rather remained as a quiet glow throughout the 1940s, before fanning into flame again in a sweeping blaze of revival fire towards the close of the decade.

CONCLUSION

IT is important to note that physical manifestations by no means accompanied all revival meetings in Lewis in 1938 and 1939. Indeed, even at the height of the movement, the numbers affected were comparatively small. MacKinnon of Garrabost estimated that only twenty or thirty in his own CoS congregation in Point were prone to manifestations, with a similar percentage in the larger neighbouring Free Church congregation. It was chiefly the striking nature and self-promotion of the phenomena along with media fascination that gave them undue prominence. What was often less emphasised was the change for good that resulted in converts' lives and the positive effect on the community at large. In Carloway, the effect on the life and conversation of the young converts was said to have been remarkable – 'a hatred of sin, an abandonment of their former life-style, a longing for holiness, with a dread of bringing any blemish of the cause of Christ'.[163]

The Lewis Presbytery of the Church of Scotland gave its official reaction to the revival in a statement released in June 1939 in which it 'unanimously resolved as a court of the church to place on record their sincere gratitude to Almighty God that ... He had visited the people of this island with such unmistakable signs of His saving power. ...'[164]

The Free Church gave a more mixed response to the revival. We have already noted the concerns of Kenneth MacRae. Several other Free Church ministers shared their views at the General Assembly in the spring of 1939. P.M. Chisholm of Lochalsh reported that, on visiting the island just a week or two earlier, he attended several services and was led to regard the whole movement as a singular marvellous outpouring of the Holy Spirit. 'I could observe nothing visionary or enthusiastic about it. I could observe without any difficulty a solemnity and reverence, with grave deportment and close attention resting upon the vast assembly such

161. Personal communication with Donald John Smith, 22 September 2006.

162. Colin and Mary Peckham, *Sounds From Heaven*, p. 223.

163. MacAulay, *The Burning Bush*, p. 34.

164. *Stornoway Gazette*, 23 June 1939.

as I have never before witnessed.'[165] Another visitor noted 'a sense of the presence of Christ everywhere ... life-long prejudices and ecclesiastical barriers have been broken down, and people are realising the deeper unity of the Spirit. ... Everyone is of the same mind, with a desire to speak about the things of Christ. It came not by preaching, but by prayer.'[166]

Murdo MacRae of Kinloch, like numerous other Lewis ministers, was reluctant to talk publicly about the subject at all, taking the view that a revival of religion was something not to be broadcast abroad indiscriminately. Like many in Lewis he was appalled at the Press for blazing accounts of the work around the country. He did go on to state, however, that there was unanimity among Free Church ministers in Lewis 'with regard to this fundamental fact – that there is a deep and profound spiritual movement in the island which has been going on for a period of four or five years. That that movement is there no one can doubt, and until recently it was a quiet and, I believe, a profoundly spiritual movement, revealing those tokens and evidence which one always expects to find when the Lord is effectively working in the hearts of men.' With regard to 'unusual occurrences', MacRae advised: 'the wise thing is to leave these matters to the test of time. The fruits of this revival will speak for themselves.'[167]

M.M. MacSween, CoS minister of Kinloch, summarised his thoughts on the awakening:

> The movement had many pleasing features. All sectarian barriers were lost sight of, and those who endeavoured to introduce or perpetuate such differences were avoided instinctively. It is a clear case of putting 'first things first'. Where unity prevailed the good work went on most effectively. Another pleasing feature was the freedom with which people generally talk about spiritual matters and the way every believer is encouraged to bring to the notice of the non-believer the truth of eternal realities. Many who were indifferent to organised religion, and men who, through having spent years abroad, had come to look upon church services as prosaic or even stupid, had come under the influence, and were among the most enthusiastic in their support of the things which they once condemned. Those influenced were ready to join the Church as members, and take an active part in witness and prayer.[168]

---

165. Ibid., 2 June 1939, p. 8.

166. *The Lewis Revival*, in *BW*, 1939, p. 156.

167. *Stornoway Gazette*, 2 June 1939, p. 8.

168. Ibid. Others tried to explain the revival in more naturalistic terms. Arthur Geddes wrote that 'some thoughtful men and women feel that the "revival" which swept their island (with the rest of the Presbyterian Hebrides) before 1939 and during the war was partly due to the excessive influence of spinsters, to whom the strict Presbyterianism offered little outlet for motherly emotion or sisterly service' (Arthur Geddes, *The Isle of Lewis & Harris: A Study in British Community*, Edinburgh 1955, p. 216).

Effects of the revival were soon to be felt on the Scottish mainland, when a number of converts went to study for the ministry in Glasgow or Edinburgh, or when they left to find work in these cities. In Glasgow, many attended services in the Partick Highland Free Church under the much respected ministry of Peter Chisholm, or in the Gardner Street CoS. When these young Lewis exiles gathered together for fellowship, they felt it was 'just like being at home', such was the unbridled enthusiasm for prayer and worship and the longing to study the Word of God. There were even some instances of manifestations occurring when these believers met together. Norman MacLeod recalled a meeting in Edinburgh while he was a student there shortly after the revival in Lewis, where certain manifestations were on display, such as one young woman raising her arms above her head, remaining in that position for an unnatural length of time.[169]

A good number of these converts went on to become valued ministers in both the Free Church and the CoS. Among them were Murdo Martin (senior minister of Paisley Free Church), Norman MacLeod (Callanish Free Church, Lewis), Murdo MacAulay (Back Free Church, Lewis), Kenneth MacKay (Bracadale Free Church, Skye), Donald Nicolson (Glendale Free Church, Skye), and Alexander MacFarlane (Shawbost Free Church, Lewis).[170]

169. Personal conversation with Mary MacRae, 20 September 2002.

170. For more information on the movements in Carloway 1934–8, Lochs 1938–9 and Barvas 1939, see www.scottishrevivals.co.uk.

CARLOWAY

John MacIver – p.325

Malcolm MacIver – p.325

Carloway Free Church – p.328

Doune, Carloway – p.328

CARLOWAY

John MacLeod ('An Cor') – p.330

Duncan John MacLeod – p.338

Murdo MacAulay – p.338 and Norman MacLeod

Donald MacIver – p.327 and Duncan John MacLeod, 2003

Norman MacLeod (right) – p.345

Loch Roag, Lewis – p.341

CARLOWAY

Roderick MacKay – p.341

Norman MacLeod and Murdo MacAulay, c1990

BERNERA

John Morrison, Bernera – p.349

LOCHS

Murdo McKinnon – p.352

House where revival began – p.353

Murdo MacRae – p.352

Donald MacLeod – p.353

Kenneth Nicolson – p.355

Gravir – p.359

POINT

Alexander MacLeod (Sandy Mor) – p.365

William Campbell – pp.346, 363

Lower Bayble, Point – p.366

BARVAS

Barvas parish – p.369

John Smith ('Gobha') – p.369

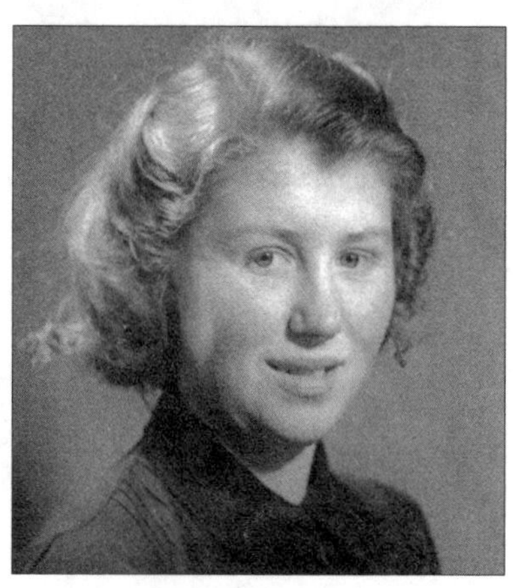

Mary MacDonald – p.377

Part Four

BAIRNS, SCHOLARS AND HOLY ROLLERS[1]

Once more, Lord, once more, Lord;
As in the days of yore;
On this dear land, Thy Spirit pour;
Set Scotland now on fire.[2]

1. Though formerly used pejoratively, this slang term for Pentecostals is in no way here intended to have any depreciative connotation.

2. A popular chorus sung by fervent crowds at meetings led by Pentecostalist George Jeffreys during his Scottish campaigns (Donald Gee, *Wind and Flame*, Croydon 1967, p. 140).

12
Work Among Children and Students

Children

THE history of evangelical revivals is replete with stories of the conversion of children.[3] A great number of remarkable cases have been documented for Scotland alone.[4] During the latter half of the nineteenth century considerable effort was placed on reaching children with the gospel. The Glasgow Foundry Boys Religious Society, formed in 1865, increased rapidly in membership, reaching a peak of 16,000 in 1886, with nearly 2,000 leaders. In 1868 Josiah Spiers left his business and, as leader of the Children's Special Services Mission (later to become the Scripture Union), began traversing the length of Britain conducting children's missions, in summer on the beaches, and at inland towns and villages for the rest of the year. His Edinburgh mission in the New Assembly Hall in January 1878 drew over 2,000 children night after night.[5] Then there was the Boys' Brigade, begun in the North Woodside Mission Hall in the West End of Glasgow in 1883 by William Smith. Influenced by Moody's 1874 campaign and the evangelical zeal of the College Church, of which he was a member, Smith adopted as the Brigade's motto 'Sure and Steadfast,' based on Hebrews 6:19.[6] Smith may also have been

3. Some of the more notable seasons of spiritual outpouring among children across the world include: no fewer than five periods of revival in the children's school in Persia where American missionary Fidelia Fiske worked in the 1840s (D.T. Fiske, *Faith Working by Love: As Exemplified in the Life of Fidelia Fiske*, Boston 1868); a most unusual move of the Spirit at an orphanage in the Yunan Province of China in the early twentieth century (H.A. Baker, *Visions Beyond the Veil*, Tonbridge 2000); a powerful outpouring upon Tamil children of Dohnavur in southern India in 1906 (Frank Houghton, *Amy Carmichael of Dohnavur*, London 1953); a remarkable awakening within both a kindergarten and a primary school at Wamba mission station during the Congo revival of 1953 (Mathew Backholer, *150 Years of Revival*, Liskeard 2007, pp. 59–60); a mighty movement at the various Sudan United Mission schools at Gindiri, Northern Nigeria in early 1972 (David and Bridget Williams, *The Wind Blowing*, Sidcup 1973, pp. 7–49); and 'days of heaven on earth' following early hostility and scepticism among pupils of a large secondary school in south-east Rhodesia in the 1980s (Michael Howard, *Recklessly Abandoned*, Kansas City 1996, pp. 99–101). For a short study of accounts of children's conversions in the ministry of John Wesley, see David Walters, *Children Aflame*, Macon, Georgia, 1996). We await a fuller study of the involvement of children in world-wide revivals.

4. For example, E.P. Hammond provides a number of examples from his own Scottish ministry in *The Conversion of Children*, Chicago, 1901.

5. John Pollock, *The Story of the Children's Special Service Mission and The Scripture Union*, London 1959, p. 24.

6. F.P. Gibbon, *William A. Smith of the Boys' Brigade*, London 1934; John Springhall, *Sure & Steadfast: A History of the Boys' Brigade, 1883–1983*, London 1983. Although Smith had devoted his life 'to the service of his Saviour', he had a life-long distaste of immediate 'decisions for Christ', believing that such a life-changing issue needed serious contemplation and a deliberate choice.

influenced by one or more of a recent 'succession of awakenings and revivals' (perhaps themselves influenced by Moody's Glasgow visit). These resulted when special efforts were made by dedicated young members of College Church to reach the inhabitants of North Woodside, during the ministry in this Glasgow church of Dr George Reith. During these periods of spiritual awakening, 'not only the young and unstained, but many who were as careless in their life as they were godless in their spirit, were born again.' [7]

Sunday schools remained the most effective form of children's outreach, however. First established in the sixteenth century by John Knox,[8] their popularity increased only in the late eighteenth century. During the following 100 years they blossomed spectacularly, reaching a high point during the twenty years between 1870 and 1890. At this latter date the Sunday school attendance of Scotland's four main Presbyterian denominations totalled at over 487,000.[9] In Glasgow they enjoyed an astonishing degree of success. At about their peak in 1891, 60 percent of children aged from 5 to 15 were enrolled in a Sunday school, and of this number as many as 75 percent attended on any given day. Thus nearly half of Glasgow's children were in attendance each Sunday. [10]

More specifically, there have occurred numerous instances of spiritual awakening among groups of children at various times in Scotland, either independent of, or simultaneous with, revival in the community at large. During the revivals in Cambuslang, Kilsyth, Baldernock and various other locations, mainly in central Scotland, in the eighteenth century, prayer meetings soon sprang up among children, and numerous conversions among peers were recorded. At a Methodist Sunday school in Kilsyth in February 1835 began a revival among the young ones, which quickly spread to the adult community. This seems to have been the precursor of the much more famous revival which overtook the town a few short years later (Kilsyth's widespread pre-Disruption revival of 1839–42), when scores more children were converted. Of the 39 prayer groups that sprang up in connection with the revival at St Peter's Church, Dundee, five were conducted by children for children. It is only in recent years that special consideration has been given to the place of children in revival. In his formative study *'Children in the Revival: 300 Years of God's Work in Scotland'*, Harry Sprange records many striking instances

---

7. W.M. Clow, *Dr George Reith: A Scottish Ministry*, London 1928.

8. Sabbath evening schools were also established in Edinburgh and crowds attended them (Rev. R.S. Duncan, *History of Sunday Schools*, Memphis 1876, pp. 80–5).

9. Callum G. Brown, *The Sunday-School Movement in Scotland 1780–1914*, in *SCHSR*, Vol. 21 (1981), pp. 17–19.

10. David Searle (Ed.), *Death or Glory: The Church's Mission in Scotland's Changing Society: Studies in Honour of Dr Geoffrey Grogan*, Fearn 2001, pp. 40–1. The role of Sunday schools in Scottish revival movements still awaits serious study.

of children's conversions and young people's prayer meetings, especially during the nationwide revival of 1859–61.[11]

Tragically, the Church has often had extremely low expectations of those of tender years. Revivals in the Western Isles rarely included instances of child-conversions. Traditionally, children in the isles did not attend church. This perhaps has a connection with the past when families were often too poor to afford 'Sunday clothes' for their kids – rather than face the embarrassment of taking them to church poorly dressed, they were kept at home. Some questioned theologically if children could understand the basic doctrines necessary for them to make genuine commitments of faith. Hence there were few conversions of children under the age of twelve.

The following narratives are restricted to instances in Scotland where spiritual blessing has appeared among children and students independent of, or prior to, any work of awakening among adults in the community (in distinction to the more numerous instances of revival in a community in which children were simultaneously or subsequently affected).

FERRYDEN 1884

THE east coast fishing village of Ferryden had a rare and fascinating spiritual history throughout the latter part of the nineteenth century. In a parish of around 2,500 people, around 1,600 had connections with the Free Church (though actual membership was around 320).[12] Dr Hugh Mitchell was licensed to preach in 1845 and was called to Ferryden Free Church three years later, in succession to Dr Brewster. At this time there were thirteen pubs in the community. Remarkably, when Mitchell retired in 1893 – two years before his death and after a prolonged period of ministry in the parish – there was only one pub in the entire locality. Playing a significant part in the moral transformation of the village was unquestionably the innumerable marked seasons of spiritual blessing that graced the congregation at various times, such as few churches have ever witnessed. It was said that additions to membership came mainly through these periodic times of awakening, when the whole place was 'shaken from end to end'.[13] The most famed of these was in 1860, but

11. Indeed more than half of the book is devoted to the work of the Spirit among the young during these exciting years, although it is to be regretted that little analysis of, or few conclusions from, his research is presented. Dramatic revival among children also marked the 1859 awakening in Ulster, as in Coleraine's Hon. Irish Society School (John T. Carson, *God's River in Spate: The Story of the Religious Awakeniong of Ulster in 1859*, Belfast 1959, pp. 55–6), and perhaps to a lesser extent, parts of Wales (Eifion Evans, *When He is Come: An Account of the 1858–60 Revival in Wales*, Denbigh 1959, pp. 67–8). The Ulster revival in fact began in connection with a Sabbath School prayer meeting in the neighbourhood of Kells, Country Antrim (Rev. Henry Montgomery, *The Children in '59*, Kilkeel 1936, p. 6).

12. 607 in 1900 (*RC-FCS-SR&M*, 1900, p. 12).

13. ARC-FCS-SR&M, 1889, p. 34.

other notable revivals occurred in 1846, 1867, 1874–5, 1893 (see pp. 206–7) and 1913 (see page 155), making Ferryden one of the most favoured locations in the history of Scottish evangelical awakenings.

In 1884 arose yet another movement, the beginning of which was both simple and touching. Mitchell told a story of a little child's death to the children in his Sabbath School, among whom it produced a profound impression, awakening in them a sense of earnestness and inquiry. From these tender ones the movement spread upward and outward, and nightly meetings were held for six weeks. More than four score young communicants were received into church fellowship at one time, the occasion being described as 'an ever memorable and impressive sight'.[14] It was truly the case that a little child did lead them (Isaiah 11:6). Further north around the same time, a marked interest was noted among Sunday school pupils at Elgin's Free Church. The minister held a list of some 56 young ones who had come to him in recent weeks in a state of anxiety.[15]

Central Scotland 1880–1904

HENRY Drummond, lecturer of natural science at the Free Church College, felt impressed to begin boys' meetings during the 1880s. He said that his work among young lads in Edinburgh, 'which was meant only to last a Sunday or two, has grown into an institution, and WILL not stop. Last Sunday, after the hour's meeting, I sent all the small boys home, and kept two or three hundred of the big ones for a private talk about decision. We did not think it wise to cross-examine them individually, or put any undue pressure upon them, but I am sure many of them are thinking most seriously.'[16] One objective of Drummond's was to encourage the boys to be religious as boys, and that they 'need not be as "pious" as their maiden aunts'.[17] His concern was based on a school football match played against a team from another public school outside Edinburgh. During the game, the strangers used some bad language. At half-time, the Edinburgh boys got together and informed the other side that such language must stop, otherwise they would never play a match with them again. 'It came on the strangers like a thunderbolt, but they gave in at once!'[18]

Drummond's experience was just one evidence of the popularity and effectiveness of children's evangelism during the 1880s. Alexander MacKeith, a Glasgow businessman described as 'probably the most significant figure in children's evangelism in Scotland at the end of the

14. Ibid. See also *RC-FCS-SR&M*, 1883, p. 47 and *The Monthly Record*, June 1895, p. 143.

15. *RC-FCS-SR&M*, 1885, p. 32.

16. George Adam Smith, *The Life of Henry Drummond*, London 1899, p. 319.

17. Ibid.

18. Ibid., pp. 319–20.

nineteenth century',[19] saw up to 1,700 boys and girls attend nightly meetings throughout Glasgow and Strathclyde in the early 1880s. A significant number of these waited to be spoken to about a personal faith, many already having sound Scriptural knowledge and being members of Sabbath Schools in their local churches. In 1882 MacKeith claimed: 'I have been in such work since 1858 and I never remember seeing such a stir in spiritual matters among the children as there is in the present day.'[20]

A couple of years later, American evangelist E.P. Hammond, who had come to enjoy a special ministry among children, paid a return visit to Scotland. He conducted a ten-week campaign in Glasgow before moving on to the Vale of Leven in Dumbartonshire. Thousands of youngsters flocked to hear him and it was claimed that the average ingathering of 'lambs' each week was over 500. Special efforts were used to verify these results; each case dealt with was probingly investigated and followed up wherever possible. According to the Rev. A.C. Fullerton, 'Many young persons who had previously been more or less awakened to concern about salvation came to Mr Hammond's meetings, and found a blessed wave of spiritual power that floated them into the harbour of assured safety.'[21] However, some questioned the restriction of meetings to just one week's duration, claiming that the work at times seemed to be unwarrantably stopped just at the moment of fullest and deepest blessing. Despite this, *The Christian* could claim that 'in all our experience we have never seen such a deep work among the young people in Glasgow'.[22]

By the 1890s children's evangelists seemed to reach a zenith, both in the numbers attending children's meetings and of those making professions of faith. During just one day of a six-week mission run by Kilsyth Methodists in the autumn of 1894, the entire Sunday school, consisting of over 300 children, rose to 'decide for Christ' following an appeal by evangelist Thomas Daniels.[23] Although many of the professions made were no doubt genuine, it seems highly probable, as Dr Bebbington has suggested, that many were playing at 'follow my leader'.[24] For little more is heard of this incredible mass turning to Christ when one would expect to hear so much. It seems that counting 'decisions' made by children was the order of the day near the turn of the twentieth century. During just one month towards the close of 1899, the newly instituted *Campaign Weekly* reported over 100 children's professions following meetings in both Trinity Free Church and

19. Sprange, *Kingdom Kids*, p. 263.

20. *The Christian*, 24 August 1882, quoted in Sprange, p. 263.

21. Ibid., 4 June 1885, quoted in Sprange, p. 266.

22. Ibid., 19 March 1885, quoted in Sprange, p. 266.

23. James Hutchison, *Weavers, Miners and the Open Book: A History of Kilsyth*, self-published 1986, p. 118.

24. Searle, *Death or Glory*, p. 44.

in Finnieston, while at a meeting for those who had accepted Christ as saviour during a week-long campaign in Parkhead, over 400 attended, most being between twelve and fourteen years of age. The same paper records that in the first fortnight of 1900 Alexander MacKeith 'dealt with 2,178 children … that made 10,765 from the start'.[25]

While there does appear to have been an overemphasis on receiving 'decisions', and little attempt in some cases to follow these up to test their genuineness and lasting effect, this period nonetheless appears to have constituted a truly fruitful season in children's evangelism. Writing in 1900, James Paterson of Glasgow's White Memorial Free Church was one who rejoiced that

> God is turning to our little ones … when all the churches are taken into account, it is found that there are some 9,000–10,000 at the meetings night after night. And the attendance is not the only hopeful element. There is found among the children a very deep conviction of sin. It is not too much to say they are weeping their way by hundreds to the foot of the cross. As an example of what is going on in this way, reference may be made to the meeting in the Kent Road UPC on the evening of Monday last. It was a wonderful meeting. Though it was the first of the mission, between 200–300 stayed behind to be spoken to about salvation. Those dealt with were under the deepest convictions. A very large number were anxiously seeking the Saviour. … Grace is sweeping in great mighty waves through the crowds of Glasgow's young people. It is a time for which Christian parents with trembling gratefulness should pour out their thanks to God.[26]

Children's meetings were also a feature of Torrey and Alexander's mission to Scotland in 1903. On the afternoon of 26 February, Edinburgh's Central Hall at Tollcross was 'packed from floor to ceiling with young people from all ages and classes'. Controversially, direct appeal for conversion was made to the audience, although precaution was taken to prevent boys and girls from simply following one another impulsively. In all, around 300 professed to accept Christ as Lord and Saviour.[27]

Alyth, Angus 1889

THE ancient market town of Alyth in Angus, situated a few miles east of Blairgowrie, is nestled at the lower end of the foothills which run from the Grampians to the plain of Strathmore. Rev. Ferguson,[28] Free Church

---

25. *Campaign Weekly*, 4 November 1899, quoted in Sprange, p. 274.

26. *Campaign Weekly*, 2 September 1900, quoted in Sprange, pp. 275–6.

27. Balfour, p. 97.

28. Rev. Ferguson is mentioned in the diary of Jessie Thain, as being a contemporary of Robert Murray McCheyne, Andrew Bonar, et al. back in the 1840s – Murdoch Campbell (Ed.), *Diary of Jessie Thain (The Friend of Robert Murray McCheyne)*, Resolis, 1955.

minister of Alyth parish, reported an interesting awakening among the young in his district in 1889, though it was not confined to his own denomination. The wife of one of his elders had long conducted in her home a prayer meeting and Bible study for young girls. By and by a number of them, including some from a non-religious background, became deeply awakened and, on professing conversion, were at once earnest about the salvation of others, especially their relatives. Soon boys were being drawn to the meetings too, and a number of them also evidenced deep change. Parents were amazed at the transformation in their children's lives, and some of them were likewise spiritually impressed and changed. By this time, the house in which they met became too small for all those wishing to attend, while, additionally, some other meetings were also initiated.[29]

General Awakening 1905–6

LARGE numbers of children were among those professing to have been savingly changed during the fruitful awakening of 1905–6, which had widespread effect throughout Scotland (see Chapter 3). In some cases the earliest and most striking work appeared among these young hearts, not least in Stenhousemuir (see pp. 134–5). In regard to the movement in Dingwall, the Rev. J.R. MacPherson wrote,

> The more striking work seemed to commence one afternoon at the close of a children's service. We were all rather troubled about some young boys and girls who waited to be talked to without apparently any real desire after Christ; but just as we were wondering about this, the spark was lighted among a few of the older girls, and there was no mistaking its bright reality. One girl followed another; a girls' prayer meeting became a new centre of work and these young women and bigger girls have, from that afternoon, been the brightest spot in Dingwall. They have helped one another, and they have brought in others; they have been the mainstay of the Christian Endeavour movement among us, but they have not been content with that. Their eagerness, their brightness, have helped us all onwards, week after week.[30]

It was also around this time that the town of Nairn received a special blessing. The Rev. John Ross of Marnoch UFC records that he had just suffered the sad loss of his eight-year-old son through illness.[31]

> I went to Inch for a mission; and when I returned home I had a wire from Rev. J.S. MacDonald, Nairn, urging me to come and help them in a work of grace there. It needed self-denial

29. *ARC-FCS-SR&M*, 1889, pp. 45–6.

30. Various, *A Wave of Blessing*, p. 42.

31. Tragically, Ross's other son also died prematurely, being killed in action in Palestine during the Great War.

> to go, yet I was glad I went, for while the meetings for adults were most encouraging, the striking thing was how the meetings for young people developed. So many remained to the after-meetings that we had to take them in groups – it would take too long to speak to them one by one. In addition, so many came to the manse seeking to know more about Jesus, that Mr MacDonald and I were at a loss to know how to deal wisely with them. The fruit of that mission was conserved by a young man – Cameron Clark.[32]

At one Sunday meeting of Motherwell's 'Boys' Own Pleasant Sunday Afternoon' – a weekly senior non-sectarian Sunday school – eighty young lads decided for Christ, with no special pleading from the speaker. Other children's meetings were also popular – at one 'a crowded audience of happy children might have been witnessed singing sacred choruses in a most hearty and joyous manner'.[33] Meanwhile, the Rev. Logan, an ardent supporter of the revival in Cambuslang, testified at a meeting in Glasgow's Tent Hall to over 200 children from the Hallside district of Cambuslang who had been recently converted. He requested those present to pray for a still greater manifestation of God's presence in that neighbourhood.[34]

Within the setting of a move of the Spirit in Gilcomston Park Baptist Church, Aberdeen in 1905, 'the whole of the Young Men's Bible Class decided for Christ over two consecutive Sundays'.[35] Following an address by the Rev. Gibb to the combined Sunday schools, most of the children were also converted and joined the Church, in time developing into workers in the Sunday schools and other departments.[36]

During the revival at Charlotte Chapel, Edinburgh in 1905, 12 out of 14 children made decisions for Jesus in one Sunday school class (see page 121). In St Paul's Parish Church, Leith, the work again first began among the young. During the first week of a mission in early 1906, a large number of youths came out. Among them were forty-five lads belonging to the Boys' Brigade – the Captain being a devout believer who had been earnestly praying that these boys would surrender. Many were broken to tears as they sought the inquiry room. The following week, nearly all the seniors in the Sunday school were also swept into the kingdom.[37]

---

32. Ross, *Reminiscences*, p. 38. Cameron Clark was later minister in St John's Church, Kilmarnock.

33. *The Lanarkshire*, 11 March 1905.

34. Ibid., 29 March 1905.

35. Anonymous, *These Fifty Years*.

36. *SBM*, 1905, pp. 87, 105.

37. *TC*, 8 February 2006, p. 24. We recall, too, the prayer movement among children in Portobello during the pre-First-World-War stage of the Pentecostal movement, after many of them 'got saved and baptised with the Holy Ghost' (see page 432).

GLASGOW 1920S

BAPTIST minister Edward Last makes mention of two small-scale movements in and around Glasgow in the 1920s.[38] In the first, a young Christian teacher was encouraged to yield her life more fully to the Lord after hearing an evangelist preach. Back at school, she took the opportunity to invite one of her pupils to the meetings. 'The boy went and was saved that night, and went again, taking a chum, and he got saved; and again and again they went, taking others, until eight were trusting Christ.' The young converts requested that their teacher assist them in reading and understanding the Bible. They were offered the use of a room in the home of one of the boys, whose mother was delighted with the change that had taken place in her son. Soon twenty-two were meeting together, all but one of whom had 'definitely accepted Christ'.[39]

STUDENTS

THE conversion of students at universities and colleges – predominantly among those in their later teens or early twenties – is common (see the many accounts in J. Edwin Orr's matchless *Campus Aflame: A History of Evangelical Awakenings in Collegiate Communities*).[40] Indeed it is well known that the great majority of people who become Christians make that life-changing decision when in this age bracket. This is true both in times of revival and during the more 'ordinary' course of life.

EDINBURGH UNIVERSITY 1884–94

EXCEPT during times of general revival,[41] evangelical awakenings at secular establishments of higher education are extremely rare.[42] This makes all the more remarkable a longstanding work of grace that began

38. It was during this decade, too – in 1924 – that Last, accompanied by Oswald J. Smith of Toronto, made a life-changing trip to Russia and Poland, where, in Latvia and also among both Russian and then German settlers in different parts of Poland, the visitors witnessed scenes of remarkable revival, later described by Smith as 'the atmosphere of a revival, the like of which I have never known anywhere before ... one of the greatest revivals of modern times' (Oswald J. Smith, *The Great Russian Revival*, Willowdale, Ontario 1964, pp. 3–19).

39. Edward Last, *Hand-Gathered Fruit, Twelve Chapters on Personal Soul-Winning*, Stirling 1950, pp. 94–5. Regarding the second movement, see page 419.

40. Wheaton 1994. See also Dan Hayes, *Fireseeds of Spiritual Awakening*, San Bernardino, 1983.

41. Such as during the extensive revival of 1859–61, when the Universities of Aberdeen, Edinburgh and Glasgow all shared in the movement. Of the general awakening of 1905–6 it was claimed, particularly regarding America, that, 'Never in the history of universities have there been so many genuine spiritual awakenings among students; in fact, some of the remarkable revivals have taken place in undenominational and non-Christian universities' (quoted in J. Edwin Orr, *Campus Aflame: A History of Evangelical Awakenings in Collegiate Communities*, Wheaton 1994, p. 133).

42. It is for this reason that Orr's *Campus Aflame* focuses almost exclusively on awakenings in academic institutions that were specifically Christian-based, and mostly located in the United States.

at Edinburgh University in 1884,[43] spreading, in time, to other centres of learning and many towns, small and large, throughout Scotland. David Cairns, a former student in Edinburgh, testified how, before the movement began, religious life within the University was at a low ebb. Indeed the only sign whatsoever of spiritual life was a sparsely attended Saturday morning prayer meeting, and the man who led it had little rapport with students. If ever the Lord's Prayer was made in class, students had to say it in Greek. After a period abroad, Cairns returned to Edinburgh in 1886 to find 'the Oddfellows Hall in Forrest Road nearly filled every Sunday night by some 600 students and not a few students met in little groups of prayer circles. The whole spiritual atmosphere was changed.'[44]

Dr D.A. Moxey, in speaking of the 'premonitory symptoms of the blessed outburst',[45] dated the distinct rise of tide to meetings evangelist Major Whittle held with students in 1880, enhanced by D.L. Moody's second visit to the city the following year, which again attracted much excitement and was attended by crowded meetings and scores of professed conversions. Since then, a number of Christian societies on campus had increased both in magnitude and interest, and a weekly men's prayer meeting was started, chiefly composed of those from the Arts Classes[46] (especially Medicine[47]) to petition God to move among fellow students and superiors and to pray for a genuine revival of religion. Visitations to the lodgings of other students were also inaugurated, whereby numerous individuals were brought to the throne of Christ.

Other factors conducive to the movement that ensued included the admission to the Establishment of several Professors who held firmly to evangelical views, replacing others 'whose Christianity was doubtful'.[48]

---

43. Although there was no general awakening in Edinburgh at this time, there do appear to have been one or two hopeful signs elsewhere in Scotland's capital city. The Rev. James Wilson Hood has the following record in his diary for 1884: '9.40 p.m. I have just come up from Fountainbridge. It is a wonderful sight. Have seen nothing like it for a quarter of a century. The area of the church was filled with genuine district people, all the front part with men – those who loaf about, stand at the corners of Thorybauk, etc. they seem more in a state of wonderment than anything else. There were 60 of the men there last night when I went in. Dr Whyte was just beginning to speak. Then I spoke' (Wells, *Life of James Hood Wilson*, p. 222).

44. D.S. Cairns, *David Cairns, An Autobiography: Some Recollections of a Long Life, and Selected Letters*, London 1950, pp. 112–17. This volume contains an appreciative critique of Henry Drummond, who became deeply involved in the movement.

45. *TC*, 19 February 1885, p. 17.

46. It is unclear to what extent the Divinity Classes were affected. A history of this department, (G. Badcock and D.F. Wright (Eds), *Disruption to Divinity: Edinburgh Divinity 1846–1996*, Edinburgh 1996), makes no mention whatever of the spiritual movement.

47. The earliest records of the Edinburgh Medical Students' Christian Association are dated 1874, when the membership was just 38. But in later years of its greatest influence, numbers were in the region of 400, over half the total number of medical students enrolled in the University at that time (Douglas Johnson, *Contending For The Faith: A History of the Evangelical Movement in the Universities and Colleges*, Leicester 1979, p. 47).

48. *TC*, 19 February 1885, p. 17.

Indeed, only one name from the long list of the University's Professors was known to have been strongly anti-Christian, thus being much in the prayers of students and fellow teachers alike. Added to this, the sudden death of the previous Principal stirred many a heart to consider eternal issues, while the appointment in his place of Sir William Muir, Indian statesman and a devoted believer, was a matter of deep gratitude to God.

Yet another link in this chain was the recent Ter-centenary Anniversary celebrations, which around 2,000 students – almost the whole University – attended. On the platform were a good number of well-known sceptics and freethinkers from the literary and scientific world, including the poet Robert Browning, Count Saffi of Italy and Professor de Laveleye of Belgium. However, things took a wholly unexpected turn when a number of speeches sounded a definite religious tone. Wrote Moxey, 'The outcome of the extraordinary gathering focussed in an unmistakable testimony (from the foremost intellects of Europe) to the truth of, and need for, the glorious revelation to man, contained in God's blessed Book. Students went off to their homes all over the United Kingdom with this testimony surviving all the excitement, and doubtless in many hearts speaking with a still, small voice.'[49]

But what helped most to fan spiritual flames at this time was the visit to the University in December 1884 of two young Christian athletes, Charles T. Studd and Stanley Smith, from Cambridge. Their visit had been arranged by a sub-committee of six medical students, all but one of whom later became medical missionaries. Studd had been a top-rate bowler in the England cricket team, and as such, a household name throughout much of Britain. His father had been converted as a result of Moody's 1874 visit to England. The young Studd, along with two of his brothers, came to Christ a few years later through the influence of a family friend. Later, after several years of backsliding, the young sportsman renewed his vows with God.

Stanley Smith was the ex-captain oarsman of the Cambridge Boat. He, too, came to Christ through Moody, this time during the American's memorable visit to Cambridge University in 1882, a mission that 'began in derision and ended with "the most remarkable meeting ever seen in Cambridge", a University transformed, and proud undergraduates humbled at the foot of the Cross.'[50] Both Studd and Smith, along with five other young converts – termed the 'Cambridge Seven' by the Press – were making headline news in respect of their decision to go out to China as missionaries. Robert Stevenson, an undergraduate at Cambridge University in 1882, gave testimony to the remarkable events

49. Ibid.

50. John Pollock, *A Fistful of Heroes*, Fearn 1998, p. 206.

that occurred with Moody's visit to the campus. He later transferred to Divinity Hall of Edinburgh University, when the revival movement was underway there. Fifty years later he still retained 'a vivid memory of scenes not unlike those beheld in Cambridge'.[51]

On their arrival in Edinburgh, Studd and Smith spent the afternoon in deep prayer in their host's drawing room, where they eventually reached a place of spiritual victory. At the evening meeting, Smith spoke eloquently and entreatingly of his redeemer's love, while the quieter Studd gave personal testimony to a powerful saviour. 'Opposition and criticism were alike disarmed, and Professors and students together were seen in tears, to be followed in the after-meeting by the glorious sight of Professors dealing with students, and students with one another.'[52]

Dr G. Purves Smith remarked in his 'Memorandum' that after Studd and Smith's speeches, there was a stampede for the platform to shake hands with the two men. Wrote Moxey: 'A great impression had been made and men were crowded round Studd and Smith to hear more about Christ. Deep earnestness was written on the faces of many. A great religious movement had had its birth and it was all so evidently the work of the Spirit of God. Many of these students were our best men.'[53] Such was the impression made by the occasion that a large procession made its way to the railway station, from where the two athletes were booked to leave for London on the overnight train. The students cried 'speech' and entreated the two sportsmen with deep sincerity to make a hasty return. One gentleman was heard asking a porter, 'Who are all these men?' The porter replied, 'Th're aa medical students, but th're aff their heeds!'[54]

All other colleges in Edinburgh were also represented on the committee of students that made arrangements for Smith and Studd's next visit. This took place in January 1885 in the Free Assembly Hall. One thousand seven hundred men attended one meeting and the impression produced was deep and widespread, with large numbers – including leading students at the University – making decisions for Christ.[55] According to John Pollock, the visits of the English students 'brought to white heat the religious revival which had begun under Moody in '81'.[56]

---

51. Various, *Moody Centenary Celebrations*, p. 34.

52. *TC*, 19 February 1885, p. 17.

53. Quoted in *The Christian*, 19 February 1985, p. 17.

54. Norman P. Grubb, *C.T. Studd: Cricketter and Pioneer*, London 1933, pp. 44–5.

55. Oswald Chambers, writer of the devotional classic, *My Utmost For His Highest*, became a student at Edinburgh University in 1885, where he entered the Arts Faculty (David McCasland, *Oswald Chambers: Abandoned to God*, Grand Rapids 1993, p. 45). It is quite likely that he was involved to a greater or lesser degree in this movement.

56. J.C. Pollock, *A Cambridge Movement*, London 1950, p. 83.

Two nights later, Professor Henry Drummond addressed around 1,000 students in Oddfellows Hall. 'Students are essentially hero-worshippers,' reflected Moxey,

> and hard muscle and fertile brain seem to be the gods they especially revere. They had already found two of their muscular heroes in vital communion with the Lord Jesus Christ, and now they listened to an intellectual giant, who looked no older than themselves, glorifying this same Jesus – a scientist preaching the Gospel. This last surprise seemed to have been the means used by God to topple over the absurd idea that Christ meant cant, and the devil meant manliness; and when Professor Greenfield, M.D., who is regarded as a man of brain-power and of scientific attainments second to none in the University, stood up, and in tearful and broken sentences, almost child-like in their simplicity, urged the students to come to Jesus, a scene ensued which everyone who saw it declares to have been unexampled in his experience. Whole rows of weeping men were dealt with, the difficulty being to find a sufficient number of workers.[57]

During the weeks that ensued the presence and power of the Holy Ghost continued to make themselves felt, and numbers more were pointed to a yet more willing Saviour. One brilliant student who exhibited an 'intense and burning zeal' during these months spoke of the revival as 'I think, the greatest blessing I ever got. … How overflowing with joy we were! It was glorious. … The Lord has opened the windows of heaven.'[58] On 8 February, Drummond's address touched hearts deeply. It was clear to the Professor that a deep move of the Holy Spirit was well underway, and despite the fact that he had been personally involved in the awakening that accompanied Moody's visit to Edinburgh in the mid-1870s, he was nonetheless taken by surprise by these latest events. 'It is a distinct work of God,' he wrote, 'such a work as I, after considerable experience of evangelistic work, have never seen before. … It haunts me like a nightmare. The responsibility I feel almost more than anything in my life.'[59] Such deepened interest required Drummond to be present in Edinburgh every Sunday, and he refused invitations to visit other universities.

Meetings, however, were set up by Professors of other learning establishments, and deputations from Edinburgh were despatched to share at these. In Aberdeen University, over 300 out of 800 students from

57. *TC*, 19 February 1885, p. 17.

58. Robert L. Bremmer, *A Child Of Faith: Memorials of Andrew Kennedy Bremmer*, London 1890, pp. 102, 106. The excitement of deputation work became too much for the young man, however, and he was forced to retire from it. Tragically, Bremmer died of kidney failure just a couple of years later, without having completed his studies. He retained a strong faith till the end and left behind a stirring spiritual diary.

59. Smith, *Life of Henry Drummond*, p. 301.

King's and Marischal Colleges attended a series of meetings before the end of session, with scores remaining to after-meetings. The result was not only the formation of a University Christian Association and a deepened consecration of many believers, but also 'the moral elevation of the whole life of the University, which … was not transitory'.[60] In Glasgow the meetings were stronger still, with hundreds attending the after-meetings, and many decisions being recorded. Soon invitations were coming in from all quarters for deputations of Glasgow students to come and speak at meetings.[61] However, for various social, ethnic and cultural reasons, no growing and permanent movement took shape in this city as it did in Edinburgh. According to Johnson, each of the Scottish universities felt the effects of these 'winds of God' for years and during them many Scottish graduates offered themselves for overseas missionary service.[62]

At this time, the 'Holiday Mission' arose, whereby sixty or seventy Edinburgh students volunteered to carry the influences of God's grace to other parts of Scotland, Ireland and England. The volunteers were carefully organised and within weeks deputations of students were holding week-long outreaches in towns such as Dalkeith, Jedburgh, Dunbar, Kirkcaldy, Bo'ness and Alloa. Meetings were addressed almost exclusively to men, and were confined to personal testimony. In some places, as in Stirling, 'The moving among young men has been so marvellous that … we felt it our clear calling to go forward.'[63] A second week's meetings were deemed necessary. In the Perthshire village of Errol, an account of the Edinburgh University work was given by the minister of the Free Church on his return from the Assembly. 'Serious results were manifest', and around twenty male converts formed the Errol Evangelistic Union, which soon began holding meetings in the neighbourhood.[64]

In Greenock, and preceded by a mission conducted by John M. Scroggie, about 2,000 packed Cooke's Circus Hall to capacity for a students' meeting, and many young men could not get in. 'The presence of the Holy Spirit was a very vivid reality from the first,'[65] noted one commentator, and a deep impression was made. In Wick, week-night audiences varied from 200 to 300 and it was recorded that, 'It is no metaphor to say that the whole town of Wick is moved just now,'[66] unanimity prevailing among all the churches. Back in Edinburgh itself, one congregation added 45

60. Ibid., pp. 301–2.

61. One of the first went to the Free Gorbals Mission, of which opening meeting one student remarked, 'I do not remember such a signal answer to prayer in connection with any meeting. We were all in raptures' (Bremmer, *A Child Of Faith*, p. 106).

62. Johnson, *Contending For The Faith*, p. 61.

63. *TC*, 23 April 1886, p. 11.

64. ARC-FCS-SR&M, 1886, pp. 60–1. For Kilmarnock 1885–86, see www.scottishrevivals.co.uk.

65. *TC*, 23 April 1886, p. 11.

66. Smith, *Life of Henry Drummond*, p. 305.

young communicants, most of them the result of deputation work. A letter from one new convert spoke of what '"joy unspeakable" came to me that night, and last night at the meeting my cup was filled to the brim, I might say, by seeing three of my own friends brought to the knowledge of Christ Jesus – two of them partly by my influence'. One of them 'went home rejoicing to tell his mother what a Christ he had found'.[67]

Meanwhile the movement among Edinburgh students continued long after any mere human excitement would have worn off. Drummond's series of addresses, begun in Oddfellows Hall, continued over a period of ten years, and became what Tatlow called 'the most famous sermon of a religious character which has ever been delivered anywhere to university men'.[68] Snippets from the preacher's diary for these years include the following:

> 26 February 1886 – 'The work is still very wide and deep, and I am still going there every Sunday.'[69]
>
> 27 January 1887 – 'Edinburgh was splendid last night.'[70]
>
> 17 February 1887 – 'Edinburgh is as good as ever, both the boys and the students.'[71]
>
> 31 March 1887 – 'Edinburgh still glows. We have not been able to stop the meetings. I had four last Sunday, and have four more next.'[72]
>
> 28 January 1888 – 'Edinburgh takes a lot of time, for we are in full sail there again, and I had three students' meetings last Saturday and Sunday.'[73]

The academic session 1889–90 saw the work as engrossing as in previous years, with the fresh crop of students who had begun their desired courses showing as much interest and response as had their predecessors. The movement continued right through the early 1890s, and a number of years later it was possible to report: 'In nearly every town of our country, in every British colony, in India, in China, in Japan, converts or disciples of this movement, who gratefully trace to it the beginnings of their moral power, are labouring steadfastly, and often brilliantly, in every profession of life.'[74]

---

67. *TC*, 23 April 1886, p. 11.
68. T. Tatlow, *The Story of the Student Christian Movement of Great Britain and Ireland*, London 1933, pp. 11–12.
69. Smith, *Life of Henry Drummond*, p. 315.
70. Ibid., p. 319.
71. Ibid.
72. Ibid., p. 321.
73. Ibid., p. 322.
74. Ibid., p. 340. For further information on the Students' Movement in Edinburgh see Agnes R. Fraser, *Donald Fraser*, Edinburgh 1934, pp. 22–30. See also Professor A.R. Simpson, *The Year of Grace, 1884 in the University of Edinburgh*, Edinburgh n.d. A further 'very real spiritual movement' developed among students of this ancient institution during 1899, climaxing with a visit from John R. Mott, General Secretary of the recently formed World's Student Christian Federation. The movement created a considerable stir throughout the University and Mott interviewed forty young men who voluntarily went to speak with him (*TC*, 1899).

GENERAL AWAKENING 1905

MEANWHILE, a 'remarkable blessing' was experienced by the students of the Bible Training Institute in Glasgow in the spring of 1905.[75] The College was founded by D.L. Moody in 1892 and John Anderson, a shipping agent from Ardrossan, was its first Principal, a post he held till 1913. News of revival in Wales came as a sweet sound to his ears and he could not refrain from visiting the country.[76] 'Extraordinary interest was manifested' at Anderson's 'welcome home' meeting in Glasgow. The large hall of the Christian Institute was full to overflowing well before the hour of meeting, so an overflow meeting was held in the Bible Training Institute, which was also packed.[77] His report quickened believers, especially in intercessory prayer.[78] Alexander Mair, a student at the Bible Training Institute at this time and later a missionary in China, records, 'The spirit of revival was among us. I'll always be grateful for finding myself in such an uplifting and inspiring atmosphere. The building was full and over-full, for a number of the students had to get quarters outside.'[79] This wave of grace raised notably the spiritual tone of the Institute, and also resulted in an unwonted degree of blessing in connection with the practical work carried on by the students. As a result, a very large number of professions of faith was recorded as a result of their labours over a relatively short period.[80] A further season of spiritual quickening came to college students towards the close of 1906, after they heard about revival at the Moody Bible Institue in Chicago, and they were quick to share this blessing when invitations came to speak at church meetings.[81]

STUDENTS' UNION MISSIONS 1920S

A FEATURE of the heightened sense of spirituality during the period of general awakening in the early 1920s (see pp. 165–90) was the

75. Revivals were common at Christian colleges in 1905, particularly in America, where such institutions were far more numerous. (Unusually, Orr makes no mention of the movement at Glasgow's Bible Training Institute in his otherwise comprehensive *Campus Aflame.*) Such movements had a notable effect on the number of students applying for missionary service abroad in the first decade of the twentieth century.

76. Anderson communicated by letter with Evan Roberts, the charismatic leader of the Welsh revival. In one message he assured Roberts that many in Scotland were praying for him.

77. *Glasgow Weekly Herald*, 21 January 1905.

78. Gibbard, *Fire on the Altar*, p. 114.

79. Mair, *Unforgettable*, p. 15.

80. On several occasions, notably 1919 and 1925, the Faith Mission Training Home and Bible College, based in Edinburgh's Ravelston suburb, experienced God's Spirit becoming manifest in a special way, although there is no mention of any resulting conversions of non-believers (Woolsey, p. 58; Peckham, *Heritage of Revival*, p. 143). Elsewhere in Britain, at another Bible college, the Bible College of Wales, founded by Rees Howells, occurred a similar 'visitation of the Spirit' in 1937, which continued in some intensity for three weeks (Norman P. Grubb, *Rees Howells: Intercessor*, Guildford 1973, reprinted 1983, pp. 231–236).

81. Balfour, *Revival in Rose Street*, p. 106.

evangelistic activity of a number of students from various universities and divinity halls, who conducted special services in towns and cities in the Lowlands. The Edinburgh Students' Evangelistic Association came into being in 1922 and the Glasgow equivalent the following year.[82] Drawn from the faculties of Arts, Science, Law, Medicine and Divinity, the members of these unions were pledged to active evangelism in towns and villages of central Scotland during university vacations, the basis of their fellowship being interdenominational.

The Glasgow Union,[83] for example, normally worked in teams of about a dozen, and lived in church halls, where they did their own catering. They had a policy of only going to districts where the local churches were prepared to give them a united invitation. The teams were generally led by older students who had served in the First World War before beginning their courses. One of their number, D.P. Thomson, said that 'these young evangelists had developed a mission technique all their own, and their work had met with a real response in many districts'.[84] A mission held in the industrial town of Armadale, West Lothian, in the spring of 1923 – already the seventeenth such mission the fledgling Glasgow Union had conducted! – was followed up by an address from Edinburgh student Eric Liddell, already the best-known athlete in Scotland. This campaign had a lasting effect on Liddell's own life and, due to it being reported in many of Scotland's newspapers, also led to increased audiences at all further union missions where this highly popular athlete was invited to speak. A large number of young people remained after each meeting, prompting some critics to assert that Thomson and Liddell were playing on the emotions of the audience.[85]

The students spoke in theatres, music halls, churches and public auditoriums of all kinds, in schools and colleges, and at least once in a public house on a Sunday morning! Thomson's diary notes that in Rutherglen, '35 came to the inquiry room'; in Kilmarnock, 'right from the opening night the interest was obvious – and the blessing manifest'; and when addressing senior boys at four leading Glasgow schools, some received impressions that had lasting results – 'sometimes bringing a change in vocation as well as in outlook and character. … At Hillhead

82. Similar Christian Unions were formed in the early 1920s at Aberdeen University (1922) and in several English universities.

83. Co-launched by D.P. Thomson as a direct result of his experience in the 'Fishermen's revival' in Fraserburgh a few years previously. Thomson referred to the Union as 'perhaps the most vital force in evangelism in Scotland in the middle twenties … what eventually remained as the permanent sphere of this new student body was the organisation and carrying through of United Evangelistic Campaigns, and in the ten years that followed … these were held all over Scotland' (D.P. Thomson, *The Road to Dunfermline*, quoted in Mair, *Unforgettable*, p. 50).

84. D.P. Thomson, *Scotland's Greatest Athlete: The Eric Liddell Story*, Crieff 1970, p. 3.

85. David McCasland, *Eric Liddell: Pure Gold*, Grand Rapids 2003, p. 111. See also John Keddie, *Running the Race: Eric Liddell, Olympic Champion and Missionary*, Darlington 2008.

High we got a tremendous ovation; at Glasgow High an almost equally exuberant and thunderous welcome; Allan Glen's however, was the best meeting – we got home there as nowhere else.'[86]

Often the students reached audiences not readily accessible to any other type of evangelist, and, writes Thomson, 'it is no exaggeration to say that thousands were deeply moved and stirred by the straight-forward manly message of student athlete (Eric Liddell),[87] and were gripped by his telling and effective illustrations, gathered largely at first hand from the chemical laboratory, the football field and the running track. Young men and boys in particular were led in larger numbers of cases, I am persuaded, than either of us was ever likely to know of, to invest their lives in the service of the Lord and master Eric set forth so winsomely.'[88] Another fruit of these campaigns came to light from a report indicating 'a notable increase of zeal and expectation among evangelical ministers of all the churches'.[89]

The Edinburgh Students' Evangelistic Association was no less active during these years. When formed in 1922, the lively missionary interest that had characterised the 1880s Edinburgh students was again strongly evident from the start.[90] As well as evangelising in nearby towns and villages, the Union launched its first full-scale mission to the University in 1925, led by Liddell.[91]

Meanwhile, around the same time, though not in connection with the Students' Union Missions, 'a real spiritual movement' began in a town just outside Glasgow when two daughters of an eminent Christian submitted themselves to the Lord and at once took a bold stand among fellow students and friends. One sister invited the girls in her sports club to tea, and, testifying to the change in her own life, led her friend to the saviour. The sisters also began prayer meetings in the respective colleges they attended, as a consequence of which forty girls started meeting for prayer in a local church.[92]

---

86. Thomson, *Scotland's Greatest Athlete*, pp. 46, 76.

87. Thomson got to know Liddell intimately, and developed a huge regard for this godly man: 'I have never known a finer character in all my varied experience,' he wrote. 'He is pure gold through and through' (ibid., p. 77).

88. Ibid. In March 1962, a fortieth anniversary gathering of former members of the Glasgow, Edinburgh and Aberdeen Christian Students Unions was held in Crieff. Among the many present were 'Professors, Principals of Theological Colleges, Convenors of Assembly Committees, Doctors, Headmasters and Ministers and Missionaries with backgrounds too numerous to classify' (ibid., p. 48).

89. *RC-FCS-RM&T*, 1925, p. 153.

90. Johnson, *Contending For The Faith*, p. 107; Alister McGrath, *Thomas F. Torrance: An Intellectual Biography*, Edinburgh 1999, p. 26.

91. Now fondly termed 'The Flying Scotsman', Liddell by this time was an Olympic Gold medallist and a national hero, having sensationally achieved a new world record for running 400 metres at the Paris Olympics the previous year. Just a month or two after this university campaign, Liddell left his homeland to work as a missionary in China, where he faithfully served till his death in a Japanese prisoner-of-war camp in 1945.

92. Last, *Hand-Gathered Fruit*, p. 94.

E.P. Hammond – p.406

Henry Drummond – p.414

Edinburgh University – p.411

Kilsyth – p.422

13
Pentecostal Movements

Introduction

ALTHOUGH there were numerous influences,[1] it is generally accepted that the more immediate origins of the hugely influential twentieth century Pentecostal movement date from meetings at a Bible Institute set up by Charles C. Parham in Topeka, Kansas, in 1898. From the first day of 1901, students, as well as their teacher, began to experience glossolalia. Transferring to Houston, Texas in 1905, Parham's teaching influenced, among others, a black Holiness evangelist named William J. Seymour. Moving to Los Angeles, Seymour began prayer meetings in a home in Bonnie Brae Street, where many more received a fresh spiritual anointing accompanied by tongues.[2] This attracted more and more people to the meetings, which were transferred to a run-down former livery-stable in Azusa Street in April 1906. Reports of intense spiritual atmosphere, profound blessing, remarkable inter-racial harmony and other extraordinary and irreverent goings-on appeared in the Press, causing thousands of pilgrims from all over the USA and beyond to be drawn to the Azusa St meetings, many out of curiosity, many hungry for the 'full gospel' experience.[3] From these humble beginnings, the Pentecostal movement rapidly spread throughout the world.[4]

The Spirit Comes – Kilsyth 1908

PRIOR to the twentieth century there occurred several marked seasons of revival in the mining town of Kilsyth, twelve miles north-east of Glasgow, particularly in the years 1742, 1839 and 1866.[5] By the turn of the twentieth

---

1. Such as the Holiness Movement, the growth of the Church of God in Christ denomination, the work of lay evangelist Frank Bartleman in Los Angeles, and the 1904 Welsh revival, which aroused much excitement and expectancy among Christians in America.

2. Larry Martin, *The Life and Ministry of William J. Seymour*, Joplin, Missouri 1999; Larry Martin, *The Topeka Outpouring of 1901*, Joplin, Missouri 2000.

3. It is of interest to note that Walter Hollenweger, who authored the most authoritative and acclaimed early study of the Pentecostal movement, wrote that the charismatic experience of Los Angeles was not 'the eschatological pouring out of the Holy Spirit (as the Pentecostal movement itself claims) but an outburst of enthusiastic religion of a kind well-known and frequent in the history of Negro churches in America which derived its specifically Pentecostal features from Parham's theory that speaking with tongues is a necessary concomitant of the baptism of the Spirit' (Walter J. Hollenweger, *The Pentecostals*, London 1972, pp. 23–4).

4. See Stanley H. Frodsham, *With Signs Following*, Springfield, Missouri 1941, for an account of its worldwide spread.

5. There was also a movement during the nation-wide revival of 1859–61, but this appears to have been less marked than the others (Thomas Brown, *Annals of the Disruption*, Edinburgh 1876, p. 776; *Falkirk Herald*, quoted in *Scottish Guardian*, 27 September 1859). In the early 1870s occurred one additional burst of spiritual blessing in this favoured town (*The Christian Herald*, 7 June 06, p. 7).

century poverty was rife in the town and its housing stock was among the worst in Britain. Established Churches were finding it difficult to integrate the predominantly mining community into church life. Partly in response to this, partly in attempt to be separated from worldliness within the churches, a small band of believers formed the Kilsyth United Evangelical Society and began services in a converted theatre and working men's club known as 'Westport Hall'. These commenced in 1897 and, as advertised in the local Press, were intended 'to meet the wants of the non-churchgoer'.[6] Surprisingly, this innovation met with the approval of other ministers in the area, and within just four years the Hall had achieved attendances of 150 and 200 on Saturday and Sunday evenings respectively.[7]

In 1902 a committee of four elders and four deacons was appointed, the church being named 'Church of God, Kilsyth'. These Christians were greatly intrigued by news that trickled in of the Pentecostal revivals in Azusa Street and then in Sunderland[8] and they began to earnestly pray for a similar revival.[9] A year later, one of their elders, Bill Hutchison, made a visit to the Humberside town to observe events for himself. When the Rev. A.A. Boddy came to Edinburgh to speak at a convention soon after, two who heard and received his message were known to those at Westport Hall and were invited to come and share information on this new Pentecostal movement and on their own experiences of baptism in the Holy Spirit and speaking in tongues. By this time – the New Year of 1908 – a Pentecostal movement had already commenced in Dunfermline, led by Andrew Bell.[10] But it was Kilsyth that was to become the main centre for the new movement in Scotland.[11]

---

6. Kilsyth is also renowned for being the birthplace of William Irvine (1863–1947), a former Pilgrim with the Faith Mission and founder of a less orthodox ministry known variously as 'The Cooneyites,' 'Two-by-Twos,' 'The Church Without a Name,' 'Christian Convention Church,' etc.

7. One mission, led by itinerant evangelist John Long in 1898, and during which some half-nights were spent in prayer, saw 'upwards of 100 souls decide for Christ. ... These were days of refreshing coming from the presence of the Lord; the fruits and results were real and lasting' (Long, *Journal of John Long*, Chapter 5).

8. This town became the original centre of the Pentecostal movement in Britain through the personal interest shown in it by local Anglican minister Alexander A. Boddy.

9. Evangelist John Long witnessed these heartfelt prayers on a visit to Westport Hall in September 1907 (Long, *Journal of John Long*, Chapter 5).

10. Here, in October 1908, it was reported that 'the work goes on steadily and growing deeper' (*Confidence Magazine*, October 1908, located in *Confidence Magazine 1908–1926*, Revival Library CD-ROM). This congregation later became part of the Apostolic Faith group of churches, with Bell as leader.

11. This was by no means, however, the first outbreak of Pentecostal manifestations in Scotland. An unusual 'charismatic' revival, centring on the Gareloch region of Dumbartonshire, commenced in the late 1820s. It became a significant precursor of the Azusa Street revival of 1906 (Stanley Burgess (Ed.), *The New International Dictionary of Pentecostal & Charismatic Movements*, Grand Rapids 2002, pp. 1189–92). Just over a century earlier, a group of 'prophets' in Edinburgh and Glasgow, the most prominent of whom were women, claimed direct inspiration from the Holy Spirit, and spoke in tongues, while one of their number, Ann Topham, even claimed to have levitated (A.M. King et al, *Warnings of the Eternal Spirit*, Edinburgh 1709, in Neill Dickson, 'Modern Prophetesses', in *SCHSR*, Vol. 25, Edinburgh 1993, p. 93). A century earlier still, John Welsh, eminent minister of Ayr, was overheard in prayer – the mainstay of his entire life – speaking 'strange words' (considered to have been tongues) about his spiritual joy (George Jeffreys, *Pentecostal Rays: The Baptism and Gifts of the Holy Spirit*, London 1923, pp. 200).

Here the meetings began in January 1908 and about a dozen received 'the blessing'. It was while praying in his own home with visiting evangelist Victor Wilson of Motherwell that church secretary Andrew Murdoch received his baptism in the Spirit, while the next night, on visiting Murdoch, and as the two men embraced, fellow-elder Bill Hutchison was also filled with the divine power. At a service on Friday 31 January, a Mr Reid raised his hand and cried 'Blood, blood, blood!' 11 people received 'the blessing'. Then, the following night, 'the fire fell and between 30 and 40 were prostrated under the power of God, and all received a scriptural Pentecost'.[12] Soon crowds were flocking to the Hall, which seated 500, while many more who could not get in climbed up to peer through the windows.

A local newspaper reporter attended a weeknight meeting within the first few weeks of the movement. 'All sects and creeds were represented,' he wrote, 'the acknowledged Christian, the avowed infidel, the thoughtless scoffer. … Studying the features of those entering the hall could be traced an expectancy or desire, on others awe was plainly depicted, but excitement was awanting.' Several cross-centred hymns were followed by earnest prayer to 'pluck brands from the burning'. Then followed direct and forceful gospel addresses by two speakers, from which were 'entirely absent any interjections'. For the duration of the meeting an earnest prayer meeting was in progress in an ante-room. It was only at the after-meeting from 10 p.m. that specifically Pentecostal activity was engaged in. Those present described the scenes as 'something they would never forget. In apparent frenzy a man or woman would stand up and make incoherent utterances, absolutely unintelligible to the hearers. There was much groaning and crying; "the travail of the soul" as one described it. Altogether the experiences were such as to lead the devout to hope that the long looked for revival in Kilsyth is at hand.'[13]

It was estimated that around 200 were 'baptised in the Spirit' at those initial meetings, and services continued every night for the following four months, with further remarkable demonstrations of God's power being evidenced. In March A.A. Boddy from Sunderland came to the Hall, and was so overcome that he lay on his face on the platform unable to speak. He told Murdoch that he had been in T.B. Barratt's meetings in Norway and that the power of the Holy Spirit was more manifest in Kilsyth than it was there; in fact more than in any place he had been.[14] Seekers came to the town from all over, including Ireland,[15] and some ventured further on to Sunderland to see for themselves the work in

---

12. *Confidence*, May 1908.

13. *Kirkintilloch Gazette, Lenzie and Campsie Reporter* (hereafter *KGLCR*), 7 February 1908.

14. Gordon Weeks, *Chapter Thirty Two (part of): A History of the Apostolic Church 1900–2000*, Barnsley 2003, p. 25.

15. On their return to Ireland, visitors established a number of Pentecostal meetings.

progress there. Soon Pentecostal centres were opening throughout central Scotland, as people brought back the 'fire' to their local communities. By April 1908 it was estimated that in the Westport Hall, 'perhaps 200 have been sealed' by the Spirit. By May the work was said to be 'quieter, but deep and true'.[16]

A considerable number of those attending meetings in Kilsyth were miners from nearby pits. Indeed, resounding detonations would shake the windows of the hall as stone was blasted in the surrounding hillside quarries. A pitman at Motherwell 'found his Pentecost' while at work on the face of the coal-pit. For two hours, 'he sat on his pile of coal, speaking in tongues as the Holy Spirit gave him utterance'. The men in the adjoining works soon heard him, and one cried: 'There's Jock through in tongues, and me no saved yet!' A number were converted just through hearing others speak in their heavenly language. One young man, a keen cycle-racer, kept away from the meetings, but when he heard his sister in the house 'speaking mysteries', praising God in an unknown tongue, he was broken down. In the Mission Hall, from three o'clock one afternoon until two the next morning, 'he dealt with God and was saved, sanctified, and baptised with the Holy Ghost'.[17]

Many children were deeply touched by the movement. Westport Hall's Sunday school, established just a year previously, exceeded 200 members by 1908. Some parents testified that 'Pentecost' had done in their homes, through love, 'what we have failed to do in years with prayer and the belt'. A number of boys at Kilsyth who had 'got their Pentecost' could now 'all be seen with their Bibles in the meeting, and little girls, too, speaking in tongues and giving out solemn messages'. However, some children had to endure not only taunts from their peers, but abuse from within their own homes. One drunk father was known to kick his young daughter for attending the meetings. Meanwhile 'a violent mother tore her girl's hat off her head as she came in (without removing the hat pins), and though it hurt she only answered, "Glory to Jesus."'[18]

S.A. Renick from Glasgow held a mission in Kilsyth in March 1908. He reported on one week's activities:

> Sunday I began with the children at 11.30 a.m. There were no less than 400 of them. At 4 p.m. I had the men's meeting. 1,400 men for just one hour, only spoke 20 minutes; short and to the point. At 7 p.m. there were about 1,000 people in the hall and some very clear conversions. Monday night we had an open air march with the children, about 1,000 strong. It was a great sight. All kinds of lights; pit lamps, anything they could get. At the

16. *Confidence*, May 1908.
17. Ibid., April 1908.
18. Ibid.

> close of this meeting over 200 asked to be prayed for. From eight to nine is the big folks. There must have been about 600 children tonight and about 100 remained for prayer.[19]

Many people testified to the necessity of making restitution for past offences before they were able to receive further blessing from God. One man could get no rest till he had repaid the twopence ha'penny that he had owed a local tobacconist for years. The tobacconist was so overcome by the gesture that he offered the man a bottle of 'Brilliantine' for his honesty! 'A young woman rose from her knees at an after-meeting and went out. She soon returned, looking happy, and received her "blessing" quickly. She had remembered someone to whom she had not spoken for long, and had been to her and put things right again.'[20]

In reply to the charge that the meetings appeared quite disorderly, Andrew Murdoch – viewed as the leader at Westport Hall – said, 'We are not yet in I Corinthians 14, only in Acts 2'; meaning that too much could not be expected in the early days of the work and that a greater degree of order would follow in due course.[21]

As might be expected with such unorthodox goings-on, considerable opposition came against the fledgling movement. Fiery letters from Christians on both sides of the 'tongues' fence appeared in the local Press, each accusing the other of being 'Satan's servants'. One anonymous correspondent railed against the 'blasphemy' promoted by the Pentecostals. 'Now there is a New Testament to guide us,' he wrote. 'Why then do we need to be baptised with the Holy Ghost?' Quoting from Mark 16, where Jesus said that as well as speaking in tongues, believers would cast out devils, heal the sick, handle serpents and drink poison with no ill effect, the writer asked why Pentecostals zoomed in on only one of these activities? 'They are too wily,' he continued. 'They are as wily as the Jewish lawyers. They are as wise as serpents, but they are not as harmless as doves.' He concluded by condemning the 'damnable heresies' of these 'so-called Christians'.[22]

Local clergymen were no less sympathetic. One Sunday morning in May 1908 two UFC ministers spoke against the movement in St David's Church. Rev. H.Y. Reyburn viewed Pentecostals' babbling, convulsions, incoherence and confusion as indicative of their vulgar nature giving way to unrestrained emotion, when what was required was a cultured nature to master the emotions. The Rev. J. Rollan MacNab regarded

---

19. 'Christian Alliance,' quoted in *KGLCR*, 3 April 1908. A correspondent challenged Renick's report for designating Kilsyth, with its 8,000 inhabitants, a 'city', and for suggesting that 1,400 people could fit into Westport Hall, which he claimed seated just 400 (ibid.).

20. *Confidence*, April 1908.

21. Ibid.

22. *KGLCR*, 24 April 1908.

tongues-speaking as 'most insignificant and practically useless'. It was an 'aberration in our midst', not Pentecostal in character, but Corinthian, i.e. unintelligible rather than intelligible. Love alone, he insisted, was the answer.[23] Meanwhile, the local Baptist minister viewed the movement as 'a kind of religious freak. ... Instead of reproducing an apostolic experience they have been trapped by something wholly fanciful and useless. ... The sooner it is damped down the better.'[24]

In August the local Press reported that meetings in Westport Hall were causing 'much clandestine inquisitiveness on the part of outsiders, who prowl about the building to hear the strange sounds' of the worshippers inside, or 'secure a peep through vantage spots' at their 'mysterious doing. ... Those listening outside have strange stories to tell ... and to them the periodic fluttering on the floor of those who take part in the proceedings is the cause of more merriment than reverence.' So great did the annoyance caused by eavesdroppers become that the police were in the habit of clearing them away from the vicinity of the building.[25]

A resident of Motherwell who had made repeated visits to Kilsyth from the start of the movement reported, on being there again in August 1908, that never 'even when the work first began here, have we had such power. We just gathered at the front, perhaps three seats full on each side, and began to pray. When the Fire fell the scene and the glory were indescribable.'[26]

It was common in these early days to hold open-air meetings to witness to what Christ, through His Spirit, had done for people. In Kirkintilloch in early September 1908, around 500 gathered while 'several of us told of Jesus' love in our own lives'. In the same month in Kilsyth, about 100 men and women of varying ages met in the prayer room in the upstairs hall, waiting upon God for guidance prior to going out to witness in the Market Square. For over an hour a large crowd listened to heart-burning testimonies from several of the converts. On one occasion, 'a young Roman Catholic, who was on the hillside putting a ferret into a rabbit-hole, heard the distant strains of the sweet singing of the open-air band. The Holy Spirit laid hold of him so strongly that he left his ferret in the hole and drew near the outskirts of the crowd. Eventually he followed the workers into the hall. Being convicted of the truth of what he heard, he was not long before he came boldly out for the Lord Jesus, and now is a bright and useful worker of our living Lord.'[27]

---

23. Ibid., 23 May 1908.

24. Ibid., 17 April 1908.

25. Ibid., 21 August 1908.

26. *Confidence*, September 1908.

27. Ibid., October 1908. John Long did a lot of house-to-house visitation and tract distribution in Kilsyth. Altogether, and in addition to his preaching work, he claimed to have distributed over 100,000 tracts in the places he visited during 1908 alone (Long, *Journal of John Long*, Chap. 5)

The Kirkintilloch Gazette reported on one Sunday evening open-air meeting, at Kilsyth's Watson Fountain. As the meeting proceeded, 'there was a decided change' when one man who was addressing the crowd 'in a startling manner, dropped into an unintelligible line of what seemed "gibberish". This happened more than once and the crowd surrounding the inner ring swelled from a handful to some hundreds.' Those outside the inner ring looked on proceedings with frequent outbursts of merriment. This annoyed the speaker, who rebuked them, saying that God was speaking to him in heavenly language. 'This statement was received with a round of cheers and "Hallelujahs".'[28]

By October 1908 it was reported from Kilsyth:

> We believe we are on the eve of a revival. Here it has begun, I believe. Some of the worst characters of the place are being saved. One case, a man who was a terror to his folk and the police. Some months ago it took five policemen to take him to jail, and not having handcuffs large enough (he is very strong) they procured ropes and bound him. That man has been saved, and was at an open-air meeting on Saturday night and caused quite a sensation, people coming from different parts of the town to see him; the very policeman had a look at him. Another case of Jesus and Lazarus. We have other cases about as bad, or better way to put it, as good. We have wonderful times of prayer. Men never prayed like this before. It would do your heart good to see nearly 100 young men and maidens in the upper room on Sabbath night all praying, sometimes nearly all in tongues. I say it to the glory of Jesus. I don't think you could see the like of it in all Scotland, and this has continued for over eight months, and is the result of Pentecost.[29]

THE MOVEMENT SPREADS THROUGH CENTRAL SCOTLAND 1908

THE movement spread quickly. As early as mid-February 1908, Renick of Glasgow led meetings in Hillhead Hall, Kirkintilloch. The local newspaper stated that, 'Following the evening meeting there was a prayer meeting which, it would seem, got into a very hysterical state. Two or three of those present began to talk in an incoherent way, similar to the manner in which the Kilsyth people are said to have been affected, and the meeting became so excited that several women were in a fainting condition. The affair has caused much speculation in the town.'[30]

---

28. *KGLCR*, 31 July 1908.

29. *Confidence*, October 1908. An article written on the centenary of the Kilsyth movement said that 'some people today speak of collective mass hysteria and the temporary nature of many of the conversions'; also that in and around the town there are still many family names that appear in accounts of both the 1908 revival and previous ones in the town (*Kilsyth Chronicle*, 22 February 2008).

30. *KGLCR*, 21 February 1908.

An unusual story was told from one village near Kilsyth in which

> the little Chapel got on Fire, and about 20 received their 'Pentecost' with signs following, and 13 have been soundly converted. They were holding a 'Fellowship Meeting' for those who had been fully anointed. Outsiders, hearing the vehement cries of praise and the speaking in tongues, gathered round. A sympathetic policeman kept the door (his wife and daughter, who had received the blessing, were inside). At last he cried, 'Lads, I can stand it no longer, here goes,' and he flung open the door, and, putting down his helmet, was soon pleading with God for the full baptism of the Holy Ghost, and he received it then and there and came through speaking in tongues.[31]

After attending meetings in Kilsyth, a group of ten people from Coatbridge waited on God from house to house every night for five weeks. In time, someone would receive 'the baptism of the Holy Ghost', then another and another, until eventually all 'came through'. Soon folk were flocking to Coatbridge from Airdrie, Motherwell and many other nearby communities.[32]

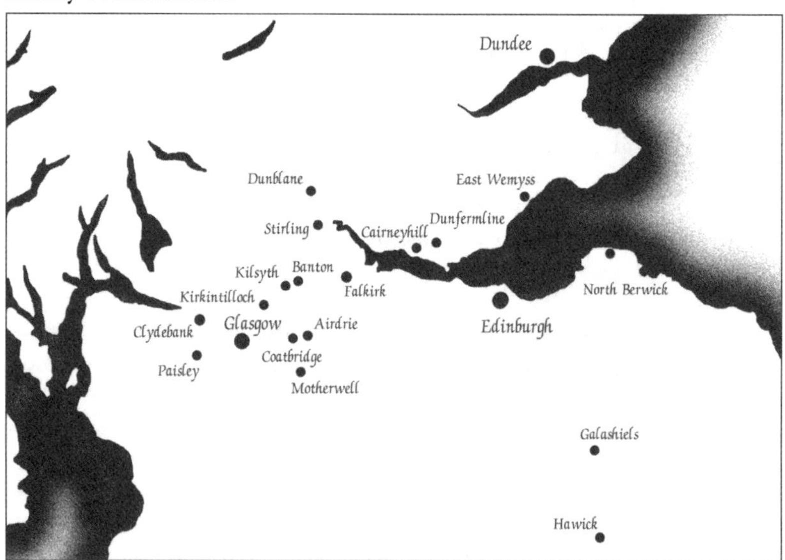

A man from Clydebank relates the story of Pentecostal beginnings in that town. His mother had been visiting friends in Kilsyth, and brought to her home church news of how God was working in that town in Pentecostal power. This greatly quickened the hearts of quite a few, and at the close of the after-meeting the following Sabbath, when the closing hymn was announced, 'not an individual made a move, for it seemed as

31. *Confidence*, April 1908.
32. Ibid., May 1908, July 1908.

if some were on their knees, and others on their faces crying, and waiting we did not really know what for'.

A small group journeyed to Kilsyth the following weekend. Greatly impressed with what they there witnessed, they returned home to set aside three nights in the week to wait upon God. 'Night after night we met, expecting God to work in a new way. But no outward manifestations were witnessed in those waiting times, only the hunger was deepening.' Then one Sabbath evening, following meetings in which 'God had fastened us to the floor' throughout the day, 'suddenly a young man in the front seat was raised to his feet and then fell on his back on the floor, and lay there under the power of Almighty God. … He lay there for a while, his jaws going, when at last God took his tongue and he began to speak and sing in an unknown tongue,' continuing in this manner for fully three hours.

By this time a curious crowd had gathered outside, followed, in the early hours of the following morning, by two policemen, who had been called upon by some anxious tenants. The officers were invited in, where they watched proceedings 'for a few moments in amazement' before taking their leave. These meetings were continued for a month or more with few further manifestations occurring. Then, in early March, a team from Kilsyth arrived. At one meeting, two or three people began to speak in tongues for the first time. This kindled an even greater yearning in the hearts of others who so longed for this gift, so after the close of the meeting a group of seekers gathered in a private home. 'We all got down on our faces before God,' said the Clydebank witness. 'I lost sight of all that was surrounding me and began to plead the Blood, and before long I began to feel myself going on to my back, and then one of the sisters from Kilsyth laid hands on me, and before long I felt my tongue going and could in no way stop from singing in an unknown tongue. It was a hallowed day … .'[33]

Further south in Scotland at the start of 1908, Welsh revivalist Fred Clarke[34] was conducting revival meetings in the Railway Mission, Hawick. As a result of this Andrew Turnbull 'was marvellously baptised in the Holy Spirit, speaking in tongues for a long time. His friends in the Railway Mission and the Baptist Church feared he was mentally unbalanced. During the year this rejection increased and towards the end of the year he was forced to resign his positions and membership in both the Church and the Mission. He then formed a Pentecostal Assembly with twelve women and two men who were all baptised in the Holy Spirit. The gifts of tongues, interpretation of tongues and healing

33. Ibid., December 1908.

34. Just a few years earlier, Clarke had received a special anointing from God during the Welsh revival. He later became a prominent revivalist in the lead-up to the Fishermen's Revival of 1921–2.

were all in use and up to 20 people attended the services. During this period his son, Thomas, aged nine, was miraculously healed of the croup.'[35]

EARLY DEVELOPMENT OF THE MOVEMENT 1909–15

THE Dunfermline, Kilsyth, Coatbridge, Clydebank and Hawick churches were among Scotland's first Pentecostal congregations, and during the year 1908 and those immediately following, the Pentecostal movement spread rapidly throughout the country, though not managing to penetrate the Presbyterian Highlands.[36] In less than three years, and generally before the end of 1908, centres had sprung up in Edinburgh, Glasgow, East Wemyss, Dundee, North Berwick, Galashiels, Dunblane, Stirling, Paisley, Airdrie and Motherwell, as well as in smaller communities such as Cairneyhill, Banton and Moffathill, near Airdrie – all of which 'had their little waiting bands whose lives God was touching with blessing and power'.[37] The first Pentecostal denomination to arise in Scotland was the Pentecostal Church of Scotland, formed by George Sharpe in 1909.[38]

In January 1908 Eilif Beruldsen, an elder at Charlotte Baptist Chapel, Edinburgh, made the journey, along with his wife, Christina, to Boddy's church in Sunderland, where they both received a baptism in the Spirit. On their return they were allowed to share their testimony in their home church – just once! 'Thenceforth,' writes Donald Gee, 'they shared the obloquy meted out to all who confessed to having spoken in tongues.' Undaunted, the Beruldsens commenced fruitful Pentecostal meetings in their large house in Murrayfield, later transferring to a beautiful home by the Firth of Forth. They also opened a Pentecostal Mission Hall in Leith, despite this area already being 'overstocked with little Mission Halls of that type'.[39] In 1911 'remarkable times of blessing' were being reported

---

35. *Confidence*, December 1908. Inflammation of the upper airway that leads to a cough that sounds like a bark. Just three years later, at the age of 12, young Thomas Turnbull 'received the gift of prophecy and later was recognised as the assembly Prophet' (Weeks, *Chapter Thirty Two (part of)*, p. 34).

36. Alex Muir recalls that in the 1960s 'a group of us, who were in Kilsyth as a deputation from Hermon Baptist Church, Glasgow, were talking to an old man who had witnessed the revival of 1908. Thrilled with the account he gave us of that wonderful time, we began to sing slowly the words of Psalm 100 to "the Old Hundredth". The experience was powerful. Heaven came down!' (Personal communication, 21 September 2003).

37. Donald Gee, in his book *Wind & Flame*, published in 1967, said that 'the work at Westport Hall has flourished to this day, and as recently as 1934 nearly 50 of the younger members of the Assembly received the fullness of the Spirit inside one week of renewed Pentecostal Revival' (Croydon, p. 32).

38. This Church united with the Pentecostal Church of the Nazarene in November 1915, bringing with it eight churches, 665 members and property worth £15,000 (Anonymous, *The Church of the Nazarene in the British Isles*.).

39. Donald Gee, *These Men I Knew: Personal Memories Of Our Pioneers*, London 1980, pp. 17–18.

from the Hall.[40] By this time the Beruldsens had five grown-up children who claimed to be filled with the Holy Ghost and keen to grow in their faith. Mrs Beruldsen said that she had tried for twenty-five years to win her children for Christ, but had failed. However, after her own 'Pentecost' she began to praise God that He was going to save every one of them, and she was absolutely delighted to report that He had done it.[41]

A Pentecostal Conference was held in Edinburgh in January 1910, the first of many led by the Beruldsens.[42] Many testimonies were shared from conference attendees. One man said he used to be a 'tramp' but now he was 'tramping on with Jesus'. An ex-actor referred to as 'Brother Michael' made the claim that he had 'seen Jesus in a vacant chair on the platform'. 'Brother Stewart' of Edinburgh said he had been twenty years an elder in the Free Church, but 'had been attracted by the face of a Pentecostal Singer in a railway carriage ... had a vision afterwards of the Saviour in the garden, with the drops of bloody sweat. ... The Book is all new to him now. Jesus has come to stay now, no longer a visitor.'[43]

Following a tour of numerous assemblies in Central Scotland in 1911, Mrs Crisp of the Pentecostal Missionary Union was 'much impressed with the steadfastness of the work. Many drunkards have been reclaimed through open-air work, and the life in many of the Assemblies seemed to be deepening all the time ... the work was most encouraging.'[44] It was in this year, too, that the testimony came from a Jessie H. Millie of Stirling that all six members of her household had received the baptism of the Holy Ghost.[45]

The work in Kilsyth, too, grew from strength to strength. A New Year's Conference in the town at the start of 1909, at which English Pentecostal leader Cecil Polhill spoke, saw twenty-eight offer themselves for the foreign mission field at one meeting. Some of these expressed a wish to go to China, following in the footsteps of a previous intrepid missionary from their locality – W.C. Burns.[46] In 1911, famous converted Bradford plumber turned 'Apostle of Faith', Smith Wigglesworth, among others, spoke at a Pentecostal Conference held in the town.

The following year Murdoch stated that the Lord was 'blessing very abundantly in our midst'. As well as a 'Band of Hope' group of over 100,

---

40. *Confidence*, August 1911.

41. Ibid., January 1910.

42. Diana Chapman, *Searching the Source of the River: Forgotten Women of the British Pentecostal Revival 1907–1914*, London 2007, pp. 84–98. A central argument of Chapman's book is that many of Britain's early Pentecostal pioneers – including Christina Beruldsen – were women, a fact largely overlooked by later Pentecostal leaders.

43. *Confidence*, November 1910.

44. Ibid., December 1911.

45. Ibid., April 1911.

46. Nearer home, outreach work was begun in Condorrat and Queenzieburn in 1913 and 1917 respectively.

they now had 103 church members, six of whom were very recently converted. 'Every week souls are being saved and added to the church, without any outside help. ... We have not received any wrong messages, they are all on the line of the Word. ... We never accept anything unless the counterpart is in the Word.'[47] In early 1913, Murdoch reported: 'Three received a real fiery baptism in our home last week, something like what took place at the beginning, and the Lord is saving souls every week. I was kneeling last night amongst the snow with a young man who called me as I passed. He pitched a bottle of whisky over the bridge, and gave himself to Jesus, then we were on the public road on our knees. ... We have now a very large congregation – 300 on Sabbath night; 80 at prayer meeting on Wednesday; Sabbath School, 300, 200 in attendance. ...'[48]

Andrew Turnbull moved from Hawick to Portobello, just east of Edinburgh, in 1912, after receiving confirmation through prayer that this was the will of God. At first a congregation met in a large room in someone's house. Here the work grew quickly, mainly due to the 'remarkable healings' that were being experienced.[49] Soon after a church was erected and Smith Wigglesworth was one who ministered at special meetings in the new sanctuary.[50] By 1914 it was reported that 'the Lord is working here. Souls are being saved and baptised ... the children – including all of Turnbull's offspring – also have got saved and baptised with the Holy Ghost. They held a little prayer meeting about a week after they got saved. They pleaded the Blood, and the Lord wonderfully spoke through five of them, ages twelve, ten, eight and seven.'[51] However, revelations given through prophecy, sometimes through these young ones, led to some agitation and disturbance, and caused a degree of concern to the church leadership.

GLASGOW 1916–33

FOLLOWING a prophecy from Andrew Turnbull's young son, Tom, in 1916, the Turnbull family moved to Glasgow as an act of faith. Here, as a result of open-air work, the room in their house became too small for

47. Ibid., April 1912. Not everyone agreed. Sadly, due to dissension over a prophecy, in 1911 many in oversight of the church resigned, and eventually Murdoch and some others established a separate assembly, as part of the Apostolic Faith Church, led by W.O. Hutchinson of Bournemouth.

48. Ibid., February 1913. John Long paid many visits to Westport Hall before and after 'the Spirit fell' in 1908. During a visit there as late as 1923, he wrote of God 'reviving His work in saving the young people, and adding them to the church' (Long, *Journal of John Long*, Chap. 17).

49. T.N. Turnbull, *Apostle Andrew*, Bradford 1965, p. 36; Weeks, *Chapter Thirty Two (part of)*, p. 33.

50. It was the author's privilege in 2006 to meet Kathleen Reeve, an elderly lady in Leytonstone, north London, who had known Wigglesworth well and, along with her late husband, used to host him during his visits to the city.

51. Weeks, *Chapter Thirty Two (part of)*, p. 39.

meetings and another home was secured.[52] The gathering – named the 'Burning Bush Assembly' – continued to prosper and a still larger hall was obtained in the city centre two years later.[53]

In 1919 the assembly joined the Apostolic Church of Wales. From that date, claimed Turnbull's biographer, and 'after many years of hard labour, through many trials, Mr Turnbull now saw wonderful progress. … Every Sunday night in that upper room from three to seven people were converted. The power of God was so real that unbelievers were coming forward at the beginning of the services, while the songs of Zion were being sung. Between 1920 and 1928 there was a minor revival in the Glasgow church. The building, which seated 250 people, was sometimes full an hour before the service started.'[54]

By 1922 the membership of the Glasgow church was 150 – 50 men and 100 women. Eventually the number rose to 200, plus 100 in Shettleston church, four miles away. During 1920, the Glasgow church enrolled 109 new members and more than 100 were added each year for the next eight years. Turnbull baptised most of these, including a backslidden woman aged 102, who served the Saviour for another five years; as well as 'doctors, lawyers, school teachers, nurses, commercial travellers, clerks, artisans of all kinds'. At one New Year Convention 76 were baptised, followed by 77 more at five further services, making a total of 153 in six months. Open-air work played an important part in this growth. Sometimes hundreds would gather round – Turnbull's voice being so distinct that it is said that a lady in a nearby cinema heard him one evening, was convicted by his words, and rose and left the building.

A united service was held each Tuesday night, when, among others, members of a dozen assemblies within a 2d. tram-ride of the Renfew St Hall came together. Some unusual healings were reported at these meetings. 'Mr Turnbull used to give his old overcoats to a member of the Glasgow church. One night this member became ill when it was too late to send for the Pastor to come and pray for him. Remembering the pastor's coat hanging in the hall, he put it on. Later he testified that he was healed instantly.'[55]

In 1929 Turnbull conducted an evangelistic campaign in the city that embraced twelve meetings a week for four weeks. Attendance was rarely less than 400 and was sometimes more than double that, and 'at times the atmosphere was charged with revival power as the Holy Spirit moved mightily among the congregation'.[56] During this period, annual conventions were held in Glasgow, usually at the very start of each year.

52. Ibid., p. 50.

53. Ibid., p. 55.

54. Turnbull, *Apostle Andrew*, p. 58.

55. Ibid., pp. 49–53.

56. Ibid., p. 79.

These became increasingly popular, till in 1933, 1,500 met at the large Communion service in the morning, 2,000 attended the divine healing service in the afternoon, and 2,500 attended the gospel service at night, all in St Andrew's Halls. On each occasion 100 people were baptised in a special tank at the front of the hall.[57]

During the 1920s and early 1930s, the Apostolic Church grew rapidly, not only in Glasgow, but throughout Scotland. This was largely due to the pioneering efforts of Turnbull, who spent six months of the year away from home, preaching around the country, usually holding three or four-week campaigns in each town he visited (as well as three more months of most years labouring abroad!). As a result, five new assemblies were established each year over twelve years. By 1933 there were 56 assemblies in Scotland, the majority in the central belt or lowlands districts. Indeed, there were only two Apostolic groups north of Perth; one in Aberdeen, the other in Stromness, Orkney. From 1920 to 1933, membership of the Apostolic Church expanded from just 30 to some 1,600.[58]

WORK OF STEPHEN AND GEORGE JEFFREYS 1924–32

PENTECOSTAL groups other than the Apostolic Church were also flourishing during this period, while some of the many congregations that remained independent of any denomination also showed signs of growth. The Assemblies of God was established in 1924 and was promoted by the campaigns led by Welsh evangelist Stephen Jeffreys. In the summer of 1926 Jeffreys visited Edinburgh[59] and his special services there concluded with a meeting of such power that one man in attendance saw men literally gripping their seats under the convicting solemnity of the warning of judgment to come.[60] Many Scots, however, considered Jeffreys' style too emotional for their liking. In Larbert, for example, public appeals were not the 'done thing' and so no-one responded to the evangelist's entreaty. At a later date Jeffreys joked that when he retired he would like to settle in Larbert, as, apparently, no sinners dwelt there! [61]

---

57. Ibid., p. 60; Weeks, *Chapter Thirty Two (part of)*, p. 135. A 1928 Convention in Airdrie saw 750 people participate in the March of Witness through the streets of the town (Weeks, p. 129).

58. Ibid., p. 58. Turnbull obediently left the flourishing work in Glasgow, however, when, at the New Year Convention of 1931 it was 'prophesied' that he and his son should immediately relocate to County Durham. From his new base, Turnbull continued to minister faithfully; even engaging in demanding – and hugely successful – campaigns as far away as Nigeria and Sierra Leone. Meanwhile, the Glasgow church never recovered from the loss of its enterprising leader, and its vigorous forward ministry all but drew to a halt.

59. Smith Wigglesworth had conducted a 'powerful campaign' here the previous year (Gee, *Wind and Flame*, p. 133).

60. Ibid., p. 134.

61. Personal conversation with Desmond Cartwright, author, historian of the Elim Pentecostal Churches and founding archivist of the Donald Gee Center for Pentecostal and Charismatic Research, 10 November 2004.

The Elim Foursquare Gospel Alliance began in Northern Ireland in 1916, but it was only after the war that new assemblies were formed on the U.K. mainland. By this time Pentecostal leaders were urging upon their followers their views that the greatest revival of modern times was underway.[62] The spring of 1926 began the first of fourteen consecutive Easter Pentecostal celebrations in London's famed Albert Hall. Star attraction at these meetings was Elim founder George Jeffreys, brother to Stephen, but Pentecostals from all groupings were influenced by these gatherings.[63]

In January 1927 George Jeffreys made his first serious attempt in Scotland with a campaign in Glasgow. He was given encouragement by 600 people who arrived by train from Carlisle, where a new church had very recently been formed. On arriving in Glasgow, these supporters marched in procession from the station to St Mungo's Hall with Jeffreys leading in his chauffeur-driven car. Says Gee, 'The stiffer Presbyterian soil did not prove so immediately responsive to the somewhat emotional and spectacular characteristics of Foursquare Gospel campaigning, and it took several weeks of steady logical preaching of the Word before the people finally became gripped with its power in the Spirit of God. The move in Scotland was all the greater when it did come.'[64] By the time the meetings ended on 28 March the estimated number of professed conversions had risen to 1,500, with many also claiming physical healing.[65] The *Daily Express* reported: 'Scenes in Glasgow and the surrounding towns during the past four weeks rival the most emotional incidents in Scottish history.'[66]

In the years that followed, Paisley, Greenock, Dundee, Aberdeen and Edinburgh all became the scenes of notable campaigns that filled the largest and most famous halls in the land.[67] Jeffreys visited Greenock in 1929. Both the editor of *The Greenock Telegraph* and the ex-Provost of the town spoke in glowing terms of the meetings. Many came out of curiosity, hearing of the healings that were taking place. These included

62. Randall, *Evangelical Experiences*, p. 211.

63. Gee, *Wind and Flame*, p. 141.

64. Ibid., p. 140.

65. Desmond W. Cartwright, *The Great Evangelists: The Lives of George and Stephen Jeffreys*, Basingstoke 1986, p. 86. Another report suggests 750 as the number who 'publicly accepted Christ as their Saviour' in this campaign, in addition to 'a number who were converted in their seats'. Whatever the actual number of 'decisions', Pentecostal historian Donald Gee wisely suggests consideration of 'the great discrepancy between the large numbers who professed conversion … and the number of permanent converts who finally remained and united in resultant congregations' (Gee, *Wind and Flame*, p. 148).

66. *Daily Express*, 24 March 1927, quoted in A.W. Edsor, *The Foursquare Revival Mirror: Principal George Jeffreys and his Revival Party*, London 1937, p. 34.

67. Part of Jeffreys' success, particularly as his popularity grew, seems to have been his magnetic personality. A journalist from Edinburgh's *Evening Dispatch* attended his 1932 campaign in the Usher Hall. 'The air was electric. It was an overwhelming feeling of vital joy. It permeated the great hall. … Every person in the audience responded to the distant figure on the platform with extraordinary precision. Mr Jeffreys was obviously the channel of the electrical pulse throbbing throughout the hall. The sheer magnetism of the man dominates.' (Edsor, *The Foursquare Revival Mirror*, p. 34.)

the dramatic healing of two boys, both of whom were partially blind. When they responded to the appeal to give their lives to the Lord, they both found that they had received physical healing too.[68] On evenings when the Town Hall was not available, a large Parish Church in the East End of town was hired.[69]

With a visit to Dundee's Caird Hall in 1932, 'unprecedented scenes of revival were witnessed at meeting after meeting, a harvest of the city's youth having been garnered for Christ'. Edwin Scrymgeour, M.P. for Dundee 1922–31, was among those 'moved by the mighty truth that "God's revival fire is falling"' on the city.[70] Following Jeffreys' visit to Dundee the Pentecostal community grew considerably. In October 1932, the church here had a congregation of 650 in the morning and 820 at night. To cope with the crowds, which included many young people, another church was opened for a short time across the Tay in Broughty Ferry. Services were held most nights during the week as well, taxing the young minister of each congregation to his utmost.

In subsequent years Pentecostal churches flourished in fishing towns and villages along the north-east coast, but they never succeeded in penetrating the Highlands and Islands. Even in places where they did succeed, they had, during the fledgling decades of the movement, to constantly battle against much suspicion and opposition. Other evangelicals generally ostracised them, viewing them as a form of cult. On top of this there were numerous splits within congregations over methods of local church government and specific words of prophecy given, while there was also some conflict between the various Pentecostal groupings. For these and other reasons, Pentecostal membership in Scotland never reached truly impressive levels.[71]

---

68. Personal conversation with Desmond Cartwright, 10 November 2004.

69. This building became redundant a year later and was purchased by the Elim congregation, serving as their home for the next fifty years. During that time the church provided the ranks of Elim with more than a dozen ministers, two of whom became national President. They also gave Greenock several members of the local council, including a Provost. One who served as minister here at a later period was Desmond Cartwright, one-time editor of the *Elim Evangel* (Cartwright, *The Great Evangelists*, p. 96).

70. Edsor, *The Foursquare Revival Mirror*, p. 38.

71. The movement was stronger south of the border. By the end of the 1930s Elim had established around 280 congregations in Britain, the Assemblies of God 400 and the Apostolics 43 (Randal, *Evangelical Experiences*, p. 212).

Westport Hall, Kilsyth – p.422

Andrew Turnbull – p.432

George Jeffreys – p.435

Jeffreys' 'Revival Campaign', Glasgow – p.435

Part Five

AN APPRAISAL

Lord, in Mercy, Look on Scotland

Lord, in mercy, look on Scotland
See the scattered bones of martyrs;
Hear again the prayers they offered
For the land in which they suffered.
Generations now forgotten
Saw your splendour, felt Your power;
Fed upon the Bread of Heaven,
Drank from springs of life eternal.
Sinners wept with deep conviction,
As the Spirit moved upon them;
Strong men bowed the knee before You,
Hearts of flint by grace were broken.
Hillsides rang with joyful praises,
City streets were filled with singing;
Villages and lonely hamlets
Shone with light that came from glory.
Christ, exalted in a nation,
Pardoned sin and banished darkness:
Send another great awakening –
Give us Scotland or we perish! [1]

1. Words by the Rev. Alex Muir, from *Songs of Prayer and Praise: Tunes for Modern Versions of Metrical Psalms and Hymns of Revival*, 2003, copyright Bandleader Publications, and used with kind permission.

14
Revival Considerations

MANY books have been written giving detailed analyses of the central features of revival – when it is needed, how it might be expected to arise, its central characteristics, possible dangers, and so on. I do not wish simply to give laborious repetition of what has previously been observed by many other authors.[2] In the following pages I will focus on many less-discussed attributes and observations of revivals that have occurred in Scotland, with particular focus on movements in the 1880–1940 period.

Facilitators of Revival

EXPLANATIONS of what brings about a revival in a community or nation vary from those adopted by secular historians, who see them in purely sociological and psychological terms, to those viewed by conservative theologians, who regard them pre-eminently as divinely-ordained phenomena, requiring no further explanation. Whatever the reality, it is clear that a number of 'natural' factors may facilitate a revival's occurrence. These may include the following.

(1) *Political and social instability.* The dawn of the Reformation in the sixteenth century was marked both by political and social instability, stemming from governmental strife between king, clergy and nobles, the renaissance of learning and the increase of individual freedom among the populace. The revival movement of the 1740s, too, occurred at a time of political and social unrest, which occasioned the quashed Jacobite rebellion of 1745. The awakenings in the north of Scotland during the early 1800s also need to be seen in light of the social uncertainties of that time, in particular the notorious Highland Clearances. The various spiritual awakenings in Lewis in the 1880s occurred within the scenario of disgruntled crofters agitating for greater rights from landlords. Similarly, it is noteworthy that the revival movement among mining communities in central Scotland (such as Plean and Blackbraes, both in Stirlingshire) in the early 1920s occurred at a time of economic depression in the coal industry and deep social unrest among miners.

(2) *Ecclesiastical tension.* The European Reformation was preceded and essentially sparked by growing resentment at corruption within the

2. For thorough biblical and historical discussions on the main distinctive features of revivals, see e.g. Roberts, *Revival*; Wallis, *In The Day Of Thy Power*; Armstrong, *True Revival*; Edwards, *Revival*; Davies, *I Will Pour Out My Spirit*; Murray, *Pentecost Today*.

Catholic Church and the bondage under its all-pervading authority. The revival movement from 1839–44 should also be viewed against the backdrop of the Disruption of 1843, when around a third of the whole membership of the Established Church left to form the Free Church of Scotland. On a smaller scale, in Lewis at the turn of the twentieth century there was considerable ingathering of converts amidst the agitation caused by the union of the Free Church and UPC in 1900.

(3) *Poverty.* As biblical records and world history amply testify, people are more likely to turn to God in times of need than times of plenty. Indeed, revivals have often occurred during seasons of extreme economic hardship.[3] Two of the most striking bursts of religious revival along the north-east coast (1859–61, 1921–2) occurred in the immediate aftermath of desperately poor fishing seasons.[4] A series of unlikely factors created the desperate conditions among fishing communities in the latter period. Government subsidies were revoked, continental markets on which the British herring industry depended became hopelessly depressed, while unusual weather patterns resulted in appallingly poor catches during both the summer and autumn seasons. The impressive congregational growth of Kilsyth's Westport Hall in the closing years of the 1890s, and the remarkable spiritual outpouring on the place in 1908, occurred at times when poverty was rife in the town and when housing stock was amongst the worst in Britain.

It is common for secular historians to explain evangelical revivals in terms of economic hardship, as if this factor alone accounted for their appearance.[5] But it is of course important to recognise that poverty does not always lead to revival. The poor herring harvest of 1908 left the fishing fleet on the Moray Firth in an unparalleled state of indebtedness. Yet no significant revival was experienced among fishing communities in that year.[6] Taking a wider perspective, during the period of economic depression in America in the 1930s following the Wall Street crash of 1929, few, if any, religious revivals took place in that vast nation.[7] The same could be said of Britain during this very same

---

3. In complete contrast to contemporary revivalism. Steve Latham points out, in his essay 'God came from Heman', that instead of occurring among 'landless peasants or dispossessed urbanites, [revivalism] occurs among the rich middle-class Westerners' (Walker and Aune, *On Revival*, p. 180). Although few reports state so explicitly, crop failure – especially of the potato – during the period 1836–46 no doubt had an influence on the increased spiritual interest in many districts of Scotland around that time.

4. It is notable in this regard that most Scottish revivals have had their deepest influence among the working class (see the section, 'Converts of Revival,' pp. 453–5).

5. e.g., E.P. Thompson famously coined the phrase 'chiliasm of despair' to explain the astounding early growth of Methodism (*The Making of the English Working Class*, Harmondsworth 1986, p. 411).

6. Conversely, the 1880 herring season enjoyed unprecedented success all along the east coast 'and a most bountiful harvest of fish has been reaped from Arbroath to Lerwick' (Robert Walker, *The Diary of Robert Walker of Richmond, 1815–1890*, The North East Folklore Archive [www.nefa.net]). Yet this did nothing to dampen revival fires that had been lit along the Moray Coast earlier in the year (see pp. 200–2).

7. McClymond, *Encyclopedia of Religious Revivals in America*: Introduction.

period. What we can say, then, is that economic uncertainties are one of many factors that contribute to religious awakenings in a community. As Donald Meek has pointed out in his essay 'Fishers of Men,' '"Portmanteau theories" which link spiritual experience to secular dislocation may be convenient, but they are often just too handy, too easy to take off the ideological shelf.'[8] A whole range of perspectives needs to be considered, including those of national, local, spiritual and cultural significance. With particular regard to the 'Fishermen's revival' of 1921–2, Meek discusses each of these influences in some detail.

(4) *Disease.* Before the days of vaccination, the spread of disease often caused alarm in communities and was likely to heighten consideration of eternal matters. The outbreak of cholera in the early 1830s had direct bearing on the revival that ensued in Granton-on-Spey, also igniting movements in other parts of the nation. Revival in Lewis in the 1920s and 1930s took place against a human background of grinding poverty, endemic tuberculosis, unemployment, emigration and the gathering clouds of another terrible war. But, as already noted, there is no clear-cut cause and effect with revival movements. Prior to the Kilsyth revival of 1742, neither an outbreak of malignant fever, nor a thunderstorm that devastated crops, livestock and houses, bringing some to the point of starvation, resulted in a turning to the Lord, despite the pastor's remonstrations. It was some time later, and after an improvement in economic conditions, that awakening came. Similarly, in many places where the dreadful cholera epidemic ran rampant, there appears to have been no consequential general spiritual awakening.

(5) *Danger and death.* In the Covenanting times of the seventeenth century, a 'plentiful effusion of the Spirit' fell upon many who gathered in conditions of secrecy and peril to celebrate the Lord's Supper at Obsdale, Kiltearn, Ross-shire.[9] The particular dangers connected with fishing and mining have had a strong bearing upon the spiritual awareness and prevalence of awakenings within these communities. James McKendrick connects stories of catastrophes in both industries, in the towns with which he had associations, to striking moves of the Spirit.[10] Indeed, the 'Great Gale' in November 1893, which led to the loss of a number of fishing boats from ports such as Buckie, Banff, Portsoy and Cullen on their return home from Lowestoft, may have had some influence on this evangelist's striking success along the north-east coast around that time.[11] Further south, in the Fife port of Cellardkye, the miraculous preservation of the crew of the *Taeping* 'had the most solemnising effect upon the people, and many came to the

---

8. Meek, *Fishers of Men*, pp. 42, 53.

9. Various, *The New Statistical Account of Scotland*, Vol. XIV, Inverness, Ross and Cromarty 1845, p. 267.

10. McKendrick, *What We Have Seen & Heard During Twenty-Five Years' Evangelistic Labours*, p. 32.

11. *Banffshire Journal*, 28 November 1893, p. 5.

meeting as "people prepared"'.[12] Sudden individual bereavements of well-loved members of a community can also play a part in the lead-up to an awakening – such occurred prior to the movements in the Bullers o' Buchan around 1880, Westray (1903), Motherwell (1904) and Cromarty (1905).

INSTRUMENTS OF REVIVAL

DUNCAN Campbell observed that 'God is the God of revival, but man is the human agent through whom revival is possible.'[13] The chief source He employs in bringing about revival is invariably men and women who are wholly yielded to Him and who therefore become conduits of His living word. A few of the most famous historical examples worldwide include John Wesley, George Whitefield, David Brainerd, Jonathan Edwards, Asahel Nettleton, Evan Roberts and Rees Howells. Very few indeed are the examples of revival where one zealous, godly individual is not a main means of heralding spiritual blessing. One apparent exception from our study appears to be the Lewis revival of 1934–9, often referred to as the 'Layman's Revival' because no specific preacher or preachers were at the centre of the movement, which was predominantly led by the laity.[14]

Revivals are invariably accompanied by preaching that is uncompromising, Christ-centred and demanding of personal commitment. Scottish Church history is adorned more than that of virtually any other nation with eminent preachers whose names are still renowned – John Knox, William Guthrie, James Haldane, John MacDonald, Alexander MacLeod, Andrew Thomson, Thomas Chalmers, William Chalmers Burns, Robert Murray McCheyne, Roderick MacLeod, and a host of others. Many of these men were of course connected with powerful moves of the Spirit in different parts of the country.

In a few instances, however, the leaders of spiritual awakenings have not been known for particularly powerful or articulate preaching.[15] So, while William McCulloch was not regarded as the most eloquent of preachers, his diligent sermons on the nature of regeneration led to 'a more than ordinary' impression on his congregation in Cambuslang in the 1740s.[16] Similarly, in

---

12. McKendrick, *Seen and Heard*, p. 177. In the same town twenty-five years previously, seven men perished at sea, making a deep impression on the villagers, and 200 of them – mainly men – turned up to the prayer meeting the following Friday, leading to a remarkable awakening (William Reid, *Authentic Records of Revival*, London 1860, reprinted 1980, p. 463).

13. Duncan Campbell, *The Lewis Awakening 1949–53*, quoted in Peckham, *Heritage of Revival*, p. 166.

14. Though, even here, we have to remember that in the narratives of this awakening, parish by parish, several ministers' names do appear repeatedly, especially those of John MacIver of Carloway and William Campbell of Point – suggesting that the ministries of these men were indeed very significant to the movements that took place in their respective districts.

15. William Couper was of the opinion that in most Scottish revivals, preachers have been men of 'ordinary gifts' (Couper, *Scottish Revivals*, p. 157).

16. Even his own son, Dr Robert McCulloch of Dairsie, said of him that he was 'not a very ready speaker; he was not eloquent … his manner was slow and cautious, very different from that of popular orators' (Couper, p. 42).

Stornoway in 1880, Donald John Martin was not 'in the front rank' regarding delivery of the Word, but yet 'made much of man's sin, man's need, and man's quest',[17] and several seasons of revival ensued. In the same town ninety years later, Murdo MacRitchie was noted more for his potent, heart-felt prayers and deep love for his congregation than for striking deliveries from the pulpit; yet attendance at his services rose steadily and a period of awakening followed.[18] It is apparent that no particular oratorical power is essential in initiating a revival. What is required is simple, direct, response-demanding and Bible-based preaching that touches the whole man – his mind, emotions and will.

The main human instruments in the vast majority of evangelical awakenings recorded in this study – and indeed in revival history worldwide – have been men.[19] In contrast, one would be hard-pushed to name a single woman who has been pre-eminent in heralding a season of spiritual blessing in Scotland during this period. This, no doubt, has much to do with the Church's traditional stance of allowing only male ministers, and a similar reluctance in accepting female evangelists. Among the few groups to break from this tradition have been the Brethren (in their early years), the Faith Mission and the Salvation Army. Thus it is that the only instances of women preachers leading a time of significant spiritual quickening during our period of study was in Stenhousemuir in 1905 (Salvation Army), West Benhar in 1922–3 (Faith Mission), in a Sunday school class (Alyth 1889) and in connection with a team of Welsh revivalists – among whom women had become prominent – in Glasgow in 1905.[20]

One cannot help remarking how often revivals in Scotland have occured as a result of one of the following three scenarios.

(1) *The arrival of a new, usually young, minister in the area.* On many occasions, awakenings have begun well within a couple of years of a new minister taking up his charge.[21] It would appear that some combination of the congregation's anticipation and expectations of the new incumbent, along

17. MacFarlane, *Donald John Martin*, pp. 78–80.

18. Personal communication with several members of the Stornoway FC congregation.

19. Many names stand out – William Ross, Donald John Martin, James McKendrick, Edward Last, Duncan MacColl, Alexander Frazer, Joseph Kemp, Kenneth MacRae, Fred Clarke, Jock Troup, David Cordiner, Roderick MacLeod, John MacIver, William Campbell, Henry Drummond, D.P. Thomson, Andrew Turnbull.

20. Even with regard to the two main groups mentioned – the Faith Mission and the Salvation Army – it is male evangelists whose names are more conspicuous in regard to Scottish awakenings; e.g., J.G. Govan, D. Campbell, Adjutant Boyce.

21. This has been evident throughout the centuries, e.g. in the case of John Balfour of Nigg (1729); John Farquerson, Breadalbane (c. 1800); John MacDonald of Ferintosh (1813); Alexander MacLeod of Uig (inducted 1824); Horatio Bonar, Kelso (1837); Alexander Somerville, Glasgow (1837); John Milne of Perth (1838); Rev. MacLean of Tobermory (1843); Andrew Bonar of Finnieston (1856); John MacLean of Carloway (1858). This is in distinction to the more exceptional experience of several ministers. David Carment of Rosskeen was well advanced in years when revival came to his parish in 1840, while, in 1846, in the last year of his life and lengthy ministry in Ferryden, Dr Brewster witnessed a movement among the fisherfolk of that village.

with the latter's own excitement and sense of bold expectation at the prospect of the new charge, plus his charisma, fresh style and new initiatives, might all play a role in the lead-up to a revival. Interestingly, this feature is less true of revival movements occurring in the Outer Hebrides, many of which have taken place during the well-established ministry of the parish minister. It also tends not to have held true for revivals in north-east coast communities, the majority of which were not inaugurated by local ministers but by visiting evangelists, or by the spread of revival from nearby communities.

In general, however, we can note that the arrival of a young, energetic minister to a parish can greatly help in bringing about a revival. Almost immediately on the arrival of young Samuel Chadwick for three years' probationary service to the Methodist circuit of Clydebank in 1897 did a dramatic burst of revival activity arise. Just a few months after George Moir of Aberdeen became pastor of the Congregational Church in Avoch in 1885, revival began in the village. The arrival of zealous revivalist William Ross at Cowcaddens Free Church in 1883 quickly led to spectacular church growth, with an incredible 1,050 new members in the three years up to the end of 1886. The youthful Alexander Frazer only went to Campbeltown Free Church for a period of six months' assistantship in October 1896, but in no time an awakening had developed in both town and country areas, which in turn spread through much of the Kintyre peninsula. A similar movement began in Queen Street Free Church, Inverness, in the late summer of 1898, after Frazer moved there for a few months as assistant minister. Similarly, within just a few weeks of Adjutant Boyce taking position as leader of the Ayr Salvation Army Corps in November 1907, a glorious revival had commenced, which continued through almost the whole of the following year, drawing hundreds to the foot of the Cross. Meanwhile, in Lewis, D.J. Martin was four years into his pastorate in Stornoway when a most significant revival took place, while it wasn't long after twenty-eight year old Roderick MacLeod was settled in Ness in 1920 that a wonderful revival swept through that Lewis parish.

(2) *The preaching of a visiting evangelist or minister from outside the area.* Especially from the turn of the nineteenth century, when itinerant preaching became more common, this phenomenon has been repeatedly evident. For example, the widespread labours of men like James Haldane, John Farquerson, William Chalmers Burns, James Turner and Duncan Matheson have all helped prepare the way for revival in Scotland. Similarly, a fascinating picture emerges from our current period of study. The great majority of revival movements in east-coast fishing ports had, as part-impetus, the ministry of visiting evangelists. Notable examples include James McKendrick, who saw repeated bursts of revival along a stretch of the north-east coast in the 1890s, and Jock Troup and Peter Connolly, who paid visits to numerous towns and villages with the hope

of igniting revival fires. Conversely, virtually none of the movements in the Outer Hebrides employed the use of evangelists from outside the islands. It seems clear that in these parts evangelical awakenings were still generally of the traditional type, led principally by the parish minister, with his emphasis on the bold preaching of the Word of God.

Elsewhere in Scotland, more than half of the revival movements discussed in this book have included as a motivating feature the preaching of visiting evangelists. Recurrent examples include the ministry of Welsh revivalists in various towns of central Scotland in 1905, the work of the 'Albatross Mission' during that same first decade of the twentieth century, and the work of many Faith Mission Pilgrims in their incessant labours throughout Scotland. A notable exception appears to be the spates of revivals within the Salvation Army in 1905 and 1908, none of which began through outside evangelists. Sometimes, of course, the influence of visiting evangelists in revivals has occurred through their invitation to speak at Communion services (see next section).

(3) *A powerful post-conversion experience of the Holy Spirit in the life of a preacher.*[22] Shortly before revival broke out under his preaching in Ross-shire and subsequently Breadalbane in the second decade of the nineteenth century, the Rev. John MacDonald came under 'a fresh baptism of the Spirit' whereby his preaching became 'instinct with life. It was now searching and fervent, as well as sound and lucid.'[23] Three years before his visit to Edinburgh in 1873, D.L. Moody wrote: 'God revealed himself to me, and I had such an experience of His love that I had to ask him to stay His hand. I went on preaching again. The sermons were not different: I did not present any new truths; and yet hundreds were converted.'[24] Four years after being born of the Spirit in 1886, teenager John Harper experienced a baptism of power and an increased passion for souls. Almost immediately he became a fiery evangelist and went on to experience 'constant revivals' in the Glasgow church that he founded.

Jock Troup experienced an infilling of the Spirit in Aberdeen in 1921 just prior to his being remarkably used during the 'Fishermen's revival'. 'Something glorious happened to Jock,' wrote a friend, 'so precious that he rarely spoke about it in subsequent years, and then only in hushed tones. He had to leave the meeting … and asked God to restrain his hand.'[25] When Duncan Campbell made a fuller yielding to God prior to the 1949–53 Lewis revival, 'a new consciousness of the love of God swept over him like waves of

22. This scenario became more apparent from the mid-1800s, and was no doubt partly influenced by the growing Holiness movement.

23. John Kennedy, *The Apostle of the North: The Life and Labours of John MacDonald of Ferintosh*, Glasgow 1978, p. 29.

24. Murray, *Pentecost Today*, p. 98.

25. Mitchell, *Revival Man*, p. 50.

the sea until he wondered if he could endure it any longer. … This night of encounter with God was felt immediately in his preaching and praying.' [26]

OTHER CHANNELS OF REVIVAL

THE LORD'S SUPPER

WHILE in the great majority of cases the main instrument of revival is a powerful, charismatic preacher, sometimes there are other conduits that channel the flow of revival power – these usually feature in addition to the main instrument rather than in place of him. In Scotland revival has often been closely associated with Communion seasons.[27] These were traditionally held bi-annually and attracted participants from far and near, creating a deep sense of spiritual expectancy among those attending. Commonly ministers from other parishes would come to help at these functions, and occasionally during such times revival would break out, or an existing awakening deepen in influence.[28]

The influence of Communions on revivals – and vice versa – is much less apparent from the 1850s onwards, except in the Hebrides. In our study Communion seasons play a prominent part in only one or two – for example, the Canisbay 1886 and Burghead 1921 revivals. The latter movement, especially, is exceptional; generally revivals along the north-east coast have showed little direct connection with Communions, being more commonly associated with the weather, occurring mainly during winter months, when fishermen were not at sea.

On the other hand, the Lord's Supper features again and again in reports of awakening in the Western Isles.[29] With regard to the Lewis revival of 1934–9, people attending Communion in a district where revival fires were burning often came under conviction or received a fresh anointing, and thus helped ignite revival in their home communities on their return. This certainly appears to have been the case regarding the commencement of revivals in Point and Barvas in 1938–9. More recently, a Communion weekend in Broadford, Skye, in 1980 played a significant role in the localised awakening taking place at that time.[30]

---

26. Woolsey, *Channel of Revival*, pp. 98, 100.

27. Or, as Couper put it, they have been 'intimately associated with the most personal, loving, and evangelical rite the Reformed Church knows' (Couper, *Scottish Revivals*, p. 154).

28. Notable historical examples include Kirk of Shotts, 1630 (under the ministry of John Livingstone); Cambuslang and Kilsyth, 1740s, under George Whitefield; and Breadalbane 1816 and Uig, Lewis, 1827 under John MacDonald of Ferintosh.

29. Movements that took place in Harris 1883–6, Back 1880s, Point 1886–8, Lewis, Harris and Uist 1888–91, Lewis 1900–1, 1905 and 1910, Arran 1916, Point 1921 and Kilmaluag, Skye 1923–4 are all cases in point.

30. Personal communication with the Rev. Jack MacArthur, CoS minister in Broadford at the time of the movement, 14 July 2001.

REPORTS AND TESTIMONIES

AMONG the most common avenues by which revivals travel are reports or direct testimony. The hearing of God's unusual work in one location can help create conditions for His Spirit to move in another. Such was the case in Kilsyth in 1839 where revival commenced after W.C. Burns related the story of the Kirk of Shotts awakening two centuries previously. Such was also the means whereby, on hearing of the astounding Moody campaign in Edinburgh and Glasgow, awakening was stimulated in many rural towns and villages throughout Scotland.[31] Again, such was the means, as this study testifies, by which the Welsh revival of 1904–5 spread to various places in Scotland – and indeed throughout many parts of the world. A localised movement occurred in mid-Antrim, Northern Ireland, in 1958, following a six-month series of Bible studies, during which accounts were shared of previous awakenings, including the dramatic Ulster revival 100 years previously, and the very recent awakening in North Uist.[32]

Very often local interest has intensified following testimonies from visiting speakers or a church member who has been to the scene of a revival. In the 1740s a number of church leaders from as far away as Ross-shire and Sutherland travelled to Cambuslang or Kilsyth at times of Communion there, bringing back accounts of revival with them and sparking off awakening in their home areas. Such was common too during the 1904–5 Welsh revival, when many made the journey to the principality to see the movement for themselves, bringing home stirring reports which quickened their own congregations. Similarly, it was after one member of Kilsyth's Westport Hall went to see the Pentecostal movement in progress in Sunderland, and after two others heard the Rev. A.A. Boddy speak in Edinburgh, that revival broke out in the Kilsyth congregation.

Preachers used in one awakening also act as heralds of that awakening in other places they visit. This was true in the life of D.J. Martin, who, having experienced revival in his own Stornoway congregation in 1880, saw the Spirit move in awakening power when he travelled to Inverness and Mull shortly after. Such was also the repeated case the following decade when revival spread along the Moray Coast in connection with the labours of James McKendrick.[33] Although Duncan Campbell is famed for his ministry in the Lewis revival of 1949–53, he also played

---

31. Couper gives numerous other examples from the pre-1880 period of the 'golden thread of connection' which has linked revivals together (Couper, *Scottish Revivals*, p. 155).

32. William Fleming, *If My People: Demonstrating the Spirit's Power in Revival*, Fearn 2000, p. 15, photos.

33. It was also especially true in the ministry of J. Edwin Orr, a life-long student of revivals, who experienced awakenings in many places in which he preached, most notably Ngaruawahia, New Zealand in 1936, at some colleges in America in 1949–50, and in Brazil, 1951.

a part in several other movements, such as in Skye (1949), North Uist (1957–8) and even, indirectly, a movement in Saskatchewan, Canada in the early 1970s.

Revival also spreads infectiously through the direct witness of those newly converted. During a West Highland movement in the 1880s, a band of young converts from the granite quarries of Argyll crossed Loch Etive to bear witness in Bonawe, where awakening was also in progress. It was notably by such means also that revival fires blazed along the north-east coast of Scotland in 1921 when fishermen, lives dramatically changed by the love of Christ, returned home from East Anglia, eager to share their new-found faith. Many became bold soul-winners in their own communities, most notably Davie Cordiner of Peterhead, whose evangelistic efforts were the means of salvation for scores of people.

Characteristics of Revival

SINCE the Great Awakening of the eighteenth century in Europe and North America, and especially since the rise of the Protestant missionary movement from the beginning of the nineteenth century – itself an outcome of revival movements – evangelical awakenings have been recurring features of Church and social history in nearly all continents of the world. Certainly they have developed in different ways, and displayed varying characteristics depending on the theological position of both the main instruments of those revivals and the people groups among which they have occurred, and depending also on a whole range of social, political and other conditions prevailing.

Certain features, however, are viewed by revival historians as holding true of virtually all such movements. It is frequently noted that they generally begin during times of declension in the spiritual life of local congregations or, in the case of a general awakening, of the Church nationally. This, indeed, is very often the case. Prior to the Scottish Awakening of the 1740s, for example, the spiritual life of a great many congregations was at a very low ebb. The same was true prior to the movement that spread across the Highlands and Islands from the turn of the nineteenth century. In fact it often transpires that the deeper the declension, the greater the spiritual blessing that ensues.

As with so many general observations, however, the reality isn't always so black-and-white. The Church in Scotland in the years prior to the 1859–61 revival – the most widespread ever witnessed in the land – was not in a state of deep spiritual poverty. Just the previous decade (c. 1843) a powerful burst of spiritual life was fanned into flame in many congregations. Then in the early 1850s a new spirit of evangelism appears to have begun to affect the Church, particularly the Free Church, where Thomas Chalmers' urban community vision was revived, leading to one of the most effective periods of urban mission in the nineteenth century.[34] There was, in this case, a steady build-up of spiritual interest and evangelistic activity for a number of years before full-blown revival transpired.

Similarly there is little evidence to suggest that in the years just prior to the general awakening of 1905–6 the Scottish Church was in a particularly low spiritual condition. In fact it is remarkable how few are the reports in this book where a state of spiritual declension is specifically noted. Among those where such *is* stated are Falkirk (1882), Cowcaddens (1883), Edinburgh University (1884), Lismore (1895), Findochty and Portessie (1893) and Ness, Lewis (1922–6). There has, of course, been some controversy regarding the state of the Church in Lewis just prior to the revival of 1949–53: islanders have widely accepted that it was in a generally healthy condition, though, especially in the shadow of the war, there was increasing apathy among the young. In general, then, we can say that while there does not always exist a state of deep spiritual declension prior to a revival, there is often an awareness among believers that things are not what they ought to be, and a longing for God to move in revival power.

Another uncontested principle of revivals is that they usually have their initial influence among existing believers, before having a further impact among the non-churched. This is often the case; believers are revived and the effect of their energised prayers and outreach efforts, combined with the labours of any prominent 'instrument' of revival, has a subsequent impact on non-believers. In Rothesay, in 1889, Faith Mission Pilgrims initially conducted a meeting for Christians. This was followed by an extended time of prayer, and 'the coming of the Spirit to His own people'.[35] Believers were thus greatly revived, and such transformation had an almost immediate effect on Rothesay's inhabitants. Before long the entire town seemed to be stirred and hundreds were converted. It is notable, too, how blessing came to believers in Motherwell in 1904–5 over a period of months, when several Christian conventions, along with news of developments in Wales, all helped stir the hearts of believers. At one convention, addresses on sanctification and heart cleansing brought much soul-searching and repentance among believers. Revival broke out in the town very soon after, and scores of the unsaved were brought to the foot of the Cross.

In perhaps the majority of cases recorded in this book, however, believers and non-believers seem to have been impacted by the Spirit at the same time and in at least one instance it was the unconverted who were first impacted. When James MacFarlane held meetings in Findochty in 1903, great anxiety was manifested by the unsaved at the

34. See Jeffrey, *When the Lord Walked the Land*, pp. 52–3.

35. McLean, *Faith Triumphant*, p. 71.

very first meeting, but believers in the congregation seemed unmoved. Words of admonition by the evangelist led to many Christians spending the night in prayer and confession, and quickly their spiritual condition was transformed.

Many other characteristics of revivals tend to be more prevalent. They have as their focus Christ-centred preaching and the authority of the Word of God.[36] Deep conviction of sin (on the part of both believers and non-believers) is a necessary outcome of such focus, followed by genuine repentance, a release of peace and joy, and a marked change in lifestyle. Restoration of relationships is another prominent feature; the example of the Findochty revival of 1903, where longstanding feuds were 'buried in the tide of saving grace',[37] is far from unique. Revivals also result in increased attention to prayer, worship, evangelism and financial giving. While some revivals solely affect a particular age or social group, most tend to be community-based movements which influence people of virtually all ages (except, often, younger children, of whom the Scottish Presbyterian Church has traditionally had low spiritual expectations – see Chapter 12).

A consequence of the joy attained by new converts is an innate desire to fellowship with other believers. Informal house-meetings might be held somewhere or other every night of the week, often continuing into the early hours of the following morning, with people even then reluctant to part. Yet it is a strikingly recurring testimony that with only a few hours' sleep, believers are entirely able to carry out a normal day's work the next day. In a few exceptional instances there existed such spiritual intensity that whole nights were spent without sleep, and labour got temporarily abandoned. This occurred in the Breadalbane area in 1802, and has also been particularly notable in fishing communities; for example, among north-east fishing villages in 1860, in Findochty in 1880 and in that same village, as well as in Ferryden and Portknockie, in the 1890s, as a result of revivals inaugurated by James McKendrick.

Evangelical awakenings have a long association with new spiritual hymns and songs. These have been effective in spreading doctrines of a particular group, and were extensively used 'during the 20 years of struggles and suffering which preceded the full establishment of the Reformed Church' in the sixteenth century.[38] Horatius Bonar, who became known as 'the Prince of Scottish hymn writers', wrote over 600 hymns, a number of which (for instance, 'I Heard the Voice of Jesus say'

---

36. As in the Carloway revival of the 1930s, which was noted for 'the eager attention to which young and old listened to the Word' (MacAulay, *The Burning Bush*, p. 32).

37. *The Christian*, 30 April 1903, p. 23.

38. Couper, *Scottish Revivals*, pp. 5–6.

and 'Blessing and Honour and Glory and Power') became known all over the English-speaking world. 'The Ninety and Nine,' Sankey's most-loved hymn, was in fact composed in Scotland during the widespread 1873–4 revival inaugurated by Moody and Sankey's first visit, and was given spontaneous melody during a meeting in Edinburgh. Many other hymns and choruses have come into being during subsequent periods of revival: for example, among fishing communities, where many new indigenous spiritual songs – characteristically awash with sea-faring metaphors – became popular.[39] New songs also characterised revivals in Tiree in 1887–8, and particularly Lewis, 1949–53, when it was said that by 1952, over eighty Gaelic songs had been written.[40]

One recurring feature of revival movements is a deep awareness of the nearness of the divine. Sometimes, not just the church, but the whole community becomes God-conscious. Duncan Campbell claimed: 'Revival is neither more nor less than the impact of the personality of Jesus Christ upon a life or upon a community.'[41] This sense of God's nearness is often felt by believers and non-believers alike, causing not only many sinners to turn to Christ in repentance, but even many who remain careless in their ways to yet feel a sense of shame. A report of the revival at Cambuslang in 1742 speaks of 'the gracious and sensible presence of God'.[42] During the Rothesay awakening of 1888–9, J.G. Govan wrote: '*He* came near, and revealed the name of Love, and oh, I felt I had so little of His love, and was quite broken down at His feet.'[43] When the Spirit fell on Edinburgh's Charlotte Chapel in December 1906, 'Quite suddenly, upon one and another, came an overwhelming sense of the reality and awfulness of His presence and of eternal things,'[44] while in a time of awakening in Ross-shire around the same time, some spoke of many prayers being wonderfully answered 'because God was so gloriously near'.[45] Jackie Ritchie relates testimony times in the fishing villages of north Scotland in 1921–2 when 'the atmosphere was charged with the presence of God'.[46] During the North Uist awakening of 1957–8, one convert said she could 'never forget the sense of God's

39. e.g., see the song at the start of Part 2 (page 195).

40. Duncan Campbell, 'The Revival in the Hebrides', in *The Keswick Week*, London 1952, p. 147.

41. Black, *Revival: Including the Prophetic Vision of Jean Darnall*, Greenock 1993, p. 83. Thus it was in 1950 that the Lewis village of Arnol became 'alive with an awareness of God', while in Harris and other places, an 'awe-inspiring sense of the presence of God' pervaded the community, one man stating, 'I haven't been to church, but this revival is in the air. I can't get away from the Spirit' (Campbell, *Lewis Awakening*, pp. 174–5; Woolsey, *Channel of Revival*, p. 122).

42. Arnold Dallimore, *George Whitefield: The Life and Times of the Great Evangelist of the Eighteenth-Century Revival, Vol. II*, Carlisle, PA n.d., p. 129.

43. McLean, *Faith Triumphant*, p. 72.

44. Kemp, *The Record of a Spirit-Filled Life*, pp. 32–3.

45. Various, *A Wave of Blessing in Black Isle and Easter Ross*, Glasgow 1906, p. 23.

46. Ritchie, *Floods Upon the Dry Ground*, p. 54.

presence that pervaded Lochmaddy. It was an awesome presence, but there was with it a sense of security, love and joy.'[47]

An important aspect of evangelical awakenings is how long they endure. This generally varies from several days to a number of years depending on the nature of the movement. The vast majority of movements studied in this book lasted for several weeks or a number of months. Their duration is generally dependent on which of the three types of revival as defined by Kenneth Jeffrey that they come under (see pp. 26–8). Thus movements such as the Torrey campaign of 1903, or that led by Chapman in 1913–14, and Jeffreys' missions between 1927 and '32, generally lasted as long as the campaigns themselves, or a little longer. When, however, the pastor of a congregation has constantly engaged in revivalist operations in his church or community, having encouraged his workers to do likewise, then almost constant revivalist activity can continue over a period of years or even decades. Thus, Edward Last's nine years' ministry in Cambridge St Baptist Church, Glasgow was accompanied by, in George Yuille's words, 'all the features of revival'.[48] Even more outstanding was William Ross's ministry in Cowcaddens from 1883 to 1904.

Intense movements led by itinerant, and often lay, evangelists who view the experience of 'new birth' as immediate and climatic – as were especially common in fishing communities – tend to be sudden, dramatic affairs which burn out fairly quickly. It has to be said that the majority of movements discussed in Parts 1, 2 and 4 of this book fall loosely within this category.[49] The blessing that came to fishermen stationed in Girvan in 1885 lasted just two weeks (although a further awakening sprang up in Lochgilphead a few months later after the fishermen returned home). Similarly, the intense bursts of revival that accompanied McKendrick's labours along the north-east coast in the 1890s were mostly of brief duration. Revivals in the Salvation Army also fit the pattern described here; most of those related in this study were short and emotional, although the Ayr revival of 1908 was so powerful that it lasted almost a full twelve months. The outpouring that descended on Charlotte Baptist Chapel in the first decade of the twentieth century might also fit into this category; in that scenario there were several dramatic bursts of blessing – usually near the start of the year – between 1905 and 1908.

---

47. Ferguson, *When God Came Down*, p. 79. It is this uncanny nearness of God that causes so many revival converts to testify, 'You can't know what it's like unless you've experienced a revival yourself.' Those whose lives have been transformed by revival movements never forget such experiences and tend to be more dissatisfied than most with any subsequent spiritual dryness in a congregation.

48. Yuille, *History of the Baptists in Scotland*, p. 172.

49. There is often, however, a degree of overlap. A few mainland movements, particularly in the north, carry features of both type 1 (spontaneous outbursts of divine favour) and type 2 (sudden, dramatic revivals of short duration). These include Canisbay 1886, Kilbrandon 1889–9, Kirkintilloch 1897–8, Nigg 1903 and the Black Isle 1905–6. A few movements among children (e.g. Alyth 1889, Glasgow 1920s) also contain a spontaneous element characteristic of type 1 revival.

A third class is the traditional concept of revival, i.e. a spontaneous outburst of divine favour, led principally by the parish minister. Common in the sixteenth and seventeenth centuries, these were fairly protracted affairs, and while largely overtaken by the late nineteenth century by other, more immediate forms, still appeared here and there, particularly in the Western Isles, and solely within the Presbyterian tradition – predominantly the Free Church. Thus, embers of the quietly pervasive awakening that spread over the Southend district of Arran from 1916 were still burning two years later. The revivals that have lasted the longest, however, were those that occurred in the Outer Hebrides. The significant movement that arose in Harris in 1925 continued over several years. In Lewis, the remarkable awakening that spread across the island with the dawn of the twentieth century continued in some places – notably Carloway – right up to the outbreak of the First World War, and even beyond. Similarly, the 'Layman's revival' of the 1930s continued in varying degrees of intensity over a number of years from the middle of the decade. In Carloway the most significant periods of blessing occurred in 1934, 1936 and 1939, in which latter year war broke out and the revival drew to a close.

Converts of Revival

EXPERIENCE has proved that in general people are more likely to make commitments of faith during their teens or twenties than at any other period of life. As they grow older, there is less likelihood, statistically speaking, of them being converted.[50] Thus it should be no surprise to find that the vast majority of cases of awakening and conversion during times of revival have been among those within this same age bracket.[51] This is so prevalent a characteristic that any movement where this does not hold true is likely to be noted for that fact – as in cases of revival among children (see Chapter 12) – and as was the case regarding an awakening in the north-east fishing village of Rosehearty in the 1890s, when most of the converts were over thirty years old and a good number over fifty (and where the proportion of married converts to unmarried was as high as 5 to 1). Conversely, the conversion of people aged seventy or over – though much less uncommon during a revival than in the ordinary course of life – is usually considered, even within the progress of a spiritual awakening, to be remarkable enough for it to be specifically highlighted.

---

50. This fact is completely overlooked by David Wells in his study of Christian conversion (David F. Wells, *Turning to God: Biblical Conversion in the Modern World*, Carlisle 1989). One of the earliest studies on this theme showed that out of 1,000 Christians questioned, nearly 70 per cent were converted before the age of 20, and over 90 per cent before the age of 30 (A.T. Schofield, *Christian Sanity*, London 1908, p. 50).

51. Jeffrey estimated from a series of studies on revivals that 'between 73 and 90% of those who were "born again" during these religious movements in the 18th and 19th centuries were less than 30 years of age' (Jeffrey, *When the Lord Walked the Land*, p. 98–9). This, he notes, is broadly comparable with studies of those who experienced an evangelical conversion in the nineteenth century generally, where 'at least ¾ were less than 20 years of age' (p. 98). As the section in this book on awakenings among students shows (see Chapter 12), some movements have taken place almost exclusively among young men and women.

A number of factors may help explain this universal phenomenon. In Christian homes – from where a great number of converts come – there may be considerable encouragement from parents to 'decide for Christ'. People in the teens-to-twenties age group tend also to be more open to new ideas; indeed they will be intentionally seeking answers to the big questions in life. Not yet being set in their ways, this younger generation may also be more willing to risk major life changes and will be in search of excitement and adventure.

Revival converts are more likely to be female than male – this to be understood in light of the fact that those who attend evangelistic services, and indeed churchgoers generally, comprise a higher proportion of women than men. It is also argued that women are more emotionally susceptible and hence more likely to be swayed by the emotion-laden appeals of evangelists. Jeffrey suggests that 'women have accounted for between at least 60 and 70% of revival converts'.[52] To counter this imbalance, by the mid-nineteenth century evangelistic campaigns specifically aimed at men were being employed by Charles Finney, while the Y.M.C.A. – whose founder George Williams was strongly influenced by Finney's 'new methods' – was set up with the same aim. Moody also used men's meetings to counter the gender imbalance of revival converts, and of his campaign in Scotland in 1873–4, it could be successfully noted that 'perhaps the most striking feature of the whole mission was the way it seized upon young men'.[53] Exceptionally, though, revivals have occured where more men were brought under its influence than women. This was a notable feature of 'Roddie's revival' in Ness, Lewis in the early 1920s, while such an outcome was even more prominent in the initial stage of the Carloway revival the following decade.[54]

Most converts of revivals are from the working classes, where community links are nearly always the strongest and whose members are more likely to be open to changes in their lifestyle.[55] The 1857 awakening in North America started through thousands of businessmen meeting daily for prayer in New York and other cities. The national and international revival

52. Jeffrey, *When the Lord Walked the Land*, p. 103. This factor would account, too, for the observation that any physical phenomena that appear during a revival are far more likely to occur among women than men. This was apparent regarding, for example, W.C. Burns' campaign in Aberdeen in 1840, numerous Scottish locations during the first phase of the 1859–61 revival, and early Pentecostal meetings in Scotland (as, too, in Azusa St meetings from 1906).

53. Couper, *Scottish Revivals*, p. 148.

54. One gets the impression (quite wrongly), from reading Murdo MacAulay's account of the Carloway revival as a whole – i.e., extending from 1934 to 1939 – that the converts were nearly all men; a host of 'prominent' men are specifically named in connection with the movement and many stories are related with regard to them, whereas no direct mention is made of any female convert (MacAulay, *The Burning Bush*, pp. 32–53).

55. This is a world-wide phenomenon, though there have been a few notable exceptions, such as in the ministry of Lord Radstock among the Russian nobility of St Petersburg in 1874, whereby many of the aristocracy were converted and a spiritual awakening ensued (Mrs Edward Trotter, *Lord Radstock: An Interpretation and a Record*, London 1914, pp. 190–4).

that resulted, however, was predominantly among the working classes. Its spread to Scotland brought to the fore a number of respected 'gentlemen preachers' such as Brownlow North and MacDowall Grant of Arndilly, but its success, even in urban Aberdeen, was again mostly among young working class folk. The awakening that swept through Lanarkshire in 1905 occurred predominantly among working class communities. Similarly, it was said that the majority of people who flocked to the campaigns of George Jeffreys, himself from a mining class background, were largely working class folk.[56] It was observed of the 'Fishermen's revival' of the 1920s that even in the towns and villages most powerfully affected, the middle classes of society, who lived in a separate part of town from the fisherfolk, were much less moved by events.

There was more of a class balance during the Moody revival of 1873–4. Couper insisted that 'all classes without exception have been represented in the enquiry meetings,'[57] and MacPherson, commenting on the work in Scotland in general, was thankful for 'the increased number of persons of the middle and upper classes that have been reached', noting that 'the evangelisation of the rich and well-to-do … is one of the hardest of all tasks'.[58] While generally this movement flourished within ordinary working class communities, even in the rural Aberdeenshire hamlet of Cornhill, 'the work of grace was most signally developed among the better-educated class and in godly families, especially the families of elders and deacons'.[59] But it was particularly in Edinburgh and Glasgow that 'those under 25 and of the more educated classes' featured notably among the registered converts.[60] The modernising and refining of revival meetings helped give them a greater sense of respectability, and thus helped attract the higher classes to subsequent revival campaigns; for example, those of R.A. Torrey, Wilbur Chapman and Billy Graham.

Some later periods of awakening also stand out for not appearing solely or predominantly among the working classes. One such movement, again in Edinburgh, was that among students in the city's University following visits from members of the 'Cambridge Seven'. This resulted in a goodly number of conversions and an intense campaign of evangelism throughout the country. Again, during the awakening that spread across the South and West End of Glasgow during the same decade (1885–6), a union was formed, which soon boasted 180 young ladies and 120 men, 'all of them of the better classes in the West End of Glasgow'.[61]

56. Randall, *Evangelical Experiences*, p. 211.

57. Couper, *Scottish Revivals*, p. 150.

58. John MacPherson, *Revival and Revival Work: A Record of the Labours of D.L. Moody & Ira D. Sankey, and Other Evangelists*, London 1875, p. 45.

59. Ibid., p. 110

60. John Pollock, *Moody Without Sankey*, London 1963 (reprinted 1995), p. 138.

61. *RC-FCS-SR&M*, 1886, p. 61.

GEOGRAPHY OF REVIVALS

CERTAIN areas of Scotland have been repeatedly favoured with divine blessing. 'Seed sown long ago', claimed Couper, 'disappeared from sight and only required the appointed conditions to germinate. … There is an evangelical succession in such experiences.'[62]

The evangelical history of Ayrshire goes back to the Lollards of the fourteenth century. Since then it has hosted numerous famous revivals.[63] Since 1860, however, awakenings in this county have been few and far between. Similarly, Easter Ross, a refuge for Covenanting refugees as well as Commonwealth troops, was described by one historian as being in a former age 'one of the most Christian areas of the world'.[64] Numerous showers of divine blessing have fallen on this favoured region, although relatively few from the late 1800s.[65]

The Western Isles, in particular Lewis, Skye and Tiree, feature prominently in Scotland's revival legacy. Tiree has known a long succession of awakenings from 1839 to 1955, many in connection with the Baptist Church. Lewis, and, to a slightly lesser extent, Skye and Harris, have a fascinating and unique history of evangelical awakenings, a legacy unparalleled anywhere in the world – especially from the 1820s to the mid 1900s. In Lewis, during our period of study, the parishes of Barvas, Ness and Point all receive repeated mention in connection with revivals – Point being blessed by a remarkable four periods of awakening in just a quarter of a century (1935–58).

Great and recurring blessing has also fallen on Scotland's fishing-ports; in particular those along the Moray Firth coast. The effects of the lay preaching of fish-curer James Turner along this stretch of coast in 1861–2 were sensational and extraordinary, igniting powerful revivals almost everywhere he travelled. Since that time there have been periodic bursts of spiritual flames, particularly in Portessie and Findochty, which latter village saw seasons of refreshing every ten or twelve years right up to the turn of the twentieth century, and again in 1921–2. Further south,

---

62. Couper, *Scottish Revivals*, pp. 156–7. Couper perhaps overstates the case, however, in saying that 'once a name appears in the narrative of any revival, its recurrence in movements of later date is almost assured' (ibid.).

63. It became a renowned area in Covenanting times, the influence of which lingered on to the seventeenth century – when Scotland's first famed localised revival arose in Stewarton – and into the eighteenth, when revival spread south from Cambuslang. Ayrshire was also one of the first areas to be affected by the nation-wide awakening of 1859–61.

64. Iain H. Murray, *The Puritan Hope*, Edinburgh 1971 (reprinted 1991), p. 25. A proud accolade of worthy men of God served in parishes in this northerly region; not least Thomas Hog of Kiltearn, John Porteous of Kilmuir, Charles MacIntosh of Tain, Hector MacPhail of Resolis, and the redoubtable John Kennedy of Dingwall. Another titan of Calvinist preaching, John MacDonald of Ferintosh, found the ground had been well-prepared for him by his predecessors, and his labours in Easter Ross were particularly favoured. Here, between 1829 and 1939, the village of Avoch, especially, repeatedly experienced times of spiritual refreshing.

65. While, by 1950, Murdoch Campbell deemed Easter Ross 'almost spiritually barren', he nonetheless observed that 'the moral tone of the community … remained on a high level' (Campbell, *Memories*, pp. 99–100).

the villages of Footdee, by Aberdeen, and Ferryden, near Montrose, along with the south Fife community of Cellardkye, and Cockenzie to the east of Edinburgh, have also received repeated mention in revival accounts. Even in more recent decades, small fishing ports like Kinlochbervie and Gardenstown have been host to notable localised awakenings.[66]

Revivals are more common in close-knit communities where there are strong cultural or occupational bonds. This goes some way toward explaining the recurrence of awakenings within crofting and farming districts, as well as in fishing and mining villages, where, as noted earlier, the 'danger' factor is also more real.

It is also for this reason that revivals have been much more common in rural areas than in larger towns and cities. Rarely has an awakening moved powerfully through an entire city – the nearest examples of this are Aberdeen (1859–60) and Edinburgh (1873–4), when this latter city became 'the religious centre of the country in a way it had not been since the days of Knox and of the Covenant'.[67] However, it has been observed that even during the Moody campaign, in proportion to population – and given that statistics can never fully gauge a spiritual work – the number of professed Christians in many rural districts was 'immensely greater than in the cities and towns'.[68] During the 'Fishermen's revival' of the 1920s, too, the towns of Aberdeen and Dundee were noticeably less affected than the smaller fishing ports located in the same or neighbouring counties.

It is true that a number of spiritual awakenings that have occurred between 1880 and 1940 have taken place in Scotland's cities. But when this has happened the spiritual blessing has generally been confined to one particular district of that city. Thus the sporadic bursts of revivalist activity reported from William Ross's Glasgow church from 1883 were confined to the Cowcaddens district. The same was true of a separate movement in Glasgow in 1885–6, the spectacular series of revivals that graced Charlotte Chapel in Edinburgh from 1905–8, and the Pentecostal work led by Andrew Turnbull in Glasgow in the 1920s. Certainly the 1905–6 movement that diffused all over the country appeared to have a more general effect on Glasgow (as too did the awakening of 1921–2),

66. Special mention might also be given to the fishing and crofting community of Westray, in Orkney, especially the Baptist presence there. This fellowship dates back to the beginning of the nineteenth century and to the remarkable pioneering ministry of William Tulloch from North Ronaldsay. The church has seen repeated blessing since that time, with 30 members being added during a time of awakening in 1830–1; 70–80 between 1840 and 1843; 75 during the great revival of 1860; and a further 60 in 1866. It is most curious to note that each of the three main periods of awakening in the British Isles in the twentieth century was preceded about a year earlier by a notable movement on this small island (1903, 1919, 1948). What is additionally noteworthy is that each of these periods of heightened spiritual activity, viz., in 1905–6, the early 1920s and the early-mid 1950s, did not find its counterpart in this already-blessed north isle.

67. Couper, *Scottish Revivals*, p. 145.

68. MacPherson, *Revival and Revival Work*, p. 116.

but only in a few specific districts of the city could it be said that marked revival fires fanned into flame. Several other sparks of spiritual blessing to have occurred in Scotland's cities – for example, at Edinburgh University in the 1880s, in Army Barracks in Glasgow in 1908, and in Edinburgh's Faith Mission College – have been of an institutional nature, and so, naturally, did not have an effect on the city's population at large.

A similar picture emerges in regard to Scotland's large towns. Thus movements that sprang up in Kilmarnock in 1885 and in Clydebank in 1905 did not have a strong influence on these towns generally. On the other hand, and exceptionally, the anticipated revival fires that burned in Motherwell in 1905, and the dramatic deluge that descended on Ayr through the work of the Salvation Army three years later, were both said to have had general effect throughout those centres of population.

It has already been noted that revivals frequently spread by report, direct testimony, or the labours of itinerant preachers. However, especially during times of general awakening, spiritual movements sometimes seem to arise quite simultaneously in various places without any of the usual methods of conveyance. While the 1873–4 revival spread quickly to many areas following reports of goings-on in Edinburgh and Glasgow, there also occurred a simultaneous and seemingly independent movement in parts of Lewis. Similarly much of the spiritual quickening in various parts of inland Scotland in the 1920s seems to have had no direct connection with activities in east coast fishing ports. More recently there was a cluster of localised awakenings in diverse locations in the north of Scotland in the early and mid-1980s, though few of the people involved in any one of them were aware of proceedings in the other districts. It was as if a spiritual susceptibility pervaded the atmosphere at such times.

When dealing with the more self-contained Outer Hebrides, however, it is questionable whether one can make much in the way of direct comparison with other parts of the U.K. Believers on these islands, so geographically removed from the Scottish mainland (not least during the period of this study, when the shortest journey there took eight hours), have also adhered to very differing church traditions from believers on the mainland. As a result, awakenings occurring in parts of mainland Britain have not always manifested in the Hebrides (for example, as a result of the Welsh revival of 1904, or in direct connection with the 'Fishermen's revival' of the 1920s). More commonly, awakening has appeared in these islands when the rest of the U.K. has felt none. Thus, significant movements in Lewis at the turn of the twentieth century, in the mid-late 1930s, from 1949 to 1953, and again in the early 1970s, saw no real counterpart in mainland Scotland.

It is difficult not to notice from the movements studied in this book that the larger share of them occurred in the north of Scotland. One entire section is taken up with an almost continual flow of revival movements in the north-west of the country – viz., the spectacular legacy of spiritual awakenings belonging to the Outer Hebrides. Another busy section concerns itself wholly with revivals along the entire stretch of Scotland's east coast, but largely concentrated on the northern coast between Inverness and Aberdeen. Certainly fishing ports further south such as Cellardyke, Cockenzie and Eyemouth make colourful appearances, but Moray coast townships (such as Fraserburgh, Findochty and Portessie) feature much more prominently.

Several clusters of revivals, however, have occurred solely or predominantly in southern districts. The movements initiated by Torrey and Alexander, and in the following decade by Wilbur Chapman, were completely confined to large urban centres in central Scotland. Although the general awakening of 1905–6 worked its way north through Aberdeen, the Black Isle and up the far north-east coast to Wick and Thurso, it left its strongest mark in many towns and villages of central Scotland, being particularly prominent in Glasgow, Lanarkshire and Leith. Both of the seasons of blessing within the Salvation Army – during the general awakening of 1905 and again in 1908 – occurred in central and southern Scotland, while the early Pentecostal movement was confined almost entirely to the central belt.

Despite this, and even leaving aside the Outer Hebrides and east coast fishing communities, the majority of revival movements within our sixty-year study have occurred in the northern half of the country. This state of affairs was not always so. The Protestant Reformation in the sixteenth century, the sporadic revivals of the seventeenth century and the great awakening that quickly spread from Cambuslang in the mid-eighteenth century were all concentrated in lowland Scotland. However, it is probably true to say that ever since evangelicalism took root throughout the Highlands and Islands from the early nineteenth century, the north of Scotland has had the greater preponderance of revival movements. This requires some explanation.

It would be easy to say that because spiritual awakenings are more common in rural than in urban areas (as noted above), they have been more prominent in the far less populated north of the country than in the south, where most of Scotland's large towns and cities are situated. But this is false reasoning. Many of the large towns of Lanarkshire have in fact experienced times of spiritual quickening – for example, Motherwell, Hamilton and Wishaw – while, of course, a large part of the south of Scotland is in fact very rural; south and west Ayrshire, Dumfries and Galloway, and the Borders are made up predominantly of rural communities. Perhaps a better explanation lies in the fact that Presbyterianism has retained a stronger influence in the north and it is within this tradition – notably the Free Church, the UFC and the evangelical wing of the CoS – that revivals in the north have been more common. It is in these peripheral areas, as David Bebbington observes, that 'the old ways lingered longest'.[69] Why movements should be more frequent within this tradition than others requires a detailed discussion of the theological doctrines that underpin each, as well as a deeper insight into the history and social and religious mores of the communities concerned. This necessitates a more detailed analysis than the present study can lend to.

Scotland's rich revival heritage is especially noticeable when compared to that of other parts of the U.K., and to nations in continental Europe. Wales, famed for its dramatic awakenings of the nineteenth century and more so for the 'Big One' of 1904–5, has seen few marked seasons of blessing in the past 100 years.[70] The same can be said for both England[71] and Ireland, while in most countries of Western Europe evangelical awakenings have been virtually non-existent in the past century. In Scotland too, however, although several widespread movements occurred between 1880 and 1925, revivals have been noticeably scarce since that time, as well as less dramatic in nature.

PRAYER FOR REVIVAL

VERY few are the books by Christian authors on revival that do not emphasise the importance of prayer as an essential prerequisite. A number of entire books have been written on the necessary connection between prayer and revival.[72] Brian Edwards states that from a human standpoint, prayer is 'the single most significant cause' of an outpouring of the Spirit.[73]

Within a Scottish dimension, times of public prayer for revival have occurred prior to awakenings in, for example, Arran (1812), Granton on Spey (1832) and Kilsyth (1839). There were also numerous instances of both individual and group prayer throughout Scotland in 1858–9 after reports came through of revival in Ulster or from other parts of Scotland where revival had already ignited. Again, times of public

---

69. Bebbington, *Evangelicalism in Modern Britain*, p. 274.

70. Although there have been a few, e.g., see page 193 fn117.

71. Main English locations playing host to revivals in the early twentieth century were Cornwall and East Anglia, both also 'peripheral areas'.

72. e.g. Brian H. Edwards, *Can we Pray for Revival?*, Darlington 2001; David Bryant, *With Concerts of Prayer*, Ventura 1985; Paul Y. Cho, *Prayer: Key to Revival*, Berkhamsted 1985; Stuart Robinson, *Praying the Price*, Tonbridge 1994.

73. Edwards, *Revival*, p. 75. Edwards lists over a dozen dramatic examples of awakenings following committed group prayer for revival. Perhaps most notable among these are the all-night prayer times of a Moravian community in Hernhut, Saxony in the 1720s, prior to the great Moravian missionary enterprise that spread across the globe; the famous Fulton Street lunch-time prayer meetings in New York in 1857, which led to widespread revival in America; and the school-house prayer meetings in Kells, Northern Ireland, that preceded the dramatic Ulster revival of 1859.

prayer were common in various places during and following Moody's campaign in 1873–4.

R.E. Davies writes that the most constant of all factors in preparing for revival is that of 'urgent, persistent prayer. This fact,' he states, 'is acknowledged by all writers on the subject,' and he cites around a dozen references in strength of his point.[74] E.E. Cairns states simply and unequivocally, 'There cannot be revival unless Christians pray for it.'[75] Most categorically of all, Reformed minister Dr A.T. Pierson writes, 'From the day of Pentecost, there has been not one great spiritual awakening in any land which has not begun in a union of prayer, though only among two or three; no such outward, upward movement has continued after such prayer meetings have declined.'[76]

This all sounds very good in theory. However, known instances of group prayer for revival in Scotland, especially during our period of study, are not nearly as common as might be supposed. The proportion of movements recorded in this study where more than the very minimal details are provided, and where prayer by local believers is specifically stated as having preceded a period of spiritual awakening, works out at around a third. In some instances, of course, it is difficult to ascertain whether the seasons of prayer mentioned in relation to a particular revival were a welcome outcome of that revival, or actually preceded it. In any case, an emphasis on prayer, both public and private, is always a fruit of genuine revival. Certainly, one would expect that if a lot of prayer had been offered prior to a revival, then that important fact would be stated in narratives devoted to its origins and progress. Of course, there may be many more examples of groups of Christians praying for God's Spirit to move in their locality – the meeting together of two or three earnest believers that may not have been known even to the minister or others in their parish – of which nothing has been recorded.

In the 1880s members of Cowcaddens Free Church engaged in 'abounding, passionate, agonising, persevering prayer for the Lord's revival in Scotland' prior to a movement that broke out there very soon after.[77] Prayer meetings were also said to have been the birthplace of the awakening that swept over the Black Isle in 1905–6. Some had prayed for months prior to droplets of blessing falling, while in Dingwall a small group of men gathered after a hard day's work and a long evening meeting to wait upon the Lord – often interceding till after midnight. Duncan Campbell was convinced that the work of grace that arose in

74. Davies, *I Will Pour Out My Spirit*, pp. 217–18.

75. Earle E. Cairns, *An Endless Line of Splendour: Revivals and their Leaders from the Great Awakening to the Present*, Wheaton 1986, p. 341.

76. Quoted in Wallis, *In the Day of Thy Power*, p. 112.

77. Ross, *William Ross of Cowcaddens*, pp. 127–8.

south Skye in 1924 came about through the prevailing prayers of two godly women who knew how to 'pray through'. On one occasion they prayed right through the night, receiving the assurance that God was about to break through in their community. On other occasions, too, times of prayer preceding revival have involved half or whole nights in intercession, for example, in Motherwell (1905), Ayr (1908), Cairnbulg (1919) and Lambhill (1927).

Where stated, these special prayers for spiritual outpouring tend to have been in operation for a period of weeks or months prior to the commencement of revival, and only in a few cases, a number of years. Such lengthier time-scale was the case in regard to the outbreak of blessing in Dunfermline in 1905, and also prior to a movement that spread along the south-east coast of Caithness in the closing years of the nineteenth century. In regard to that movement, George Morrison of Thurso noted that over the course of many years he had rarely heard the public prayer of any believer throughout the county that failed to include simple, heartfelt petition for a season of spiritual harvest.

In a number of cases where revival has succeeded an evangelistic campaign, believers came together in the weeks leading up to that campaign to pray that a spiritual outpouring on their district would be a consequence of such mission. This was the case prior to the visit of Welsh revivalist Maggie Condie at Tolcross Baptist Church, Glasgow in 1905, and prior to a campaign in Cockenzie in 1921. Meanwhile, R.A. Torrey went as far as equating the quantity of prayer offered prior to his 1903 campaign with the quality of 'revival' subsequently experienced.[78]

It is specifically stated that in Findochty in the weeks prior to the 'Fishermen's revival' that swept along the east coast in late 1921, at least one or two earnest believers spontaneously cried out to God to bless their sin-stained neighbourhood. Interestingly, however, there are virtually no other reports of believers in east coast communities coming together to plead for a spiritual outpouring at that time. Indeed, in many towns and villages along the north-east coast, the situation seems to have been similar to that in Eyemouth, where it was said that revival broke out suddenly.[79] 'There had been little of what is usually called preparation, and as little organisation' prior to the revival, yet 'one day it was not and the next day it was.'[80] Meanwhile, while we're not told how much prayer preceded the burst of blessing that came upon

78. Janice Holmes, *Religious Revivals in Britain and Ireland 1859–1905*, Dublin 2000, pp. 172–3.

79. However, it is notable that six months prior to the outpouring of the Spirit in Lowestoft a few months earlier (which movement was, of course, a precursor of the revival that sprang up among Scottish fishermen later that year), around sixty Christians had met in that town every Monday evening to pray exclusively for revival.

80. *MR-UFC*, 1922, p. 47.

Cairnbulg in the same year, an immediate fruit of the awakening was the commencement of early morning prayer meetings from 6.30 to 9.30 each day.

An unexpected observation from our study is that only occasionally do records of spiritual awakening in the Outer Hebrides make mention of believers coming together to plead such an outpouring before God. It might seem that the central place for prayer in Hebridean Presbyterian congregations was either individually and within families, or within existing church structures, which included appointed prayer meetings, for instance, on a Thursday evening. Nevertheless, instances of communal prayer for revival did occur among UFC congregations in Lewis in 1900–1 and 1903–4, while in Harris (1925) awakening arose from a prayer meeting held in a small community. Similarly, a study of the famous revival of 1949–53 reveals that its outbreak in Barvas was preceded by numerous small groups of believers throughout the parish – not just the two Smith sisters that are singled out in many narratives – pleading with God together in cottages for another outpouring of His Spirit. Lastly, prayer preceding outbreaks of 'Pentecostal' blessing that sprang up in many areas of central Scotland from 1908 seems generally to have been on an individual basis; that is, believers praying specifically for themselves and their loved ones to be 'baptised in the Spirit'.[81]

It would appear that the connection between fervent, continual prayer by a group of believers in a community, and resultant revival in that locality has often been overstated. In many cases, especially in regard to periods of general awakening throughout a wider area, revivals often spread quickly from community to community, taking many people by surprise. This is what W.J. Couper says happened with the 'Moody revival' of 1873–4. 'There were no particular indications that the land was to be specially visited. … On the whole there were no general preparations, no special desire over the country, and no special expectancy among the people.'[82]

The same lack of expectation appears to have existed in districts of Glasgow affected by a spiritual awakening in 1885–6, as well as many east coast fishing towns and villages in the closing months of 1921, when revival descended suddenly on these communities. It also appears to have been true of many – though by no means all – districts that were affected by the general awakening of 1905, where, time and again, there is no mention of persistent prayer in the months prior to spiritual blessing being received. Of course it is very probable that in almost every community there will be at least someone who is praying for a blessing to

81. In Coatbridge a group of ten people waited on God from house to house every night for five weeks in the hope of receiving divine blessing.

82. Couper, *Scottish Revivals*, p. 141.

come to that district in any given season. In such cases it is impossible to prove or disprove any cause and effect pattern. And it must be noted that in some places faithful believers have prayed for decades for a spiritual outpouring, with no evidence of any resulting blessing.[83]

Better attested are the prayers of individual ministers or evangelists who became the main instruments of ensuing revivals.[84] Christian biographies are replete with examples of godly men pouring out their hearts to God for an outpouring of the Spirit on their congregations or upon the people-group to which they are acting as missionaries. John Welsh, who experienced times of remarkable blessing in Ayr in the late sixteenth century, was known to spend as much as eight hours a day in private prayer. Duncan MacBeath, the Lewis minister in whose Ness parish occurred a notable awakening in the 1880s, was said to have lived much of his life in the habit of prayer. D.J. Martin, under whose ministry revival came to Stornoway in 1880 and again in 1887 and 1896, was said to have been steeped in prayer. He prayed on his knees in his study, as he walked to church, in the vestry prior to a service, and in the pulpit while the congregation was singing. 'It was in prayer he developed the burning for souls which rose to a passion,' records his biographer.[85] James McKendrick, who preached on average 450 times a year for thirty years, could still say, 'I have spent more time upon my knees alone before God than I have spent on the platform before men.'[86] Jock Troup and Peter Connolly, both used powerfully during the 'Fishermen's revival' of the 1920s, 'would spend days and nights in prayer, even fasting when the heavens seemed as brass'.[87]

The ministry of the Faith Mission, whose Pilgrims have been the instruments of many localised awakenings in Scotland since its inception in 1886, was also bathed in intense, soul-searching intercession. Time and again, reports tell of pilgrims wrestling in deep heartfelt prayer for days, whole nights and even entire weeks from a spiritually dark location before at last a breakthrough was reached. One night in Balintore in 1923, after evangelising for five weeks with little apparent success, the two male pilgrims felt unable to return to their temporary caravan home until, with tears, they claimed the villages for God in deep intercession.

---

83. R.T. Kendall admits that despite a prophecy from the charismatic world's most renowned 'prophet' of a coming 'revival in Westminster Chapel like in Jonathan Edwards' day', and despite a longstanding prayer covenant whereby church members agreed to pray daily for true revival, '300 people praying daily for years and years didn't bring revival, nor did our days of prayer and fasting do it' (R.T. Kendall, *In Pursuit Of His Glory: My 25 Years at Westminster Chapel*, London 2002, pp. 102, 255).

84. Other scenarios also emerge: e.g., a group of 'office bearers and workers' entering into 'a solemn covenant of daily private prayer' (Glasgow's Kinning Park, 1905); or local ministers meeting together for monthly prayer times (Dunrossness, Shetland, 1912).

85. MacFarlane, *Donald John Martin*, p. 91.

86. McKendrick, *Seen and Heard*, p. 259.

87. Ritchie, *Floods Upon the Dry Ground*, p. 94.

A dramatic move of God immediately followed. Prior to the North Uist revival in 1957, Faith Mission Pilgrims 'repeatedly … were brought low before God to see our nothingness and complete dependence on His sovereign power. … We had times of brokenness, followed by times of great joy and rejoicing, with power and liberty in prayer.[88]

Of course we must not assume that prayer for revival will automatically lead to that result. As Iain H. Murray rightly states, our trust needs to be, not in prayer, nor in revival itself, but 'in the God who is himself the prime mover. … God has chosen to make prayer a means of blessing, not so that the fulfilment of his purposes becomes dependent upon us, but rather to help us learn our absolute dependence upon him.'[89] Thus, as Puritan Matthew Henry famously observed, 'When God intends great mercy for his people, the first thing he does is to set them a-praying.'[90] The above examples suggest that it is not so much how many people are praying that is important, nor necessarily how long they pray, but the utter yielding of even just one person's life to God that accompanies such urgent, heart-searching prayer.

Impact of Revivals

THE impact of revivals on congregations caught up in them is clearly considerable, and often wholly transforming. Not only are the lives of new converts radically changed, but the faith of existing believers is also strengthened – notable, for example, as a result of the 1886 movement in Dunblane, or the work in Kilmarnock in 1892, which was said to have revitalised the spiritual life of Brethren Assemblies across the west of Scotland. Another important impact of revivals is that commonly they result in converts leading friends and families to Christ – a particularly significant feature of the movements in Alyth in 1889 and in Cromarty, 1905–6.

Revivals always result in a steady advance in the ordinary work of the Church, as occurred in numerous Glasgow congregations following the movement of 1885–6, when groups such as Sunday schools, Bible classes, Prayer Unions and Y.M.C.A. meetings all grew in both numbers and enterprise. Revivals also lead many into full-time Christian service, as was notable in Rothesay (1889), Inverness (1898), Harris (1925) and Skye in the early 1930s. In some cases permanent changes to the structure of church services are begun; for example, during the Ness revival of the 1920s, week-long winter evangelistic services – *orduigean beagan* – were

88. Ferguson, *When God Came Down*, pp. 40, 41.

89. While 'cocks crow thickest towards the break of day,' he reminds us, 'it is neither cocks nor prayer which causes the dawn'. Murray, *Pentecost Today*, pp. 68, 69.

90. John Greenfield, *Power From on High: The Story of the Great Moravian Revival of 1727*, 1928 (reprinted Bethlehem, PA 1995), p.19.

introduced. Revivals can often necessitate, also, the erection of new church buildings or meeting halls, as followed the 1925–9 awakening in Harris, the rise of new fellowships, a consequence of the Benhar revival of 1922, or even new denominations, as followed the Pentecostal movement of 1908.

But in many cases revivals also make an impact on the wider community in which they occur. Indeed, this is often regarded as a necessary consequence of such movements, to the extent that if no significant impact is made on the community at large, then it is deduced that no real revival has occurred.[91] Clearly the stronger a revival, the more likelihood of it having a significant impact on neighbouring districts. Walker and Aune, however, in their identification of six different types of revival (see page 24), show that it is generally only in the higher orders of the term that society is impacted; for example, as a result of societal or cultural awakenings, such as the 'Great Awakening' of the mid-1700s, or, to a less enduring degree, the Welsh revival of 1904. Scottish examples would include the Reformation, the results of which Couper succinctly stated as 'nothing less than the after-history of Scotland'.[92] Similarly the Lowland revival of the mid-1700s had a powerful effect on the state Church and helped to modify and mould its history for more than a century afterwards.[93]

In many of the case studies in this book, little or no mention is made of the impact made on society at large. Instead the blessing appears to have been largely confined to the congregation(s) directly caught up in the movement. Even the general awakening of 1905, although the most extensive spiritual movement examined in this study, seems to have made no real impact on Scottish society as a whole, although in several locations it did leave a mark on particular communities (for example, Motherwell, Thurso, and Cockenzie). This feature appears to be true not only of smaller, less intensive movements, but also of some more remarkable revivals.

No one can legitimately question the genuineness of the revival that hit Charlotte Baptist Chapel on Edinburgh's Rose Street in various phases between 1905 and 1908. Yet the reports of this dramatic revival make no mention of it influencing the nearby community at large. One can question to what extent there really existed a 'community', as close as the Chapel was to Princes St and the city centre. But to the north and west of Rose St was the New Town – a largely prosperous residential

---

91. For example, Arthur Wallis wrote: 'Revival must of necessity make an impact upon the community…' (Wallis, *In the Day of Thy Power*, p. 23). Stuart Piggin insists that genuine revivals are 'always accompanied by … the diminution of sinful practices in the community' (Stuart Piggin, *Firestorm of the Lord: The History of and Prospects for Revival in the Church and the World*, Carlisle 2000, p. 11).

92. Couper, *Scottish Revivals*, p. 159.

93. Ibid.

district. It was with this area in mind that a Tract Society, initiated in 1886, was revived in 1903, so that four-page tracts were distributed each month to homes in the vicinity. However, Kemp's favourite stand for open-air meetings was on the corner of South Charlotte St and Princes St, and this proved the birthplace of many souls. The majority of those who traversed Princes St, of course, would not have lived in the immediate vicinity. Thus, the church was very much a 'gathered' congregation,[94] consisting of people from different parts of Edinburgh and even beyond.[95] Rose St itself was the haunt of drunks and prostitutes, and contained no fewer than nineteen public bars. There is no suggestion that the revival had a noticeable impact on this state of affairs. Indeed, Dr Balfour still speaks of 'the spiritual darkness of Rose St and its 19 public houses' in the aftermath of the revival period.[96] Although hundreds of people from outwith the congregation were wonderfully converted between 1905 and 1908, Kemp made it clear towards the close of the movement that 'the work has been chiefly confined to the saints of God'.[97]

In many other cases, however, specific note is made of the effect a revival has had on the non-churched community. Again and again, revivals lead directly to a significant reduction in drinking (Kintyre 1897, Westray 1903, Motherwell 1905, Balintore 1923) and activities such as gambling, sporting, dancing and theatre-going (Nairn 1886, Tiree 1887, Westray 1903, Thurso 1905), all considered by evangelicals of the time as worldly amusements.

Perhaps the most remarkable lasting effects of Scottish revivals have been along the Moray Firth coast. Repeated bouts of revival blessing in these close-knit communities were said to have resulted in a greater sense of responsibility and diligence among villagers, leading, as was observed in 1874, to outward prosperity and progress. Where income had previously been squandered on drinking and other worldly amusements, it was now spent more wisely. The roads had been greatly improved. Handsomely-built public schools now existed in both Findochty and Portessie. Scores of fine two-storey houses had been erected in recent years.[98] Lewis's legacy of revivals no doubt similarly played a significant part in the generally healthy state of morality (compared to the mainland) that existed on the island in the immediate post-First World War period – near empty prisons, no licence for the sale of alcohol, and an almost complete absence of pornographic literature.

---

94. Balfour, *Revival in Rose Street*, p. 159.
95. One man made a return journey on foot all the way from Balerno, some eight miles distant.
96. Balfour, *Revival in Rose Street*, p. 118.
97. *Charlotte Chapel Record*, 1907, quoted in Balfour, ibid., p. 108.
98. *Times of Blessing*, 21 May 1874, pp. 83–4.

In a number of revival cases the police reported a reduction in crime (Rothesay 1889, Cockenzie 1905, Ayr 1908), while a revival among the miners of south Kintyre in 1897 was similar in effect to that among the same class of worker in the 1904–5 Welsh revival – the coalmines now resounded with psalms and hymns. During the revival in Cromarty in 1886, every household was said to have shared in the blessing, while in Avoch the same year, the whole village was more or less interested. An even stronger effect was made by the 'Fishermen's revival' in Cairnbulg in 1921, which was said to have had a profound impact on the village and surrounding districts. Similarly, in Stornoway in 1880, the whole town was said to have been caught up in the movement then in progress, while in Cockenzie in 1905, a spirit of revival was said to have filled the whole village. Then, strikingly, in a few cases it was reported that the entire life of the community was transformed by an awakening: as in the south Lanarkshire mining village of Haughead in the early 1880s; in Balintore in 1923; and in Portsoy in the same year.

Impressive as reports like these sound, it has to be admitted that in many cases any beneficial impact of revivals on society – and even within the churches in which they occur – is short-lived. It is almost impossible to make judgment on this from the accounts considered in this book, as very few of them give indication of any lasting impact (many were written too soon after the events described to ably comment on lasting impressions). This was particularly true when itinerant evangelists wrote accounts of revivals that they led. They may have been able to provide details of immediate results, but because of the nature of their ministry they rarely stayed around long enough to establish whether there were any enduring impressions. Thus McKendrick is unable to comment on any long-term results of the dramatic revivals that occurred in the stream of east coast fishing villages he visited in the 1890s, although he does confirm that on return visits to two of these places – Ferryden and Cellardyke – some years later, many of the converts were holding strong to their faith.

A further case in point appears in the Westray revival of 1903–4. While there is no question that the movement had a lasting effect on scores of converts, one short-lived result was that virtually no one turned up for that year's 'Harvest Home', an important annual social celebration in every Orkney parish. A year later, however, and the 'Harvest Home' was back in full swing! [99]

---

99. This story is strongly reminiscent of a consequence of the 1860 revival on the same island. On New Year's Day 1861, not a soul turned up for the rough, rugby-type game known as 'The Ba' played on the first day of each year, although no efforts had been made to stop it. Indeed 'the aspect of the day was completely changed from its usual appearance … no amusement of any kind was engaged in' (*Orkney Herald*, 22 January 1861). Yet Jocelyn Rendall records that this 'mirthless New Year was never repeated; 1862 was brought in in traditional fashion' (Jocelyn Rendall, 'The Orkney Revivals,' in *The Orkney View*, 1993, pp. 24–5).

We should not forget either the simple fact that in the two regions given specific focus in our study, namely the Outer Hebrides and east coast fishing villages, revivals have made repeated appearance. In Findochty an initial, dramatic burst of revival activity occurred in 1860. This was followed by other movements in 1863, 1866–7, 1870, 1880, 1893, 1903 and again in 1921 – no fewer than eight times in around sixty years. It could be said that the effects of these movements, both upon the churches involved and the surrounding communities, couldn't have been very enduring or there would have been little need of a further awakening a few short years later! Yet some reforms did last (see above).

Revivals, then, vary significantly not just in nature, but also in overall lasting impressions made on the wider community. While some, especially in their initial stages, are dramatic and loud, many others are characterised by being, as Couper puts it, 'pervasive, quiet and unnoticed'.[100] In all cases, revivals make a significant impact on local church attendance and an enduring impact on the spiritual quality of a great many lives. But while some have indeed become imbedded in local and regional historical lores,[101] many others are quickly forgotten, if noticed at all, by society at large and are often ignored in secular histories.[102]

REVIVAL AND THE DENOMINATIONS

A NOTABLE feature of the awakenings that occurred in Scotland between 1880 and 1940 is that they embraced virtually all the Protestant denominations. This said, some groups have played a more prominent role than others. The Free Church clearly comes out on top for having experienced the greatest number of revivals, receiving repeated mention in virtually every chapter of this volume. 'The Glorious Eighties,' in particular, abounds with spiritual awakenings within the Free Church. Revivals in this denomination have been especially notable in the Western Isles, where virtually all the movements related in this book have occurred within its bounds (the exceptions being the 1913–17 and 1925–9 awakenings in Harris, which occurred predominantly within the United Free Church).

More widespread blessing fell upon the United Free Church during the active years of 1905–6 and 1921–2, while they also enjoyed great favour

100. Couper, *Scottish Revivals*, p. 159.

101. A number of earlier famed revivals are referred to, albeit briefly, in regional or national historical texts; examples include Cambuslang and Kilsyth 1742, the general awakening of 1859–61, occurrences among north-east fisherfolk, and the Moody campaign of 1873–4. General histories of Lewis would be lacking if they failed to note the awakening that spread through the island from the 1820s, because of the permanent changes such revival (and subsequent movements) had on the island's spiritual and social identity. Other revivals that variably receive a mention in Highland histories are those of Breadalbane 1816 and Skye 1812.

102. The main exception in regard to the present period of study is the 'Fishermen's revival' of 1921–2, which has, on occasions, attracted the attention of secular historians.

during their first decade-and-a-half of operations in Lewis (1900–1916). Baptist movements also feature repeatedly – except in the Outer Hebrides, where this group never managed to take root. Especially from the turn of the century, Baptists show up prominently in the general awakenings of both 1905 and the early 1920s. The Salvation Army experienced three main bouts of revival activity north of the border – in the days of their early advance (Peterhead 1880s), in the years 1905 and 1908, and later in fishing villages like Findochty (1921–2) and Portsoy (1923).

Methodist congregations were partakers of several seasons of revival: for example, Samuel Chadwick's work in Clydebank in 1887–8, and movements along the Moray Coast prior to and during the 'Fishermen's revival' of 1921–22. It was during this latter period that the Primitive Methodists were the main recipients of a wonderful spiritual deluge, viz., in the Borders' fishing town of Eyemouth. The most salient revival to occur among the Brethren between 1880 and 1940 was in parts of South Lanarkshire in 1905. Additionally, this group featured in movements led by Alexander Marshall in Dumfries and Kilmarnock in 1891 and 1892 respectively, and in the same county and in Glasgow in the immediate post-First World War period.

Only one movement in our period of study has centred on the Congregational Church – this the dramatic revival that overtook Avoch in 1886. But Congregationalists were participants in various other movements; for example, in Fraserburgh and some Fife ports in 1921–2. The United Presbyterian Church similarly makes a brief appearance (not least because it ceased to exist twenty years after the commencement of our period of study), sharing in the revival that came to Stornoway in 1880 and being one of several Presbyterian Churches that participated in the Campbeltown movement of 1897. Disappointingly, Scotland's Free Presbyterian Church has known no notable revival within its ranks since its inception in 1893.[103]

Independent churches crop up now and again: for example, the Mission Hall in Camelon, near Falkirk, in the 1880s; numerous Glasgow Missions in the period 1905–06 (such as the Tent Mission and the Highland and Open Air Gospel Mission); Carrubbers Close Mission, which hosted a revival in 1919–20; and Lambhill Evangelistic Mission, where a significant work went on in 1927. Another independent group that saw revival fires burn in their midst was Kilsyth's Westport Hall from 1908, from which central base the fledgling Pentecostal movement spread throughout central Scotland and beyond – spawning, in time, a number of new denominations (such as the Assemblies of God, Elim

103. The Rev. Donald A. Ross, Moderator of the Free Presbyterian Church Synod at the time of writing, stated that in no sense, however, was his Church against revivals, and there had indeed occurred seasons of unusual growth within individual congregations at different times (personal communication, 6 February 2008).

and the Apostolic Church). Meanwhile, in regard to a few movements, such as Lochgilphead 1885 and Arran 1897–8, we are not told what church groups were especially affected.

The focus of only two revival movements in this study has been the Church of Scotland – these the awakening in the south of Shetland in 1912 and that in Barvas in 1921–2, of which latter movement many converts went on to become the nucleus of the Barvas CoS during later revivals. But a few Established Church congregations did participate in a number of other revival movements, such as in Tiree in 1903–4, in the Black Isle in 1905–6, in Fraserburgh in 1921–2 and in Brora during the same period. A few CoS congregations also shared in various other movements, such as the general awakening of 1905–6, although it has to be said that in hardly any reports are they specifically mentioned. The national Church also partook of revival blessings that rained repeatedly upon Lewis. While most of these had prominence among Free Church congregations, we know that some CoS congregations were also revived at such times: for example, during the revival in Stornoway in 1897, that in Ness 1922–26, and particularly in the 'Layman's revival' of 1934–9. Here two CoS ministers particularly caught up in the work were Harry MacKinnon of Point and M.M. MacSween of Kinloch.

One of the most marvellous features of times of revival is that evangelical Christians are much more likely to come together, setting aside denominational differences and past disagreements, and working in unity for the sake of the gospel. In this way, as we have seen, a number of churches in a locality are likely to reap from the harvest, although it is often said that any unity achieved is usually of a temporary nature. The season of blessing that came to Dunkeld Free Church in 1882 was shared in by other Presbyterian churches in the town, and even, to a lesser extent, unusually, by the local Episcopal congregation. A spirit of co-operation has particularly marked times of widespread blessing, having united churches of different denominations during the general awakening of 1905; for example, in Motherwell and Thurso, and again during the 'Fishermen's revival' of 1921–22. In Fraserburgh, in which district the latter movement was perhaps felt the strongest, the Baptist, Congregational, United Free and Free Churches all worked together harmoniously, while the Established Church joined in to a lesser degree. In Hopeman, the Baptist and UFC ministers stood jointly at the forefront of the movement, while in Brora joint services among the Free and United Free congregations took place. Such harmony along the east coast was not to be taken for granted – it was said of Portknockie in the late nineteenth century that, despite the frequent times of blessing the village had enjoyed, 'the spirit of separatism has greatly marred the result'.[104]

104 ARC-FCS-SR&M, 1882, p. 26.

In Lewis, while some revival movements have been characterised by a wonderful coming together of members of various churches, there has at times been considerable division. No stronger spirit of disunity existed in Lewis within our sixty-year study than that which surrounded the union of the Free Church and UPC in 1900. Remarkably, in the immediate aftermath of such controversial operation, a spirit of awakening spread across the island, affecting both opt-out Free Church congregations and the newly-formed UFC. While, in general, disharmony continued between the two groups, on a few rare occasions – notably in Leurbost in 1912 – adherents of the two Churches came together to share in the Lord's blessing.

In the Ness revival of 1922–6, too, those of differing church traditions fellowshipped together, while such spirit of cross-denominational harmony was particularly evident during the widespread revival of the 1930s. Time and again, members of both the Free Church and CoS met together in homes to fellowship, worship and pray. Relations were probably closest in Point, where the two churches were said to be 'as one'. Indeed, it was said that if a service in one church ended before the other believers would wait for one another and walk home together. Again, during the famed 1949–53 revival in Lewis, there was generally much unity between the laity of the two main denominations, any spirit of division that arose being mainly confined to several church leaders.

REVIVAL CONCERNS

OPPOSITION FROM WITHIN

THERE is no prototype for revivals, specifying how they should begin, progress, or come to a close. Because they are exceptional experiences, usually accompanied by multiple and varied expressions of intense human emotions, revivals tend to be messy affairs, and rarely, if ever, are all who observe them satisfied with their progress. Invariably, they come in for a lot of criticism. Sometimes those outside the Church look at them askance, viewing them as outbursts of mass hysteria and thinking that those transformed as a result of them have become at best deceived and at worst mentally deluded. Occasionally within our period of study believers came under forms of physical attack from non-believing opponents; for example, Faith Mission Pilgrims being treated to volleys of rotten eggs, or Salvationists being attacked on their arrival in a town.

It is perhaps ironic, however, and most hurtful to those at the receiving end, that the strongest and most bitter attacks on revivals and those leading them has often come from fellow-believers. Sometimes individual ministers, fellowships, or whole denominations may oppose an awakening that is occurring in their area or elsewhere in the country. This may be on theological grounds, due to denominational rivalry, or because of jealousy of other individuals or churches experiencing blessing. It may also come from church leaders being afraid of not being in control of events (that is, fear of allowing the Spirit to take over) and a dislike of the often messy elements that accompany revival. At other times there is no direct opposition, but rather an indifference (as McKendrick found in Portessie in 1893), or such a love of tradition as leads to resistance to anything that might bring about change (as Duncan Campbell encountered in Skye in 1924).

Opposition from within the Church has been a hallmark of a great many Scottish revivals. Perhaps the most notorious were the vehement attacks meted out to George Whitefield and his supporters by erstwhile friends in the Secession Church during the Cambuslang revival of 1742. A century later, in a foreword to reports of the 1859 revival in Ireland and Scotland, Horatius Bonar felt compelled to pen an essay on 'Modern Hostility to Revivals'.[105] Many of a Calvinist persuasion, particularly John Kennedy of Dingwall, strongly opposed the ministry of Dwight Moody in 1873–4. As a consequence, relatively few pulpits were open to him in the Highlands, and the revival, which also affected many places the American evangelist did not visit, did not touch these resistant areas. D.J. Martin's work in Stornoway in the last two decades of the nineteenth century was also criticised because of his supposedly Arminian views (which he denied), and for his 'revival methods'. Indeed, the very thing 'which closed some pulpits in Lewis against him was this revival (of 1880) that now filled him and hundreds in Stornoway with joy'.[106] The Faith Mission came in for a lot of attack in the early decades of its existence; again, particularly in the Highlands and Islands. When Pilgrims concerted efforts on Rothesay, causing much excitement among locals and leading to a powerful awakening, local minister C.A. Salmond wrote an attack on the Mission's emphasis on sanctification and perfectionism. From other sources came criticism of the Faith Mission's use of the penitent form, song tunes as hymns, using musical instruments in church services and the engagement of women preachers.

New groups other than the Faith Mission also faced bitter opposition. The arrival of the Salvation Army in Peterhead in the 1880s was received with much suspicion from believers. The Army work during the Ayr revival of 1908 also came under attack from other churches – this time for being too exclusive. Perhaps the strongest opposition within our period of study was levelled at the early Pentecostal movement. Some were forced to leave their churches when it was found that they spoke in tongues. One man who became a Pentecostal was considered by other believers he fellowshipped with to have become mentally imbalanced. Pentecostal historian Donald Gee had evidence to suggest that 'in Britain

105. Reid, *Authentic Records of Revival Now in Progress in the United Kingdom*, pp. 1–9.

106. MacFarlane, *Donald John Martin*, p. 91.

the Pentecostal Movement received the most determined, capable and prejudiced opposition that it encountered anywhere in the world'.[107]

With regard to the Lewis revival of the 1930s, opposition was sparked by a number of ministers against the physical manifestations that became a feature of some cottage meetings. Opposition also attended the later revival of 1949–53, which was almost totally confined to Church of Scotland congregations, being rejected by all but one Free Church minister on the island.[108] The opposition, led fiercely by Kenneth MacRae, was ostensibly on the grounds of theology, both Duncan Campbell and the Faith Mission which he served repeatedly being accused of Arminianism.[109] In the face of opposition from their pastors, many Free Church members attended Campbell's meetings, and a good number were converted. Meanwhile, leaders of the strict Free Presbyterian Church were extremely wary of any outward expression of emotion, and therefore voiced strong opposition to both the 1930s and the 1949–53 movements.

Sometimes church splits have occurred as a result of a revival. Those whose lives have been radically changed and are abounding in new spiritual enthusiasm do not always sit comfortably alongside other, long-serving church members who have not been so affected. New points of doctrine can also be opened up to revival converts to which other members of the congregation may not adhere.[110] This can lead to a parting of ways, which may be amicable, though often leads to distrust and dissension. Church splits may also occur in a church for reasons unconnected with a revival it has recently experienced.[111]

What is perhaps just as common as individual church splits occurring in the aftermath of revival is the formation of whole new denominations or church networks. It has been observed that many of Scotland's main denominations were begun in times of awakening.[112] There are occasional examples

107. Donald Gee, *The Pentecostal Movement*, quoted in John Thomas Nichol, *The Pentecostals*, Plainfield 1971, pp. 71–2.

108. Rev. William Campbell of Point.

109. Many agree that other factors also played a significant part, for example: (1) resentment of an outside evangelist coming to an island awash with evangelical teaching; (2) longstanding distrust between the FC and the CoS; and (3) jealousy.

110. e.g., the setting up of new charismatic fellowships occurred after localised awakenings in several areas in the North of Scotland in the 1980s.

111. This occurred in Point, Lewis following the 1956–7 awakening, when suspicion concerning financial matters, along with personality clashes, resulted in a new fellowship being established.

112. Numerous converts of the Cambuslang and Kilsyth revivals left the Established Church a number of years later to join the Relief Church, founded by Thomas Gillespie, himself a preacher in these former awakenings. Congregational and, soon after, Baptist congregations began to appear and subsequently flourish in Scotland as a result of awakenings that followed the itinerant preaching of men like the Haldanes at the turn of the nineteenth century. In 1839, the same year that the powerful pre-Disruption revival spread across the land, James Morison founded the Evangelical Union of Churches in Scotland after being dismissed from the United Secession Church for espousing Finneyite views. The FC, too, arose in the midst of a general awakening throughout much of Scotland. The Salvation Army began operations following the 1859–61 awakening, while the Scottish Brethren movement came into prominence in the same period.

in the post-1880 period: Pentecostal churches came into being as a result of the Azusa Street revival in Los Angeles in 1906, while a whole range of new charismatic networks were one notable outcome of the charismatic renewal of the 1960s–1970s.[113] As with new individual fellowships, so too with new network structures, it would appear that the pouring out of new wine necessitates new wineskins to contain them. Whether the appearance of new 'denominations' is a good thing will depend on the issues concerned in each case.[114] Certainly they have provided a broad spectrum of spiritual colour to the Scottish Church, although with new church structures comes the possible accusation of 'sheep-stealing', as has been demonstrated again and again in Church history.[115]

Opposition from within the Church has been a hallmark of most major revivals worldwide. Indeed in modern revivalist scenarios, criticism is often taken as de facto evidence of a movement's authenticity! Revivals are messy events and those involved in them, however pure their motives, are imperfect at best. Far from constituting quenching of the Spirit,[116] criticism of certain features of a revival may often be positive and helpful.

Revival Statistics

ESTIMATING the number of converts in an awakening is always a precarious task. Even the author of the Acts of the Apostles could say only that 'about 3,000 were added to their number' on the day of Pentecost (Acts 2:41), that figure later increasing to 'about 5,000' (Acts 4:4). 'Near 500' is the well-known number who were said to have had 'a discernible change wrought on them' during the famed Communion season at Shotts,[117] while Orr estimated the increase in Scottish Presbyterian church membership following the 1859–61 awakening to be around 10 percent (although frequently quoted, many regard this as grossly over-optimistic).

Many revival reports do not even begin to estimate converts, it being considered injudicious to proclaim with any degree of certainty who is and isn't among God's elect. Additions to church membership are

113. Including Harvestime (later Covenant Ministries International), Pioneer, and more recently Vineyard. Many of these church streams developed congregations in Scotland.

114. A.W. Tozer, in his book *God Tells the Man who Cares*, argues that church 'divisions are not always bad' (Quoted in *Best of Tozer*, compiled by Warren W. Wiersbe, 1978, reprinted Nottingham 1993, pp. 73–5). Iain H. Murray makes the same argument in his chapter *The Churches and Christian Unity*, in *A Scottish Christian Heritage*, Edinburgh 2006, pp. 277–310.

115. e.g., with the emerging Brethren movement, there were charges of proselytising, most notably, perhaps, from Baptist ranks.

116. As commonly claimed by many revivalists; e.g., note the pungent attacks on those who questioned any aspect of the Pensacola 'outpouring' by two of its former leaders (Stephen Hill, *God Mockers*; Michael L. Brown, *Let No One Deceive You: Confronting Critics of the Brownsville Revival*, both Shippensburg 1997).

117. Couper, *Scottish Revivals*, p. 37. I.H. Murray states that, characteristic of the Puritan age in which he lived, Livingstone, the preacher under whose sermon such changes were wrought, gave no indication of numbers when recounting this event in his life-story (Murray, *Puritan Hope*, p. 268).

a helpful indicator but by no means always an accurate guide. Some converts, especially from a Calvinist tradition, are unwilling to join a church due to a fear of appearing presumptuous regarding their salvation. Others may be inadvertently accepted to membership without having undergone a saving change (the degree of discipline in regard to assessions to membership naturally varies from church to church and from denomination to denomination). There is also the problem of backsliding. This is an almost invariable consequence of periods of multiple conversions. Many writers give no details of whether or not converts stood the test of time, while in other instances they make rather vague reports on the lasting fruits of an awakening.

More helpfully, on repeated visits to the village of Ferryden following a revival led by McKendrick in 1893, his colleague James MacFarlane reported that 'most' of the fruit of that movement were still holding fast to their faith. It was reported a year after the 1886 revival in Avoch that of the hundreds of professions of faith, a mere two or three were known to have turned back. Similarly favourable reports emerge from numerous other scenarios – such as Glasgow 1885, Ardrishaig 1886, Cromarty 1886, Ness 1880s and Campbletown 1897. Sixteen months after an awakening in the Ardnamurchan districts of Sanna and Kilchoan in the early 1920s, an older believer in the district was asked how the lambs of the flock were getting on. His quaint reply was, 'There's none lame yet!'

Unfortunately, however, compilers of the majority of revival records in this book either ignore or were not yet in a position to report on backsliding. More transparent in this regard are reports from denominational deputies, who sought to glean detailed information on the congregations they visited. Around sixteen months after a burst of revival in Portknockie Free Church in 1880, deputies visited the congregation. They found that kitchen meetings, which had risen to six during the revival, were back down to two or three, while the weekly prayer meeting attracted on average just twenty people.[118] Kenneth MacRae, in his diary, also confessed frankly to 'seasons of terrible backsliding and sad trials' following spiritual awakening in the north of Skye in the early 1920s.

Similarly, while follow-up visits among converts of the 1905–8 revival at Edinburgh's Charlotte Chapel revealed that 'the larger percentage of those visited were found to be genuinely saved,' Joseph Kemp was honest anough to admit that 'periods of declension almost invariably follow' times of spiritual refreshing. 'By and by a cooling process begins, the exuberance of feeling is dulled, activity slackens, and meetings lose their freshness and power; the blessing ebbs, conversions are less and less

118. *RC-FCS-SR&M*, 1882, p. 26.

frequent, rivalries appear, and in the end many fall back into apathy and some into sin.'[119] While it is clear that much abiding fruit blossomed from the extended movement in Kemp's church, it is sobering to read that just months after revival had drawn to a close, Kemp, with his emphasis on high standards, could complain that 'in many departments our workers are thinning out. … Some have grown weary and have fallen out, while not a few have made over their energies to outside causes.'[120] There is good reason to believe that similar cases of declension are far from uncommon. This said, there is a vast supply of evidence testifying that the lasting good wrought from revivals greatly outweighs the bad, and it is also universally accepted in evangelical circles that there tends to be much less falling away as a result of revivals than there is from evangelistic campaigns.

An interesting story was recorded in the Faith Mission's monthly journal, relating to a revival in the mining town of Whitburn, midway between Edinburgh and Glasgow, in the summer of 1890. In a village of 1,200 inhabitants, a hall holding 660 people was crowded night after night, with up to forty deciding for Christ on many evenings. By the end of just one week 100 converts were marching through town proclaiming the joy of their new-found salvation. Subsequently, however, the same magazine had to bring the unfortunate news of a large number of backsliders in the months following the awakening, to the extent that only 'a small remnant kept true to God'[121] – although, thankfully, a prayer meeting was still being continued.[122] Considerable backsliding was also an aspect of a school-camp revival in Abington, Lanarkshire, in 1952.[123]

Part of the problem may be in counting as converts everyone who has shown deep interest and evidence of soul-concern. As William Burns noted in 1840, it is 'almost inevitable' that there will be 'a great falling away of those merely alarmed, or but partially awakened, and never savingly changed'.[124] Less and less distinction has been made between these two very different spiritual states in the period since Burns made his observation, with much resulting confusion and disappointment. Lines are particularly blurred in evangelistic campaigns, when converts to Christ are often calculated simply by counting those who raise their

---

119. Balfour, *Revival in Rose Street*, p. 111.

120. Ibid., p. 116.

121. *BW*, 1890. I.R. Govan, in the biography of her father, J.G. Govan, speaks of the 'great missions' held in Whitburn in 1890, but makes no mention of the subsequent backsliding (Govan, *Spirit of Revival*, p. 79; cf. Peckham, *Heritage of Revival*, p. 31).

122. Longing to 'see God glorified where He had been dishonoured', and relying on a Scriptural 'word' from the Lord, it was felt appropriate to hold another mission in the town at the start of 1892 (*BW*, 1892).

123. Black, *Revival: Personal Encounters*, pp. 83–115.

124. Sprange, *Children in Revival*, p. 15.

hands following a direct appeal. R.A.Torrey came under considerable attack in this regard during the city missions he held in 1903. The immediate results of George Jeffreys' mission in Glasgow in 1927, when 1,500 made profession of faith, are also open to interpretation.

A problem also emerges where more dramatic manifestations accompany revivals, in that people of an emotional disposition may be more attracted to meetings, and therefore in a group setting may appear as one of 'the number'. Peer-pressure may also influence some in seeking to convince both themselves and others that they have taken the same step of faith as their friends or family members. This tendency has perhaps been most prevalent among children (see Chapter 12).

BIASED REPORTING

IN estimating the number of converts in an awakening, and in reporting events generally, there is always a temptation to exaggerate. Exaggeration, of course, is more likely to flourish when the reporter has a strong personal bias in favour of or against the subject he is writing about. For this reason, and those noted in the above section, we should always be careful about statistics quoted. While separate reports suggest the number of converts from revivals in Avoch in 1886 and 1906 as between 300–400 and 'about 200' respectively, a third (and probably more accurate) account suggests the 1906 awakening as being the 'greater one'.[125] As American evangelists have been prone to do, R.A.Torrey rather overstated the case when he spoke of 'two and a half years of revival work in Great Britain' following his U.K. missions in the early years of the twentieth century. In reality, Torrey's overall efforts constituted no more than a highly successful evangelistic campaign.

Duncan Campbell had to request the withdrawal of a book on the Lewis revival of 1949–53 by an American author, whom, Campbell lamented, 'had more imagination than facts at his disposal'.[126] One gets the impression from some accounts of this awakening that intense revival spread through the entire isle, converting thousands, and dramatically altering island life. One writer said, 'So tremendous was the supernatural moving of God in conviction of sin, not a home, not a family, not an individual escaped fearful conviction, and even the routine of business was stopped that the island might seek the Face of God like Nineveh of Bible days.'[127] In fact, while a dramatic and powerful awakening certainly occurred, its greatest influence was along the entire stretch of the west

125. W.D. McNaughton, *Alexander Dewar's Testimony: The Origins of Avoch Congregational Church*, Glasgow 1994, p. 13.

126. Woolsey, *Channel of Revival*, p. 146.

127. Owen Murphy, *When God Stepped Down from Heaven*, Portland n.d.

of Lewis and parts of Harris, but hardly moving certain districts, such as Back parish or the main centre of population, the town of Stornoway (this largely because of the opposition in these areas).[128] Further, it did not have a strong influence on the largest denomination on the island. Campbell himself was known at times to exaggerate or to inadvertently mix up one story with another, and as a result, there is to this day disagreement over some of the stories related.[129]

An equally intriguing scenario attends the occasion, recorded on tape a number of years later, of an awakening in Skye in the early 1950s.[130] It was claimed that, after spending a day waiting on God, Duncan Campbell, Charles Henderson (the local minister) and others made their way to that evening's meeting in church, only to find that it was packed to capacity, and included the presence of a busload of people from fifteen miles away. That evening, revival broke out in the community. However, Henderson claims that while Campbell's visit indeed constituted a successful mission, and there were a number of converts, there was no revival in the area at the time. It was, rather, a 'very fine spiritual experience'.[131]

Revivals and the Charismata

IT is interesting to note how often periods of awakening are preceded by a premonitory dream or vision, or by strong spiritual discernment concerning a coming season of blessing to the community. This occurred, for example, prior to a revival in Westray in 1903, when a church elder strongly predicted a season of spiritual refreshing on the island; and in Edinburgh's Charlotte Chapel in 1905, when, independent of each other, both the church secretary and Joseph Kemp's future mother-in-law felt certain that God was about to pour out His blessing. Awakening in Motherwell the same year was

---

128. One recent title has the New Hebrides as the location of this movement, where, near 'Barvis', close to the 'town of Lewis', two women were 'the human instruments responsible for revival', which came after Campbell, a grandfather, suddenly left the Keswick Bible Conference to come and minister (Elmer Towns and Douglas Porter, *The Ten Greatest Revivals Ever: From Pentecost to the Present*, Ann Arbor, Michigan 2000, pp. 144–6). There are a number of inaccuracies here.

129. For example, a number of the remarkable stories related in a recent account of this revival, many of which are transcribed from audio tapes of Campbell's sermons, are noticeably absent from converts' own testimonies, as collected by the Peckhams in *Sounds From Heaven*. In my own research I was unable on a number of occasions to obtain verification of stories that Campbell himself related.

130. Duncan Campbell audio tape, as transcribed by Brad Allen in *Catch the Wind*, pp. 201–3. There were several other inaccuracies in Campbell's account, e.g. regarding the birthplace of Henderson's parents.

131. Personal conversation with the Rev. Charles Henderson, November 2002. It has been said of J. Edwin Orr, too, that he sometimes saw revival where there was none (e.g. Davies, *I Will Pour Out My Spirit*, p. 13). I have to say, though, that from my own reading of numerous of Orr's works, I have found him to be careful to reserve the word 'revival' to a set of conditions that truly deserve that denotation. A more serious charge of Orr's work, and one of which he himself became aware, was that he wasn't analytical enough (Richard Owen Roberts, *Event of the Century: The 1857–1858 Awakening*, Wheaton 1989, pp. viii–ix).

preceded by an emphatic 'word' that revival would come to the town soon. Jock Troup and David Cordiner both got 'visions' while in East Anglia concerning work they were to attend to in their homeland, where a significant harvest was subsequently reaped. Prior to the movement that came to Carloway, Lewis in 1934, John MacIver was convinced by a dream that revival was on its way, while his colleague in Point, William Campbell, sensed in a time of prayer that God was also about to move in his congregation. Subsequent movements in Back (1959) and Orkney (early 1980s) have been preceded by similar premonitory signs, while in advance of various times of spiritual blessing experienced through the work of Faith Mission Pilgrims, 'victory' was assured through prolonged periods of intercession (for example, in Skye 1924 and North Uist 1957–8).

As can be seen, a number of the above instances occurred in the Highlands and Islands, where for centuries premonitions have been a curious feature of social life. A number of examples of these taking place, not just prior to, but during, times of awakening are to be found in the pages of this book (for example, Ness 1880s, Carloway 1902, Ness 1922–6), as well as in stories of more recent movements (for example, Skye 1949, Lewis 1949–53, Kinlochbervie 1966–7). Several other examples of the supernatural occurred during both the 1930s and 1949–53 revivals in Lewis, such as the shaking of a house in which people were praying, and people seeing a strange glow above certain houses. Meanwhile, other unusual phenomena have attended subsequent movements in the north; for example, a beautiful and naturally inexplicable fragrance was repeatedly experienced by believers at house meetings during a localised awakening in Skye in 1980.

Interestingly, nearly all these experiences were received by people with a non-Pentecostal theology, and the terminology they would normally use to describe such extraordinary occurrences would differ from typical charismatic descriptions of the same events; viz., 'prophecies', 'words of knowledge'. It is ironic that in the strongly Presbyterian culture of Lewis, during at least one or two prominent revival movements, notably those of 1934–9 and 1949–53, numerous unusual phenomena were accompanying features; while among early Pentecostals, one of whose central foci was outward manifestations, relatively few substantiated testimonies of the miraculous were reported.[132]

---

132. Where, e.g. a prophecy was given, as to a group of Pentecostals in Portobello in 1916, that they should relocate to Glasgow, there is no way of establishing or disproving its authenticity. Meanwhile, Iain H. Murray states as a clear historical fact that 'great revivals have occurred without the presence of any ... gifts, while excitement and interest in them may abound where there is no revival.' Controversially, he claims that all charismatic claims for the present operation of the gifts – 'tongues, healings, prophecies and "slaying in the Spirit" – far from preparing for revival, have rather been a distraction from the great truths which the Spirit has always honoured in the heralding of awakenings' (Murray, *Pentecost Today*, pp. 197–9).

The Pentecostal movements covered in this book are considered worthy of inclusion because they appear to have been marked by a genuine move of the Spirit accompanied by the conversion of significant numbers of individuals. They are not, however, 'traditional' revivals in that they tend to focus on one or other aspect of charismatic gifting as much, if not more, than on the salvation of souls.[133] While speaking in tongues was paramount to the early Pentecostal movement, the 'interpretation of tongues' and physical healing were also prominent features.[134] It is noteworthy, conversely, that in the more traditional revivals covered in this study, tongues and healing have been almost entirely absent.[135] Lastly, it is significant to note that even since the introduction of Pentecostalism in Scotland, the vast majority of community-based evangelical revivals, large and small, to have occurred in the country has taken place within a non-Pentecostal framework.[136]

---

133. The Kilsyth movement of 1908 centred, as did the Azusa Street and Sunderland movements immediately preceding it, on tongues-speaking and being 'slain in the Spirit' (an extra-biblical term, to indicate a person falling down, apparently under the power of the Holy Sprit, to his or her back on the floor). A main focus of the Charismatic movement of the 1960s and 1970s was 'baptism in the Spirit', while that of meetings associated with the 'Toronto Blessing' in the mid-1990s was phenomena such as jerking, falling, laughing and unusual noises.

134. Though there is virtually no mention in early accounts of Scottish Pentecostalism of the practise of various other biblical gifts, such as those of miracles or words of knowledge.

135. Just one or two individual cases of healing are recorded, while the only reported instances of glossolalia were individual occurrences during both the 1930s and the 1949–53 Lewis revivals (Black, *Clash of Tongues*, p. 156; *Revival: Personal Encounters*, p. 65).

136. Equally intriguing is the fact that nearly all of the most popular and comprehensive historical studies of worldwide revivals have been written by authors who pertain to a non-charismatic theology (e.g., Gillies, *Historical Collections of Accounts of Revival*; Cairns, *An Endless Line of Splendour*; Edwards, *Revival*; Davies, *I Will Pour Out My Spirit*; McDow and Reid, *Firefall;* and J. Edwin Orr, who has around a dozen published revival works to his name, as well as masses of as yet unpublished material). Orr's friend and 'successor' as world authority on evangelical awakenings, Richard Owen Roberts, along with John H. Armstrong, former editor of *Reformation & Revival* Journal, both also hold to a non-Pentecostalist theology (Roberts, *Revival Literature*, pp. 32–3).

Epilogue

THE period covered in this book represents the end of an era in the history of evangelical awakenings in Scotland. The early 1920s witnessed the last revival movement not confined to one geographical area that the country has experienced. That does not mean, of course, that there were no revivals after that time. We have already noted a powerful spiritual awakening in Lewis through the latter half of the 1930s. But the 1920s did turn out, additionally, to be the last decade in which numerous significant revivals occurred. Ironically, the Second World War helped bring a change in the spiritual climate. In the later 1940s and throughout the 1950s there developed a considerable deepening of spiritual interest across the land, in part caused and in part taken advantage of by American evangelist Billy Graham, with his mass rallies centred on Glasgow in 1955, which drew tens of thousands to Hampden Park Stadium. This was also the period when yet another powerful revival ignited in Lewis, sweeping through the island as well as adjoining Harris, and quickly becoming one of the best-known evangelical revivals in the world.

Despite the excitement created by movements like these, the spiritual tone in Britain was changing, and changing at an accelerating rate. In Scotland, a peak in church membership in most Protestant denominations came around 1956 (when, in numerical terms, it was still 6 percent lower than in 1900). Church membership started to decline again within two years of Graham's visit, although in Glasgow church attendance was still 50 per cent higher in 1960 than in 1954. However, by the early 1960s, a free-fall in church attendance had set in, which continued throughout the remainder of the century and into the new millennium. While evangelical awakenings still occurred from time to time in various places, they were much less frequent than in the 1880–1940 period. In addition, they were generally much less powerful and influential then their predecessors (some were referred to as 'mini-revivals'), and they were largely confined to the north and north-west of Scotland, where there existed a stronger sense of community (though not as strong as in the 'olden days'), and where the Church played a more prominent part in community life (though here, too, the Church's influence was gradually eroding). It is interesting to note, however, that while spiritual 'movements' of varying intensity and duration were relatively common in the Outer Hebrides right up to and including the 1980s, Scotland's other favourite revival hot-spot, the fishing communities of the north-east coast, played host to no major period of awakening after the 'Fishermen's revival' of the 1920s (although several communities were swayed by a burst of revivalist activity in the late 1960s). A consideration of this and many other factors are contained in the author's forthcoming book, *Fire On The Heather: A History of Evangelical Awakenings in Scotland 1945–2000.*

We close our study with a concluding remark from William Couper, which is no doubt even more relevant today that it was when he penned it in 1918: 'Revivals in the past have done much to strengthen the Scottish character and to provide the land with those men who have carried its name for integrity and industry over the world. At the present time, as in former years, there is need for the urgent cry to go up: "O Lord, revive Thy work in the midst of the years, in the midst of the years make it known; in wrath remember mercy."' [1]

1. Couper, *Scottish Revivals*, p. 160, quoting Habakkuk 3:2.

Bibliography

Primary Sources

Books

Anonymous, *'It Happened in Peterhead': Extracts from The Peterhead Sentinel and The Corps History Book*, Peterhead n.d.

Anonymous, *These Fifty Years,* Anniversary Booklet of Gilcomston Park Baptist Church (1886–1936), Aberdeen n.d.

Anonymous, *Thirty Years of Broughton Place Church*, Edinburgh 1914.

Anson, Peter F., *Fishing Boats and Fisher Folk on the East Coast,* London 1930.

Baikie, J.M., *Revivals in the Far North,* Wick n.d.

Brown, A. Douglas, *Revival Addresses*, London 1922.

Bryson, N.W., *History of the Lanarkshire Christian Union, Instituted 1882*, Strathaven 1937.

Campbell, Duncan, *The Lewis Awakening 1949–1953,* Edinburgh 1954.

Campbell, Murdoch, *Memories of a Wayfaring Man*, Glasgow 1974.

Clark, Alexander, *Cambridge Street Baptist Church: A Historical Sketch*, Glasgow 1924.

Crossman R.H.S., et al (Eds.), *Oxford and the Groups: The Influence of the Groups*, Oxford 1934.

Davis, George, *Torrey and Alexander: The Story of a World-wide Revival*, London 1905.

Govan, J.G., *In the Train of His Triumph: Reminiscences of the Early Days of the Faith Mission,* Edinburgh n.d.

Hammond, E. Payson, *The Conversion of Children*, Chicago 1901.

Jeffreys, George, *Pentecostal Rays: The Baptism and Gifts of the Holy Spirit*, London 1923.

Last, Edward, *How the Churches Grew in the Olden Days*, London 1932.

MacAulay, Murdo, *The Burning Bush in Carloway*, Carloway 1984.

MacDonald, Donald, *Christian Experience: A Selection of Sermons*, Edinburgh 1988.

McLean, J.B., *Faith Triumphant: A Review of the Work of the Faith Mission, 1886–1936, by Those Who Have Seen and Heard*, Edinburgh 1936.

MacLean, John K., *Triumphant Evangelism: The Three Years' Missions of Dr Torrey and Mr Alexander in Great Britain and Ireland*, London 1906.

MacRae, Alexander, *Revivals in the Highlands & Islands in the 19th Century*, Stirling 1906 (reprinted 1998).

MacRae, Kenneth, *The Resurgence of Arminianism*, Stornoway 1950.

McIver, Rev. Daniel, *An Old-time Fishing Town – Eyemouth: Its History, Romance, and Tragedy*, Edinburgh 1906.

MacKenzie, William C., *The Book of the Lews: The Story of a Hebridean Isle*, Paisley 1919.

MacLean, J. Kennedy, *A Revival Among Soldiers*, London c. 1915.

Mitchell, Alexander H., *The History of Lothian Road United Free Church Congregation*, Edinburgh 1911.

Murray, Iain H. (Ed.), *Diary of Kenneth A. MacRae*, Edinburgh 1980.

Newton, John W., *The Story of the Pilgrim Preachers and their Tours throughout Britain*, London 1939.

Peckham, Colin and Mary, *Sounds From Heaven: The Revival on the Isle of Lewis 1949–1952*, Fearn 2004.

Ritchie, Jackie, *Floods Upon the Dry Ground*, Peterhead n.d.

Ronald, John, *History of the Cairns United Free Church*, Stewarton, Ardrossan 1926.

Salmond, C.A., *Perfectionism: The False and the True: A Lecture Delivered by Rev. C.A. Salmond, M.A., Rothesay, on 30th December 1888, with Special Reference to the Teaching of the 'Faith Mission Pilgrims'*, Glasgow 1889.

Stewart, Ruth, *James Stewart: Missionary*, Asheville, NC 1927.

Various, *A Wave of Blessing in Black Isle and Easter Ross*, Glasgow 1906.

Walker, Norman, *Chapters From the History of the Free Church of Scotland*, Edinburgh 1895.

Watson, Mrs J.T.S., *Pathmakers in the Isles 1850–1949*, Edinburgh 1919.

Wood, John, *The Story of the Evangelisation Society*, London 1907.

Biographies

EMILIA BAEYERTZ – Evans, Robert Owen, *Emilia Baeyertz, Evangelist: Her Career in Australia and Great Britain*, Hazelbrook 2007.

ANDREW BONAR – Bonar, Marjory, *Andrew A. Bonar: Diary and Life*, Edinburgh 1893 (reprinted 1961).

JOHN S. BOWIE – White, Robert, *Semi-Jubilee of Rev. John S. Bowie: Sketch of his Life and Work*, Edinburgh 1900.

ANDREW KENNEDY BREMMER – Bremmer, Robert L., *A Child Of Faith: Memorials of Andrew Kennedy Bremmer*, London 1890.

DAVID CAIRNS – Cairns, D.S., *David Cairns, An Autobiography: Some Recollections of a Long Life, and Selected Letters*, London 1950.

HECTOR CAMERON – MacAulay, Murdo, *Hector Cameron of Lochs and Back: The Story of an Island Ministry*, Edinburgh 1982.

DUNCAN CAMPBELL – Woolsey, Andrew A., *Channel of Revival: A Biography of*, Edinburgh 1974 (reprinted 1982).

MURDOCH CAMPBELL – Campbell, Rev. Murdoch, *The King's Friend: Memorial of Norman MacDonald or 'Tormod Sona'*, Glasgow n.d.

OSWALD CHAMBERS – McCasland, David, *Oswald Chambers: Abandoned to God,* Grand Rapids 1993.

PETER CHISHOLM – Chisholm, Peter M., *Wandering in Fields of Dreams*, Inverness 1952.

G.N.M. COLLINS – Collins, G.N.M., *The Days of the Years of my Pilgrimage*, Edinburgh 1991.

JOHN COLVILLE – Colville, Mary A., *John Colville of Burnside, Campbelton: Evangelist: A Memoir of his Life and Work by his Widow*, Edinburgh 1888.

HENRY DRUMMOND – Smith, George Adam, *The Life of Henry Drummond*, London 1899.

D.J. FINDLAY – Gammie, Alexander, *Pastor D.J. Findlay: A Unique Personality*, London 1949.

LIONEL FLETCHER – Fletcher, Lionel B., *Mighty Moments*, London 1931.

DONALD FRASER – Fraser, Agnes R., *Donald Fraser*, Edinburgh 1934.

ALEXANDER FRAZER – Carson, John T., *Frazer of Tain: The Rev. Alexander Frazer,* Glasgow 1966.

DONALD GOLAN – Various, *Leaves of Remembrance of the Life and Work of the Rev. Donald Charles Campbell Gollan*, Coatbridge 1930.

J.G. GOVAN – Govan, I.R., *Spirit of Revival: Biography of J.G. Govan, founder of the Faith Mission,* London 1938.

JOHN HARPER – Climie, John, *John Harper, a Man of God,* Glasgow 1912.

WILLIAM IRVINE – Cropp, Cherie, *The Life and Ministry of William Irvine*, 2000.

GEORGE and STEPHEN JEFFREYS – Cartwright, Desmond W., *The Great Evangelists: The Lives of George and Stephen Jeffreys*, Basingstoke 1986.

FRANK and SETH JOSHUA – Fielder, Geraint, *Grit, Grace and Gumption: The Exploits of Evangelists John Pugh, Frank and Seth Joshua*, Fearn 2000; Rees, T. Mardy, *Seth and Frank Joshua, the Renowned Evangelists*, Wrexham 1926.

JOSEPH W. KEMP – Kemp, Mrs W., *Joseph W. Kemp: The Record of a Spirit-Filled Life*, Edinburgh, n.d.

OLIVE LAST – Last, Edward, *Olive: The Story of a Brief but Beautiful Life*, Glasgow c. 1911.

ERIC LIDDELL – McCasland, David, *Eric Liddell: Pure Gold,* Grand Rapids 2003; Thomson, D.P., *Scotland's Greatest Athlete: The Eric Liddell Story*, Crieff 1970.

JOHN LIVINGSTONE – Anonymous, *A Faithful Minister: Being Memorials of the Rev. John Livingstone, Gallowgate U.F. Church, Aberdeen*, Aberdeen 1910.

JOHN LONG – Long, John, *Journal of John Long*, 1927.

DUNCAN MACCOLL – Stirling, H. Austin, *Duncan MacColl, an Apostle to Highlanders. Memoirs of the Founder of the Highland Mission, Glasgow*, Edinburgh 1932.

JOHN MACKAY – MacKenzie, Rev. Alexander, *The Rev. John MacKay, M.A., Student, Pastor, General Assembly's Highland Evangelist*, Paisley 1921.

JAMES MCKENDRICK – McKendrick, James, *What We Have Seen & Heard During Twenty-Five Years' Evangelistic Labours*, Arbroath 1914.

HECTOR MACKINNON – Mrs MacKinnon, *Hector MacKinnon*, London 1914.

ALEXANDER MACLENNAN – Jenkins, Hugh, *Alexander MacLennan of Dunfermline: Memoir and Sermons*, Leith 1906.

DONALD JOHN MARTIN – MacFarlane, Rev. Norman C., *Life of the Rev. Donald John Martin: Preacher, Soul Winner, Social Reformer*, Edinburgh 1914.

ALEXANDER MAIR – Mair, Alexander, *Unforgettable*, London 1966.

ALEXANDER MARSHALL – Hawthorn, John, *Alexander Marshall : Evangelist, Author and Pioneer*, Glasgow 1929 (reprinted1988).

ALEXANDER MURRAY – Murray, Isabella B., *In Remembrance: Rev. Alexander Murray*, Edinburgh 1921.

GEORGE MURRAY – MacLeod, A. Donald, *George Murray of the 'U.P.'*, Newton Corner, Massachusetts 1996.

W.P. NICHOLSON – Barnes, Stanley, *All For Jesus: The Life of W.P. Nicholson*, Belfast 1996.

GEORGE REITH – Clow, W.M., *Dr George Reith: A Scottish Ministry*, London 1928.

EVAN ROBERTS – Jones, Brynmor P., *Instrument of Revival: The Complete Life of Evan Roberts 1878–1951*, South Plainfield 1996.

JOHN ROSS – Ross, Rev. John, *Reminiscences*, Kilmarnock n.d.

WILLIAM ROSS – Ross, J.M.E., *William Ross of Cowcaddens: A Memoir*, London 1905.

GEORGE SHARPE – Rev. George Sharpe, *This is My Story*, Glasgow n.d.

GIPSY SMITH – Lazell, David, *Gypsy From the Forest: A New Biography of the International Evangelist Gipsy Smith* (1860–1947), Bridgend 1997; Smith, Gipsy, *Gipsy Smith: His Life and Work*, London 1903.

JAMES STEWART – Jenkins, T. Omri, *Five Minutes to Midnight: James Stewart and Mission to Europe*, Darlington 1989.

C.T. STUDD – Grubb, Norman P., *C.T. Studd: Cricketter and Pioneer*, London 1933.

REUBEN A. TORREY – Martin, Roger, *R.A. Torrey: Apostle of Certainty*, Murfreesboro, Tennessee 1976.

JOCK TROUP – Mitchell, George, *Revival Man: The Jock Troup Story*, Fearn 2002.

ANDREW TURNBULL – Turnbull, T.N., *Apostle Andrew*, Bradford 1965.

JAMES HOOD WILSON – Wells, James, *The Life of James Hood Wilson D.D. of the Barclay Church, Edinburgh*, London 1904.

SECONDARY SOURCES

Aitchison, Peter, *Children of the Sea: The Story of the Eyemouth Disaster*, East Linton 2001.

Allan, Ian M., *West the Glen: A History of the Free Church Just West of the Great Glen*, Drumnadrochit 1997.

Allen, Brad, *Catch the Wind: The Story of Spiritual Awakening on The Hebrides Islands*, Tarentum, Pennsylvania 2002.

Allen, Dr Brad, *The Land God Chose to Love [An Tir a Roghnaich Dis a Ghradhachadh]*, Tarentum, Pennsylvania 2004.

Anonymous, *The Church of the Nazarene in the British Isles*, n.d.

Anonymous, *A History of Burra Isle Baptist Church 1816–1990*, Shetland 1990.

Anonymous, *Together with God*, Centenary Booklet of Gilcomston Park Baptist Church, n.d.

Armstrong, John H., *True Revival: What Happens When God's Spirit Moves?* Eugene 2001.

Badcock, G. and Wright, D.F. (Eds), *Disruption to Divinity: Edinburgh Divinity 1846–1996*, Edinburgh 1996.

Baker, H.A., *Visions Beyond the Veil*, Tonbridge 2000.

Balfour, Ian L.S., *Revival in Rose Street: Charlotte Baptist Chapel 1808–2008*, Edinburgh 2007.

Bardgett, Frank D., *Devoted Service Rendered: The Lay Missionaries of the Church of Scotland*, Edinburgh 2002.

Beattie, David, *Brethren: The Story of a Great Recovery*, Kilmarnock 1940.

Bebbington, D.W. (Ed.), *The Baptists in Scotland: A History*, Glasgow, 1988.

Bebbington, D.W., *Evangelicalism in Modern Britain: A History From the 1730s To the 1980s*, London 1989.

Bennett, Peter and Dorothy, and Harris, Courtenay B., *Do We Consider the 1904/05 Revival as Just Water Under the Bridge?: Read the Reports From the Newspapers of the Day*, Llanfairfechan n.d.

Black, Hugh B., *The Clash of Tongues with Glimpses of Revival*, Greenock 1988.

Black, Hugh B., *Revival: Personal Encounters*, Greenock 1993.

Black, Hugh B., *Revival: Including the Prophetic Vision of Jean Darnall*, Greenock 1993.

Blakey, Ronald S., *The Man in the Manse*, Edinburgh 1978.

Brierley, Peter and MacDonald, Fergus, *Prospects for Scotland 2000: Trends and Tables from the 1994 Scottish Church Census,* Edinburgh 1995.

Brown, Calum G., *The Social History of Religion in Scotland*, London 1987.

Brown, Stewart J. and Newlands, George (Eds), *Scottish Christianity in the Modern World*, Edinburgh 2000.

Brown, Thomas, *Annals of the Disruption*, Edinburgh 1876.

Burgess, Stanley (Ed.), *The New International Dictionary of Pentecostal & Charismatic Movements*, Grand Rapids 2002.

Cairns, Earle E., *An Endless Line of Splendour: Revivals and their Leaders from the Great Awakening to the Present,* Wheaton 1986.

Cameron Nigel M. de S. (Ed.), *Dictionary of Scottish Church History and Theology*, Edinburgh 1993.

Campbell, Murdoch (Ed.), *Diary of Jessie Thain [The Friend of Robert Murray McCheyne]*, Resolis 1955.

Campbell, Murdoch, *Gleanings of Highland Harvest*, Fearn 1989.

Carson, John T., *God's River in Spate: The Story of the Religious Awakening of Ulster in 1859*, Belfast 1959.

Carwardine, Richard, *Transatlantic Revivalism: Popular Evangelicalism in Britain and America 1790–1865*, Westport 1978.

Chapman, Diana, *Searching the Source of the River: Forgotten Women of the British Pentecostal Revival 1907–1914,* London 2007.

Clark, Rufus W., *Moody & Sankey in Great Britain*, London 1875.

Collins, G.N.M., *The Heritage of our Fathers: The Free Church of Scotland: Her Origin and Testimony*, Edinburgh 1976.

Couper, W.J., *Scottish Revivals*, Dundee 1918.

Dallimore, Arnold, *George Whitefield: The Life and Times of the Great Evangelist of the Eighteenth-Century Revival, Vol. II*, Carlisle, PA n.d.

Davies, R.E., *I Will Pour Out My Spirit: A History and Theology of Revivals and Evangelical Awakenings,* Tunbridge Wells 1992.

Devine, T.M., *The Scottish Nation 1700–2007*, London 1999 (revised 2006).

Dickson, Neil T.R., *Brethren in Scotland 1838–2000: A Social Study of an Evangelical Movement*, Carlisle 2002.

Duncan, Rev. R.S., *History of Sunday Schools*, Memphis 1876.

Edwards, Brian H., *Can we Pray for Revival?,* Darlington 2001.

Edwards, Brian H., *Revival : A People Saturated with God*, Darlington, 1990.

Evans, Eifion, *The Welsh Revival of 1904,* Bridgend 1969.

Evans, Eifion, *When He is Come: An Account of the 1858–60 Revival in Wales*, Denbigh 1959.

Ferguson, John (Ed.), *When God Came Down: An Account of the North Uist Revival 1957–58*, Inverness 2000.

Fish, Henry C., *Handbook of Revivals, For the Use of Winners of Souls*, London 1873.

Fiske, D.T., *Faith Working by Love: As Exemplified in the Life of Fidelia Fiske,* Boston 1868.

Fleming, William, *If My People: Demonstrating the Spirit's Power in Revival,* Fearn 2000.

Frodsham, Stanley H., *With Signs Following*, Springfield, Missouri 1941.

Geddes, Arthur, *The Isle of Lewis & Harris: A Study in British Community,* Edinburgh 1955.

Gee, Donald, *These Men I Knew: Personal Memories Of Our Pioneers*, London 1980.

Gee, Donald, *Wind and Flame*, Croydon 1967.

Gibbard, Noel, *Fire on the Altar: A History and Evaluation of the 1904–05 Welsh Revival,* Bryntirion 2005.

Gibbard, Noel, *On the Wings of the Dove: The International Effects of the 1904–05 Revival*, Bryntirion 2002.

Gibbon, F.P., *William A. Smith of the Boys' Brigade*, London 1934.

Gibson, W.M., *Fishing In Old East Lothian: Cockenzie, Port Seton, Fisherrow and Prestonpans*, Haddington 1994.

Gillies, John, *Historical Collections of Accounts of Revival,* Kelso 1845 (reprinted 1981).

Grant, James Shaw, *The Gaelic Vikings*, Edinburgh 1984.

Greenfield, John, *Power From on High: The Story of the Great Moravian Revival of 1727,* 1928 (reprinted Bethlehem PA 1995).

Griffin Stanley C., *A Forgotten Revival: East Anglia and NE Scotland – 1921,* Bromley 1992.

Grubb, Norman P., *Rees Howells: Intercessor,* Guildford 1973 (reprinted 1983).

Guillebaud, Meg, *Rwanda: The Land God Forgot? Revival, Genocide & Hope,* London 2002.

Hayes, Dan, *Fireseeds of Spiritual Awakening*, San Bernardino, 1983.

Hollenweger, Walter J., *The Pentecostals*, London 1972.

Holmes, Janice, *Religious Revivals in Britain and Ireland 1859–1905,* Dublin 2000.

Horridge, Glenn K., *The Salvation Army: Origins and Early Days: 1865–1900*, Godalming 1993.

Houghton, Frank, *Amy Carmichael of Dohnavur*, London 1953.

Howard, Michael, *Recklessly Abandoned*, Kansas City 1996.

Howie, John, *The Scots Worthies*, 1870 (reprinted Edinburgh 1995).

Hutchison, James, *Weavers, Miners and the Open Book: A History of Kilsyth*, Self-published 1986.

Jeffrey, Kenneth S., *When The Lord Walked The Land: The 1858–62 Revival in the North East of Scotland,* Carlisle 2002.

Johnson, Douglas, *Contending For The Faith: A History of the Evangelical Movement in the Universities and Colleges*, Leicester 1979.

Jones, Brynmor P., *Voices from the Welsh Revival 1904–1905: An Anthology of Testimonies, Reports, and Eyewitness Statements from Wales's Year of Blessing,* Bridgend 1995.

Jones, R.B., *Rent Heavens: The Revival of 1904,* London 1931.

Jones, R. Tudur, *Faith and Crisis of a Nation: Wales 1890–1914,* Cardiff 2004.

Kennedy, John, *Days of the Fathers in Ross-shire* 1861 (reprinted 1979).

King, J.D., *Written Not with Ink But With the Spirit: Introduction to Revival Literature with Anotated Bibliography*, Kansas City 2005.

Last, Edward, *Hand-Gathered Fruit: Twelve Chapters on Personal Soul-Winning,* Stirling 1950.

Lloyd-Jones, D. Martyn, *Revival: Can We Make It Happen?,* London 1986.

Lynch, Michael (Ed.), *The Oxford Companion to Scottish History*, Oxford 2001.

M., J., *Recollections of Mr D.L. Moody and his Work in Britain, 1874–1892,* Edinburgh 1901.

Martin, Larry, *The Topeka Outpouring of 1901*, Joplin, Missouri 2002.

McClymond, Michael J. (Ed.), *Encyclopedia of Religious Revivals in America,* Westport, Connecticut 2006.

MacColl, Allan W., *Land, Faith and the Crofting Community: Christianity and Social Criticism in the Highlands of Scotland 1843–1893,* Edinburgh 2006.

McDow, Malcolm and Reid, Alvin L., *Firefall: How God has Shaped History through Revivals* Nashville 1997.

MacFarlane, Rev. Norman C., *Apostles of the North*, Stornoway, n.d.

MacFarlane, Norman, *Scotland's Keswick: A Sketch of the Message and of the Men,* London 1916.

MacFarlane, Rev. Norman C., *The 'Men' of the Lews*, Stornoway 1924.

McGibbon, John, *The Fisher-Folk of Buchan: a True Story of Peterhead,* London 1922.

McGrath, Alister, *Thomas F. Torrance: An Intellectual Biography*, Edinburgh 1999.

MacInnes, Rev. David, *Kilmuir Church, North Uist 1894–1994*, Kilmuir 1994.

MacLeod, John, *A Brief Record of the Church in Uig (Lewis), up to the Union of 1929*, Stornoway 2001.

MacLeod, John, *Banner In The West: A Spiritual History Of Lewis And Harris,* Edinburgh 2008.

MacLeod, Rev. John, *Happy Norman (Tormod Sona) + Gleanings of Early Days of Gospel Power in Lewis,* Stornoway n.d.

MacLeod, Rev. Norman, *Lewis Revivals of the 20th Century*, Lewis 1989.

McNaughton, W.D., *Alexander Dewar's Testimony: The Origins of Avoch Congregational Church*, Glasgow 1994.

McNaughton, William D., *Early Congregational Independency in the Highlands and Islands and the North-East of Scotland*, Glasgow 2003.

MacPherson, John, *Revival and Revival Work: A Record of the Labours of D.L. Moody & Ira D. Sankey, and Other Evangelists*, London 1875

MacRae, Alexander, *Revivals in the Highlands & Islands in the 19th Century*, Stirling 1906 (reprinted 1998).

Mair, Graham, *The Fisherman's Gospel Manual*, London 1994.

Martin, Larry, *The Life and Ministry of William J. Seymour*, Joplin, Missouri 1999.

Matheson, Alistair J., *Highland Pentecost*, Portree 2001.

Maxwell, Victor, *A Mission to Millions: The Story of Ernie Allen and the Every Home Crusade,* Belfast 1999.

Meek, Donald E., *Island Harvest: A History of Tiree Baptist Church 1838–1988*, Tiree 1988.

Mitchell, George, *Comfy Glasgow: An Expression of Thanks*, Fearn 1999.

Montgomery, Rev. Henry, *The Children in '59*, Kilkeel 1936.

Mowat, W.G., *The Story of Lybster*, Lybster 1959.

Murphy, Owen, *When God Stepped Down from Heaven,* Portland, n.d.

Murray, Derek, *The First 100 Years: The Baptist Union of Scotland*, Glasgow, n.d.

Murray, Iain H., *Pentecost Today: The Biblical Basis for Understanding Revival*, Edinburgh 1998.

Murray, Iain H., *The Puritan Hope*, Edinburgh 1971 (reprinted 1991).

Murray, Iain H., *Revival & Revivalism: The Making and Marring of American Evangelicalism 1750–1858*, Edinburgh 1994.

Murray, John J., *The Church on the Hill: Oban Free High Church: A History and Guide*, Oban 1984.

Nichol, John Thomas, *The Pentecostals*, Plainfield, New Jersey 1971.

Orr, J. Edwin, *An Appenticeship of Faith,* Wheaton 1993.

Orr, J. Edwin, *A Call for the Re-study of Revival and Revivalism*, Los Angeles 1981.

Orr, J. Edwin, *Campus Aflame: A History of Evangelical Awakenings in Collegiate Communities,* Wheaton 1994.

Orr, J. Edwin, *The Flaming Tongue: The Impact of Twentieth Century Revivals,* Chicago 1973.

Patrick, Belle, *Recollections of East Fife Fisher Folk*, Edinburgh 2003.

Peckham, Colin N., *Heritage of Revival: A Century of Rural Evangelism*, Edinburgh 1985.

Peckham, Colin, *The New Faith Mission Bible College*, Edinburgh 1994.

Penn-Lewis, Jessie, *The Awakening in Wales*, London 1905 (reprinted 2002).

Piggin, Stuart, *Firestorm of the Lord: The History of the and Prospects for Revival in the Church and the World*, Carlisle 2000.

Pollock, John, *A Fistful of Heroes*, Fearn 1998.

Pollock, John, *Moody Without Sankey*, London 1963 (reprinted 1995).

Pollock, John, *The Story of the Children's Special Service Mission and The Scripture Union*, London 1959.

Porter, James (Ed.), *After Columba – After Calvin: Religious Community in North East Scotland*, Aberdeen 1999.

Presbytery of Aberdeen, *Evidence on the Subject of Revivals, Taken Before a Committee of the Presbytery of Aberdeen*, Aberdeen 1841.

Randall, Ian M., *Evangelical Experiences: A Study in the Spirituality of English Evangelicalism 1918–1939*, Carlisle 1999.

Reid, Rev. William (Ed.), *Authentic Records of Revival Now in Progress in the United Kingdom*, London 1860 (reprinted 1980).

Roberts, Richard Owen, *Revival*, Wheaton 1991.

Roberts, Richard Owen, *Revival Literature: An Annotated Bibliography with Biographical and Historical Notices*, Wheaton 1987.

Roberts, Richard Owen (Ed.), *Scotland Saw His Glory: A History of Revivals in Scotland*, Wheaton 1995.

Royle, Trevor, *The Flowers of the Forest: Scotland and the First World War*, Edinburgh 2006.

Sanders, J. Oswald, *This I Remember; Reminiscences*, Eastbourne 1982.

Schmidt, Leigh Eric, *Holy Fairs: Scotland and the Making of American Revivalism*, Grand Rapids 1989.

Searle, David (Ed.), *Death or Glory: The Church's Mission in Scotland's Changing Society – Studies in Honour of Dr Geoffrey Grogan*, Fearn 2001.

Sheils, W.J. and Wood, Diana (Eds.), *Voluntary Religion: Papers Read at the 1985 Summer Meeting and the 1986 Winter Meeting of the Ecclesiastical History Society*, Oxford 1986.

Shirra, Robert, *Remains of the Rev. Robert Shirra*, Kirkcaldy 1850.

Smith, Angus, *An Eaglais Mhor*, Ness 1992.

Smith, Rev. J.A., *Sinclair Thomson: The Shetland Apostle*, Lerwick 1969.

Smith, Oswald J., *The Great Russian Revival*, Willowdale, Ontario 1964.

Smith, Robert, *One Foot In The Sea*, Edinburgh 1991.

Sprange, Harry, *Kingdom Kids: Children in Revival,* Fearn 1993 (revised and reprinted as *Children In Revival: 300 Years of God's Work in Scotland*, Fearn 2002).

Springhall, John, *Sure & Steadfast: A History of the Boys' Brigade, 1883–1983,* London 1983.

Stewart, I.R. Govan, *Abundance of Grace: The Story of Margaret Livingstone,* Edinburgh 1967.

Stewart, James A., *Opened Windows: The Church and Revival*, Asheville, NC 1958.

Struthers, Gavin, *History of the Rise, Progress and Principles of the Relief Church,* Glasgow 1843.

Synan, Vinson, *The Holiness-Pentecostal Tradition: Charismatic Movements in the Twentieth Century,* Grand Rapids, Michigan 1997.

Talbot, Brian R., *Standing on the Rock: A History of Stirling Baptist Church, 1805–2005*, Stirling 2005.

Tatlow, T., *The Story of the Student Christian Movement of Great Britain and Ireland,* London 1933.

Taylor, Steve, *Lewis Revival 1934–1941,* Kensaleyre n.d.

Thomson, D.P., *Iona to Ardnamurchan by Mull, Coll, and Tiree: A Pilgrimage Through the Centuries*, Crieff 1956.

Thompson, E.P., *The Making of the English Working Class*, Harmondsworth 1986.

Towns, Elmer and Porter, Douglas, *The Ten Greatest Revivals Ever: From Pentecost to the Present*, Ann Arbor, Michigan 2000.

Towsey. Kate (Ed.), *Orkney and the Sea*, Kirkwall 2002.

Wakefield, Gavin, *The First Pentecostal Anglican: The Life and Legacy of Alexander Boddy*, Cambridge 2001.

Walker, Andrew and Aune, Kristin (Eds.), *On Revival: A Critical Examination* Carlisle 2003.

Wallis, Arthur, *In the Day of Thy Power,* Alresford 1956.

Walters, David, *Children Aflame*, Macon, Georgia 1996.

Weeks, Gordon, *Chapter Thirty Two (part of): A History of the Apostolic Church, 1900–2000*, Barnsley 2003.

Weisberger, Bernard, *They Gathered at the River*, Chicago 1958.

Wells, David F., *Turning to God: Biblical Conversion in the Modern World,* Carlisle 1989.

White, Rev. R.E.O., *History of Rutherglen Baptist Community Church,* 1954.

Whyte, Rev. William, *Revival in Rose Street: A History of Charlotte Baptist Chapel, Edinburgh*, Edinburgh n.d.

Wiersbe, Warren W. (Ed.), *Best of Tozer*, 1978 (reprinted Nottingham 1993).

Williams, David and Bridget, *The Wind Blowing*, Sidcup 1973.

Various, *Report of the Proceedings at a Great United Meeting Held Under the Auspices of the Glasgow United Evangelistic Association, the Christian Churches and the Christian Organisations for Youth Welfare in the St Andrew's Hall, Glasgow on Monday, 8th February, 1937 to Celebrate the Centenary of the Birth of Dwight L. Moody* (*Moody Centenary Celebrations*), Glasgow 1937.

Yuille, Rev. George, *History of the Baptists in Scotland*, Glasgow 1926.

NEWSPAPERS AND JOURNALS

Associated Presbyterian Church Magazine, Vol. 37 (Nov/Dec 1996).

The Ayrshire Post, 1908.

The Banffshire Journal, 1893–95 (partial).

The Border Telegraph, 1905.

Bright Words, 1890–1940.

Buchan Observer and East Aberdeenshire Advertiser, 1905.

The Cambuslang Advertiser, 1905.

The Campbeltown Courier, 1897.

The Christian, 1880–1939.

The Christian Herald And Signs of Our Times, 1905–6, 1921–2.

The Coatbridge Express, 1905.

Dumfries-shire and Galloway Courier & Herald, 1905.

Foursquare Revival Mirror: Principal George Jeffreys and his Revival Party, 1937.

Fraserburgh Herald and Northern Counties' Advertiser, 1921.

The Glasgow Weekly Herald, 1905, 1921.

The Highland News, 1924.

The Kilsyth Chronicle, 2008.

The Kirkintilloch Gazette, Lenzie and Campsie Reporter, 1908.

Kirriemuir Free Press and District Advertiser, 1884.

The Lanarkshire, 1905, 1921–22.

Lanarkshire Examiner and Upper Ward Advertiser, 1905.

Life Indeed, 1996.

Missionary Record of the United Free Church of Scotland, 1905–6.

The Monthly Record of the Free Church of Scotland, 1880–1940, 1974.

The Moray and Nairn Express, 1893–1896.

Northern Ensign and Weekly Gazette for the Counties of Caithness, Ross, Sutherland, Orkney & Shetland, 1921.

The Oban Times and Argyllshire Advertiser, 1885–86.

The Orcadian, 1904.

The Orkney Herald, 1861.

The Orkney View, 1993.

Perthshire Constiutional & Journal, 1905.

The Revival, 1860–1, 1905–14.

The Ross-shire Journal and General Advertiser for the Northern Counties, 1885–7, 1905.

The Scotsman, 1921–2.

Scottish Baptist Magazine, 1904–22.

Scottish Church History Society Records, Vol. 20, 1980; Vol. 21, 1981; Vol. 25, 1993; Vol. 36, 2006.

The Stornoway Gazette, 1934–9.

The Scottish Guardian, 1859.

Times of Blessing, 1874.

The War Cry, 1905–8.

Wesleyan Methodist 'Spectator', Melbourne, Australia 1894.

The Wishaw Herald, 1905.

ARTICLES

Brown, Callum G., 'The Sunday-School Movement in Scotland 1780–1914' in *SCHSR*, Vol. 21, 1981.

Campbell, Iain D., 'Revival in Lewis,' on www.backfreechurch.co.uk, 2001.

Dickson, Neil, 'Modern Prophetesses,' in *SCHSR*, Vol. 25, 1993.

Dickson, Neil, 'Scottish Brethren and the Welsh Revival,' unpublished paper 2004.

Duthie, John Lowe, 'The Fishermen's Religious Revival,' in *History Today*, December 1983.

MacLeod, Kenina, 'Testimony,' in *Associated Presbyterian Church Magazine*, Vol. 37 (Nov/Dec 1996).

Muirhead, Ian A., 'The Revival as a Dimension of Scottish Church History,' in *SCHSR*, Vol. 20, 1980.

Ridholls, Joe, 'Spark of Grace: The Story of the Haldane Revival,' Unpublished Paper 1967.

Roxburgh, Kenneth B.E., 'The Fundamentalist Controversy Concerning the Baptist Theological College of Scotland,' in *Baptist History and Heritage*, January 2001.

Thomson, Elizabeth P., 'The Impetus Given to the Use of Instrumental Music in Scottish Churches by the Visit of Moody and Sankey to Scotland in 1873–74,' in *SCHSR*, Vol. 36, 2006.

Church Reports and Year Books

Baptist Home Missionary Society Records.

Proceedings of the General Assembly of the Free Church of Scotland.

Report of the Committee of the Free Church of Scotland for the Highlands & Islands.

Proceedings of the General Assembly of the United Free Church of Scotland.

Proceedings of the General Assembly of the Free Church of Scotland for the Highlands & Islands.

Report of the Committee of the Free Church of Scotland for Morals & Temperance.

Report of the Committee of the Free Church of Scotland on the State of Religion and Morals.

Report of the Committee of the United Free Church of Scotland for the Highlands & Islands.

Report of the Free Church of Scotland on Services for Scottish Workers in the English Fishing Ports 1922.

Report of the Home Mission and Church Extension Committee of the Free Church of Scotland.

Report of the Home Mission and Church Extension Committee of the United Free Church of Scotland.

The Scottish Baptist Year Book 1904.

Local Church Minutes and Communion Rolls

Allars United Free Church, Hawick 1903–6.

Alyth Free Church 1889–90.

Avoch United Free Church 1905–6, 1922.

Brandon Street United Free Church, Motherwell 1905–6.

Buckie Wesleyan Methodist Church 1903–23.

Burray Baptist Church 1904.

Cowcaddens Free Church 1885–1903.

Cromarty Free Church 1886–7, 1905–6.

Dumfries Buccleuch Street United Presbyterian Church 1900–2.

Dunkeld Free Church 1882.

Eyemouth United Free Church 1919–23.

Eyemouth United Presbyterian Church 1880–97.

Fraserburgh United Presbyterian Church 1880–96.

Henderson Free Church, Kilmarnock 1883–6.

Kilbrandon & Kilchattan Free Church 1888–90.

Kirkapol Church of Scotland, Tiree 1902–4.

Lambhill Evangelistic Mission, 1927–8.

Ness Free Church, Lewis 1921–8.

Nigg Free Church 1901–6.

Portgordon Wesleyan Methodist Church 1898–1906.

Portsoy United Presbyterian Church 1880–7.

Rathven United Free Church 1920–4.

Rosemarkie Church of Scotland 1880–1922.

St Andrews Church of Scotland, Fraserburgh 1919–23.

St Mark's United Free Church, Glasgow 1904–6.

St Monance United Free Church 1905–6, 1921–2.

Tain United Free Church 1903–5.

Tarbert Free and United Free Church, Harris 1882–1910.

Westray Baptist Church 1880–1930.

Other Sources

Confidence Magazine 1908–1926, Revival Library CD-ROM.

Craigie, John (Westray Baptist Church Secretary), Letter to Rev. J.B. Frame, 4 November 1919.

Innes, John, 'Ye Sons of the Main,' song.

MacAulay, M. and MacLeod, Rev. M.A., 'Discussion on Revival,' audio tape.

MacLeod, Alexander (*Sandy Mor*), 'Revival in Point,' audio tape.

Muir, Rev. Alex, 'Lord, Look on me in Mercy,' from *Songs of Prayer and Praise: Tunes for Modern Versions of Metrical Psalms and Hymns of Revival*, 2003.

Murray, Rev. John J., 'Revivals in Scotland,' Carey Conference 1990, audio tape.

Nicolson, Kenneth, 'Revival At Garry-Bhard,' poem.

Taylor, Steve, 'Skye Revival,' CD-ROM.

Places Index

References to footnotes: e.g. 418/82 refers to page 418, footnote 82

People Index

Where applicable, the abbreviations (a), (c), (e) and (m) are used to signify the subject's principal role in the narrative - as author, convert, evangelist or minister, respectively.

Christian Focus Publications
publishes books for all ages

Our mission statement –

STAYING FAITHFUL
In dependence upon God we seek to help make His infallible Word, the Bible, relevant. Our aim is to ensure that the Lord Jesus Christ is presented as the only hope to obtain forgiveness of sin, live a useful life and look forward to heaven with Him.

REACHING OUT
Christ's last command requires us to reach out to our world with His gospel. We seek to help fulfil that by publishing books that point people towards Jesus and help them develop a Christ-like maturity. We aim to equip all levels of readers for life, work, ministry and mission.

Books in our adult range are published in three imprints.

Christian Focus contains popular works including biographies, commentaries, basic doctrine and Christian living. Our children's books are also published in this imprint.
Mentor focuses on books written at a level suitable for Bible College and seminary students, pastors, and other serious readers. The imprint includes commentaries, doctrinal studies, examination of current issues and church history.
Christian Heritage contains classic writings from the past.

Christian Focus Publications, Ltd
Geanies House, Fearn,
Ross-shire, IV20 1TW, Scotland, United Kingdom
info@christianfocus.com

Our titles are available from
www.christianfocus.com